Poles

PSYCHOLOGICAL ANTHROPOLOGY

Approaches to Culture and Personality

THE DORSEY SERIES IN ANTHROPOLOGY AND SOCIOLOGY

EDITORS

PETER H. ROSSI
University of Chicago

WILLIAM FOOTE WHYTE
Cornell University

ARGYRIS   *Understanding Organizational Behavior*

ADAMS & PREISS (eds.)   *Human Organization Research*   (Published for the Society for Applied Anthropology)

HSU (ed.)   *Psychological Anthropology: Approaches to Culture and Personality*

Psychological Anthropology

APPROACHES TO CULTURE AND PERSONALITY

Edited by *FRANCIS L. K. HSU*

CHAIRMAN, DEPARTMENT OF ANTHROPOLOGY
NORTHWESTERN UNIVERSITY

THE DORSEY PRESS, INC.

Homewood, Illinois • 1961

First Printing, July, 1961

Library of Congress Catalogue Card No. 61–15062

PRINTED IN THE UNITED STATES OF AMERICA

FOREWORD

THE PURPOSE of this volume is twofold. On the one hand, it is an assessment of the up-to-date gains in the field of culture-and-personality. Each of the contributors tries to achieve comprehensiveness within the scope of his particular assignment. Insofar as possible each brings together materials from diverse sources, from obscure journals to their own yet unpublished field notes. On the other hand, each of them also attempts to indicate some of the most important problems yet to be tackled. All the contributors outline some of these problems, the hypotheses and methods most relevant to their investigation, and possible solution.

The American tradition in textbooks is that they contain materials from the beaten paths and are exercises in facts and principles generally endorsed by most or all scholars. Such a tradition fails to introduce the student to the vitality of an expanding and exciting discipline. This book is a textbook, but there will be many controversial spots in it. The reader will find no complete agreement among the contributors, nor between the contributors and the editor. This is a text in which differences in facts, theories, and points of view are not only pointed out, but also explored at some length, leading, in some instances, even to almost diametrically contrasting conclusions between the authors.

Another reason for our approach to this text is that, since the subdiscipline of culture-and-personality is only about twenty-five years old, we are severely limited by the availability of well-established facts and principles. If we only aim at the beaten paths, then we would have either to confine ourselves to the obvious or have little to say. Culture-and-personality has simply not had the accumulation of scholarly heritage enjoyed by older subdisciplines of the science of man such as archaeology or linguistics.

These two reasons are interrelated. The paucity in culture-and-personality of beaten paths points to the need for growth. And growth is impossible without strong efforts to explore new and unsure grounds. In an interdisciplinary subject such as ours, exploration of new and unsure grounds will by definition be a major part of its endeavour for years to come.

Throughout this enterprise I am fortunate in having a group of colleagues as collaborators who have spared no pains in giving me their generous support and gracious cooperation. In particular I would like to acknowledge my indebtedness to Thomas Gladwin, Anthony F. C. Wallace, and Donald T. Campbell, who are also contributors to this book, and to Paul J. Bohannan. But my gratitude to all contributors to this volume is very considerable. Their intellectual distinction as scholars is a matter of public knowledge in the professions and needs no advertising from me. But I, for my part, am compelled to express my gratitude to all thirteen contributors to this volume for their forbearance in the face of my many requests, demands, and even, at times, impudence. As a person born and brought to adolescence in traditional China, I know I am open to the suspicion (on the part of those who have read Chapter 14) that, still prompted by my early culture pattern of mutual dependence, I protest gratitude merely as a matter of good form. In the present instance, however, my contributors completely and truly deserve my gratitude. As a result of laboring as Editor of this volume I have the great satisfaction not only of seeing our joint efforts come to fruition, but also of receiving invaluable intellectual benefits.

I wish also to express my indebtedness to Mrs. Elizabeth E. Reed, Mrs. Sharon Horine, and Mr. Robert Hunt, who have most ably assisted me in the final preparation of the manuscript for publication.

F. L. K. H.

TABLE OF CONTENTS

LIST OF CONTRIBUTORS

DAVID ABERLE, Professor of Anthropology and Chairman of the Department, Brandeis University

ROY D'ANDRADE, Instructor of Anthropology, School of Education, Harvard University

DONALD T. CAMPBELL, Professor of Psychology, Northwestern University

GEORGE DEVOS, Associate Professor, School of Social Welfare, Associate Research Psychologist, Institute for Human Development, and Research Associate, Center for Japanese Studies, University of California at Berkeley.

THOMAS GLADWIN, Social Science Consultant, National Institute of Mental Health

JOHN J. HONIGMANN, Professor of Anthropology, University of North Carolina

FRANCIS L. K. HSU, Professor of Anthropology and Chairman of the Department, Northwestern University

ALEX INKELES, Professor of Sociology, Harvard University

BERT KAPLAN, Professor of Psychology, University of Kansas

ROBERT A. LEVINE, Assistant Professor of Anthropology, Committee on Human Development, University of Chicago

EDWARD NORBECK, Professor of Anthropology and Chairman of the Department, William Marsh Rice University

MELFORD SPIRO, Professor of Anthropology, University of Washington

ANTHONY WALLACE, Professor of Anthropology and Chairman of the Department, University of Pennsylvania

JOHN W. M. WHITING, Professor of Anthropology, School of Education, Harvard University

Chapter 1

PSYCHOLOGICAL ANTHROPOLOGY IN THE BEHAVIORAL SCIENCES

FRANCIS L. K. HSU
Northwestern University

AT THE beginning of our joint efforts the contributors to this volume were of the opinion that attempts at delineating boundaries for culture-and-personality would do more harm than good. Too often precise boundaries have been used as excuse for lack of data, methods, and results. What we need in culture-and-personality is not orthodoxy but more specific research and discussion. Some opinions were milder than others but the direction of our comments was similar. One commented in the following vein:

I feel that any area of study which is still as formative as ours can readily deal itself out of important areas of inquiry by a premature setting of limits. Anthropology itself supplies a classic example. The respective areas of study of archaeology, physical anthropology, and ethnology were so neatly defined and separated that it took years of effort and the pressure of great intellectual need to reconstitute the connective tissue which had been unthinkingly destroyed by the classificatory surgery once fashionable. We are not an exclusive society which needs entrance requirements for members.

Others expressed themselves as follows:

My advice is not to worry about these demarcation problems but to go where our interests and talents lead us. Anthropology has always been distinguished by amoeba-like extensions into any discipline where its problems or interests have pushed it.

The virtues of anarchy and chaos are many—the pains of efforts to achieve unity are usually without compensatory gain.

Finally, I do not think we should repeat the errors of many in the standard academic disciplines by taking the boundaries of our field too seriously. A recent article begins with a comment that is relevant here: "It is perhaps a reflection of the intellectual insecurity of social scientists that they spend an inordinate amount of time and energy defining the boundaries of their respective fields as if these were holy lands which had to be defended against expansive, barbaric, and heathen invaders."

1

I received more reactions on this subject than I have reproduced here. They do not all state the point as strongly but there is none which upholds the opposite view. In the circumstances it is natural that our ideas as to what should be the proper concern of culture-and-personality vary a good deal. As I scan our correspondence and the sometimes copious notes of our various meetings, I find the following general trends of thought:

1. A work of culture-and-personality is one by an anthropologist who has a good knowledge of psychological concepts or by the member of another discipline who has a good knowledge of anthropological concepts.

2. Any work that deals with the individual as the locus of culture.

3. Any work that gives serious recognition to culture as an independent or a dependent variable associated with personality.

4. Any work by an anthropologist which uses psychological concepts or techniques or by a scholar in a psychological discipline which provides directly pertinent data in forms which are usable by anthropologists.

5. The field of culture-and-personality is equivalent to the cross-cultural study of personality and sociocultural systems and includes such problems as (a) the relation of social structure and values to modal patterns of child rearing, (b) the relation of modal patterns of child rearing to modal personality structure as expressed in behavior, (c) the relation of modal personality structure to the role system and projective aspects of culture, and (d) the relation of all of the foregoing variables to deviant behavior patterns which vary from one group to another. The theories used and hypotheses tested can come from any of the behavioral sciences, but the characteristic mark of culture-and-personality research is the emphasis on natural group differences as the subject matter. Studies of individual differences are not, therefore, works of culture and personality. Nor are studies of the experimentally produced group differences of many social psychologists. Studies of many role personalities within a particular society are on the borderline, but group differences within a society are, in my opinion, squarely within the culture and personality field. Thus, Marvin Opler's studies of types of schizophrenia in two American ethnic groups are culture and personality work.

6. The conception of personality-culture as emergent from intereaction is fruitful. To this it should be added that students of culture-and-personality are concerned with behavior always with reference to its antecedents and cannot be satisfied simply to describe its characteristics—as social psychologists are wont to do.

The possible differences between culture-and-personality and social psychology will be touched upon later. Our own lack of agreement is probably reflective of the perennial seesaw discussion among many anthropologists on the same question. At one end is Kroeber's concept of the *Superorganic*, and the perhaps more extreme position of Leslie A. White in his *Culturology*, which comes close to asserting that the march of history is independent of the birth of particular personalities and that cultures transcend the minds and bodies of the individuals living in them (Kroeber 1948:253–255 and White 1949). This view has been criticized on the ground that culture cannot exist without the individual, since "to objectify a phenomenon that can have no manifestation except in human thought and action is to argue a separate existence for something that actually exists only in the mind of the student" (Herskovits 1948:25). At the other end are students who note individual differences and cultural variation in each society. Herskovits shows how the same song, "John Crow," prevalent in the northwestern part of Jamaica, is rendered into many different versions by many different singers (Herskovits 1948:565–569). John Gillin demonstrates the intrasocietal differences among many nonliterate societies (Gillin 1939:681–702). Bert Kaplan has revealed similar differences in four American Indian cultures (Kaplan 1954). Hart perhaps pushed the importance of individual personality differences to a greater extent than most others (Hart 1954).

Needless to say, Kroeber was not unaware of the fact that cultures have to be expressed through individuals, for in his major textbook he did devote a whole chapter to "Cultural Psychology" (1948:572–621). On the other hand, it is equally obvious that no science of man is possible if we merely concentrate on individual differences. Perhaps it is to satisfy both extremes that Kluckhohn and Mowrer found it desirable to introduce an extensive analysis of all the components of personality, from the biological, the physical-environmental, the social, and the cultural, on the one hand, and the universal, the communal, the role, and the idiosyncratic on the other (Kluckhohn and Mowrer 1944:4).

In the 1948 edition of their anthology entitled *Personality in Nature, Society and Culture,* Kluckhohn and Murray reformulated the four determinants which were then designated as constitutional, group membership, role, and situational. The two editors concluded in the second edition of this book that "the differences observed in the personalities of human beings are due to variations in their biological equipment and in the total environment to which they must adjust, while the similarities are ascribable to biological-environmental regularities" (Kluckhohn and Murray 1953:65).

In a later publication Kluckhohn leaned more strongly toward the cultural factor in human behavior, but modestly guarded himself as follows:

In all these, and other, secondary categories the basic determinants are confounded—as the statisticians would say or, in other words, behavioral scientists
must deal with a complex field structure. There is, at best, a vague recognition
that all are involved, but, in practice, scientists from different disciplines and with
different temperamental biases tend to operate as if motivation were, after all,
simply biological or situational or cultural. We lack the techniques, quantitative
or otherwise, for dealing with systems of organized complexity. And so, for the
time being at least, we must do the best we can with crude, first approximations.
Each of us must continue to insist that the particular variable he is most interested
in be taken fully into account. If there is a reasonable of "give" on every side, if
each specialist fully accepts the fact that his discipline can explain not everything
but something, the results are not too bad. One may compare a game in which
the high card or combination is crucial. Other cards in the hand have a value but
a secondary importance for that deal. Some hands are dealt by science where the
winning combination is certainly held by biology, others where psychology, sociology, geography, or anthropology can do the calling. So I shall here unashamedly
concentrate upon the hands where, it seems to me, anthropology can bet high
upon the significance of cultural factors for understanding and explanation.
(Kluckhohn 1954:3–4)

The Core of Culture-and-Personality

Though as a group we eschew boundaries, I think it is quite appropriate for the editor at least to offer some thoughts on the central concerns of culture-and-personality. In this venture I do not
expect to settle anything. In such a fuzzy area no clarification is
likely to meet with universal acceptance. What I shall try to do is
not more than to offer some material to feed further discussion.

It is probably as trite to observe that all human behavior is mediated through the minds of individual human beings as it is to observe
that all human individuals live in social groups each governed by a
specific pattern of culture. All human behavior, except random
movements and reflexes, is, therefore, at once psychological and social in nature. However, the same psychosocial data may be approached from different angles. The angle of approach would seem
to be the primary difference between cultural anthropology and
social anthropology, and between them and culture and personality.

Social anthropology began in Britain. The British view is that
social anthropology is synonymous with anthropology and sociology
combined. That is to say it deals with all aspects of human behavior
from kinship and political organizations to economies and religions.
The American definition is that social anthropology is confined to
the study of social or political organizations. Therefore, some
American students are surprised that E. E. Evans-Pritchard, a well-

known social anthropologist, should have "left" his field to write a book on *Nuer Religion* (1954). There are perhaps two ways of seeing the real difference between them. First, the British social anthropologists really have distinguished themselves in the intensity of their field work and of analysis of the data, a trend first begun with Rivers and Williams in the Torres Straits and later Malinowski in the Trobriands. Thus, Evans-Pritchard carried out his field work in the late twenties and spent the next thirty years publishing primarily on the two societies he studied. This is more or less true of other well-known British social anthropologists such as M. Fortes, R. Firth, and Max Gluckman, though most of them have studied more than one people. This contrasts with the less intensive pattern of field work among American anthropologists, characterized by shorter periods of sojourn, lack of emphasis on thorough familiarity with the native language, and even among many students of the Historical School, a relatively greater emphasis on problem orientation.

The other way is to see cultural anthropology as largely dealing with human behavior in terms of products (culture traits, rituals, dances, techniques, and so forth) while social anthropology, in terms of relationships (such as kinship, inheritance, law, and government). According to this view cultural anthropology studies the end results—cultures, including their diffusion from area to area and their development from epoch to epoch; and social anthropology studies the interpersonal mechanisms through which human beings learn, manipulate, and produce cultures.

Neither of these distinctions is complete in itself. The British and American patterns of field work reflect no real difference in scope, only, with many obvious exceptions and to a certain extent, in thoroughness and depth. They are, in fact, complementary approaches to the same objective. The British way often leads the field worker into a displaced ethnocentrism in which Bongo ethnocentrism takes the place of English ethnocentrism. The American way sometimes leaves the field worker with many factual details but with possibly less sensitivity to the feelings and the views of the peoples he has studied. The product versus relationship distinction is equally without finality. For as the student intensifies his researches, his concern for the mechanisms will inevitably lead him to the end results and vice versa. Many anthropologists will probably deny the existence of either of these distinctions.

It is in this context that we must view culture-and-personality.

Culture-and-personality deals with human behavior primarily in terms of the ideas which form the basis of the interrelationship between the individual and his society. On the one hand, it deals with ideas shared by a considerable portion of any society: the "shame" or "guilt" feelings among the Japanese, the belief in immanent justice among some children of Ghana, the anxiety about food in excess of the actual danger of going hungry among some Oceanic peoples, and even the world view of the Chinese; how these and other ideas held by the individuals are rooted in the diverse patterns of culture in which they grow up. On the other hand, culture-and-personality deals with characteristics of societies: reactions to conquest and disaster, internal or external impetuses to change, militarism and pacificism, democratic or authoritarian character; it deals with how these and other characteristics consistently associated with some societies may be related to such things as the aspirations, fears, and values held by a majority of the individuals in these societies.

With these thoughts on the central concerns of culture-and-personality, I would like to propose a new title for our subdiscipline: psychological anthropology.

For over twenty years culture-and-personality has retained its cumbersome title. I think the time has probably come for us to give it a less cumbersome and more logical title. The concept of personality, which anthropologists have borrowed from psychologists, leads to some difficulties. For example, some anthropologists, though resorting to psychological explanations at many crucial points of their arguments, tend to regard the personality concept either as indistinguishable from culture or as much deeper than what the anthropologist can usually deal with. In his book *The Foundations of Social Anthropology* Nadel expresses the following thoughts:

> We may take it for granted that there is some connection between the make-up of a culture and the particular personality (or personalities) of its human carriers. Yet in taking this connection to be a simple and obvious one, so simple and obvious that one can be inferred from the other, we run the risk of arguing in a circle and of using the word "personality" in an ambiguous sense. For by "personality" we can mean two things. We can mean, first, the sum-total of the overt modes of behaviour of an individual, in which we discern some integration and consistence, and which we thus understand to be facets or "traits" of that total, patterned entity. Or secondly, we can mean some basic mental make-up underlying the pattern of overt behaviour and accounting for it in the sense of a "hidden machine" or a causally effective set of factors. (Nadel 1951:405)

Nadel then refers to a distinction made by the psychologist, R. B. Cattell, between "surface traits" "which give us 'clusters' of intrinsically related characteristics of behavior observable in everyday life," and "source traits" or "factors," "which are extricated by analysis and have a causal significance, being possible explanations of how the actually existing cluster forms may have originated" (Cattell 1946:4). Nadel's reasoning goes as follows: If the anthropologist operates with the personality concept and wishes to ascertain the mental make-up of a group possessing a certain culture, he should resort only to tests and other techniques developed by psychology. If he wishes to "define the cultural patterns in terms of 'basic' psychological agencies," he "must examine them where they are ultimately rooted—in the individual" (Nadel 1951:407). But if the anthropologist approaches the personality merely from cultural observation, by means of direct inference, he can only reach the "surface traits." Even though he may infer the desires, motivations, and so forth, prompting the overt behavior he "penetrates, as it were, only a short distance beneath the surface;" for the desires and so forth are "simply implicit in the cultural mode of behavior," or "are merely its sustaining energies, and have no causal and explanatory significance" (Nadel 1951:405). Nadel concludes:

As long as we are inferring personality types from cultural observation we cannot legitimately claim any explanatory value for the personality concept; if we did, we should be committing the cardinal sin in science, namely, of pronouncing upon invariant relations between facts which are not "demonstrably separate." (Nadel 1951:407)

I think Nadel is wrong here. Psychological constructs, by virtue of the fact that they have to be inferred from linguistic data or other indirect evidences supplied by the actors, are certainly "demonstrably separate" from behavior which can be directly observed. Furthermore, gravitation is inferred from falling apples, rises and falls of tides, and movements of the moon, earth, and other heavenly bodies. Gravitation can never be seen anywhere except in terms of what it does, through the behavior of the objects which it controls or influences. Similarly physical hunger can only be inferred by stomach contractions, nausea (if the hunger is severe enough), or malnutrition of the body (as a result of prolonged hunger). No one can see hunger except through these and other concrete expressions of it. I have yet to hear from a scientist who denies the usefulness of the concept of gravitation or hunger, and who insists that correlating certain movements of the heavenly bodies with gravitation, or correlating certain physiological phenomena with hunger, is equivalent to commiting "the cardinal sin in science, namely, of pronouncing upon invariant relations between facts which are not demonstrably separate." As our knowledge progresses, we may conclude that the concept of gravitation or hunger is no longer adequate to account for certain phenomena, but we cannot deny that during a certain period of our scientific development these concepts have played crucial and organizing roles.

However, Nadel's arguments do point up one important matter, namely the personality which psychological anthropologists deal with is not the same as that of the individual psychologists. At least conceptually, the latter deal with the unique personality of the individual, but the former deal only with those characteristics of the individual's mind which are shared as part of a wider fabric of human minds. In Chapter 8 Kaplan discusses various attempts to conceptualize and understand the differences between the two kinds of reality, for example, by introducing the term "socially required" personality patterns as distinguished from the "actual modal" personality patterns. Yet the term "personality" possesses connotations that often lead the student to regard it as a complete entity in itself. Instead of seeing personality as a life-long process of interaction between the individual and his society and culture, he thinks of it as being some sort of reified end-product (of very early experiences according to orthodox Freudians, of somewhat later sociocultural forces according to many Neo-Freudians and social scientists), which is ready to act in this or that direction regardless of the sociocultural fields in which it has to operate continuously. It is true that the scholars have never quite said so in exact words. It is also true that "field theory" of Kurt Lewin or others has many advocates. But given the social scientist's individualist culture heritage of hero and martyr worship, and a Judaeo-Christian theological background of absolute conversion and final salvation, the one-sided finished-product view of personality would seem too "natural." Such a view must be resisted and the beginning of such a step is to eliminate the word personality from the title of our subdiscipline.

Some anthropologists may object to the new title of psychological anthropology on several grounds, though I see no insurmountable obstacles against it. One argument is that it may lead to proliferation of subdisciplines. But giving the subdiscipline a more logical name should not cause any more proliferation than culture-and-personality has done. In the second place, division of any large single discipline into subdisciplines is inevitable as our knowledge in that area grows. Seventy-five years or so ago it was as sufficient simply to be an anthropologist as it was to be a sinologist. But soon anthropology was divided into cultural anthropology, physical anthropology, and so forth, and we no longer find the term sinologist except in some ultraconservative academic pockets. The same phenomenon has occurred in biology, physics, chemistry, and even such subdisciplines as linguistics and geometry. The only caution that we must exercise in branching out is that we must make sure that the advances of knowledge are ahead of the subdivision and not vice versa.

Another argument against the new title is that it will turn out to be neither psychology nor anthropology, that it is a no man's land. This is not a fruitful argument. We have textbooks on physiological psychology, biochemistry, astrophysics, and psychosomatic medicine. There is not the slightest indication that the separate disciplines which have been so allied with each other have suffered intellectually. On the contrary psychosomatic medicine has enriched both psychology and medicine; and, without biochemistry, biology and chemistry would both have been poorer. The psychological anthropologist should certainly make use of the results not only in psychology but also in psychoanalysis, sociology, and even experimental psychology and philosophy wherever these are relevant and applicable. This is the way all sciences grow, like so many amoebae which extend a pseudopodium here and another there, retracting them here and there while their nuclei remain more or less constant.

Psychological Anthropology and Related Disciplines

To clarify our thoughts further, it may be advantageous to examine the relationship between psychological anthropology and a few other disciplines. In the short history of psychological anthropology as a subdiscipline the clinical sciences have figured largely. In fact the indebtedness of psychological anthropology to psychiatry and psychoanalysis is immeasurable. Anyone who knows anything about psychological anthropology can easily call to mind the significant roles of such clinicians as Abram Kardiner, Erik Erickson, Alexander Leighton, Karen Horney, Erich Fromm, Geza Roheim and associates, and of course the master himself, Sigmund

Freud. These students have, either singly or in collaboration with anthropologists, helped to make psychological anthropology grow immensely in stature, concepts, and volume of research.

However, psychological anthropology is not a clinical science and, while it has benefited from the clinical sciences, it has its own ways. In objectives, psychological anthropology is concerned with large numbers of individuals who are normal and functioning members of their societies. In methods of approach psychological anthropology follows the usually accepted scientific procedure of hypothesis formation, testing of hypothesis, cross-cultural validation of the result, and further refinement of the hypothesis. In this it must first be emphasized that psychological anthropology is not simply the psychology of the individual, and it must shun psychoanalysis of whole cultures in the manner that Freud arrived at his conclusion on the origin of totem and taboo (Freud 1919).

What psychological anthropology deals with are (*a*) the conscious or unconscious ideas shared by a majority of individuals in a given society as individuals (which can be subsumed under such terms as basic personality or modal personality (Linton 1945:130), both statistical or nearly statistical concepts) and (*b*) the conscious or unconscious ideas governing the action of many individuals in a given society as a group (sometimes described as group psychology, mob psychology, or collective conscience). Both of these are different from the unique psychology of the individual. It is not maintained that the ideas underlying the life pattern of a group and those of the actions of an individual are two distinct entities. In fact they form a continuum. There is much evidence to indicate that many individuals evaluate national or international affairs in terms of their own personal likes and dislikes, anxieties, or aspirations. But before the psychological anthropologist can conclude that one is rooted in the other, he must make sure that he is not arguing merely from analogy, that he has made sure he is not confusing broad trends of cultural development, which may be psychologically propelled, with specific institutional details, which are usually historically determined.

The damage to psychological anthropology by the failure to differentiate the normal from the abnormal is great. Admittedly the demarcation line between the normal and the abnormal is not clear. Nevertheless, even after allowing cultural differences, there is still undeniable evidence for certain core differences between them (Hsu 1952:238–248). The extension of the abnormal psychology of the individual into the normal pattern of the group was, I think, responsible for Freud's lopsided emphasis on the death instinct, and its continued lopsided emphasis by modern Freudians of many hues. That all human beings die is as indisputable as the fact that all human beings live. The extent to which some human beings apparently seek self-destruction in wars, suicides, alcoholism, and psychotic behavior, and the possible psychological mechanisms underlying such patterns of action have been brilliantly outlined by Jules Masserman (1955:647–649).

However, while the evidence in support of the universality of the life instinct among humans and animals is overwhelming, the evidence in support of the death "instinct" comes chiefly from the relatively abnormal. This is why the self-destructive tendencies are not common among the majority of any society. Furthermore, the incidence of suicide and homicide no less than delinquency and adventure vary from culture to culture. Clearly another type of explanation than a universal postulate of death instinct is indicated. It will probably be well for psychological anthropologists to be on guard against generalizing from the psychology of a minority of the relatively abnormal to that of a majority of the relatively normal when they make use of the psychiatrically derived resources, insights, and data.

Among all the behavioral sciences, psychological anthropology and social psychology have the future potentiality of developing the closest and most mutually enriching relationship with each other. Both disciplines deal with society and both deal with psychology, but they have been separated from each other so far in significant ways. We have seen that two of the points made in the preliminary discussions among the contributors to this volume were: (*a*) that the characteristic mark of culture-and-personality research is the emphasis on natural group differences along ethnic or societal lines, and so forth, as the subject matter, whereas social psychology often deals with experimentally produced group differences; and (*b*) that culture-and-personality scholars are concerned with behavior always with reference to its antecedents, while social psychologists are satisfied simply to describe its characteristics. I do not think the second distinction to be valid, for many studies in social psychology are attempts to discover the antecedents of behavior; and I think the first distinction is only partially valid, since psychological characteristics due to role, sex, and occupational affiliations are also problems of psychological anthropology.

What have so far differentiated psychological anthropologists from the social psychologists are found in three areas. First, psychological anthropology is cross-cultural in approach from its inception while social psychology has traditionally drawn its data from Western societies. Second, social psychology is quantitative and even, to a certain extent, experimental in orientation, while psychological anthropology has paid little attention to research designs and only lately awakened to the need for rigor in the matter of hypothesis formation and of verification.

In both of these connections the distance between the two disciplines is narrowing, and rightly so. Social psychologists have become increasingly more interested in cross-cultural validity of their generalizations. This anthropological contribution to psychology is well recognized by Campbell, a social psychologist, in Chapter 11 of this volume. A comparison of the earlier and later editions of many texts on social psychology shows far greater use of cross-cultural data in the later than in the earlier works, though some such as Klineberg (1940 and 1954) have always led among the pioneers in interdisciplinary thinking and research, while others such as Bogardus (1950) are less inclined in that direction. In fact, it is a rare textbook on social psychology today which does not contain at least references to Margaret Mead, Ruth Benedict, Geoffrey Gorer, Clyde Kluckhohn, Ralph Linton, M. J. Herskovits, John Whiting, or some other anthropologists. Psychological anthropologists, on their part, have become increasingly more sensitive to the importance of sophistication in research designs and quantification. The chapters by Wallace, Whiting, Aberle, Spiro, and D'Andrade in this volume and the works of Hallowell, Kluckhohn, Gillin, and others are, in different ways, objective evidence in this new direction. The psychological anthropologist may not agree with (or may not be able to do much about it at the moment even if he does agree with) some of the methodological points raised by Campbell in Chapter 11, but there is no doubt about the importance of such thinking to psychological anthropology. Psychological anthropology has already derived no small part of its methodological inspiration from social psychology and, as time goes on, its indebtedness to social psychology is likely to be even greater than its previous indebtedness to the clinical disciplines.

The third area in which psychological anthropology differs from social psychology thus far is that it deals not only with the effect of society and culture on personality (a basic concern of social psychology) but also with the role of personality characteristics in the development, formation, and change of culture and society. Chapters 7, 8, 12, 13, and 14 of the present volume touch upon this in different ways. Finally, in Chapter 15 the reader will find a hypothesis to investigate the mechanism underlying the mutual influences between the individual society and culture. For a sound theory which aims at explaining the relationship between man and culture must not only account for the origin of psychological characteristics as they are molded by the patterns of child rearing, social institutions, and ideologies but must also account for the origin, development, and change in these child-rearing practices, institutions, and ideologies. It is a well-known fact that societies and cultures do change, often slowly but sometimes drastically. Since human beings are not so many helpless creatures simply being pushed by external forces such as geographical calamities, foreign conquests, fate, gods, or the unaccountable vicissitudes of some superorganic, we must at least find part of the explanations for cultural and social changes in the interaction between the human minds and the societies and cultures in which they operate.

❧   ❧   ❧   ❧   ❧

At the beginning of this attempt at clarifying our thoughts on psychological anthropology, I noted the difficulties besetting such a venture. What I hoped to do was not to close the discussion but to keep it going. Furthermore, just as a mere matter of emphasis or point of view separates cultural anthropology from social anthropology, so psychological anthropology is similarly differentiated from its related disciplines. For example, a cultural anthropologist will ultimately come to analyze the ideas behind the diffusion of certain cultural traits and complexes; a social anthropologist will ultimately look at the material wealth involved in the different forms of social organization, exactly as the psychological anthropologist will ultimately relate the conscious or unconscious ideas to both particular cultural end results and particular human relationships. It is probably desirable, however, for the student from one viewpoint to hold on to his particular viewpoint as he probes deeper and deeper into his data, or else he may be hopelessly enmeshed in them without guideposts to go forward or backward. The significance of such a viewpoint to the field worker is comparable to that of the "ego" to the maker of a kinship chart. As the maker of a kinship chart cannot change the "ego" in it without getting lost, the field worker who shifts from one viewpoint to another, or has no viewpoint at all, is likely to bring back little that is of coherent significance.

BIBLIOGRAPHY

BOGARDUS, E. E.
    1950   Fundamentals of social psychology. New York, Appleton-Century-Crofts.

CATTELL, R. B.
    1946   Description and measurement of personality. Yonkers, N.Y., World Book Co.

EVANS-PRITCHARD, E. E.
    1954   Nuer religion. London, Oxford University Press.

FREUD, SIGMUND
    1919   Totem and taboo. London (reprinted in The Basic Writings of Sigmund Freud, 1938, The Modern Library, New York, Random House).

GILLIN, JOHN
    1939   Personality in preliterate societies. American Sociological Review 4:681–702.

HART, C. W. M.
    1954   The sons of Turimpi. American Anthropologist 54, 2, Part I, 242–261.

HERSKOVITS, M. J.
    1948   Man and his works. New York, Alfred Knopf.

HSU, F. L. K.
    1952   Anthropology or psychiatry: A definition of objectives and their implications. Southwestern Journal of Anthropology 8:227–250.

KAPLAN, BERT
    1954   A study of Rorschach responses in four cultures. Papers of Peabody Museum of Archaeology and Ethnology, Harvard University, Vol. 42, No. 2.

KLINEBERG, OTTO
    1954   Social psychology. New York, Henry Holt (1st ed., 1940).

KLUCKHOHN, CLYDE and O. H. MOWRER
    1944   Culture and personality: A conceptual scheme. American Anthropologist 46:4.

KLUCKHOHN, CLYDE, HENRY A. MURRAY, and DAVID SCHNEIDER
    1953   Personality in nature, society, and culture. 2d ed., New York, Alfred Knopf.

KLUCKHOHN, CLYDE
    1954   Culture and behavior. In handbook of social psychology, Gardner Lindzey (ed.), Cambridge, Mass., Addison-Wesley Press.

KROEBER, A. L.
    1948   Anthropology. New York, Harcourt Brace & Co.

LINTON, R.
   1945   Cultural background of personality. New York, D. Appleton Century Co.

MASSERMAN, JULES
   1955   Dynamic psychiatry. Philadelphia, W. B. Saunders Co.

NADEL, S. F.
   1951   Foundations of social anthropology. Glencoe, Ill., Free Press.

WHITE, LESLIE A.
   1949   The science of culture. New York, Farrar, Strauss & Co.

INTRODUCTION TO PART I
AREA

THE TREATMENT of the subject of psychological anthropology by area presents some difficulties. Culture and personality differences between tribal groups and national groups within these large areas are sometimes so great that the contributors will either have to generalize on a relatively superficial level or else have to confine themselves to a few selected studies which already possess intensity and depth.

There is no adequate answer to these difficulties. In a work of this scope it is simply not possible to gain the intensity and depth attainable in a field report on a single tribe or community. A general picture of the psychology of a region like North America or even Japan is bound to contain fewer details than a monograph on the culture and personality of Polish peasants inhabiting a village in Ruthenia. The contributors themselves are keenly aware of the danger of overgeneralization, or generalization based on scanty data. LeVine has indicated, with reference to Africa, some of the clearest instances of fallacies resulting from such procedures; Honigmann has assembled a fine array of studies among the North American Indians in which more refined designs and techniques have yielded composite psychological characteristics of peoples each scattered over a large area that bear out the purely qualitative and inferential pictures arrived at years earlier. There are many social and cultural mechanisms which, on closer inspection, make for psychological standardization of large communities. Communal, tribal, or national myths are some of these. Communication and diffusion processes are others.

However, even in this section of the book, our interest is only partially areal. The areal arrangement is convenient in providing the reader with a panorama of the most significant works of psychological anthropology in the area of his curiosity. But a problem orientation is present in this section of the book, as in the subsequent sections. Norbeck and DeVos discuss personality factors affecting differential Japanese acculturation on different continents. LeVine summarizes problems of infant experiences and the family environment; psychocultural interpretation of ritual, witchcraft, and dreams; and the problem of differential incidence and types of mental illness. Honigmann treats the problems of values and of model personality. Gladwin analyses the contributions of Mead and co-workers and their use of a broadly framed learning theory, and of the Kardiner-Linton group and their use of a revised Freudian psychology. In these and other materials the problem-minded reader will find much that is informative and stimulating.

The last two chapters analyze the composite psychological characteristics of some large, modern, and complex societies, relating the individual aspirations to the over-all thought and action patterns of each group. On the one hand, they indicate fresh approaches to the question of generalization on huge societies. Too often national character studies have been attacked on *a priori* grounds, that it is "impossible" to gauge the psychological characteristics underlying complex civilizations, with hundreds of millions of individuals living in them. But the basic problem is surely one of level of generalization. If we look for individual differences, there is no shortage of data which compel us to observe that no two individuals are identical. But if we raise our sights to a different level, we shall at once see that millions of human beings interact with each other, voluntarily or involuntarily, in any large society on any one day, often sight unseen, apparently without any significant difficulties. This relatively smooth interaction among strangers in any large, modern society is a remarkable reality, which will be impossible without some high degree of uniformity, not merely in externally visible laws, customs, procedures, and usages but also in externally invisible ideas, emotions, expectations, and faiths. Yet these two analyses arrive at very different conclusions. Is this due to the differences in point of view of the two authors? Is this due to differences in the kinds of fact upon which the two authors based their generalizations? Are the two papers products of different levels of abstraction? Or are they evidence that we must employ more precise methods?

Chapter 2

JAPAN

EDWARD NORBECK,
William Marsh Rice University, and

GEORGE DE VOS,
University of California

THE objectives of this chapter are to review research in the field of
Japanese culture and personality, and to appraise it from the standpoint of the contribution it has made to theory and the promise of
future contribution that it holds.

Anthropological interest in Japan and the Japanese is old, but
until World War II it was left principally to native Japanese
scholars, whose publications rarely reached the Western world. For
decades before the war, Western writers had made many impressionistic observations on the character of the Japanese, but writings
on this subject by scholars trained in psychology, sociology, and
anthropology are principally postwar. Entry of the United States
into the war served in several ways to direct the attention of American social scientists to Japanese culture, and it is during the war
years that research on Japan using modern techniques of person-
ality-and culture-began, principally under the sponsorship of the
United States government. The first published studies are papers
by LaBarre (1945), Gorer (1942, 1943), and others which attempt
to describe the Japanese personality and relate it to cultural institutions of child training. As is well known, Ruth Benedict's *The
Chrysanthemum and the Sword* also sprang from research conducted during the war under governmental subsidy.

Since the end of the war, the number of American social scientists engaged in research on Japan has grown, and scholarly writings
on Japanese culture have increased greatly. We no longer regard
Embree's *Suye Mura* as modal for Japanese communities. As a result of sociological and ethnological research, we have become aware
of many regional distinctions in Japanese culture and differences

along lines of occupation and social class. We have also become increasingly aware that Japanese culture is in a state of rapid transition so that observations made at one point in time are often quickly outdated.

Research on Japan concerned with the relationship between personality and culture began with American scholars. Since the end of World War II, Japanese scholars have also engaged in research in this field on their own culture, and interest in the subject among native scholars is growing. Publication of a Japanese journal concerned with studies using projective techniques (*Japanese Journal of Projective Techniques*) began in 1954. A society composed of approximately 30 psychologists and anthropologists called *Nihon Bunka to Nihonjin no Shinrigakuteki Kenkyū no Kai* (Society for the Psychological Study of Japanese Culture and the Japanese People) was formed in 1958. During the past decade many relevant publications in the Japanese language have appeared, and several research projects concerned with Japanese personality and culture are now being conducted by Japanese social scientists. The combined research of native and foreign scholars makes a surprisingly large total, and Japan is probably unique in the field of culture-and-personality in being the focus of fairly extensive study by both natives and foreigners.

We shall review both Western and Japanese research that has been completed and discuss projects now under way. As a matter of convenience we shall classify these studies under five major headings that are not mutually exclusive:

1. Broad Approaches to Understanding National Character
2. Content Analyses of Forms of Expressive Behavior
3. Studies Using Projective Techniques
4. Studies of Early Socialization Patterns
5. Studies of the Japanese Overseas

Judgment as to the kind of research and the specific studies to include has, of course, been in part arbitrary. We have not limited ourselves to research conducted by anthropologists, but have included publications in social, clinical, and child psychology, in psychiatry, and in other fields when these studies have dealt with questions of the relationship between culture and personality. No attempt will be made to review all publications relevant to Japanese culture and personality. Many publications, especially in the fields of psychology and psychiatry, have been omitted or mentioned only in passing because they make no attempt to relate traits of personality to cultural determinants. For lack of space, a very large group of studies of Japanese culture prepared by ethnologists, sociologists, historians, economists, and political scientists, both Japanese and Western, are not discussed. Omission is made with full awareness that these publications are relevant to an understanding of Japanese culture and personality, as they provide vital information on such matters as differences in culture by region and class and trends of cultural change.

Studies of National Character

Ruth Benedict's *The Chrysanthemum and the Sword* is probably the only major Western publication on Japan that consensus would place under the heading of studies of national character. The impact of this work upon both the scholarly world and the general public of Japan was surprisingly great. Translated into Japanese, it was widely read and served as a strong stimulus to Japanese scholarly interest in personality and culture. An indication of the importance of Benedict's work is afforded by the fact that it served as the topic for a series of seminars, well publicized in scholarly circles, in which prominent Japanese scholars participated. A summary of the Japanese critique of Benedict's methodology and conclusions has been given us by John Bennett and Michio Nagai (1953), and we shall mention here only the chief criticism that her study presents a static picture of ideal upper class patterns of a time gone by, and ignores distinctions by social class and changes through time. Jean Stoetzel's postwar study, *Without the Chrysanthemum and the Sword,* points up change and indicates that much of what Benedict describes does not apply to the modern youth of Japan. Benedict's work not only stimulated interest in Japanese character but also led to field research by Japanese scholars, notably T. Kawashima (1951), on modes and differences in conceptions of the values in interpersonal relations (*chū, on, giri*) with which her study had dealt. This research summarizes interviews with country people showing that these cultural ideals are less strongly held by them, especially by young people, than Benedict reports.

Benedict's attempt to delineate Japanese character stands out also from the standpoint of methodology. As one of the pioneer studies of "culture at a distance," it points out the potentialities of this approach. As a result of subsequent field research in Japan and the critique of the study by Japanese scholars, we are given a better idea of its limitations.

Since the publication of *The Chrysanthemum and the Sword*, the most extensive research aimed at understanding Japanese national character has been the interdisciplinary studies conducted from 1953 to 1955 by the Human Relations Research Group, headed by Tsuneo Muramatsu, Professor of Psychiatry at Nagoya National University. Included in the group were Japanese scholars from various disciplines and one American, George De Vos. The principal objective of this project was to determine both modes and regional differences in cultural values as these are related to types of personality. With the efforts of as many as 30 researchers, samples were taken of attitudes and customs of urban and rural populations of central and southwestern Japan. Data were also gathered on social and economic backgrounds, and a number of families selected as modal were subjected to intensive interviews. Principal test instruments used were the F Scale, derived from American studies of the authoritarian personality; two opinion scales devised to test attitudes toward familial relations and "liberal-traditional" attitudes toward Japanese values; the Rorschach test; the Thematic Apperception Test modified for Japanese culture; a problem situation test; figure drawings; a "child-parent problem" test, and questionnaires on customs of child training. Photographs were also taken to illustrate mother-child relations during the first few years of life.

Samples totaling 250 individuals were obtained from three rural settlements, a mountain community depending for subsistence on farming and forestry, a fishing community, and a lowland rice-farming community, which represent the spectrum of the conventional scholarly Japanese classification of types of rural communities.

A sample of over 2,000 individuals was obtained in the cities of Nagoya and Okayama, although not all persons of this group were subjected to the entire battery of tests. Data gathered under this research project are still in the process of analysis and interpretation. Although no generalizations concerning modal traits of the Japanese personality have as yet emerged, a series of publications presenting interpretations of smaller scope have appeared or are now in press.[1] Results of these studies will be discussed in this paper.

A second major research project aimed at determining regional variations in traits of personality and the cultural factors which have brought them into existence is now in progress under the direction of Seiichi Izumi of Tokyo University. This project is also

---

[1] These include articles by Marui, Murakami, De Vos, and Wagatsuma, cited in bibliography.

interdisciplinary. It makes extensive use of projective tests and includes among its objectives an assessment of national character. Research is centered upon northeastern Japan and other areas which have not previously been subjected to intensive investigation using the techniques of culture-and-personality.

A number of studies by Japanese scholars, some of which are discussed below, touch in varying degree upon Japanese national character. A recent book (Sofue and Wagatsuma 1959), based upon Benedict's work and other published accounts, compares traits of personality of Japanese, Americans, and Europeans. No synthetic analysis approaching the stature of Benedict's work has, however, yet emerged. Conservative scholars, both Japanese and foreign, are well aware that the present state of knowledge of regional, class, and occupational differences makes generalizations on the Japanese personality difficult, but the objective of an over-all characterization has not been cast aside.

Content Analysis of Forms of Expressive Behavior

Postwar publications by Japanese social psychologists have presented a number of content analyses of Japanese movies, popular songs, life-counseling columns in newspapers, novels, and common folk-sayings, attempting to determine the values which stand out most strongly in these forms of expressive behavior.[2] The technique is American derived, and in some instances the Japanese analysts have made comparisons with similar research in the United States. All of these studies have bearing on the subject of national character, although none attempts to be comprehensive in the manner of Benedict. We shall here present only a sample of the conclusions of these reports.

The most ambitious of these impressionistic studies is Hiroshi Minami's *Nihonjin no Shinri* (Psychology of the Japanese), which attempts to outline "those modes of feeling, thinking, and expressing which are peculiar to the Japanese." Minami uses in a highly intuitive way popular songs, ideas expressed in fiction, common sayings, writings on army life, essays by successful men, and similar nonscholarly sources to deduce a number of themes or motifs. One wonders whether the themes are, in fact, inferred or whether the raw data are used to buttress preformulated themes. The work nevertheless contains observations that seem apt and, like others of its kind, provides information and interpretations that might serve

[2] Many of these have been translated into English. See Kato, ed. 1959.

as starting points for future research. In a rather lengthy discussion of conceptions of happiness and unhappiness, for example, Minami observes that the Japanese seldom express happiness. Words conveying this idea are few, and when they are used, the turn of expression sounds awkward. The Japanese vocabulary is, however, rich in words denoting unhappiness. Many aphorisms, songs, writings, and personal philosophies of life contain as their central theme ways to cope with unhappiness, and attempts are made to justify unhappiness on the grounds that it serves a useful purpose, as in ensuring the proper ordering of familial relations. Other major sections of Minami's work are entitled The Conception of the Self, Rationality and Irrationality, Spiritualism versus Sensualism, and Patterns of Human Relationships. No attempt is made to present a systematic characterization of the Japanese.

An analysis of life-counseling columns in newspapers (Kato 1959) reports that letters from the lovelorn are much fewer than is characteristic of similar columns in American papers. Letters are placed under three classifications: those concerned with group or international situations; those which center on human relations with one other individual; and those expressing concern with height, weight, looks, and other physical features of the individual. Among adults the greatest source of distress is interpersonal relations in the family. Letters concerning relations between two individuals are principally between a young male and a young female. Among young girls the greatest concern is expressed over their own physical features. A majority of letters from mature adults consist of complaints made against persons of higher social status than the writers. Wives complain more about husbands than husbands do about wives. This observation, it may be noted, seems contrary to the stereotype of the uncomplaining Japanese woman.

An analysis of the lyrics of 61 postwar songs (Kato 1959), judged to be the most popular on the basis of sales of phonograph records, reports that the majority are sentimental, sometimes telling of love but never expressing happy sentimentality. The authors find in the songs four prevailing motifs: pessimism, fatalism, "existentialism" (explained as unexpressed feelings of loneliness and helplessness), and "premodern humanism" (feudal values in interpersonal relationships).

A useful review and critique of early postwar Japanese writings of similar kind that relate to traits of the Japanese personality has been made by Dore (1953).

Studies Using Projective Techniques

Among the techniques of personality and culture research, Japanese scholars have made by far the greatest use of projective tests.[3] Unfortunately, analysis has generally been confined to interpretation of the tests themselves with little or no attempt to relate findings to elements of culture. Results of most studies using the Rorschach, for example, are relatively crude statistics on the types of responses, giving means and percentages of color, movement, animal content, and whole responses. During World War II and shortly afterward a number of studies were conducted by Japanese scholars with a Rorschach in which certain standard blots were modified and new ones added. It is, of course, highly doubtful that the results of these studies can be directly comparable with those based upon the standard Rorschach. For lack of other opportunity to learn, many Japanese researchers using the Rorschach and other projective tests in normative, nonclinical studies have been self-taught from reading American publications, and their interpretations often indicate a lack of familiarity with the potentials and limitations of the techniques. It must be added that these scholars were sometimes emulating the manner of use of projective tests followed by a number of American anthropologists some years ago.

Another weakness of Japanese scholars employing projective tests has been a general reluctance to interpret findings of the tests. Even when interpretation is made, the basis for the conclusions presented is seldom clearly stated. Thus, although a number of studies attempt to depict modal personalities for individual villages or occupational groups, and many others describe types of responses, they are generally of little value except insofar as they might constitute acceptable raw data.

Recent research using projective tests appears to be more promising, and we have already noted two of the major projects which employ them. The Human Relations Research Group at Nagoya University is presently preparing a report of the Rorschach tests of over 700 urban and rural residents. This report is probably unique

---

[3] Formosan natives were given Rorschach tests by a Japanese psychologist in 1930. This is said to constitute the earliest trial of the Rorschach on a primitive people. A fairly extensive program of psychological testing of Formosan aborigines was conducted from that time until World War II. Projective tests have also recently been given to the Ainu by Japanese researchers. In very recent years research by Japanese social scientists has again expanded into areas outside Japan, and projective tests have been used on native populations of Nepal, Thailand, Brazil, Peru, and several other countries. Analyses of most of these data have not as yet been made or have not been published.

in the field of culture and personality because it is based upon research using many projective and nonprojective techniques, and is the first large sample of its kind that crosscuts occupational groups and social classes of a culturally elaborate, highly stratified society. Findings with the Rorschach (T. Murakami and others, personal communications) indicate that regional and class differences within the area tested, central and southwestern Japan, are generally slight. On other tests, however, certain significant differences appear—as noted in the pages that follow. Reports by Japanese scholars on smaller Rorschach samples from other regions of Japan support the interpretations of the Nagoya group. A recent report (Kodama 1953) listing popular responses to the Rorschach by Japanese adolescents of the Tokyo area, for example, is strikingly similar to the findings of the Nagoya University Human Relations Research Group. Japanese responses to the Rorschach indicate characteristics markedly different from those regarded as general for the population of the United States. They may be summarized briefly as follows:

The number of responses is low in all social groups. Rejections are very high (from 20 to 25 per cent) on colored card 9, and black and white cards 6 and 7. There is a relatively high rate of rejection of card 10, which seems related to an inability or reluctance to use the details on this complex card. Difficulty in handling color freely and other indications attest to difficulty with spontaneous affect. Although markedly lower among urban residents than among rural residents, personal rigidity is generally very high in comparison with norms for the United States. A great deal of organizational drive in the use of intellectual functions is indicated; the Japanese subjects are prone to push for complex, integrated whole responses. The sense of reality is generally very adequate. Although sometimes imaginative, responses include little fantasy of an extreme sort in directions considered primitive or psychopathological. The form level is characteristically quite high. Labile color responses are usually perceptually tolerated when they are incorporated in some complex overall concept. Pure color by itself is almost completely lacking. These and other signs attest to the effectiveness of ego control that appears to be characteristic throughout the population.

Although less commonly used than the Rorschach until recently, other projective tests have been employed to interpret Japanese values and attitudes as well as personality dynamics, and they have yielded interesting results. Basing his arguments principally on responses to the Thematic Apperception Test and a problem-situation test, De Vos (1960a) argues against the widely held view that Japanese culture may best be regarded as a "shame" culture in a guilt-shame dichotomy. He holds that the strong achievement drive so often noted among the Japanese is not to be understood solely in terms of shame-oriented concern with community standards, but is also linked with a deep undercurrent of guilt. The Japanese seem to suffer from guilt which is not associated with any complex of supernatural sanctions, but is instead derived from the system of loyalties which cements the structure of their traditional society. Guilt in Japanese is hidden from Western observation because we do not understand Japanese familial relationships, and because conscious emphasis on external sanctions helps to disguise the underlying feelings of guilt which, severely repressed, are not obvious to the Japanese themselves. The keystone toward understanding Japanese guilt is held to be the nature of interpersonal relationships within the Japanese family, particularly the relations of children with the mother. The Japanese mother, without conscious intent, has perfected techniques of inducing guilt in her children by such means as quiet suffering. She takes the burden of responsibility for their behavior and, as also with bad conduct on the part of her husband, will often manifest self-reproach if her children conduct themselves badly or in any way fail to meet the standards of success set for the community. If one fails to meet social expectations, he thereby hurts his mother, and he also hurts other familial members; as a result, he suffers unhappiness and feelings of guilt.[4]

Another study based upon responses to the Thematic Apperception Test (De Vos and Wagatsuma 1959) reports a high incidence of concern over death and illness, which the authors interpret as introjection of guilt. Death and illness of parents, as seen in cards of the Thematic Apperception Test by respondents, is very often related by them in stories to failure of a child to comply with parental wishes in entering an arranged marriage, or in meeting other standards of behavior and achievement. Another recurrent theme found in responses is that of expiation; achievement of honor or success on the part of a child atones for egocentric or profligate behavior. The manner of introjecting guilt among the Japanese is thus seen to be related to the strong drive toward achievement that Western observers have long noted and pondered upon. The Japanese interpretation of the meaning of illness is also contrasted by the authors with that of various groups of American Indians who, in attributing illness to witchcraft, make use of the mechanism of projection.

An unpublished report on Japanese attitudes toward arranged marriages (Wagatsuma and De Vos) analyzes responses to the

---

[4] For another approach to the subjects of shame and guilt, see Hsu (1949).

Thematic Apperception Test and compares them with data derived by techniques eliciting more consciously controlled attitudes. Although current public opinion in Japan is increasingly lenient toward love marriage, as opposed to the traditional arranged marriage, individuals who have contracted love marriages are often reported to feel considerable guilt and inner restriction. Dependent upon the level of consciousness involved, attitudes and emotional reactions toward the two forms of marriage differ. A phenomenon labeled "psychological lag" appears to exist. In responses to the Thematic Apperception Test many respondents give clear evidence of strong internalized feelings against love marriage, although, as revealed by opinion surveys and direct interviews, when speaking on a conscious level these individuals express approval of this form of union.

The Thematic Apperception Test has also indicated differences in attitudes between occupational and social groups that conform with and amplify observations made by ethnologists using traditional techniques of interviewing and observation. A farm community, in which the so-called "traditional" Japanese pattern of hierarchical authority according to age, sex, order of birth, and status in the household is well established, is compared with a fishing community, where social relationships within the family do not follow such a strict hierarchy (De Vos & Wagatsuma, in press). Responses to tests indicate markedly less rigidity, freer expression of aggression between the sexes, and less guilt in connection with intrafamilial relations among people in the fishing community.

Projective tests have also been put to use in the study of Japanese communities abroad, and, to a lesser extent, in research on child training. Discussion of these studies follows.

Studies of Early Socialization

Japanese customs of rearing and socializing children have been the focus of more research in the field of personality-and-culture than any other subject. Perhaps the outstanding feature of published accounts resulting from this research has been conflict of opinion. The principal controversy in the entire field of Japanese culture-and-personality has revolved about interpretations of the influence of practices of child rearing on the adult personality. Early wartime studies conducted in the United States emphasized customs of toilet training and weaning, and contended that Japanese practices, particularly in toilet training, were harsh and strongly influenced the adult personality. In this as well as other instances where interpretations have conflicted, differences by region and class, changes in practices, and cultural influences other than child training were overlooked or ignored. Haring's (1953) observation seems noteworthy here. The Japanese personality, he states, is what might be expected of the people of a police state.

The pioneer studies of Gorer and LaBarre, long looked upon with question, were based upon information drawn from a limited number of informants residing in the United States who appear to have held middle-class ideas of child training current at that time. The results of an investigation of practices of toilet training among Hawaiian Japanese (Sikkema 1948) presented conflicting data, and cast further doubt on the idea that severity of toilet training contributed to the compulsive personality traits of the Japanese. The sample in this instance was composed of individuals stemming principally from rural Japan, who had presumably been exposed to American ideas.

More recently, Betty Lanham (1956) has reported on a fairly extensive investigation in a community of southwestern Japan on practices of weaning, toilet training, and forms of sanctions used to discipline children. Her statements, based upon a questionnaire devised and administered by Japanese associates, generally agree with unquantified observations made by Margaret and Edward Norbeck (1956) in a fishing community approximately 200 miles from Lanham's community. Miss Lanham concludes that although there are a number of sharp differences between Japan and the United States in other customs of child training, practices of toilet training differ little.

Lanham's report has been criticized by Japanese scholars, who report different findings. The greatest point of dispute has been practices of weaning. Japanese scholars (e.g., Hoshino, Sofue, and others 1958) have expressed doubt about Lanham's information. Basing their statements upon field investigations of their own in Nagano Prefecture and, especially, upon huge samplings by pediatricians in the Tokyo area, they find that weaning begins and ends earlier than Lanham reports. Part of the argument here appears to hinge on the definition of weaning. Japanese scholars hold the view the weaning begins with the *introduction* of supplementary "solid" foods, and thus the span of time from the beginning of "weaning" until the child ceases to nurse is long. Research planned or presently under way by Lanham, Sofue, Hoshino, and others should do much to clear up points of contention in this and other matters of child training.

One of the more noteworthy of the Japanese studies that does take cognizance of differences by social class (Ishiguro 1955) describes practices of child training in three Japanese social strata called "old middle class," "new middle class," and "lower class," and compares these practices with those reported for the United States. As Lanham also notes, the nursing period in Japan is reported to be longer than in the United States, and nursing tends to be on demand rather than on a fixed time schedule. Toilet training begins and ends earlier in Japan, but, unlike circumstances in the United States, control over urination precedes bowel control. In both countries weaning is abrupt in approximately 20 per cent of the cases reported. Practices of the American lower class are reported to resemble most those of the Japanese "old middle class," and practices of the American middle class are most similar to those of the Japanese "new middle class" and "lower class." Although this study recognizes that change has occurred in customs of child training (the category "new middle class" is composed of salaried men in industry, commerce, and public service, a relatively new social group in Japan), it is dependent upon the recall of the mothers who served as informants, and is thus subject to distortion—probably in the direction of modern trends of change in these practices.

A subject of recent investigations by Japanese scholars has been the psychological effect of the *ejiko*, a type of cradle for children used over a wide area of rural Japan. The most common type of *ejiko* is made of straw and is bowl-shaped. When it is necessary for the mother to leave the child unattended, it is placed in a squatting position within the cradle, wrapped in a quilt, and tied by a rope so that hardly any movement of the body is possible. Preliminary papers on the distribution and local varieties of the *ejiko* have been published (Sofue 1958; Sue 1958; Sofue, Sue, and Murakami 1958). An intensive study directed toward determining its psychological significance was conducted in 1958 and 1959 by Sofue and others in a hamlet of Nagano Prefecture. It is interesting to note that practices of child training differ with social class even in this small rural community (Sue, personal communication). This project includes the use of projective tests, and the data gathered will be compared with those obtained from other communities. It is not clear how the researchers intend to relate the findings of the tests to the custom of using the *ejiko*, or how the possible effects of use of the *ejiko* may be distinguished from those of other childhood experiences.

Increasingly, both Japanese and American scholars engaged in research on Japanese practices of child rearing, as related to the adult personality, have come to realize the weaknesses of an approach that deals with formal customs such as toilet training or the use of the cradle. They have looked to multiple and less formalized factors, including the identity of the adults concerned in the socialization process and affective relations between the socializers and the socialized. Greater attention is now given to such questions as the length of time the child sleeps with its parents, who bathes a child or accompanies it in the bath, and the manner of gratifying impulses (e.g., Caudill 1959c).

An indication of the multiplicity of factors involved in the formation of the adult personality is provided by the results of a psychological testing of *Kibei*, American-born Japanese who, after spending their early childhood in the United States, are taken to Japan for a number of years for schooling, and then return to the United States (De Vos 1955). From the standpoints of personality rigidity and maladjustment, the *Kibei* were generally intermediate to the *Issei* and *Nisei*. If the earliest practices of socialization are in fact the most powerful, little difference should of course be found between *Kibei* and *Nisei*, as they appear to have been exposed to essentially identical practices of training in infancy and early childhood. Assimilation of Japanese values later in childhood and during adolescence seems to be the source of conflict for the *Kibei*.

Although not focused directly on the subject of customs of child rearing, research presently being conducted by Ezra Vogel on the linkage between intrafamilial social relations and emotional disturbances has much relevance. The project consists of the intensive study of familial relations among the members of twelve Japanese families of comparable social and economic backgrounds, of which six have "normal" children and the remaining six have one or more emotionally disturbed children under intensive treatment at the Japanese National Institute for Mental Health. Vogel reports that the emotional attachment of the Japanese child to his family is greater than that of the American child and is maintained for a longer period, and that tensions arising out of relationships with kin are more common in Japan. Conflicts within the family follow a limited number of characteristic patterns, such as tension between a man's wife and his mother, and tension on the part of the wife because of the husband's habit of seeking sexual and other gratifications outside the home. The degree and type of conflict among adults are related to the intensity and type of emotional disturbance of the children. This research is organized so as to allow direct comparison with similar studies of the Harvard Psychological Clinic on familial relations among Irish-Americans, Italian-Americans, and old Americans.

Somewhat more peripheral to the subject of child rearing is William Caudill's current research on the subject of impulse gratification and restraint. Basing his statements on responses to a picture test similar to the Thematic Apperception Test, Caudill (1959c) reports that there are differences between Japanese and Americans in what is ego-syntonic (consciously acceptable to the ego and needing no repression). For example, a Japanese mother's sensual gratification in nursing her infant is consciously acceptable to her, whereas the feeling of gratification is generally repressed by the American mother. The Japanese are also described as being more ego-syntonic with reference to certain forms of mutual dependency within the family. A young man, for example, may remain dependent upon his mother for many satisfactions long past the age that would be considered appropriate in the United States. The Japanese are said to be much less ego-syntonic than Americans in direct expression of aggression. Caudill (1959b) relates the hypochondriasis manifest in the Japanese to their inability to express direct aggression toward others easily and the consequent deflection toward the self in various forms including hypochondriasis.

An interesting and useful film on child rearing gives a visual comparison of Japanese, Indian Hindu, French, and Canadian practices (National Film Board of Canada 1959). The Japanese section, prepared with the advice of William Caudill, depicts the events of a day in the life of an infant girl, 10 months of age, from a farming family of the Kantō Plain, near Tokyo.

Other current research using a personality and culture approach and bearing upon the subject of child training is De Vos's study of juvenile delinquents in the Tokyo area (1960b). Data were gathered by means of conventional interviews, Q-sort cards, the Thematic Apperception Test, and the Rorschach on the attitudes of juvenile delinquents toward their parents and their conceptions of the social roles of mother and father. These data will be compared with findings on a control group of nondelinquent Japanese youth and with similar material previously gathered on delinquent and nondelinquent groups of juveniles, including Negroes and Mexican-Americans, in the United States.

Japanese child psychologists and pediatricians have carried out a considerable number of studies of child training, but these are often fragmentary, and they have not attempted to analyze systematically the interrelationships between child rearing and the formation of personality. Little consideration is given in these studies to the social class of the informants used. The studies are also characterized by some degree of "culture-blindness." Much that is pertinent to an understanding of the relationships between personality and culture is overlooked simply because it is so familiar to the scholars themselves that it escapes notice or is deemed unworthy of it.

Although they have wider significance, a group of unique papers by the Japanese psychologist Takeo Doi (1956, 1958, 1960) touch indirectly upon child training. Doi calls attention to Japanese words and concepts as illustrative of Japanese psychology, and states that terms referring to the emotions and interpersonal relationships often have no suitable English equivalents. He cites as an example the noun *amae,* derived from the verb *amaeru,* which he defines in English (1958, writer's English abstract) as *to depend and presume upon another's love or indulge in another's kindness.* (A popular Japanese-English dictionary [Masuda 1957] translates this word, dependent upon context, as: *to baby; to act like a spoiled child; to coax, to be coquettish; to fawn upon; and to avail oneself of another's kindness.*) In Western psychological terms, Doi holds, the word *amae* (or *amaeru*) has a central meaning referring to dependancy needs. To Japanese minds it usually means what a child feels about or how he acts toward his parents, particularly his mother, and thus it distinctly relates to the nursing period. Thinking in terms of this familiar Japanese concept, Doi states, easily led Japanese psychoanalysis to formulate theories about the importance of oral dependency in the formation of neuroses, an interpretation which has only recently become the focus of psychoanalytic workers in Western nations.

Studies of Japanese Overseas

A group of studies which give promise of being particularly useful in a number of respects is that conducted on Japanese immigrants to foreign countries and their descendants. Sociologists, educational psychologists, anthropologists, and scholars in other disciplines of social science have engaged in research of this kind, which has been concerned principally with Japanese in the continental United States and Hawaii. Interest has grown to include Japanese in South America and Canada, where field research has recently been conducted or is now in progress.

One of the earliest studies was an investigation by educational psychologists of school behavior of *Nisei* children on the Pacific coast. An extensive series of studies, most of them summarized by E. K. Strong (1934), compares Caucasian-American and Japanese-American grade school and high school children in intellectual functioning and related features of personality. These studies fail to make any explicit use of the concept of culture and for this reason appear naive in the light of present-day theory and knowledge in the social sciences. They bring out distinctly, however, a number of traits that characterize the *Nisei*. Psychological tests indicated no differences in the intellectual functioning of *Nisei* and Caucasian-American children, although they did indicate different artistic sensibilities. The sense of composition and the use of line of the *Nisei* was found to be superior; their use of perspective inferior. Other traits noted are of greater interest. One of these is close conformance with middle-class American norms of behavior. Behavior of the *Nisei* children in the schools is described as characteristically docile, patient, and respectful and obedient to the teachers. Motivation to achievement is strong, and it is clear that parents of the *Nisei* exerted strong pressure to inculcate in their children the idea that meeting American standards of achievement and other norms of behavior is desirable. *Nisei* students tended to earn higher grades for school work than others and to receive greater recognition from teachers for exemplary conduct.

Interest in the Japanese of the Pacific coast and elsewhere in the United States was heightened during World War II, when many were sent to relocation centers. A number of published accounts deal with the adjustment of the Japanese to life in these camps and the new surroundings to which they moved when the war ended and the camps were closed (e.g., Leighton 1945), but they do not relate directly to the Japanese personality.

Postwar interdisciplinary research on the acculturation of Japanese in the Chicago area has yielded publications on acculturative changes in personality and on the nature of psychological conflicts which the bridging of Japanese and American cultures has produced among the Japanese-Americans. Among these is Caudill's (1952) extensive analysis of psychological aspects of the drive toward achievement and other value attitudes of the *Nisei*. A study, based on Rorschach tests, of acculturative changes in structural aspects of personality of *Issei* and *Nisei* (De Vos 1955) reports a high level of rigidity and certain indications of maladjustment among the

Issei. Nisei were much lower in rigidity, and displayed fewer indications of maladjustment. Comparison with data on Japanese in Japan of the same social backgrounds (i.e., rural residents) revealed equally high rigidity, but indications of severe maladjustment were found only among the American *Issei* and appear to be related to stress in adjusting to the alien American culture.

A focus of continuing interest in the study of the Japanese in America has been attempts to analyze their drive toward achievement. The question has been asked why *Issei* and *Nisei* have apparently adopted the attitudes and values, including the strong motivation to achievement, of the American middle class when certain other immigrant groups under comparable circumstances have not done so to the same degree (*see*, for example, Norbeck 1959 on ethnic groups in Hawaii). Scholars have also asked why the Japanese have made such apparently successful adjustments to life in the United States when other minority groups, some of them suffering less social discrimination, have failed to do so.

Similarities and compatibilities in certain American and native Japanese values and attitudes have been offered in partial explanation (Caudill and De Vos 1956). Japanese are described as extremely sensitive to stimuli from the outer world and as having a superego structure that depends strongly on external sanctions for reinforcement. Cultural values are internalized in a socialization process that emphasizes long-range goals, perseverance, obedience to authority, and a sense of obligation to parents. Socialization takes place within the family, but the drive to achievement is satisfied by conforming with expectations of the outer society. (This observation, it may be noted, is in keeping with opinions expressed by numerous other scholars. For example, a study comparing the vocational aspirations of American and Japanese schoolchildren [Goodman 1957] describes the Americans as "self-oriented" [egocentric] and the Japanese as "others-oriented.") Attitudes and community values to which the *Nisei*, as a minority group, are most strongly exposed in extrafamilial contacts, and which the *Nisei* internalize, are those of the American middle class. Thus native Japanese and American attitudes of valuing conformance and achievement and stressing long-range goals reinforce each other. Success for the *Nisei* differs from success for the non-Japanese American, however, in being closely related to the fulfillment of filial obligations. The feeling of necessity to succeed as a means of satisfying obligations to parents is brought out in clinical studies of individual Nisei (e.g., Babcock and Caudill in G. Seward, ed. 1958). A tendency toward psychological depression among *Nisei* is well documented in a collection of papers on culture conflict related to psychiatric problems of the *Nisei* (G. Seward, ed. 1958), which includes a particularly pertinent paper by Marvin Opler on psychological stress as related to filial obligations in the case history of an individual *Kibei*.

A study which compares acculturating Arabs in Algeria and other minority groups with Japanese-Americans reports that certain indications of intrapsychic stress appear in the Rorschach record of all groups, although they are less marked among the *Nisei* than among the *Issei*. Stress is seen to be connected with acculturation or status as members of minority groups because the indications do not appear in the records of individuals when they are members of a majority group (De Vos, in Kaplan, ed. 1961).

Data on immigrant and South American-born Japanese in Peru and Brazil that will allow comparison with studies in the United States have recently been collected under the direction of Seiichi Izumi of Tokyo University. Results of Rorschach, Thematic Apperception Tests, and problem situations tests are now in the process of analysis, and promise to allow direct comparison of personality traits and problems of acculturation among Japanese of the United States and these two South American countries. Preliminary analysis (Hiroshi Wagatsuma, personal communication) indicates that results of projective tests administered in Peru differ from those obtained in Brazil and the United States as well as Japan. Japanese-Peruvians appear to be less strongly motivated toward personal achievement than Japanese-Brazilians, Japanese-Americans, or Japanese in Japan, and, as indicated by the Rorschach, to be more pragmatic, presenting less emphasis on the integrated conceptions characteristic of the Japanese in the United States and at home.

An interdisciplinary study under the direction of R. P. Dore of the University of British Columbia and Masao Gamō of Meiji University on a fishing community of British Columbia populated by Japanese immigrants and their descendants is worthy of note. The aims of this study include investigation of problems of acculturation and research on personality, and the project includes projective tests among its tools.

Although the Ryukyu Islands are hardly "overseas" in the same sense as North and South America, research in personality and culture on the inhabitants of these islands is of significance for comparison in quite the same way as data on Japanese in faraway lands. Although to some degree culturally and perhaps physically distinct from the residents of Japan proper, the Ryukyu Islanders speak a Japanese dialect, regard themselves as Japanese, and are so regarded by the people of the principal islands of Japan. The Ryukyus were a part of the Japanese nation for many centuries before the end of World War II, but because of their isolated geographic position the islands escaped or were only lightly affected by many cultural innovations that swept Japan proper. In a provocative short article on the island of Amami Ōshima, Douglas Haring (1954) describes the islanders as having more "open" personalities than the residents of Japan proper. He suggests that the lack of sustained direct contact with Japan proper prevented the spread to this small island of attitudes and values which permeated the principal islands during the Tokugawa era (1603—1868). The modern Amami Oshima islanders, more impulsively labile and directly expressive of emotions than modern mainland Japanese, may represent a type of personality that characterized the whole nation before Tokugawa times.

J. Moloney's controversial writings on the Okinawans describe them as relatively free of conflict and assert that as a result of permissive practices of nursing there is little mental illness among them. A detailed field study of child-rearing practices in an Okinawan community conducted in 1957 by T. W. and H. S. Maretzki (personal communication) casts much doubt on the statements of Moloney. Research by the Maretzkis centered on dependence-independence, aggression, and internalization of values with the objective of relating measures of children's personality to antecedent factors of socialization. They observe that both adults and children indulge in a great deal of verbal aggression, and they report many traits that differ from observations made on Japanese in the main islands. Notable among these is less parental stress upon achievement by their children. Tightly knit social relationships throughout the whole community, encouraged by the customs of community endogamy, are tied in with the high sociability and little concern with competitiveness which characterize the children. Outstanding features in Okinawan socialization include an emphasis on nurturance, a high diffusion of caretakers of children, and the importance of the role of peers in every stage of child development. The community as a whole is almost an extension of the household environment. Additional research by the Maretzkis in 1960 is focussed on the adult personality and will provide data for more detailed comparison with Japan proper as well as other countries.

A study of another Ryukyu community on Ishigaki Island by Allan H. and Ann Gertrude Smith now in press (American Philosophical Society) provides additional data on Ryukyuan practices of child rearing, including mechanisms of social control.

Pertinent investigations that fall outside the classifications we have used here, but are worthy of notice, include research on patterns of suicide in Japan and types of therapy used in Tokyo hospitals to treat psychopathology. Seiichi Kato of the National Institute for Mental Health (of Japan) has been conducting research for ten years on Japanese suicides and attempted suicides with the objective of determining their patterns and social correlates. It is interesting to note that statistics since 1882 show that incidence by age groups has been essentially constant until the end of World War II. Postwar statistics reveal a rise in suicides among young males and, although figures for this group are still high, a decrease among young women. Caudill has completed field research (1959) on the psychiatric techniques and social environment of three Tokyo mental hospitals, one of which emphasizes organic therapy, another psychoanalytic treatment, and the third a distinctively Japanese form of treatment named Morita therapy after its founder and derived in part from Zen Buddhism.

Summary and Conclusions

An over-all view of research in Japanese culture and personality reveals both strengths and weaknesses. The absolute number of foreign and native scholars engaged in research on Japan in this field is not great, yet few if any foreign cultures have been the subject of study by so many individuals. The total of published studies, many of them in the Japanese language, is impressive in volume, but it is weak or deficient in a number of respects, some of which we have noted. The techniques and theories of modern culture and personality research have as yet hardly had adequate testing in Japan— but it is extremely doubtful that they have had adequate testing in any other culture. Considerable progress has been made in determining differences in culture and traits of personality according to region and social class in Japan, but much more is required before generalizations on the nation may be made with assurance. A conspicuous failing of Japanese scholars has been concentration on minute problems and a reluctance to go beyond mere description.

It must be added that research by Japanese scholars has been greatly inhibited by lack of funds, and their emphasis on studies of small scope is in part due to this circumstance. Japanese scholars have also been at a serious disadvantage for lack of opportunity to receive training in the techniques of personality and culture research. Only in very recent years have a few had the opportunity to take professional training.

Despite these negative comments, research in Japanese culture-and-personality has not been merely a spotty repetition of techniques and interpretations borrowed from scholars of the United States and Europe. It has made its own contributions of theoretical significance and it holds unusually great promise of making future contributions. Subjects of research have been examined in such a way that their conclusions concern and shed light on issues of general interest in the field of culture-and-personality and the social sciences as a whole. Past or present research in Japanese culture-and-personality has special relevance to the following subjects of general interest:

1. The nature of human drives to achievement.
2. Variations in the cultural conditioning of basic psychological mechanisms: shame versus guilt as motivating forces; different uses of introjection and projection.
3. Processes of acculturation: factors involved in making acculturation easy and successful or difficult and unsuccessful; the relationship between acculturation and psychic stress.

Motivation toward achievement has long been a subject of scholarly interest, and the practical value of an understanding of factors that inhibit and encourage the growth of drives to achievement is obvious. Explanations have been sought through examination of religiously sanctioned ideals of behavior and in many other ways. The eagerness and speed with which Japan assimilated Western culture, the startling rapidity with which it rose to a position as a major international power, and the remarkable recovery of the nation after devastating defeat and economic collapse in World War II have stimulated much curiosity and theorizing. Historians have pointed to the long-established receptiveness of the Japanese to items of foreign culture and their equally long record of successful adaptation of borrowed items. Other scholars have held that the hierarchical ordering of Japanese society, especially the former tight control of ruler over subject, has made the industrialization and "modernization" of Japan easy. Robert Bellah's recent and in-

teresting *Tokugawa Religion* (1957) approaches the problem so-
ciologically after the manner of Max Weber. He concludes that an
equivalent of the Protestant ethic, evident in Tokugawa times,
served as a spur to Japanese economic growth. T. C. Smith (1959)
has argued effectively that the road to industrialization was paved
by indigenous developments during Tokugawa times.

All of these studies leave off where culture-and-personality begins. The pattern of psychological integration of the personality
that encourages diligence and self-denial for the purpose of attaining long-range goals is of particular interest in understanding the
achievements of Japan as a nation. It is here that research in culture-
and-personality can be very helpful. As we have noted, much evidence from studies in culture-and-personality indicates that strong
motivation toward success exists among the Japanese of Japan and
Japanese-Americans. Other research has suggested the means by
which motivation is inculcated and reinforced. Research under way
on intrafamilial relations gives promise of telling us more about
motivation as it is related to Japanese social structure as well as
contributing to our understanding of psychological stress arising
from social living. These theoretical matters are, of course, highly
relevant to the problem of understanding other Asian countries
where economic developments have followed quite different courses,
and to the understanding of motivation and achievement for all
mankind.

In connection with the problem of understanding the drive to
achievement of the Japanese, published studies in personality and
culture have presented hypotheses that should stimulate re-
examination of theories of the relationships between superego and
ego ideal as these are related to guilt and shame. Perhaps all scholars
working in the field of culture-and-personality would agree that
theorizing on the subject of guilt versus shame has often been oversimplified. Certainly, the Japanese studies suggest strongly that
shame and guilt are not necessarily antithetical or mutually incompatible. The question of the weighting of the sanction of shame
versus that of guilt in any society cannot be investigated satisfactorily without consideration of several other related subjects, including the mechanisms of introjection and projection. Research
on Japan on this latter subject points up the necessity of re-
examination of theories and of further cross-cultural comparison.

Perhaps the most promising avenue of research in Japanese personality and culture bears on the subject of acculturation. The fact

that Japanese citizens of similar backgrounds have migrated to several nations with quite different cultures provides a unique opportunity for cross-cultural comparison of processes of acculturation. Research completed to date indicates that the Japanese of the United States differ considerably in traits of personality from those who have settled in South America. Studies of the Japanese in these areas suggest that compatibility rather than duplication of values between the minority and majority group are necessary for successful acculturation, and that quite different patterns of psychological reinforcement of values may yield results that are similar. Delineation of the values as well as interpretation of associated psychological mechanisms are problems which appear to yield best results when approached through the methods of personality and culture.

Research conducted to date on the Japanese also indicates that projective tests are useful instruments for detecting intrapsychic stress arising from difficulties of acculturation. Further comparison with data on Chinese-Americans, American Negroes, Puerto Ricans, Filipinos, and other minority groups and acculturating peoples in the United States in this and other matters should be extremely fruitful.

The promise which future research holds seems particularly great. Japan is a large and culturally complex society with many social strata representing subcultures, and many regional differences. This circumstance provides an unusually fine opportunity for comparison to aid in gaining understanding of many questions concerned with personality and culture. The Japanese abroad offer another useful avenue of comparison. Japan is, moreover, a highly literate society with much recorded history. During the past century it has undergone tremendous cultural change, proceeding at an accelerated rate since the end of World War II, and much of the change is well documented. In these respects, Japan offers an exceptional opportunity for observation of sociocultural change and its relationship to personality. In all of these matters, the prospect of future contributions to knowledge is particularly favored by the fact that both native and foreign scholars in several disciplines are engaged in research directed toward solving the same problems.

BIBLIOGRAPHY

(Titles of Japanese works have been Romanized, and English translations are given. When Japanese journals and serials have official English as well as Japanese titles, both are cited. English abstracts are published with some Japanese articles, and these have been noted.)

BABCOCK, CHARLOTTE, and WILLIAM CAUDILL
    1958   Personal and cultural factors in treating a nisei man. In Clinical studies in culture conflict, Georgene Seward, ed. New York, Ronald Press.

BELLAH, ROBERT N.
    1957   Tokugawa religion; the values of pre-industrial Japan. Glencoe, Free Press.

BENEDICT, RUTH
    1946   The chrysanthemum and the sword: patterns of Japanese culture. Boston, Houghton Mifflin.

BENNETT, J. W. and MICHIO NAGAI
    1953   Echoes: reactions to American anthropology—Japanese critique of the methodology of Benedict's "Chrysanthemum and the sword." American Anthropologist 55:404–411.

BUCHANAN, D. C.
    1954   Japanese character and personality as revealed in their culture. In Understanding other cultures, William A. Parker, ed. Washington, American Council of Learned Societies.

CAUDILL, WILLIAM
    1952   Japanese-American personality and acculturation. Genetic Psychology Monographs 45. Provincetown, Mass., Journal Press.
    1959a The relationship of anthropology to psychiatry in the study of culture and personality. Seishin Bunseki Kenkyū (The Japanese Journal of Psychoanalysis) 6:57–65.
    1959b Similarities and differences in psychiatric illness and its treatment in the United States and Japan. Nagoya University, Seishin Eisei (Mental Hygiene) 61/62:15–26.
    1959c Watakushi no pikuchā intabyū gijutsu (The use of a "Picture Interview" technique in the study of impulse gratification and restraint). Yokohama, Hiyoshi Byoin, Seishinbunsekigaku no Susume 3:1–13.

CAUDILL, WILLIAM and GEORGE DE VOS
    1956   Achievement, culture and personality: the case of Japanese Americans. American Anthropologist 58:1102–1126.

COLTON, H. A., JR. and F. G. EBAUGH
    1946   Japanese neuropsychiatry. American Journal of Psychiatry 103:342–348.

DENING, WALTER
    1891   Mental characteristics of the Japanese people. Trans. and Proc. of the Japan Society, old series, 19(1):17–36.

DE VOS, GEORGE
    1954   A comparison of the personality differences in two generations of Japanese Americans by means of the Rorschach test. Nagoya Journal of Medical Science 17(3):153–265.
    1955   A quantitative Rorschach assessment of maladjustment and rigidity in

acculturating Japanese Americans. Genetic Psychology Monographs 52 (First Half) :51–87. Provincetown, Mass., Journal Press.

1960a The relation of guilt toward parents to achievement and arranged marriage among the Japanese. Psychiatry: Journal for the Study of Interpersonal Processes Vol. 23, No. 3.

1960b Psycho-cultural attitudes toward primary relationships in Japanese delinquents—a study in progress. Seishin Eisci (Mental Hygiene), No. 66.

1961 Symbolic analysis in the cross-cultural study of personality. *In* Studying personality cross-culturally, Bert Kaplan, ed., Evanston and White Plains, Row Peterson.

DE VOS, GEORGE and H. WAGATSUMA

1959 Psychocultural significance of concern over death and illness among rural Japanese. International Journal of Social Psychiatry 5:5–19.

1961 Variations in traditional value attitudes toward status and role behavior of women in two Japanese villages. American Anthropologist, in press.

DOI, TAKEO

1956 Japanese language as an expression of Japanese psychology. Western Speech 20:90–96.

1958 *Shinkeishitsu no seishinbyori* (Psychopathology of *"shinkeishitsu"*). Seishinshinkeigaku Zasshi (Psychiatria et Neurologia Japonica) 60:733–744 (English abstract).

1960 *Jibun to amae no seishinbyori* (Psychopathology of *"jibun"* and *"amae"*). Seishinshinkeigaku Zasshi (Psychiatria et Neurologia Japonica) 62:149–162 (English abstract).

EMBREE, J. F.

1939 Suye Mura, a Japanese village. Chicago, University of Chicago Press.

FUJIOKA, Y.

1952 Rorschach test *ni yoru* personality *no chōsa* (I)—*Nara-ken, Seiki-gun, Hirano-mura no baai* (An investigation of personality by means of the Rorschach test, I, Hirano Village, Seiki-gun, Nara Prefecture). Kyōto Daigaku Jimbun Kagaku Kenkyūsho Chōsa Hōkoku (Social Survey Report of The Research Institute for Humanistic Studies, Kyoto University), 8.

1957 A statistical approach to group comparison based on the distribution of Rorschach responses. Memoire of The Research Institute for Humanistic Studies, Kyoto University.

1958 *Jinruigaku ni okeru* personality *no mondai*—Rorschach test *ni yoru hikaku kenkyū* (Some problems of personality studies in anthropology—comparative research by means of the Rorschach test). Shisō 412:34–44.

1959a Rorschach *hannō no sūgakuteki bumpu ni yoru* group *hikaku no kokoromi* (An attempt to compare groups by means of the mathematical distribution of Rorschach responses). Shinrigaku Hyōron (Psychological Review) 1:35–49.

1959b Rorschach *hannōshū*—*Nihon nōsanson dansei shotaishu no baai* (Tables of Rorschach responses of male house-holders in Japanese farming and mountain communities). Kyōto Daigaku Jimbun Kagaku Kenkyūsho Chōsa Hōkoku (Social Survey Report of the Research Institute for Humanistic Studies, Kyoto University), 18.

FUJIOKA, Y., Y. MAKI, T. IKEDA, and M. OKANO
1956 Rorschach test *ni yoru* personality *no chōsa* (III)—*Nara-ken, Yoshino-gun, Totsugawa-mura no baai* (An investigation of personality by means of the Rorschach test, III, Totsugawa Village, Yoshino-gun, Nara Prefecture). Kyōto Daigaku Jimbun Kagaku Kenkyūsho Chōsa Hōkoku (Social Survey Report of The Research Institute for Humanistic Studies, Kyoto University), 14.

GOODMAN, M. E.
1957 Values, attitudes and social concepts of Japanese and American children. American Anthropologist 59:979–999.

GORER, GEOFFREY
1942 Japanese character structure and propaganda: a preliminary survey. Prepared for the Committee on National Morale and the Council on Human Relations. Yale University (mimeo).
1943 Themes in Japanese culture. Trans. New York Academy of Sciences, Series II, 5:106–124.

HARING, D. G.
1943 Comment on Japanese personal character. *Excerpts from* Blood on the rising sun, by D. G. Haring.
Reprinted in Personal character and cultural milieu, D. G. Haring, ed. Syracuse, Syracuse University Press.
1946 Aspects of personal character in Japan. Far Eastern Quarterly 6:12–22.
1949 Japan and the Japanese. *In* Most of the world, Ralph Linton, ed. New York, Columbia University Press.
1953 Japanese national character; cultural anthropology, psychoanalysis and history. The Yale Review 42:375–402.
1954a Comment on field techniques in ethnography; illustrated by a survey of Amami Ōshima. Trans. New York Academy of Sciences 16:271–276.
1954b Comment on field techniques in ethnography; illustrated by a survey of the Ryukyu Islands. Southwestern Journal of Anthropology 10:255–267.

HOSHINO, AKIRA, TAKAO SOFUE, HIROKO SUE, and YOSHIKAZU IMAI
1958 *Ikuji yōshiki to paasonaritei* (Infant training and personality) (I), International Christian University, Kyōiku Kenkyū 5:148–216.

HSIAO, H. H.
1939 Mentality of the Chinese and Japanese. Journal of Applied Psychology 13:9–31.

HSU, F. L. K.
1949 Suppression versus repression: a limited psychological interpretation of four cultures. Psychiatry 12:223–242.

IMANISHI, K.
1952 *Mura to ningen* (Villages and people). Tokyo, Shinhyōronsha.

IMANISHI, K., Y. MAKI, and Y. FUJIOKA
1955 Rorschach test *ni yoru* personality *chōsa* (A study of personality by means of the Rorschach test). *In Tachikuiyō no kenkyū—gijutsu, seikatsu, ningen* (Studies on a pottery-making village, Tachikui—technology, way of life, the people), K. Yabuuchi, ed. Tokyo, Kōseisha Kōseikaku.

ISHIGURO, TAIGI
1955 *Haha-ko kankei no shinrigakuteki kenkyū (sonoichi)—Nyūyōji-ki no shitsukekata no jittai* (Psychological study on mother-child relations (I)—actual circumstances in child training). Nagoya Daigaku Kyōiku Gakubu Kiyō (Bulletin of the Faculty of Education, Nagoya University) 1:74–86 (English abstract).

KAPLAN, BERT, ed.
1961 Studying personality cross-culturally. Evanston and White Plains, Row Peterson.

KATO, SEIICHI
1956 Suicide. *In* Annual Report of Mental Health of the National Institute of Mental Health, Chapter IV, Section 22. Tokyo.

KATO, HIDETOSHI, ed. and trans.
1959 Japanese popular culture. Tokyo and Rutland, Vt., Charles E. Tuttle.

KAWASHIMA, TAKEYOSHI
1951a *Giri no kannen ni tsuite* (On the concept of *giri*). *Shisō*, Sept., 21–28.
1951b *On no ishiki no jittai* (The nature of the concept of *on*). Chūō Kōron 56:119–129.
1957 *Ideorogii to shite no kazoku seidō* (The family system as ideology). Tokyo, Iwanami Shoten.

KERLINGER, F. N.
1953 Behavior and personality in Japan: a critique of three studies of Japanese personality. Social Forces 31:250–258.

KIDA, MINORU
1956 *Nihonbunka no kontei ni hisomumono* (What lies at the bottom of Japanese culture). Tokyo, Kōdansha.

KODAMA, HABUKU
1953 *Nihonjin no ryōrushyakku hannō no kenkyū* (A study of Rorschach responses of Japanese). Shinrigaku Kōza 7:1–92.

KYŪGAKKAI RENGŌ TSUSHIMA KYŌDŌ CHŌSA IINKAI
1954 *Tsushima no shizen to bunka* (Nature and culture in Tsushima). Sōgō Kenkyū Hōkoku, 2. Tokyo, Kokinshoin.

LABARRE, WESTON
1945 Some observations on character structure in the Orient: the Japanese. Psychiatry 8:319–342.

LANHAM, BETTY B.
1956 Aspects of child care in Japan: preliminary report. *In* Personal character and cultural milieu, D. G. Haring, ed. Syracuse, Syracuse University Press.

LEIGHTON, ALEXANDER H.
1945 The governing of men; general principles and recommendations based on experience at a Japanese relocation camp. Princeton, Princeton University Press.

MARETZKI, T. W.
1957 Child rearing in an Okinawan community. Yale University, Ph.D. dissertation.

MASUDA, K.
1957 Kenkyusha's new pocket Japanese-English dictionary. Tokyo, Kenkyusha.

MEADOW, ARNOLD
    1944 An analysis of Japanese character structure. Prepared for and distributed by the Institute for Intercultural Studies, New York City (mimeo).
MINAMI, HIROSHI
    1954 Nihonjin no shinri (Psychology of the Japanese). Tokyo, Mainichi Shimbunsha.
MOLONEY, J. C.
    1945 Psychiatric observations on Okinawa Shima. Psychiatry 8:391–399.
    1951 A study of neurotic conformity: the Japanese. Complex 5:26-32.
    1953 Understanding the paradox of Japanese psychoanalysis. International Journal of Psychoanalysis 34 (part 4):1–13.
    1954 Understanding the Japanese mind. New York, Philosophical Library.
MORI, SHIGETOSHI and TADASHI MIWA
    1958 Okinoerabutō-tōmin no paasonaritei (Personality of Okinoerabutō Islanders). Jinruikagaku, 10.
NATIONAL FILM BOARD OF CANADA
    1959 Four families (film on practices of child rearing). Box 6100, Montreal, Quebec.
NORBECK, EDWARD
    1959 Pineapple town—Hawaii. Berkeley, University of California Press.
NORBECK, EDWARD and MARGARET
    1956 Child training in a Japanese fishing community. In Personal character and cultural milieu, D. G. Haring, ed. Syracuse, Syracuse University Press.
OKANO, M.
    1956 Shūdan kōzō to personality (Group structure and personality). Shinrigaku Kenkyū (Japanese Journal of Psychology) 27:8–14.
SELIGMAN, C. G.
    1930 Japanese temperament and character. Trans. and Proc. of the Japan Society. London. 28:123–142.
SEWARD, G. H., ed.
    1958 Clinical studies and cultural conflict. New York, Ronald Press. [Chapters pertaining to Japan]: C. G. Babcock and W. Caudill, Personal and cultural factors in the treatment of a Nisei man; T. E. Bessent, An aging Nisei anticipates rejection; N. L. Farberow and E. S. Schneidman, A Nisei woman attacks by suicide; L. B. Olinger and V. S. Summers, The dividing path: psychocultural neurosis in a Nisei man; and M. K. Opler, Cultural dilemma of a Kibei youth.
SIKKEMA, MILDRED
    1947 Observations on Japanese early training. Psychiatry 10:423–432.
SILBERFENNIG, JUDITH
    1945 Psychological aspects of current Japanese and German paradoxa. Psychoanalytic Review 32:73–85.
SMITH, T. C.
    1959 The agrarian origins of modern Japan. Stanford, Stanford University Press.

SOFUE, TAKAO
1954 Patterns of the Japanese personality indicated by the Rorschach test. Japanese Journal of Projective Techniques, 1.
1958 *Ejiko ni tsuite—sono bumpu to jinruigakuteki igi* (Ejiko: its distribution and anthropological significance). Shōnika Shinryo (Journal for Pediatric Practice), 21.

SOFUE, TAKAO, HIROKO SUE and TAIJI MURAKAMI
1958 *Ejiko ni kansuru bunkajinruigakuteki kenkyū—bumpu oyobi chiikiteki heni ni tsuite* (Anthropological study of the *Ejiko*, a Japanese cradle for child: its distribution and areal varieties). Jinruigaku Zasshi (Journal of the Anthropological Society of Nippon) 66:77–91 (English abstract).

SOFUE, TAKAO and HIROSHI WAGATSUMA
1959 *Kokumin no shinri—Nihonjin to Ōbeijin* (National character—Japanese, Americans, and Europeans). Tokyo, Kōdansha.

SPITZER, H. M.
1947 Psychoanalytic approaches to the Japanese character. *In* Psychoanalysis and the social sciences, Vol. 1, G. Roheim, ed. New York, International Universities Press.

STOETZEL, JEAN
1955 Without the chrysanthemum and the sword; a study of the attitudes of youth in post-war Japan. New York, Columbia University Press.

STRONG, E. K.
1934 The second-generation Japanese problem. Stanford, Stanford University Press.

SUE, HIROKO
1958 *Ejiko ni kansuru bunkajinruigakuteki kenkyū—Miyagi-ken no ejiko shiyō chiiki ni okeru chōsa* (Anthropology study of *ejiko* (cradle)— intensive study of an *ejiko*-using community in Miyagi Prefecture). Jinruigaku Zasshi (Journal of the Anthropological Society of Nippon) 66:128–136 (English abstract).

TSUKISHIMA, KENZŌ
1954 *Nōmin no paasonaritei—Kitakami-gawa chūryūiki no nōson no baai* (The personality of farmers, as seen in the farming villages of the middle reaches of the Kitakami River). Tokyo University, Tōyō Bunka Kenkyūsho Kiyō (The Memoirs of the Institute for Oriental Culture) 5:1–76.
1955 *Gyomin no paasonaritei—Nanao-wangan no gyoson no baai* (The personality of fishermen, as seen in the fishing villages of Nanao Bay). Tokyo University, Tōyō Bunka Kenkyūsho Kiyō (The Memoirs of the Institute for Oriental Culture) 7:147–190.
1957 *Nihon kōzan buraku no ningenkankei ni kansuru bunka shinrigakuteki chōsa hōkoku* (A study of human relations in Japanese mining communities from the standpoint of cultural psychology). Tokyo University, Tōyō Bunka Kenkyūsho Kiyō (The Memoirs of the Institute for Oriental Culture) 13:149–188.

WAGATSUMA, HIROSHI, and GEORGE DE VOS
In press "Attitudes Toward Arranged Marriage in Rural Japan," *Human Organization*.

Chapter 3

AFRICA*

ROBERT A. LeVINE
University of Chicago

Introduction

SUBSAHARAN Africa is one of the world's great strongholds of non-literate peoples. Its ethnographic literature is vast, yet studies of culture and personality are exceedingly few. There has probably been less research on socialization processes, the psychodynamics of cultural behavior, the application of projective techniques, personality and culture change, and culture and mental disorder in Africa than in any major continental area of the world. Anthropologists working there have generally eschewed such research, leaving it to psychiatrists, educators, and missionaries. The latter, many of whom were untrained in anthropology or scholarly research of any kind, have produced works which are at best straightforward descriptions of childhood or psychotic behavior, at worst racial stereotypes with scientific window dressing. All too often such studies concern *The African Mind* or *The African Mentality,* ignoring cultural differences among Africans. We are told that *The African* is impulse-driven, fear-ridden, incapable of long-range planning, and unable to distinguish between himself and his kin group.

The case of J. C. Carothers, whose works are among the most widely read on the subject of mental disease and personality in Africa, is illustrative. Dr. Carothers is a psychiatrist who practised in Kenya for many years and was in charge of the Mathari Mental Hospital (for Africans) there. His articles have appeared in *Psychiatry* (1948) and the *Journal of Mental Science* (1951); a monograph by him was published by the World Health Organization (1953), and a topical report, *The Psychology of Mau Mau,* was

* Prepared with the assistance of National Institute of Mental Health Grant No. M-4037 (A).

48

published by the Kenya Government (1954). The following quotations are characteristic of his writings.

The native African in his culture is remarkably like the lobotomized Western European and in some ways like the traditional psychopath in his inability to see individual acts as part of a whole situation, in his frenzied anxiety and in the relative lack of mental ills (1951:47).

In summary, by the nature of African experience in infancy and childhood, no firm foundation is laid for clear distinction of the subject and object, or for a proper balance in regard to those of love and hate. Tendencies to later readjustment (especially in the field of impersonal intelligence) of this distorted state are consistently frustrated, so that in later life there is little approach to a total personal integration, and, in dealing with any situation for which no pattern of behavior is prescribed by local custom, such behavior is impulsive and is marked by concentration on immediately presenting aspects of that situation, without regard for the sum of stored experience, of present perception, or of implications for the future (1953:107).

If one scans the faces of the passers-by in any town in Western Europe it is clear that most of the people observed are impelled by some continuing inner purpose and yet are also alert to the events around them. If one leaves the ship for a moment at any African port, it is equally clear that most of the faces observed express either exclusive interest in some immediate affair or complete apathy (1953:108).

In *The Psychology of Mau Mau*, in which Carothers was forced by the nature of the subject to consider the Kikuyu apart from other Africans, two factors adduced specifically to explain Kikuyu behavior are their "forest psychology" which comes from living near the edge of the forest and explains their willingness to return to it in Mau Mau bands, and the fact that "in Kikuyuland authority lacked strength" (1954:5).

Equally ethnocentric and unscientific as the writings of Carothers, and more Freudian, are the works of J. F. Ritchie (1943) and S. Davidson (1949). These authors seek to discover why *The African* is irrational, lacking in curiosity, and so forth; Ritchie, a school principal in Barotseland, attributes it to excessively late and traumatic weaning; Davidson, a psychiatrist among the Bemba, sees adolescent sexual promiscuity as the cause. Such analyses are primarily relevant, not to culture-and-personality investigations, but to the sociology of knowledge as examples of the use of psychological concepts to support race prejudice.

Although many British social anthropologists specializing in Africa observe what Richards has called a "psychology taboo" (1958:118), their field reports contain much data of interest to the student of culture-and-personality, particularly on family relationships, sexual behavior, the life cycle of the individual, and religion. That they have so rarely availed themselves of psychological theory in the analysis of their data is perhaps attributable to the persistence of a tradition concerning the separation of social and psychological facts. Like Durkheim and Radcliffe-Brown, the present upholders of that tradition reject explicitly psychological explanations of sociocultural phenomena but often interpret field data in terms of individual sentiments and attitudes. Gluckman's *Custom and Conflict in Africa* (1955) is an example of this; much of what he terms conflict is equivalent to culturally patterned ambivalence within individuals. Another example is *Nuer Religion;* in it Evans-Pritchard makes the following comments on psychological theories of primitive religion:

> The psychological explanations were very varied, changing with changes in psychological theory. Intellectualist interpretations were succeeded by emotionalist interpretations and they by psycho-analytical interpretations. Religion was discussed and explained in terms of association of ideas, of personification of natural phenomena, of awe, of thrill, of fear, anxiety and frustration, of projection, and so forth. Most of these theories have long ago been discredited as naive introspective guesses (1956:312).

In spite of this strong statement, Evans-Pritchard also rejects strictly sociological explanations of primitive religion and subsequently concludes, "Though prayer and sacrifice are exterior actions, Nuer religion is ultimately an interior state" (1956:322). He discusses the Nuer "sense of guilt" which he claims "is not just fear but a complex psychological state" and which "varies in intensity from one situation to another" (1956:312–313). At another point it is stated "Nuer religious conceptions are properly speaking not concepts but imaginative constructions" (1956:321). This seems to approach a psychological view, as does his general characterization of Nuer religion:

> We can say that these characteristics . . . of Nuer religion indicate a distinctive kind of piety which is dominated by a strong sense of dependence on God and confidence in him rather than in any human powers or endeavors . . . this sense of dependence is remarkably individualistic. It is an intimate personal relationship between man and God. This is apparent in Nuer ideas of sin, in their expressions of guilt, in their confessions, and in the dominant piacular theme of their sacrifices. It is evident also in their habit of making short supplications at any time. This is a very noticeable trait of Nuer piety, and my conclusions are here borne out by Dr. Lienhardt's observations. He tells me that when he was in western Dinkaland he had in his household a Nuer youth whose habit of praying to God for aid on every occasion of difficulty greatly astonished the Dinka (1956:317–318).

This description of a modal habit pattern as characteristic of a religious system is similar to one that might be written by a behavioristically oriented student of personality and culture. The difference is that Evans-Pritchard believes that the underlying processes are better analyzed by a theologian than a psychologist (1956:322). In any event it is apparent that, though personality theory as such is either rejected or ignored by most British Africanists, even some of the most antipsychological of them do not overlook the individual and his response patterns in their ethnographic analyses.

Culture and personality studies are not entirely missing from the anthropological literature on African peoples. Indeed, such studies can be found among the writings of some of the most eminent Africanists—Melville J. Herskovits, S. F. Nadel, Audrey I. Richards, Meyer Fortes—though rarely in their best-known works. Furthermore, a few younger scholars such as S. G. Lee combine psychological training with cultural sophistication to produce culture-personality studies of high quality. At the Fifteenth International Congress of Psychology at Brussels in 1957, several papers were presented reporting African personality research of variable quality. The number of papers was encouraging, as was the attitude expressed by Dr. S. Biesheuvel of the National Institute of Personnel Research, Johannesburg, in his introduction to their published form:

> Psychology owes a considerable debt to social anthropology for its elucidation of the social systems and functions that govern African community life. . . . Psychological research . . . should be social in its orientation, closely related to the work of social anthropologists, and preferably conducted on a team basis (1958a: 161).

In the remainder of this paper I shall outline the cultural background to personality in Africa and then review African studies of culture and personality under the headings of infant experience and the family environment, personality development in childhood and adolescence, the T.A.T. in South Africa and the Congo, personality and acculturation, psychocultural interpretation of ritual, witchcraft, and dreams, and culture and mental disease.[1] The review is not exhaustive; works of primary interest and relevance are

---

[1] I am indebted to my wife, Barbara B. LeVine, for an extensive search of the psychological literature for relevant sources, to Igor Kopytoff for bringing to my attention studies conducted in the Congo, and to Hans Panofsky of the African Studies Library, Northwestern University, for invaluable bibliographical assistance.

discussed. Works on African intelligence (e.g., Biesheuvel 1943) and many psychiatric studies have necessarily been omitted. My intention has been to select for discussion those studies which, by their insights or their errors, help to point the way for future research.

The Cultural Background to Personality in Africa

Cultural variation among the millions of people and hundreds of linguistic groups in subsaharan Africa is so great as to defy any attempt to describe "African Culture." Ignorance of this variation has vitiated the attempts of many nonanthropologists to contribute to culture and personality studies. The culture area classifications of Herskovits (1948) and Murdock (1959) provide means of comprehending cultural similarities and variations at an intermediate level of generality between the particular culture and the entire continent. There are numerous cultural characteristics, however, which may be said to be distinctively African, although they are neither limited to Africa nor universal throughout it. For purposes of comparison with other areas of the world, I present a list of those distinctively African characteristics which have demonstrable or potential relevance to personality variables.

1. *Pastoralism.* Cattle, camels, sheep, and goats are raised in many parts of Africa, sometimes along with agricultural activities, less frequently as the sole subsistence activity. A distinctive ethos or attitude has often been attributed to strictly pastoral and nomadic peoples, such as the Masai and pastoral Fulani, and to peoples such as the Nuer among whom pastoralism is highly valued but not exclusively practised. Herding is an important childhood occupation in many areas of Africa.

2. *Large and Dense Populations.* African ethnolinguistic units tend to be large by comparison with nonliterate societies in other parts of the world. There are numerous African ethnic groups of more than a million persons (e.g., Zulu, Xhosa, Kikuyu, Ibo, Mossi) and many more over a quarter of a million in population; linguistic groups of less than 100,000 are often considered small by local standards. Within those large groups there is local variation in cultural practices which makes comparative studies of communities or districts both feasible and valuable. Population densities are high among many of the sedentary peoples, ranging up to 2,000 per square mile. In West Africa there are indigenously urban and infra-urban communities.

3. *Highly Developed Prestige Economy and Acquisitive Culture Patterns.* Indigenous economic institutions are varied, but acquisitive values and status distinctions based on wealth are common throughout Africa. In west and west central Africa these patterns are related to trading and markets; on the eastern side of the continent they most frequently involve livestock. Plural wives are almost everywhere items of conspicuous consumption.

4. *Centralized Political Institutions and Institutionalized Leadership.* Stateless societies outnumber centralized states in Africa, but the latter are found in greater abundance there than in any other nonliterate area of the world. Chiefs, headmen, and royal and aristocratic lineages play an important part in the functioning of many African social systems.

5. *Unilineal Descent Groups.* These are not only the most widespread form of kin group, but serve political functions in stateless societies and form the basis of local organization in many areas.

6. *Bridewealth.* Marriage payments are customarily made to the family of the bride, although bride service and sister exchange are found in some societies.

7. *Polygyny and the Mother-child Household.* Polygyny is extremely common in Africa on the whole (see Dorjahn 1958b) and has important consequences for patterns of sexual behavior and child rearing. In many societies each wife occupies a separate house with her children.

8. *Initiation Rites and Genital Operations.* Male and female initiation rites at or around puberty can be found in every major region of Africa, with groups lacking the rites interspersed among those that practise them. Circumcision and clitoridectomy are also widely distributed, sometimes associated with initiation, often not.

9. *Ancestor Cults.* Beliefs and practices pertaining to ancestors are often associated with unilineal kin groups and are the most prevalent single form of African religion. The worship of nature deities and other gods and spirits is also found, however.

10. *Witchcraft and Sorcery.* Beliefs and practices concerning magical aggression by humans against one another are extremely widespread, though their form and intensity vary. Exuvial magic is common.

11. *Importance of Proverbs in Folklore.* In most African societies much traditional wisdom, both moral and cynical, is summarized in proverbs which are used in everyday life and taught to children.

Infant Experience and the Family Environment

Much of what has been written on childhood in Africa by researchers and casual observers has emphasized the closeness of the mother-child relationship, the prolonged indulgence of infants, and the traumatic character of weaning. One of the few observational studies of African infants is that of Geber (1958), whose work was part of the research program organized by the International Children's Centre and carried out in four European cities as well as Africa. The children whose psychomotor development she tested consisted of 308 in Kampala, Uganda (cultural group unspecified but apparently all Ganda), 16 in Johannesburg, South Africa, and 30 in Dakar, Senegal (cultural groups unspecified). The published conclusions do not distinguish between the groups in different parts of the continent but contrast them as a whole with European children.

Using Gesell tests for infants past the neonate stage and methods devised by André Thomas for testing neonates, Geber found striking evidence of precocity in African infants. Nine-hour-old infants drawn into a sitting position were able to prevent their heads from falling back, which European children cannot do until six weeks after birth; two-day-olds looked at the examiner's face and seemed to focus their eyes, a feat not performed until eight weeks by European infants.

... up to the fifth month, the motor precocity was remarkable, especially in regard to posture. Between the fifth and seventh months, adaptivity, language and personal-social relations came to equal the motor development: the level was that of European children two or three months older (1958:186).

Geber suggests that the initial motor precocity might be due to the attitude of the pregnant mother: "The arrival of a baby is always looked forward to with great pleasure . . . and is not a source of anxiety. . . . The mother . . . is active up to the moment of delivery" (1958:194). Her "happy acceptance of motherhood may be related to the slight degree of tonic flexion in her new-born child" (1958:195). The continued precocity of older infants is attributed to the fact that the African children live "surrounded by affection," especially the "loving and warm behavior of the mothers." Geber states, "Before the child is weaned, the mother's whole interest is centered on him. She never leaves him, carries him on her back—often in skin-to-skin contact—wherever she goes, sleeps with him, feeds him on demand at all hours of the day or night, forbids him nothing, and never chides him" (1958:194). In support of this hypothesis, she cites (without specifics) the cases of some African children whose westernized parents kept them in cots most of the time and fed them on schedules; they "did not show similar precocity after the first month, and later were inclined to be quiet and subdued" (1958:195). Furthermore, children examined before and after weaning are said to have shown "marked differences" in their behavior and test results; afterwards they were less lively and precocious. This is attributed to the withdrawal of the mother's love and attention at the time of weaning; the Ganda custom of sending the child away to grandparents for months at the time of weaning is mentioned here. But "children for whom weaning had not caused a sudden break in the way of life retained their liveliness after the weaning, and developed without interruption" (1958:195).

Despite the brevity of the article by Geber and its lack of detailed evidence, she does raise some intriguing hypotheses concerning the effect of desire for children, maternal love, and mother-infant contact on infant development. Like many nonanthropologists, however, she assumes cultural uniformity for Africans, so that the patterns of infant care found among the Ganda of Kampala are generalized by implication to her South African and Senegalese samples. Although our knowledge of infant care in Africa is somewhat scant, several relevant pieces of information are reliably reported and should not be overlooked:

1. *Not all African women desire motherhood.* Among the Ila of Northern Rhodesia, where childbirth is followed by a 2½- to 3-year prohibition on female sexual activity, young married women induce abortions so that they can go on with their marital and extramarital sexual lives.[2] Furthermore, in those groups which disapprove of childbirth before marriage, the unwed mother often endures pregnancy in anxiety and disgrace.

2. *The close and constant relationship between mother and unweaned child is far from universal in Africa.* In much of East and South Africa the infant is introduced to gruel within the first month by forcefeeding, and is left in the care of an older sibling during the day while the mother is working in the fields. This contrasts sharply with the pattern of unbroken mother-infant contact found not only among the Ganda but in numerous Central African societies. Such variation provides the conditions for natural experi-

---

[2] I am indebted for this information to Arthur Tuden, who did field work among the Ila in 1956–57.

ments within Africa on the effects of mother-child relationships.

3. *There appears to be considerable variation among African societies in the degree of maternal warmth and affection.* My own observations indicate that there are groups in which mothers play with and praise their children, and others in which they ignore them even when ministering to their needs for nourishment and physical comfort. If the findings of Harlow (1958) concerning monkeys apply to humans, it may be that affection is a less important variable than the simple availability of the mother for physical contact with the infant.

4. *In at least some African groups mothers and other adults do punish and scold unweaned children for wandering too near the fire, for crying too much, for masturbation, for striking an adult, and so forth.* The picture of total indulgence may hold for some societies but is often exaggerated by persons who have not observed African families at length.

5. *Weaning from the breast is not a "stage" which occurs at the same age or with the same effects in all African societies.* The mean ages of weaning for African groups probably range from less than a year to well over two years, which is a substantial segment of the world-wide range of variation. Evidence marshaled by Whiting (1954:524–525) suggests a curvilinear relationship between age at onset of weaning and amount of emotional disturbance the child shows. The greatest amount of emotional disturbance occurs in societies where weaning is begun between thirteen and eighteen months; weaning beginning before one year or over two years results in much less emotional disturbance. This evidence is consistent with the common finding of traumatic weaning in African societies, since so many of them wean in the second year of life, but it also suggests greater variation in amount of weaning disturbance (when the early-weaning and late-weaning societies are included) than has been recorded to date for Africans.

Age of weaning in African societies is related to degree of polygyny, since women whose husbands have other wives tend to give birth at less frequent intervals (see Dorjahn 1958a) and are thereby able to nurse each child longer. The length of customary restrictions on the postpartum sexual activity of women is also involved in the determination of child spacing and hence often age of weaning as well. In some societies the postpartum taboo is justified on grounds of allowing the mother to devote a long time to the care of a particular child without getting pregnant again.

6. *Methods of weaning vary among African groups.* Although some, like the Ganda mentioned by Geber, send children away to relatives to be weaned, others slap, frighten, or smear repellent substances on the breast while keeping the child at home.

In sum, there is variation in attitude toward motherhood, mother-infant contact, maternal warmth, punishment of infants, age of weaning, and method of weaning among African societies. They constitute a ready-made laboratory for the investigator who wishes to explore the effects of such variations on personality development.

Albino and Thompson (1956) have carried out a study of Zulu weaning which could well serve as a model for future research on African infants. The Zulu wean suddenly, on a day set in advance, and this culture pattern provided the investigators with an opportunity to observe the immediate effects of this alleged trauma on infant behavior. A group of sixteen Zulu infants from a single rural neighborhood were selected for intensive study before, during, and after weaning, and they were compared with a control group of ten urban Zulu children of roughly the same age who had been weaned considerably earlier. The sixteen children were given full nutritional examinations before and after weaning (no signs of marked malnutrition were found), and they were also provided with a more than adequate daily ration of milk for three weeks, beginning a week before weaning, in order to eliminate nutritional discontinuity as a factor in behavior change. The mothers were interviewed and the children observed for seven weeks after weaning. They were tested one day before weaning, one day after, and one week after, on a modified Gesell Development Schedule, which was administered at similar intervals to the urban control group.

The Zulu children were allowed almost unlimited access to the breast before their weaning, which took place at an average age of 18.9 months by the smearing of the breast with the bitter juice of the aloe in their presence. When the aloes were applied to the breast, immediate reactions of the children took two forms: "apathetic" bewilderment with no attempt to run away, and running away from the mother without attempting to approach her again. During the first few hours, only one child accepted the breast to suck more than once again, though most of them touched the mother's breasts. Negativistic, aggressive, and fretful behavior was common in the first two hours after weaning. In the following days, the child's relationship with his mother was disturbed, going through three distinct stages in ten of the cases: (1) a period of alternately attacking and ignoring mother, attacks occurring mainly at night in connection with attempts to nurse, and avoidance of mother occurring in the daytime; (2) a stage in which the child makes attempts to gain his mother's attention and to be constantly near her; (3) a period of increasing independence of the mother, with the child spending more time with other persons and showing no anger toward her or other signs of disturbance.

Other changes following weaning included the following: closer relationship to members of the family other than mother, with increasing aggressiveness directed against a sibling; increasing maturity of behavior—helping in domestic tasks, imitating elders, speaking more distinctly with a larger vocabulary; apathy and anxiety during the first week, disappearing gradually thereafter; a marked increase in aggressive behavior, continuing in some cases to the end of the investigation; a marked increase in behavior disapproved of by mother, such as spilling water and playing with fire; disturbed sleep; increase in appetite and food-demanding behavior. Although no change in developmental level was observed, on the Gesell test, the children changed from cooperative before weaning to negativistic or quietly uncooperative on the second administration. This change did not occur in the control group. The authors conclude that weaning causes a temporary disturbance in the child's emotional and social life but that in the longer run it facilitates the development of sociability, self-reliance, and socially valued aggressiveness, and is therefore adaptive, rather than merely traumatic.

Several anthropologists have analyzed the termination of infantile dependency on the mother in African societies by invoking hypotheses adapted from the psychoanalytic theory of the Oedipus complex. M. and F. Herskovits discovered that the classic Oedipal theme of killing the father "does not figure significantly in the corpus of Dahomean mythology," but that, "invariably, it is the father who initiates the hostility. His fear of eventual replacement by his offspring, usually made known to him through some form of supernatural revelation, causes him to have the son exposed, or killed outright." (1958:10–11). They also found sibling rivalry to be an important theme in Dahomean myths. They relate this to the life of the infant in Dahomey, who is "constantly with its mother" until she gives birth again; the replaced child has "a sense of rejection and neglect" out of which develops hostility toward the younger sibling. When the male grows up and becomes a father, his "jealousy of the son can be conceptualized as that aspect of the sibling rivalry complex which, through projection, reactivates the infantile competition for the mother in terms of competition for the affections of the wife" (1958:14). Thus the mythological theme of fathers killing their sons to avoid replacement by them is explained as the expression of intergenerational competition which began "in infancy on the intragenerational level in the situation of sibling rivalry" (1958:1).

A somewhat more orthodox Freudian view of the Oedipus complex provides the basic hypotheses for a cross-cultural study of male initiation in fifty-five societies (twelve of them African) by Whiting, Kluckhohn, and Anthony (1958). They take as their cultural consequent the presence or absence of male initiation ceremonies at puberty involving painful hazing, tests of endurance and manliness, seclusion from women, and genital operations. They find that such ceremonies are more likely to occur in societies where mother and infant sleep together for at least a year to the exclusion of the father, or where the mother is prohibited from sexual intercourse for at least a year after the birth of her child. In the latter case, it is suggested that the mother may obtain some "substitute sexual gratification" from nursing and caring for her infant. This intense relationship and/or the exclusive mother-child sleeping arrangement is seen as leading to a great emotional dependence of child on mother which is frustrated by the father's resumption of sexual relations with the mother. The child becomes hostile and envious toward his father, and though these feelings may be latent in childhood, when the boy reaches adolescence, it is necessary for the society to have an initiation rite of the type mentioned above "to put a final stop to (1) his wish to return to his mother's arms and lap, (2) to prevent an open revolt against his father who has displaced him from his mother's bed, and (3) to ensure identification with the adult males of the society" (1958:362).

Six African societies (Azande, Chagga, Dahomey, Nuer, Thonga, Tiv) are classified as having the male initiation rite and its hypothesized childhood antecedents. While M. and F. Herskovits focus on the Dahomean child's replacement in the mother's affection by the next child, Whiting *et al.* go farther back to the point at which the mother resumes sexual relations with her husband; they view this as the crucial replacement, which has an impact on the child even before his mother is pregnant again. It is true that in Dahomey "the cultural ideal dictates her complete abstinence from sexual relations for two years at the least; a year's abstinence is still generally observed" (Herskovits 1958:5), so that the hypothesized conditions for an exclusive mother-infant relationship are present, and this relationship is terminated in part when the period of abstinence ends. On the other hand, the custom in Dahomey is for each nonlactating wife to live with the husband in his house for four days at a time, leaving the children in her own house, so that they "do not witness the sexual act of their parents." This appears to weaken the point of Whiting *et al.*, since they have mentioned the presence of the newly replaced child at the scene of parental intercourse by which means "the child may truly become aware of his replacement" (1958:362). It may be, however, that the mother's leaving the child for four days at a time, may function equally well to make him aware of his replacement and jealous of his father. The Herskovits hypothesis has the support of evidence from Dahomean culture that sibling rivalry is more important than jealousy of the father; the hypothesis of Whiting *et al.* is strengthened by the fact that it could "predict" patterns of childhood experience in Dahomey from a knowledge of its male initiation rites.

A third analysis based on the notion of the Oedipus complex is that of LeVine (1959), who attempts to explain the high frequency of rape among the Gusii and the culture pattern of sadomasochistic heterosexuality in terms of structural and psychological factors. Within the Gusii family there are four kinds of parent-child relationships with varying degrees of sex avoidance (i.e., verbal and physical modesty): father-daughter, which is strictest; father-son, which is next strictest; mother-son; and mother-daughter, respectively. The mother is more nurturant to all children than the father, who is rather aloof and described (by the mother) to the children as a strict disciplinarian. If, according to an Oedipal hypothesis, the relationship of child to cross-sex parent determines his later heterosexual adjustment, then we would expect the Gusii boy, whose mother was nurturant, to seek heterosexual experience, and the Gusii girl, whose father was modest in her presence and fear-inspiring, to fear heterosexual experience. This does not help explain the apparently sadistic motivation of Gusii men but it is consistent with the fact that Gusii girls are more sexually inhibited than boys.

Both Dahomey and Gusii, among whom father-son hostility or avoidance is pronounced, are patrilineal peoples. The matrilineal Ashanti as described by Field (1960) are characterized by an extremely warm and affectionate father-son relationship beginning in infancy, while it is the mother's brother-sister's son relationship which involves hostility and tension: "They say that a son loves his father too much to kill him for the sake of inheritance, whereas he has no such sentiments regarding his uncle" (1960:27). This contrast between patrilineal and matrilineal peoples in regard to father-son relationships, and the role of the mother's brother in the matrilineal situation, constitute another confirmation of Malinowski's assertion that the Oedipus complex is differently structured in matrilineal societies.

Sibling rivalry is a prominent feature of polygynous families in Africa; it is mentioned not only by Herskovits for Dahomey but by anthropologists describing many other groups (for example, Evans-Pritchard 1953, on the Nuer). There is a close connection between sibling rivalry and the co-wife rivalry which is engendered by certain types of polygynous family structure. In many societies each wife has her own house, is allotted her own fields, and is, with her children, a subfamily unit operating under the more or less frequently exercised authority of her husband. In those groups which have what Gluckman (1951) has called "the house-property complex," each mother-child unit is termed "a house" and is semi-autonomous for purposes of property holding and inheritance. Thus, the cattle that are paid in bridewealth for a woman's daughter are to be used for the marriage of one of her sons. If the family head decides to use the cattle to marry another wife, the bride establishes her "house" owing the amount of her bridewealth to the "house" of the older wife, and the debt should be paid from her own daughter's bridewealth. These debts cause friction among co-wives and are often carried down one or two generations, causing dissension between the children and grandchildren of the co-wives. Furthermore, in societies of this type, inheritance is patrilineal but the sons of each "house" inherit much of their wealth through their mother, to whose cattle and habitually used fields they have a legitimate claim. The more property assigned to their mother's "house" during the father's lifetime, the more the sons will inherit. This is also a factor in co-wife rivalry which becomes translated into the rivalry of half-brothers. In those societies where the family head appoints his successor or can disinherit a son, the wives vie with each other to have their own sons obtain paternal favor. The mother not only wants to see her sons prosper for their own sake and for the elevation in status it will give her, but also because she will be dependent on their support in her old age.

What impact does this "interhouse" rivalry have upon the child? He often grows up in a family in which relations between his mother and her co-wives are tense or even hostile; accusations of witchcraft and sorcery among the father's wives may be among his earliest memories. Children understand these hostile relationships while still young, and boys come to feel their personal stake in the struggle. Usually, good surface relations among half-siblings are maintained so as not to antagonize the family head, but there is likely to be considerable underlying aggression. A strong, affectionate, and mutual loyalty develops between mother and sons. Members of the family outside his own "house," including his father, are likely to be viewed by the son with suspicion and treated with respect (for the father) or courtesy. This constellation of familial attitudes does not die easily in the individual who has acquired it. In many societies with segmentary patrilineages, it becomes a principle of social organization. When a lineage divides, it is often descendants of different wives of the founder (through their sons) who form the separate (and sometimes hostile) segments, which are frequently named after the founder's wives. In such groups the rivalry of co-wives and half-brothers is considered the normal pattern of social life, represented as it is in the group structure and mythology as well as in family interaction.

Personality Development in Childhood and Adolescence

There is a good deal of scattered information on the training of African children between weaning and puberty, but few noteworthy analyses. Fortes (1939) emphasizes how much the Tallensi child learns by observation without instruction by adults, and how a strong and early identification develops which results in spontaneous imitation of adult sex role behavior, in play and, insofar as possible, in real life situations. Raum (1940) graphically describes the punitive discipline of Chagga parents. Simmons (1960) has provided a brief but careful description of childhood and adolescence among the Efik. In a previous work (LeVine 1960) I have contrasted the Nuer and Gusii with respect to aggression training. The Nuer encourage children to fight for themselves, while the Gusii train their young to report quarrels and attacks to adult authority. The difference is seen as related to the greater tendency of the contemporary Nuer to settle quarrels by the feud, and of Gusii to resolve them in litigation. Another comparison is that by Biesheuvel (1959:11–14) of the

Pedi and Lovedu in the Northern Transvaal. These two Bantu groups are closely related and similar in many aspects of culture, but they differ in the requirements of their social systems. The Pedi are warlike, group oriented, and accord a low place in society to women. The Lovedu, protected from attack by geographical features, are peace loving and individualistic, with women having high status in their society. Child training among the Pedi involves "frequent and severe corporal punishment," with the education of boys being "directed towards the development of aggressive virtues," while the Lovedu consider corporal punishment an "insult to personality." This concomitant variation, not elaborated by the author, is seen by him as illustrating the importance of social structure and values as causal factors in the socialization process. He endorses the view of Barry, Child, and Bacon (1959) that child rearing practices are adaptations to the socioeconomic environment as well as formative influences on the individual.

The monograph by Read (1960) on Ngoni childhood is the first extended analysis of traditional African education in terms of values and personality. She sees values as determinants of child training practices, operating through an "ideal personality" or cultural self-image which the Ngoni aristocrats with whom she worked hold up to their children as a standard. Socialization is viewed as a conscious attempt to shape children's behavior in the direction of cultural ideals, and Read does not deal with unconscious processes of learning and personality development. Her mode of analysis is illustrated by the following quotation.

> Two other qualities were emphasized in child training since they were expected of all Ngoni people in interpersonal relations. One was generosity in sharing anything a person had. It was a quality demanded of everyone, from the small child who was made to unclench his fist in which he was hiding three ground-nuts and give two of them to his fellows, to the big chief whose duty at a feast was to see that everyone had enough and to send food from his own portion to anyone who looked hungry (1960:155).

An outstanding characteristic of childhood among the Ngoni aristocrats as described by Read is their emphasis on training in respect, obedience, and formal politeness, which is clearly related to the requirements of roles in their political system. I have also described the learning of authority relationships, contrasting childhood experience among the "authoritarian" Gusii with that of the "egalitarian" Nuer (LeVine 1960). The entire problem of how the dominance-submission patterns—which are so striking a feature of many African political systems—are learned by individuals, deserves more attention and comparative analysis than it has received.

Some of Piaget's hypotheses concerning child development have been reviewed and tested on West African children by Jahoda (1958a, 1958b, 1958c). The most relevant of these studies is that of immanent justice in 120 school children of Accra, Ghana (cultural group unspecified). Jahoda criticizes the study by Havighurst and Neugarten (1953), which found that the belief in immanent justice (i.e., that punishment by the physical world is an automatic consequence of wrongdoing) increases with age in Southwestern American Indian children, on the grounds that their scoring procedures were too "mechanical" and tended to inflate their results. In his Accra study, Jahoda found that "pure immanence" decreases significantly with age, naturalistic explanations (of accidental injuries following wrongdoing) increase significantly, and there is also a marked but not significant increase in explanations classified as "acts of god." He cites a study done in the Belgian Congo which found a steady decrease in punishment of unspecified origin ("immanent justice"), and an increase in "simple accident" and "punishment by God." Since considerable difference in age trends remain even when the Havighurst and Neugarten data are scored according to Jahoda's criteria, it would seem that the African children are being socialized to a different moral and cosmological order than Indians of the Southwestern United States. The paucity of cultural data in the African study allows no further conclusions.

M. H. Lystad (1960a) asked eighty-three Ashanti secondary school boys, aged thirteen to seventeen, to paint pictures of their choice. Although the pictures were analyzed primarily in terms of the predominance of western or traditional values, the author proposes antecedents to the form characteristics of the pictures as a group:

> The Ghanaian pictures are free rather than restrained in form and design. Ghanaian children are brought up casually. They live in an extended family setting where there is always some family member available for their needs and for play. Adult roles are assumed gradually as the children become more and more physically capable of assuming them. The relative freedom afforded them by the adults around them thus appears to be related to the relative freedom expressed in these paintings (1960a:241).

This freedom is compared with the rigidity of paintings by French children described by Wolfenstein, who related it to the rigidity of behavior demanded of the French child. The correlation between amount of behavioral demands and amount of "freedom" in graphic expression, though vaguely defined, is susceptible to cross-cultural testing on a larger sample of cultural groups.

Puberty rites and other initiation rituals in Africa offer a fertile field for culture and personality study, but relatively little has been done to relate such ceremonies to individual development. The world-wide analysis of male initiation at puberty by Whiting, Kluckhohn, and Anthony (1958) has been mentioned. The female initiation ceremony of the Bemba has been analyzed by Richards (1956), who points out the multifunctional character of such rites. They can be recognition of sexual and/or social maturity; they can sever mother-child bonds and serve as a vehicle for the expression of ordinarily repressed emotions by adults. Richards concludes her analysis by stating:

> Bemba evidence supports the suggestion that there is a correlation between matrilyny and girls' initiation ceremonies which emphasize the importance of fertility. In any society in which it is believed that women provide all the physical substance from which the foetus is formed, this would be natural; it is the case in Bemba society. Moreover, the connection between matrilyny and girls' initiation ceremonies has been observed in a number of other African communities. . . . I have also suggested, very tentatively indeed, that in this particular matrilineal society there may be a connection between the lack of open hostility between the sexes and an unconscious feeling of guilt at robbing the man of his children, which is expressed in fears on the part of the women that the men will leave them, and on the part of the men that their wives will not respect them unless taught to do so by the Chisungu (initiation ceremony) (1956:160).

In a valuable appendix, Richards surveys the literature on female initiation rites in Central Africa and finds that:

> . . . the correlation between girls' individual puberty rites and matrilineal organization is very marked in Central Africa, and that both the glorification of the role of the nubile girl and the praise of the man from another clan who gives her fertility, are consonant with the beliefs on which matrilineal organization rests in this area (1956:185).

This areal survey indicating an association between matrilyny and girls' initiation rites in Central Africa suggests a method that could be used to gain a better understanding of the psychocultural aspects of initiation rites in many parts of Africa. In every major culture area, societies that have certain types of initiation ceremonies live right next to groups that do not have them. In western Kenya, for example, there are groups that have initiation and genital operations for both sexes (e.g. Kipsigis, Gusii, Kuria), peoples having initiation and genital operations for boys but not girls (Logoli and other Luhyia peoples), and one large cultural group, the Luo, with no initiation or genital operations for either sex. In Nigeria there are regions with an even greater variety of practises; one group may perform clitoridectomy on infants without ceremony, while in the next group clitoridectomy may be an elaborate ceremonial prelude to marriage, and so forth. Such variation within regions provides the student of culture and personality with a laboratory. If our hypotheses linking puberty rites to child rearing on the one hand and social structure on the other are of any value, they should be able to predict from areal data on puberty rites, what differences in child rearing and social structure should be found in the area. If they cannot make valid predictions, then new hypotheses must be developed. In Africa there are even enough recorded instances of societies adopting and giving up initiation practices to enable the analyst to make comparative studies of the correlated factors involved in changes of this type.

The T.A.T. in South Africa and the Congo

Although few projective technique studies have been carried out in Africa, the past decade has seen at least four adaptations of the Thematic Apperception Test (T.A.T.) for use with African subjects, and some published studies, mostly of a methodological nature so far. Lee (1953) has designed a set of twenty-two T.A.T. cards (eight for each sex and six for both sexes) and published a manual for its use with African subjects. The subject matter for the pictures was based on fantasies collected from "Bantu inmates" of a South African mental hospital. Lee indicates that the pictures were originally made for use with Zulu subjects "but have since been found to serve their purpose adequately among Sutho, Zulu, Ovambo, Fingo, Xosa, Tswana, Griqua, and Swazi" (1953:preface), as well as among both educated and uneducated subjects. He recommends that the test be administered by an African, to eliminate the telling of stereotyped stories which the subjects consider will gain the approval of a European, and that it should be written or spoken in whatever language the subject finds easiest for the purpose. The procedure includes a follow-up interview, conducted a day or two after the test, in which the subject is asked to explain the sources of his plots, in particular whether they have been derived from his own experience or from folktales, myths, legends, books, and so forth.

The comments by Lee on sources of the plot illustrate the importance of knowing the history and folklore of the people to whom the T.A.T. is administered. For example, a certain type of folktale concerning a character named Cakyana is common among the stories told by the Zulu and Xosa subjects. If the analyst knows the traditional version of the story, he can interpret the idiosyncratic distortion (if any) which the subject has made; otherwise he confounds cultural norm with individual response pattern. In another case Lee identifies a very dramatic plot as "the stereotyped story of Nongquase, the Xosa prophetess" (1953:14). One can easily imagine a psychologist who lacks knowledge of the culture and who has not interviewed concerning sources of the plot making incorrect interpretations of such responses.

In his manual Lee gives detailed suggestions for the analysis of the form and content of stories elicited by his T.A.T. cards. One of the most valuable sections is that giving the two most common responses (in brief) of Zulu adults to each of twenty-two pictures. The author cautions that these common stories are not norms, that they vary considerably from one culture to another, and that particularly noticeable differences appear with variations in age and degree of Westernization of subjects. Much of the content analysis is in terms of Murray need-press categories. A fifteen-page specimen analysis of the stories of one subject (an educated Tsonga male from the Transvaal) is presented, using the subject's autobiographical material and sentence completion test responses as confirmatory evidence for specific interpretations. One of the major findings of the specimen T.A.T. analysis is as follows.

There is a certain conflict engendered . . . between the Western and tribal roles of the subject. His usual solution is to give unquestioning obedience (in deference) to those in authority in the tribe. This reaction is probably a reflection of Gilane's attitude to his father, whom he feels to be a better man than himself, both from the point of view of effectiveness and that of morality (1953:38).

Biesheuvel, who has done a great deal of psychological testing on South African subjects, expresses some skepticism concerning the use of T.A.T. pictures.

The rules of perspective drawing are not understood. . . . Conventional graphic details in the postural or facial representations of persons frequently suggested mutilation or blindness. Whether the latter association symbolizes the state of cultural confusion experienced by many Africans today, whether it is an expression of their preoccupation with a scourge which is common in Southern Africa, or whether it is merely a misinterpretation, at a purely perceptual level, of conventional pictorial cues, it is not possible to say in the present state of our knowledge concerning African perceptual habits (1958b:176).

One of the few publications reporting in detail the results of a T.A.T. study in Africa is the monograph by Ombrédane (1954). In a brief trip to the Belgian Congo, Ombrédane administered his "Congo T.A.T." to twelve Basuku subjects, seven Bapende of Mbata-Kondo, ten Bapende of Gungu, and five workers of "varied races" in the town of Tshikapa. He regrets not having large enough samples to use statistical analysis. His analysis consists largely in searching for content characteristics, some of which serve to differentiate the cultural groups. For example, the Basuku often mentioned food in their stories, while the Bapende, who occupy a more fertile and abundant environment, rarely mention food. There are many methodological difficulties with this study. Of the eleven pictures reproduced in the monograph, eight are drawings by a Belgian artist. The human figures are grotesquely elongated and in most cases suggest violent activity or macabre events; in fact they seem to be outpourings of aggressive impulses rather than the somewhat ambiguous stimuli which most researchers recommend. Leblanc (1958a), in a critique of the Ombrédane study, reports the shock with which her Congolese subjects reacted to the same pictures. She criticizes Ombrédane on a large number of points including sample size, administration, and failure to consider form in his analysis.

Leblanc (1958a, 1958b, 1960) has had T.A.T. pictures made up and has used them in a study of women in Katanga Province of the Belgian Congo. Her pictures, in contrast with those of Ombrédane, were drawn by a Congolese artist and are schematic and two dimensional. The hypotheses and results of her published study will be discussed below; at this point the methodology is of primary interest. The tests were administered by the European researcher herself in Swahili, which is not the native tongue of any Congolese. This violates the rules laid down by Lee (1953) on two counts. Furthermore, nowhere in her 1958 report does she mention the cultural groups to which her subjects belong; she refers to them as "Katangese," but the Katanga is a province containing numerous cultures.

One of the most sophisticated contributions to T.A.T. methodology in Africa has been made by E. T. Sherwood, who has devoted a long article (1958) to the problem of designing a set of pictures for acculturation studies in South Africa. His own preference is for pictures which are structured in the sense of being aimed at particular variables. The criteria he sets up for picture design, on the basis of much experimenting with different kinds of stimuli, may well serve as a guide to researchers in other areas. His substantive study was a comparison of the responses of Swazi adults who had been in Johannesburg less than four years with those of Swazi who had been there for a much longer time; it is not yet published at this writing.[3]

Personality and Acculturation

More and more of the psychological studies being carried out in Africa have to do with acculturation. This is particularly true of personality testing and attitude research, in part because amount of education and place of residence (rural-urban) are readily available indices of acculturation and provide the researcher with a source of variation on which to test hypotheses. Unfortunately, some investigators using acculturation as an independent variable have completely ignored differences in traditional culture in the samples being surveyed or tested. They make the bland assumption that more educated or urbanized Africans have more of "Western culture" and less of "African culture," which they characterize as fear-ridden or secure, restrictive or undisciplined, as they happen to imagine it. With the increasing number of ethnographic accounts of African urban life, such as Southall and Gutkind (1956) on Kampala, Uganda, and Longmore (1959) on sex and marriage in the Johannesburg metropolitan area, ignorance of the sociocultural context in studies of urban respondents is becoming less excusable; yet such studies continue to be produced.

An example of such a study is that of Leblanc (1958b, 1960) cited above. Subjects were drawn from the most "advanced" sections of the Congolese populations of Elisabethville, a city of 130,-000 Congolese settled there since the 1930's, and Kolwezi, a smaller city with 30,000 Congolese settled there since World War II. A sentence completion test was administered to 137 subjects of both sexes from both cities, and a T.A.T. to 29 women from both cities. The sentence completion test concerned "the tribal traditional attitude toward women" as measured in areas of behavior "governed by a number of strict native customs and rituals: marital and extra-marital relations, sources of marital conflicts, such as aggressiveness, arguments about food, fecundity, sex separation, woman's infer-

---

[3] An unpublished version of the Sherwood study (1961) became available too late for discussion in the present article.

iority" (1958b:258). The author does not take into account the possibility that the various cultural groups represented in her samples might have different traditional attitudes toward extramarital relations and woman's inferiority, for example. She finds that men showed a more traditional attitude toward women than did women in her sample, and that Kolwezi subjects (less acculturated) also had a significantly more traditional attitude toward women than Elisabethville subjects (more acculturated).

In the T.A.T. section of the study, Leblanc selected fourteen women from Elisabethville and fifteen from Kolwezi, and formulated the unusual general hypothesis that acculturation would have the effect of "bringing about better personality adjustment." The only significant differences she found between the Elisabethville and Kolwezi samples were greater productivity (length of stories), optimism, and characterization (mentioning sex, age, and role characteristics of individuals as opposed to "someone" or "people"), in the former. If one considers that the tests were administered by a European in Swahili, a foreign language to all subjects, it is evident that most of the differences could be attributed to greater fluency in Swahili and more experience in contact with Europeans on the part of the Elisabethville women. Leblanc states that the sentence completion test "is a valid measure to differentiate the attitude of groups . . . in accordance with degree of acculturation," while "the T.A.T. produced more doubtful results" (1958b:263). But she devises a new substantive hypothesis to explain the difference: "The tribal traditional attitude toward women which is unacceptable to the white man tends to disappear before the deeper personality variables which determine it are really modified" (1958b:263). Considering the inadequacy of the research instruments employed, this generalization cannot be said to have received confirmation in the study.

Two studies of the changing values of African students are relevant here, although they do not directly involve personality. Powdermaker (1956) analyzed the imagery in essays written by students of the Northern Rhodesian copperbelt; M. H. Lystad (1960b) analyzed, in sociological terms derived from Parsons and Levy, the favorite stories recounted by students in a secondary school outside of Accra, Ghana. In both cases, many of the students had been born in rural areas, and the predominance of traditional themes and values over urbanized western ones was a major finding in both studies, as it was in Lystad's (1960a) analysis of paintings by Ashanti schoolboys. Both the copperbelt and Accra samples, however, contained individuals from numerous tribal groups with contrasting cultures, and no attention is paid to differences in cultural background.

In a study by Doob (1957) account is taken of cultural differences among Africans. One of the numerous hypotheses tested concerned the relation between amount of Western education and deviation from traditional beliefs and practices concerning the family. Differences between responses of more and less educated groups were great (.01 level of significance) for the Zulu, weak for the Ganda (.10 level), and nonexistent for the Luo. This finding is consistent with the duration and intensity of Western influence in the areas in which these three cultural groups are located: Natal, South Africa (Zulu), Buganda, Uganda (Ganda), and Central Nyanza, Kenya (Luo). Doob concludes:

> Psychologically . . . the person (African) who is like a European in many respects because during or after adolescence he has learned European ways may resemble only superficially the person who was raised like a European in the same respects by his acculturated parents (1957:156).

Thus, as in many acculturation studies outside of Africa, childhood experience is seen as a crucial factor leaving persistent marks on the individual's response patterns. Although Doob compares samples of persons from differing cultural groups, he does not attempt to relate the content of traditional cultures to the attitudes or personality characteristics of his subjects. This remains to be done by students of culture and personality in Africa.[4] Some of the studies discussed in the following sections take acculturation into account, but concentrate on interpreting culture content.

Biesheuvel (1959) is alone in having attempted to generalize in broad outline about the psychological consequences of culture change, particularly urbanization and industrialization, in Africa. His analysis, which applies primarily to South Africa, is that urbanization has weakened traditional African norms and sanctions without replacing them with other means of social and psychological control. The majority of township dwellers are portrayed as lacking the kinship bonds, the effective child training practices, and the conformity of traditional life, so that they are "directed only by impulse" and approach being "devoid of culture." This explains the lawlessness, violence, and laxity of sexual morals among urban

---

[4] E. T. Sherwood (1961) has done this in his recent study of Swazi personality.

Africans. Biesheuvel considers this similar to developments in Europe during the dissolution of medieval society, and finds hope in viewing the "id-directed self" a phenomenon of transition. The smaller group of middle-class Africans are portrayed as closer to the Western values, which they learn not from their parents but from teachers, supervisors, and employers of European descent at a fairly late stage in life. Their anxiety level is high. Citing evidence from Rae Sherwood (1958a, 1958b) and using Riesman's typology of character structure, Biesheuvel concludes concerning middle-class Africans:

> The circumstances under which they grow up and function in the Union of South Africa encourage the development of the other-directed personality type, in which conformity is normally regulated by anxiety. Hence it would appear that African personality development is proceeding straight from tradition- to other- direction, and that the historical stage where behavior was controlled by an internalized code, by guilt rather than by shame as it used to be, or by anxiety, as it is now, has passed them by (1959:18–19).

Turning his attention to industrialization, Biesheuvel asserts that traditional subsistence economies favored personal qualities which are not particularly adaptive for work performance in a wide range of industrial settings. The least westernized South African workers have been found to prefer the lot of a migrant mine worker because it allows traditionally valued leisure (even if only sporadically) and because of its paternalistic protection from the hazards of urban life. However, industrial workers with a long period of urban residence

> ... no longer look upon work as an interruption of the more meaningful and satisfying life of the African areas. They are committed to their daily task and hope to be able to advance in it. It is evident that within this group a new motivation has made its appearance, in which the need to work is recognized as an enduring feature of life, capable of creating and satisfying other needs beyond the mere subsistence level (1959:27).

Biesheuvel asks whether there is a unique element in the personalities of Africans, and tentatively concludes he has found it in *négritude* as expounded by Leopold Senghor.

> Négritude ... is in keeping with the concept of vitality which I consider to be characteristic of the behavior of African peoples. A culture in which this concept concerning the meaning of life reigns, can dispense with an excess of activity, ... such activity is required mainly for sustained effort in pursuit of some self-imposed duty or goal. It has no need of the inner-directed personality structure which Africans are not now likely to develop to any extent, and it repudiates the drive element in work motivation, which is relatively lacking in Africans, as

destructive of the main purpose of life. Though essentially a West African creed and in keeping with limitations imposed on human effort by the tropical climate, it is by no means inappropriate to certain features of African personality development at all cultural levels as we have found it here in the South. Indubitably, the philosophy of *négritude* is far more likely to provide the black masses, in their transition from traditionalism, with a meaningful new culture than is provided by the more alien model of the West (1959:36–37).

It would be easy to criticize this lecture by a usually rigorous psychologist for its facile generalizations, its awkward applications of social theory to African situations, and its occasional ethnocentrism, but these faults seem less important than the service he has performed by raising a number of important problems concerning the psychological dimension of culture change in contemporary Africa. Social control in urban society, adaptation to new economic circumstances, and the development of nontraditional motives are problems relevant to culture and personality which are becoming increasingly important in the African scene.

Psychocultural Interpretation of Ritual, Witchcraft, and Dreams

For many years ethnographers have been describing African culture patterns which allow the occasional expression of feelings usually kept strictly in check. In one of the earliest attempts to apply psychoanalytic theory to African data, Herskovits stated that "socially institutionalized release constitutes an outstanding characteristic of the Negro cultures of West Africa and of the New World" (1934:77). He described the Dahomean institution of the *avogan*, the market place dance at which people are obliquely ridiculed in song, and the calumnious songs which co-wives sing against one another. Rattray was quoted to the effect that West Africans, by incorporating into their folklore descriptions of behavior ordinarily forbidden, "had discovered by themselves the truth of the psychoanalysts' theory of 'repression'," and "sought an outlet for what might otherwise have become a dangerous complex" (Herskovits 1934:77).

More recent reports indicate similar phenomena in cultures of South Africa, Kenya, Northern Rhodesia, and Nigeria, among others. The institutionalized expression of ordinarily repressed hostilities and other emotions is seen by anthropologists as a safety valve, functional for the maintenance of institutions which require restraint of individuals. Most commonly these culturally patterned outlets involve the expression of political hostility or antagonism between the sexes. In both cases, the form is frequently one of status reversal: the subject or vassal reprimands his chief or lord; the submissive female dons male clothes, swaggers, insults men. Gluckman (1955) has discussed these phenomena at length in sociological terms; he considers them prime illustrations of the positively functional nature of conflict in African societies. Mayer (1950) has described the noisy, demanding behavior of the usually obedient Gusii wife toward her husband at the *enyangi* ceremony which completes their marriage rites. Richards notes that in many girls' initiation rites "the women, who are bound to be submissive and humble to men at other times, are allowed to be quite outrageous in the ceremony, to swagger, to shout obscenities or to attack the men" (1956: 60). This is true for the Gusii as it is for many other societies, but not among the matrilineal Bemba. Among the Nupe of Nigeria, each community has one of three annual ceremonies which allow "cathartic release" for impulses which are repressed in secular life (Nadel 1954). All three of the ceremonies concern adolescence, though in varying degrees, and two of them, *gunnu* and *gani*, have periods of sexual license as well as the imitation and caricature of women by boys. The third, *navu*, involves (or did involve before it was banned by the government) an all-night battle with torches, sticks, and stones, between the adolescent boys of opposing village factions, in addition to some licentious heterosexual activity and the good-humored "kidnaping" and ransoming of women and old people by gangs of young men. Nadel uses psychoanalytic terminology in his analysis of these rituals, concluding that Nupe religion "in providing these outlets . . . anticipates as well as canalizes the working of psychological mechanisms, which might otherwise operate in random fashion or beyond the control of society, in the 'private worlds' of neuroses and psychopathic fantasies" (1954:274).

In analyzing witchcraft and ritual, Nadel formulated his own version (apparently influenced by Kluckhohn's analysis of Navaho witchcraft) of psychoanalytic theory in relation to culture. Briefly, this theory is that magico-religious beliefs and practices reflect the anxieties and unconscious desires of a people, but that the anxieties and desires thus expressed have their origins in adult roles (sex and age roles in the context of family and kinship relations) rather than childhood experiences. Although it is the contemporaneous frustrations and tensions of adult life which are viewed as the starting points, their expression in religious phenomena are discussed in terms of standard psychoanalytic defense mechanisms such as projection, displacement, and compensation.

Nadel's position, particularly his rejection of the importance of child rearing, is most clearly illustrated by his comparative analysis of the Nupe and Gwari, two closely related tribes of Northern Nigeria (1952). Both have witchcraft beliefs, but the Nupe invariably accuse women of witchcraft, while the Gwari accuse individuals of both sexes. Nadel attributes this difference to the fact that marriage "is without serious complications and relatively tension-free in Gwari, but full of stress and mutual hostility in Nupe" (1952:21). The stress in Nupe stems from the ideal of masculine domination contrasted with the reality that many women are successful itinerant traders, usurping economic dominance in the family and engaging in independent behavior which is considered immoral. This explanation is adopted by Nadel only after he has searched for differences in child rearing. The only difference uncovered is that, among the Nupe when the two to three-year postpartum taboo on maternal sexual behavior is terminated, the woman visits her husband in his hut, leaving her children behind in her own hut, while the Gwari husband visits his wife so that cohabitation takes place in the presence of the young children. On the assumption that Freudian psychology would predict witnessing the primal scene to be the cause of sex antagonism, Nadel rejects this hypothesis on the grounds that the Nupe have sex antagonism but no primal scene, while the Gwari have the primal scene but no sex antagonism.

An alternative explanation in terms of childhood experience is overlooked. It could be asserted that the Nupe child feels abandoned by his mother, who leaves him at night for the paternal hut, while the Gwari child sees his father as an intruder upon his relationship with the mother. One would then predict that the Nupe male would hate women and the Gwari male would hate men older or more powerful than himself. This is consistent with Nadel's statement that "Gwari informants in fact claimed that a marked hostility between father and son was a common feature of their family life" (1952:21). Furthermore, there is considerable evidence of maternal rejection among the Nupe: women practise abortion and use alleged contraceptives to continue their trading activities, and they tend to leave their children for itinerant trading when the latter are four or five years old. Nupe women may antagonize their husbands by their economic activities and sexual independence, but they also reject motherhood and abandon their children. Thus it can be argued with equal cogency that the mother-child or husband-wife relationship is the significant antecedent to sex antagonism in witch beliefs. For a more crucial test than was provided by the Nupe and Gwari, one would need a society, or sample of societies, in which maternal rejection and female usurpation of male dominance in the conjugal relationship, were not associated. In any event, the evidence presented by Nadel is not convincing support of his rejection of child-rearing determinants for supernatural beliefs.[5]

In the same article on witchcraft, Nadel contrasts the Korongo and Mesakin, neighboring matrilineal peoples in the Nuba Mountains of the Sudan. The Korongo have no witchcraft beliefs at all; the Mesakin are obsessed with fears of witchcraft and frequently accuse each other of it, a man's mother's brother being most commonly suspected. In both groups masculine vigor in youth is emphasized, and at the first sporting contest after puberty there is a ceremony and a presentation of a gift in livestock—an "anticipated inheritance"—made to the youth by his mother's brother. The difference is that among the Korongo, the gift is given spontaneously, while among the Mesakin, the mother's brother always refuses to give it at first and it often must be taken by force, a socially accepted procedure. Quarrels over the gift between the Mesakin youth and his mother's brother are frequent. If the former should fall ill, the latter would be suspected of witchcraft. Nadel relates this difference to the contrasting age-class systems of the two groups: the Korongo have six age classes in which the valued masculine physical activity is gradually given up, while the Mesakin have only three from birth to death, so that a man relinquishes his sporting life abruptly at a fairly young age. For the Mesakin, "the resentment and refusal . . . express the older man's envy of youth and virility, the loss of which is brought home to him by the very request for the anticipated inheritance" (1952:26). This resentment is allowed acceptable expression only in the sphere of witchcraft, and "every man projects his own frustrations of this nature into the allegations that others are guilty of witchcraft" (1952:26).

As in the comparison of Nupe and Gwari, so for the Korongo and Mesakin, Nadel examines child-rearing practices, finding them in this case "identical in the two tribes." He does mention, however, that among the Korongo premarital and highly promiscuous sex relations are fully accepted and openly engaged in, "while the Mesakin conceal such activity and recognize an ideal of premarital chastity." This suggests the possibility, on which Nadel makes no

---

[5] An extended analysis of the relation of sex antagonism to witchcraft beliefs among the Nupe, complete with four case histories, can be found in Nadel (1954:172–206).

comment, that the sex training of children may differ in the two groups. His role analysis is again plausible, but his attempts to eliminate childhood experience as a factor are not.

Comparing two other Nuba groups, Nadel (1955) finds that the religion of the Heiban is more pessimistic and fear-ridden than that of the Otoro. He relates this to the greater degree of order in the Otoro role system: wives are incorporated into their husband's lineages, adolescence is regulated in a series of stages, male homosexuals are allowed an accepted role as transvestites. All of these traits are lacking in Heiban culture, where role ambiguity is pronounced. Such ambiguity is seen as fostering tension which finds an outlet in religion. In sum, Nadel's comparative analyses are some of the most stimulating studies of culture and personality based on African material. They illustrate the advantages of taking a point of view wider than the single society, and the difficulties of achieving conclusive results when comparing only two societies. Future students of culture and personality would do well to carry on the investigations of religion and age and sex roles which he pioneered.

In a different methodological vein, but equally concerned with sex and age roles, is Lee's study of Zulu dreams (1958). Dreams are important in Zulu culture, being interpreted by diviners who forecast the future and diagnose misfortunes from them. Lee collected dreams from 600 Zulu men and women and made an intensive study of another 120 women to whom he administered the T.A.T., as well as interviewing on their dream life. He found that women reported a much greater amount of dream activity than men, and that the former dream more of intrinsically terrifying objects such as "monsters," while the latter enjoy dreaming more. In terms of central imagery, the number of different Zulu dreams was found to be very restricted. A general conclusion was that "dream content, for the particular sex, is derived almost exclusively from areas of social experience permitted by the culture *in the indigenous system of sanctions* of some 50 to 75 years ago" (1958:270, italics in original). Thus, women, "acting under a very strong cultural imperative," dreamed of babies and children but not cattle, while men dreamed of cattle, their chief economic goal and source of prestige. This is significant since Zulu women were formerly prohibited from handling cattle, but now (in the absence of migratory-laboring husbands) do so more than men. More males also dream directly of fighting, which Lee interprets as related to the traditional warrior role of men. In his intensive study of females, Lee found that traditional imagery and folklore were more accurate in dreams than in T.A.T. responses. He tentatively concludes that "the unconscious minds of individuals are very stable repositories of the past, and can be used as a valuable source of ethnographic material" (1958:280). The cultural lag of the unconscious is attributed to its being acquired in childhood, while living in comparatively traditional circumstances and before exposure to European culture. This is similar to Bruner's finding in his study (1956) of acculturation in an American Indian group.

In his study of Zulu females, Lee was able to obtain evidence relevant to the Freudian theory of dream interpretation. He found that the contents of women's dreams tend to vary with their age: young women dream of sex and childbearing more than older women, unmarried women dream of weddings more than married women. Many women reported dreaming of "a baby," while others mentioned a recurrent dream of still water, considered by Freud and by Zulu diviners to symbolize childbirth. Adopting from Freud the hypothesis that high motivation yields directly wish-fulfilling dreams, while ambivalent or weaker motivation yields symbolic dreams, Lee compared the motivational state of women who reported baby dreams with those who mentioned still water dreams as more frequent. He found that baby dreams, interpreted as directly wish-fulfilling, were more common among young married women "on whom the social pressure to prove their fertility is very great" (1958:274). Both unmarried girls, who look forward to childbirth but fear the social disapproval of premarital pregnancy, and married women with two or three children, who want to have more but have proved their fertility, dream of still water more frequently. Thus those who were assumed on grounds of social role to be more highly motivated toward childbirth had less symbolic dreams than those with weaker or ambivalent motivation in the same direction. Lee takes this as confirmation of the Freudian hypothesis.

Like Nadel, Marwick (1952) has related witch beliefs and accusations to aspects of social structure which generate or direct the hostilities of individuals. He presents quantitative data to show that the Cewa, a matrilineal group of Northern Rhodesia, tend to accuse their own matrilineal kin of witchcraft, in contrast to the outgroup scapegoating found by Kluckhohn in Navaho witchcraft. Marwick suggests that the difference may be due to the fact that Cewa local groups are not as small, isolated, or crucial for subsistence as those of the Navaho; in fact "it may even be that among the Cewa witch-craft accusations have the adaptive function of being catalytic to the natural process of lineage segmentation" (1952:123):

Cewa seem to have an almost neo-Freudian recognition of the inevitable danger of repressing hostility for the sake of loyalty to one's close relatives. They express this recognition neatly by saying that members of the same matrilineage tend "to practice witchcraft against one another" because when they quarrel they are inclined "to leave unspoken words of speech with one another" (1952:217).

Marwick interprets the Cewa data in terms of his hypothesis that interpersonal competition is generated by nonascriptive status relationships, that it develops into tension and conflict if the object competed for is intensely desired and if there are no structural means for regulating the competition, and that the "tension will be projected into witch beliefs... if there are no adequate institutionalized outlets for it" (1952:129). He concludes that witch beliefs and accusations are positively functional for the Cewa social system in that they destroy old social relationships, clearing away the ground for new ones.

The studies reviewed in this section indicate some of the potentialities of African research for work on sex roles, sex personality, and the expression of culturally patterned anxieties and hostilities in ritual and supernatural beliefs. It is to be hoped that the excellent beginnings made by investigators such as Nadel and Lee will be followed up by systematic, comparative research into the same theoretical problems.

Mental Illness

There is a body of psychiatric literature on Africans, much of it authored by psychiatrists with little anthropological sophistications who fail to distinguish one African cultural group from another and who at best make comparisons between urban and rural Africans.[6] One common finding is that "depressive" conditions are rare among Africans and "schizophrenic" disorders frequent, relative to Europe and the United States. In light of recent challenges to traditional diagnostic categories among U.S. psychiatrists, and the drastic changes in psychodiagnosis which appear to be taking place, these older studies of Africans are of dubious value. In any event, there was rarely any attempt to relate the incidence or form of mental disease to culture patterns in specific African groups.

---

[6] An exception is the description by Brelsford (1950) of concepts and treatment of psychopathology among the Bemba.

The most relevant of the strictly psychiatric studies is that by Tooth (1950), who surveyed mental illness in the Gold Coast (now Ghana). He found a correlation between the amount of European contact (and traditional motives) in a region and the delusional content of schizophrenics in that region.

In the North and among the "bush" peoples the delusional content was almost invariably concerned with the ramifications of the fetish system. The fact of lunacy means that an offense has been committed either against the nature spirits, who then trouble the offender in the form of dwarfs or fairies, or against the ancestral hierarchy who appear and influence the sufferer in person. Although it is not unusual for the insane from this section of the population to speak of themselves as under the control of God, no example was found of identification with the Deity. It is possible because of the concentration of missionary activity in the South that the identification of the insane with an anthropomorphic God is so common there. Messianic delusions were not met with outside the asylum, where identification with Christ was sometimes combined with one or more of the leading figures of international politics. Delusions of grandeur were not found among the "bush" people but among the insane in Ashanti, delusions of great wealth were common and often associated with claims to royal birth and connections with powerful chiefs. It was only in the more sophisticated South that living individuals or groups, usually connected with the government and operating by means of electricity, wireless or television, took precedence in the delusions of the insane over the traditional supernatural agencies (1950:52).

Tooth hypothesizes that the situations of personal choice introduced under Westernization lead to mental disorder, but he is unable to find quantitative evidence of more psychosis among Westernized segments of the population. With respect to treatment of psychotics, he mentions the frequent sight of them at market places (a possible locus for ethnopsychiatric field work!) and contrasts the attitude toward psychosis in three regions of the country. He concludes that "the Africans have evolved a system which cares for quite 80 per cent of their insane under conditions which compare favorably with those provided by the European authorities" (1950:65).

Among the few studies of culture and mental disease carried out in Africa are those on related Nguni groups by Laubscher (1937) and Lee (1950). Laubscher, a psychiatrist who did field work among the Tembu and related Fingo of South Africa, describes the role of mythical beings in their traditional explanations of psychotic behavior, in the delusions of hospitalized psychotics, and in the dreams of normals. The beings include hypersexual dwarfs, blood-eating and hypersexual birds, and snakes harbored in the female organs. In many cases these creatures are viewed as gratifying the extramarital sexual cravings of females. The imagery itself and interpretations of it by diviners are so suggestive of Freudian concepts that one might almost say that psychoanalytic theory is part of the Tembu-Fingo belief system.

Lee has analyzed almost identical phenomena among the Zulu, a closely related Nguni people, and his analysis is freer of a heavy-handed early Freudianism than that of Laubscher. He describes the syndrome known as "Bantu disease" or *ufufunyana,* which is recognized by the Zulu as a nonorganic condition similar to the state of possession manifested by a "witch doctor" during his apprenticeship (This is true of the Tembu and Fingo as well).

Stereotyped dreams involving the above-mentioned supernatural beings and, among present-day Zulu, involving Indians (many of whom live in Natal), are an integral part of the syndrome. The disease is most commonly found among women, who complain of pains in their lower abdomen, sometimes develop paralysis, and also have seizures during which they talk incoherently in what their neighbors assume to be an Indian language. The women often dream of "tokoloshe," the bearded dwarf with a huge penis, and believe that he rapes them at night. Lee describes three rather different cases of *ufufunyana,* two of which he considers "pure cases of conversion hysteria." The women afflicted suffer from obvious sexual fears and frustrations and their disorders were precipitated by sexual crisis, in one case desertion by a husband, in the other a threat by a rebuffed lover. The third case, that of an old man, appeared to be related to sexual jealousy. Lee states his conviction that this disease, its high frequency among women, and its apparent increase in recent years, are related to the "heavy anxiety load" of Zulu culture, and indicates that he will carry out further studies "directed at the discovering of specific reasons for the obviously insecure personality pattern which seems to be so common among the Zulu people" (1950:18). Loudon (1960) has speculated on the correlates of *ufufunyana,* but without any convincing evidence.

Nadel (1946) has attempted to relate shamanism among the Nyima and other peoples of the Nuba mountains in the Sudan to the incidence of mental disease among them. The shamanism he describes is similar to that found in Central Asia, is highly institutionalized, and plays an important part in the medical and religious aspects of Nyima culture. The shaman must be capable of spirit possession which is similar in overt behavior to cataleptic seizures; instances of possession observed by Nadel appeared to him to vary in their degree of "sincerity" and conscious fakery, but he was convinced that a majority of them resulted in seizures over which the shaman had little conscious control. "Insanity" (not defined) is said to be rare among the Nyima, but epilepsy is widespread (estimated at one in 100) and is recognized as frequent by the people themselves and by medical officers in the district. Epilepsy is not regarded by the Nyima as spirit possesssion or as a qualification for the role of shaman, but six of the shamans interviewed had epilepsy in their families and, of eight hereditary shamans, only two claimed that none of their relatives had been epileptic. The shamans themselves are not epileptics and have no histories of mentally deranged behavior.

The possibility is considered that shamanism in the Nuba mountains is associated with a low incidence of "insanity" and a high incidence of epilepsy. However, the Dilling, who also have shamanism, are estimated to have a relatively high incidence of insanity (one in 300) but little or no epilepsy; the Koalib, another shamanistic group, have much less of both conditions (one in 500 for insanity, one in 1000 for epilepsy). Furthermore, nonshamanistic Nuba groups have incidences of insanity both lower and higher than those estimated for the shamanistic groups. Thus this simple hypothesis is rejected. Taking into account the fact that shamanism is increasing in intensity and frequency among shamanistic groups and is also spreading to nonshamanistic groups, Nadel suggests its relationship to the "psychologically unsettling" impact of culture change brought about by contacts with Western civilization. This change "among the Nyima as among all primitive communities . . . must create and foster emotional instability, neurotic and hysterical leanings, that is, the constitutional qualifications of a shaman" (1946:36). The hypothesis is formulated that shamanism is a preventive measure for mental health:

> Shamanism still leaves in existence and without a social "niche," the deviant and abnormal personality, though the borderline between normal and abnormal differs from that valid in non-shamanistic groups. But it remains an open question whether shamanism does not in a different sense "absorb" mental derangement; the institutionalized catharsis which it offers may well have the therapeutic effect of stabilizing hysteria and related psycho-neuroses, thus reducing a psychopathic incidence which should otherwise be much larger (1946:36).

Thus the shamanistic groups may be able to cope with the general psychological disturbance resulting from acculturation without a higher incidence of mental disease. In other words, Nadel rejects a synchronic hypothesis, that shamanistic and nonshamanistic groups differ in their incidence of mental disease, in favor of a diachronic hypothesis to the effect that the groups will differ in the amount of increment in mental disease under changing conditions.

Thus the hypothesis I suggest is verifiable . . . for if it is true, it must be possible to show that psychoses and kindred disorders are increasing among the non-shamanistic groups, while in the shamanistic groups the increase of shamanism would go hand in hand with a relatively undisturbed mental stability (1946:37).

Nadel did not have the data to test this hypothesis, but his study provides an excellent example of research design for future students of the relation between culture patterns and mental disease in changing African societies.[7]

Messing (1958, 1960) has analyzed the Zar spirit-possession cult of the Amhara of Ethiopia as group psychotherapy for a wide range of emotional disturbances "ranging from frustrated status ambition to actual mental illness." Married women are the most frequent patients, and the cult functions not only to mitigate symptoms, but also to provide a group context in which deviants are reintegrated into society. The sexual symbolism of the relation between the patient and his Zar, and the manner in which the cult reflects Ethiopian social stratification, are some of the fascinating aspects of the study. Spirit-possession phenomena of a similar type occur in West Africa and the Caribbean; their comparative analysis in sociopsychological terms would contribute greatly to our understanding of the psychiatric functions of religion.

The most thorough investigation of mental illness in a single African culture is that by Field (1960) among the rural Ashanti. Utilizing her previous experience as an ethnographer, Field returned to the Ashanti as a psychiatrist and set herself up near a shrine where troubled people come to receive help from a deity whose priest becomes possessed and communicates advice from the god. It was possible for her to observe and obtain case histories on those supplicants who were mentally ill, and she conducted some local surveys as well. The troubles and desires which normal people bring to the shrine are described in detail before the psychiatric data are presented. For the most part, standard diagnostic categories are used, and the emphasis is on similarities between behavior patterns observed in the field and those found among Europeans.

One of Field's findings illustrates perfectly the need for intensive

---

[7] Another excellent example is provided by Scotch (1960) in relating essential hypertension to changes accompanying urbanization in a quantitative study of rural and urban Zulu.

community study outside the mental hospital to get a valid picture of the incidence of various mental disorders in a given population. As mentioned above, the older psychiatric studies (including that of Tooth, who worked in Ghana) are unanimous in stating that depression is extremely rare, and they present quantitative data to prove it. However, Field states:

> Depression is the commonest mental illness of Akan rural women and nearly all such patients come to the shrines with spontaneous self-accusations of witchcraft. . . . The depressive personality is, in sickness and health, self-effacing and is seldom a disturbing nuisance. She is therefore the last type of patient who would ever find her way to any kind of European hospital unless she had some concurrent and conspicuous physical trouble. . . . It is not surprising therefore that psychiatrists and other doctors who see patients only in hospitals and clinics should have the idea that depression in Africa hardly exists (1960:149).

This discovery of depressive disorders is an important one and is adequately documented in the case histories, but there is no discussion of the psychocultural determinants of guilt in Akan individuals. In fact, Field appears to regard the guilt and depression as a tendency not produced by the conditions of Akan culture but occurring equally among all peoples who actively believe in witchcraft. She claims that only the confessions of depressives can keep such beliefs alive in a group; the fantasies of paranoids are not sufficient. This is contrary to fact, for there are numerous African societies in which witchcraft is a major preoccupation but no one ever confesses to being a witch. Field does not take into account the variation of witch beliefs among African societies, and this leads her away from investigating the peculiar conditions in Ashanti which make confession a pronounced pattern.

Cultural norms *are* considered in the section on paranoid reactions: "In a country where nobody looks twice at a lorry announcing in big letters, 'Enemies all about me,' or '*Suro nnipa*' (Be afraid of people), it is clear that our ideas of what constitutes a morbidly paranoid attitude must be revised" (1960:296). Nevertheless, Field asserts that it is quite possible to distinguish the controlled paranoia of the normal Ashanti from abnormal paranoid reactions. The valuable contribution of the study is that it presents psychotic behavior in cultural context, with the element of supernatural belief, which is so important in these disorders, clearly delineated in its relation to precipitating social circumstances and organic factors. The etiology of the psychoses described is considered as being outside the limits of the study, in part (I suspect) because the author believes that the Akan do not differ significantly from other peoples in their mental illnesses but only in the cultural forms which these disorders take.

Although Field's monograph contains the largest number of published psychiatric case histories from a single African group, it should be noted that Tooth (1950) also includes numerous case histories, and Sachs (1947) did a book-length case history of a Johannesburg witch doctor. The study by Bohannon (1960) of homicide and suicide in seven African societies, although it is not a psychological analysis, does contain case histories and is important as the first comparative study of deviant behavior in Africa.

Conclusions

The foregoing survey bears out the initial assertion that relatively little culture-and-personality research has been carried out in Africa. In fact, considering how little has been done, it is remarkable that there are studies of the quality of Albino and Thompson (1956) on weaning, Lee (1950, 1953, 1958) on adult personality and projective techniques, and Field (1960) on mental illness. The still untapped and largely unrecognized potentialities of Africa as a field for culture and personality study necessitate attention to the possible lines of future research. In the recommendations which follow, emphasis is placed on types of research which utilize the peculiar advantages of Africa as a major ethnographic area. Thus the large number of distinct ethnic groups suggests the feasibility and importance of comparative studies; the vast accumulation of published ethnographic material, particularly on social organization, makes analysis of existing literature valuable, with personality and social structure a natural emphasis; the recency of Western contact in many groups is conducive to studies of culture change, and the differential exposure to Western culture of persons with the same traditional culture (in the rural-urban and educated-uneducated dichotomies) makes controlled comparisons possible; the migrant labor situation creates the conditions for studies of the impact of absent fathers on personality development; variations in the presence and content of initiation rites present themselves as a problem for psychocultural investigation, and so forth.

Comparative Analysis of Existing Ethnographic Materials.   No area of the world has as much reliable information on social organization in as many different societies. Correlational studies of personality and social structure could include relationships between family roles and sociopolitical roles, between the economic and social position of women and mother-child relationships, among different forms of culturally patterned aggression, such as warfare, the feud, sorcery, and so forth, and between sex roles and patterns of sexual behavior.

Comparative Socialization Studies. We need basic material similarly collected on a large number of traditional African cultures. The kinds of data required range from motor development and infant nutrition through parent-child and sibling relationships to the socialization of sex, aggression, and dependence, and training in achievement, responsibility, and skills. Only by the collection of comparable materials on traditional child-rearing patterns will it be possible to find the conditions under which traditional culture patterns were learned and adapted to individual needs, and to establish baselines for studies relating to socialization and culture change. Feasible studies of special significance include: (1) the effect of structural variations (different polygynous arrangements, virilocal versus uxorilocal marriage, more and less authoritarian extended family patterns, varying divorce rates, high and low status position of women) on child experience and behavior; (2) the effect of economic factors (pastoral versus agricultural subsistence patterns, differentiated versus undifferentiated economic role systems) on child experience and behavior; (3) the effect of mother-child separation (at termination of postpartum sexual taboo, weaning, or replacement by a sibling) on children conditioned to varying amounts of initial nurturance by mother, with dependency weaning varying in its abruptness from one group to another; (4) the effect of differential severity of sex and aggression training on cultural behavior in those motivation systems; (5) the differing courses of adolescent development in cultures with and without male and female initiation rites at puberty; (6) the connection between varying political values (for example, authoritarian versus egalitarian) and the values concerning interpersonal behavior which are transmitted to children.

Urbanization and Education. These two processes are of fundamental importance in contemporary culture change in Africa and can be expected to have their correlates in personality change. In one kind of research design, urban and ural, or educated and uneducated, individuals belonging to the same ethnic group can be compared on indices of culture stress (mental illness, psychosomatic disorders, suicide, crime), patterns of child rearing, and values concerning interpersonal relations, supernatural phenomena, political behavior, achievement, and ethnic parochialism. Another approach, increasingly feasible under contemporary conditions, is to study differences on these variables between the first urban or Western-educated generation and later generations whose parents have been urbanites or educated persons. The varying reactions of different cultural groups to the same urban or school environment provide another possibility for personality study, with the emphasis on the extent to which traditional behavior patterns are persisting under changed social conditions. The effect of labor migration on child experience and identification processes, adolescent adjustment in urban settings, and changes in female roles brought about by economic development, are examples of specific topics which deserve study.

Comparative Psychiatry.   Primary attention must be paid to the collection of basic data concerning the incidence of mental illnesses of various types and their cultural contexts, in variety of African populations. This is a tremendous task in itself, and will necessarily involve medical investigators to distinguish functional disorders from the behavioral effects of trypanosomiasis and nutritional deficiencies, as well as anthropologically sophisticated personnel to concentrate on cultural reactions to behavioral deviance. Some special problems which the African studies to date suggest include: the development of sexual disorders such as impotence and conversion hysteria in societies which set a high value on fecundity, but which vary in the requirements of their sex roles; the particular relation of cultural stresses affecting women to their development of depressive conditions (as in Ashanti) and various forms of dissociative behavior which involve spirit possession as a psychotherapeutic technique; the differential incidence of mental illnesses in Westernized and non-Westernized segments of the population (mentioned above); the relation of sorcery and witchcraft beliefs to paranoid conditions.

In making these suggestions I have avoided suggesting particular techniques to be used. I assume that investigators will choose behavioral observation, projective techniques, interviews, questionnaires, dreams, or life histories, according to the problem under study and their own assessment of the validity and reliability of these research instruments.

In the long run, systematic studies of culture and personality in Africa will benefit not only this developing subdiscipline but also the new nations of Africa in their attempts to modernize themselves while meeting the needs of their culturally heterogeneous populations. This difficult task cannot be accomplished without an understanding of the behavior patterns and motivations of the changing but still mainly traditional ethnic groups within their borders.

BIBLIOGRAPHY

ALBINO, RONALD C. and V. J. THOMPSON
1956   The effects of sudden weaning on Zulu children. British Journal of Medical Psychology 29:177–210.

BARRY, H., I. L. CHILD, and M. K. BACON
1959   Relation of child training to subsistence economy. American Anthropologist 61:51–63.

BIESHEUVEL, SIMON
1943   African intelligence. Johannesburg, South African Institute of Race Relations.
1958a   Objectives and methods of African psychological research. Journal of Social Psychology 47:161–168.
1958b   Methodology in the study of attitudes of Africans. Journal of Social Psychology 47:169–184.
1959   Race, culture and personality: The Hoernlé Memorial Lecture 1959. Johannesburg, South African Institute of Race Relations.

BOHANNON, PAUL (ed.)
1960   African homicide and suicide. Princeton, N.J., Princeton University Press.

BRELSFORD, W. V.
1950   Insanity among the Bemba of Northern Rhodesia. Africa 20:46–54.

BRUNER, EDWARD M.
1956   Cultural transmission and cultural change. Southwestern Journal of Anthropology 12:191–199.

CAROTHERS, J. C.
1948   A study of mental derangement in Africans and an attempt to explain its peculiarities, more especially in relation to the African attitude to life. Psychiatry 11:47–86.
1951   Frontal lobe function and the African. Journal of Mental Science 97:12–48.
1953   The African mind in health and disease, a study in ethnopsychiatry. Geneva, World Health Organization Monograph Series, No. 17.
1954   The psychology of Mau Mau. Nairobi: The Government Printer, Colony and Protectorate of Kenya.

DAVIDSON, S.
1949   Psychiatric work among the Bemba. Rhodes-Livingstone Journal 7:75–86.

DOOB, LEONARD W.
  1957 An introduction to the study of acculturation. Journal of Social Psychology 45:144–160.

DORJAHN, VERNON R.
  1958a Fertility, polygyny and their interrelations in Temne society. American Anthropologist 60:838–860.
  1958b The factor of polygyny in African demography. *In* Continuity and change in African cultures, W. Bascom and M. Herskovits, eds., Chicago, University of Chicago Press.

EVANS-PRITCHARD, E. E.
  1953 Kinship and marriage among the Nuer. London, Oxford University Press.
  1956 Nuer Religion. London, Oxford University Press.

FIELD, M. J.
  1960 Search for security: an ethno-psychiatric study of rural Ghana. Evanston, Ill., Northwestern University Press.

FORTES, MEYER
  1939 Social and psychological aspects of education in Taleland. London, International African Institute Memorandum. XVII.

GEBER, MARCELLE
  1958 The psycho-motor development of African children in the first year, and the influence of maternal behavior. Journal of Social Psychology 47:185 195.

GLUCKMAN, MAX
  1951 Kinship and marriage among the Zulu of Natal and the Lozi of Northern Rhodesia. *In* African systems of kinship and marriage, A. R. Radcliffe-Brown and C. D. Forde, eds., London, Oxford University Press.
  1955 Custom and conflict in Africa. Glencoe, The Free Press.

HARLOW, HARRY
  1958 The nature of love. The American Psychologist 13:673–685.

HERSKOVITS, MELVILLE, J.
  1934 Freudian mechanisms in primitive Negro psychology. *In* E. E. Evans-Pritchard, Raymond Firth, Bronislaw Malinowski, and Isaac Schapera, Essays presented to C. G. Seligman. London, Kegan, Paul, Trench, Trubner and Co.
  1948 Man and his works. New York, Alfred A. Knopf and Co.

HERSKOVITS, M. J. and FRANCES HERSKOVITS
  1958 Sibling rivalry, the Oedipus complex, and myth. Journal of American Folklore 71:1–15.

JAHODA, GUSTAV
  1958a Child animism: I. A critical survey of cross-cultural research. Journal of Social Psychology 47:197–212.
  1958b Child animism: II. A study in West Africa. Journal of Social Psychology 47:213–222.
  1958c Immanent justice among West African children. Journal of Social Psychology 47:241–248.

LAUBSCHER, B. J. F.
1937   Sex, custom, and psychopathology, a study of South African pagan natives. London, Routledge.

LEBLANC, MARIA
1958a La problematique d'adaptation du T.A.T. au Congo. Zaire 12:339–348.
1958b Acculturation of attitude and personality among Katangese women. Journal of Social Psychology 47:257–264.
1960   Personnalité de la femme Katangaise Louvain Publications Universitaire.

LEE, S. G.
1950   Some Zulu concepts of psychogenic disorder. Journal for Social Research, Pretoria, 1:9–18.
1953   Manual of a thematic apperception test for African subjects. Pietermaritzburg, University of Natal Press.
1958   Social influences in Zulu dreaming. Journal of Social Psychology 47: 265–283.

LeVINE, ROBERT A.
1959a Gusii sex offenses: a study in social control. American Anthropologist 61:965–990.
1960   The internalization of political values in stateless societies. Human Organization 19:51–58.

LONGMORE, LAURA
1959   The dispossessed: a study of the sex-life of Bantu women in and around Johannesburg. London, Jonathan Cape.

LOUDON, J. B.
1960   Psychogenic disorder and social conflict among the Zulu. In Culture and mental health, M. K. Opler, ed. New York, Macmillan.

LYSTAD, MARY HANEMANN
1960a Paintings of Ghanaian children. Africa 30:238–242.
1960b Traditional values of Ghanaian children. American Anthropologist 62:454–464.

MARWICK, M. G.
1952   The social context of Cewa witch beliefs. Africa 22:120–35, 215–33.

MAYER, PHILIP
1950   Privileged obstruction of marriage rites among the Gusii. Africa 20: 113–125.

MESSING, SIMON D.
1958   Group therapy and social status in the Zar cult of Ethiopia. American Anthropologist. 60:1120–1126.
1960   Group therapy and social status in the Zar cult of Ethiopia. In Culture and Mental Health, M. K. Opler, ed. New York, Macmillan.

MURDOCK, GEORGE PETER
1959   Africa, its peoples and their cultural history. New York, Macmillan.

NADEL, S. F.
1937a Experiments on culture psychology. Africa 10:421–435.
1937b Field experiments in racial psychology. British Journal of Psychology 28:195–211.

1946 A study of shamanism in the Nuba mountains. Journal of the Royal Anthropological Institute 76:25–37.

1952 Witchcraft in four African societies: an essay in comparison. American Anthropologist 54:18–29.

1954 Nupe religion. London, Routledge & Kegan Paul Ltd.

1955 Two Nuba religions: an essay in comparison. American Anthropologist 57:661–679.

OMBRÉDANE, ANDRÉ

1954 L'exploration de la mentalite des noirs congolais à moyen d'une épreuve projective: Le Congo T.A.T. Memoire d'Institut Royal Colonial Belge, T. 37.

POWDERMAKER, HORTENSE

1956 Social change through imagery and values of teen-age Africans in Northern Rhodesia. American Anthropologist 58:783–813.

RAUM, O. F.

1940 Chagga childhood. London, Oxford University Press.

READ, MARGARET

1960 Children of their fathers; growing up among the Ngoni of Nyasaland. New Haven, Yale University Press.

RICHARDS, AUDREY I.

1956 Chisungu: a girl's initiation ceremony among the Bemba of Northern Rhodesia. London, Faber & Faber.

1958 Review of Custom and Conflict in Africa by Max Gluckman. Man 58:117–118.

RITCHIE, J. F.

1943 The African as suckling and as adult (a psychological study). Livingstone, The Rhodes-Livingstone Papers, No. 9.

SACHS, WULF

1947 Black Hamlet. Boston, Little, Brown.

SCOTCH, NORMAN A.

1960 A preliminary report on the relation of sociocultural factors to hypertension among the Zulu. Annals of the New York Academy of Sciences 84:1000–1009.

SHERWOOD, EDWARD T.

1957 On the designing of T.A.T. pictures, with special references to a set for an African people assimilating Western culture. Journal of Social Psychology 45:162–190.

1961 Swazi personality and the assimilation of western culture. Unpublished Ph.D. dissertation, University of Chicago.

SHERWOOD, RAE

1958a The Bantu civil servant. Unpublished report to the National Council for Social Research, South Africa.

1958b The Bantu clerk: a study of role expectations. Journal of Social Psychology 47:285–316.

SIMMONS, DONALD C.

1960 Sexual life, marriage, and childhood among the Efik. Africa 30:153–165.

SOUTHALL, A. W and P. C. W. GUTKIND
  1956   Townsmen in the making. East African Studies No. 9. Kampala, Uganda, East African Institute of Social Research.
TOOTH, GEOFFREY
  1950   Studies in mental illness in the Gold Coast. London, His Majesty's Stationery Office, Colonial Research Publication No. 6.
WHITING, JOHN W. M.
  1954   The cross-cultural method. *In* Handbook of social psychology, Gardner Lindzey, ed. Vol. 1. Cambridge, Mass., Addison-Wesley.
WHITING, JOHN W. M., R. KLUCKHOHN, and A. ANTHONY
  1958   The function of male initiation ceremonies at puberty. *In* Readings in social psychology (3d edition), E. E. Maccoby, T. M. Newcomb, and E. L. Hartley, eds. New York, Henry Holt and Co.

Chapter 4

NORTH AMERICA*

JOHN J. HONIGMANN,
University of North Carolina

Introduction

THE distinction between ethnology or cultural anthropology and that subdiscipline of anthropology, culture and personality, rests on which of two ideally distinct points of view an observer adopts. Paraphrasing Sapir (1932; *cf.* Kluckhohn 1944:602–604), an ethnologist looks at a segment of behavior as a culture pattern, while the student of culture and personality studies the same segment from the standpoint of the persons whom it directly involves. The behavior has "person-defining value." Using other words, in culture and personality an observer focuses on the subjective side of culture, that is, culture as experienced or manifested by a composite (or typical) individual—*the* Hopi child, *the* Sioux Indian, or *the* U.S. American. Or an observer studies a real individual or categories of people to see how they experience a way of life. Culture and personality implies sustained concentration on the explicit and implicit meanings which cultural traits (artifacts, ceremonies, legal norms, or epic poems) possess for *persons* in the community. In a somewhat different approach, demonstrated by Ruth Benedict (1932:24), the student of culture and personality may choose to see culture as the personality of its carriers writ large. True, all cultural anthropology gives attention to persons, meanings, and to the subjective. In culture and personality there is simply more emphatic or explicit recognition of the social actor *as a person,* often to the relative exclusion of social structure, technology, ideological systems, and historical

* Several years ago with the assistance of Lewis Binford and under the auspices of the Institute for Research in Social Science, University of North Carolina, I gathered material for a history of culture and personality. A portion of that material has been used for this essay. I am grateful to the Institute for assistance in preparing the present work for publication; a brief version was presented at the 1958 meeting of the American Anthropological Association.

background. In a work of culture and personality, whether it is a record of children's development, a life history, or an interpretation of Rorschach tests, the individual looms very large.

My object in this chapter is to review culture and personality research which has been conducted in native North America and, though somewhat more incidentally, below the border. I do not propose to write an all-inclusive history but, rather, a judicious record of general accomplishments. My emphasis will be on the bench marks which reveal new interests, methods, or levels of sophistication. The chapter is divided into three parts: an introduction, which is herewith concluded; an evaluative review of research on North American Indians; and a final section of assessment and discussion. In this last part I realize that I go beyond reviewing North American Indian studies.

Review and Evaluation

Aboriginally North America was a continent of varied lifeways, traces of which still remain. Practically all over the continent, however, missions, schools, traders, and government administrators have churned up culture change. The displacement of war, hunting, and ceremonies brought about a profound alteration in the traditional roles of men and women and in all other interaction patterns. The socially standardized milieux in which children were aboriginally socialized have been substantially transformed. In the United States, as well as in southern Canada, Indians cluster on reserves and occupy a special status as far as the larger community is concerned. Someone might regard these conditions as evidence that the American Indians, with a few exceptions, no longer possess truly exotic cultures. He might believe that the Indians could hardly be worthwhile subjects to study in order to learn something about the diverse systems of personality that occur under differing cultural conditions. He might believe that, while the Indians who live under reservation conditions might at best reveal traumatized personalities, casualties of culture change, they will not provide the kinds of insights that it is possible to obtain, say, in parts of Africa and the Southwest Pacific. One could conceivably interpret some of the works to be reviewed in this chapter as supporting such extreme expectations. Anthropologists have indeed found some Indian social personalities to be laden with conflict and uncertainty. But it is worth remembering that the theoretical point from which much culture and personality research departs has been almost deliberately concerned with discovering *pathology* in people's world- and self-views. Anthropologists who employed a crisis-oriented approach when they studied personality were much more responsive to evidence of conflict and stress than to behavior that indicates personal wellness (Honigmann 1954:104; Maslow 1950; Dunn 1959). Such personality stress need not have been produced by acculturation. Acculturation or, to be more exact about the variable that is probably crucial, uneven culture change (*cf.* Mead 1956), undoubtedly encourages personal stress, but stress is also evident in American Indian personality as it became known in very early contact times (Hallowell 1946). Characterological stress continues to be found among remote northern people like the Kaska Indians who adhere to a way of life not grossly changed from aboriginal times (Honigmann 1949). I do not suggest that the American Indians have from prehistoric times been subjected to more personality conflict than other people.

How far anthropologists' accounts of American Indian personality have been influenced by factors such as reservation life remains a question worth investigating in detail. The restricted range of occupations, atmosphere of paternalism, and social arrangements that relieve the Indian of considerable responsibility for creatively solving his problems undoubtedly help to standardize behavior in adults and children. Behavior, overt and covert, that is so standardized is what the anthropologist observes. Hence, reservation life must have personal repercussions, but its influence need not be predominantly pathological. My own experience also leads me to believe that the transformation of the American Indian personality has been less pervasive than superficial evidence of assimilation (in clothing, housing, jobs, language, and other elements of reservation life) leads some people to believe. Iroquois Indians in New York State, Cherokee in North Carolina, Sioux in North Dakota, and Makah in Washington do not structure experience precisely like their Euro-American neighbors even though they may in some cases speak the same language. Anthropology, of course, devotes itself to more than the study of only highly exotic cultures or personalities. However, to an extent truly exotic data are valuable and even essential in order to accumulate comparative material on which to base universal generalizations. Exotic material can still be secured in our continent by someone capable of close, clinical observation that dives below the superficial veneer of Americanization. One or two summers of field research are insufficient to discover the social personality of a community. Culture and personality research requires an intensive understanding of individuals who must be seen over long periods in their environment. With them the anthropologist must develop intensive rapport.

Culture and personality studies began among North American Indians with the collection of personal documents, a category in which I include autobiographies, biographies, and psychological analyses such as *Gregorio, The Hand-Trembler* (Leighton and Leighton 1949) or Devereux's (1951) account of a psychoanalysis. American Indians have provided some notable personal documents, including Radin's (1920) account of Crashing Thunder, Dyk's story of Son of Old Man Hat (1938), Simmon's (1942) rendering of Sun Chief's own life, and Ford's *Smoke from Their Fires* (1941). However, the exploitation of this channel to present "person-defining" behavior has not been very widely pursued. It is much to be regretted that in most cases we do have no more than one first-rate life history per culture. Nor have many innovations appeared within the life-history approach. Oscar Lewis (1959) is responsible for a new departure in his portrayal of five family cultures in Mexico, though his approach departs somewhat from the strictly personal document. Life histories, as Kluckhohn (1945) points out, are valuable for the insight they provide into the meaning which social forms possess for the members of a given community. They are analogous to the case histories which psychiatrists collect from patients and study carefully because in those communications the patient's style of life is revealed. But anthropologists are ultimately interested in more than the record of a specific individual's experiences. They note Sun Chief's attitudes toward sex not merely as one individual's way of handling of a universal situation, but for what they tell us about how that aspect of Hopi culture is generally experienced—hence, the importance of accumulating personal documents from a number of people who occupy different statuses in a particular community.

Culture and personality research has not remained identified with life histories. To understand how it came to apply theories from child development, psychology, and psychiatry in the study of culture, we must note the emergence at the end of the nineteenth century of psychology as a science.[1] Twentieth century psycholo-

---

[1] Wundt's *Voelkerpsychologie* is only indirectly related to the origins of the culture and personality movement which, however, shows definite traces of the *Volksgeist* School of German historians like Ranke and Grimm (Kluback 1956:24). For other antecedents see Meggers 1946:178–179.

gists showed increasing interest in the relationship of personality development (including the breakdown of personality organization) to social conditions (Burt 1957). Meanwhile, anthropologists noted that culture after all is manifested only through individuals. This conclusion occurred to Boas, for example, though he did little to pursue it. He did, however, transmit his interest to a number of his students who were to become extremely influential in the new movement (*cf.* Kluckhohn 1944:596; Mead 1959:14).

Among those students was Edward Sapir, who, in his paper "Culture, Genuine and Spurious" (1924), distinguished between the concept of culture as applied to man's whole material and spiritual social heritage and to "those general attitudes, views of life, and specific manifestations of civilization that give a particular people its distinctive place in the world." Sapir was offering a new version of an orientation that had long interested certain historians, like those of the *Volksgeist* group in nineteenth century Germany. In subsequent papers (for example, "Cultural Anthropology and Psychiatry," 1932), Sapir advanced the germ of the definition of culture and personality which I have offered at the start of this chapter. Cultural anthropology, he said, emphasizes the group and its traditions but pays little regard to the individuals who make up the group and who actualize its traditions in individual variations of behavior. Anthropology might focus on persons and see culture in its "true locus," namely "in the interactions of specific individuals and, on the subjective side, in the world of meanings which each one of these individuals may unconsciously abstract for himself from his participation in these interactions"—in much the same way as psychiatry focuses on a whole individual and observes him in his world of social relationships.

If I had to date the actual beginning of culture and personality field research conducted in this spirit, I would choose the year 1928, the year in which Margaret Mead—a student of Boas—published *Coming of Age in Samoa.* However, we are concerned with North American Indians. Here the signal event emerged from Ruth Benedict's (1928, 1932, 1934) preoccupation with characterizing cultures in psychological terms. In 1934 this brilliant student of Boas published *Patterns of Culture.* The book attempts to characterize several cultures in terms of contrasting psychological orientations. One chapter of the book, in which she contrasts the Indians of the Great Plains with the Pueblo people (Zuni) of the Southwest, will illustrate Benedict's approach.

The Plains way of life reveals a Dionysian quality. In personal experience the Plains Indians seek to press beyond the commonplace toward excess in order to achieve a certain psychological state. The Pueblo Indians in contrast are Apollonian, meaning that they distrust excess, prefer to keep to the middle of the road, and avoid meddling with disruptive psychological states. Benedict saw Plains and Pueblo cultures as two configurations. The Dionysian and Apollonian emphases reveal themselves in many parts of the configuration, for example, in response to death. The Plains Indians give way to uninhibited grief when a kinsman dies; mourning is prolonged, and some people even mutilate their bodies in a form of self-torture. The Apollonian Pueblos also react to death with sorrow, but people seek to make as little, rather than as much, of the event as possible. In each culture area the ideal personality type reflects the dominant psychological orientation. The Plains value the self-reliant man. By showing initiative in war or hunting, such a man achieves honor. The Pueblos have a different ideal. They value the mild-mannered and affable man who acts in moderate rather than in grandiose or spectacular terms.

In another chapter of her book, Benedict describes the Kwakiutl Indians of the North Pacific Coast of North America. She views them not only as Dionysian, but characterizes them as obsessed by megalomaniac ideas of grandeur, ideas which express themselves in furious competitive feats (potlatches) and in the way chiefs seek to gain the best of one another through boasting and mutual ridicule.

The inspiration for Benedict's brand of configurationalism came not from anthropology, nor from a school of psychology that was already current, Gestalt psychology, but from a historian, Oswald Spengler (1926). Note that Benedict's interpretations of cultures in psychological terms omits intensive, firsthand study of the people whose behavior she describes. The Plains Indian and Kwakiutl ways of life which she characterizes had long vanished and Benedict relied on ethnographers' earlier accounts. Culture and personality rarely again followed this method but instead put great reliance on firsthand field work. For if personality is interpreted solely from ethnographic materials which describe a culture, there is danger that the actual underlying psychological organization of the people who live that culture will be falsified. Explanation will be circular: the cultural datum—people behave peaceably and co-operatively—will be explained in terms of underlying peaceful, restrained, and co-operative motivations. This danger is inherent in Benedict's approach, though mostly she avoids falling into circularity because she does not essay a direct account of personality. She tends to say people act *as if* they had such motives. The safe position is never to assume that overt peaceableness or any other cultural trait is motivated by a similar state, like absence of hostility. It may or may not be. The point is that the existence of motives cannot be directly inferred from the outward form of behavior. Motivation and culture are not isomorphic. Motives must be assessed through studying living individuals in depth using clinical methods. Or else the various myths, films, and fictions of a community may be interpreted in a clinical manner (see Margaret Lantis' approach described below).

How shall *Patterns of Culture* be evaluated? Some anthropologists have condemned the book as subjective and unscientific. In some instances such condemnation is motivated by anthropologists' unwillingness to admit that their discipline includes a strong humanistic tradition. Benedict, however, clearly thought of her work as scientific. One reason why she may have identified with science is that in her day, as in ours, categorizing a piece of research as scientific surrounds it with greater authority. *Patterns of Culture* does partake of science, provided we are not too narrow in how we define the concept and do not make science identical with the experimental testing of hypotheses. Any attempt to generalize knowledge fits into the scientific tradition. Benedict offered a method for generalizing many specific bits of behavior in order to see cultures as wholes.

Patterns of Culture contributed much to stimulate thought concerning method and interpretation (*cf.* Nadel 1937; Li An-Che 1937). The very fact that people distrusted Benedict's interpretations and felt that she was too subjective made them refer back to the same evidence she too had used. Her accounts of Pueblo and Kwakiutl life have been found to be incomplete. She selected facts to draw a picture that would be in accord with the way the Pueblo and Kwakiutl themselves ideally view life. She ignored some instances of behavior that were incongruent with the configuration of dominant, ideal interests. Nevertheless *Patterns of Culture* remains timelessly important and in a certain sense indisputably valid in the same way that any great interpretation of reality remains valid because it expresses fully the aims of its creator. So too a judicious historian's work remains viable even after subsequent works are written that contain more complete evidence and more up-to-date interpretations.

One paper, written by John Bennett (1946) to review recurring disagreements over the interpretation of Zuni and adjacent Pueblo cultures, raises methodological implications that go quite beyond the field of culture and personality. Bennett examines the interpretations of Pueblo life made by Benedict and others and sets them in opposition to another view of Pueblo culture, one that he calls the "repressed" approach. His conclusion is that in each case the values of the observer to a certain extent necessarily govern the way he structures his data. We cannot determine on empirical grounds once and for all which point of view is "right."

The publications that appeared in the latter part of the decade and in the forties reveal that actual field research was already under way in the thirties. In 1937 came the first of Landes' reports on the Ojibwa (1937, 1938a, 1938b) and Hallowell's (1936, 1937; also see 1942, 1946, 1951, 1952) work on another branch of the same ethnic group. Hallowell's research among the Ojibwa indicates that, although personality development is undoubtedly influenced by cultural change, in some respects the personality system is also highly autonomous and persists. In eastern North America, his evidence indicates, the fundamental organization of personality persisted through two centuries of culture contact. Hallowell's (1946, 1952) method was to compare the reports of seventeenth and eighteenth century missionaries and explorers with the people as he knew them. In the early period Europeans characterized the Indians as emotionally restrained, stoical, strongly inhibited in the expression of aggression, mild in the face of provocation to anger, and suppressive of open criticism. In "deeper" or more nuclear terms, Hallowell finds in the reports evidence that the aboriginal northeastern Indian was anxious lest he fail to maintain the required standards of fortitude, express anger and resentment, or provoke the anger of others. Essentially the same characteristics still existed in the relatively unassimilated Ojibwa Indians whom Hallowell observed along the upper banks of the Berens River which flows into Lake Winnipeg and even in the more assimilated Ojibwa who live farther down the river. Indians who had been in more intense contact with Euro-Canadians did differ in some respects from their more isolated contemporaries. For example, they were more extroverted. But the personality core, Hallowell found when he scored responses to the Rorschach test given by both Berens River groups, was fundamentally the same. No radical psychological shift had occurred in the course of acculturation. Later Hallowell moved

to the still more acculturated Lac du Flambeau Indians in northern Wisconsin, another branch belonging to the same ethnic group
of Ojibwa. Here, in spite of heavy culture change and cross breeding between Indians and whites, he found that the Lac du Flambeau
people psychologically remained Indians. Obviously these people
who were being encouraged to live as Euro-Americans would have
a difficult time adjusting to the demands of their social environment.
Characterologically they were in another cultural world, says
Hallowell, anticipating one of the main conclusions of the U.S. Indian Education Research Project which will be described more
fully below. Presumably the core structure of the aboriginal personality was able to resist change because it could get along with the
traditional characterological system, though this cannot be accepted as a full explanation of how that traditional character structure manages to be transmitted from one generation to another.

Certain methodological aspects of Hallowell's work deserve special note. In effect he applied to his three communities a variant of
the experimental method—actually the only kind of experimental
method that can be applied in studying living groups of people
(Chapin 1947). His procedure involved a fruitful adaption to culture and personality research of the method of intercultural comparison, a method which has a long history in anthropology. His
groups illustrate three levels of acculturation. On Level One were
the least acculturated, pagan inland Ojibwa of Berens River. Then
came the Christian lakeside people, among whom aboriginal dwellings had disappeared along with the old songs and ceremonies. About
20 per cent of this group were of mixed racial ancestry. On Level
Three we find the highly acculturated Lac du Flambeau Indians of
Wisconsin, 80 per cent of whom were racially mixed and all spoke
some English. The Lac du Flambeau children attended school, their
families had radios, and in general the people maintained a close
association with whites. However, at Lac du Flambeau the Mide-
wewin ceremony had been carried over from precontact times.

The Rorschach test offered Hallowell a common device which
he could apply in each group to measure differences in response. He
tested over 200 people with this instrument, recognizing, of course,
that it had never been fully validated for cross-cultural use (Hallowell 1951). One of his findings we have already stated: persistence
of personality independent of degree of assimilation to Euro-Cana-
dian or Euro-American culture. Another finding comes from
counting the number of signs of adjustment that appear in the

Rorschach responses of each group. Differences in adjustment are not significant when the two Berens River communities are compared to one another, but there is a significant increase in personal maladjustment in the records of Lac du Flambeau. For example, 9 per cent of the Level One records show signs of bad integration compared to 18 per cent of the Lac du Flambeau subjects.[2] We should also recognize Hallowell's lasting interest in social psychiatry, a field he has pursued with the aid of North American cultural data. He was one of the earliest anthropologists to distinguish between normal and abnormal anxiety (1936).

Hallowell revealed new possibilities in using the ethnohistorical method to reconstruct aboriginal personality. One other example of this method may be mentioned, Esther Goldfrank's (1943) work on the Teton Dakota. She shows how aspects of Dakota interpersonal behavior—notably aggression—altered in pace with other changes in the way of life. Before 1850 the Dakota were horse-mounted buffalo hunters and warriors. Ingroup violence was fairly common and sprang partly from ingroup rivalries. The rich competed with displays of wealth. The introduction of liquor by early fur traders intensified violence toward the end of this early period. Between 1850 and 1877 increasing contact occurred with the white man and there was a growing decimation of the wild buffalo, the Indian's mainstay. Aggression was turned outward as wars broke out between the Indians and Euro-Americans over the latters' encroachment on the land and on account of broken treaties. When the Indians' aggressive energies began to be deflected against enemies, a need for increased responsibility and in-group co-operation arose. It is largely for this reason that ingroup aggression began to decline, though competitive displays of wealth by the rich continued. What pressures were used to alter personality with respect to aggression? The chiefs, whose position had grown stronger, gave sermons on the importance of ingroup co-operation. Blood money rather than blood revenge was used to settle murder. To borrow terms which Anthony F. C. Wallace (1959) has introduced, the periodic expression of impulses normally suppressed gave way to an emphasis on the *lasting* suppression of incongruent motives and behavior. A similar phenomenon occurred among the Iroquois after their disorganizing contact with Euro-American civilization. For a time the Dakota managed to release aggression outward, against rival tribes and the United States' troops, but their power to do so

[2] For other Ojibwa research see Caudill 1949, and Barnouw 1950.

was broken following Custer's massacre. Between 1877 and 1885 the Indian was "crushed." In this third period the buffalo disappeared and the old economy was wrecked. Most of the horses had been taken by the victorious army. With the external threat removed, acute internal aggression again broke forth. The chiefs' injunctions were ignored. But now a strong, foreign, legal system was on hand to curb the disruptive trends that had almost free play prior to 1850. From 1885 onward the people reluctantly turned to making a living as farmers and also to religion. Chiefs entered the ministry and became pastors of their people. The Indians eagerly adopted one feature of Christianity, the blessedness of giving. Religion and law restored ingroup peace and generosity became an ideal.[3]

Goldfrank's work exhibits one difficulty encountered with the ethnohistorical method: it too rarely permits psychologically sophisticated inferences of motivation. The nature of the available data forces the student to deal largely with the overt features of personality or interpersonal relations.

For most workers the dominant aim in culture and personality research has been to throw light on motives and feeling states which underlie overt behavior. Applying the Rorschach test in field work and interpreting the responses with the aid of Rorschach theory constitute one way of reaching the covert area of personality. Of course, a person who relies solely on the test and ignores clues to covert states present in other instances of overt activity is basing his understanding on a very narrow foundation. One cannot infer covert phenomena from outward forms without some kind of theory, the purpose of which is to specify how to proceed with interpreting in covert terms what people say, do, make, or write. Some form of the psychoanalytic theory (usually not in its most extreme, orthodox form) is still the most widely employed adjunct to culture and personality research, though the utility of the theory for cross-cultural research has been questioned at certain points, for example, concerning the universal existence of an Oedipus complex. However, with regard to defense mechanisms, the importance of childhood in personality formation, the overdetermined nature of behavior, the motivated nature of dreams, and other subjects, psychoanalytic theory has been confidently and on the whole successfully utilized.

I shall not trace the somewhat complicated history of the appli-

---

[3] For other studies of Dakota (Sioux) personality see Erikson 1939, and Macgregor 1946.

cation of psychoanalytic theory to culture and personality. The psychoanalytic approach in anthropology came to maturity with the publication of *The Individual and His Society,* a book written by Abram Kardiner, psychoanalyst, in collaboration with Ralph Linton, anthropologist (Kardiner 1939). The same year saw publication of another psychoanalyst's "Observations on Sioux Education" (Erikson 1939). *The Individual and His Society* is not based on deliberately organized field work in North America, although the authors do briefly examine the Zuni and Kwakiutl Indians and also the Eskimo in terms of their theory. The book grew out of a seminar jointly conducted at Columbia University by Kardiner and Linton. The seminar continued and provided Kardiner with material for a second volume, *The Psychological Frontiers of Society* (1945). In this book one American Indian group, the Comanche, receives intensive consideration though no fresh data were collected for the purpose of this analysis. As a matter of fact, the interpretation pertains exclusively to the aboriginal Comanche personality, that is, to the period when the Indians were warriors and buffalo hunters on the southern plains.

Since a comprehensive statement of Kardiner's theory is given by Thomas Gladwin in another chapter of this book (Chapter 5) I need not do so here. We should, however, recognize the emphasis which most schools of psychoanalysis put on the early years of life. Childhood is the period when the meanings in terms of which individuals carry out other aspects of their culture—war, religion, child rearing, and many other activities—are established in the personality. Ideally, psychoanalytic theory aims to predict the way an adult will regard his world and himself in terms of the way he was reared. But it is doubtful if an adult social personality can really be predicted in this way except in very general and not very useful terms. What customarily happens is that the adult covert personality—what Kardiner calls the "basic personality type"—is interpreted using knowledge of how children are currently being socialized and also by drawing simultaneous inferences from adult activity. Instead of really predicting, the researcher attempts to develop a plausible explanation which will tie into a neat package both certain events of early life and certain selected features revealed by adults' overt behavior.

In 1945 I was enough impressed with the potentialities inherent in Kardiner's work and Karen Horney's (1939, 1945) version of psychoanalytic theory to apply this approach to the Kaska Indians who live in northern British Columbia and southern Yukon Territory (Honigmann 1949). My intentions among the Kaska were to identify the emotional qualities which people revealed as they acted their cultural roles and account for such qualities in terms of underlying, dominant motivations. I also hoped to explore the conditions of early life under which the dominant motivations are learned.[4]

Kaska social personality is characterized by seven, very much interrelated, dominant motivations, or value orientations, each of which must be understood in terms of its context and not by other definitions which the terms may have. The first of these motives is egocentricity, defined here as a high evaluation of personal independence in which interests are self-centered rather than group-centered. This motivation colors the way Kaska Indians resist direction from sources outside the family. It enters into the positive evaluation of work, which guarantees independence and self-sufficiency in this trapping-hunting economy, and also into the masculine striving of women, some of whom appear to be in part dissatisfied with their sex role.

A second dominant motivation is utilitarianism, a concept that refers to a practical and resourceful attitude toward the problems of living, an interest in concrete rather than abstract thinking. The Kaska are present-oriented and little concerned with a remote future. Deference is a third guiding tendency in the nuclear area of Kaska social personality. The word denotes an attempt to maintain frictionless human relationships and a concern lest one becomes disliked and rejected. In conformity with this value orientation, people make requests obliquely, thereby not risking open rejection and also not pressing on other people too aggressively. More directly, deference is expressed by the avoidance of face-to-face quarrels. Hostility is, however, expressed indirectly and covertly through gossip. In other words, hostility is not lacking in Kaska social personality. Evidence for it appears in dreams and more overtly in how some people act when they are intoxicated, for example, threatening others and themselves with violence. The normal suppression of interpersonal hostility is very useful for people who live in an atomistic social system, one without strong social controls.

The next dominant motivation, flexibility, is difficult to define positively. It denotes a state of mind in which external necessity,

---

[4] For a study of the Aymara Indians of Peru which employs a similar approach to the core personality see Tschopik 1951.

duty and hurry are subordinated to personal inclination. This state reveals itself in an absence of rigidity and in tolerant, even indecisive, attitudes toward the demands of living. The absence of hurry or of rigorous timetables, the people's easy conscience, the noncompulsive way in which children are reared and dogs trained, and the lack of obsessiveness all express this motive. In certain crisis situations flexibility combines with dependence, another dominant motivation, to produce procrastination and hesitation. As a result of these behaviors, the critical state that confronts the individual may grow worse instead of being resolved. The motivating state of dependence needs little explanation, though it should be noted that this tendency in the character structure is at variance with the emphasis characterologically placed on egocentricity and resourcefulness. It is quite possible for a social personality to reveal inconsistent trends which people themselves occasionally have difficulty reconciling in their day-to-day living.

Finally there is emotional isolation, perhaps the most dominant note in Kaska Indian social personality. The concept includes a strong desire to maintain aloofness from emotional experience and emotional involvement as well as a tendency to suppress all feeling. It is based on a characterological inability to tolerate strong emotion, including affection. Egocentricity is quite congruent with a social organization in which for much of the year families engaged in trapping live in relative isolation from one another in the bush and under a social system that is without superordinate authorities. Sexual constriction is one specific mode in which emotional isolation is expressed in interpersonal behavior. This form of expression shows up in the ambivalence that marks the relations of men and women, in the absence of public display of affection between couples, in the reluctance to marry (that is, to enter a strong emotional—even dependent—relationship), and, most dramatically, in the behavior accompanying premarital sexual relations. Premarital sexuality includes considerable preliminary teasing that culminates in a chase, capture, struggle, and, finally, coitus. Such a sequence, I discovered when I lived among the Indians, is often difficult to distinguish from actual rape. Girls and also married women conceive of the sex act as a hostile encounter, a perception they reveal in dreams and in the associations spontaneously given to dreams. The promiscuity of adults, since it offers the opportunity for sexual satisfaction without risk of emotional involvement, also reveals emotional isolation.

In general the Kaska world-view wavers between the idea that experience is manageable and the idea that life is difficult as well as uncertain. The self-view also comprises two conflicting attitudes: value placed on self-reliance and a tendency to abandon striving and revert to passivity. The former is far more conscious, and much more acceptable, than the second. Passivity particularly manifests itself in crises, when there is eager reaching out for help (cloaked, of course, by virtue of the tendency here called emotional isolation) and surrender of active striving.

Emotional isolation is the motivation whose grounding in early socialization is easiest to perceive. This value orientation is rooted in the way a Kaska mother withdraws emotionally from her child when the youngster is between two and three years old. She does not outrightly reject the child but spontaneously withdraws show of warmth and affection. The mother becomes more impersonal, more concerned with herself, or more preoccupied with a younger sibling. She shows herself less patient and indulgent to the youngster. In this situation the child unconsciously makes a decision never again to invest strong affection in others. The significance of growing up and spending all one's life with relatively affectless people who serve as role models must not be ignored in understanding how the Kaska style of life is acquired.

Psychoanalytic theory suggests that the striving for independence, which also makes up Kaska social personality, is founded on the indulgent care of infants. In this highly favorable period of life, the Kaska baby develops an unverbalized attitude of confidence in himself and hopeful expectations toward the world. These expectations are only loosely entrenched, however. They are contradicted by the emotional withdrawal that comes as an early shock. The passivity of Kaska personality in certain crisis situations can be explained as it derives from this traumatic episode and also as it reflects the hold which the passive-receptive state of infancy continues to exert in the personality.

The major test of truth that can be applied to this kind of interpretation is the test of consistency. Is the explanation sufficient, reasonable, clear? Does the explanation offered explain the facts in noncontradictory fashion? Does the evidence hold together sensibly? Are contradictions between facts, if they occur, adequately accounted for in terms of the theory that is being used? For reasons that I shall examine more closely at the conclusion of this chapter, anthropologists have become shy of research whose validity can be assessed mainly on evidential grounds, that is, by applying tests of consistency and reasonableness.

Culture-and-personality studies directed to the American scene thrived in the forties. One development that added enormously to our knowledge of American Indians as persons began in 1941 with the start of the Indian Education Research Project (also called the Indian Personality and Administration project). This was a co-operative venture in which the Committee on Human Development of the University of Chicago was allied with the United States Office of Indian Affairs where John Collier was Commissioner (Havighurst and Neugarten 1955:v–vi; Thompson 1951:12). Their general purpose was to examine the whole development of Indian children in six American Indian tribes in order to derive practical, useful lessons for Indian education. What was happening to the personalities of Indians under the impact of American civilization? An answer to this question, it was believed, would help to define the "real needs" and resources of American Indians and would serve as a guide for administrators. In other words, although the results of the project were expected to contribute substantially to general knowledge, the project was designed as action research or applied anthropology. Indian Service personnel, mainly teachers, nurses, and school administrators, were recruited to do much of the field work, but professional anthropologists were also assigned to the six groups selected for intensive study. In addition to anthropologists the project was carried through psychologists, psychiatrists, public administrators, linguists, and other specialists. The groups for which monographs of findings have been published are the Hopi (Thompson and Joseph 1944), Sioux (Macgregor 1946), Navaho (Leighton and Kluckhohn 1947; Kluckhohn and Leighton 1946), and Papago Indians (Joseph, Spicer, and Chesky 1949). The reports on Zia and Zuni Pueblos have unfortunately never appeared.

The approach which these works follow may be called psychogenetic or developmental. With a variety of methodological aids (Emotional Response, Moral Ideology, Rorschach, Thematic Apperception, and other tests) as well as direct observation, the intellectual and emotional development of children is followed from birth to adolescence. The underlying theory draws from psychoanalysis, but the various workers are concerned with more than the earliest years of life and base interpretations on experiences that occur considerably later than feeding, toilet training, or early sexual training.

It is beyond the scope of this chapter to summarize and evaluate the whole project. Fair evaluation especially would be difficult, for clear evidence concerning how the results of the research entered into the administration of the United States' Indians is hard to come by. Laura Thompson (1951) has written on the significance of the project for which she co-ordinated research activities. Six years of field work, she says, were required before a general solution of the welfare problem peculiar to each tribe could be formulated. The research involved far more than the relationship of personality to culture change. Other variables also had to be taken into account: ecology, health, social organization, language, arts, crafts, ceremonies, and the core values of the people. The main findings were, first, that a program of administration which was oriented primarily to assimilating the Indians into the general American population was highly detrimental to the welfare of Indian communities and Indian personality. Second, a substantial increase in costly schools, health services, and technological aid will not bring about rapid assimilation of the Indians into the general population. Thompson writes: "We may predict with assurance that the current Indian Bureau policy of rapid assimilation and 'liquidation,' in so far as it is effectively implemented at the reservation and the community levels, will be detrimental to Indian personality development and community welfare." On the other hand, her findings support the wisdom of the Indian Reorganization Policy which had been adopted under the early administration of Commissioner Collier.

Perhaps the best way to give some conception of this research is to take a specific tribe and describe findings which are relevant to culture and personality there. For this purpose I have selected the Hopi Indians (Thompson and Joseph 1944: Thompson 1950).

The birth of the Hopi child occurs in the mother's home. Shortly thereafter rites introduce the newborn individual to his father and to the Sun and also initiate a life-long series of gift exchanges between the child and his father's clanspeople. The infant spends practically all of the first three months of life in a supine position on a cradleboard. After this time the cradle is used only as a place to sleep until it finally becomes discarded between six months and a year. The cradle, it is suggested, probably contributes to the baby's feeling of security and also conditions the newborn individual to expect restriction. But many other, less physical restrictions will appear as the child matures. Weaning comes with little difficulty, usually around the age of two years. Cleanliness training is introduced gradually, without shock. Up until the age of six in boys and throughout youth in girls the mother and other females of the matrilocal household act as the primary agents of socialization. The mother's brother is a source of stricter discipline. The general character of early life is permissive but the freedom of the youngster is firmly limited in the interests of his physical safety. From such limitation every Hopi probably gains an early conception of how hazardous the environment is in his village. Adjustment is more difficult for boys than for girls, a generalization that is revealed in boys' behavior problems, like thumbsucking, temper tantrums, and stealing. The explanation lies in the fact that girls grow up in a house where they are expected to remain even after marriage. Boys, already by the age of four or five, begin to break away from the family group and spend more and more time in the kiva (a religious structure) or in the fields and on the range. Eventually a young man will marry into a strange house and there assume a very marginal position. Actually, the boy also gains freedom by breaking away from his family around the age of five. In contrast, the girl's role remains restricted. She must stay close to home and help her mother, and she too experiences conflicts that show up in temper tantrums, stealing, and fighting. Psychological tests show that five-year olds among the Hopi are more relaxed and spontaneous than older Hopi children. For one thing, they are not yet fully disciplined. The girl's inner life at this age is simpler than the boy's; he is already quite introverted and shows a pervasive, vague anxiety.

Initiation into the Kachina cult marks the transition from childhood to youth. The ceremony introduces the child to the Kachinas, his ancestors, who send rain and food in exchange for prescribed ritual behavior. Initiation means a ceremonial whipping for some children, depending on the sodality into which they are initiated. Naughty boys, it is said, are usually initiated into the sodality that calls for the more severe whippings. The boy is whipped while he is stripped naked, but a girl initiate wears her clothes and is beaten less severely. Following initiation, public opinion to a considerable extent replaces the matrilocal household as the main control over the child's behavior. The father remains a source of happiness to youngsters but, tests show, the larger community becomes a source of fear, punishment, anger, and shame. The tests also reveal the child's conception of his family as a source of reward and praise. Economic responsibilities also increase for the initiated boy. Both sexes restrict their play to the evening. From six to twelve children attend day school, an experience that girls particularly welcome because it liberates them from the house. At fourteen some boys go on to boarding school. As seen in psychological tests, the period from eight to ten is a time when outside contacts increase for both sexes. Girls are finally aroused from their simple, unquestioning, walled-in existence; their imagination develops; their personality becomes more complex, more like the boy's. Just before puberty, however, boys and girls reveal a tendency to withdraw into themselves, much of the earlier spontaneous responsiveness to outside impressions disappearing.

The transition to adulthood in Hopi life is not clearcut, though marriage marks a profound change in role. Tests probe below the surface to reveal what happens in adolescence as the sexual impulse rises in consciousness. However vaguely sex is defined by the young person, it is not perceived as evil. The force of the sex impulse now halts the introversive trends so apparent at the threshhold of puberty. An easier acceptance of outside contacts takes place. Boys achieve sex indulgence more easily than girls. Hopi girls are not allowed to roam around and must avoid showing themselves to be boy-crazy. Hence, girls continue to demonstrate more emotional withdrawal than boys.

The Hopi and other Indian samples of children were compared to a Midwest, white sample in order to establish differences (Havighurst and Neugarten 1955). In contrast to the latter, Hopi children derive little happiness from personal achievement. This is understandable for they have been taught to avoid any demonstration of achievement. Yet the Hopi youngsters are consciously proud of being praised and respected. Tests also show that aggression makes Hopi children anxious, perhaps because of the enormous pressure that the community exerts against fighting. Work is important in their young lives; in how well or poorly he performs it, an individual demonstrates whether he is of good or evil character. Conscience is reflected through belief in immanent justice—belief that morality is sanctioned by an all-knowing unchangeable, and unchallengeable external moral power. Belief in immanent justice in Hopi children does not decline with age as it does in Midwest children. In fact, the belief increases with age! Belief in animism decreases more slowly among the Hopi than in the Midwest sample.

The Rorschach test reveals near-adolescent Hopi children to possess a deeply disciplined character structure. These youngsters are carefully selective with regard to their emotions; they are cautious and restrained. Yet they recognize pleasurable aspects of the world, though these must be accorded their due place. Exuberance is toned down. The children have average good imagination but it is seldom richly fluid, lively, or vivacious. Here again appears the all-pervasive note of restraint. (Compare how closely these findings correspond to Ruth Benedict's [1934] characterization of the Pueblo Indians as Apollonian! Remember, Benedict achieved her insight without the benefit of gathering her data clinically.) Instead of being primarily concerned with the emotional aspects of impressions and events, Hopi children approach the world intellectually and imaginatively, though without abandoning themselves to fantasy. The Hopi child is cautious, especially in his approach to a new situation. He does not become confused by something new. He rather firmly accepts or declines what is offered; his behavior sometimes makes the Hopi youngster appear stubborn or unshakeable to his teachers. The personality reveals a vague, free-floating anxiety which is unattached to definite, fear-provoking objects. In this character structure we see reflected the "price" that the Hopi child pays in order to survive in an environment which he has been taught is filled with potential danger and one which for these desert farmers is actually perilous. The Hopi adapts by limiting his desires, emotions, and ambitions. Limitation in turn generates an "inside pressure" that lacks any definite outlet. The child feels discomfort and fear without understanding that the source of the disturbing force is his own overdisciplined self. Such fear is expected in the Hopi community and is socially "normal." One area of personality remains unaffected by discipline, the area of the instinctual (including sexual) urges—the id. These impulses remain unusually vivid and spontaneous.

Adult Hopi are much given to malicious gossip and frequently suspect one another of witchcraft. Such behavior probably originates from hostility and anxiety. From whence do hostility and anxiety arise? They arise from social relations carried on in a small, town-dwelling group, a group that is vulnerable to danger of famine and epidemics and whose pressure is a source of anger, shame, and punishment. The role of the mother plays a part. As a disciplinarian she is a source of anger, shame, and discipline—more to the boy than to the girl. Hostility and anxiety are also rooted in the inability of the child to form deep, emotional attachments with anybody, except the mother, a person with whom his relationship is ambivalent.

Two further developments that brought culture and personality to maturity in the forties must be mentioned. First, criticism began to be leveled against the new movement. Particularly did critics object because, they thought, too much was being claimed for the formative years of childhood in the process of personality formation. Anthropologists doing such research, themselves deplored the excessive weight that, under the inspiration of psychoanalytic theory, was sometimes given to early disciplines (Goldfrank 1945; Underwood and Honigmann 1947). But this was only one controversial feature of the vigorous, new approach. Others too received a full, frank, and sometimes hostile airing. In her review of "Recent Trends in American Ethnology" Betty J. Meggers (1946:186) looked with alarm at the way Sapir had been heeded and attention was being diverted from cultural to psychological problems. Censure, Meggers said, was being met by anthropologists who chose to study culture. "That this trend will continue for some time to dominate anthropology cannot be doubted," she wrote. "In the meantime, however, the province of culture is being neglected."

Critical notice was not the only indication of the maturity which culture and personality had achieved. A second was the appearance of two collections of mainly reprinted readings (Haring 1948; Kluckhohn and Murray 1948). These, naturally, did not limit themselves to data from North America. Both quickly went into new editions and were joined by a textbook in culture and personality (Honigmann 1954).

The new decade opened with two contributions from Latin America which marked new levels of development. Holmberg's (1950) study of the Siriono is essentially ethnographic, but the underlying problem derives from psychological theory. Where a sparse and insecure food supply exists, do frustrations and anxieties centering around the hunger drive have major repercussions on behavior? Holmberg found overwhelming evidence for strong anxiety responses toward food among the Siriono and he traced their development back to Siriono childhood. In the other work, John Gillin (1951) examined cultural sources of threat and security affecting Indians and Ladinos in a Guatemalan community. Rorschach analyses had already appeared comparing these two populations and had also examined the motivational makeup of six witch doctors (Billig, Gillin, and Davidson 1947–48). In the same year as Gillin's publication, Oscar Lewis (1951) published his study of Tepoztlan, a book important as much for the questions it poses pertaining to the re-examination of already studied cultures as for itself being a meticulous approach to personality conceived of largely as manifesting itself in interpersonal relations.

One major development of the fifties transcends the North American culture area. This is a comparative approach that utilizes statistical techniques to test *cross-culturally* the relationship between aspects of child rearing (the antecedent variables) and subsequent personality or cultural variables. The principal work of this type is Whiting and Child's (1953) *Child Training and Personality: A Cross-Cultural Study*. Several other publications followed in the late fifties (Child, Storm, and Veroff 1958; Spiro and D'Andrade 1958; Barry, Child, and Bacon 1959). Quantitative inquiries and correlation analyses have a long history in cultural anthropology. In this case they have been facilitated by the existence of the Human Relations Area Files developed at Yale University.

The comparative method, relying on statistical tests of relationship, coincided with a continuing and mounting wave of criticism directed against what is still sometimes called the "excesses" of culture and personality studies. Orlansky's (1949) literature search had already assembled much material showing that, contrary to psychoanalytical theory, no consistent or meaningful relationship linked early forms of nursing and personality traits in latter childhood. In the next year, further searching questions were asked by an anthropologist, psychologist, and two sociologists (Goldman 1950; Farber 1950; Lindesmith and Strauss 1950), not to speak of Roheim's (1950) strictures directed against members of the "culturalist school" for rejecting pure Freudian theory as being too biological! Against this background let us examine briefly some recent methodological innovations in North American research, particularly those introduced by the Harvard Values Project (Kluckhohn 1951); by Spindler (1952, 1955) in his careful research design for studying personality variation as correlated with differential assimilation of a foreign culture among the Menomini, and by Wallace (1952), who demonstrates how the Rorschach test can help in deriving a true modal personality type.

All research in values is not equally concerned with studying personality. For example, Northrop's (1946) and Albert's (1956) interests hardly seem to be. But the Harvard Values Project has tended to keep its focus on individuals, and Clyde Kluckhohn (1954:691) said that the work of his colleagues is partly in the field of culture and personality. The special attraction of values research lies in the fact that it provides a procedure promising a higher measure of objective reliability than many people would see residing in the more subjective approach keynoted in *Patterns of Culture,* or in the diagnoses of psychoanalytically oriented workers. Projective tests it is true also did much to reduce subjectivity and heighten reliability (as far as test protocols, not interpretations, are concerned) but they still leave unanswered the question of the validity of the test itself. Note that George Spindler (1955), in a work to be reviewed, sharply separates his *interpretation* of Rorschach data from the scored responses which he analyzes statistically. His first and main proof of personality differences between categories of people is in the objective and statistically defensible scores (pp. 122–123). Wallace's modal Tuscarora personality, too, we shall see, is first constructed out of test scores. In using the Rorschach technique, it is the validity of the interpretations that presents the problem.

Vogt's (1951) work among the Navaho can be taken as a fair example to illustrate the contribution that the values approach makes to understanding people. Some Navaho men who served in the U.S. Armed Forces significantly shifted their value orientations (*cf.* Florence Kluckhohn 1950), for example, dropping the Navaho orientation that views man to be subjugated to nature and adopting the position that man controls nature. Some veterans also adopted a future outlook in place of being primarily oriented to the present. All veterans, however, did not assimilate Euro-American values. Vogt shows that sociocultural variables, like disruption of the family of orientation as well as the size and structure of that family, are conditions which governed the veterans' acculturation. Large extended families, to take another specific instance, tended to conserve Navaho values, exerting a negative influence on assimilation. The individual's personality adjustment also related to his readiness to alter his values. Those Navahos who accepted white values tended to be characterized by stronger personal conflicts and insecurity.

The experimental method that Hallowell pioneered when he examined personality and acculturation cross-culturally was advanced by Spindler (1955) in his well-designed study of the Menomini Indians on their Wisconsin reservation. He too relied on the Rorschach test. Spindler graded a sample of 68 male Menomini Indians (all at least half Indian in ancestry) in terms of degree of assimilation. At one extreme of his five-point continuum are the native-oriented population, people who obtain subsistence from wage work but also continue with hunting and fishing. They consciously maintain kinship ties and traditional ceremonies. All persons in this category speak Menomini. In character structure they show a passive but not hopeless orientation toward life unmarked by strong threat. This narrowly defined personality is hardly suited to competitive struggle or to the expression of aggression. They keep a damper on emotional expressiveness.

Next come the peyotists, the members of the peyote ritual group who practice a ceremony that is not traditional and in which visions are a key feature. They are people over whom the old culture maintains a substantial hold although they do not fully endorse its traditions. Characterologically they reveal a quality of hopeless, passive soul searching that expresses individual anxiety.

Then come the reservations' transitional people who have no overt ties with the old culture and have adopted a full measure of the new way of life. On a deeper level, however, nostalgia for the past reveals itself along with identification with Euro-American culture. Transitionalists are less passive and more aggressive than the native-oriented population. They do not deal with anxiety through hopeless soul searching. In them aggression sometimes takes explosive forms.

In fourth place are the lower-ranking, assimilated Indians who obtain their living from lumbering and belong to the Catholic Church. People on this level of assimilation are no longer passively oriented but the character structure is deeply disturbed.

Most assimilated are the members of the elite-assimilated category, Spindler's fifth category of reservation people. The men hold supervisory jobs in lumbering and other fields and also belong to the Catholic Church. Personality reveals a quality of ready emotionality. There are no signs of disturbance as in the previous group and little evidence of passivity.

Spindler's study is notable for several things. It confirms and amplifies the thesis that acculturation has been detrimental for some American Indians. Instead of speaking globally of all Menomini men, it divides the population into categories based on degree of assimilation and demonstrates meaningful psychological differences between the categories. This represents a degree of refinement in culture and personality research though it does not invalidate generalizations based on a community as a whole, generalizations that for some purposes continue to be very useful. Principally, Spindler's work is meritorious for the precision and objectivity it reveals, qualities that it has not been possible to demonstrate adequately here in this small summary. But the Menomini study is mainly descriptive. We miss in it the painstaking examination of socialization that would enable us to understand how each of the five categories achieves its particular behavior style. The almost complete reliance on the Rorschach is unfortunate in one respect. Good clinicians do not rely exclusively on one test. There are characteristics of behavior that the Rorschach test cannot pick up but which a sensitive observer could bring out. The loss in objectivity would to my way of thinking be balanced by the enriched picture of personality produced.

Anthony Wallace's (1952) work with the Tuscarora demonstrates how the Rorschach test and appropriate statistical procedures allow a strictly modal-personality type to be constructed. The term "modal personality," of course, was used before Wallace but there is a substantial difference between usages. The usual constructs of so-called modal personality (for example, by Honigmann 1949; DuBois 1944) or of what Kardiner calls "basic personality" are really ideal types and not constellations of traits most frequently (modally) appearing together in a community (*cf.* Aberle 1954: 669). Wallace sampled deliberately and his work deals with true modal types. If culture and personality have usually been delineating ideal types, then doesn't it follow that certain criticisms of national-character studies must be reconsidered? I have in mind particularly the criticism which condemns such research as invalid when it does not sample a national population by class, region, and similar attributes. The heterogeneity of a modern nation need not be incompatible with the construction of an ideal personality type of the country as a whole, although the usefulness of such a type may be queried.

Bert Kaplan's monograph, *A Study of Rorschach Responses in Four Cultures* (1954), is a very astute, experimental appraisal of culture and personality method and of the Rorschach test applied in such research. In a sense it is a reply to the critics of culture and personality research. Kaplan asks whether, objectively, there is such a thing as social personality. Specifically, can the Rorschach test pick up personality differences between the culturally different communities? Comparing Zuni, Navaho, Mormon, and Spanish-American Rorschach records Kaplan proves that, generally speaking, each of these groups does perform differently in the Rorschach test situation and concludes that systematic differences in personality do occur from one community to another.

As we come up to the present it is hard to gauge the long-range significance of a given piece of work. But the new, good sense that Anthony F. C. Wallace (1955, 1956) makes out of certain of the ethnohistorical data pertaining to North American Indian acculturation will probably count in future anthropology. He has introduced the concept of "revitalization" to designate the psychological processes that operate in persons during certain kinds of nativistic movements. Such movements, he shows, can be interpreted in psychological terms quite meaningfully. The sequence of a typical revitalization movement, according to Wallace, begins with a period of constantly mounting stress. Over the years people look for a way out, for some way to restore a more satisfactory culture. Some people "succeed" in effecting rather narrow-base, personal "solutions" for their stress through such behaviors as alcoholism or neurosis. War and changes in political leadership are also tried, and new economic doctrines are advanced, but generally without much success. At one point a prophetic leader appears. He announces a solution that came to him, perhaps from a divine source. At this point, assuming that the leader is indeed heeded, revitalization sets in as order is restored in the community's world of meanings. People become more satisfied and hopeful; the stressful conditions of their existence are alleviated, at least for a time. The prophet shows an intense concern for cultural reforms. The changes he prescribes range from minor ritual innovations to institutional rearrangements that add up to a substantially new culture. Wallace focuses on the prophet and tries to account dynamically for his behavior. Typically prophets have been disturbed people exposed to intense personal and social stress. Wallace looks to the level of physiological functioning for much of the explanation of the prophets' personality resynthesis. When the prophet's stress reaches a critical point "the physiochemical milieu for resynthesis is automatically established." A convulsive effort to redesign his perception of the situation occurs and becomes the basis of his teaching. Of course, what message the prophet hears and what lines of action he recommends cannot be explained physiologically. They depend on his prior experience and intelligence.

Wallace's work is notable for the courageous way in which he attempts to fuse social and physiological levels of analysis. He opens himself to the charge of being reductionistic, that is, of explaining phenomena on one level by phenomena belonging to another system of events. But for many people such criticism carries little weight, provided that the explanation which is offered really explains what is being studied. His explanation, of course, is hypothetical, and we may not know for a long time, if ever, whether physiochemical changes are indeed associated with prophetic revelations. (For a related work of the American Indians' response to the United States civilization, see Voget 1956, though he does not write primarily from the psychological point of view.)

We have said several times that the prevailing tendency in culture and personality research is to observe with the aid of appropriate theory and with clinical exactness living people in their normal environment in order to infer the underlying psychological states by which they can be characterized. But we have also noted that Goldfrank, Hallowell, and Wallace utilized ethnohistorical data in pursuing personality studies. The work of Margaret Lantis (1953, 1959) demonstrates well how theory can be applied to a rich mythology in order to assess personality. Her work with Nunivak Island Eskimo mythology draws on a close and detailed knowledge of the people, knowledge based on long-term acquaintance. Lantis offers theoretical justification for using myths as evidence of psychological processes. Mythology, like folklore, brings out people's objective view of reality and also offers insight into their subjective perception of what that reality means to them. The sharing of myths in a community offers all members an opportunity to standardize their views of human behavior and of the rest of the natural world. Myths, in other words, constitute an amalgamated body of science, philosophy, and religion through which people give structure to reality. Radcliffe-Brown (1930–31:63), a British anthropologist, in similar terms speaks of a social structure that includes not only human society but also that society's relationship with its total environment.

Elimination, sex, intercourse, and other bodily functions are referred to very casually in Nunivak Eskimo myths. Their relative de-emphasis may, of course, be due to repression, but such an interpretation is not confirmed by other evidence (for example, extant cultural patterns). Apart from sex, myths indicate that the relationship of men and women is quite a complex problem for the Eskimo. Men pursue in women an idealized mother image. Yet the terms in which the myths portray women (that is, the way men perceive them) suggests that men are often disappointed in their quest.

Nunivak Eskimo individuals seem to possess a firm idea of what they want to be and a clear image of the world in which they realistically strive to attain desired ends. The characters in the myths are persistent; usually they are cautious and judicious observers, rational beings, willing to admit defeat while at the same time trying to overcome it. They are responsible, diligent, and methodical beings who in most cases prove to be effective in their goal-oriented behavior. All these traits, says Lantis, indicate that the Eskimo himself has a "good orientation to reality." Yet, on the ego level of functioning the Eskimo personality, judging from the myths, is not quite what at first glance it seems to be. The readiness of the people in the stories to accede to others' desires and the tendency to be submissive suggest a restricted ego. Particularly does ego restriction reveal itself in the way the individual in myths is unable to be aggressive when he has to further his competitive ambition or satisfy some other desire. Toward some interpersonal problems the characters maintain a laissez-faire attitude; they are afraid of impinging on others and therefore restrict their own area of assertive activity. Close examination of the stories makes it clear that the characters obtain objectives not solely by their own efforts but also through magic. When a defense is needed against a feeling of inferiority or against real ineffectiveness in a tough situation, the people in the stories submit to supernatural power. In psychological terms, this suggests that the feeling of inadequacy that the Eskimo experiences in some situations motivates him to objectify his wishes and to rely on relatively passive forms of coping. Such a readiness to inhibit vigorous self-assertion may be acquired early in life, Lantis suggests, explaining that her evidence for this hunch comes not from the myths but from observation of child rearing among the Nunivak people. Submissiveness and only the gentlest signs of physical assertion suffice to bring the child satisfying rewards.

We have looked briefly at the id and ego, and now come to material from myths bearing on the superego level of the Eskimo personality. A strong superego is evident in phenomena such as repression, subconscious compulsion, and other defenses that appear in mythology. Furthermore, restraint on a person's physical drives is made into an acceptable positive value. Hostility is often expressed deviously, that is, by magical means, rather than through direct aggression. More clues to superego functioning come from examining the many emotional threats that confront the characters. One, especially, is significant: being bitten or eaten. Lantis finds an explanation for this anxiety in the guilt and fear of retaliation that

Eskimo probably feel for killing and eating the soul-bearing animals on which their life depends. Lantis reasons cogently in order to support this interpretation:

. . . these people who are among the world's most effective hunters, that is, among the greatest human predators against animals, feel continuous guilt for this very effectiveness and so must enter into the myriad small rituals, must observe the tabus, load themselves down with amulets, rush to confess what seem trivial offenses, practice the magic, in order to reduce their anxiety. . . . The hunter must have sensed his own deep hostility against these creatures that so often eluded and frustrated him.

The myths reveal a large stock of defenses that presumably also operate in Eskimo personality, including wish fulfillment, avoidance, denial of reality, projection, rejection, displacement, undoing, and others. Yet, in her final assessment, Lantis finds this personality not to be a morbid one. Destructive forces in the myths are after all combated successfully. The death of a protagonist is rare and so, too, are unhappy endings. The myths show "an objective and effective people, much too busy meeting the world to think about the emotional conflicts within themselves."

Lantis reports a brief analysis of thirty-two Rorschach records from Nunivak Eskimo men and women that at many points corroborates interpretations derived from the myths. Subjects who took the Rorschach are shown to be of "high average" intelligence and given to careful, meticulous observation, almost to the point of compulsiveness. They reveal high energy, persistence, and extroversion. There is a real tendency to conform but no direct evidence of submissiveness. The subjects are preoccupied with sex but without conflict or guilt (preoccupation seems to be concentrated in the Rorschach records of adolescents). The test records reveal signs of frustrated aggression, dependence, and oral aggression, for example, revealed by biting and eating). Repression, too, is shown to be a fairly common defense. Lantis's work, unusual for the intensive exploration which she devotes to a relatively neglected source of data is also noteworthy because it is the only full-scale appraisal we have of Eskimo social personality.[5]

Assessment

Practically all culture and personality research in North America (and, for that matter, in Latin America as well) has been done

---

[5] For relevant materials on other Eskimo see Honigmann and Honigmann 1953 and 1959 and Ferguson 1960. For quite a different use of folktalks in culture and personality research see Child, Storm, and Veroff 1958.

anthropologists from the United States working in their own
k yard. They have experimented with a variety of frameworks,
hods, and techniques, including the use of autobiography, depth
iewing, psychoanalytical formulations, projective tests, and
nstruction of statistical modal types. Anthropology in gen-
always encouraged methodological innovation and experi-
n. Innovation in culture and personality research has been
by the desire to do better work. Research workers have
cure more objective data, penetrate "deeper" after elu-
, and by-pass the superficial for the presumably richer
vealed conscious or unconscious thought. In general,
s have only exceptionally trusted themselves to make
th   sweeping interpretations that psychiatrists (especially
tho analytically oriented) make with such confidence. Increasingly, anthropologists doing culture and personality research have
come to resemble the clinical psychologists, who, when they advise
a psychiatrist, rely closely on their scores and are often diffident,
cautious, and embarrassed as far as the subjective tenor of their
diagnosis goes. It is as if their role as interpreters of personality
conflicts with values they acquired while apprenticing in the experimental laboratory. Anthropologists studying personalities have
also rarely been subjective in the manner of men like De Madariaga
or Maurois who put great reliance on their intuitive skills and sensitivity.

Thirty years of field work gave time to try many approaches, but
they have scarcely been sufficient (considering the available manpower) to investigate more than a small fraction of the indigenous
New World population. A few culture areas are well represented
in culture and personality literature but for many our knowledge
is spotty indeed. The Southwest has been well studied, but all tribes
have not received the same amount of attention (Kluckhohn 1954:
689). People like the Navaho and Hopi have been repeatedly visited.
They are our best laboratories for future problem-oriented research. Considerably less thoroughly studied in the Southwest are
groups like the Papago and Apache. California, the Great Basin,
Plateau, and North Pacific Coast have been sampled out only exceptionally by more than one field worker. No matter how reliable
his methods may be, no man can go very far in one short season.
Quite a bit of work has been done on the Plains; enough for Gladwin (1957) to suggest that the cultural unity of the area may not
be accompanied by much homogeneity of basic personality. He ad-

mits that he has compared only two typical tribes, the Comanche and Cheyenne, and is aware that for the second of these, very limited personality data are available. Ethnohistorical data pertaining to New York State Iroquois Indians have been intensively utilized for research—more perhaps than the surviving Iroquois themselves. Several anthropologists have recently been studying personality among the North Carolina Cherokee and we should soon know how that community fits into the continental picture. (For a synthesis that does not, however, incorporate all available material see Gulick 1960: Ch. 8–9.) The Seminole represent a continuing, viable cultural enclave, although one that is hard to work with. In the far North the situation is striking: a number of excellent Algonkian studies (mostly of Ojibwa-Chippewa communities), one detailed Athapaskan monograph, and, apart from Lantis's work, little concerning the popular Eskimo! For Latin America the total picture is far more spotty.

Just as culture areas have been spottily covered and with varying degrees of intensity so methodology has been divergent from one group to another. If we are really to compare the Navaho, Hopi, and Ojibwa, don't we have to do among the Hopi and Ojibwa what has been done among the Navaho and apply to the Navaho some of the questions asked in the other groups? Against this suggestion runs the preference to approach each new piece of work with a fresh mind (Mead and Wolfenstein 1955:5). The whole issue may revolve around personal inclination. Why not restudy the Berens River Ojibwa using the life-history or Kardiner's psychogenetic approach? How about a thorough study of the Kwakiutl using Rorschachs? This brings up the value of revisits, preferably by different anthropologists, to communities that were studied some time ago. Sixteen years had passed since the Kaska Indians were studied. It would be appropriate to discover what has happened on the covert and overt levels of Kaska personality and in Kaska culture. Indications are that tremendous theoretical advances will come in anthropology when research workers who possess different methods, or at any rate a healthy skepticism concerning some of their predecessors findings, systematically re-examine the dozens of intensively studied communities of the world.

Having complained about spotty coverage in North America, let us admit that we know enough to begin to develop wider generalizations and comparisons (*cf.* Kluckhohn 1954:693). A number of reports, for example, suggest quite convincingly that a high degree of psychological homogeneity characterizes the American Indian. Recently a portion of the available data was assembled in an admittedly undocumented form by George D. and Louise S. Spindler (1957). The psychological features which they discovered to be most widely exhibited among Indians are: "nondemonstrative emotionality and reserve" accompanied by a high degree of control over in-group aggression; autonomy of the individual; ability to stoically endure deprivation and frustration; high value on bravery; "a generalized fear of the world as dangerous" a proclivity for practical joking; "attention to the concrete realities of the present" (in Rorschach argot, the large D approach), and dependence on supernatural power that one strives purposefully to obtain. The picture of homogeneity is even more clear cut if we limit ourselves to northern forest people, Algonkians and Athapaskans. Emotional restraint, for example, appears to be a highly reliable characterization of these Indians. Other common traits include a high value placed on deference in interpersonal relationships, personal resourcefulness, and individualism. People do not attempt to tell others what to do. Authoritarian attitudes and leadership behavior are suppressed.

Another line of constructive synthesis for which we are ready is to relate particular personality syndromes to technology, social structure, and other segments of culture. Hallowell and I have suggested a relationship between the relatively atomistic social systems of northern hunters and their personality. He also perceives consistency between the inhibition of overt aggression and use of sorcery. Laura Thompson (1948) relates Indian world-views to bases of subsistence. In the hunting world-view, man conceives of himself as a helpless supplicant for power on which he depends for success. It comes to him from a universal power pool through disparate nonhuman entities, chiefly animals, whom he obtains as personal guardians. This world-view persists even among agriculturalists in North America but there it is altered. Where people develop a more systematic control of the food supply, they no longer conceive of themselves as helpless supplicants of power which derives from disparate power sources. They become power entities in their own right and the power source also becomes more clearly structured.

Assessment of culture and personality research in any area of the world can scarcely fail to note the plethora of theoretical problems which have been generated by culture and personality research (*cf.*

Inkeles and Levinson 1954). The discussion which follows in part reflects thinking that developed while work was being done with North American personality materials, but it also applies to work done in other areas of the world.

For example, there is the question of how child rearing leads to the formation of adult personality configurations. Not that anybody doubts the learned nature of personality or would any longer ignore the significance of the later years for socialization. But *what* is learned in early childhood? Before the child can verbalize, how can we know what cognitive and emotional learning occurs? How does early, basic learning continue to influence later learning and direct the individual's world and self views? (The theory of cognitive dissonance, while it doesn't say wholly new things, speaks systematically and might fruitfully be applied to the process of personality development.) The accumulated materials on personality from North American Indians and other areas of the world are sufficient for at least beginning to develop an anthropologically satisfactory theory of socialization.

How certain core areas of personality are able to persist despite change in other areas of culture is a theoretical problem directly instigated by research conducted with North American Indians. To what extent is such persistence bound up with socialization, language, or mode of ecological adaptation? The solution to the problem may well lie in an imaginative theory such as Friedl's (1956) designed for the Chippewa (Ojibwa). Incessant change was characteristic of the aboriginal culture. It has continued with culture contact and supports the persistence of personality.

In noting possibilities for research in North American culture and personality—people to be visited or revistied and generalizations to be drawn—we must also assess whether the flow of manpower is adequate for this research. Anthropology in this country does not want for serious graduate students and creative minds. But are they turning to problems of culture and personality in proportion to their growing number? I have noted diminishing enthusiasm for culture and personality research since the thirties and forties.[6] In the balance of this paper, I shall examine some reasons

---

[6] The editor of the *American Anthropologist* (Vol. 61, p. 498) reports that 47 manuscripts falling into the category of culture and personality were submitted (not all were published) between 1955 and 1958 or 10 per cent of the total (498). Social organization was in top position (101 manuscripts, 20 per cent) and then came ethnology—ethnography, method-theory, and acculturation with 82, 81, and 57 articles each (the percentages are 17, 16 and 11 respectively). The criteria used in classification are not given. In a survey that I recently did

for this withdrawal of interest and also attempt to resolve some of the methodological problems that may be discouraging students from entering this field.

Part of the reason for the lack of support of culture and personality research is given in these words of Nadel (1957:189):

The advance of any science is punctuated as much by the disappearance of old problems as by the emergence of new ones. This is little better than a truism if we have in mind problems disappearing and discussions or controversies ceasing because the issues in question have been resolved. But often it is not a question of solution; rather it is a question of changes of viewpoint and interest. The old problems are abandoned because they no longer seem important; the controversies cease because all that can be said has been said; and if certain questions still remain unanswered, they are yet shelved in spite of it, or perhaps because of it— because one realizes that they are unanswerable and should be replaced by other, more profitable, ones.

The change of interest came when new problems opened up in adjacent areas of the discipline, particularly with regard to social structure and linguistics. These new problems attracted graduate students faced with choosing thesis topics as well as full-fledged professionals. But this explanation makes us want to know what caused culture and personality to lose appeal. Why couldn't it meet competition?

Several things succeeded in promoting dissatisfaction with culture and personality. Instead of proving a challenge, the barrage of criticism released in the forties and early fifties proved to be a deterrent. Why did it have a deterring reaction? The answer lies in the growing climate of empiricism and operationalism, the high evaluation of objectivity, and the stress put on objective reliability. The positivist conception of science which had long captivated anthropology and had become the dominant intellectual force in American academic life was incompatible with certain aspects of the new approach (*cf*. Kroeber 1915, 1935, 1936). Foundation support could best be commanded by establishing that one's problems were amenable to treatment by procedures generally accepted to be scientific. The notion that anthropology is a humanity as well as a social science has been lost (Honigmann 1959b). If, as is generally assumed, scientific method is a unitary thing, then anthropology must conform as closely as possible to the methods used in those disciplines that were indisputably in the scientific tradition as currently con-

---

for a biennial review, I came across many papers that took a psychological view of cultural phenomena (Honigmann 1959a). But many of those papers hardly represent what I would call culture and personality research and are not by anthropologists.

ceived. To the extent that culture and personality could not be re-directed along new lines, it lost ground.

Recently I listened to a discussion concerning two variant inter-pretations of the same data from an American Indian community. The anthropologists agreed on the facts, but they disagreed when it came to ascertaining their psychological meaning for the Indians. For one thing, the researchers probably did not really know the people very well and hence were handicapped for interpreting their data. They also lacked a sufficiently powerful theory in which they believed enough to apply it to their facts. But more pertinent is the question they faced of proving any one interpretation to be objectively more true than the other. How could any reconciliation between interpretations be verified empirically? This is an unhappy state of affairs for men to contemplate who wish to model them-selves after campus colleagues who follow more rigorous methods. (Note that this particular difficulty would not have arisen had the psychologically minded ethnologists retained faith in one theory, say psychoanalysis. Their deductions would have been guided by psy-choanalytical principles. Logical reasoning would have brought back someone who went beyond the basic postulates of the theory. The fact that the insights obtained by psychoanalytical formula-tions could not be checked operationally would also not have been unduly distressing. But, very likely, back in the twenties and thirties it was these very characteristics of psychoanalytical psy-chology that made anthropologists decide against following Freud exclusively!)

One might properly argue that somebody who really wishes to study personality as it develops and functions in one set of cultural conditions or another doesn't care what his work is called—whether science, history, or art. Furthermore, according to some philoso-phers, no hard and fast line separates science from other modes of understanding (Polanyi 1958). Everybody agrees that experimen-tation is not the essence of science. Nor is the central criterion even prediction—what can the paleontologist predict? The field worker in anthropology is mainly concerned with communicating his un-derstanding of the way of life he researches. His work, then, should be appraised by how meaningful is the understanding which it offers and what it contributes to the wider understanding of man. I have long thought that novels are among the most perceptive means of gaining insight into ways of life that a skillful or sensitive writer authentically grasps.

Rival interpretations of personality by men who really know their people might receive the same kind of attention that is accorded to rival views of events in history. The final resolution of the dispute would have to wait until fresh data are accumulated, new field work is undertaken, or a better theory comes to hand. I am convinced that we need more perceptive studies of persons whose behavior is standardized in different fashions. To obtain such information, we need sensitive students willing to immerse themselves thoroughly in exotic ways of life and, by whatever means recommend themselves, come to know the covert and overt sides of the people they study. The care, thoroughness, authenticity, level of interpretation, and the underlying degree of understanding which such studies will achieve will greatly vary from one case to another, but they should not be judged by standards foreign to the problem in hand.

BIBLIOGRAPHY

ABERLE, D. F.
 1954 Comments on Southwestern studies of culture and personality, by Clyde Kluckhohn. American Anthropologist 56:697–700.

ALBERT, E. M.
 1956 The classification of values: a method and illustration. American Anthropologist 58:221–248.

BARNOUW, V.
 1950 Acculturation and personality among the Wisconsin Chippewa. Memoirs of the American Anthropological Association No. 72.

BARRY, H., III, I. L. CHILD, and M. K. BACON
 1959 Relation of child training to subsistence economy. American Anthropologist 61:51–63.

BENEDICT, R.
 1928 Psychological types in the cultures of the southwest. Proceedings of the International Congress of Americanists 23:572–581.
 1932 Configurations of culture in North America. American Anthropologist 34:1–27.
 1934 Patterns of culture. Boston, Houghton Mifflin Co.

BENNETT, J.
 1946 The interpretation of Pueblo culture: a question of values. Southwestern Journal of Anthropology 2:361–374.

BILLIG, O., J. GILLIN, and W. DAVIDSON
1947–48 Aspects of personality and culture in a Guatemalan community: ethnological and Rorschach approaches. Journal of Personality 16:153–187, 326–368.

Burt, Cyril

1957   The impact of psychology upon education. *In* The yearbook of education 1957. London, Evans Brothers Ltd.

Caudill, W. A.

1949   Psychological characteristics of acculturated Wisconsin Ojibwa children. American Anthropologist 51:409–427.

Chapin, F. S.

1947   Experimental designs in sociological research. New York, Harper & Bros.

Child, I. L., T. Storm, and J. Veroff

1958   Achievement themes in folk tales related to socialization practice. *In* Motives in fantasy, action, and society, J. W. Atkinson, ed. Princeton, D. Van Nostrand Co., Inc.

Devereux, G.

1951   Reality and dream: psychotherapy of a Plains Indian. New York, International Universities Press.

Du Bois, C.

1944   The people of Alor. Minneapolis, University of Minnesota Press.

Dunn, H. L.

1959   What high-level wellness means. Canadian Journal of Public Health 50:447–457.

Dyk, W.

1938   Son of Old Man Hat. New York, Harcourt Brace & Co.

Erikson, E. H.

1939   Observations on Sioux education. Journal of Psychology 7:101–156.

Farber, M. L.

1950   The problem of national character: a methodological analysis. Journal of Psychology 30:307–316.

Ferguson, F.

1960   Eskimo personality in the light of nine Rorschachs from Great Whale River Eskimo. Research Previews (Institute for Research in Social Science, University of North Carolina) 8, No. 1:8–13.

Ford, C. S.

1941   Smoke from their fires. New Haven, Yale University Press.

Friedl, E.

1956   Persistence in Chippewa culture and personality. American Anthropologist 58:814–825.

Gillin, J.

1951   The culture of security in San Carlos. Middle American Research Institute, Publication 16.

Gladwin, T.

1957   Personality structure in the Plains. Anthropological Quarterly 30:111–124.

Goldfrank, E. S.

1943   Historic change and social character: a study of the Teton Dakota. American Anthropologist 45:67–83.

1945   Socialization, personality, and the structure of the Pueblo society (with particular reference to Hopi and Zuni). American Anthropologist 47: 516–539.

GOLDMAN, I.
1950   Psychiatric interpretation of Russian history: a reply to Geoffrey Gorer. The American Slavic and East European Review 9:151–161.

GULICK, J.
1960   Cherokees at the crossroads. Chapel Hill, Institute for Research in Social Science, University of North Carolina.

HALLOWELL, A. I.
1936   Psychic stresses and cultural patterns. American Journal of Psychiatry. 92:1291–1310.
1937   Temporal orientation in western civilization and in a preliterate society. American Anthropologist 39:647–670.
1942   Acculturation processes and personality changes as indicated by the Rorschach technique. Rorschach Research Exchange 6:42–50.
1946   Some psychological characteristics of the northeastern Indiana. *In* Man in northeastern North America, F. Johnson, ed. Papers of the Robert S. Peabody Foundation for Archaeology, 3.
1951   The use of projective techniques in the study of the socio-psychological aspects of acculturation. Journal of Projective Techniques 15:27–44.
1952   Ojibwa personality and acculturation. *In* Acculturation in the Americas, proceedings and selected papers of the XXIXth International Congress of Americanists, Sol Tax, ed. Chicago, University of Chicago Press.

HARING, D. G. (ed.)
1948   Personal character and cultural milieu. Syracuse, University of Syracuse Press.

HAVIGHURST, R. J. and B. L. NEUGARTEN
1955   American Indian and white children: a sociopsychological investigation. Chicago, University of Chicago Press.

HOLMBERG, A. R.
1950   Nomads of the long bow. The Siriono of Eastern Boliva. Smithsonian Institution, Institute of Social Anthropology, Publication No. 10.

HONIGMANN, J.
1949   Culture and ethos of Kaska society. Yale University Publications in Anthropology, No. 40.
1954   Culture and personality. New York, Harper & Bros.
1959a Psychocultural studies. *In* Biennial Review of Anthropology 1959, B. Siegel, ed. Stanford, Stanford University Press.
1959b The world of man. New York, Harper & Bros.

HONIGMANN, J. J. and I. HONIGMANN
1959   Notes on Great Whale River ethos. Anthropologica n.s. 1:106–121.

HORNEY, K.
1939   New ways in psychoanalysis. New York, W. W. Norton & Co., Inc.
1945   Our inner conflicts. New York, W. W. Norton & Co., Inc.

INKELES, A. and D. J. LEVINSON

1954 National character: the study of modal personality and sociocultural systems. *In* Handbook of social psychology, Gardner Lindzey, ed. Two volumes. Cambridge, Mass., Addison-Wesley Publishing Co.

JOSEPH, A., R. B. SPICER, and J. CHESKY

1949 The desert people: a study of the Papago Indians of southern Arizona. Chicago, University of Chicago Press.

KAPLAN, B.

1954 A study of Rorschach responses in four cultures. Papers of the Peabody Museum of American Archaeology and Ethnology, Vol. 42, No. 2.

KARDINER, A.

1939 The individual and his society. New York, Columbia University Press.

1945 The psychological frontiers of society. New York, Columbia University Press.

KLUBACK, W.

1956 William Dilthey's philosophy of history. New York, Columbia University Press.

KLUCKHOHN, C.

1944 The influence of psychiatry on anthropology in America during the last 100 years. *In* One hundred years of American psychiatry, J. K. Hall, G. Zilboorg, H. A. Bunker, eds. New York, Columbia University Press.

1945 The personal document in anthropological science. *In* The use of personal documents in history, anthropology and sociology, L. Gottschalk, C. Kluckhohn, and R. Angell, eds. Social Science Research Council Bulletin 53.

1951 A comparative study of values in five cultures. *In* Navaho veterans: a study of changing values, by E. Z. Vogt. Papers of the Peabody Museum of American Archaeology and Ethnology, Vol. 41, No. 1.

1954 Southwestern studies of culture and personality. American Anthropologist 56:685–697.

KLUCKHOHN, C. and D. LEIGHTON

1946 The Navaho. Cambridge, Harvard University Press.

KLUCKHOHN, C. and H. A. MURRAY (eds.)

1948 Personality in nature, society, and culture. New York, Henry A. Knopf.

KLUCKHOHN, F.

1950 Dominant and substitute profiles of cultural orientations. Social Forces 28:376–393.

KROEBER, A. L.

1915 Eighteen professions. American Anthropologist 17:283–288.

1935 History and science in anthropology. American Anthropologist 37:539–569.

1936 So-called social science. Journal of Social Philosophy 1:317–340.

LANDES, R.

1937 The personality of the Ojibwa. Character and Personality 6:51–60.

1938a The abnormal among the Ojibwa Indians. Journal of Abnormal and Social Psychology 33:14–33.

1938b The Ojibwa woman. Columbia University Publications in Anthropology, No. 31.

LANTIS, M.
1953 Nunivak Eskimo personality as revealed in the mythology. Anthropological papers of the University of Alaska 2:109–174.
1959 Alaskan Eskimo cultural values. Polar Notes 1:35–48.

LEIGHTON, A. H. and D. C. LEIGHTON
1949 Gregorio, The hand-trembler: a psychobiological personality study of a Navaho Indian. Papers of the Peabody Museum of American Archaeology and Ethnology, Vol. 40, No. 1.

LEIGHTON, D. C. and C. KLUCKHOHN
1947 Children of the people. Cambridge, Harvard University Press.

LEWIS, OSCAR
1951 Life in a Mexican village: Tepoztlan restudied. Urbana, University of Illinois Press.
1959 Five families: Mexican case studies in the culture of poverty. New York, Basic Books, Inc.

LI AN-CHE
1937 Zuni: some observations and queries. American Anthropologist 39: 62–76.

LINDESMITH, A. R. and A. L. STRAUSS
1950 Critique of culture-personality writings. American Sociological Review 15:587–600.

MACGREGOR, G.
1946 Warriors without weapons. Chicago, University of Chicago Press.

MASLOW, A. H.
1950 Self-actualizing people: a study of psychological health. Personality Symposium 1:11–34.

MEAD, M.
1928 Coming of age in Samoa. New York, William Morrow & Co.
1956 New lives for old. New York, William Morrow & Co.
1959 An anthropologist at work: writings of Ruth Benedict. Boston, Houghton Mifflin.

MEAD, M. and M. WOLFENSTEIN (eds.)
1955 Childhood in contemporary cultures. Chicago, University of Chicago Press.

MEGGERS, BETTY J.
1946 Recent trends in American ethnology. American Anthropologist 48: 176–214.

NADEL, S. F.
1937 The typological approach to culture. Character and Personality 5:267–284.
1957 Malinowski on magic and religion. In Man and culture, Raymond Firth, ed. London, Routledge & Kegan Paul.

NORTHROP, F. S. C.
1946 The meeting of east and west. New York, The Macmillan Co.

ORLANSKY, H.
1949   Infant care and personality. Psychological Bulletin 46:1–48.

POLANYI, MICHAEL
1958   Personal knowledge: towards a post-critical philosophy. Chicago, University of Chicago Press.

RADCLIFFE-BROWN, A. R.
1930–31 The social organization of Australian tribes. Oceania 1:34–63, 206–246, 322–341, 426–456.

RADIN, P.
1920   The autobiography of a Winnebago Indian. University of California Publications in American Archaeology and Ethnology 16:381–473.

ROHEIM, G.
1950   Psychoanalysis and anthropology. New York, International Universities Press.

SAPIR, E.
1924   Culture, genuine and spurious. American Journal of Sociology 29: 401–429.
1932   Cultural anthropology and psychiatry. Journal of Abnormal and Social Psychology 27:229–242.

SIMMONS, L. (ed.)
1942   Sun Chief, the autobiography of a Hopi Indian. New Haven, Yale University Press.

SPENGLER, O.
1926   The decline of the west. 2 vols. New York: Alfred A. Knopf.

SPINDLER, G. D.
1952   Personality and peyotism in Menomini Indian acculturation. Psychiatry 15:151–160.
1955   Sociocultural and psychological processes in Menomini acculturation. University of California Publications in Culture and Society, No. 5.

SPINDLER, G. D. and L. S. SPINDLER
1957   American Indian personality types and their sociocultural roots. Annals of the American Academy of Political and Social Science 311: 147–157.

SPIRO, MELFORD and R. G. D'ANDRADE
1958   A cross-cultural study of some supernatural beliefs. American Anthropologist 60:456–466.

THOMPSON, L.
1948   Attitudes and acculturation. American Anthropologist 50:200–215.
1950   Culture in crisis. New York, Harper & Bros.
1951   Personality and government. Mexico, D. F., Ediciones del Instituto Indigenista Interamericano.

THOMPSON, L. and A. JOSEPH
1944   The Hopi way. Chicago, University of Chicago Press.

TSCHOPIK, H., JR.
1951   The Aymara of Chucuito, Peru. 1. Magic. Anthropological Papers of the American Museum of Natural History, vol. 44, pt. 2.

UNDERWOOD, F. and I. HONIGMANN
  1947   A comparison of socialization and personality in two simple societies. American Anthropologist 49:557–577.

VOGET, F. W.
  1956   The American Indian in transition: reformation and accommodation. American Anthropologist 58:249–263.

VOGT, E. Z.
  1951   Navaho veterans: a study of changing values. Papers of the Peabody Museum of American Archaeology and Ethnology, Vol. 41, No. 1.

WALLACE, A. F. C.
  1952   The modal personality structure of the Tuscarora Indians, as revealed by the Rorschach test. Bureau of American Ethnology, Bulletin 150.
  1955   Stress, personality change, and cultural creativity. Paper read at meeting of the American Anthropological Association, Nov. 17, 1955. Mimeographed.
  1956   Revitalization movements: some theoretical considerations for their comparative study. American Anthropologist 58:264–281.
  1959   The institutionalization of cathartic and control strategies in Iroquois religious psychotherapy. *In* Culture and mental health, M. K. Opler, ed. New York, The Macmillan Co.

WHITING, J. W. M. and I. L. CHILD
  1953   Child training and personality: a cross-cultural study. New Haven, Yale University Press.

Chapter 5

OCEANIA

THOMAS GLADWIN
National Institute of Mental Health

Introduction

Much of Oceania is comprised of islands, islands which are characteristically fairly small, tropical, and separated from adjacent lands by open ocean, sometimes by vast stretches of ocean. Obvious exceptions to this generalization are the great land mass of Australia and the large islands of New Guinea and New Zealand. The preponderance of smallish tropical islands has inevitably created both limitations and challenges to the pursuit of anthropological studies in the area.

The most severe limitation is set by the thinness of the archaeological record, at least as it has been revealed thus far. In part at least this must be ascribed to the high rates of oxidation and biotic decay characteristic of warm climates, heavy rainfall, and proximity to the sea. Even artifacts tough enough to survive such conditions are likely to find the ground washed away beneath them. Although some recent archaeological work has been more encouraging, Oceania is far from having the solid foundation of prehistory found elsewhere in the world. Added to this is a short and very fragmentary historical record. The result is a focus primarily on the here and now, on the present characteristics of populations and cultures rather than on their antecedents.

Granting an inadequate or nonexistent developmental perspective, the islands of the Pacific frequently provide the challenge of a nearly ideal research setting. The physical anthropologist can find a relatively stable, isolated, and homogeneous breeding population on which to base his studies. Cultural homogeneity within an island can bring similar clarity to the study of social structure and cultural dynamics. Furthermore, the small size and isolation of many

135

island communities permit the detailed description of the totality of a finite population. Within a setting of this sort it is often possible to define and examine *all* of the interpersonal and intergroup relationships which determine the relevant social environment of an individual.

Finally, if one disregards the large land masses of New Zealand, Australia, and New Guinea, the ecology and basic economy of the smaller islands of Polynesia, Micronesia, and Melanesia have many common, almost uniform, attributes. They are tropical, with abundant rainfall at least part of the year, and are favored with trade winds. In all three areas there are islands which are clustered together, and some which are widely scattered and isolated. There are flat, sandy coral islands on atolls ("low" islands) and steeper, usually larger, volcanic ("high") islands. On all of them the soil is relatively poor, favoring principal reliance on root and tree crops, and discouraging domestication of animals for meat. This leaves the ocean as a primary source of protein. Metal is generally lacking. This is only a partial list, which could be extended to include technology, health conditions, transportation, etc. On this common ecological base one finds a wide range of social and political organizations, value systems, and personality types. A special opportunity thus exists for comparisons between one group and another with a number of variables fairly well controlled.

A particularly fruitful comparison might be made with respect to the response of these various island peoples to foreign, especially European, contact. The circumstances of this contact were again rather uniform. After the early explorers came traders and missionaries, and in many areas whaling ships from New England seeking provisions and release from shipboard life. The traders were followed by more stable commercial arrangements, especially the exploitation of coconut and other crops through foreign-operated plantations, or through resident traders. Despite the relative similarity of this experience, the response to it appears to have been markedly different. Here the differences can be mentioned in only a general and impressionistic way.

The Micronesians, with few exceptions, retained their core culture—especially their social organization, values, and economy—while adopting a wide array of superficial technological changes. In Polynesia the changes were more sweeping, often devastating. This was especially true on the larger island groups such as Hawaii, Tahiti, or the Marquesas. Even on the smaller atolls, foreigners—missionaries, traders, or administrators—were granted more leadership, and therefore more opportunity to effect pervasive changes in values, in political structure, and in other ways. In Melanesia there was frequently hostility, suspicion, and bloodshed, with minimal acceptance of foreign leadership except when imposed by force. Yet Melanesia has also experienced the sweeping fantasy of embracing foreign culture, or at least material culture, in the cargo cults. These are bizarre outbursts in which a whole population may, for example, destroy its possessions and await a ship full of foreign goods—a ship which of course never comes.

Even though these characterizations are obviously overgeneralized, it is clear that there were striking differences in response. There were of course special factors. Polynesian girls looked especially attractive to American men. Melanesia was a source of slave labor for "blackbirders." And so on. But these factors do not obscure the fact that the people themselves responded differently. Personality differences must have played a major role. Conversely, the psychological impact of these changes must have varied widely. Oceania is therefore an unusually inviting area in which to make systematic, comparative studies of culture change, including its psychological dimensions. Culture change, however, is only one of many ways in which the special character of this area lends itself to research, and particularly to research in culture and personality.

In evaluating the work that has been done to date, we must bear these conditions in mind. It is thus particularly legitimate to ask what real contributions to our understanding of personality (as well as of culture) have emerged from Oceania. After reviewing what has been done, I will return to this question in the assessment.

The review of the literature which follows will be concerned with noting the landmarks. It is not in any sense an encyclopaedic inventory of all work done thus far. Nor does the supporting bibliography pretend to exhaust the literature.[1] In particular, I will not dwell upon those studies which, while developing data potentially useful for the elucidation of personality dynamics, have not been developed in this way either by the authors or by others. The monograph of the Berndts (1951) on sexual behavior in Western Arn-

---

[1] I have been greatly aided by a quite complete bibliography through 1954 prepared by the University of Hawaii Pacific Islands Studies Committee (Vinacke *et al.* 1955). To the serious student of the area this three-part bibliography can be invaluable. Taylor's (1951) Pacific bibliography is a standard reference; at the present writing an expanded and updated edition is in preparation. The *Journal de la Société des Océanistes*, published by the Musée de l'Homme in Paris, provides an annual bibliographic review of Oceania.

hem Land or Warner's *Black Civilization* (1937) would be cases in point.

Geographically and culturally I include work done in Australia, New Guinea, and the broad expanses of Melanesia, Polynesia, and Micronesia. Among these, Micronesia is a late entrant. During the formative years of culture and personality research, Micronesia was under the exclusive political control of Japan. The few Japanese anthropologists who worked in these islands were seemingly not interested in this new field of study, so the first culture and personality studies began in Micronesia only after the Second World War.

Obviously, inclusion in this survey is based on the locus of field work, not on the nationality of the researcher. With the exception of Ernest Beaglehole of Victoria University and his students, and possibly of Stanley Porteus of the University of Hawaii, none of the researchers whom I discuss are residents of the area under consideration. Reo Fortune is a New Zealander, but no longer lives there.

Chronological Review and Evaluation

Oceania can claim a twenty-year beat on the rest of the world. It was the locus of the first systematic field work among non-European peoples designed to enrich the interpretation of ethnology by the insights of psychology. This comprised one of the explicitly stated aims of A. C. Haddon in organizing the Cambridge Anthropological Expedition to the Torres Straits. The published report (Myers and McDougall 1903) deals almost entirely with the sensory modalities and would not now be included within the purvey of culture and personality as the field has evolved. But its undeniable historical significance rests on the fact that Haddon sought, as collaborators for Rivers (who was himself trained in psychophysiology) and Seligman, two psychologists who were felt to be competent in the most fruitful procedures of the scientific psychology of the day. However, at the time the Torres Straits Expedition was in the field in 1898, Sigmund Freud was at work on the manuscript of *The Interpretation of Dreams*. It is an historical fact, but not necessarily a stroke of undiluted good fortune, that the study of culture and personality has come to depend almost exclusively upon the line of inquiry being initiated sixty years ago by Freud rather than that envisioned by Haddon.

Certainly considerable credit for determining this trend is due to Géza Róheim, the most orthodox and loyal of Freudian psychoanalysts to concern himself with non-European personality. As early as 1925 he published a book entitled *Australian Totemism: a Psycho-analytical Study in Anthropology*. Some years earlier, in 1913, Freud had completed his first major work on religion, *Totem and Taboo*. This drew heavily upon the secondhand ethnographic data assembled by Frazer, Robertson Smith, and others, especially as these pertained to Australia. Among other things, Freud assumed that Oedipal conflicts were shared by all peoples. These conflicts had their beginnings in primitive family groups wherein at intervals the sons banded together to kill and sacrifically eat their father. The tabooed totem animal survives as a substitute for the father. In the literature of the day both totemism and primitiveness were emphasized as characteristic of the Australian aborigines, hence Róheim's early interest in Australia. After publishing the book noted above, which was based on published accounts, Róheim set out to see for himself. He undertook field studies in several parts of the world (Róheim, 1932), but spent the longest time with the Aranda of Central Australia. He explored at first hand the symbolic residue of the primal feast and the conflicts arising from living in a primitive horde dominated by an older male. Róheim deserves credit for being willing to test his beliefs under rugged field conditions, not a fashionable pastime in his day. Furthermore, because Malinowski had denied the existence of Oedipal conflicts in matrilineal societies (see below), Róheim also went to matrilineal Normanby Island near Malinowski's Trobriands, gathering evidence to refute Malinowski (*cf.* Róheim 1950). For all his enthusiasm, Róheim's work is no longer cited with any frequency by anthropologists. He was willing to go so far in attributing symbolic and historical significance to cultural acts that many anthropologists find it difficult to take his work seriously, and therefore tend to dismiss his conclusions (e.g., Lessa 1956). But the lack of continuing attention to Róheim's published writings is deceptive. His early work was widely read and initiated or expanded an interest in psychoanalysis in many of the influential pioneers in the field of culture and personality. Among others, Edward Sapir, Margaret Mead, and Clyde Kluckhohn have acknowledged Róheim's important impact on their thinking. Róheim's contribution to the field, then, is paradoxical: practically no one accepts his conclusions, but their stimulating effect was nevertheless very great.

Róheim also undoubtedly provided part of the impetus for the writing of the first monograph which undertook systematically to examine a hypothesis of personality dynamics in the light of solid ethnographic data, and in accordance with acceptable anthropological standards of interpretation. This was Bronislaw Malinowski's *Sex and Repression in Savage Society* (1927). Malinowski drew upon his extensive data from the Trobriand Islands to re-examine some aspects of *Totem and Taboo*. As noted above, he rejected the universality of the father-son Oedipal conflict, essentially on the ground that, in the Trobriands at least, discipline is in the hands of the mother's brother and not the father. He also discussed Freud's more anthropologically acceptable development of the psychological and social dynamics which support exogamy and the incest taboo. Róheim was undoubtedly justified in criticizing Malinowski for an incomplete understanding of Freud's writings. Malinowski was unfortunately the first of many anthropologists who have over the years criticized psychoanalytic theory on the basis of an inadequate and watered-down understanding of its implications (*cf.* La Barre 1958). But Malinowski's excursion into psychoanalytic theory nonetheless established a precedent for anthropologists. It was, in effect, the first anthropologically "respectable" substantive study in culture and personality.

Malinowski's encyclopaedic and highly literate ethnographic accounts of the Trobriander Islanders (1922, 1929, 1935) have also made important contributions to culture and personality through their use by others in developing new lines of analysis. As we shall note later, Kardiner started with these materials (as summarized by Du Bois) in developing his particular approach (Kardiner 1939). More recently Dorothy Lee (1950) made a major contribution to cognitive theory and psycholinguistics in her paper on "Lineal and Nonlineal Codifications of Reality," based entirely on Malinowski's published accounts of the Trobriands.

Meanwhile, Margaret Mead had gone to Samoa and in 1928 published on the basis of this field work the first of a series of studies of personality development and integration in Oceania. This was followed by a comparable monograph on Manus in 1930, and then in 1935 by a book describing and comparing personality in three contrasting New Guinea cultures—Arapesh, Mundugumor, and Tchambuli (the three monographs appeared together in Mead 1939). Accompanying her books on personality, in most cases, were solid ethnographic monographs in the best anthropological tradition. Concurrently, the impact of Mead's approach was clearly evident in Reo Fortune's study of Dobu (1932). Bateson's (1958) book centered upon the *naven* ceremonies of the Iatmul, first published in 1936, marked the beginning of a long collaboration with Margaret Mead. Especially to be noted is the large-scale 1936–39 team study of Bali (especially Bateson and Mead 1942, and Mead and Macgregor 1951; a full bibliography is to be found in Mead and Wolfenstein 1955:95–98). The many publications resulting from the Balinese research reflect a deliberate attempt to develop more effective techniques and more rigorous methodologies in support of the lines of inquiry established in Margaret Mead's earlier work. Aspects of this research which can only be mentioned here, but which deserve careful examination, range from systematic exploitation of photographic techniques, through detailed studies of music, dance, ritual, and drama, to theoretical analysis of social equilibrium (Bateson 1949). Finally, there is the account of Manus upon her return there in 1953 (Mead 1954b, 1956) when she found and described an extraordinarily successful cultural transformation and reintegration. This transformation, as analysed by Theodore Schwartz (Mead and Schwartz 1960), comprises a valuable addition to the literature on messianic movements; they found a complex interplay between a long-term transformation movement and a short-term cargo-type cult. These publications, of course, comprise only a small fraction of the contributions of Margaret Mead and her colleagues, and are concerned only with work in the Pacific area. But they perhaps define the substantive core of her work and methodological influence. The point of view reflected throughout her research is effectively (and often charmingly) synthesized in *Male and Female* (1949).

A more systematic statement of Mead's methodological premises is to be found in her retrospective evaluation of the national character studies undertaken during World War II (Mead 1953). Margaret Mead was one of the leaders in this challenging attempt to construct, at a distance, a basis for predicting the behavior of peoples of foreign nations (Mead and Métraux 1953). Anthropologists have always been notably reluctant to make predictions, and now they were asked to do so by extrapolation from a few informants and such documentary materials as could be collected. Mead based her approach upon the conception of the individual in his culture developed throughout her work and Bateson's in the Pacific: "Any member of a group, provided that his position is properly specified, is a perfect sample of the group-wide pattern on which he is acting as an informant." (Mead 1953:648) The discussion, and sometimes controversy, surrounding this methodological approach served to make explicit many of the assumptions hitherto lying below the surface of stated culture and personality theory.

Since it would obviously be impossible to summarize separately even the few works listed above, it is useful to attempt a general evaluation of her work to provide a basis for comparison with that of others. Special aspects of some of these studies will be considered later in this chapter.

In evaluating Margaret Mead's work, one fact scarcely needs underlining: she is a pioneer. From the outset she did field work in Oceania explicitly directed toward the understanding of the varieties of human personality and the mode of their development (*cf.* Mead 1959). She returned to write monographs of major and lasting value years before any other anthropologist (excepting her own colleagues) undertook a comparable task. True, Malinowski's field work was done during the first World War, and Linton was in the Marquesas in 1920–22. But the psychological implications of their data were only elucidated as afterthoughts—useful and intelligent, but still afterthoughts—many years subsequent to leaving the field.[2]

A striking example of Mead's pioneering receives too little attention, especially in view of the current surge of interest among social scientists in the work of Piaget. A primary purpose of Mead's 1928–29 field work in Manus (Mead 1932) was to examine the assumptions of Piaget (and of Lévy-Bruhl) that the less "logical" (by European standards) thought of children was a function of their immaturity, and that the thought processes of primitive people were analogous to those of children in our society. Using a variety of ingenious psychological measures, she found that Manus children actually analysed situations in a far more matter-of-fact ("logical") fashion than characterized the animistic reasoning of their

---

[2] Margaret Mead is also an effective and dedicated crusader in the cause of bringing anthropological insights to bear on the problems of our society. She has translated and focused anthropological material upon education, mental health, child development, technical assistance, and a variety of other fields. There are scores of journals in other professional and popular fields to which she has been the first anthropological contributor. Furthermore, her contribution has frequently had a clearly discernable effect on the thinking in that profession. Bridging the gap between anthropology and a variety of other fields of endeavor often requires a daring leap, a leap which some anthropologists feel frequently ends with an agonizing wrench. Without laboring this point, I will only suggest that when Margaret Mead is, for example, talking to educators she is concerned with improving and enriching our schools, not with meeting the canons of anthropological rigor. Her contributions to the anthropological literature provide a quite ample basis for judgment of her work as an anthropologist, and I will confine myself to these. But I offer my personal cheers to a person willing to balance research with an equal commitment to translating the insights so derived into the language and problems of any activity concerned with helping mankind.

elders. She offered several possible explanations and then arrived at the well documented conclusion that, Piaget and Lévy-Bruhl to the contrary, "Animistic thought cannot be explained in terms of intellectual immaturity."

Mead's work in culture and personality rests upon the same conceptual underpinnings of psychodynamics which are common to other workers in the field. Her interest in the possibilities of using this body of theory in anthropological research was first stimulated in the early 1920's by the writings of contemporary psychoanalysts. As her own theoretical position was developing she worked intensively, among others, with Erik Erikson, Lawrence K. Frank, Kurt Lewin, John Dollard, and Edward Sapir. Her approach is perhaps most differentiated by the biological and social matrix within which she sees these forces operating. She is concerned with the biological endowment and biological changes which shape a person's being, with the total social environment which surrounds the growing child and the adult, with how the child perceives and interprets this environment, with how the environment is interpreted, explicitly and implicitly, to the child, and with those figures in the social environment who are the agents of interpretation and learning. The structure of a particular society not only channels all relationships and activities within it, but also determines the manner in which an individual lives and learns his life. In this approach she hews more closely than many to a view of socialization and personality development as a process of enculturation, of the gradual learning of the integrated totality of attitudes and feelings and behaviors which comprise the culture. Inherent in this is a concern with the process and nature of learning, and with the consistency between the patterns of experience in a variety of learning situations (Mead 1953). Related also to this is the intriguing methodological exercise of Mead and Macgregor (1951) in their photographic analysis of the learning by Balinese children of a single facet of behavior, patterns of motor activity. In addition to its methodological emphasis, this monograph examines the psychoanalytic concept of body zones. Analytic theory posits successive concern of the individual with the oral, anal, and genital zones. Mead and Macgregor accept this formulation for our culture. The Balinese, however, have a greater focus on the total body, and in particular on the visual and tactile stimulus of the skin. This question is thus raised of how other cultures shape the interpretation by each individual of his own biologically given body.

In this monograph Mead also succinctly characterizes her approach to the study of socialization: "Cultural analysis of the child-rearing process consists in an attempt to identify those sequences in child-other behavior which carry the greatest communication weight and so are crucial for the development of each culturally regular character structure" (Mead and Macgregor 1951:27). Communication is a two-way process, involving interaction in both directions. Mead believes the interactive nature of socialization represents one of the major new concepts which anthropology brought to the study of personality:

> From the cultural anthropologist has come the recognition that cultural forms emerge from other cultural forms. Stated genetically, this means that parents and children are a continuously interactive system, not a one-way system in which the child (impelled upward by a set of specific drives) simply meets a series of obstacles (in the form of institutions) that, if it is sufficiently mutilated by them, it will then proceed to alter. (Mead and Métraux 1953:39)

Mead's view of socialization studies, her own as well as others', is well summarized in her chapter in the *Manual of Child Psychology* (Mead 1954a).

Inherent also in Mead's approach is the premise that learning is continuous. A person who is growing old, for example, changes in behavior not only because of the physiological changes taking place within him, but also because he learns to behave in the way the culture expects old people to behave. She shares the common focus on childhood as the time in which the major dimensions of personality are established, but her scheme equally permits substantial changes in these constellations through the years which follow.

Mead's analytic and descriptive procedure has sometimes been referred to as "configurational," thereby implicitly identifying her work with that of Ruth Benedict. Benedict and Mead were close collaborators, and Benedict often followed an approach very close to that of Mead, as in her notable paper on "Continuities and Discontinuities in Cultural Conditioning" (Benedict 1938). But Mead is not typically concerned with delineating the broad themes of a culture as exemplified in Benedict's *Patterns of Culture* (1934), the epitome of configurationalism. Mead does point up the consistency in feeling tone and attitude from one nexus of interpersonal behavior to another, where such consistency is discernable, but she makes no assumption that a common theme must necessarily be sought in all important arenas of action in a culture. Benedict's approach is global and open-ended. Mead, on the other hand, constantly reverts back to the social system and structure, and to the biological determinants of behavior.

The distinctive significance of Margaret Mead's work, outside of its pioneering nature and the substantive contributions to knowledge it represents, can best be considered after reviewing the approaches developed by later workers in the culture and personality field.

Another "first" in the study of personality falls in the still largely neglected area of intelligence and cognition. In 1929 Stanley D. Porteus, a clinical psychologist trained in Australia but with most of his professional career in the United States, undertook field work with the Arunta in Central Australia, and more limited work in Northwest Australia (Porteus 1931). He administered, primarily to children, a variety of intelligence and performance tests, principal among these being his own Maze Test. This test, as its name implies, consists of a series of mazes on paper which the subject is asked to trace. Porteus later did comparable work among the Bushmen of the Kalahari Desert in South Africa (Porteus 1937), and also utilized the test extensively in obtaining comparative data among the various ethnic groups available to him at the University of Hawaii. Of all the tests of mental ability thus far generally available for use in cross-cultural settings, there is some reason to feel that the Porteus Maze is the "fairest" in the sense that it appears to be the least strange and confusing to non-Europeans (cf. Masland, Sarason, and Gladwin 1958:271–72).

As a result of this work Porteus was able to formulate a formidable list of cautions to be observed by anyone attempting cross-cultural intelligence measurement, cautions which, despite later elaboration by Klineberg and others, were more often than not ignored in the years to follow. He also devoted considerable thought to the nature of mental ability and its measurement. He concluded that any test designed to measure the kinds of mental ability valued in our culture would fail to tap those intellectual resources which would be useful to a person in another culture where the approach to thinking and problem solving might take different directions. This applies as much to the Maze as to any other test. However, he also made an important but usually overlooked distinction with respect to the purposes of measurement: if one is concerned with making comparisons between the essential intelligence of two groups in an absolute sense, a test built around the concepts of thinking taught in one culture cannot be used validly in another. But if one is interested in identifying those persons in another culture with the greatest potential for being trained to think *our* way, as for example in recruiting for schooling, a test devised for our culture can be valid. Furthermore, in the latter context, it becomes crucial to minimize the degree of strangeness which the test and the testing situation evoke among people who are unfamiliar both with the materials used and with the whole idea of a test. The Porteus Maze perhaps best meets this latter criterion. It would appear useful for anthropologists interested in cognitive development to explore whether this is really so, and if it is to develop further the potentialities of this approach. Thus far, however, the Maze has received only passing attention from anthropologists.

As noted earlier, two monographs appeared in the early 1930's which reflected Margaret Mead's influence, but which were also of major importance in their own right. One was Reo Fortune's *Sorcerers of Dobu* (1932). Dobu is a Melanesian island near Malinowski's Trobriands. The society is so riven with hostility and suspicion that Ruth Benedict labeled it "paranoid." Fortune was trained as a psychologist and strongly influenced by Freud and W. H. R. Rivers, especially the latter's *Conflict and Dream* (1923). Before going to Dobu, Fortune himself had published a book on dream interpretation, *The Mind in Sleep* (1927). In spite of this background, Fortune did not systematically address himself to personality as such, although he did pay consistent attention to psychologically relevant aspects of Dobuan culture. His psychodynamic orientation, however, made his work highly appropriate for use by Ruth Benedict in counterpoint to Zuni and Kwakiutl in *Patterns of Culture*. It is, in fact, in the latter context that Dobu is probably most widely known.

The other monograph is Gregory Bateson's *Naven*, recently republished with additional theoretical discussion (1958). Bateson did not attempt a full descriptive ethnography, concentrating instead on exploring the implications of several ceremonies, especially the *naven* ceremony, among the Iatmul of New Guinea. His analysis of these ceremonies led to the formulation of two important new constructs. One of these, *eidos*, will be discussed later in this chapter. The other is *schizmogenesis*. Schizmogenesis describes those forces in society which are centrifugal, that is, which increase the social distance between individuals or groups. Schizmogenesis can be complementary, as in dominance-submission relationships, or symmetrical, as in rivalry. The centrifugal effect of schizmogenesis derives both from social dynamics and from personality, and both these factors are culturally determined. Marriage in Iatmul, for example, is socially defined as a dominance-submission relationship (complementary schizmogenesis). It also brings together two people with culturally defined different male and female personalities. Yet marriages persist (sometimes) in spite of the forces which tend to drive the couple apart. However, whereas in Iatmul schizmogenic forces are strong enough to make any equilibrium precarious, a comparable analysis of Bali (Bateson 1949) revealed that stabilizing forces are so effective that schizmogenic sequences can never get started. Bateson therefore became interested in these counterforces which keep centrifugal tendencies from going to the extreme of destroying all social relationships. This led him to seek controlling stabilizing mechanisms which would return the social system to balance. In collaboration with a number of persons in various fields he turned to theories of mechanics, physics, and mathematics concerned with feedback and other mechanisms responsible for maintaining systems in a steady state of dynamic equilibrium. This field of inquiry is now referred to as cybernetics. Collaboration with persons in fields so exotic to anthropology seems to have created a lack of communication between Bateson's thinking and that of all but a handful of anthropologists. If this is true, it is a matter we should view with alarm. Anthropologists who are content merely to feed their cultural data into equations provided for them ready-made by personality psychologists can remain union members in good standing, but why should a person who reaches out to develop radically new equations of human behavior move beyond the pale of anthropological discourse?

In the later 1930's Ernest Beaglehole began a series of field researches in Oceania which he and his students at Victoria University are continuing to the present. Although trained in his native New Zealand and in London primarily as a psychologist, Beaglehole studied with Sapir and others at Yale in 1931–34 and became a well-qualified anthropologist. He has consistently provided general cultural data quite as full as that adduced by other anthropologists working in culture and personality. His first field work was accomplished prior to his return to the Pacific, with the Hopi of Second Mesa (Beaglehole and Beaglehole 1935). In 1936 he returned to the Pacific, first to the University of Hawaii and then to Wellington. He initiated a series of ethnographic and culture and personality studies in Polynesian societies, including Pukapuka (Beaglehole and Beaglehole 1938, 1941), native Hawaiians (Beaglehole 1939),

Tonga (Beaglehole 1940, 1941), Maori in New Zealand (Beaglehole and Beaglehole 1946), and Rarotonga and Aitutaki (Beaglehole 1957). In addition he has published a number of important theoretical papers in culture and personality. He has directed a group of his students in a large-scale interdisciplinary study of personality development in Rakau, a Maori community in somewhat different circumstances than Kowhai, the New Zealand community studied by the Beagleholes themselves. The Rakau study is notable for its extensive experimentation with various methodological approaches to the use of projective tests (Beaglehole and Ritchie 1958). Five monographs, in addition to several short papers, have appeared on the Rakau research thus far: James E. Ritchie 1956, Mulligan 1957, Jane Ritchie 1957, Earle 1958, and Williams 1960.

Beaglehole's contribution to culture and personality in Polynesia would be notable alone for the sheer quantity of solid, insightful research he has contributed to the literature. He has, in addition, made a number of clarifying theoretical observations, especially his 1944 paper on "Character Structure." Here he considered the cultural directives governing interpersonal behavior, and their relationship to individual personality and behavior deviation, observing that when a person

> . . . is acting according to the major directives he is really acting according to a personal organization or structure of his own needs, emotions and thoughts which is in congruence with the emphases of the major directives themselves. In other words the person has developed a character structure in response to the specific pressures of his own culture. When a person acts idiographically, he is determined by a personal variant on this character structure, that is, by the specific drives of unique personality. A person's integrations can be predicted when it is known that his personality corresponds rather exactly to the character structure of the group. One is often at a loss to predict the course of a person's integrations when how different or how alike his personality is to this character structure is not known. (p. 148)

This position is in many respects similar to that of Margaret Mead; in each case attention is directed to the shaping of personality by the totality of expectations and pressures exerted on and communicated to a person by other persons sharing the same culture. Explanatory concepts must then emphasize the conditions under which behaviors, attitudes, and feelings are learned by living with others who already share such attributes. This is in contrast to explanations which lay stress on individual emotional reactions to a succession of experiences shared with others in childhood.

Beaglehole has also gone considerably deeper than most psychologists or anthropologists into questions of cognitive structure raised by the administration of intelligence and other tests to non-European people. The following discussion of his findings on Aitutaki bears on this.

In the cross-cultural measurement of intellectual capacity the psychologists' skill and techniques do not yet appear to be adequate to measure differences in quantitative amounts of latent intelligence. But test results are still valuable in so far as they can be used to indicate the existence of cross-cultural qualitative differences in intellectual or cognitive organization. Two aspects of Aitutaki cognitive organization seem to be suggested by the present results. The first concerns the fact that the culture itself does not place value on problem-solving. In its technological aspect Aitutaki culture is extremely simple. Results are achieved by the simple application of rules traditionally inherited. This is not to say that judgment is not required of the successful fisherman or cultivator, but the number of variables within his control are so few that complicated judgments are hardly ever required. Success in farming and fishing or even in many aspects of social life is more likely to be achieved by the application of rules learned by rote, rather than by the use of principles applied by reason. Cognitive organization, therefore, is likely to be rather simple in structure and largely formed by experience derived through the rote learning of repeated lessons. (1957:221)

The second characteristic aspect of Aitutaki thinking is the fact that it functions mainly at a perceptual, rarely at an abstract level, and at a perceptual level which may be significantly different from the perceptual level thinking of the Western European. . . . The way perceptual relations are noticed will be a function of a given culture. How the relations, once noticed, will be abstracted and generalized about will also depend on the interests and training available in the culture concerned. The children of Aitutaki have plenty of experience of coloured objects or variously shaped objects, but their culture teaches them to be interested mainly in the objects and not in their abstracted shapes, colours and patterns. Therefore the quality of their thinking will reflect this perceptual orientation, and imaginative thinking either of a controlled or a free fantasy type will be rare. This quality of Aitutaki thought again receives confirmation from the limited use of imagination in Rorschach records. (1957:222–223)

We shall return to the discussion of cognitive process and problem solving in the final portion of this chapter. For the present it will suffice to note that whereas Porteus and others went no farther than to note factors in the tests which interfere with the performance of non-Europeans, Beaglehole's discussion goes beyond this to consider the differences in learning and thinking which actually create differences in performance. He is also concerned with how these are related to the demands of the culture. I would myself raise a further question, whether the concept of "learning rules by rote" does not itself imply more European-type verbalization of the learning process than in fact obtains. At very least, the descriptive label "rote learning" is almost certainly an oversimplification.

In 1939 a book was published which had a large share in crystallizing anthropological thought on the relationship between personality and culture, and setting the pattern of research for much of the present generation of students of the field. This was Abram Kardiner's *The Individual and His Society*. Ralph Linton was a collaborator in Kardiner's seminar at Columbia University at the time this and subsequent books developed (e.g., Kardiner *et al* 1945, Du Bois 1944, West 1945). He contributed ethnological reports based on his own earlier field work in the Marquesas in Polynesia, as well as in Madagascar. The high point of this undertaking was the study of the village of Atimelang on Alor, an island in eastern Indonesia, by Cora DuBois (1944). This was the first anthropological field work explicitly designed to employ an array of personality assessment techniques of psychologists in a non-European culture. These included the Rorschach, the Porteus Maze, word associations, children's drawings, autobiographies, and systematic observation of behavior sequences. Most of these techniques had been used singly by earlier investigators, but their coordinated use was a distinct milestone. The methodological groundwork for the Kardiner-Linton collaboration was laid in Kardiner's earlier work, including seminars participated in by Ruth Benedict and Ruth Bunzel. Since preliminary exploration of the method was worked out with Malinowski's Trobriand material, and the first full-scale analysis utilized Linton's Marquesan data, this collaboration can legitimately be claimed as Oceanic in origin. However, its impact was sufficiently great that it could not in any event be ignored in any review of the field.

Although clearly psychoanalytic in his orientation, Kardiner recognized cultural reality and cultural imperatives. Briefly, his analysis began logically with primary institutions, the cultural systems devoted to meeting essential needs. Adaptation and socialization in accordance with the dictates of the primary institutions requires the control of natural impulses. This control leads to frustration, and then to reactions to frustration, especially the formation of aggressive tendencies. The anxieties so created give rise to secondary institutions, which are projections of anxiety in a variety of forms. The working out of anxiety is examined primarily at the level of the ego and of the superego in people, and through the analysis of projective systems in culture.

This thumbnail summary obviously does not do justice to Kardiner's conceptual scheme of analysis, but it is sufficient to make clear the difference in emphasis in his approach from that adopted by

Mead, or by Beaglehole. Both Mead and Beaglehole treat personality development in the broader framework of the learning of culture and its appropriate behaviors. Mead adds to this constitutional temperament and the effect of biological changes in maturation. Kardiner, in contrast, accounts for the same phenomena primarily in terms of psychological response to emotionally important experiences. In Kardiner's scheme the observable congruence in adult personality necessarily requires the assumption that each individual who shares a culturally determined socialization experience will respond to it in substantially the same fashion as his fellows. Similar anxieties in a large number of people will then give rise to projective systems which serve to comfort them all. In the final section of this chapter we will return to an examination of this extremely crucial assumption.

Without raising questions for the present regarding the usefulness of either mode of analysis, the difference between Kardiner's approach on the one hand, and the emphasis partially shared by Mead and Beaglehole on the other, can perhaps be exemplified by parallel examples. Each deals with a culture in which older children have extensive responsibility for the care of their younger siblings during the day. The cultural behavior, and the reason for its existence, are highly comparable in both instances, but the significance seen in it differs sharply.

First, Kardiner's discussion of Alor (Kardiner *et al*. 1945, p. 155) :

In late childhood . . . both sexes are prematurely inducted into the role of taking care of their younger siblings. The performance of this role is undoubtedly subject to much variation. In general, however, a child who is robbed of the care essential for growth and development will not bestow such care upon a younger claimant without resentment. The result is that the older child, who is now the mother surrogate, is no more dependable than the mother herself. So the situation for the younger child is not greatly ameliorated by this institution. On the other hand, the older sibling is likely to be given attributes which were prevented expression toward the mother by the strong ambivalence to her. This attitude is furthermore facilitated by both older and younger sibling having a common claim. This is a factor which in some would tend to ameliorate the situations of sibling rivalry and render the hatred toward the parent still greater. In others it might terminate in intensified sibling rivalry and hatred.

Contrast this with the view of James Ritchie, a student of Beaglehole, of essentially the same behavior in Rakau (Ritchie 1956:47) :

The Maori child is typing himself against an older sibling's concept of the adult world. His perceptions of adult behavior and adult roles are being strained through the perceptions of his older sib. The latter will only be approximately varying in their degree of conformity according to the age, sex, intelligence and experience variables of the older child. In this transmission of percepts from a child's view of the world, the value structure is thrown into sharp relief. The limited comprehension of the older child requires that the values he sees around him be used in modifying the behaviour of younger children; he cannot therefore make do with a tentative approximation but must resolve his percepts into a formal structure from which he is able to direct and instruct younger children.

Originality departs. The value-structure sets hard, prematurely, and the child enters onto a plateau in value-learning. The organized model with which he has been presented will do for all situations right up to the time he assumes direct adult behaviour and even then a rigid conformity based on the simplicity and absolutism of the middle years will be a ready source of certainty in conflicting or incipiently dangerous social situations.

Although Beaglehole's students, and indeed Beaglehole himself, are not always consistent in viewing personality as learned rather than as shaped by emotional response, they do represent a minority who are carrying forward and developing this approach. As the citation from Ritchie indicates, they are especially concerned with when, and from whom, a person learns his culture, his attitudes, and his ways of behaving.

However, it is the work of Kardiner and his associates which one finds most commonly cited as methodological models for subsequent monographs in culture and personality. This is somewhat paradoxical, because practically no one has been able to make effective use of his central concept of primary and secondary institutions. Reference is made instead to some techniques he has employed—especially the use of projective tests and life histories. This is perhaps the key to the paradox. Kardiner's books (1939, 1945) and DuBois' *The People of Alor* (1944) were available at the time, shortly after the war, when clinical psychologists in large numbers became interested in cultural differences. Undoubtedly Kardiner's work spurred this trend, but its real impetus derived from the participation of psychologists in wartime intelligence analysis and psychological warfare. When psychologists then began to collaborate with and train anthropologists they found Kardiner's tools were the ones with which they were themselves familiar. Kardiner was not the first to use any of these tools, but he brought them together in a persuasive and effective manner.

The psychologists were also comfortable in accepting Kardiner's assumption of the primacy in personality development of the individual's intrapsychic integration of emotional experience. Yet while citing Kardiner to legitimize their focus on emotional determinants of behavior, the psychologists and their anthropological colleagues disregarded the one solid tie to culture in Kardiner's scheme —his concept of primary and secondary institutions. The latter concept may or may not be useful. But the net effect has been an uncritical acceptance of both the theory and the tools of clinical psychology in culture and personality studies, an acceptance more wholehearted even than Kardiner's (*cf.* Hsu 1952, 1955).

A final landmark can be identified with the late 1930's, John W. M. Whiting's *Becoming a Kwoma* (1941). This arose from a ferment of interest at Yale in the anthropological implications of the theories of learning and behavior developed by Clark Hull and his students (*cf.* Miller and Dollard 1941), largely on the basis of learning experiments with rats. Whiting wrote a standard ethnography of the Kwoma, a mountain tribe in the Sepik River area of New Guinea, with considerable attention devoted to personality development. He then reanalysed his material in terms of drive, cue, response, and reward as an exercise in the application of Hull's theory of learning to a set of concrete ethnographic data. A brief example will suffice to illustrate the mode of analysis:

> In adolescence a boy learns to carry on secret love affairs with adolescent girls. The drives are sex, sex appetite, and anxiety (sex impells him to seek girls, sex appetite leads him to choose a girl culturally defined as attractive, and anxiety impells him to do so secretly); the response is the complex of behavior which leads to and includes sexual intercourse in the bush; the cues are the sight of an attractive girl, verbal permission from her, the environmental scene which has both public and secluded spots, etc.; the reward is sexual orgasm, satisfaction of sex appetite, and anxiety reduction. (pp. 176–177)

Whiting's application of Hull's concepts to the Kwoma was so literal that it was almost a tour de force. The exercise has therefore not been repeated by others. But it was an instructive undertaking. It undoubtedly contributed to the explicit and scrupulous approach to theory which has since been characteristic of Whiting and his students. It also served to refine and make more effective the use of Hull's theory in culture and personality studies.

During the early 1940's much of Oceania became a theater of war. Field work necessarily ceased, and most anthropologists were in any event otherwise engaged. Monographs based on earlier field work were published during this period, but there was a break in the continuity of research effort. After the close of World War II, several people who had worked in Oceania earlier returned to the field; their work has been discussed above. But a new and more numerous generation of anthropologists also came into the area, among them quite a few interested in culture and personality. Their work differed in two important respects from that of their predecessors. One was a shift in locale. The majority of new field work was undertaken in Micronesia. Not only was this an area formerly almost entirely closed to anthropologists, it was also comprised primarily of the small insular communities characterized in the introduction to this chapter as ideal for some types of research. Many correspondingly small island societies in Polynesia had of course been studied in the past, but their cultural transfiguration through foreign contact was generally much greater than in Micronesia. Furthermore, a good deal of money became available for field work in Micronesia, and this had the not surprising effect of tipping the scales in favor of doing research in this area.

The other difference is more subtle, and hopefully will prove transitory. This is a sharp reduction in the amount of methodological pioneering displayed by students of culture and personality in postwar Oceania. The account thus far has been highlighted by a series of "firsts," of often rather daring developments of new methods or new theories which have had a widespread impact on the field. Any field of study tends to crystallize as it matures, but culture and personality theory has certainly not yet fully stabilized. New approaches—the use of projective tests or photographic analysis, for example—have since the war had their primary development elsewhere and then been applied later with variations in Oceania. The remainder of this account will therefore be more brief and selective than that which has preceded, confined essentially to major monographic contributions. Virtually all of these, excepting those already discussed which stem from the continuing activity of persons already in the field in the 1930's, are based on work in Micronesia.

In particular, the Coordinated Investigation of Micronesian Anthropology (CIMA), sponsored by the Pacific Science Board of the National Research Council, put a large number of anthropologists and related scientists into the field in 1947. Among these were four persons primarily interested in studying culture and personality: Joseph and Murray on Saipan, Spiro on Ifaluk, and the present writer on Truk. In addition Lessa, on Ulithi, had a strong secondary interest in the field.

Alice Joseph and Veronica Murray (1951) undertook to see how much useful information could be derived from a relatively short study of Chamorro and Carolinian children (and a few adults) on

Saipan. Although both are physicians, Joseph in particular was already well known to anthropologists for her work with the Hopi. In this study they placed primary reliance on projective and performance tests administered to one hundred children of each of the two ethnic groups. The Bender-Gestalt test was interpreted by its author, Lauretta Bender. The Rorschach, Arthur Point Performance Scale II, and the Porteus Maze were treated exclusively by the authors, using conventional scoring and interpretive procedures. This study did not, therefore, make any new contributions to methodology. Nor can it be said to have validated a field procedure for economical personality delineation. Numerous subsequent studies in which ethnographic and projective interpretations have been compared for cross-validation show the clear danger of accepting projective test results at face value. In fact, the authors' own findings tend to confirm this danger. They conclude their discussion of the Rorschach results with the prediction that "either large scale antisocial behavior with unconscious self-destructive aims or death-like apathy might be expected from the younger generation." (p. 202) Bender found that the normal Saipanese Gestalt patterns corresponded to those found in confusional states elsewhere, and speculated whether "environmental influences can, in a people with strong primitive tendencies, produce a state of intellectual perplexity and disorientation which will manifest itself in a disturbance of Gestalt function similar to that produced by toxic influences." (p. 142) As of this writing the children so delineated now range in age from 18 to 30 years and thus far show no external evidence of crippling psychopathology. Actually, it is quite plausible to conclude that differences in perceptual orientation and in style of cognitive thinking were responsible for almost the entirety of the response patterns the authors found so bizarre. This is not the appropriate place in which to examine the manner in which these differences can produce such distortion in the particular tests used. But one would certainly feel more comfortable had the authors addressed themselves to this possibility rather than accepting at face value conclusions based on interpretive criteria developed with European and American subjects.

Melford Spiro's study of Ifaluk was undertaken in conjunction with the late Edwin Burrows. A number of projective and attitudinal measures were used, coupled with a full ethnography and psychological interpretations of individual and group behavior. Unfortunately, although Spiro has published a number of important theoretical papers based on this work (e.g., 1951, 1959, 1960), only the ethnographic account has been published in full (Burrows and Spiro 1957). It is therefore not possible to review the culture and personality study here.

It should be noted that both Spiro (1959) and Joseph and Murray in their book contributed substantially to the accounts available in the literature of psychotic personalities on non-European cultures. Spiro presented three detailed case studies, and Joseph and Murray ten short summaries, plus brief coverage of disorders of other kinds.

The Truk study undertaken by myself and Seymour Sarason, a clinical psychologist (Gladwin and Sarason 1953), was also intended to develop a relatively quick method of personality assessment, aided in this case by the presence of other anthropologists on the team who covered areas not directly relevant to personality development. The method was an evolution of that used by Du Bois (1944) on Alor. Rorschach and Thematic Apperception Tests were used in conjunction with life histories and some dreams of 23 individuals selected to include both "average" and deviant persons. These data were combined with a standard ethnography. "Blind" interpretations of the Rorschachs and TAT's were undertaken by Sarason, using a clinical mode of interpretation rather than placing reliance, as is more customary in such studies, on scoring categories and frequencies. It was felt that a clinical interpretation, while admittedly more subjective, permitted fuller exploitation of the material produced by the subjects. This procedure also made possible explicit examination of the ways in which culturally determined perceptual modes affected the response pattern in all subjects, a factor which is obscured in interpretations based upon the scoring of responses. The interpretations in this study appeared to have considerable face validity. The methodology used here was perhaps more rigorous and self-conscious than that usually found in culture and personality studies, at least those which attempt to collate a variety of sorts of data. But essentially very little in this monograph is really new methodologically or theoretically. More recently, I have re-analysed some of my data in an attempt to define the cognitive structure of Trukese thinking (Gladwin 1960).

William Lessa undertook on Ulithi an even more abbreviated method than those described above (Lessa and Spiegelman 1954). He administered the Thematic Apperception Test to 99 persons well distributed by age and sex, and scored the resulting stories in accordance with procedures developed by William E. Henry. His psychologist collaborator, Marvin Spiegelman, then interpreted the results solely on the basis of the comparative frequencies of different responses in the various age and sex groups. This was the first time the TAT had been used in this way, and Lessa found a quite satisfying congruence between Spiegelman's conclusions and those based on the ethnographic data. This congruence held throughout a wide range of behaviors, including general motivational structure, handling of aggression, attitudes toward sex, food anxieties, etc. This does not necessarily mean that the TAT can be assumed to yield valid personality measures when used as a basis for quantitative interpretation in a culture other than Ulithi. However, an accumulation of similar evidence might encourage those anthropologists who are still interested in using projective tests to shift their emphasis away from the Rorschach. Interpretation of the Rorschach in any setting necessarily requires more inference than the TAT because the Rorschach presents a less structured stimulus. Rorschach interpretation rests on a larger series of assumptions about unconscious psychological processes derived from clinical experience in our own culture than does the TAT. Its cross-cultural application is therefore inherently more hazardous—although by no means necessarily invalid if the instrument is used with due caution.

With these few Micronesian studies by newcomers to the field, our review can be considered completed. Increasingly, of course, persons primarily interested in other ethnological specialties nonetheless include psychological constructs in their observations and hypotheses, but this is true of anthropology as a whole and need not be detailed for Oceania. We may therefore turn to an assessment of the work here reviewed within the broader perspective of the field of culture and personality as a whole.

Assessment

Oceania, as noted at the outset of this chapter, has held out an almost unparalleled opportunity and challenge for students of culture and personality. We have seen the challenge well met. Much pioneering field work has taken advantage of the unusual research settings afforded by island populations, and the data so derived have inspired a number of bold but cogent new theoretical modes of interpretation. It would probably be justifiable to claim some of these new concepts as genuine anthropological contributions, in the sense that they could only have arisen from the necessity for explaining differences between cultures. Margaret Mead's exploration of the interrelationships between personality and social structure and maturational levels might be an example. The examination by Beaglehole, Ritchie, *et al.*, of the mechanisms of transmission of the psychological aspects of culture from one generation to the next is another. We might also cite the development by Porteus of the Maze Test for cross-cultural use, and Bateson's concept of schizmogenesis. Each of these approaches I would judge has the potential of making really new contributions to personality theory.

However, few if any of them are to be found in the main stream of culture and personality theory as it is taught and used today. The field has come to place almost exclusive reliance upon theory and psychodynamic concepts derived from clinical psychiatry and psychology. The clinician undertakes to cope with and modify the emotional disturbances he finds in his patients, and he can understand the source and nature of these disturbances most readily by recourse to explanatory concepts derived from psychoanalysis. Years of research and clinical experience have modified, enriched, and elaborated this theoretical system since it was first set forth by Freud. The psychiatrist or psychologist finds here a handy and effective set of tools. Although he is urged to tinker with the system and perhaps improve a little upon it, he sees no reason to question its basic premises.

It is not surprising that anthropologists, seeing psychology unanimous in its support of a coherent and rather glittering body of theory, should accept from psychology the promise that this is *the* way to describe and account for personality and its development. However, the brief historical review just completed shows clearly that the relative unanimity on this score among anthropologists is of rather recent origin. I have suggested that the crystallizing event was the publication of Abram Kardiner's first book based on his collaboration with Ralph Linton. Whether or not others would agree upon this landmark, I believe few would disagree that psychoanalytic theory (as it is interpreted by clinical psychologists) now dominates the thinking of anthropologists in culture and personality (*cf.* Kluckhohn 1944:590). It would therefore seem most appropriate in this assessment to take a second look at some of the earlier divergent views which arose from field work in Oceania, to see whether we have perhaps not been overly hasty in brushing them aside in our rush to leap upon the Freudian bandwagon.

The most thoroughly documented and elaborated position is that of Margaret Mead, in many respects seconded as we have seen by Ernest Beaglehole. Mead does not, of course, reject the concepts of current personality theory. In fact, she draws heavily upon them and has ever since her earliest work, done at a time when most anthropologists were scarcely aware of the existence of a man named Sigmund Freud. However, analytic theory has two aspects. First, it is a conceptual scheme for the description of the emotional structure of personality, of the forces within the individual which shape his behavior. But beyond this it also embraces a developmental scheme which undertakes to account for the formation, primarily in early childhood experience and on an emotional basis, of the psychological forces it has described. In psychiatry these two components of theory are thoroughly intertwined, to such a degree that the formal diagnostic criteria for most disorders require both behavioral and etiological determinations. However, Mead has in effect drawn upon the descriptive concepts while at the same time placing very minor reliance upon the developmental theory.

Although Mead's difference is quite fundamental, and consistent throughout her work, it has probably received so little explicit attention largely because she has been content to be quietly selective rather than to attack the Freudian developmental premises. She has elaborated her own position while coexisting peacefully with the clinicians, being satisfied to show them the importance of cultural differences without attempting to force them to alter their basic theory. In her early work in Samoa and the New Guinea area she demonstrated the great differences in adult personality which result from growing up and living in different kinds of social environments. Although she noted the stresses and strains of socialization in various types of life experience, she tended not to evaluate the importance of such crises or conflicts in terms of the significance attributed to them by a predetermined theoretical system. Rather she examined their consistency and congruence with other experiences which preceded, followed, and surrounded the situation under consideration. As has already been pointed out, this approach views personality as a system of thinking, feeling, and behaving which is learned through continuing experience. In her view, people learn to conform to the norms not merely to avoid punishment or gain rewards, but also because in this way life becomes more predictable and meaningful.

The learning process is central to Mead's scheme, and by learning she means not merely the factors which may stimulate and affect the permanence of learning, but also the context and content of learning. Learning for Mead is therefore a more inclusive and descriptive concept than it is in the learning theory derived from Hull, but by the same token less subject to experimental manipulation and verification. In her scheme, the learning which culminates in adult personality is the end product of an infinity of small experiences shared with other people. The process is consequently much more difficult to capture and define than one which is postulated as a response to a more limited array of emotionally charged critical situations or relationships. In her early work Mead was content to describe the social environment and the manner in which it was interpreted by the individual and by the persons about him, leaving unexamined the detailed process whereby this cultural transmission took place. In Bali she tried to actually document the process, largely through photography, and in one study already referred to (Mead and Macgregor 1951), she undertook to spell out all the nuances of learning of one component of behavior.

I have risked redundancy in restating here the development of Margaret Mead's theoretical position in order to underscore the consistency of its development, and its completeness. She has not only a point of view, but also a research method consistent with her point of view. Furthermore, this is a point of view which is essentially anthropological. Personality, to Mead, is part of the cultural heritage to be passed on from one generation to the next. It is learned by each generation in much the same way as is canoe building, speaking, or social etiquette. Because it is learned, and because it is learned through living the culture, it necessarily develops, with variations, in essentially similar form from one person to the next. No two individuals in a given society are identical in the way they build a canoe or in the way they feel toward their mothers, but within each society everyone does these things, and many others, in a fashion sufficiently uniform and distinctive to be characteristic of the culture they share. If people did not learn to behave with this essential uniformity, anthropologists would not be warranted in speaking of culture and cultural differences. Mead in effect sees no reason why anthropologists should then not consider personality simply as another component of culture, to be studied as far as possible in the same way.

Let us now examine briefly the contrasting but currently more popular view, that represented by the personality theory of the clinical students of human behavior. This approach, as befits one tailored in the first instance to the needs of individual patients, stresses the integration of the personality within the individual. This integration is developed through adaptive response to experience as it is emotionally perceived and interpreted by the individual. People learn to behave and feel in certain ways because this will defend them from anxiety or other distressing psychological experiences, or will bring them love and reward. With this view is associated a conviction that the experiences of early childhood are more crucial and lasting in their impact than later ones. However, it should be noted that this emphasis on early experience is in no way theoretically required by the primary focus on emotional integration (*cf.* Hsu 1952).

Studies in culture and personality which use this scheme account for the similarities of adult personality found in a given society by the culturally determined similarities in (early) socialization experience. As stated, this does not differ from Mead's scheme. The difference lies in the fact that in the psychoanalytic framework the intervening operative variable is emotional integration within each developing individual. Thus, for example, in a society in which adults characteristically reveal strong anxieties about food in excess of the actual danger of going hungry, and where the nursing of babies is inconsistent or otherwise frustrating, analytic theory might lead to explanations of adult anxieties in terms of unfulfilled oral needs (despite the lack of thumb sucking observed in several such societies). In contrast Mead would probably also say that if young children see strong capable adults worried about food, they are most likely to learn to worry also. She would look at the social structure, perhaps finding that the mutual responsibilities of kin groups are so arranged that food which is objectively obtainable at all times is in fact frequently hard to get. And she would look at the biological rhythms and nutritional needs of the people to inquire whether these created special conditions or problems. Similarly, the commonly felt fear of heights in our culture can be attributed either, on the one hand, to a symbolic fear of loss of support by a loved person, or, on the other, to the fact that mothers in our society usually show a panic reaction when they find their children climbing trees, buildings, etc., and thus teach the child to be frightened of falling. There may even be inherited differences in different population groups with respect to perception and balance, as these affect reactions to height.

With this outline of the differences between the available methodological strategies before us, how can we assess their respective validity and utility? No definitive evaluation is possible, and what follows must necessarily represent only my own opinion.

The research objective of culture and personality studies employing conventional analytic personality theory is essentially to test the validity of the concepts subsumed under that theory in a variety of cultural contests. A plausible explanation of some aspect of personality development in another culture serves to buttress the validity of the particular explanatory formulation derived from our own culture. If our explanation does not "fit" the other culture, the original concept must be discarded or reinterpreted. Anthropology becomes the handmaiden of psychology, testing a secondhand theory without any real opportunity to lead the way to new and different understandings of personality development.[3]

Irrespective of the productivity of using analytic theory in culture and personality research, the more serious question of validity must be examined. In the first place, it should be noted that the interpretative substance of a monograph written in this vein is not the exposition of an observed ongoing process such as anthropologists usually favor. Rather it is a series of post hoc explanations of developmental processes, working back from adult personality. The plausibility of such interpretations can be attributed equally to their inherent validity or to the ingenuity of the explainer. Post hoc interpretations are of course appropriate to the theory used because psychoanalytic case studies, upon which the theory has largely been built, are usually of adults and therefore retrospective. However, insofar as this theory is clinically validated, its validation rests upon a successful therapeutic outcome. Such an outcome is likely to depend as much or more upon the skill of the therapist than upon the accuracy of the theory. A developmental history which will serve well in therapy will not necessarily serve science.

If we look at these same clinical tools in the hands of those psychiatrists who have elected to work with children, the picture becomes quite different. It must be remembered that, as used in culture and personality studies, analytic theory posits that similar early life experiences are integrated similarly by a large number of people to produce a distinctive adult personality common to all of them. Yet no responsible child psychiatrist, even when faced with a young

---

[3] For what interest it may have, it might be mentioned that some years ago I discussed precisely this same research approach and arrived at an opposite and much more enthusiastic conclusion (Gladwin and Sarason 1953:21–22).

patient who has experienced several clearly traumatic years, will use his clinical concepts to predict this child's adult personality with nearly the precision which is taken for granted in accounting for culturally determined basic personality structure. The child psychiatrist may feel safe in saying the child will probably always be maladjusted. But he would consider it foolhardy in any one case, to say nothing of hundreds, to state in just what form the child's anxieties will become crystallized, how his defense mechanisms and projective systems will be structured, what sorts of behaviors this will lead him to adopt in a variety of adult situations, and so on. In other words, the same body of clinically derived theory which permits psychiatrists to make post hoc explanations *for therapeutic purposes* becomes unthinkable, even in a clinical context, as a basis for the very sort of prediction of outcomes of childhood experience which are essential to their valid use in culture and personality studies.

Therefore the comparison between, on the one hand, Margaret Mead's view of personality as simply an aspect of culture and biology, and on the other, the more analytically oriented view of most workers in the field today, leads, in my opinion, to a discouraging view of the latter. Stated in extremes, we have surrendered our anthropological birthright to the clinicians, and received in return a methodology which is both limited in productivity and suspect in validity. Obviously, the situation is not that bleak. If nothing else, the work done thus far has provided a thorough exploration of one approach, and has unquestionably served to enrich the theory it has borrowed. Increasingly, however, not only anthropologists, but also psychologists and sociologists, are wondering where all this work leads.

If the answer is to be hopeful, it is my conviction that anthropologists must be prepared to make a commitment to their own theory of culture as full as their present commitment to the psychologists' theory of personality. As Hsu (1955) has observed, the predictable similarity in behavior between members of any single society has been noted by travelers ever since Herodotus. This striking phenomenon obviously cannot be accounted for solely by the psychodynamics of development within each individual in that society. It is a cultural phenomenon, and anthropologists must view it as such. It is of the same order as similarities in house types or agricultural methods. This, of course, does not mean that psychological theory should be discarded. One cannot speak of houses without attention to architectural principles, or of agriculture without considering the chemistry of soils and nutrition. What is needed is real collaboration, not one-sided borrowing, in the relationship between anthropology and psychology.

One other aspect or component of personality remains to be considered: cognitive process, or the style of thinking and problem solving which characterizes a culture. Cognitive development has been almost entirely overshadowed in culture and personality research by the emphasis on emotional development. This is doubtless in part because of a heavy reliance on analytic theory in which cognition plays a very small role. But it is also because psychology does not itself have an agreed upon body of cognitive theory. Anthropology has edged into this field of inquiry largely through linguistics. Explicit attention to cultural differences in logical process as such is rare in anthropology. Surprisingly, almost all of this work has been based on data from Oceania, and has been cited above (Bateson 1942, 1958; Beaglehole 1957; Gladwin 1960; Lee 1950; Porteus 1931, 1937; see also Margaret Mead's [1932] analysis of Manus animism).

In 1936, in the first edition of *Naven*, Bateson emphasized the distinctness and importance of cognitive processes. He characterized the usual grist for the culture and personality mill as *ethos*, "the expression of a culturally standardized system of the organization of the instincts and emotions of . . . individuals" (1958:118). Complementary to ethos is *eidos*, "a standardization [and expression in cultural behavior] of the cognitive aspects of the personality of individuals" (p. 220). Eidos embraces such matters as the nature of memory, the perception and structuring of external reality, the possibility of a positive valuation of intellectuality (e.g, expert knowledge of genealogy or folklore), and preferred strategies in problem solving. Subsequently, he carried eidos one step farther, evolving the concept of *deutero-learning*, or learning how to learn, referring to the context or intellectual tools of learning (Bateson 1942). In neither instance did Bateson carry through with a full review of his ethnographic material to demonstrate the potentialities of an analysis in these terms. His concepts, however, are important in that they point to culturally determined differences in the basic intellectual tools available to persons reared in different societies. When one remembers that *Naven* first appeared over 25 years ago, it is hard to understand why so few have been moved to pick up this line of inquiry.

The significance of Bateson's insight, and also the fact that it could come only to an anthropologist trying to account for observed cultural differences, is apparent if one looks at the efforts of psychologists to grapple with the nature and development of intellect. The often brilliant studies of such psychologists as Bartlett, Bruner, Guilford, Hebb, Piaget, and others, have one characteristic in common: they make the assumption that real intelligence consists in the ability to integrate information in symbolic and relational terms, and thus subsume large amounts of data through abstract generalizing principles. This assumption is entirely reasonable for persons working within our culture. Virtually all our major intellectual achievements are predicated upon just this mode of abstract thinking.

However, as anthropologists we must raise the question whether it is not culturally parochial to view abstract thinking as the only, or even the best, form of intelligence. Here we may refer to Beagle-hole's conclusion, cited earlier, that the Aitutaki do not think abstractly, and in fact do not value problem-solving ability in the terms we know it, that is, in terms of conscious rational processes. Yet they and their forebears have developed a complex and adaptive technology. To mention another example, Sarason and I found the Trukese to have a highly concrete nonabstract style of thinking.[4] Yet the Trukese also not only have a very useful technology, but can be demonstrated in their highly evolved techniques of interisland navigation to be accomplishing entirely in their heads some truly extraordinary feats of data reduction and problem solving (Gladwin 1960). The Trukese navigator is clearly not equipped to embrace the logical systems analysed and studied, for example, by Piaget, but it is hard to say that he is not being distinctly intelligent.

Piaget, of course, and the other psychologists mentioned are not studying the totality of intelligence, but only intelligence-in-our-culture.[5] Or, to be more correct, they are studying intelligence-as-valued-by-middle-class-intellectuals-in-our-culture. The latter phrasing points up the problem more sharply. Even if he had available a detailed analysis of Trukese thinking it is doubtful that Piaget would or should change his research approach. It is in the evaluation

---

[4] The distinction between concrete and abstract thinking refers, of course, to differences in emphasis in basic problem-solving strategy. It is doubtful that any thought process could be totally concrete or totally abstract.

[5] For views of Piaget, Margaret Mead, and others on this issue, see World Health Organization (1957).

of the full range, rather than the upper reaches, of intelligence that a cross-cultural perspective can have the greatest impact.

Psychologists essentially concern themselves with only one criterion of fully developed intelligence—abstract symbolic manipulation of information. They therefore tend to measure—and indeed define—intelligence in terms of tests which at each higher age level require more ability in abstraction. It is disturbingly suggested by work in our own culture, and often obvious when the tests are tried out in other cultures, that some people are ill equipped to cope with our intelligence tests even though they can meet the mental problems posed by their culture and environment with assurance and success. Furthermore, identifiable groups of people (e.g., lower-class Italians in the U.S.) have characteristic sorts of difficulties with tests (cf. Masland, Sarason, and Gladwin 1958, chap. 14). Psychologists have been troubled by this situation, and have attempted to develop a variety of culturally fair tests. Best known are the Davis-Eells Games, and the Cattell Culture-Free Test. However, what they have generally done is to make the content revolve about familiar situations and reduce or eliminate the explicit verbal skills required, while leaving essentially intact the kind of reasoning ability required for effective performance.

Meanwhile, anthropologists have done little to help them other than to insist piously that all groups and classes of men, regardless of cultural origin, must have equal intellectual potentialities. Anthropologists have contributed very little toward giving psychologists an understanding of the meaning of intelligence-in-our-culture as against intelligence-in-another-culture. With respect to emotional factors, personality and culture studies have assuredly given psychologists a valuable perspective. As a consequence, psychologists feel comfortable in looking for rather fundamental differences in personality development in the various subcultures of our society. Quite aside from the theoretical importance of cognitive theory, it is high time anthropology lent a similar helping hand to psychologists in the study of thinking and intelligence. Psychology is in the troubled position of lacking the theoretical and practical tools to disprove the racial inferiority its own tests are constantly being cited to "prove." It appears that only a wide cross-cultural perspective can provide a foundation of knowledge upon which to develop such tools.

Summing up, it seems fair to say that the challenge of unusual research opportunities offered by Oceania has indeed proved stimulating. As was noted, practically the entirety of explicit anthropological contributions to the study of cognitive process has stemmed from this area. Two major approaches to a genuinely anthropological—i.e, cultural—theory of personality development have been developed by Mead and by Beaglehole and their colleagues. Yet there seems at present to be a slackening in leadership in Oceania. Hopefully this is illusory, or at least temporary. The challenging opportunities remain. The relationship between personality and culture change, mentioned earlier in this chapter, is only one of several lines of inquiry which have scarcely been exploited at all, but which can fruitfully be pursued in the Pacific area.

BIBLIOGRAPHY

BATESON, GREGORY

    1942   Social planning and the concept of "deutero-learning." Conference on Science, Philosophy, and Religion, Second Symposium. New York, Harper & Bros.

    1949   Bali: the value system of a steady state. *In,* Social structure: studies presented to A. R. Radcliffe-Brown. Meyer Fortes, ed. 35–53. Oxford, Clarendon Press.

    1958   Naven. 2d ed. Stanford, Stanford University Press.

BATESON, GREGORY and MARGARET MEAD

    1942   Balinese character: a photographic analysis. Special Publications of the New York Academy of Sciences II.

BEAGLEHOLE, ERNEST

    1939   Some modern Hawaiians. University of Hawaii Research Publications 19.

    1940   Psychic stress in a Tongan village. Proceedings of the Sixth Pacific Science Congress. Berkeley, University of California Press 4:43–52.

    1941   Pangai village in Tonga. Memoirs of the Polynesian Society 18.

    1944   Character structure: its role in the analysis of interpersonal relations. Psychiatry 7:145–162.

    1957   Social change in the South Pacific: Rarotonga and Aitutaki. New York, Macmillan.

BEAGLEHOLE, ERNEST and PEARL

    1935   Hopi of the Second Mesa. Memoirs of the American Anthropological Association 44:1–67.

    1938   Ethnology of Pukapuka. Bulletins of the Bernice P. Bishop Museum 150:1–420.

    1941   Personality development in Pukapukan children. *In* Language, culture, and personality. Leslie Spier, A. Irving Hallowell, and Stanley S. Newman, eds., pp. 282–298. Menasha, Sapir Memorial Publication Fund.

    1946   Some modern Maoris. New Zealand Council for Educational Research. Wellington, Whitcombe and Tombs.

BEAGLEHOLE, ERNEST and JAMES E. RITCHIE
    1958   The Rakau Maori studies. Journal of the Polynesian Society 67:132–154.

BENEDICT, RUTH
    1934   Patterns of culture. New York, Houghton Mifflin.
    1938   Continuities and discontinuities in cultural conditioning. Psychiatry 1:161–167.

BERNDT, R. M. and CATHERINE H.
    1951   Sexual behavior in Western Arnhem Land. Viking Fund Publications in Anthropology No. 16. New York, Wenner-Gren Foundation for Anthropological Research, Inc.

BURROWS, EDWIN G. and MELFORD E. SPIRO
    1957   An atoll culture: ethnography of Ifaluk in the Central Carolines. 2d ed. Behavior Science Monographs. New Haven, Human Relations Area Files.

DU BOIS, CORA
    1944   The people of Alor: a social psychological study of an East Indian island. Minneapolis, University of Minnesota Press.

EARLE, MARGARET JANE
    1958   Rakau children: from six to thirteen years. Wellington, Victoria University of Wellington Publications in Psychology 11. (Monographs on Maori Social Life and Personality 4.)

FORTUNE, REO F.
    1927   The mind in sleep. London, Kegan Paul.
    1932   Sorcerors of Dobu: the social anthropology of the Dobu islanders of the Western Pacific. New York, Dutton.

GLADWIN, THOMAS
    1960   The need: better ways of teaching children to think. *In* Freeing Capacity to Learn: papers and reports from the Fourth ASCD Research Institute, pp. 23–39. Washington, National Education Association.

GLADWIN, THOMAS and SEYMOUR B. SARASON
    1953   Truk: man in paradise. Viking Fund Publications in Anthropology No. 20. New York, Wenner-Gren Foundation for Anthropological Research, Inc.

HSU, FRANCIS L. K.
    1952   Anthropology or psychiatry: a definition of objectives and their implications. Southwestern Journal of Anthropology 8:227–250.
    1955   An anthropologist's view of the future of personality studies. Psychiatric Research Reports 2:155–168.

JOSEPH, ALICE and VERONICA F. MURRAY
    1951   Chamorros and Carolinians of Saipan, personality studies. Cambridge, Harvard University Press.

KARDINER, ABRAM
    1939   The individual and his society: the psychodynamics of primitive social organization. New York, Columbia University Press.

KARDINER, ABRAM, et al.
    1945   The psychological frontiers of society. New York, Columbia University Press.

KLUCKHOHN, CLYDE

1944   The influence of psychiatry on anthropology in America during the past one hundred years. *In* One hundred years of American psychiatry. pp. 589–617. New York, Columbia University Press.

LA BARRE, WESTON

1958   The influence of Freud on anthropology. American Imago 15:275–328.

LEE, DOROTHY M.

1950   Lineal and nonlineal codifications of reality. Psychosomatic Medicine 12:89–97.

LESSA, WILLIAM A.

1956   Oedipus-type tales in Oceania. Journal of American Folklore 69:63–73.

LESSA, WILLIAM A. and MARVIN SPIEGELMAN

1954   Ulithian personality as seen through ethnological materials and thematic test analysis. University of California Publications in Culture and Society 2:243–301.

MALINOWSKI, BRONISLAW

1922   Argonants of the Western Pacific, an account of native enterprise and adventure in the archipelagoes of Melanesian New Guinea. London, Routledge.

1927   Sex and repression in savage society. London, Kegan Paul.

1929   The sexual life of savages in North-Western Melanesia. New York, Halcyon.

1935   Coral gardens and their magic, a study of the methods of tilling the soil and of agricultural rites in the Trobriand Islands. New York, American Book, 2 vols.

MASLAND, RICHARD L., SEYMOUR B. SARASON and THOMAS GLADWIN

1958   Mental subnormality: biological, psychological, and cultural factors. New York, Basic Books.

MEAD, MARGARET

1932   An investigation of the thought of primitive children, with special reference to animism. Journal of the Royal Anthropological Institute 62:173–190.

1937   Cooperation and competition among primitive peoples. New York, McGraw-Hill.

1939   From the South Seas: studies of adolescence and sex in primitive societies. New York, Morrow. (Comprises reprints of Coming of age in Samoa, 1928; Growing up in New Guinea, 1930; Sex and temperament in three primitive societies, 1935.)

1949   Male and female: a study of the sexes in a changing world. New York, Morrow.

1953   National character. *In* Anthropology today, A. L. Kroeber, ed., pp. 642–667. Chicago, University of Chicago Press.

1954a Research on primitive children. *In* Manual of child psychology. Leonard Carmichael, ed., 2d ed., pp. 735–80. New York, Wiley.

1954b Cultural continuities and personality transformation. Journal of Social Issues, Supplement Series No. 8. Kurt Lewin Memorial Award Issue.

1956   New lives for old, cultural transformation: Manus 1928–1953. New York, Morrow.

1959　Reply to Kardiner. Science 130:1728, 1732.

MEAD, MARGARET and FRANCES COOKE MACGREGOR
1951　Growth and culture: a photographic study of Balinese childhood. New York, Putman's.

MEAD, MARGARET and RHODA MÉTRAUX
1953　The study of culture at a distance. Chicago, University of Chicago Press.

MEAD, MARGARET and THEODORE SCHWARTZ
1960　The cult as a condensed social process. *In* Group Processes: Transactions of the Fifth Conference, Oct. 12, 13, 14 and 15, 1958, Princeton, N.J. Bertram Schaffner, ed., New York, Josiah Macy, Jr. Foundation, 85–187.

MEAD, MARGARET and MARTHA WOLFENSTEIN, eds.
1955　Childhood in contemporary cultures. Chicago, University of Chicago Press.

MILLER, NEAL E. and JOHN DOLLARD
1941　Social learning and imitation. New Haven, Yale University Press.

MULLIGAN, D. G.
1957　Maori adolescence in Rakau. Wellington, Victoria University College Publications in Psychology 9. (Monographs on Maori Social Life and Personality 2.)

MYERS, CHARLES J. and W. McDOUGALL
1903　Reports of the Cambridge Anthropological Expedition to Torres Straits II, Physiology and Psychology. Part 2. Cambridge, Cambridge University Press.

PORTEUS, S. D.
1931　The psychology of a primitive people: a study of the Australian Aborigine. New York, Longmans, Green.
1937　Primitive intelligence and environment. New York, Macmillan.

RITCHIE, JAMES E.
1956　Basic personality in Rakau. Wellington, Victoria University College Publications in Psychology 8. (Monographs on Maori Social Life and Personality 1.)

RITCHIE, JANE
1957　Childhood in Rakau: the first five years of life. Wellington, Victoria University College Publications in Psychology 10. (Monographs on Maori Social Life and Personality 3.)

RIVERS, W. H. R.
1923　Conflict and dream. New York, Harcourt, Brace.

RÓHEIM, GÉZA
1925　Australian totemism: a psycho-analytical study in anthropology. London, Allen and Unwin.
1932　The psychoanalysis of primitive cultural types. International Journal of Psychoanalysis 13:1–224.
1950　Psychoanalysis and anthropology. New York, International Universities Press.

SPIRO, MELFORD E.

1951   Culture and personality: the natural history of a false dichotomy. Psychiatry 14:19–46.

1959   Cultural heritage, personal tensions, and mental illness in a South Sea culture. *In* Culture and mental health, Marvin K. Opler, ed., pp. 141–171. New York, Macmillan.

1961   Social systems, personality, and functional analysis. *In* Studying personality cross-culturally, Bert Kaplan, ed.

TAYLOR, C. R. H.

1951   A Pacific bibliography. Wellington, N. Z., The Polynesian Society.

VINACKE, W. EDGAR, et al.

1955   Bibliography of sources on personality and culture of the Pacific region. Honolulu, University of Hawaii (mimeographed).

WEST, JAMES

1945   Plainville, U.S.A. New York, Columbia University Press.

WHITING, JOHN W. M.

1941   Becoming a Kwoma: teaching and learning in a New Guinea tribe. New Haven, Yale University Press.

WILLIAMS, JOHN SMITH

1960   Maori achievement motivation. Wellington, Victoria University of Wellington Publications in Psychology 13. (Monographs on Maori Social Life and Personality 5.)

WORLD HEALTH ORGANIZATION

1957   Proceedings of the Fourth Meeting, Study Group on Psychobiological Development of the Child, Sept. 20–26, 1956, Geneva. Mimeographed. (To be published by Tavistock Press.)

Chapter 6

NATIONAL CHARACTER AND MODERN POLITICAL SYSTEMS*

ALEX INKELES
Harvard University

THE method of analysis which yields studies in "culture and personality" when applied to "primitive" peoples has its analogue among studies of large-scale societies in a varied assortment of investigations on what is called national character. If, under this heading, we allow impressionistic, introspective, and loosely evaluative works to qualify, then for the United States alone—from De Tocqueville to Brogan and Gorer—the articles and books depicting the American character will be numbered in the hundreds (Commager 1947). Were we to extend our coverage to the major nations of Europe and Asia, the number of relevant studies would be in the thousands. To review even the most important of these would strain the limits of our allotted space even while permitting only the driest catalogue of their contents. Yet if we were to insist on the more rigorous standards of empirical social science, and were to consider only more systematic investigations based on representative samples and utilizing standard psychological tests, then not more than two or three studies in the relevant literature could qualify. There is a third alternative. By selecting a specific problem focus we may simultaneously escape the boundlessness of a general review and the confining restrictions forced on us through the adoption of a rigorous methodological canon. A topic suitable to our purpose, one of interest and importance, is the relation of national character to the political systems found in modern national states, and more specifically, to the establishment and maintenance of democracy. Be-

* Revised and expanded version of a paper read at the Fourth World Congress of Sociology, Stresa-Milan, 1959. The aid of the Social Science Research Council is gratefully acknowledged, as well as the support of the Russian Research Center at Harvard. Professors S. N. Eisenstadt and Daniel J. Levinson were kind enough to offer numerous excellent suggestions.

fore we examine this relationship, we must clarify the meaning of our concepts.

WHAT IS NATIONAL CHARACTER AND HOW CAN IT BE MEASURED?

Problems of Definition

The confusion about the term *national character* is pervasive and enduring. Yet arguing about what a concept *should* mean can be utterly sterile. What is important is that we designate some empirical phenomenon which has concrete reference, which can be effectively distinguished from other phenomena, and which can conceivably be investigated by standard replicable, reliable, and valid methods. For purposes of this discussion I will adopt the definition of national character presented in the *Handbook of Social-Psychology* (Inkeles and Levinson 1954) which, I believe, is now widely accepted: "National character refers to relatively enduring personality characteristics and patterns that are modal among the adult members of a society."

The other meanings given to national character, and related terms such as people's character, folk character, national (or "racial" or popular) psychology, are almost as numerous as the roster of political essayists from Plato to Pareto and from Pareto to Potter. Some treat national character as simply "the sum total" of all the values, institutions, cultural traditions, ways of acting, and history of a people. However useful this idea may be for popular discourse, it is sadly lacking for purposes of scientific analysis, since the failure to differentiate the elements of the phenomenon makes an impossible task of measurement, obfuscates issues of cause and effect, and precludes systematic study of the relations between elements. With most other definitions we have no quarrel, so long as those using the different terms are appropriately aware that each has a special and restricted meaning, and that no one of these concepts exhaustively describes the phenomenon under investigation. The following main types of definition may be discerned (*cf.* Herz 1944, and Klineberg 1944):

National Character as Institutional Pattern. In this approach, most common among political scientists, the national character is epitomized by the dominant, or typical and representative, institutions, particularly those concerned with politics and economics. The choice between dominant as against typical or representative institutions as the basis for characterizing a nation is a difficult one, and has led to much confusion in those studies in which the distinction was not precisely made or rigorously adhered to. Outstanding examples of the genre are to be found among numerous studies of the American character, such as those by Andre Siegfried (1927) or D. W. Brogan (1933, 1944).

National Character as Culture Theme.   Broadly similar to the preceding approach, this genre gives prime emphasis not to political and economic institutions but to the family, friendship, the local community, and to values, attitudes, philosophy of life, religion and the like. Themes are often selected as cutting across or as infusing these and other social realms. Most common among anthropologists, this approach is also typical for many historians, political scientists, and essayists who speak in terms of spirit or *folkgeist,* world outlook, life-ways, and similar themes. Perhaps the best known of the more or less modern efforts of this type would be de Madariaga's *Englishmen, Frenchmen, Spaniards* (1929), and the most impressive of the recent statements, Ruth Benedict's *The Chrysanthemum and the Sword* (1946).

National Character as Action.   In this approach stress is placed on behavior and its consequences, with special reference to political and economic *action.* In this view both formal institutional patterns and informal cultural norms, in and of themselves, are not regarded as very reliable guides to a nation's "character." Those adopting this approach stress particularly the history of peoples or societies, and on this basis may characterize them as warlike or peaceful, enterprising or backward, trustworthy or deceptive, pragmatic and industrious, or idealistic and impractical. Germany is a case often discussed in this context. Many have emphasized the contrast between Germany's outstanding institutional creations and cultural achievements on the one hand, and on the other its historic role in Europe in the first half of the twentieth century. Hearnshaw's *Germany the Aggressor Throughout the Ages* (1940) may serve as an example. This mode of analysis should not be confused with a more sophisticated type in which national character is recognized to be a property of persons, and is treated as an independent variable contributing to an explanation of some form of political action considered as a dependent variable. An outstanding example is Gabriel Almond's (1950) use of materials on the American character to explain certain persistent tendencies in the conduct of foreign policy by the United States.

National Character as Racial Psychology. The identification of national character with the allegedly "inborn" and presumably biological characteristics (generally defined as superior or inferior) of a group is one of the oldest and most common approaches, and in modern social science the one most severely criticized if not actively abhorred (*cf.* Benedict 1945). A typical illustration, by no means the most extreme, may be found in Jaensch's (1938) study, published under Hitler, in which he asserted that the French were usually erratic and unreliable, the Germans consistent and stable.

The belief in racial psychology is by no means restricted to racist theoreticians. As tolerant and democratic a man as Andre Siegfried (1951), for example, attributes one of the two main qualities he finds in the French mind—its being "extremely practical and matter of fact"—to a Celtic heritage which he says is found wherever "Celtic blood prevails," including places as widely separated as northern Spain and the west of the British Isles. And Brickner's (1943) analysis of the German character as one essentially paranoid struck many students of the problem as verging on racism in psychology, even though it certainly did not suggest that the allegedly typical paranoid behavior was biological in origin. Although the pendulum may have swung too far in the opposite direction, there is today general agreement that the biologically given properties of what are in any event extraordinarily mixed national populations are *not* a significant influence in shaping the institutions, culture, or behavior of those national populations. Yet the altogether proper discrediting of racial psychology has perhaps had the unfortunate unintended effect of discouraging serious scientific research on a basic question of social science.

In most of the better known general essays on national character, such as those by Sforza (1942) on Italy, Siegfried (1930) on France, and Ortega y Gasset (1937) on Spain, more than one of these definitions or approaches will be used simultaneously and generally without any special note being taken of this fact. Typically, no distinction is made between character as something already formed and acting, and those forces such as climate and geography, history, biology, or child rearing which may be designated as the causes or consequences of the observed national character. If progress is to be made in the field, we need to make our investigations more systematic. There is no one line of development which can do full justice to the complexities of the problem. We feel, however, that great advantages inhere in the concentration on *modal adult personality* characteristics as a central problem in national character study. We therefore pose the question: whether produced by common heritage, common upbringing, the sharing of common culture, the exposure to common institutional pressures, or other causes, are there in fact any clearly demonstrated important differences in the psychological characteristics of the populations who make up modern national states? The question is more difficult to answer with confidence than many imagine it to be.

The Problem of Measurement

No matter how we conceive of national character, a scientific approach to it must face the problem of its assessment—or to use a less evasive word, its measurement. This subject generates as much confusion and malaise as does the issue of definition. The different approaches to national character based on institutional structure, and on national action or behavior, involve virtually no common understanding, standard techniques, regular procedures, or canons of reliability and validity. The situation is only slightly less variable in the racial psychology and the culture-pattern approaches. Each study proceeds almost entirely independently of all others, utilizes unique perspectives, draws on distinctive materials, follows idiosyncratic rules of evidence, and observes only its own standards of reliability and validity. The result is, if not intellectual chaos or anarchy, at least a great buzzing, blooming confusion which defies representation. Under the circumstances, a systematic comparative perspective is almost impossible.

It is argued by some, not without cogency, that institutional arrangements are so varied, culture patterns so unique, national psychologies so distinctive, that no common or standard language can hope to encompass this infinite diversity. Under these circumstances, it is said, we cannot do justice to the unique character of any people unless we develop a special battery of concepts and a new glossary of terms to describe them. This claim may be somewhat exaggerated. In any event it suggests that systematic analysis of national character as a field of scientific investigation is blocked. The same basic difficulty does not, at least in equal degree, attend efforts to deal with national character as modal personality patterns. There is good reason to believe that the range of variation in human personality, however great, can be adequately encompassed by a conceptual scheme, with a sufficiently limited set of terms to make for manageable research designs without sacrifice of essential richness or variety. We also maintain that, despite the many methodological and conceptual problems involved, this scheme and its measuring instruments can be developed so as to permit reliable and valid applications across national lines.

Harold Lasswell once claimed it would be an exaggeration to say that in two thousand years of studying politics we had made no advances whatsoever beyond Plato and Aristotle. Perhaps an exaggeration, but not a great one. At least so it seems when we recognize that the genius of political analysis has gone mainly into the invention of new terms for old ideas which were never made operational, never tested, and therefore never developed. For how else is one to choose between Plato's theory of the desiring, spirited, and reasoning parts, Pareto's "residues of combination" and "residues of persistence of aggregates," Spranger's six types of men, or Thomas and Znaniecki's Philistine, Bohemian, and Creative Man. These approaches must meet the criticism, as Spranger acknowledged, that they "abandon the concrete ground of experience and reduce psychology to mere speculation" (1928:xi).

As Harold Lasswell went on to say, however, our chief contemporary advantage over Plato and Aristotle lies "in the invention and adaptation of procedures by which specific individuals and groups, operating in specific historic and cultural settings, can be understood. . . . In a word, the modern approach is toward the building of scientific knowledge by perfecting the instrumentalities of inquiry" (1951:468–469). For the first time in the history of the study of politics we actually have within our grasp the means for systematic study of such conceptions as those developed by Plato, Pareto, and Spranger. I refer, of course, to the great strides made in this century in our understanding of personality dynamics and in the means for personality testing, measurement, and assessment. However, the concepts of Plato and others must first be clarified. They must be made operational, that is, transformed into possible research procedures of testing and measurement.

In some cases this has already been attempted, and it has been found possible and useful to devise formal measures of these classic typologies. Spranger's types, for example, were an important influence in shaping the widely used Allport-Vernon Scale of Values. In the process the old concepts may be found wanting. For example, Lurie's (1937) factor analysis to ascertain which generalized attitude clusters, if any, conform to Spranger's types, located several fitting Spranger's definition fairly closely—the theoretical, the religious, the social, and the economic-political. Several others, however, could not be empirically distinguished. As we test and perhaps discard some of these "classic" concepts, they will be replaced by others which are proving important in our study of personality and have obvious relevance to politics, such as: the needs for power, affiliation, and achievement; the authoritarian and ethnocentric syndrome; dominance drives; alienation and anomie; dogmatism and rigidity; tough- and tender-mindedness. It is in the nature of science and the inevitable path of its advance that concepts are replaced as empirical research advances. If for sentimental reasons we are unable to abandon the old familiar concepts, we may do ourselves honor as classicists, but we disqualify ourselves as scientists.

POLITICAL SYSTEMS AS OBJECTS OF STUDY

The definition and classification of political systems is a more familiar and less ambiguous task, although it too has its vicissitudes. The sturdy old distinctions among political forms such as democracy, oligarchy, and tyranny which come down from Plato and Aristotle still serve us well today, although some may prefer a more contemporary classification, such as that proposed by Gabriel Almond (1956) who identifies the Anglo-American, the Continental European, the pre- or partially industrial, and the totalitarian political systems. Whatever scheme we might choose, we would probably not have great difficulty in agreeing on the defining characteristics of each type and could probably attain fair agreement in classifying particular societies.

Such classifications are, however, deceptively easy, and for many purposes they may be misleading. We generally accept the Greek city-state as the epitome of the democratic political system, but we should not forget that internally it rested squarely on a large slave class, and in external affairs was characterized by almost continuous intercity warfare motivated by nothing more noble than the desire for power and gain. Tsarist Russia was perhaps the most absolute autocracy in Europe in the eighteenth and nineteenth centuries, yet the village *mir* was a self-governing community observing some of the purest principles of egalitarian democracy. Germany was an outstanding example of relatively absolute monarchy before World War I, although intellectually and spiritually one of the freest nations in Europe. The Weimar Republic which followed represented the embodiment of the most advanced democratic principles, but it was succeeded by one of the blackest of totalitarian regimes—which again is followed by a West German Republic which seems one of the stablest and most genuine of Europe's democracies. The rule of Ataturk in Turkey was a dictatorship, yet he used his dictatorial powers to foster democratic institutions against the resistance of the traditional religious oligarchy and the peasant masses. Soviet Russia under Stalin had what was nominally the most democratic constitution in the world, while in fact it closely approximated a regime of absolute totalitarian terror.

The obvious point is that we must differentiate the components of political systems just as we must distinguish the diverse elements in, and the different bearers of, national character. As a minimum we must make a distinction between: the relatively enduring and the more fleeting or transitional features of a nation's political system (cf. Lipset 1960 on stable and unstable democracies); the formal, exoteric system from the informal, esoteric, operational patterns (cf. Leites 1951 on the *Politburo*); the politics of central government from that which characterizes vital institutions such as the local community, the church, trade union, or family (cf. Michels 1949 on the iron law of oligarchy); the principles embodied in constitutions and other venerated documents and those commonly held by the populace (cf. Stouffer 1955 on civil liberties in the United States); the political orientation of the elite as against that of the rank and file of the population (cf. Stouffer 1955 and Mills 1956 on the power elite).

Only if we recognize both politics and national character as highly differentiated systems of variables can we hope to do any justice to the complex phenomena we are studying. Unfortunately many, indeed most, studies which seek to relate character to political systems fail to make these necessary distinctions. They treat political systems as undifferentiated and more or less unchanging units rather than as complex variables.

REVIEW OF SYSTEMATIC EMPIRICAL STUDIES

Despite the efflorescence of the field of culture and personality during the last three decades,[1] and a parallel growth of interest in

---

[1] The point at which a new field of exploration begins can as a rule be designated only on an essentially arbitrary basis. Most authorities acknowledge Franz Boas as the father of this movement (see especially Boas 1910), and many date its formal beginning with the publication in 1934 of Ruth Benedict's *Patterns of Culture*. Ruth Benedict and Margaret Mead were, of course, students in the seminars on Individual and Society which Boas gave at Columbia in the late twenties. Boas himself gave great credit to Theodore Waitz, of whose *Anthropolgie der Naturvolker* he said "[this] great work is an inquiry into whether there are any fundamental differences between the mental make-up of mankind the world over, racially as well as socially."

the empirical study of modern political systems, we can point to very few systematic empirical studies of the relations between personality patterns, or psychological factors in general, and the rise, functioning, and change of political systems. As usual the history of intellectual disciplines reveals much of the story. Modern studies of the relations between personality and sociocultural systems have been developed almost exclusively by cultural anthropologists. Perhaps because most nonliterate (or primitive) people rarely have a formal or specialized political organization, all but a few cultural anthropologists have shown little interest in political structure. In this respect, at least, the students of personality and culture have followed the dominant pattern in their discipline. Benedict's book on Japan (1946) and Hsu's comparison of the Chinese and American culture (1953) each give a chapter or more to politics and government, and Mead (1957) devoted an entire book to Soviet attitudes toward authority, particularly political authority. But these are outstanding exceptions. The early editions of the two standard and massive American collections of articles on culture and personality do not contain a single item which deals directly with the relation of personality patterns to the political system.[2] Similarly, the standard anthropological textbook in the field contains a chapter on psychiatric disorders and one on "personality in class, caste, region, and occupation," but none on politics.[3] Linton's (1945) little classic on *The Cultural Background of Personality* makes no mention of government or politics. The same may be said of the works of Abram Kardiner (1939, 1945) which have done so much to shape the field. Geoffrey Gorer's study of the English character has chapters on "friends and neighbors," on "people and homes," on "religion," and on "marriage," but none on those political in-

---

[2] Clyde Kluckhohn and Henry Murray (1953); Douglas Haring (1948). The former did contain an article on personality under the Nazis, but rather than having a political focus it was designed only to show that personality remained unchanged despite changes in the individual's political security. The latter had an article on the armaments race, but only as illustrating a type of mechanism in interpersonal relations. Later editions gave somewhat, but not much more, attention to the political process. The later edition of the Kluckhohn, Murray (and Schneider) volume (1956) included a new article by R. Bauer, "Psychology of the Soviet Middle Elite." In addition, the third edition of the Haring volume (1956) included materials on the role of character in postwar Japanese sociopolitical development and one by Gorer which, while not explicitly dealing with political structure, discussed the role of the police in the apparent modification of the English character in modern times.

[3] John Honigmann (1954). The index does call attention, under the heading "political relations," to two pages which discuss the evidence that organizational atomism in a community is related to the degree of ingroup sorcery, and two pages on the relations of family patterns to political structure.

stitutions and attitudes about parliaments, elections, local government, civil liberties, and personal rights which most people regard
as the truly distinctive political features of English society.[4]

These comments are, of course, not meant to ignore the substantial contribution of the British anthropologists to our understanding of primitive political systems, but in this case the hiatus is complementary to that found in the culture and personality studies.
In their exceptionally fine work on African political systems Fortes,
Evans-Pritchard, and their associates (1940) say virtually nothing
about the characterological qualities which may be important to
the development and maintenance of stable political orders in these
important underdeveloped regions.

Unfortunately the situation is not markedly changed when we
consider the work of political scientists, to whom one might appropriately assign greater responsibility for this line of work.
Although Plato and Aristotle both stressed the role of character in
shaping political forms and processes, the person tends periodically
to disappear from political theory. Early in this century Graham
Wallas made a plea for a return to the study of human nature in
politics. He deplored the books by American university professors
as useless, because the writers "dealt with abstract men, formed on
assumptions of which they were unaware and which they had never
tested either by experience or by study" (1908:10). Very little was
done to take up the challenge. More than two decades later Charles
E. Merriam (1925) was still pleading the same needs, but in a more
focused and hopeful manner with emphasis on personality, measurement, large-scale statistical studies, and correlational analysis
of the relations between political conduct and psychological characteristics of the political man. In the same year Henry Moore
(1925) published a pioneering study of psychological factors associated with holding radical and conservative political opinions.
Moore's analysis, utilizing tests for resistance to majority opinion
and of readiness to break old habits, anticipated much of the recent
research on personality and politics. Unfortunately it failed to become the start of an active research tradition in psychology.

Merriam's role in fostering the application of psychology to
politics is comparable to that played by Franz Boas in the development of culture and personality studies. It was under Merriam's

---

[4] Gorer's (1955) book does contain a chapter on "law and order," but it deals exclusively
with two questions: the popular image of the police and the attitude toward "fiddling," a
term used to describe minor infractions of the rationing regulations.

influence that Harold Lasswell wrote what was probably the first modern, systematic, and broad application of psychology to contemporary politics. In *Psychopathology and Politics* (1930) Lasswell broke new ground in going beyond the usual hypothetical classification of political types to develop the detailed study of life histories. Guided by psychoanalytic theory, he showed quite explictly and empirically the connection between personality traits and the choice and style of political roles such as the agitator, the propagandist, and the administrator. In the same volume he sketched one of the first systematic schemes for describing personality in politically relevant terms. Although he worked mainly with the individual case study, Lasswell was not unaware of the implications of this mode of analysis for the study of political patterns characteristic of classes and national populations. "What matters to the student of culture," he said, "is not the subjective similarities of the species but the subjective differences among the members of the same and similar cultures" (1930:261). He did not, however, follow through to undertake the systematic research this statement implied.

A decade elapsed before the next really major event in the field occurred with the publication of Erich Fromm's *Escape from Freedom* (1941). Fromm took the step that Lasswell had anticipated but failed to make himself. He held that the typical character types prevalent at any given time were different, that these differences varied systematically with changes in the socioeconomic system, and that character types could serve either as a cement holding the system together or as an explosive tearing it apart, depending on the degree to which a given character type fit the demands of the system and found satisfaction in it. He traced this interaction through the history of medieval Europe and the Reformation, sought to explain the appeal of Hitler by the widespread prevalence of the authoritarian character in Germany, and sketched some of the forces in democratic society—such as the sense of aloneness, the loss of individuality and spontaneity—which he saw as inducing an "escape from freedom."

Fromm's theory has been extraordinarily stimulating to all concerned with the study of personality and politics. We should appreciate his theoretical sophistication, his clinical intuition, and his clear recognition of the most vital problems. His use of historical documents and contemporary sources, such as political speeches and party platforms, represented a commendable improvement over the efforts of those who were content to rely more or less ex- clusively on their clinical experience with psychoanalytic patients. Nevertheless, many students of the problem would insist that Fromm's analysis did not present more than suggestive hypotheses. It was yet to be demonstrated by objectively verified testing based on adequate samples that the modal personality types in different socioeconomic systems were significantly different from each other, or that within any nation the form and content of political action varied according to the personality traits typical for any group.

Considering that the conflict of political principles played so central a role among the issues in World War II, it is rather striking that the series of books on national character which anthropologists contributed to the war effort gave such incidental, indeed almost casual, treatment to the relations between national character and democratic government. There are important limitations on the justice with which this characterization can be applied in one or another case, yet it fairly well fits the work of Gorer on Japan (1943), Russia (1950), and the United States (1948), Mead on the United States (1942), and Benedict on Japan (1946). Insofar as they did deal with governments, they did not with any rigor specify the personality traits of politically active adults which might con- duce them to support democratic or autocratic government. In- stead, their method was to highlight the analogy between the po- litical system and other features of the culture, most notably the family. Thus Gorer notes the characteristic division of power in the United States as contrasted with greater centralization in Euro- pean governments, then points to the typical American nuclear family council, and concludes that "to a certain extent the pattern of authority in the state is reflected in the family" (1948:44–45). Similarly, Benedict notes that the Japanese father is not a martinet, but rather exercises his authority as the representative of the larger family. The attitude thus "learned by the child in his earliest ex- periences with his father" is then invoked to explain why in Japa- nese governmental affairs "the officials who head the hierarchy do not typically exercize the actual authority" (1946:301).

These are undoubtedly important insights. Nevertheless, to con- ceive of the family as the mirror of the state, and of the state as a reflection of the pattern of relations in the family, establishes a circle without any suggestion as to how change can and does come about. In the case of the Japanese, Benedict sought to meet this challenge by stressing the Japanese "ethic of alternatives." But what of the Germans and Russians who presumably do not have such an ethic? Are they doomed to perpetual authoritarian government as the cycles of family and state patterns ever renew themselves?

The basic difficulty with this approach, one pervasive in the culture and personality literature, is its failure to take adequate account of the differentiation within large national populations. It emphasizes the central tendency, the existence of which it presumes but does not prove, and neglects the range of variation within and around the average or typical. Once we begin to deal with distributions, with variation and range, we must recognize that a second weakness of this approach is that its descriptive language, the technical terms on which it is based, does not easily permit the precise measurement and quantitative expression necessary to the study of a distributive phenomenon. These deficiencies were largely remedied in another set of the wartime studies, particularly those by Henry Dicks (1950) and David Levy (1951), which represent an important landmark in the development of our understanding of how personality relates to political action.

Dr. Dicks' work was in the main line of culture and personality studies in that it considered personality in psychoanalytic terms and was based on a general model of the German personality drawn from a variety of cultural sources. In his case, however, what is generally the conclusion of many studies was only the starting point. He went beyond previous studies in three important respects: (1) the personality of each subject was explicitly scored on clearly specified and carefully defined variables; (2) the political orientation of each person was also carefully measured in concrete terms; and (3) the personality measures and the indices of political orientation were systematically related to each other by standard statistical procedures. All this was done with clinical sensitivity, with use of general theory, and without loss of contact with the more traditional but impressionistic description of the German national character.

Dicks worked with a sample of 138 German soldiers taken as prisoners of war between 1942 and 1944. On the basis of *politically* focused interviews each man was classified on a five-point scale running from "fanatical, wholehearted Nazi" to "active, convinced anti-Nazi." In addition, on the basis of nominally free but in fact highly focused *psychiatrically* oriented interviews, each man was rated on 15 different psychosociological variables ranging from degree of religiosity to presence or absence of schizoid features. Relationships attaining a high degree of statistical significance (at the .01 level or better) were obtained between Nazism and six of the fifteen psychosocial variables. For example, those high on the scale of Naziism showed a marked taboo against tenderness, were more sadistic or antisocial, and were much more likely to engage in projection.

It is important to recognize that Dicks did not prove these or any other characteristics to be *generally* present in German nationals. He proved only that Nazis and near-Nazis were different from non-Nazi Germans in a number of important respects. This is not to say that Dicks did not attempt a general characterization of the German personality. He could hardly have undertaken his study without some such hypothetical model which, he assumed, the Nazi "embodied in more exaggerated or concentrated form." The typical German he described as having "an ambivalent, compulsive character structure with the emphasis on submissive dominant conformity, a strong counter-cathexis of the virtues of duty, of 'control' by the self, especially buttressed by re-projected 'external' super-ego symbols." Even though such individuals might be highly susceptible to the propaganda themes and the style of leadership offered by the Nazis, it is also apparent that this character type could freely support any one of a number of different sociopolitical orders. Dr. Dicks' study is of particular value, therefore, in keeping before us the awareness that in any national population there is likely to be substantial variation in modal personality patterns, even though for any given nation this variation may cover only a narrow part of the world-wide range. Dicks' study also suggests that the extreme political positions are those which are most likely to be attractive to the extremes on the personality continuum. If the extremists seize power, the resulting political forms may or may not be congruent with the dominant personality tendencies in the population at large. It seems likely that this congruence was greater in Hitlerite Germany than in Stalinist Russia.

Inkeles, Hanfmann, and Beier (1958) administered a battery of tests including the Rorschach, TAT, sentence-completion test, and others to a small sample (51 cases) of refugees from Soviet Russia who departed during and just after World War II (*cf.* Dicks 1952). On this basis they constructed a composite national character portrait, differentiating a main modal pattern, a variant on it, and a residual group. The subjects were also divided into four social classes. The authors did not, unfortunately, relate the personality characteristics of each individual directly to his mode of political orientation. For the group as a whole, however, they related its adjustment to the Soviet political system to each element of the modal personality pattern—which included a strong need for affiliation, marked dependency needs, emotional expressiveness and responsiveness, and resistance to being shamed for failures in impersonal performance. The authors found, for example, that the persistent shortages of food, shelter, and clothing which characterized Soviet life under Stalin, aggravated the anxieties about oral deprivation which were frequently manifested in the Russian character. In general, they concluded, "there was a high degree of incongruence between the central personality modes and dispositions of many Russians and . . . the behavior of the regime." This was most marked, however, for those who represented the basic personality mode, and was much less true for those whose personality reflected a substantial departure from the modal pattern common to the mass of peasants and workers.

Postwar Developments

Research in the period after World War II has been characterized by two important developments: (1) improvements in the methods for assessing personality on a large scale and (2) the application of such methods on a cross-national or comparative basis.

If we require that national character studies be based on systematic and objective study of personality, that they represent all the diverse elements of national populations, and that they permit meaningful comparison with results from other studies, we are in effect calling for a transformation of the standard methodology of the field. Such a demand made before 1940 would have been perhaps not visionary, but hardly reasonable as a practical matter. The postwar period, however, has seen the development and application of means for the assessment of personality which enable us to measure it with relative ease, and to do so with large representative samples. There is reason to believe that at least some of these instruments may be effectively used cross-nationally.

The effort to measure with some precision the personality traits of entire national groups has a longer history than many suppose. One of the earliest ventures in the use of a standard psychological test to assess personality trends in a significantly large population was the Bleulers' (1935) application of the Rorschach Ink-Blot test to Moroccans in the thirties. The Bleulers administered the Rorschach to an unspecified number of "simple country folk" (half

Arab, half Berber) living in the vast plains of West Morocco. Their characterization, based on the Rorschach records as measured against their experience with the test in Europe, is full of comments of the following order: the Moroccan lacks the typical European "tendency to abstractive generalization;" his extroversion emerges mainly in "a marked enthusiasm under the influence of momentary events . . . but he lacks the systematic, energetic, and persevering striving after outward success."

Of course we will wonder whether we can safely generalize these comments to other Moroccans, and how much these patterns reflect not Moroccan culture but rather the low level of education and the relative isolation of these people. But more important for our purposes is the question of the relevance of such qualities of character for the ability to act as a good citizen in a stable political order of a national state. The Bleulers' description typically makes no mention of images of authority, civic consciousness, or other traits of obvious political relevance, and we do not have the knowledge to judge whether the lack of a tendency to abstractive generalization is conducive to good democratic citizenship or not. That these defects of the typical Rorschach analysis of group personality are relatively persistent may be observed by comparing the Bleulers' study with later ventures, such as the study of the Chinese by Abel and Hsu (1949). Indeed, the Rorschach has come into serious question as an instrument for systematic research into group traits (Carstairs, Payne, and Whitaker 1960).

Probably the greatest influence on our thinking and practice in the measurement of personality dimensions relevant to politics is exerted by the now classic study of the authoritarian personality by the Frankfurt Institut fur Sozialforschung (Horkheimer 1936). Erich Fromm played a major role in this group's development of the concept of the authoritarian personality, which Adorno (1950) and his associates carried forward in the United States both theoretically and methodologically. The main fruit of the California group's investigation was the isolation, definition, and measurement of a particular personality type, but the conception of that type was initially derived from ideas about the distinctive psychological coloration of authoritarian political creeds and movements. Although the F scale [5] has been severely criticized because it can

---

[5] The letter F was used with the scale to designate "susceptibility to Fascism." This sounds more like a specifically political than a psychological measure, although the authors intended it mainly as a measure of personality. This use of the term Fascism for the scale unfortunately clouded the issue by seeming to prejudge the relation between measures of personality and those of political orientation, or worse to suggest they were perhaps one and the same thing.

distinguish right authoritarians but permits left authoritarians to escape notice (Christie 1954), there can be no serious question but that the psychological syndrome thus isolated is highly correlated with extreme right-wing political attitudes.

The semipsychiatric interview which Dicks used requires special talent to conduct, is difficult and expensive to code or score, and must therefore be restricted to very small samples. By contrast the F scale has the special virtue of great simplicity as a test instrument, something unusual in the earlier efforts to measure personality variables of theoretical interest and proved clinical significance. The F scale thus made possible for the first time the simultaneous collection of data on personality and on political orientations from a fully representative national sample. Using a modified version of the F scale, Janowitz and Marvick found that in the United States those whose personality tended more toward authoritarianism were also more markedly isolationist in foreign affairs (*cf.* Levinson 1957). The more authoritarian also revealed a sense of political ineffectiveness, that is, they believed themselves powerless to influence government action. The conclusion reached by Janowitz and Marvick is particularly noteworthy: "Personality tendencies measured by [an] authoritarian scale served to explain political behavior at least as well as those factors [such as age, education, and class] traditionally included in political and voting behavior studies." (1953: 201; also see Lane 1955.)

In addition to the F scale, there are other personality measures suitable for administration to large samples and relevant to political orientations, such as Rokeach's (1956) dogmatism scale and Eysenck's (1954) classification of the tender minded and tough minded. In their study of American automobile workers, Arthur Kornhauser (1956) and his associates utilized measures not only of authoritarianism but also of life satisfaction and social alienation or "anomie." Those characterized by anomie showed little interest in politics, and were much less likely to vote. When they did vote, they tended to vote contrary to the prevailing sentiment among their fellow workers. Among numerous important findings in this rich and interesting study was the discovery that authoritarianism is related to political extremism *whether of the right or left*. This assumption gains support from a study of political orientations in Iran. Despite their fundamental differences in political position, the extreme rightists and extreme leftists were more like each other in many social and behavioral characteristics—such as "level of social detachment" and "breadth of social horizons"—than they were like the more moderate groups of the political center (Ringer and Sills 1953).

In summarizing their detailed results, Kornhauser and his associates reach a conclusion which accords well with the requirements of our model of the democratic personality. They say: "The problem of democracy . . . is partly the problem of maintaining an adequate proportion of members who are capable of engaging in the market place of proposals and counter-proposals, immune from the feeling that 'the leader knows best' and from the temptation to condone, or to resort to, desperate measures in times of social and political crisis" (1956:249–250).

Perhaps the most systematic effort to relate personality to political inclinations is to be found in the pioneering study by Herbert McClosky (1953) in which he sought to define the personality characteristics of those taking positions along the continuum from conservative to liberal politics. He unfortunately defines conservatism not by party affiliation, but on the basis of agreement with a set of normative propositions drawn from the works of leading, modern, conservative spokesmen. These statements include items such as: you can't change human nature; no matter what people think, a few people will always run things anway; duties are more important than rights. Using a rich battery of personality scales developed at the University of Minnesota and elsewhere, he finds that the extreme conservatives are sharply differentiated from both the "liberals" and "moderate liberals" in being more submissive, anomic, alienated, pessimistic, guilty, hostile, rigid, paranoid obsessive, intolerant of human frailty, and extremely ego-defensive. It will be immediately apparent that the personality traits of the extreme conservative or "reactionary" bear a very close relation to those of the authoritarian personality, and at every point are polar to the qualities described below in our model of the democratic personality.

It is unfortunately characteristic of McClosky's study, and many others in this field, that they are not comparative. This necessarily leaves us in doubt as to whether in other countries or environments the same traits of personality would also be associated with the same kinds of political orientation. For example, Dr. Dicks' (1950) study raises at once a question as to the uniqueness of the Nazi pattern and the degree to which we can generalize his findings. Since all of Dicks' comparisons were made within the German sample, he is quite justified in saying that in Germany certain individual characteristics are more associated with fascist political leanings than others. But his assumption that the Nazis are only extreme variants of a more general or typical German character cannot be taken as proved. On the basis of his sample he could hardly establish what the average or typical German is like, if he exists at all. In any study restricted to one sample, we may easily be led into assuming that the response which fits our preconception of the group is distinctive to it, when in fact that response is quite common in other populations as well. For example, we would have much more confidence in Schaffner's (1948) finding of extreme authoritarianism in the typical German conception of the family had he given his sentence completion test to at least one other comparable national group.

This defect was remedied in a number of studies conducted after World War II. Indeed the postwar period is outstanding for the development of more systematic comparative research. For example, D. V. McGranahan (1946) put a number of questions on basic issues—such as obedience to authority under duress, and freedom of the press even when not "for the good of the people"—to comparable samples of American and German boys. In the latter case he made a distinction by political orientation between Nazis, neutrals, and anti-Nazis. The German youth distinctly favored obedience to authority more often than the Americans, showed less faith in the common man, and were more admiring of people with political or military power. In general these findings fit our expectation with regard to the greater emphasis on democratic values in American as against German society. But it is crucial to note that *within* the German group, those classified as anti-Nazi were on some questions closer to the Americans than to their Nazi-oriented compatriots.

Of course, no simple conclusions can be drawn from one such study standing alone. For example, when the same questions were given by Stoodley (1957) to a more or less comparable group of youths from the Philippines, he found that on some dimensions they were closer to the Germans, on others, to the Americans, thus yielding a distinctive national profile. Unfortunately, he did not inquire into the relation of these attitudes to political orientation, which would have enabled us to judge whether the same value orientations which made for Nazism in Germany made for comparable antidemocratic leanings in the Philippines.

Gillespie and Allport (1955) studied hopes for the future among college students in several countries. Although they did not inquire directly into political beliefs, several of the topics they dealt with are clearly relevant to an evaluation of the strength of tendencies toward various forms of active "citizenship." They reported the Japanese to be outstanding in their "sense of obligation to the social group in which they live." The Japanese were, for example, first among all countries in saying they would seek to inculcate in their children such qualities as good citizenship, social usefulness, and service to society (*cf.* Stoetzel 1955). On this and similar questions Americans were near the bottom of the list. They "emphasized their rights rather than their duties and in all presented a picture of individuality, separation from the social context of living, and privatization of values and personal plans" (1955:29). The New Zealanders presented a profile quite similar to that of the Americans, but we cannot say whether this results from their common Anglo-Saxon heritage, the common experience of settling a new continent, or some combination of these and similar influences. These findings are well in accord with the conclusions of earlier, more impressionistic studies of American and Japanese character. They are none the less welcome for providing firm confirmation of these hypotheses.

Despite such promising starts there seems to be great hesitation to undertake systematic comparative studies. The hesitation to apply methods of personality testing cross-nationally arises not merely from the magnitude and cost of the task, admittedly substantial, but in large part from resistance, skepticism, and outright rejection of the possibility of reliable and valid cross-national testing of opinions, values, and personality traits. We should not minimize the substantial technical difficulties facing any such effort. But the objections often offered to such attempts seem exaggerated, and in any event the appropriate response is to accept the challenge and attempt the necessary methodological innovation. By way of encouragement we may note that a number of studies have shown that certain tests can be used cross-nationally with a high degree of reliability. In a study for UNESCO (Cantril and Buchanan 1953) conducted in nine countries it was found that most questions had the same meaning in all the countries studied, and that the opinions related to each other in one setting were similarly correlated in the others. For example, in each country those who believed human nature can be changed were also more likely to believe that national characteristics arise from the way in which people are brought up. Indeed the same syndrome, or complex pattern of attitudes, was represented in all countries. One group in each country, who might be called the optimists, believed human nature perfectible, national character pliable, world peace attainable, and world organization desirable. The pessimists, or fatalists, believed there would always be wars, human nature cannot be changed, and that efforts at improving the international situation are bound to fail.

The UNESCO study, of course, dealt more with opinions than with deeper lying attitudes and facets of personality, but we are not limited to that level. In an important study of values which Charles Morris (1956) conducted in the United States, India, and China, he discovered that in each country the ratings of individual questions were made along the same common value dimensions and that "there is thus revealed an underlying value structure (or value space) which is very much the same in the culturally diverse groups of students." In addition, the relation of the value factors to other issues was much the same in each culturally distinct group. For example, those individuals whose values centered on receptivity to and sympathetic concern for others tended, in all three countries, to dislike or reject the operative values of the political world, as measured by the Allport-Vernon scale.

Similar results are reported in the use of a personality test which presumably taps deeper-lying strata of the personality. In a comparative study of teachers in seven European countries it was found that the same items of the F scale designed to test authoritarianism tended to cohere and form a pattern in all of the countries studied.[6] In addition, the research uncovered high consistency in the way in which orientations toward threatening situations in both domestic and international politics were patterned in the several countries. But at the same time the authors offer us some sobering words of caution regarding the difficulties facing such comparative studies. They found "many of the relationships vary in size, direction, and significance in different countries . . . modified by specific national and international situational factors—by the historically given structures of political forces, by the dominant policies, by majority-minority relations, by the ongoing communication processes in the mass media and in the larger organizations" (Aubert et al. 1954: 38).

---

[6] Personal communication from Drs. D. J. Levinson and Stein Rokkan. The data were collected in the study reported in Aubert, 1954.

TOWARD THE DELINEATION OF THE DEMOCRATIC CHARACTER

It is apparent that we have made at least a modest beginning in studying the relation of personality patterns to the development and maintenance of political systems. There is substantial and rather compelling evidence of a regular and intimate connection between personality and the mode of political participation by individuals and groups within any one political system. In many different institutional settings and in many parts of the world, those who adhere to the more extreme political positions have distinctive personality traits separating them from those taking more moderate positions in the same setting. The formal or explicit "content" of one's political orientation—left or right, conservative or radical, pro- or antilabor—may be determined mainly by more "extrinsic" characteristics such as education and social class; but the form or style of political expression—favoring force or persuasion, compromise or arbitrary dictation, being tolerant or narrowly prejudiced, flexible in policy or rigidly dogmatic—is apparently largely determined by personality. At least this seems clear with regard to the political extremes. It is not yet certain whether the same characteristics make for extremism in all national groups and institutional settings, but that also seems highly likely.

Prominent among the traits which make for extremism appear to be the following: exaggerated faith in powerful leaders and insistence on absolute obedience to them; hatred of outsiders and deviates; excessive projection of guilt and hostility; extreme cynicism; a sense of powerlessness and ineffectiveness (alienation and anomie); suspicion and distrust of others; and dogmatism and rigidity. Some of these terms have been or will be shown to be merely alternative designations of the same phenomenon, but some such general syndrome of authoritarianism, dogmatism, and alienation undoubtedly is the psychological root of that political extremism which makes this type actively or potentially disruptive to democratic systems.

If political extremism is indeed an accompaniment—and even more a product—of a certain personality syndrome, and if this syndrome produces the equivalent extremism in all national populations and subgroups, that fact poses a considerable challenge to the student of national character in its relation to political systems. At once we face this question: Are the societies which have a long history of democracy peopled by a majority of individuals who possess a personality conducive to democracy? Alternatively, are societies which have experienced recurrent or prolonged authoritarian, dictatorial, or totalitarian government inhabited by a proportionately large number of individuals with the personality traits we have seen to be associated with extremism? In other words, can we move from the individual and group level, to generalize about the relations of personality and political system at the societal level?

Almost all the modern students of national character are convinced that the answer to this question is in the affirmative. Systematic empirical evidence for this faith is unfortunately lacking. To prove the point we would be required to show that the qualities of personality presumably supportive or less destructive of democracy are more widely prevalent in stable democracies such as the United States, England, Switzerland, or Sweden than in Germany, Japan, Italy, or Russia. At the present time we cannot offer such proof. We will continue to be unable to settle this question until we undertake nation-wide studies of modal personality patterns—such as we do of literacy or per capita income—and test their relation to the forms of political organization in various countries. Before we undertake such studies we must have some conception of the character types for which we are looking.

The problem of defining anything as broad as "the democratic character" may be much like the problem of locating the Manchester economists' "economic man" who Unamuno somewhere described as "a man neither of here nor there, neither this age nor another, who has neither sex nor country, who is, in brief, merely an idea—that is to say, a 'no-man.'"

The danger of excessive generality in defining the democratic character is not greater than the danger of "misplaced concreteness," that is, defining the characterological requirements of *any* democracy as identical with those of some particular people who have a strong democratic tradition. For example, it has been true of the great majority of commentaries on the people of the United States, going back to its earliest days, that "practicality" and "emphasis on religion" have been consistently cited as American traits (Coleman 1941). Yet it would be difficult to argue that either quality is a sufficient or even a necessary requirement for effective citizenship in a democracy. The same may be said of other traits frequently cited as characterizing the American people, such as valuing success and achievement, which are also strongly emphasized in Japanese culture, or the marked emphasis on activity and work, which is also commonly cited as typifying the German character.

While observing these cautions, we should not avoid postulating certain qualities which are probably indispensable to the long-run maintenance of a democratic political order. In holding this view we do no more than did De Tocqueville. De Tocqueville weighed the role of geography and climate, of religion and political institutions, and finally of what he called "manners," meaning thereby "various notions and opinions current among men . . . the mass of those ideas which constitute their character of mind . . . the whole moral and intellectual condition of a people." Comparing Mexico, South America, and the United States in these terms, he concluded: "The manners [character] of the Americans of the United States are the *real* cause which renders it the only one of the American nations that is able to support a democratic government . . . I should say that the physical circumstances are less efficient than the laws, and the laws very subordinate to the manners [character] of the people" (1947:213).

De Tocqueville's insistence that the maintenance of democracy depends upon the primacy of certain popular values, and what we would today call character traits, has often been reaffirmed since by numerous authorities including men as widely separated in formal philosophical allegiance as Sidney Hook and Jacques Maritain.[7] What specific qualities do we then require in a people as a necessary condition for the maintenance of a democratic political order? Even a casual content analysis of any sampling of opinion on the democratic society reveals an extraordinary degree of agreement about the values, attitudes, opinion and traits of character which are important to its maintenance. The various formulations may be summed up by reference to conceptions about others, about the self, about authority, and about community and society.

Values about the Self.   All authorities are agreed that democratic societies require widespread belief in what Maritain calls the "inalienable rights of the person," and Hook "the belief that every

---

[7] Hook has said, for example, "Democracy is an affirmation of certain attitudes and values which are more important than any particular set of institutions" (1950:294). Maritain argues that "the democratic impulse burst forth in history as a temporal manifestation of the gospel" and says directly that the democratic ideal "is the secular name for the ideal of Christianity" (1944:65). It does not seem necessary or desirable to clutter the text in the remainder of this section with source and page citations for each of the numerous quotations. In addition to the cited works of Hook and Maritain the main sources are Lasswell (1951) and De Tocqueville (1947).

individual should be regarded as possessing intrinsic worth or dignity." "Where low estimates of the self are permitted to develop," says Harold Lasswell, "there the democratic character cannot develop."

Orientation toward Others.   The basic dignity not only of the self but of all others is an essential ingredient cited by virtually every theory on the democratic character. This particularly manifests itself in the concept of equality, under which Hook includes recognition "that equal opportunities of development should be provided for the realization of individual talents and capacities." To hold this view one must have a basic acceptance of other people. In Lasswell's words: "The democratic attitude toward other human beings is warm rather than frigid, inclusive and expanding rather than exclusive and constricting . . . an underlying personality structure which is capable of 'friendship' as Aristotle put it, and which is unalienated from humanity." Underlying these attitudes is a fundamental conception of the perfectibility of man, which De Tocqueville phrased as the belief "that a man will be led to do what is just and good by following his own interest rightly understood."

Orientation toward Authority.   At the core of the democratic personality lies a stress on personal autonomy and a certain distance from, if not distrust of, powerful authority, or, to put it negatively, an absence of the need to dominate or submit such as is found in the authoritarian personality. As Sidney Hook phrased it: "a positive requirement of a working democracy is an intelligent distrust of its leadership, a skepticism stubborn but not blind, of all demands for the enlargement of power, and an emphasis upon critical method in every phase of social life . . . Where skepticism is replaced by uncritical enthusiasm . . . a fertile soil for dictatorship has been prepared." Almost identical language is used by Maritain. Maritain described the democratic philosophy as one insisting on the "political rights of the people whose consent is implied by any political regime, and whose rulers rule as vicars of the people . . . it denies to the rulers the right to consider themselves and be considered a superior race and wills nevertheless that their authority be respected on a juridical basis. It does not admit that the state is a transcendent power incorporating within itself all authority and imposed from above upon human life . . ." The same idea is stressed by Lasswell who says: "the democratic character is multi-valued rather than single valued . . . disposed to share rather than to monopolize. In particular, little significance is attached to the exercise of power as a scope value . . . [for] when the demand for respect is the consuming passion, other values are sacrificed for the sake of receiving symbolic acknowledgments of eminence."

Attitudes toward the Community. Although overweening authority may be controlled, there is always the danger of that tyranny of the majority which De Tocqueville early warned might undo democracy. This realization has repeatedly led those who sought to define the democratic character to stress the importance of openness, ready acceptance of differences, and willingness to compromise and change. De Tocqueville early anticipated this point, as he did so many others. Stressing the belief "that every man is born of the right of self-government, and that no one has the right of constraining his fellow creatures to be happy," he went on to say we must recognize "society as a body in a state of improvement, [and] humanity as a changing scene in which nothing is or ought to be permanent." Hook also speaks of the importance of "a belief in the value of differences, variety, and uniqueness in a democracy [where] differences of interest and achievement must not be merely suffered, they must be encouraged." According to Hook this requires that the ultimate commitment of a democracy must be in some method by which value conflicts are to be resolved, which in turn means that policies must be treated as hypotheses, not dogmas, and customary practices as generalizations rather than as God-given truths.

It will be apparent from this extremely brief review that there is substantial agreement about the core personal beliefs and values which have been frequently identified as important to the maintenance of a democratic order. The relevant "themes" can, of course, be integrated into the personality at different levels. They may reflect opinions publicly held, but not vitally important to the person. They may represent basic attitudes or central values in the belief system, typical "ideologies" to which the individual has deep allegiance. Or they may be even more "deeply" embedded in the personality at the level of character traits and modes of psychodynamic functioning. Most of the outstanding writers on the democratic character do not trouble to distinguish these "levels." I have not attempted above to sort them out, and merely note here that most of the characterizations given above are statements at the level of ideology. We can, however, translate or transform the classic portrait of the democratic character to present it in the language of clinical psychology, expressed in terms of character traits, defenses, ways of dealing with wishes and feelings, and the like. In those terms, the democratic character emerges at the opposite pole from the authoritarian personality syndrome. The citizen of a democracy should be accepting of others rather than alienated and harshly rejecting; open to new experience, to ideas and impulses rather than excessively timid, fearful, or extremely conventional with regard to new ideas and ways of acting; able to be responsible with constituted authority even though always watchful, rather than blindly submissive to or hostily rejecting of all authority; tolerant of differences and of ambiguity, rather than rigid and inflexible; able to recognize, control, and channel his emotions, rather than immaturely projecting hostility and other impulses on to others.

This model of the democratic personality represents only a very rough first approximation. Although it is based on a great deal of philosophical wisdom and historical experience, by the standards of modern social science it rests on an extremely narrow and uncertain base of empirical research. Indeed, it might be argued that at the present moment there is no relevant evidence which meets the standards set by contemporary social science research. It is largely to the future that we must look for refinement of the model, and for testing of its actual relevance for political systems and popular participation in them. No doubt some elements in the model will be discarded, others added. It may even be discovered that some one element is critical, all the others incidental or even irrelevant. In the present stage of our work it is important to avoid premature closure through the exclusive concentration on one conceptual scheme for analyzing personality. It is true that earlier efforts which accepted publicly offered opinions, attitudes, and values as guides to the individual's probable political action were often naive and misleading. Nevertheless, an analysis couched exclusively in terms of psychodynamic depth psychology, of defenses, projective tendencies, and the like may also leave out much which is of great significance in shaping the pattern of political life. We cannot be satisfied with a scheme of personality analysis which is insensitive to themes such as self-centeredness or "privatism" which Gillespie and Allport (1955) found so important in distinguishing the students from different countries in their study. Nor can we be content with an analysis of the "compulsive" German character (Kecskemeti 1947) if it leads us to neglect the feelings of obligation to self and society (McClelland 1958).

Whatever the defects of the available scheme, the use of some explicit model is essential to focus our studies in this area. It is also a necessary condition for the meaningful comparison of different studies, and particularly for our efforts to cumulate the results in ever firmer generalizations or conclusions. We must particularly regret, therefore, that so few of the empirical investigations into the relations of character and political systems have sought systematically to test the model of the democratic character presented above, or, for that matter, any other explicit model.

SOME PROBLEMS AND PROSPECTS

With very few exceptions, the available studies of modal or group personality unfortunately suffer from several defects which make them poor evidence in support of *any* systematic proposition. As a rule they are not designed to test any theory or validate any model. They are usually based on very small and haphazardly selected samples, making it extremely difficult to generalize with any confidence beyond the sample itself or the narrow circle from which it is drawn. In addition, the analysis is usually based on the total sample, without basic differentiation of the characteristics of subgroups, whether deviant or merely variant. More serious for our purposes is the fact that the description of personality is generally cast in clinical or psychodynamic terms which are difficult to relate to social structure. Even in the rare cases when a study has given attention to the more politically relevant realms of personality such as attitude toward authority, tolerance of ambiguity, acceptance of differences, and the need for power, it generally fails to record information on the political attitudes and opinions, the party affiliation, or other political characteristics of the subjects. Most of these studies, therefore, are obviously of limited usefulness to the student of politics. Only in the last few years have we attained the first, limited personality inventory of a representative sample of the national population of the United States—and this applies only to the F scale, as we have already noted, and more recently to the TAT variables of n affiliation, achievement, and power.[8] There are apparently no comparable results on these or any other dimensions for any other modern nation, and it will undoubtedly be many years

[8] The test was administered in connection with the national survey sponsored by the Joint Commission on Mental Illness and Health and conducted by the Survey Research Center of the University of Michigan. Reports on this material are in preparation by Gerald Gurin, Joseph Veroff, and John Atkinson.

before we have such results for a number of major nations simultaneously.

Even when we attain good data on the distribution of personality traits in a number of national populations, a great many questions will remain. For example, we will need to understand better the relation between personality dispositions in the rank and file of a population, and their orientation to different kinds of leadership. The decisive factor affecting the chances of preserving democracy may not be the prevalence of one or another undemocratic personality type, but rather the relation between the typical or average personality and that of the leaders. It is highly unlikely that any character type will be found to be invariably associated with a single form of political system. Nevertheless, certain personality types may indeed be more responsive to one than to another form of government. Their character, then, may be an important determinant of their susceptibility to certain kinds of influence. Thus, Dicks does not argue for the propensity toward authoritarian government *per se* in the German character. The typical German character delineated by Dicks was a type highly susceptible to the style of leadership the Hitler movement offered and extremely vulnerable to the kind of propaganda appeals it utilized. Much the same conclusion is suggested by Erikson's (1950) analysis of the German character and Hitler's appeal to it. Neither analysis should be interpreted as suggesting that the German character, as described, could not under any circumstances adjust to or function in *any* democratic political order. McClelland's analysis (1958) of the distinctive structure of obligations to self and society in Germany and the United States is particularly interesting for the light it throws on this question.

Whatever the distribution of personality types, including leaders, in any population, we will want to know what produces the types. This enormously complex problem is one I have been obliged by limits of space to ignore almost entirely, although it is one of the most fundamental facing the field. The predominant opinion among students of national character is that these types arise mainly out of the socialization process, and that in democratic societies the family structure is one which generates individuals adapted to life in a democracy. The typical argument was forcefully stated by Ralph Linton when he declared: "Nations with authoritarian family structure inevitably seem to develop authoritarian governments, no matter what the official government forms may be. Latin American countries with their excellent democratic constitutions and actual dictatorships would be a case in point" (1951:146).

Linton's opinion is not uniformly held. On the basis of a thorough review of a great deal of relevant empirical research, Herbert Hyman (1959) poses a formidable challenge to this assumption and suggests a number of other factors—particularly experiences in adulthood—which may account for the political orientations we observe in certain groups. Even after we secure data on the distribution of personality characteristics in large populations, there will be much work to be done in discovering what produces the propensity to extremism, how it operates, and what—if anything—changes or modifies it.

Another problem we must face is the relation between personality factors and other forces which affect the political process (cf. Levinson 1958). To analyze political participation and political structures through a study of personality and its statistical distribution is, of course, only one of the possible avenues of approach to the problem. Clearly, political institutions and political action can not be comprehended exclusively or even predominantly by reference to attitudes and values. The history of a people obviously plays a major role in shaping the basic structure of their political institutions. And institutional frameworks, once established, may have an endurance much greater than the formal allegiance to their principles would have indicated. Indeed, once firmly established, institutions have the capacity to develop or generate support among those whose early disposition would hardly have led them to move spontaneously in that direction.

A recent extensive comparative study by S. M. Lipset (1959) of the relation between a complex of factors including industrialization, urbanization, literacy, education, and wealth, reveals that they are highly correlated not only with each other, but also with the existence of stable democratic systems.[9] None of these factors cited by Lipset is at all psychological or attitudinal, but it is interesting to note that in seeking to understand why these factors play such a role, Lipset had to fall back from these more "objective" to more subjective causes, in particular to such concepts as the "effectiveness" and the "legitimacy" of a political system in the eyes of its constituents. By effectiveness he means the capacity to satisfy the

---

[9] De Tocqueville made the same point: "Their ancestors gave [the people of the United States] the love of equality and of freedom, but God himself gave them the means of remaining equal and free by placing them on a boundless continent . . . When the people rules it must be rendered happy or it will overthrow the state, and misery is apt to stimulate it to those excesses to which ambition rouses kings" (1947:185).

basic interests of most members of society, or of the most important groups in it, and by legitimacy "the capacity of a political system to engender and maintain the belief that existing political institutions are the most appropriate or proper ones for the society" (1960:77). Surely the tolerance of ambiguity, the readiness for compromise, the level of projectivity characteristic of a people or important subgroups, will play a major role in shaping the "effectiveness" of the political system and even its freedom of action *to be* effective. The value placed on autonomy versus control and direction, the strength of needs for power or achievement, the wish for dominance or subordination, the orientation toward authority figures, will all clearly play an important part in determining whether a particular political system is felt by people to be legitimate or not.

Although further refinements are needed, it is not likely that we will make any further unusual leaps along the line of analysis which Lipset has so diligently pursued. By contrast, the role of psychological factors—of attitudes, values, and character traits—in influencing the political process is an almost virgin field which promises a rich harvest. To secure it we must overcome imposing but by no means insuperable obstacles. We need to clarify our concepts, isolating or delineating those personal characteristics which, on theoretical grounds, seem to have the greatest relevance for the development and functioning of the political system. We must also refine our analysis of the political system, so that our descriptive categories are maximally analytical and conducive to comparative study. Our next step must be to assess systematically the distribution of these qualities in different national populations and in important subgroups of those populations. This poses one of the most difficult methodological problems, since the meaning of important terms, the pattern of response to tests, and the interpretation of those responses are highly variable as we move from country to country. On this base we can then proceed to correlational and causal analyses of the relations between opinions, values, and personality on the one hand, and the quality of political participation and the stability of political structures on the other. We may thus develop a comparative social psychology of the political process to support and supplement our traditional study of politics.

BIBLIOGRAPHY

ABEL, THEODORA M. and FRANCIS L. K. HSU
   1949   Some aspects of personality of Chinese as revealed by the Rorschach test. Rorschach Research Exchange and Journal of Projective Techniques 13:285–301.

ADORNO, T. W., E. FRENKEL-BRUNSWIK, D. J. LEVINSON and R. N. SANFORD
   1950   The authoritarian personality. New York, Harper and Bros.

ALMOND, GABRIEL A.
   1950   The American people and foreign policy. New York, Harcourt Brace.
   1956   Comparative political systems. The Journal of Politics 18:391–409.

AUBERT, VILLEM, B. R. FISHER and STEIN ROKKAN
   1954   A comparative study of teachers' attitudes to international problems and policies. Journal of Social Issues 10:25–39.

BAUER, RAYMOND A.
   1953   Psychology of the Soviet middle elite. In Personality in nature, society, and culture, Kluckhohn, Murray, and Schneider, eds. New York, Alfred Knopf.

BENEDICT, RUTH
   1934   Patterns of culture. Boston, Houghton Mifflin.
   1943   Race: science and politics (rev. ed.). New York, Viking Press.
   1946   The chrysanthemum and the sword. Boston, Houghton Mifflin.

BLEULER, M. and R.
   1935   Rorschach's ink-blot test and racial psychology: mental peculiarities of Moroccans. Character and Personality 4:97–114.

BOAS, FRANZ
   1910   Psychological problems in anthropology. American Journal of Psychiatry 21:371–384.

BRICKNER, RICHARD M.
   1943   Is Germany incurable? Philadelphia, J. B. Lippincott.

BROGAN, D. W.
   1933   Government of the people, a study in the American political system. New York, Harper and Bros.
   1944   The American character. New York, Alfred Knopf.

BUCHANAN, W. and H. CANTRIL
   1953   How nations see each other, a study in public opinion. Urbana, Ill., University of Illinois Press.

CAMPBELL, ANGUS, G. GURIN and W. E. MILLER
   1954   The voter decides. Evanston, Ill., Row, Peterson.

CARSTAIRS, G. M., R. W. PAYNE and S. WHITAKER
   1960   Rorschach responses of Hindus and Bhils. Journal of Social Psychology 51:217–227.

CHRISTIE, RICHARD and M. JAHODA, ed.
   1954   The authoritarian personality: studies in continuities in social research. Glencoe, Ill., Free Press.

COLEMAN, LEE
    1941   What is American: a study of alleged American traits. Social Forces
            19:492–499.
COMMAGER, HENRY STEELE, ed.
    1947   America in perspective, the United States through foreign eyes. New
            York, Random House.
DAVIES, JAMES C.
    1954   Charisma in the 1952 campaign. American Political Science Review
            48:1083–1102.
DICKS, HENRY V.
    1950   Personality traits and national socialist ideology, a war-time study of
            German prisoners of war. Human Relations 3:111–154.
    1952   Observations on contemporary Russian behavior. Human Relations
            5:111–175.
EYSENCK, H. J.
    1954   The psychology of politics. London, Routledge and Kegan Paul.
FORTES, MEYER and E. E. EVANS-PRITCHARD, ed.
    1940   African political systems. London and New York, Oxford University
            Press.
FROMM, ERICH
    1941   Escape from freedom. New York, Farrar and Rinehart.
GILLESPIE, JAMES M. and GORDON W. ALLPORT
    1955   Youth's outlook on the future: a cross-national study. Garden City,
            New York, Doubleday.
GORER, GEOFFREY
    1943   Themes in Japanese culture. Transactions of the New York Academy
            of Sciences Ser. II, 5, 106–124.
    1948   The American people, a study in national character. New York, W. W.
            Norton.
    1955   Exploring English character. London, Cresset Press.
GORER, GEOFFREY and JOHN RICKMAN
    1949   The people of Great Russia, a psychological study. London, Cresset
            Press.
HARING, DOUGLAS G.
    1948   Personal character and cultural milieu. Syracuse, N.Y., Syracuse Uni-
            versity Press. (3d ed. 1956.)
HEARNSHAW, F. J. C.
    1940   Germany, the aggressor throughout the ages. London, W. and R.
            Chambers.
HERZ, FREDERICK
    1944   Nationality in history and politics. London, Routledge and Kegan Paul.
HONIGMANN, JOHN J.
    1954   Culture and personality. New York, Harper and Bros.
HOOK, SIDNEY
    1950   Reason, social myths, and democracy. New York, Humanities Press.

HORKHEIMER, MAX, ed.
1936   Studien uber authorität und familie. Paris, Alcan.

HSU, FRANCIS L. K.
1953   Americans and Chinese: two ways of life. New York, Schuman.

INKELES, ALEX and D. J. LEVINSON
1954   National character: the study of modal personality and sociocultural systems. *In* Handbook of social psychology, vol. II, G. Lindzey, ed. Cambridge, Addison-Wesley.

INKELES, ALEX, EUGENIA HANFMANN and HELEN BEIER
1958   Modal personality and adjustment to the Soviet socio-economic system. Human Relations 11:1–22.

JAENSCH, ERICH R.
1938   Der gegentypus. Leipzig, Barth.

JANOWITZ, MORRIS and D. MARVICK
1953   Authoritarianism and political behavior. Public Opinion Quarterly 17:185–201.

KARDINER, ABRAM
1945   The psychological frontiers of society. New York, Columbia University Press.

KARDINER, ABRAM and L. OVESEY
1951   The mark of oppression: a psychosocial study of the American Negro. New York, Norton.

KECSKEMETI, PAUL and NATHAN LEITES
1947   Some psychological hypotheses on Nazi Germany. Journal of Social Psychology, I 1947 26:141–183; II 1948 27:91–117; III 1948 27: 241–270; IV 1948 28:141–164.

KLINEBERG, OTTO
1944   A science of national character. Journal of Social Problems 19:147–162.
1951   Psychological aspects of international relations. *In* Personality and political crisis, Alfred H. Stanton and Stewart E. Perry, eds. Glencoe, Ill., Free Press.

KLUCKHOHN, CLYDE and HENRY MURRAY
1953   Personality in nature, society, and culture. New York, Alfred Knopf. (Rev. ed., with David Schneider, 1956.)

KORNHAUSER, ARTHUR, H. L. SHEPPARD and A. J. MAYER
1956   When labor votes, a study of auto workers. New York, University Books.

KORNHAUSER, WILLIAM
1959   The politics of mass society. Glencoe, Ill., Free Press.

KROUT, MAURICE H. and ROSS STAGNER
1939   Personality development in radicals: a comparative study. Sociometry 2:31–46.

LANE, R. E.
1955   Political personality and electoral choice. American Political Science Review 49:173–190.

LASSWELL, HAROLD D.
  1930   Psychopathology and politics. *In* The political writings of Harold D. Lasswell. Glencoe, Ill., Free Press, 1951.
  1951   Democratic character. *In* The political writings of Harold D. Lasswell. Glencoe, Ill., Free Press.
  1959   Political constitution and character. Psychoanalysis and the Psychoanalytic Review 46:3–18.

LEITES, NATHAN C.
  1948   Psychocultural hypotheses about political acts. World Politics 1: 102–119.
  1951   The operational code of the politburo. New York, McGraw-Hill.

LERNER, DANIEL
  1958   The passing of traditional society; modernizing the Middle East. Glencoe, Ill., Free Press.

LEVINSON, DANIEL J.
  1957   Authoritarian personality and foreign policy. Conflict Resolution 1: 37–47.
  1958   The relevance of personality for political participation. Public Opinion Quarterly 22:3–10.

LEVY, DAVID M.
  1951   Anti-Nazis: criteria of differentiation. *In* Personality and political crisis, Alfred H. Stanton and Stewart E. Perry, eds. Glencoe, Ill., Free Press.

LINTON, RALPH
  1945   The cultural background of personality. New York, D. Appleton-Century.
  1951   The concept of national character. *In* Personality and political crisis, Alfred H. Stanton and Stewart E. Perry, eds. Glencoe, Illinois, Free Press.

LIPSET, S. M.
  1959   Some social requisites of democracy: economic development and political legitimacy. American Political Science Review 53:69–105.
  1960   Political man: the social bases of politics. Garden City, New York, Doubleday.

LURIE, WALTER A.
  1937   A study of Spranger's value-types by the method of factor analysis. Journal of Abnormal and Social Psychology 8:17–37.

MADARIAGA, SALVADOR DE
  1929   Englishmen, Frenchmen, Spaniards: an essay in comparative psychology. London, Oxford University Press.

MANNHEIM, KARL
  1950   Freedom, power and democratic planning. New York, Oxford University Press.

MARITAIN, JACQUES
  1944   Christianity and democracy. New York, Scribners.

McCLELLAND, DAVID, J. F. STURR, R. H. KNAPP and H. W. WENDT
  1958   Obligations to self and society in the United States and Germany. Journal of Abnormal and Social Psychology 56:245–255.

McCloskey, Herbert
1953 Conservatism and personality. American Political Science Review 52: 27–45.

McGranahan, Donald V.
1946 A comparison of social attitudes among American and German youth. Journal of Abnormal and Social Psychology 41:245–257.

McGranahan, Donald V. and I. Wayne
1948 German and American traits reflected in popular drama. Human Relations 1:429–455.

Mead, Margaret
1942 And keep your powder dry. New York, William Morrow.
1951 Soviet attitudes toward authority. New York, McGraw-Hill.

Merriam, Charles E.
1925 New aspects of politics. Chicago, University of Chicago Press. Selections reprinted in H. Eulau, S. J. Eldersveld and M. Janowitz, Political behavior. Glencoe, Ill., Free Press, 1956.

Michels, Robert
1949 Political parties. Translated by Eden and A. Paul. Glencoe, Ill., Free Press.

Mills, Charles W.
1956 The power elite. New York, Oxford University Press.

Moore, Henry T.
1925 Innate factors in radicalism and conservatism. Journal of Abnormal and Social Psychology 20:234–244.

Morris, Charles W.
1942 Paths of life; preface to a world religion. New York, Harper and Bros.

Morris, Charles W.
1956 Varieties of human value. Chicago, University of Chicago Press.

Ortega y Gasset, José
1937 Invertebrate Spain. New York, W. W. Norton.

Peak, Helen
1945 Observations on the characteristics and distribution of German Nazis. Psychological Monographs vol. 59, no. 6, whole no. 276.

Ringer, Benjamin B. and David L. Sills
1952–53 Political extremists in Iran. Public Opinion Quarterly 16:689–701.

Rokeach, Milton
1956 Political and religious dogmatism: an alternative to the authoritarian personality. Psychological Monographs vol. 70, no. 18, whole no. 425.

Schaffner, Bertram H.
1949 Father land: a study of authoritarianism in the German family. New York, Columbia University Press.

Sforza, Carlo
1942 The real Italians: a study in European psychology. New York, Columbia University Press.

SIEGFRIED, ANDRÉ
   1927   America comes of age. New York, Harcourt Brace.
   1930   France: a study in nationality. New Haven, Yale University Press.
   1951   Approaches to an understanding of modern France. *In* Modern France,
          Edward M. Earle, ed. Princeton, Princeton University Press.

SPRANGER, EDUARD
   1928   Types of men. Tübingen, Max Neimeyer, Verlag-halle.

STOETZEL, JEAN
   1955   Without the chrysanthemum and the sword. New York, Columbia
          University Press/UNESCO.

STOODLEY, BARTLETT H.
   1957   Normative attitudes of Filipino youth compared with German and
          American youth. American Sociological Review 22:553–561.

STOUFFER, SAMUEL A.
   1955   Communism, conformity and civil liberties; a cross section of the
          nation speaks its mind. Garden City, N.Y., Doubleday.

TOCQUEVILLE, ALEXIS DE
   1947   Democracy in America. New York and London, Oxford University
          Press.

WALLAS, GRAHAM
   1908   Human nature in politics. London. Selections reprinted in H. Eulau,
          S. J. Eldersveld, and M. Janowitz, Political behavior. Glencoe, Ill., Free
          Press, 1956.

WOLFENSTEIN, M. and N. LEITES
   1950   Movies: a psychological study. Glencoe, Ill., Free Press.

Chapter 7

AMERICAN CORE VALUE AND NATIONAL CHARACTER*

FRANCIS L. K. HSU
Northwestern University

IN APPROACHING the subject of American national character, students have experienced some unusual difficulties. What they have done so far is either to present pictures of contradictions with little or no attempt to reconcile the opposing elements, or to construct models of what, in their view, ought to be, with little or no attempt to deal with what actually occurs. In this chapter I shall try to show that the difficulties are not insurmountable, that the contradictions, though numerous, are more apparent than real, and that, even the models of what ought to be, though different from reality, can be meaningful once we achieve a proper perspective.

A Picture of Contradictions

After comprehensive sampling of the literature from early times down to 1940, Lee Coleman lists the following as "American traits": "associational activity, democracy and belief and faith in it, belief in the equality of all as a fact and as a right, freedom of the individual in ideal and in fact, disregard of law—direct action, local government, practicality, prosperity and general material well-being, puritanism, emphasis on religion and its great influence in national life, uniformity and conformity (Coleman 1941:498).

It is clear at once that this list of traits not only fails to give cognizance to such obvious facts as racial and religious prejudice, but the different traits mutually contradict each other at several points.

---

* This chapter is based on a paper presented at the American Psychological Convention, 1959, Cincinnati, Ohio, as part of a symposium under the chairmanship of Dr. Fred J. Goldstein of Los Angeles Psychiatric Service. I am greatly indebted to Donald T. Campbell, Millard Hoyt, Thomas Gladwin, and Melford Spiro for their valuable criticism of this chapter.

For example, values attached to "local government" and "democracy" are in direct contradiction to that of "disregard of law" leading to "direct action." The beliefs in "equality" and in "freedom" are in direct contradiction to the emphasis on "uniformity and conformity."

Cuber and Harper, writing nearly ten years later in a book entitled *Problems of American Society: Values in Conflict,* have reduced the total number of American values enumerated but not done much else. Their list is as follows: "monogamous marriage, freedom, acquisitiveness, democracy, education, monotheistic religion, freedom and science" (Cuber and Harper 1948:369). Cuber and Harper recognize that some of these values are inconsistent with each other and with social reality. But they attempt to explain such inconsistencies as follows:

On the surface it might seem relatively easy for a society, and especially for some one person, to discover such inconsistencies as these, evaluate the two positions, choose one, and discard the other . . . . But in practice it seems not to be so easy an undertaking. In the first place, logical inconsistency may constitute social consistency—that is, a person whose values seem inconsistent when analysed by a third party may regard himself to be quite consistent. Both values seem to him to be quite tenable because he can point out the other persons in the society as authority for the rightness of each position. (Cuber and Harper 1948:372)

As we shall see later, their explanation contains the germ of truth as to why the individual is not free to act as he sees fit, to make his value orientation more self-consistent, but it has not gone far enough. If every individual adheres to his inconsistent values because he can resort to "other persons in the society as authority for the rightness of each position," then we cannot possibly explain how values in America would ever undergo change, and how some individuals are more affected by the inconsistencies than others, enough for them to espouse certain "causes" and throw their weight behind crusades for emancipation of the slaves or to bust up saloons.

Over the years the analysis of American values has remained stagnant at this level. Thus, in *American Society* Robin Williams again gives us no more than a catalogue of American values as follows: "achievement" and "success," "activity" and "work," "moral orientation," "humanitarian mores," efficiency and practicability, "progress," material comfort, equality, freedom, external conformity, science and secular rationality, nationalism-patriotism, democracy, individual personality, racism and related group-superiority themes. (The quotation marks applied to seven of these values are Williams') (Williams 1951:388–440; 1960:415–470).

Williams does realize, perhaps more than the other authors, that the values are not of equal importance and that they have to be somehow related and reconciled with each other. Accordingly, in his conclusion on value orientation, he makes a summary classification to emphasize some and to de-emphasize others:

a) Quasi values or *gratifications:* such as material comforts.
b) *Instrumental interests* or means values: such as wealth, power, work, and efficiency.
c) *Formal universalistic values of western tradition:* rationalism, impersonal justice; universalistic ethics, achievement, democracy, equality, freedom, certain religious values, and values of individual personality.
d) *Particularistic, segmental or localistic values:* best exemplified in racist-ethnic superiority doctrines and in certain aspects of nationalism (Williams 1951:441; 1960:468–469).

This classification accomplishes little. It is not simply a question of differences between professed values and the actual reality. Such differences are likely to be found in any society. More specifically the question is one of unresolved and unaccounted for differences between certain professed values and other professed values. We may reconcile "efficiency" as a value with the continuous blocking of modern improvements in the building trades as a matter of difference between theory and practice. But how do we reconcile the "value of individual personality" with the oppressive and increasing demand for "conformity"? The most glaring contradiction exists between "equality," "freedom," and so forth on the one hand and "racist-ethnic superiority doctrines and certain aspects of nationalism" on the other. Williams tries to expunge the "ethnic superiority doctrines and so forth" by inaccurately classifying the latter as "particularistic, segmented or localistic values."

It is easy to see how Williams errs here. If the belief in racist-ethnic superiority were truly segmental or localistic (by which I think Williams means that it is particular to the South), how can we explain the racism that is also prevalent in the North? In fact, it has been aptly observed, and I think with some justification, that the only difference between the South and the North in the matter of racial attitudes is that the South is more open and honest about it, while the North is more covert and hypocritical about it. Of course, this view fails to consider the fact that the law by and large still supports racism in some Southern states, while the law is against it in the North. Besides, practically all the broad legislative and judiciary improvements affecting race relations have originated from the North. These legal changes do not, however, erase the widespread social, economic, and other forms of discrimination which are practiced in the North as well as in the South. Furthermore, even if we say that the racist attitude is only characteristic of the South, we must inevitably be confronted with the question: How does the South reconcile its racist attitudes with its professed belief in democracy? Are the North and the South two fundamentally separate cultures?

Some students frankly take the line of least resistance by characterizing the American culture as "Schizoid" (Read Bain 1935: 266–76), or inherently "dualistic," that is to say, full of opposites (Harold J. Laski 1948:738). This is the same sort of conclusion reached by Gunnar Myrdal who, after a mammoth investigation of the Negro-White relations, left the entire matter as *An American Dilemma* (1944). Apart from presenting many factual details on racial discrimination in this society, Myrdal said nothing more than that there is the problem of a psychological conflict between the democratic ideal of equality, on the one hand, and the existing inequalities in race relations, education, income distribution, health benefits, and so forth, on the other. The few anthropologists who have bothered to study American values have hardly improved on this state of affairs. Thus, Kluckhohn expressed himself in 1941 on this subject:

While the relative unanimity over some kind of aid to Britain demonstrates that at least in a crisis a nexus of common purposes is still effective, the diagnostic symptom of the sickness of our society is the lack of a unifying system of canons of choice, emotionally believed in as well as intellectually adhered to. (Kluckhohn 1941:175)

When Kluckhohn gave us his more intensive analysis of the American culture six years later, we can readily understand why his early conclusion on American values was as it was. Because his analysis consists of another list of "orientations" and "suborientations" that are very much in the manner of Robin Williams' treatment detailed above on pages 211 and 212 (Kluckhohn and Kluckhohn 1947).

Thus, our understanding of American values is today no better than it was several decades ago. Periodically we note the conflicts and inconsistencies among the different elements, but we leave them exactly where we started.

An American Blind Spot

I have taken so much time to come to this futile point because I do not wish to be accused of setting up a nonexistent straw man and then, with the flourish of discovery, knock him down.

The reason for this lack of progress in the scientific analysis of value conflicts inherent in American culture is, I believe, to be found in the fact that many Western and especially American scholars have been too emotionally immersed in the absolute goodness of their own form of society, ethic, thought, and religion that it is hard for them to question them, even in scientific analyses. Consequently, they cannot see anything but the eventual triumph of their cultural ideals such as freedom and equality over realities such as racism and religious intolerance. Some frankly see the former as the basic American values and the latter as outright deviations which need not even be considered. This attitude is most decidedly characteristic even of eminent scholars of American history such as Henry Steele Commager. In his book *The American Mind* he practically dismisses the Negro and, in fact, all nonwhites with one sentence:

Nothing in all history had ever succeeded like America, and every American knew it. Nowhere else on the globe had nature been at once so rich and so generous, and her riches were available to all who had the enterprise to take them and the good fortune to be white (1950:5).

I would have regarded the last sentence quoted here to be Commager's satire on the prevailing attitude of the American public, if not for the fact that, in the rest of his 443 pages, he makes no more than a few passing references to the treatment of Negroes (in one of which the word "Oriental" is inserted). Furthermore, in these references, the Negroes might well have been as important as the wayside flowers trampled on by the horses drawing westward wagons driven by white Americans. When Commager comes to twentieth century America, he seems to be most exasperated by the adverse manifestations of the American mind in the form of crime, racial and religious bigotry, lawlessness, irreligion, looseness of sex mores, conformity, class formation, and so forth. He seems so intent upon denying them, yet cannot, that he speaks in the following confusing vein:

All this presented to the student of the American character a most perplexing problem. It was the business of the advertisers to know that character, and their resources enabled them to enlist in its study the aid of the most perspicacious sociologists and psychologists. Yet if their analysis was correct, the American people were decadent and depraved. *No other evidence supported this conclusion.* Advertisers appealed to fear, snobbery, and self-indulgence, yet no one familiar with the American character would maintain that these were indeed its predominant motivations, and statesmen who knew the American people appealed to higher motives, and not in vain. The problem remained a fascinating one, *for if it was clear that advertisers libeled the American character, it was equally clear that Americans tolerated and even rewarded those who libeled them.* (Commager 1944:419; italics mine)

Besides its obvious one-sidedness (for example, his statement that "the statesmen who knew the American people appealed to higher motives, and not in vain" is about as true as another which reads, "the statesmen who knew the American people appealed to *baser* motives, and not in vain,"), Commager contradicts himself badly. Unable to deny the reality of facts uncovered by scientists, facts which are used profitably by advertisers, yet unable to bring himself to see them in their true perspective, he solved his academic dilemma by branding the facts as "libel."

Gordon Allport commits the same error in his book *The Nature of Prejudice.* In its entire 519 pages Allport theorizes about mankind and religion, but his mankind is Western mankind (where he occasionally refers to Negroes and Orientals, he is merely speaking about to what different extents the different Western groups reject them), and by religion he means Protestantism, Catholicism, and Judaism, with nothing even about Eastern Orthodoxy and one sentence on Islam. Limited by such a culture-bound framework Allport is not unnaturally inconsistent (1954). In discussing racial prejudice, Allport relies heavily on experimental psychology. There is a great deal of evidence that the more prejudiced personality tends to be one which is more in need of definiteness and more moralistic. For example, "he is uncomfortable with differentiated categories; he prefers them to be monopolistic" (Allport 1954:175, 398–408). Here Allport apparently accepts the conclusion to which his evidence leads him. However, in connection with religious bigotry Allport seems to adopt a different procedure altogether. Here he first admits that religions which claim to possess final truths are bound to lead to conflicts, and that individuals who have no religious affiliations tend to show less prejudice than do church members. But these are, in his words, too "distressing" to him and so demands "closer inspection" (Allport 1954:451).

To the student, what Allport means by "closer inspection" turns out to be a surprise, for Allport departs from the acceptable principle of science by purposely attempting to negate stronger evidences in favor of much flimsier facts. He admits that, quantitatively, the correlation between greater church affiliation and greater prejudice is correct, but he also insists that it is not correct because there are "many cases" where the influence of the church "is in the reverse dirction" (Allport 1954:451). In other words, Allport finds the evidences too distressing because they show the Christian churches and the Christian values in an unfavorable light. He simply cannot tolerate the fact that the absolutist Christian faith and the exclusive Christian church membership do lead to greater prejudice. Under the circumstances, Allport has no alternative but to throw overboard the quantitative evidence in favor of some qualitative statements.

Yet even so sophisticated a social scientist as Lloyd Warner is no exception. In his book *American Life, Dream and Reality* he finds the Jonesville *grade school* children's evaluation of one another to be so strongly reflective of social-class values as to blind them to the actual reality (for example, children from the top classes were rated 22 times cleaner than those from the bottom, but in fact the latter as a whole came to school cleaner and neater than the former). However, he also finds that the Jonesville *high school* children, though following a similar pattern, do not make such categorical and rigid judgments by class values. Warner's explanations of this difference are most revealing:

Since the older children are presumably more the products of their culture than the younger ones, there appears to be a contradiction here. . . . Actually, the reasons for the differences in judgment help verify our hypothesis. The children in the high school, being products of American society, have learned to be less open and more careful about what they say and how they feel on the tabooed subject of status. *Furthermore, they have learned to use American values of individualism and are able to make clearer discriminations about the worth of an individual than are the younger children.* (Warner 1953:182–3; italics mine)

The interesting thing is that Warner's second explanation here not only contradicts the one preceding it but contradicts his entire thesis, which is that social class values strongly influence American behavior and ideas. It is as though this second explanation came out by accident, perhaps a Freudian slip of his research pen, for in sentiments like "the worth of the individual" many Americans find real emotional security.

What we have to see is that in the minds of a majority of our scholars the idea of democracy and Christianity, with their respective attributes of freedom and equality in one case and of love and mercy in the other, are the over-all American values par excellence. They are so consciously upheld that all explanations of American behavior must somehow begin and end with it. Any evidence contrary to this mold is therefore treated as deviation or as "regional phenomena," as "libel," as creating a "schizoid" situation, a "dilemma." This in my view is the blind spot to many of our Western social scientists today. Given this blind spot, our scientists have consistently confused what ought to be with what is. It leads many scholars to explain the kind of American behavior they deem desirable by one theory, and another kind of American behavior, which they abhor and which contradicts the first kind, by another and contradictory theory. Some even misuse the eclectic approach by pleading the multiplicity of correlates or causation in complex human affairs.

The fundamental axiom of science is to explain more and more facts by fewer and fewer theories. Anyone can explain all characteristics of a given situation with as many different theories, but his explanation will not be of value as a piece of work of science. It might be close to a factual description. Or it might be close to fantasy or rationalization. The axiom of explaining more and more facts by fewer and fewer theories is especially crucial if the facts are obviously related, as when they occur in the same organized society and often among and in the same individuals.

Once this is admitted it becomes obvious that, when confronted with contradictions in the object of his inquiry, the scientist's first duty is, instead of trying to treat them as discrete entities and explaining them with contradictory hypotheses, to explore the possibility of a link between the contradictory phenomena. In doing so the scientist is not presuming that values in any given society must be totally consistent with each other and that all contradictions must be resolved. It is perfectly possible that many societies, being large and complex, have inconsistent or contradictory values. But what our scientists so far would seem to fail or even refuse to do is to concede even the possibility of any positive connection between these contradictory values.

Self-Reliance, Fear of Dependency, and Insecurity

What we need to see is that the contradictory American "values" noted by the sociologists, psychologists, and historians are but manifestations of one core value. Furthermore, many scholars must have been aware of this core value in one way or another but, because of their blind spot, have failed to recognize its importance. The American core value in question is *self-reliance*, the most persistent psychological expression of which is the fear of dependence. It can be shown that all of the "values" enumerated thus far, the mutually contradictory ones and the mutually supportive ones, the evil ones as well as the angelic ones, spring or are connected with self-reliance.

American self-reliance is basically the same as English individualism except that the latter is the parent of the former while the former has gone farther than the latter. However, self-reliance possesses no basic characteristics which were not inherent in individualism. Individualism developed in Europe as a demand for political equality. It insists that every individual has inalienable and God-given political rights which other men cannot take away and that every man has equal right to govern himself or choose his own governors. Self-reliance, on the other hand, has been inseparable in America from the individual's militant insistence on economic, social, and political equality. The result is while a qualified individualism, with a qualified equality, has prevailed in England and the rest of Europe, what has been considered the inalienable right of every American is an unlimited self-reliance and an unlimited equality.

It is not suggested here that all Americans do in fact possess the unlimited economic and social equality in which they firmly believe. But it is easy to observe how strongly and widely the belief in them manifests itself. For example, the English have been able to initiate a sort of socialism in reality, as well as in name, but Americans, regardless of social security, farm subsidies, and other forms of government planning, intervention, and assistance, are as firmly as ever committed to the idea of free enterprise and deeply intolerant toward other social systems. Similarly, the English still tend to respect class-based distinctions in wealth, status manners, and language, while Americans tend to ridicule aristocratic manners or Oxford speech, and resent status so much that Lloyd Warner, for example, describes it as being a "tabooed" subject in discussing Jonesville high school students. Finally, the English still consider the crown a symbol of all that is best and hereditary, Americans criticize the personal taste of their highest officials and at least have the common verbal expression that everybody can be president.

This self-reliance is also very different from self-sufficiency. Any Chinese or European village can achieve self-sufficiency as a matter of fact. The average self-sufficient Chinese farmer will have no feeling whatever about other people who are not self-sufficient. But American self-reliance is a militant ideal which parents inculcate in their children and by which they judge the worth of any and all mankind. This is the self-reliance about which Ralph Waldo Emerson has written so eloquently and convincingly in some immortal pieces. This is also the self-reliance taught in today's American schools. The following is a direct quotation from a statement of "basic beliefs" given to the students by the social science department of one of the nation's best high schools in 1959:

Self-reliance is, as it has always been, the key to individual freedom, and the only real security comes from the ability and the determination to work hard, to plan, and to save for the present and the future.[1]

American self-reliance is then not new. As a concept it is in fact well known and well understood. Yet such is the power of the blind spot that its over-all and basic importance has so far escaped our scientific attention. How the individualism of Western Europe has been transformed into American self-reliance is a question outside the scope of this paper. It has been dealt with elsewhere (Hsu 1953:111–114). Suffice it to say here that under this ideal every individual is his own master, in control of his own destiny, and will advance and regress in society only according to his own efforts. He may have good or bad breaks but,

> Smile and the world smiles with you,
> Cry and you cry alone.

It is, of course, obvious that not all Americans are self-reliant. No ideal of any society is uniformly manifested in all its members. But a brief comparison will make the point clearer. A man in traditional China with no self-reliance as an ideal may not have been successful in his life. But suppose in his old age his sons are able to provide for him generously. Such a person not only will be happy and content about it, but is likely also to beat the drums before all and sundry to let the world know that he has good children who are supporting him in a style to which he has never been accustomed. On the other hand, an American parent who has not been successful in life may derive some benefit from the prosperity of

---

[1] A mimeographed sheet issued to its pupils by a school in the Greater Chicago area, 1959.

his children, but he certainly will not want anybody to know about it. In fact, he will resent any reference to it. At the first opportunity when it is possible for him to become independent of his children he will do so.

Therefore, even though we may find many individuals in traditional China and elsewhere who are in fact self-sufficient, and even though we may find individuals in America who are in fact dependent upon others, the important thing is to realize that where self-reliance is not an ideal, it is neither promoted nor a matter of pride, but where it is an ideal, it is both. In American society the fear of dependence is so great that an individual who is not self-reliant is an object of hostility and called a misfit. "Dependent character" is a highly derogatory term, and a person so described is thought to be in need of psychiatric help.

However, it is obvious that no individual can be completely self-reliant. In fact, the very foundation of the human way of life is man's dependence upon his fellow men without which we shall have no law, no custom, no art, no science, and not even language. It is not meant that an individual human being cannot be trained, from the beginning of his life, to form no relationship with any fellow human being. But if an individual wishes to lead a human existence, in this society or any other, he is bound to be dependent upon his fellow human beings intellectually and technologically as well as socially and emotionally. Individuals may have differing degrees of needs for their fellow human beings, but no one can truly say that he needs no one. It seems that the basic American value orientation of self-reliance, by its denial of the importance of other human beings in ones' life, creates contradictions and therefore serious problems, the most uniquitious of which is insecurity.

This insecurity presents itself to the individual American in a variety of ways. Its most important ingredient is the lack of permanency both in ones' ascribed relationships (such as those of the family into which one is born) and in one's achieved relationships (such as marital relationship for a woman and business partnership for a man). Its most vital demand on the individual is to motivate him in a perpetual attempt to compete with his fellow human beings, to belong to status-giving groups, and, as a means of achieving these ends, to submit to the tyranny of organization and to conform to the customs and fads of the peer group which are vital to his climbing and/or status position at any given time and place. In other words, in order to live up to their core value orientation of self-reliance, Americans as a whole have to do much of its opposite. Expressed in the jargon of science, there is, for example, a direct relationship between self-reliance and individual freedom on the one hand and submission to organization and conformity on the other (Hsu 1960:151). Exactly the same force can be seen to link:

  a) Christian love with religious bigotry.
  b) Emphasis on science, progress, and humanitarianism with parochialism, group-superiority themes and racism.
  c) Puritan ethics with increasing laxity in sex mores.
  d) Democratic ideals of equality and freedom with totalitarian tendencies and witch hunting.

These four pairs of contradictions are not exclusive of each other. For example, Christian love is in sharp contrast with racism as with religious bigotry. Similarly emphasis on science, and so forth, is as opposed to totalitarian tendencies and witch hunting as to parochialism and group superiority themes. In fact, we can contrast the first half of any of the above pairs with the second half of any other.

Christian Love versus Christian Hate

For the purpose of this paper we shall consider some of these contradictions in a composite whole: the American emphasis on Christian love, and freedom, equality, and democracy on the one hand, and racism and religious bigotry on the other. This is a contradiction which has tested the energy of some of the best euphemistic orators and the ingenuity of some of the most brilliant scholars. Especially in the religious area they try to write off the religious wars. They try to forget about the Holy Inquisitions. They try to ignore the hundreds of thousands of witches convicted and burned on the stake. They try to deny any connection between any of these and the Nazi Germany slaughter of the Jews, especially the anti-Semitism, anti-intellectualism, and racial persecution found, here covertly and there openly, in the United States. But when some scholars do realize that the past patterns are very much alive at present, though the specific techniques have changed, they tend to make harmless observations of which the following is a typical example:

> Worship in common—the sharing of the symbols of religion—has united human groups in the closest ties known to man, yet religious differences have helped to account for some of the fiercest group antagonisms. (Elizabeth K. Nottingham 1954:2)

Williams, who quotes the above passage, goes a little further by suggesting two clues to the riddle as to why some worship in common has united people and some has divided them: (a) "Not all conflicts in the name of organized religion are actually "religious" and (b) there may be different degrees of involved commitment actually at work in "nominal religious affiliations" (Robin M. Williams 1956:14–15). But there is no observable basis for distinction between "true" religious conflict and religious conflicts which are only nominally religious. Are theological controversies purely religious or nominally religious? The truth is that, even if the conflict is over nothing but liturgy, or over the question of virgin birth, they are still fought between human beings each with personal, emotional involvements in specific issues.

Williams' second clue is a more sound one. Put it differently, this is that the more "involved commitment" actually at work in nominal religious affiliations the more religious dissension and bigotry there will be. Since the stronger one's commitment to an object or issue the more inflexible this commitment becomes, it is natural that more "involved commitment" will lead to more dissension and bigotry. Certain data quoted by Allport, referred to before, directly support this proposition.[2] It is interesting to note that Williams, after stating this proposition, dismisses it as "extreme." Instead he collects a conglomeration of twenty divergencies in value—orientation which, he believes but does not demonstrate, are partially the basis of religious conflicts in the United States (Williams 1956: 14–17).

It is unnecessary to probe into the reasons why Williams attaches so little significance to his second clue. It is also beyond the scope of this paper to detail the irrelevancy of some of his "divergencies" to this problem on hand. We can, however, indicate how the link be-

---

[2] "Over four hundred students were asked the question, 'To what degree has religion been an influence in your upbringing?' Lumping together those who report that religion was a marked or moderate factor, we find the degree of prejudice far higher than among those who report that religion was a slight or non-existent factor in their training. Other studies reveal that individuals having no religious affiliation show on the average less prejudice than do church members." (Allport 1954:451)

And again, "First, it is well to be clear concerning the existence of certain natural, and perhaps unresolvable, conflicts inherent in various aspects of religion.

"Take first the claim of certain great religions—that each has absolute and final possession of Truth. People who adhere to different absolutes are not likely to find themselves in agreement. The conflict is most acute when missionaries are actively engaged in proselytizing divergent sets of absolutes. Moslem and Christian missionaries in Africa, for example, have long been at odds. Each insists that if its creed were completely realized in practice, it would eliminate all ethnic barriers between men. So it would. But in actuality, the absolutes of any one religion have never yet been accepted by more than a fraction of mankind.

"Catholicism by its very nature must believe that Judaism and Protestantism are in error. And varieties of Judaism and Protestantism feel keenly that other varieties of their own faith are perverse in many points of belief." (Allport 1954:444–445)

tween the degree of involved commitment in nominal religious affiliations and the extent of dissension and bigotry is the source of the
contradiction: Christian love versus Christian hate. It is not hard
for the trained social scientist to note that religious affiliation in the
United States today has become so largely a matter of associational
affiliation that "the values that inhere in group affiliation and participation" far and above overshadow "the specific values espoused"
by the religious body (Williams 1956:17). The overwhelming proof
of this is to be found in well-known works such as the Lynds' on
"Middle Town" and Lloyd Warner and associates on "Yankee City"
and "Jonesville,"[3] but particularly in the results of a poll of 100,000
Protestant ministers in all parts of the United States by the *Christian Century* magazine in 1951, to determine the "outstanding" and
most "successful" churches. This poll showed twelve to be the
chosen ones. One of the twelve was the First Presbyterian Church
of Hollywood.

The applauded "qualities" of this church have been analyzed elsewhere (Hsu 1953:273–277). Suffice it to say here that the "successful qualities" of this church seem to be that the "happiness" of the
parishioners revolves about the social and material endeavors which
rebound to their benefit alone but that the spiritual faith and the
quality of the ministers' teachings receive practically no attention.

All this is understandable once we appreciate the persistent demands that the core American value of self-reliance makes on the
individual. The churches must compete and, in order to exist and to
be "successful," must satisfy the status quest of its members. To
achieve that "success," the churches not only have to conform to
the trend toward organization, but they must try to find new ways
of increasing their memberships so as to reach greater "successes."

In this psychology we can now find the common ground between
religious bigotry and racial prejudice. Western religious dissensions
have been associated with many things but their principal and perennial feature has been the search for original purity in ritual and
belief. The Reformation was based on it. The entire evolution of
Protestantism from the Lutheran church to Quakerism has had it
as the central ingredient. The Holy Inquisition was instituted to
ferret out impurity in Christian thought and practice. This fervent

---

[3] Commenting on religion George C. Homans says: "We are apt to think that the choice
of a church among people brought up in the Protestant tradition is a matter of individual
conscience. No doubt it is. But it is certainly also true that the membership of churches, in
Hilltown as in Boston, tended to correlate roughly with that of certain social groups" (1950:346).

search for and jealous guard over purity expresses itself in the racial scene as the fear of genetic mixing of races which feeds the segregationist power in the North as well as in the South, no matter what rhetoric and other logic are employed. When religious affiliations have become largely social affiliations, this fear of impurity makes religious and racial prejudices undistinguishable. Religion is not the question. The point of the greatest importance is affiliation. The neighborhoods and clubs are as exclusive as the churches and church activities tend to be, in spite of all protestation of equality, democracy, worth of the individual, Christian love, and humility.

The individual who is enjoined to be self-reliant, unlike one who is taught to respect authority and external barriers, has no permanent place in his society. Everything is subject to change without notice. He is always anxious to look above for possible openings to climb, but he is at the same time and constantly threatened from below by possible upward encroachment. In his continuous effort at status achieving and maintaining, the self-reliant man fears nothing more than contamination by fellow human beings who are deemed inferior to him. This contamination can come about in diverse forms: sharing the same desks at the same schools, being dwellers of the same apartments, worshipping in the same churches, sitting in the same clubs, or being in any situation of free and equal contact.

In this context, as in others, individuals will vary in the extent to which they are pressed by the fear of inferiority. Some will join hate organizations, lynching mobs, and throw stones at Negro residences or paint swastikas on Jewish synagogues. These are violent acts of prejudice. Others will do everything they legally or by devious means can do to keep individuals of certain religious, racial, or ethnic groups out of residential areas, certain occupations, and social fraternities. These are active nonviolent acts of prejudices. Still others will quietly refuse to associate with members of religious, racial, or ethnic minorities and teach their children to observe this taboo because one just does not do such things. These are passive nonviolent acts of prejudice.

Under such circumstances many, perhaps most, individuals find it impossible to act in the same way as they have professed and been taught. It is not that they love contradiction or that they are, according to their critics, hypocritical. It is simply that they are oppressed by fears for losing satus—fears deeply rooted in a relatively free society with a core value of self-reliance. This is also why integration of minorities, be they racial or religious, cannot reach a satisfactory destination either along the line of total assimilation into the majority way of life or along that of pluralism. There is some factual indication that Jewish youngsters who are raised as non-Jews have a much harder time to adjust to their peers in college than those who have been raised consciously and militantly to cultivate their identity in Judaic tradition and church life. In other words, their complete identity and assimilation as Americans is always subject to rejection (Samuel Teitelbaum 1953).[4] On the other hand, the rationalization in support of anti-Oriental legislation was that the Oriental standard of living was too low and that they were incapable of assimilation to the American way of life.

A reverse proof of the hypothesis advanced in this paper is not hard to find. We have only to look at societies where obedience to authority and dependence relationship are encouraged and where the individual is not subject to such pressures coming with self-reliance and, therefore, more sure of his place in society. Individuals in such societies tend to have much less need for competition, status seeking, conformity, and, hence, racial and religious prejudices. For example, religious dissentions, persecutions, and conflicts have always been prominent in the West as they have alway been rare in the Orient. In Japan and China, the few occasions on which religious persecutions took place were invariably of short duration, always tied to the insecurity of political rule and never involved masses of the people except as temporary mobs (Hsu 1953:246–248). The case of Hindu-Moslem violence and casteism in India is considered elsewhere (Hsu 1961). Again, religious dissensions, per-

---

[4] This is based on two groups of answers to a questionnaire. The first group of answers was from 230 Northwestern University students in 1951 of whom 210 were undergraduates. A condensed version of the same questionnaire was sent to a random sampling of 730 undergraduates at nine midwestern universities and colleges in 1952–53, from which 325 undergraduates responded. The results, though quantitatively inconclusive, are qualitatively suggestive. First, students of Jewish background experience relatively little anti-Semitism at high school level when mixed dates are frequent, but at the university level their social contacts bcome much less diversified. Second, there is more open identification with Jewish culture and institution as the generation of Americanization advances. That is to say, the second and third generation American Jews tend to be more openly Jewish than the fresh immigrants or first generation Americans. Coupled with this, Jewish students from families of higher social statuses (such as proprietary and professional) show more open identification than those from families of lower social statuses (such as sales). Third, in spite of these facts, students of Jewish background do not seem to prefer exclusive Jewish friendship and association in college. Fourth, with the term "normal adjustment" meaning acceptance by Gentile students, "the conscious (but not self-conscious) and self-identifying Jews among the students are those most integrated with their own people and the most normally adjusted on the college or university campus" (209). These results correspond amazingly to my personal observations but any final conclusion on the subject must, of course, await further research.

secutions, and racial conflicts are today more intense and widespread in Protestant-dominated societies of the West (see Chapter 14) than in their Catholic counterparts. In this dichotomy we are contrasting the United States, Canada, Australia, Union of South Africa, and so forth, as one camp and the Latin American republics, as well as Portuguese, Belgian, and French African possessions as the other. What has happened in Protestant-dominated societies is that, by and large, persecution in the form of bloody racial and religious outbreaks has been consistently driven underground while the manifestations of prejudice have become diffused, one almost may say democratized if not for the fact that the expression smells of sarcasm. But even in the most advanced Protestant societies racial and religious violence is always around the corner, ready to erupt now and then, here and there, as indicated by the recent anti-Negro outbreaks in England and the recurrent anti-Semitic flare-ups in Europe and the United States.[5]

Three Uses of Value

It will have been clear to some readers that this analysis of the psychosocial origin of racial and religious prejudices bears some resemblance to that of Kurt Lewin on the problems of the Jews as a minority group in many a western society. But it has significant differences. According to Lewin the most basic problem of the Jews is that of group identity. Often repudiated in the country of his birth and upbringing, yet having no homeland which he can claim as his own, he suffers from "additional uncertainty," thus "giving" him "some quality of abnormality in the opinion of the surrounding groups." He concludes that the establishment of a Jewish homeland in Palestine (which was not yet a reality at the time of his writing) might "affect the situation of Jews everywhere in the direction of greater normality" (Kurt Lewin 1935:175–187).

The Jewish minority certainly shares the central problem, with other minorities, of uncertainty of group identity. But our analysis also shows that the degree of this uncertainty depends, in the first place, on the basic value orientation of the host majority and, in the second place, on that of the minority groups themselves. There is, for example, every reason to expect the Jewish minority to have far less of a problem of identity in Latin American countries than in North American countries. As far as North America is con-

---

[5] The place of Mohammedanism with reference to this analysis will be considered in another publication.

cerned, the Jews, like other minority groups, will always have the problem of identity whether or not they have a homeland. The Latin American peoples have less of the value orientation of self-reliance and, therefore, the individual has less psychosocial need to reject minority groups to maintain his status in society. On the other hand, within the United States, there is good reason to expect the Jewish minority to have a little more of a problem of identity than the Chinese and Japanese minorities even after the establishment of Israel. This is despite the fact that the Orientals possess much greater physical distinctiveness than the Jews as a whole from the Caucasoid majority. For the Chinese and Japanese have stronger ties with their families and wider kin groups than do the Jews, and are, therefore, less self-reliant and less free but more protected from the uncertainty of identity.

In this chapter I have not differentiated the different uses to which the term value may be put. Charles Morris, in a book entitled *Varieties of Human Value,* postulated three such uses: "Operative" values refer to the "actual direction of preferential behavior toward one kind of object rather than another." "Conceived" values refers to the "preferential behavior directed by 'an anticipation or foresight of the outcome' of such behavior," and "involves preference for a symbolically indicated object." He illustrates this meaning of value by the example of the drug addict who firmly believes that it is better not to be a drug addict because "he anticipates the outcome of not using drugs." "Object" values refer not to the behavior preferred in fact (operative value) or as symbolically desired (conceived value) but to what is preferable if the holder of the value is to achieve certain ends or objectives (1956:10–12).

While it is obvious that the three usages of the term "value" are not mutually exclusive and must influence each other, it is equally obvious that they are not hard to distinguish. Applying this scheme to the American scene we shall realize that self-reliance is an operative value as well as a conceived value. It expresses itself in two directions. In the positive direction it expresses itself as the emphasis on freedom, equality in economic and political opportunities for all, Puritan virtues, Christian love, and humanitarianism. These values are far more conceived than operative. On the negative side self-reliance expresses itself as the tendency toward racial prejudice, religious bigotry, laxity in sex mores, and totalitarianism. These values are far more operative than conceived. Values which are more conceived than operative are of great symbolic importance, and will be militantly defended by the people cherishing them. The less they live up to such conceived values the more they are likely to defend them, because their failures are associated with feelings of guilt. Values which are more operative than conceived are of great practical importance, and will be strenuously pursued by the people needing them. The more they have to act according to such operative values, the less they will admit their reality, since their actions also lead to feelings of guilt. At one extreme we shall find men who will openly fight to guard these operative values most flagrantly. At the other extreme we shall find men who will practice them by devious means. Those who hold on to these operative values openly and those who do so by subterfuge will share one common characteristic: both will deny their actions are motivated by prejudice and Christian hate. They will both insist that their actions are based totally on other reasons. In the South one ubiquitous reason is states' rights. In the North a widespread reason is property value or fear of intermarriage. When the real operative values are divulged accidentally, as it were, by one of those who share them, the reaction of the rest will be resentment against the simpleton who spoke out of turn and angry denial of everything he disclosed. These mechanisms are repeated so often on so many occasions, including the most recent (1959–60) Deerfield and Park Forest, Illinois, outbursts, that they need no further illustration or elaboration.

However, the ideas of equality, freedom, and Christian love inevitably affect all Americans because they are values that are conceived more than operative. They might even be described as the conscience of the American society. That is why failure to live according to them or outright opposition to them will both lead to guilt, denial, and subterfuge. There are men and women who champion the cause of the more conceived values just as those who desperately cling to and fight for the more operative values. The attitude of both sides toward their respective values tends to turn the values they champion into object values. That is to say, the champions of equality, freedom, and Christian love can consciously use their values as tools for their ends, just as the champions of prejudice, bigotry, and Christian hate can also consciously use their values as tools for their ends.

In the hands of some politicians and all demagogues the relationship between these values and the objects they desire often becomes transparently clear and undisguisedly selfish. It has been suggested that Hitler's hate campaign against the Jews was a major secret of his power. It is not surprising, therefore, that in the recent (1959–60) Chicago area integration outbursts, as with similar scenes elsewhere before, the opponents to integration charged their adversaries for promoting integration as a means of wooing Negro votes. But the link between the more conceived American values and the more operative values is the core American value of self-reliance. The supporters of both desire social arrangements in which their own particular nests will be feathered in their own particular ways.

As the emphasis on democratic equality and freedom and Christian love increases with self-reliance, totalitarian racial prejudice and bigotry and Christian hate will also increase with it. When the individual is shorn of all permanent and reliable moorings among his fellowmen, his only security must come from personal success, personal superiority, and personal triumph. Those who are fortunate enough to achieve success, superiority, and triumph will, of course, bask in the sunshine. To them democratic equality and freedom and Christian love are extremely laudable. But success, superiority, and triumph on the part of some must of necessity be based on the failure, inferiority, and defeat on the part of others. For the latter, and even for some of those who are in the process of struggling for success, superiority, and triumph, the resentment against and fear of failure, inferiority, and defeat must be widespread and often unbearable. To them totalitarian prejudice and bigotry and Christian hate can be means to a flitting security. By pushing others down they at least achieve the illusion of personal success, personal superiority, and personal triumph.[6]

The Problem of Pessimism

If the conclusions of this analysis seem to lend themselves to pessimistic inferences, I wish to assure the readers that this is neither intentional nor desired. But the rule of science is that we must contemplate whatever conclusions our evidences lead us to, whether they are pleasant or unpleasant.

In attentuation of certain pessimistic notes in the conclusions reached we need, however, to realize that the contribution of Western self-reliance to human development has been great and that even the chains of conformity and organization have their salutary

---

[6] Additional substantiation for this analysis is found in Carl J. Friedrick (ed.), *Totalitarianism*, which contains the results of a conference of scholars in 1953 under the auspices of the American Academy of Arts and Sciences. Its conclusion is that totalitarianism is a new disease peculiar to *modern* culture. *Modern* culture here refers, of course, to Western culture.

aspects. What gave the Western man his superiority over the rest of the world during the last 300 years was not his religion or his romanticism but his self-reliance and his competitive organization. It was his self-reliance which led him to discard the shackles of paternal authority, monarchical power, and medieval magic, in favor of wider organizations such as church and state, mercantile fleets, and industrial ventures. When the West met the East, it was the Western man's well-organized armed might which crushed the East. As late as 1949 one high-ranking United States official attributed civil war-torn China's plight, in a *Harper's* magazine article, to the fact that the Chinese were "organizationally corrupt." It is instructive to note that today, the two giants of the West, the U.S.A. and U.S.S.R., are still most attractive to the rest of the world by their skill in organization. In various parts of the world their experts are helping peoples of other nations to organize their educational systems, or their marketing arrangements, or their agricultural practices, or their industrial efforts, or their military capabilities, or their national finances.[7]

The purpose of this paper is neither optimistic nor pessimistic. It is to place the much-lauded American values in their proper genetic perspective. When this is done, we find that the best of America is directly linked with her worst, like Siamese twins. The way out of the worst is not to deny it but to recognize it for what it is.

---

[7] The problem of why some individuals assume some aspects of the value orientation of their society more than other aspects is outside of the scope of this chapter. That problem is treated intensively in the works of Mering (1961), Kluckhohn and Strodbeck (1961), and others.

BIBLIOGRAPHY

ALLPORT, GORDON
  1954 The nature of prejudice. Cambridge, Addison-Wesley Publishing Company, Inc.
BAIN, READ
  1935 Our schizoid culture. Sociology and Social Research 19:266–276.
COLEMAN, LEE
  1941 What is American: a study of alleged American traits. Social Forces, Vol. XIX, No. 4.
COMMAGER, HENRY STEELE
  1950 The American mind. New Haven, Yale University Press.
CUBER, JOHN F. and ROBERT A. HARPER
  1948 Problems of American society: values in conflict. New York, Henry Holt & Co.
FRIEDRICK, CARL J. (ed.)
  1954 Totalitarianism. Cambridge, Mass., Harvard University Press.

HOMANS, GEORGE C.
  1950   The human group. New York, Harcourt Brace & Co.
HSU, FRANCIS L. K.
  1953   Americans and Chinese: two ways of life. New York, Abelard-Schuman, Inc.
  1960   Rugged individualism reconsidered. The Colorado Quarterly 9:143–162.
  1961   Clan, caste and club: a comparative study of Chinese, Hindu, and American ways of life. Princeton, N.J., Van Nostrand Co.
KLUCKHOHN, CLYDE
  1941   The way of life. Kenyon Review, Spring, pp. 160–180.
KLUCKHOHN, CLYDE and FLORENCE R. KLUCKHOHN
  1947   American culture: generalized orientation and class pattern, Chapter IX of Conflicts of power in modern culture, 1947 Symposium of Conference in Science, Philosophy and Religion, New York, Harper and Bros.
KLUCKHOHN, FLORENCE and FRED STRODBECK
  1961   Variations in value-orientations. Evanston, Ill., Row Peterson and Co.
LASKI, HAROLD J.
  1948   The American democracy. New York, The Viking Press.
LEWIN, KURT
  1948   Psycho-sociological problems of a minority group, *In* Character and Personality, Vol. III, 1935, 175–187. (Reprinted in Kurt Lewin: Resolving Social Conflicts, New York, Harper & Bros.)
MERING, OTTO VON
  1961   A grammar of human values. Pittsburgh, University of Pittsburgh Press.
MORRIS, CHARLES
  1956   Varieties of human value. Chicago, University of Chicago Press.
MYRDAL, GUNNAR
  1944   An American dilemma. New York, Harper & Bros.
NOTTINGHAM, ELIZABETH K.
  1954   Religion and society. New York, Doubleday & Co.
TEITELBAUM, SAMUEL
  1953   Patterns of adjustment among Jewish students. Northwestern University, Ph.D., dissertation.
WARNER, LLOYD
  1953   American life: dream and reality. Chicago, University of Chicago Press.
WILLIAMS, ROBIN M.
  1951   American society, a sociological interpretation. New York, Alfred Knopf. (1960, 2d ed.).
  1956   Religion, value-orientations, and intergroup conflict. The Journal of Social Issues 12:14–15.

INTRODUCTION TO PART II

METHODS AND TECHNIQUES

Two PROJECTIVE instruments, the Rorschach and the Thematic Apperception Test, have practically become standard stock-in-trade of many anthropologists. However, the popularity of projective tests in anthropological studies has waned greatly in the last few years. All sorts of objections and doubts have been raised about their cross-cultural validity, or their validity as an instrument of studying anything other than individual differences, or, among psychologists, even their validity for their original purpose of diagnosing individual maladjustment.

Being the editor of two volumes containing Rorschach and TAT protocols collected by anthropologists from many parts of the world, and having intensively used the Rorschach as an instrument in the anthropological field situation, Kaplan is perhaps the most qualified psychologist to analyse the role of projective testing in psychological anthropology. Kaplan considers the merits or demerits of projective testing in psychological anthropology from two broad aspects. The first aspect is more general and concerns the efficiency of projective instruments in fathoming personality. It is understood that no projective test, by itself, pretends to be a complete measure of personality. But there are indications that the Rorschach or any other single projective test may add little to the description of a personality beyond that provided by life history materials and observation studies. On the other hand, it is clear that, since all individuals must live as members of social groups, the most important things are not the total psychological characteristics of an individual but his functioning or "socially required" motivational characteristics. It is the latter characteristics which the tests, in conjunction with other sources of data, help to reveal, and which are the primary concern of the psychological anthropologist.

The other aspect of Kaplan's chapter is concerned with several specific problems in the cross-cultural use of the Rorschach (and in a secondary way other tests) by psychological anthropologists. For example, the average number of Javanese responses to the Rorschach cards is very much larger than that of Thai responses, and so forth. How do we interpret such differences? Another problem Kaplan deals with is the possibly greater importance of the content of Rorschach responses than of the formal characteristics in the traditional scoring procedures.

Wallace's chapter will surely spearhead a renewed interest among anthropologists in the physical and biological factors in abnormal behavior. For many decades the anthropologist, like the psychiatrist, has tended to favor environmental rather than genetic determinants; and within the environmental, to favor almost exclusively social rather than physical determinants. Wallace spells out the philosophy underlying a new organic approach to mental illness and points the way to a possible synthesis between this and the functional approach which has dominated the psychosocial tradition in psychiatry and the social sciences. In this trail blazing effort, Wallace explores one of the well-known yet most puzzling of mental illnesses found among Polar Eskimos: *Pibloktoq,* sometimes translated as arctic hysteria, with two alternative hypotheses—one based on calcium deficiency and the other on the Eskimo cultural pattern of withdrawal when the individual's confidence in his own ability to carry out a struggle is shaken. In the last part of his chapter Wallace constructs one of the most sophisticated models of the intricate relationships between type of organic illness, the victim and his society's responses to the illness, and the culture of the victim and his society.

Man's attempt at reading dreams goes back as far as any cultural records, but his scientific understanding of the phenomenon is of very recent origin. Have dreams influenced the development of human thought? What do we know about universal symbolism in dreams? What are some of the interpretations of dreams in non-Western cultures? Are cultural differences correlated with differences in types of dreams? What is the significance of the diverse attitudes and practices regarding dreams in different cultures? These are questions dealt with in D'Andrade's chapter on dreams. The foundation of modern scientific dream study remains Freudian in theory: that dreams reveal some motivational characteristics of the individual which are otherwise hidden, but the Freudian view that dream language is obscure is largely giving way to the view, based on much modern research, that the most important contents of dreams tend to be manifest. The last part of D'Andrade's chapter deals with the conditions affecting dream usages. Here he summarizes the results of his own cross-cultural study of the relationship between presence or absence of the anxiety about being alone and involvements with particular types of use of dreams.

Campbell gives us a summary, from the point of view of a social psychologist, of two outstanding anthropological contributions to personality psychology: cultural relativism and the human "laboratory" situation. But the major purpose of Campbell's chapter is to outline some of the important methodological issues in anthropological research so far as he sees them, and to offer suggestions regarding alternative procedures. Some anthropologists may regard some of Campbell's indictments as being unfair. Some may object to some of Campbell's methodological suggestions on the ground that he wants us to fly before we can crawl. Others may not share to the same extent Campbell's enthusiasm for the Whiting and Child approach, represented in Chapter 10 by D'Andrade and explained in Chapter 12 by Whiting himself. But there is no doubt that Campbell has put his fingers on a number of methodological problems which sorely need systematic attention by those psychological anthropologists who hope for greater scientific gains.

Chapter 8

CROSS-CULTURAL USE OF
PROJECTIVE TECHNIQUES

BERT KAPLAN

University of Kansas

DURING the past decade a somewhat violent argument has arisen concerning the role of projective techniques in anthropological studies. Since the whole culture and personality area has somehow become prominently identified with these tests, it is of some importance that the value and significance of the tests be assessed and that an understanding of their particular role and function be achieved. The use of projective tests in cross-cultural settings has flourished over the past two decades, and one may estimate that there have been as many as 150 studies in more than 75 societies. There appears to be sufficient work done so that the usefulness of the tests can be evaluated and their main difficulties and problems delineated.

Since it is my belief that the ultimate judgment about the tests will be based on demonstrated utility or lack of it in relationship to the purposes of research workers, I shall attempt to make these purposes explicit, thereby specifying the theoretical and methodological issues that projective test studies are relevant to. My plan is to discuss both the demonstrated values and difficulties of empirical studies in relation to each of the purposes described. I shall in addition present my own position with respect to the kinds of personality data required in the culture and personality field and discuss the prospects of obtaining them by using projective techniques.

The Delineation of Modal Personality Processes

It is fairly clear that the great majority of cross-cultural projective test studies are concerned with describing the personality characteristics that are most prevalent in particular cultural groups. The concept of "modal" or "basic" personality as introduced by Kardiner and Linton in the late 1930's has been perhaps the most influential theoretical conception in the culture and personality field, and there has been widespread acceptance of the notion that in each culture there exists a core of personality characteristics which are found in most members of the group. Until relatively recently the existence of this core of homogeneity has been regarded almost as axiomatic, and it has seemed very natural to culture and personality workers to begin with the idea that they should describe these typical or "modal" characteristics. That this aim prejudges an empirical issue which has perhaps not been adequately settled, has not seemed to trouble the scientific conscience of culture and personality workers. At the present time there is beginning to be more respect for the variability that exists within societies which has, whenever it was studied, been found to be embarrassingly large (Inkeles and Levinson 1956, Kaplan 1954, Wallace 1952, Vogt 1951, DuBois 1944), and it even seems respectable to voice a doubt about the existence of modal characteristics. (See Adcock and Ritchie's factor analytic study, 1958, which found that all of the Rorschach differences between groups of white and Maori subjects could be explained by one factor, imaginative thinking. However, these writers appear to attribute the paucity of differences to the failure of the Rorschach test rather than to accept the findings of the test.)

In part the prejudgment of the issue of homogeneity has arisen from the failure to make explicit distinctions between the two main concepts—culture and personality. The most popular and widely accepted opinions (Spiro 1951, Smith 1954) tended to obscure the distinctions between these terms. Some (Kluckhohn, for example) have asserted that culture and personality are simply abstractions from the same behavior and have used such phrases as "culture in personality" or "personality in culture." When modal personality is regarded as synonymous with learned cultural behavior, there can be no question about its existence since the very concept of culture implies the existence of uniformities and regularities.

Projective techniques have fit the purposes of workers attempting to describe modal personality processes. The Rorschach has been particularly easy to work with since no matter what subjects did with the test, responses could be scored and scores averaged to get measures of central tendency. When such averages are unaccompanied by measures of variability, they are worse than worthless since they have left the worker satisfied and pleased with his errors. Unfortunately the addition of measures of variance complicates the situation since there is no standard criterion which will tell the worker when his group is homogeneous enough to be characterized validly by the mean or mode. It is perhaps not necessary to comment at this late date on the dubious practice of pooling Rorschach scores of individuals to arrive at a combined psychogram which is then taken to represent the group modal pattern. This yields a very tidy result but unfortunately one that very often seems to have no relationship to the patterns that are found in any of the individuals in the group. The derived pattern is a completely synthetic one, and the fact that such patterns have been found to be related to cultural factors is testimony to the ingenuity of research workers in being able to find relationships between almost any variables under the sun.

Wallace has made a serious and sophisticated attempt to deal with the problem of deriving a modal pattern (1952). In analyzing Rorschach records of the Tucarora group, Wallace computed the modal score for each of 21 scoring variables and then set confidence limits of 2 S.D.'s around each mode. He defined responses that fell within these limits as members of the modal class and then asserted that subjects whose scores fell within these limits on all 21 variables were members of the modal group. He found that 37 per cent of the Tuscarora were in this group while only 5 per cent of the Ojibwa were. Our admiration for the ingenuity of this attempt to develop some basis for defining modality is perhaps qualified by the arbitrariness of the limits that were set, and one is left with the question of whether Wallace's modal class is too large or too small or is nothing more than a statistical accident.

The existence of wide variability is not an insurmountable obstacle to modal personality analysis. It is merely necessary to follow the derivations of the modal picture with a second step which checks back to assess the applicability of the modal picture to each of the individuals in the group in something of the manner of Wallace's study. While this may appear to be an unwelcome complication and an addition to the labor of the research, it does seem fair to say that in the absence of some such back checking, validity cannot be claimed for one's conclusions.

Projective tests do have a particular appropriateness to the task of drawing up modal personality pictures. In using them one approaches the task in the simplest and most direct way possible. A series of individuals, hopefully a representative and unbiased sample of the population to which one wishes to generalize, is studied one by one by means of a standardized procedure. The question is asked: what is this person like? And the answer, uncontaminated, it is hoped, by knowledge of other individuals or by the expectations one has about the findings, is based upon concrete and more or less standardized interpretations of specific pieces of information. The tests allow one to reduce what is obviously a task of great complexity and difficulty to manageable proportions. It is perhaps not too much to say that culture-and-personality study could not proceed without these or equivalent techniques. And, the availability of this method has resulted in a plethora of research.

Nevertheless, one sometimes has the feeling that the problem has been made deceptively simple. The first assumption, for example, that the projective test samples adequately the personality processes of the individual in whom one is interested is an extremely hazardous one. There is ample reason to believe from intensive studies of individuals using many techniques (Murray 1938), or from studies of successive administrations of a single test (Kaplan and Berger 1956), that the data obtained from a single test is little more than a fragment which may on occasion have some central importance but which at best is only part of the story of personality. A single Rorschach, TAT or both, even when augmented with life history materials and extensive observation studies such as in Vogt's (1949), must yield an incomplete account of the person. To the extent that the anthropologist or psychologist believes that personality is encapsulated in the microcosm of the test protocol, he is undoubtedly in error and in particularly serious error because he isn't likely to be aware of it. When the protocols are sparse and inexpressive as is sometimes the case, it is even more foolish to believe that one has the truth or some substantial portion of it. When the worker knows that his sample is seriously incomplete, as most psychologists do, but treats it as though it were not, he is equally in error.

In addition to the "sampling error" in personality study, there is the very difficult problem of interpretation. Characteristically, projective techniques yield very interesting but somewhat cryptic responses. These responses, whether they are Rorschach responses or TAT stories, are difficult to interpret even under the best conditions. When a drastic cultural difference exists, which the interpreter because of his inadequate knowledge of the culture and language of the subject cannot take into account, the responses are often completely uninterpretable. Unfortunately in this situation where the interpreter has had the choice of either admitting his helplessness or of going ahead and making the interpretation he would if the response had been given by someone in his own culture, the latter course has been followed. The result has been that modal personality pictures have often had little more meaning than fairy tales.

Perhaps the most usual solution to the problem of Rorschach interpretation has been to apply one of the standard systems for scoring responses and for interpreting the scores, the Klopfer and Beck systems being the main ones in use. Since these scoring systems make it possible to score any response whatever its origin, it becomes possible, once the score has been obtained, to ignore the exotic nature of the response and average, summarize, and interpret the scores in the usual manner. Quite aside from the doubtful validity of applying these interpretative categories cross-culturally, it appears that Rorschach practice has, in the past decade, been swinging slowly away from preoccupation with scoring, toward an interest in the content of the responses. Formerly, content analysis was treated as an adjunct to the interpretation of the scores. Today, however, the situation is reversed and the principal approach is usually to an understanding of the expressive imagery of each response; the pattern and sequence of such expressions enable the worker to form a picture of some aspects of the emotional life of the subject. George DeVos (1952, 1955) has been the principal exponent of content analysis in cross-cultural work with the Rorschach. His system for analyzing and scoring the content of the responses provides a welcome technique for summarizing the emotional imagery of the responses in a relatively objective way, and makes possible at least rudimentary quantative analysis of differences between groups.

It is unfortunate that one cannot have greater confidence in the more usual scoring categories. They provide very tempting material for numerical manipulation. The scores of persons in a particular group can be averaged, for example, and the averages for each category can be taken as a pattern representative of the whole group. Other techniques, such as range, the various indices of variability, the analysis of variance, and the various correlational techniques, all yield measures that are directly relevant to questions that culture and personality workers are concerned with, such as degree of variability or homogeneity within groups or subgroups, differences between groups and between subgroups, the identification of factors accounting for variability or homogeneity, the relationship between scores in different groups, and many others. However, until it is possible to apply these techniques to reliable scores which are valid measures of what they purport to measure, it seems wisest to forego their use, especially since their spurious exactness may lead us to be content with findings of uncertain correctness.

In the face of these difficulties which probably apply to some extent to all modal personality studies it is obvious that research to date must be treated with great tentativeness. Whether it is better to proceed doing the best one can with the limited capacity one has or to retreat from tasks that are too formidable is difficult to say. In either case, the proper attitude is one which makes very limited claims and is explicitly aware of limitations.

My judgment thus far has probably been somewhat harsh and has overlooked the positive values in these studies. I have suggested that most if not all modal personality studies utilizing projective techniques have most probably been arriving at incorrect descriptions of the people they are concerned with. However, it might equally well be suggested that they have also been correct in some part of their descriptions. While the shotgun approach in which some of the wildly fired shots hit their mark is not a method to be advocated, it will yield a slow accretion of sound facts if the unsound ones are gradually culled out in the course of repeated studies. But it is very likely that much more than this is achieved. Many of the descriptions are coherent with impressions gained otherwise, in fact so much to the mark that anthropologists who have used projective tests have come to feel considerable confidence in them (see Lessa and Spiegelman 1954, Gladwin and Sarason 1953, and DuBois 1944). The tests apparently do provide descriptions which in part at any rate satisfy the needs of anthropologists for deeper insights into the people they are studying and further have a certain amount of congruence with materials derived independently.

The Delineation of Cross-Cultural Differences in Personality

Closely related to the assumption that modal personality patterns actually do exist is the belief that peoples in different cultures vary considerably from each other in their personality characteristics. While this belief has been so strong that most workers have not felt it necessary to study the matter empirically, there are a few studies which have utilized projective techniques in relation to it. Projective tests offer a particularly sound approach to this question since they provide relatively standardized stimuli to which the reactions of different peoples may be compared. Perhaps the study which most directly treats the question of cross-cultural differences is my own (Kaplan 1954).

In this study Rorschachs from 170 young men in four cultures, Zuni, Navaho, Spanish American, and Mormon, were compared with respect to fourteen variables. It was found that there was statistically significant variability from culture to culture in five of the fourteen variables. However, it was noted that within each of the four groups the variability was very great and this coupled with the fact that the between-group differences were smaller than expected, led to the conclusion that there is less variability among cultures than was expected. It should be noted that a severe limitation of this study is that it never went beyond the scores to consider the psychological traits that are presumed to underlie them. A number of other studies have done this in the context of descriptions of cross-cultural differences. Such studies include those of Billig, Gellin and Davidson (1947, 1948), Abel and Hsu (1949), Joseph and Murray's comparison of Chamorro and Carolinian Rorschachs (1951), Strauss and Strauss' comparison of Sinhalese and American children's Rorschachs (1956–57), and Hsu, Watrous, and Lord's comparison of Hawaiian Chinese adolescents and Chicago White adolescents (1961).[1] Each of these studies noted some differences between the groups they studied but also a great many variables in which no differences were noted. Although comparative studies have been relatively sparse, my general impression is that the projective test is a useful if not essential technique and that further explorations of this method are warranted. The difficult problem of interpreting the significance of various differences remains with us, but the method, by pointing out differences, can indicate many interesting and significant problems.

During the past three years the publication in large quantities of the original protocols of Rorschach and TAT studies in *Primary Records in Culture and Personality* (Kaplan (ed.) 1956, 1957), a Microcard publication, has made possible the conduct of large-scale comparative studies for the first time. With the publication of Volume III of this series in 1961, the raw data of more than 65 studies will be available and studies comparing Rorschach responses in 20 societies will be possible. To date more than 12,000 pages of personality materials have appeared.

---

[1] Henry and Spiro (1953) made a complete survey of such studies up to 1952.

The Analysis of the Role of Personality Processes in Societal Functioning

Under this heading we consider what is perhaps one of the two most theoretically and scientifically significant contexts in which projective tests are used cross-culturally, the other being the influence of cultural factors on personality functioning. This problem is subsumed by the framework of the social scientist which is concerned with understanding the bases of social order and integration. An outstanding hypothesis which has been put forward by such eminent sociologists as Weber, Parsons, Merton, Fromm, and Riesman holds that the motivational processes of individuals play a key role in societal functioning, the role having to do with the motivation of socially required performances. In this connection, Inkeles and Levinson (1954) have urged that a distinction be made between the actual modal personality patterns that are empirically determined to exist in members of a society and the "socially required" personality patterns that are needed for optimal societal functioning. The latter consists of the core of motivations which lead individuals to perform the socially necessary jobs and act in appropriate ways.

Until the last few years systematic distinctions between these two concepts had not been made and in most theoretical schemes the modal personality model did service as the socially appropriate character structure also. At the present time a number of writers including Riesman, Parsons, Spiro, Devereux, Singer, Inkeles, and others have suggested that the appropriate social behavior is not a function of the total personality pattern of individuals but of particular and specific motivational structures. Consequently the problem is to describe these specially relevant characteristics rather than to describe personality characteristics or motivations which interfere with social functioning. The remainder, which neither facilitate nor interfere with society, can from the point of view of this problem be eliminated from consideration.

A second point that might be made is that, from the point of view of society, the crucial matter is, as Parsons and Shils (1951:158) have stated "to get the patterns (of behavior) whatever their functional significance to the person.... it does not matter whether there are important differences among types of personality possessing this need-disposition (to behave in the required way) as long as it exists."

Thus it appears that it is not necessary to posit shared motivational orientations or modal personality characteristics in order to account for social behavior. The motives of individuals may vary considerably. The important matter is that the jobs get done.

What is the role of the empirical investigation of personality in this theoretical problem? It is clear that it is not simply the study of personality. Perhaps the best entering wedge is through the concept of the conformity-deviance dimension; that is, to define the problem as having to do with the discovery of the actual motivational bases which lead to conformative behavior. While from one point of view it may not seem important to have any knowledge of what these motivational supports are, since obviously they exist or the society would not function at all, from another viewpoint it seems probable that problems of culture change, inadequate role performance and of deviance, to mention only a few, all demand a knowledge of what the motivations of the person are relative to the demands that are made on him for social behavior.

In another paper (Kaplan 1957) considering what some of these motivations might be, I have suggested that these bases do not lie in point-for-point isomorphism with specific social requirements and values, so that, for example, competitive behavior is supported by motives toward competition, since these can be understood as being primarily instrumental in nature and in a means-end relationship to other motives of a more generalized nature. We have posited instead the view that what we must look for are the generalized dispositions which are involved in the total relationship of the person to the social reality in which he acts, a reality which is to a considerable extent organized in normative terms—that is, which specifies what he should be doing and how. These generalized dispositions are probably of a few main types which are widely distributed. Riesman and Fromm especially have been concerned with the nature of these generalized dispositions and term them "social character." "Other directedness" is a perfect example of the kind of generalized disposition we are talking about, and Riesman has given a very rich account of the consequences that flow from a society's general reliance upon this type of motivational orientation. His discussion indicates that what is at stake is the very core and basis of social integration, and the essence of social order itself.

The description of the dominant type of motivational orientation is an empirical matter, and in line with a bias toward individual study in matters in which traits are ascribed to individuals, I believe that the most valid approach to this task is through the study of individuals. Riesman's *Faces in the Crowd* (1952) provides this kind of study but it is perhaps more of an illustration of his theory than an analysis of the facts. Can projective technique studies supply us with relevant information? My belief that it can is based on the following theoretical analysis.

If we choose to understand personality processes as social action, that is, as being in the realm of what the person is doing rather than as something he has, the pattern which is established in a projective test protocol becomes an act or series of them which bears explaining. My view of action is that it is a function of a social reality which is organized around certain normative components and a motivational orientation relative to this reality. If we regard the projective test protocol as a personality pattern which the person establishes for the moment through his action, the two main kinds of information that we require to understand or explain it are the delineation of the normative aspects of the situation which define the legitimate expectations that are perceived by the person and the motivational orientation which prescribes the position or stance which is taken relative to these expectations. The first is a matter for the social scientist since it has to do with the character of the social situation, while the second is a problem for the psychologist whose main interest is or should be in the analysis of motivation. Each response in the projective test can be analyzed from these two points of view. This, of course, places a very heavy burden on the test analyst and perhaps it will appear to the reader that the task is too difficult or impossible. The gains to the social scientist, however, are very large since they involve nothing less than an understanding of the relationship of the actor to the phenomenal reality in which he exists.

Although there probably has been little or no interpretation of projective techniques in this vein to date, there has been a certain amount of work that is concerned with the relationship of modal personality processes to the functioning of social patterns. Inkeles and Levinson (1954) discuss the problem of "congruence" between modal personality traits and social requirements. Inkeles, Hanfmann, and Beier (1959) are concerned especially, in studying the Soviet social system, with determining the fit between the personality traits that were determined in an extensive personality study utilizing projective techniques, principally the Sentence Completion Test, and the present requirements of the Soviet system. They suggest that there is a considerable degree of noncongruence, almost inevitable in any rapidly changing society, that has serious consequences for the functioning of the Soviet system. Dicks' (1952) study of Soviet personality, although not utilizing projective techniques, is in a similar vein. Erickson (1950) is another writer who has been concerned with this kind of problem.

While we have discussed the problem of determining the motivational characteristics that are involved in conformative behavior, similar questions might be asked with respect to deviance. What is the nature of the motivational orientation which leads to a negative relationship to the normative aspects of a situation? Again this is an empirical matter of the greatest importance which should be studied with projective techniques and all other available methods. The method suggested above in relation to the problem of conformity, of viewing the response or story as an action which stems from a particular relationship of the person to the normative, can be applied in the analysis of deviance as well. In one sense a considerable part of the problem of action lies in the necessity of making a choice between the deviant and conformative alternatives that are present in the situation.

Something might be said about the merits of the Rorschach and TAT relative to this problem. For any attempt to describe and analyze motivational processes it would appear that the TAT has important advantages. As the test has been used by Murray and his associates and by most other psychologists, the primary focus has been on describing the hierarchy and patterning of motives and their relationship to the perceived social environment. Since the stories are ordinarily comprised primarily of actions rather than descriptions of qualities or feelings, and psychologists have held that motives are inferable from actions, this instrument seems especially pertinent to the requirements of the worker in psychological anthropology. The Rorschach, on the other hand, ordinarily provides a series of highly condensed and often cryptic visual images from which motivations are only indirectly inferable. One has the impression that these images pertain more to the cognitive organization of the emotional life than to the motivational or volitional elements. However, this is not the exclusive focus but rather one that is relatively stronger.

Learning More about Projective Techniques Themselves through Cross-Cultural Studies

One of the main motivations for many cross-cultural studies has been simply to see what Rorschachs or TATs or other tests look like in exotic societies. This has involved a mixture of wanting to see more of what the people are like and wanting to see what the Rorschachs of people who differ so much from ourselves would look like. Thus many sets of test protocols have been presented almost as fascinating curiosities not necessarily having any great scientific value.

One aspect of this curiosity is practical. Clinical psychologists are continually faced with the problem of cultural diversity in their subjects. Class, ethnic, and regional differences are an ever-present part of the situation in which they work. While these factors are for the most part ignored, there is an uneasy feeling that they are significant and something should be done about them. Feeding into this is the uneasiness about the norms in terms of which tests are ordinarily interpreted. Rorschach workers have fairly clear and well-established ideas about normal performances and their interpretations are generally made in relationship to these norms. Subcultural differences in subjects raise a question about the general applicability of these norms. In this situation the psychologist looks toward the worker in psychological anthropology for guidance and help in establishing the importance of cultural factors for his own interpretations and for clarifying the ways in which these factors can be taken into consideration.

Studies in perhaps seventy-five societies have not, unfortunately, served to settle these questions. The finding has been that societies do vary considerably in the typical performances that are given by their members, ranging from the sparseness and brevity of the Ojibwa Rorschachs, for example, to the richness and expressiveness of the Algerian, Japanese, and Hindu records and the cryptic and almost impossible to interpret records of the Melanesian peoples. The TAT records range from the two and three sentence records of Navaho and Hopi children to the fifty and seventy-five pages given by Javanese young men. What is perhaps most obvious is that the way the test works varies considerably from group to group. A large and important question is whether these differences result simply from the subject's approaching the test in a different framework and with different cultural conventions or whether they reflect genuine differences in personality processes. The difficulty of separating these two possibilities is one of the chief obstacles of Rorschach interpretation in cross-cultural settings.

The discovery of this great variability which clearly transcends the individual variability that exists in our own society has been of great interest, however, to the extent that it reveals to us new modes of reaction and presents us with concrete examples of personality functioning which have radically different bases than exist in Western society. The understanding and appreciation of these differences should widen our understanding of the human species and of the possibilities that are open to it.

What is the Best Way to Study Personality

It is clear that projective tests "work better" in some societies than others in the sense that in some groups they yield more extensive and richer information. This seems to be analogous to the fact that the tests work better with some individuals than with others. A general problem thus raised, might be phrased, "How do the characteristics of the people being studied influence the way that they should be studied?"

The TAT study of Lucien Hanks, Jr. (1956) utilizing a set of specially drawn pictures paralleling the Murray cards, is most notable for the sparseness of the stories told. The subjects, who were mostly agricultural workers from Bang Chan in Thailand, gave almost no fantasy material. Hanks, in trying to account for the briefness of the stories, raises the interesting question of whether the test situation has created inhibiting anxiety in his subjects or whether the ability to fantasy was undeveloped in his subjects. An examination of the records suggests that the key to their sparseness lies in the fact that the subjects, without exception, were not telling stories but simply describing what seemed to them to be happening in the pictures at the moment. While it seems possible that the Thai cannot tell stories or are reluctant to do so; that they did not understand what was required of them or, understanding, did not know how or did not wish to comply, it is clear that both cognitive orientation and motivation are essential factors in the projective test situation and that without understanding them, it is almost hopeless to attempt an interpretation of materials from societies other than our own. While these factors can frequently be inferred from the records themselves, more often they remain unclear, and we are uncertain whether the variation of the records from those of some other culture is the result of differences in what the subjects were trying to do, differences in how hard they were trying, or actual differences in the personality and intellectual characteristics of the subjects. Of course, these three factors are not independent since what we mean by personality characteristics is sometimes only that the subject prefers to do one thing rather than something else or that he has a tendency to understand things in some particular way.

It is interesting to note, in line with this same research and in vivid contrast to the Thai's performances, the fantastically lengthy and intricate stories collected from young men in Java by Hildred Geertz (1957). Using a specially constructed set of TAT cards and recording the stories in the native language, Geertz obtained protocols averaging over fifty typewritten pages in length. It seems very possible that contrary to Hanks' findings, the Javanese have the capacity to give very rich, imaginative, and revealing fantasies. These conditions undoubtedly vary from culture to culture and from individual to individual. Their discovery requires a high degree of ingenuity and flexibility from the test administration, and an acknowledgment that the standard instructions and testing situation must sometimes be abandoned in the search for the better conditions under which it is possible to elicit significant personality data. It also requires that the tester investigate the subject's understanding of the test situation and the nature of his motivations and concerns about the test. Since this kind of research has hardly been done in our own culture, it is perhaps optimistic to expect that it can be done in cross-cultural studies. However, it does seem to be the very minimum needed.

The general principle which should hold for all projective technique interpretation is that the absence of some particular kind of material should not be regarded as indicating the absence of the ability necessary to produce the material. Instead, one should interpret what has been given as the preferred style or mode of the subject under the particular circumstances of the existing situation. This principle is specially important in cross-cultural studies. The Rorschach study of Carstairs (1956) is very relevant to this issue. His extensive series was collected in Delwara village in Udaipur and in the Bhil tribe, also in Udaipur. Despite the fact that most subjects in the Delwara group were unsure of themselves and showed many signs of anxiety, these records are rich and interesting. Although a great many of the subjects seemed reluctant and anxious and felt that they were not doing what was required of them, they were appropriately oriented toward the task and gave the kinds of expressive responses which Rorschach workers expect and hope for. Perhaps something in the cultural situation and in the "modal personality" characteristics of the group is appropriate to the requirements of the Rorschach test.

Carstairs' Bhil Rorschachs were collected under much more favorable circumstances than were the Hindu records. He reports that the Bhils seemed to enjoy the test and had an easy relationship with the tester. Despite this, they had a much more difficult time in giving responses and the responses are much less revealing. There is more stereotypy, vagueness, and rejection of cards. The content seems less emotionally charged and less symbolic in nature. A comparison of the two sets of Rorschachs suggests that far deeper and more profound factors than the immediate test situation are involved in the differences between the Bhil and Hindu records. The former, despite a great readiness to respond freely and spontaneously, gave comparatively little; while the latter, despite considerable reticence, caution, and anxiety, were extremely expressive. It is difficult to say why this is so. One might speculate that two different kinds of actions are involved: the personality of the subjects and their characteristic modes of cognition. It is not possible to specify at this time how these factors operate in the Hindu and Bhil groups. Conceivably, however, the greater anxiety and involvement of the Hindu group could stem from unsolved personality problems which were being worked out very near to the surface of consciousness. If this were the case, the Rorschach situation might have greater functional significance for the subjects. The Bhils, on the other hand, whose anxieties and problems apparently are considerably more repressed, did not find the situation of psychological use since they were not "working through" their problems, but were suppressing them.

A number of studies suggest that the acculturation variable has something to do with expressiveness on projective tests, the general finding being (see Hallowell 1942, Spindler 1955) that acculturation is associated with greater expressiveness. An obvious point is that as nonliterate peoples become more and more influenced by western culture and become more like the population for whom the tests were devised, the tests will work better, in the sense of yielding richer and more valid data. As has been suggested above, the difficulty in using projective techniques cross-culturally is not only a matter of increased uncertainty about the validity of the tests but involves the sparseness of some of the materials and the inability to obtain rich, imaginative, personal, and expressive data in contrast to brief, superficial, and stereotyped responses with a minimum of personal involvement. Although the latter are certainly not unknown in our society and in some parts of the population may even predominate, it does appear that the Rorschach and TAT generally do yield better materials in our own society than in most others. The reasons for this are not completely obvious, especially where the Rorschach test is concerned. The success of these tests in our own society seems not to be based on an explicit recognition of the features of our culture and its people that make us more permeable to particular kinds of personality study procedures, but rather to be based either on pragmatic grounds or an intuitive understanding of what is appropriate in a personality study.

One factor of importance to personality study is an openness and willingness to be known by others, the exact opposite of what Lerner (1961) finds in the French, who speak of the "refus de s'engager," who answer the telephone by saying, "Je vous ecoute," and who answer the greeting on the street, "Comment va?" with the ironic reply, "On se défend." Western society is not the only one in which this openness to personality study is found. Geertz's lengthy Javanese TATs and many other sets of data indicate that the quality of openness is widely distributed. However, it would probably be premature to state that openness to personality study is a general quality of any people.

I have conducted informal studies with a group of young Navaho men which make it clear that certain techniques yield more information about personality in this group than others. These very shy, noncommunicative individuals proved to be very difficult subjects despite their apparent eagerness to co-operate and be of help. Rorschach responses and TAT stories were sparse and unrevealing. On the other hand, the Rosenzweig Picture Frustration test yielded very good data. Perhaps most interesting were my attempts to get life history materials. Individual after individual gave the briefest and most impersonal possible account of his life. In varying the conditions of the study in an attempt to get more expressive materials, I found that if the subjects were allowed to write their life stories, they furnished quite lengthy and expressive accounts, despite considerable difficulty with pencil and written English. It seems, therefore, that two different problems exist, one having to do with the reasons for the differences in the general tendency to permeability in different societies, and the other dealing with the variations in the conditions under which individuals in different societies are willing and able to be personally expressive.

With respect to the first of these problems, we might speculate that conceptions of personality and individuality prevalent in the culture are among the relevant factors. For example, in a culture in which there is considerable concern about self and where thought about differentiated individuality is high, Rorschach materials may be specially rich and revealing. Hallowell's (1954) analysis of concepts of self and of kinds of self-awareness as cultural variables influencing persons' self-images and experience of self is very relevant to this problem and offers many exciting leads.

What Has Cross-Cultural Use of Projective Techniques Taught Us about Personality Development

One of the great hopes and aims of cross-cultural personality study has been the feeling that a better understanding of personality functioning itself might be achieved if cultural factors could be given more serious consideration. It is difficult to say whether anything of real value has been accomplished along these lines. Perhaps the best criteria that can be utilized is whether any new conceptions of personality functioning have emerged as a result of these studies. Here my impression is that they have not. Of the theoretical work of anthropologists only A. I. Hallowell has made any significant contributions; his work on the self and some of his theoretical writing being in my opinion of great importance for psychologists. However, while his work with projective techniques may have added to his psychological orientation and sophistication, it has in itself been of no great importance.

Of the psychologists who have been influenced by anthropological work, Erik Erikson, Abram Kardiner, and Erich Fromm have made perhaps the only significant additions to our conception of personality functioning, the remainder of neo-Freudian social thinking coming fairly directly from Freud and Adler and not being related to postwar empirical work at all. One might say that psychoanalytic theory has had a much greater influence on the culture and personality field than this field has had on psychoanalytic or other personality theory. Projective test studies have in the main been used to support and bolster conceptions which have emerged from these theories, principally the notion that child-rearing practices have a crucial role in the development of adult personality characteristics. Considerable support for this hypothesis has been developed by empirical studies, although it is perhaps not completely conclusive as yet. However, important influences of these studies on theories of personality functioning have not yet occurred.

Nevertheless, there is perhaps some reason to be optimistic that such influence may not be too long in coming. Perhaps the fact that psychologists themselves have been very slow in coming into the culture-and-personality field is responsible. While anthropologists have shown a high degree of sophistication in the use of psychological concepts and a few like Hallowell have become first-rate psychological theorists, their contribution to what are essentially psychological problems is necessarily limited. If, as perhaps can be anticipated in the not too distant future, psychologists in substantial numbers take up the problem, further theoretical development can be expected.

A Summing Up

My judgments about the cross-cultural use of projective tests have been very harsh. I have looked for the positive values in these tests and found them very scant. I have looked at the difficulties in their use and found them to be enormous, and have concluded that as these tests are being used and interpreted at present, only a modicum of validity and value can be obtained from them.

Nevertheless, cross-cultural personality study is one of the most rewarding, exciting, and important areas in the social sciences. The difficulties that have been noted are not in the least discouraging but on the contrary add to the feeling that this is an extremely productive field which is just at the beginning of making a great contribution to the development both of social and psychological theory. My criticisms of current practices have been aimed mostly at those who would suggest that the problems do not exist or can be ignored. If there is any general moral to my remarks, it is that psychological anthropology in the next decade must center around research in how to study personality and how to use these tools with depth and validity.

BIBLIOGRAPHY

ABEL, THEODORA M. and FRANCIS L. K. HSU
    1949   Some aspects of personality of Chinese as revealed by the Rorschach test. Journal of Projective Techniques 13:285–301.

ADCOCK, C. J. and J. E. RICHIE
    1958   Intercultural use of Rorschach. American Anthropologist 60:881–892.

BILLIG, D., J. GILLIN, and W. DAVIDSON
    1947–48   Aspects of personality and culture in a Guatemalan community. Journal of Personality 16:153–187, 326–368.

CARSTAIRS, G. M.
    1956a   Rorschachs of forty high caste Hindus and ten Moslem men from Delwara, Udaipus, India. In B. Kaplan (ed.), Primary records in culture and personality. Madison, University of Wisconsin Press, Vol. 1.

CARSTAIRS, G. M.
    1956b   Rorschachs of twenty-two Bhil men from Udaipus, India. In B. Kaplan (ed.), Primary records in culture and personality. Madison, University of Wisconsin Press, Vol. 1.

DeVos, G.

1952 A quantitative approach to affective symbolism in Rorschach responses. Journal of Projective Techniques 16:133–150.

1955 A quantitative Rorschach assessment of maladjustment and rigidity in acculturating Japanese Americans. Genetic Psychology Monographs 52:51–87.

Dicks, H. V.

1952 Observations on contemporary Russian behavior. Human Relations 5:111–175.

DuBois, C.

1944 The people of Alor. Minneapolis, University of Minnesota Press.

Erickson, E. H.

1950 Childhood and society. New York, Norton.

Geertz, H.

1957 Modified TAT's of thirty-three Japanese men and women. *In* B. Kaplan (ed.), Primary records in culture and personality. Madison, University of Wisconsin Press, Vol. 2.

Gladwin, T. and S. B. Sarason

1953 Truk: man in paradise. New York, The Viking Fund.

Hallowell, A. I.

1942 Acculturation processes and personality changes as indicated by the Rorschach technique. Rorschach Research Exchange 6:42–50.

1954 The self and its behavioral environment. Explorations, Vol 2. Reprinted in A. I. Hallowell, Culture and experience. Philadelphia, University of Pennsylvania Press, 1955.

Hanks, L.

1956 Modified TAT's of forty-seven Thai children and adults. *In* B. Kaplan (ed.), Primary records in culture and personality. Madison, University of Wisconsin Press, Vol. 1.

Henry, Jules and Melford E. Spiro

1953 Psychological techniques: projective tests in field work. *In* A. L. Kroeber and Others, Anthropology today, pp. 417–429. Chicago, University of Chicago Press.

Hsu, Francis L. K., Blanche Watrous and Edith Lord

1961 Culture pattern and adolescent behavior. International Journal of Social Psychiatry, Vol. VII, No. 1, 33–53.

Inkeles, A., E. Hanfmann, and H. Beier

1959 Modal personality and adjustment to the Soviet socio-political system. Human Relations, Vol. 2, No. 1. Reprinted in B. Kaplan (ed.), Studying personality cross-culturally. Evanston, Row, Peterson, and Co., 1961.

Inkeles, A. and D. J. Levinson

1956 National character: the study of modal personality and socio-cultural systems. *In* G. Lindsey (ed.), pp. 977–1020. Handbook of social psychology. Cambridge, Addison-Wesley.

Joseph, Alice and Veronica F. Murray

1951 Chamorros and Carolinians of Sapian: personality studies. Cambridge, Harvard University Press.

KAPLAN, B.
  1954 A study of Rorschach responses in four cultures. Papers of Peabody Museum of Archeology and Ethnology. Harvard University, Vol. 42, No. 2.
  1956–57 Primary records in culture and personality. Madison, University of Wisconsin Press, Vols. 1–2.
  1957 Personality and social structure. *In* J. B. Gittler, Review of sociology: analysis of a decade. New York, Wiley and Sons.

KAPLAN, B. and S. BERGER
  1956 Increments and consistency of performance in four repeated Rorschach administrations. Journal of Projective Techniques, Vol. 20, No. 3.

LESSA, W. A. and M. SPIEGELMAN
  1954 Ulithian personality as seen through ethnological materials and thematic test analysis. University of California Publications in Culture and Society. Berkeley and Los Angeles, University of California Press, Vol. 2.

LERNER, D.
  1961 Interviewing Frenchmen. *In* B. Kaplan (ed.), Studying personality cross-culturally. Evanston, Row, Peterson and Co.

MURRAY, H. A.
  1938 Explorations in personality. New York, Oxford Press.

PARSONS, T. and E. A. SHILS
  1951 Toward a general theory of action. Cambridge, Harvard University Press.

RIESMAN, D.
  1952 Faces in the crowd. New Haven, Yale University Press.

SMITH, M. B.
  1954 Anthropology and psychology. *In* J. Gillin (ed.), pp. 32–66. For a science of social man. New York, Macmillan.

SPINDLER, G.
  1955 Socio-cultural and psychological processes in Menomini acculturation. University of California Publications in Culture and Society. Berkeley and Los Angeles, University of California Press.

SPIRO, M.
  1951 Culture and personality: the natural history of a false dichotomy. Psychiatry 15:19–46.

STRAUS, M. A. and J. H. STRAUS
  1956–57 Personal insecurity and Sinhalese social structure: Rorschach evidence for primary school children. Eastern Anthropologist, Vol. 10, No. 2.

VOGT, E. A.
  1951 Navaho veterans: a study of changing values. Papers of Peabody Museum of Archeology and Ethnology. Harvard University, Vol. 41, No. 1.

WALLACE, A. F. C.
  1952 The modal personality structure of the Tuscarora Indians as revealed by the Rorschach test. Smithsonian Institute, Bureau of American Ethnology, Bulletin 150.

Chapter 9

MENTAL ILLNESS, BIOLOGY, AND CULTURE

ANTHONY F. C. WALLACE

The University of Pennsylvania

Introduction

Do DIFFERENT cultures encourage different styles of mental illness? Are there societies in which mental illness is absent, or at least rare in comparison with our own? Have either style or frequency of mental illness, or both, changed during the history of Western civilization? These and similar questions, prompted by practical concern with the mental health of our contemporary world populations, have evoked answers from anthropologists. *Yes*, different cultures do encourage different styles of mental illness, *but* the major categories of mental illness (the organic psychoses, the functional psychoses, the neuroses, the situational reactions, etc.) seem to be universal human afflictions. *No*, there are no societies of whom it can be said with confidence that mental illness is absent or, with certainty, that it is even rare, *but* there are certainly differences in the frequencies of illness and in the readiness of different social systems to recognize what Western psychiatry would call illness as significant disorder. *Yes*, styles and frequencies of various mental illnesses have changed in recent western history (hysteria, for instance, is now a relatively rare diagnosis, and devils and demons have been replaced by radio and radar in paranoid delusions), *but* we do not know all of the reasons for such changes over time nor for the differences between social classes and between regions.

Thus, the relation between culture and mental health remains an intriguing problem for anthropologists, a promising field for research, and perhaps some day a richly rewarding field for application. At the present time, like other scientists interested in mental illness, anthropologists are still searching for more adequate concepts, more powerful theories, and more effective techniques of observation. One of the avenues of research which has been under rapid construction outside of anthropology is biological in concept and method; and since this approach is relatively unexploited by anthropologists, yet is potentially of great significance for anthropological theory, a considerable part of this chapter will be devoted to considering the ways in which the current cultural-anthropological work in this area can assimilate and exploit what may be regarded, in the context of anthropology, as a physical-anthropological position.

CERTAIN LIMITATIONS OF CONVENTIONAL ANTHROPOLOGICAL THEORIES OF MENTAL ILLNESS

The culture and personality tradition in anthropology has borrowed its models of personality development, its characterology, and its conceptions of mental illness almost exclusively from a combination of learning, *Gestalt*, and psychoanalytic theories. This is in part a historical accident: these functional approaches were developing most vigorously in American psychology and psychiatry just at the time, in the late 1920's and early 1930's, when cultural anthropologists were first turning their attention seriously to the individual. Anthropologists found these psychologies readily applicable to an understanding of the individual in culture; and the psychologists and psychoanalysts found in cross-cultural materials useful corroborative evidence for their theories. But the more recently developed biological approach, while it has not as yet (anymore than the functional approach) provided a spectrum of "cures" of such refractory disease clusters as schizophrenia and cerebral arteriosclerosis, has already yielded a considerable body of knowledge of processes (in this case, of organic mechanisms) which are implicated in one or another type of psychopathology. This knowledge should be incorporated without delay, in general outline, into the conceptual armamentarium of every anthropologist concerned not only with mental disease but also with normal personality development and function.

At the present time, anthropological treatments of mental disease topics, particularly by culture and personality scholars, generally depend on a simple paradigm: the symptomatology of the illness under scrutiny is assumed to be motivated behavior expressive of psychological conflicts and to some degree effective in reducing tension and anxiety; the symptoms are "interpreted" in terms of some deductive schema intended to lay bare the (usually assumed to be unconscious) conflict; cultural *Anlagen* in the symptomatic behavior are pointed out; and finally, the source of the conflict is sought in traumatic emotional and/or cognitive dilemmas imposed by the victim's culture. This procedure almost completely neglects the victim's body; or, rather, it attributes to the victim's psyche a virtually magical ability to control the state of its body, by uncritically assuming that almost any somatic expression can be satisfactorily explained merely by asserting a plausible concomitant intrapsychic conflict. Even the "psychosomatic" position, it must be emphasized, is not "organic" in the sense indicated above, for it seeks the explanation of both somatic and behavioral disorder in antecedent psychological and cultural rather than in antecedent physiological conditions: thus the ulcer is explained by reference to the autonomic discharge attendant upon intrapsychic conflict, and the existence of intrapsychic conflict is explained by reference to culturally enjoined learning experiences rather than by any neurophysiological process.

Thus, even with regard to syndromes familiar to Western clinicians and conventionally (if not invariably) conceived as functional in etiology, the assumption that biological determinants are negligible is becoming an increasingly hazardous one to make. But the anthropologist is peculiarly vulnerable to criticism when he utilizes the functional paradigm without qualification to explain exotic forms of mental illness, such as the *pibloktoq* of the Polar Eskimo and the *windigo* psychosis of the northern Algonkian hunters. Here, in addition to the difficulties engendered by the fundamental ambiguity of current psychiatric theory over the respective causal roles of psychological and organic factors in clinically familiar syndromes, there are (or ought to be) serious uncertainties introduced by recognition of the extreme climatic, epidemiological (in respect to infectious diseases), and nutritional conditions to which technologically primitive populations are at times exposed (see, for example, Tooth's discussion of the difficulty even psychiatrists experience, when using purely behavioral criteria, in making the differential diagnosis between schizophrenia and certain types of trypanosomiasis in West Africa) (Tooth, 1950).

This paper is not intended, however, as an admonition to anthropologists to abandon an obsolete dogma for the sake of embracing a new scientific faith. Rather, the necessity for incorporating a new viewpoint into an existing tradition is pointed out. That this incorporation will entail modification of some beliefs and procedures may be expected; but the new theoretical position should be a strong synthesis rather than a weak substitute.

THE ORGANIC APPROACH IN PSYCHIATRY

The year 1927 may be taken as the beginning of codification of the culture and personality position in anthropology, for in that year Sapir's pioneer paper, "The Unconscious Patterning of Behavior in Society," was published in a symposium on *The Unconscious* (Mandelbaum 1949). Sapir's paper, probably the first major piece of theoretical writing in the culture and personality tradition, set, or at least prefigured, the frame of reference of later anthropological work in this area. This frame of reference was predominantly psychological rather than biological: it implied that the fundamental, and often unconscious, organizations of individual behavior which are conventionally labeled "personality" are molded, not by physical constitution, but by a combination of cultural milieu and individual experience. The correspondingly functional character of the conventional culture and personality view of mental disorder, as it developed in the next few years in the work of Sapir, Benedict, Mead, and others, can be readily explained by the absence of any substantial competing body of thought; for the biological approach in psychiatry did not even begin to make headway until after 1927.

The most impressive body of psychiatric theory in 1927 was psychoanalytic. This theory, although it gave lip service to biological thinking, and although its builders were well grounded in neurology, was in operation uncompromisingly psychological. Accordingly, the published case histories provided very little information concerning the physiological status of the patients. The analyst sometimes used physical metaphors (like "the economy of psychic energy"), invoked constitutional predispositions, and made assumptions about organically grounded instincts, erogenous body zones, and stages of sexual maturation. Freud, himself a neurologist of distinction, even asserted that behind the analyst stood the man with the syringe. But the psychoanalytic physiology, as it grew beyond Freud's control, was increasingly a pseudophysiology. Biological man was for all practical purposes constant in the psychoanalytic equation, and "psychological" events (learnings, communications, fantasies, motives, defense mechanisms, etc.) were the variables.

Most of the currently prominent "organic" methods of treatment were developed after psychoanalysis reached its theoretical maturity. In 1927 psychiatry had little else to offer in treatment beyond psychological (including psychoanalytic) methods for the well-to-do and custodial care (eked out by sedatives, hydrotherapy, and work therapy) for the poor. The insulin coma treatment for schizophrenia was introduced about 1930 and metrazol convulsive therapy in 1936; electroshock was not developed until 1938 (and all of these treatments were first publicly described in Europe). Psychosurgery was seriously developed in Portugal about 1935 and in this country in 1936. Psychopharmacology, hitherto a somewhat exotic specialty, began to flourish only during World War II. The use of drugs for abreaction of emotional conflict in combat neuroses became prominent during the early years of the war; and the intensive study of the psychotomimetic drugs (principally hallucinogens) and their experimental use for therapeutic purposes has developed chiefly since World War II. The new tranquilizing (or "ataractic") drugs were first offered to the medical profession in 1952, and the energizers (or "psychostimulants") have come even later.

Basic science contributions, apart from psychoanalytic theory, were equally uninspiring in 1927. Inspired by the discovery of the role of syphilis in paretic psychoses, early speculations about the role of focal infection in the etiology of the other psychoses were failing to find clinical confirmation. Berger's first report on the use of the electroencephalograph (EEG) for recording "brain waves" (electrical potentials originating in the cerebral cortex and in other parts of the brain as well) was not published in Germany until 1929; not until 1935 did American scientists publish confirmatory findings. Clinical chemistry had only in the preceding fifteen years developed the basic techniques for analysis of small samples of blood; prior to World War I, investigations of human metabolic processes had had to depend largely on studies of diet and urine, because the quantities of blood required for chemical analysis were so large as to prohibit their use as routine clinical procedures. The application of these new techniques of blood analysis to problems of psychiatric research, and the biochemical findings based on their use, came almost entirely after 1927. Thus, for instance, endocrinology was still in its infancy in 1927. The importance of the hormones of the adrenal cortex, which play a role in regulating the carbohydrate metabolism and the balance of mineral electrolytes in the body fluids, and which in excess can precipitate psychotic states, was not realized until the late 1920's. Research in that area was so slow in diffusing into other branches of knowledge that as late as 1944, in a widely read two-volume symposium entitled *Personality and the Behavior Disorders* (Hunt 1944), the adrenal cortex is given one paragraph (and no mention in the index.) Thus Selye's first publication on the celebrated stress or general adaptation syndrome concept was first published in *Nature* in 1936 (*vide* Selye 1956); and the "cortisone psychoses" did not even exist until cortisone was isolated, synthesized, and finally used in the treatment of arthritis about 1945. Franz Kallman's early report on his genetic studies of schizophrenia utilizing pairs of identical twins was published in 1938 (Kallman 1938). The more modern theories of nerve impulse transmission emerged during and after World War II, some of them stimulated by investigations into the action of the so-called "nerve gases" by the Army Chemical Center.

But there is no reason to continue the demonstration farther. The major point is clear: a large part of the modern knowledge of the physiological parameters of the behavior of the central nervous system in man has been accumulated since the original conceptual structure of the culture and personality viewpoint was built by Sapir, Mead, and other pioneer scholars. Whole literatures, rivaling in size the entire body of culture and personality writings, now exist on such topics as the relation between the adrenal hormones and mental function, the localization of labor in the brain as revealed by electroencephalographic and derivative techniques, and the effects of drugs on mood and cognitive process. And the major portion of all of these fields of knowledge has been contributed well after culture and personality committed itself to a functional approach.

As yet, the various special lines of the new organic approach have not achieved synthesis either among themselves or with the (actually older) psychosocial tradition in psychiatry and the social sciences. Nevertheless, a general philosophy would seem to animate the approach and to determine the nature of any future synthesis with the functional position. This philosophy would seem to reside in four principles:

1. Statements about "behavior," "mind," "personality," "psyche," "mental illness," and other "psychological" entities are statements about physical systems which include brain (for the brain *is* the mind).

2. Any physical disfunction of brain implies some mental disfunction.

3. Some physical disfunctions will produce disorganizations of neural systems most of whose components will remain individually undamaged.

4. Most cases of chronic, and many of acute, behavior disorders (including the functional psychoses) are the symptomatic consequences of chronic, or acute, physical disfunctions of brain.

The reader will note that the organic approach, as thus stated, does not claim that every socially undesirable mental state, attitude, or motive necessarily implies a physical disfunction; thus, evidences of hostility and anxiety, " neurotic" defenses, suicide, antisocial acting out, and so forth may in principle be produced by brains which function perfectly well but have been subjected to environmental pressures (including faulty communication) to which these "symptoms" are "normal" responses. But the organic approach would differ from the functional approach in claiming that an adequately functioning brain will be able to adapt to, or reduce, environmental pressures, and that *chronic* mental disfunctions are therefore preponderantly the consequence of a chronic physical disfunction which existed prior to, or independently of, the organism's embarrassment by environmental pressures. A radical functional theory, by contrast, would ascribe a far smaller role to organic factors as causal agents in all except the gross and obvious types of organic brain damage; but most functionalists would probably concede that chronic psychogenic stress can on occasion elicit physiological alterations, sometimes irreversible, which aggravate functional mental disorders (just as chronic psychogenic stress can lead to nonmental organic disorders such as duodenal ulcer).

More specifically the organic approach can be divided into such main topical areas as:

1. The study of the anatomy and physiology of the central nervous system (including the autonomic system) considered as an entity.

2. The study of the localization and organization of labor in brain (including the logical structure of nerve nets).

3. The study of nerve and nerve impulse.

4. The study of the relation of metabolic (including digestive, excretory, circulatory, endocrine, and intracellular biochemical) processes to cerebral function.

5. The study of the genetics of mental disorders.

6. The study of the effect of hypoxia, hypoglycemia, and electrolyte imbalance on cerebral function and the various processes responsible for hypoxia, hypoglycemia, and electrolyte imbalance.

7. Psychopharmacology (including the study of tranquilizers, energizers, and psychotomimetic agents).

8. The study of the effect of nutritional variables on cerebral function.

9. The study of the shock therapies (principally insulin coma and electroshock).

10. The search for blood fractions containing suspected psychopathogenic (toxic) substances spontaneously produced by the body.

The disciplines involved in these and other studies of psychopathology range from mathematical physics and computer design, through such laboratory sciences as physical chemistry, biochemistry, clinical chemistry, physiology, experimental psychology, and neuropsychiatry, to those areas of anthropology and sociology which can contribute data, method, or theory to organically oriented investigations.

A major problem in the organic approach has, of course, been its relative insularity from psychosocial knowledge (this has not been a problem of the functional approach alone). Accordingly a major need of both approaches is a better understanding of how knowledge and speculation concerning the physical aspects of human systems can best be related to knowledge and speculation concerning the psychological and social aspects of these systems. This is imperative because, although cases of mental illness are usually first identified in the community by laymen using social criteria rather than criteria of physical science, and although some part of the total disease process is invariably a function of social system interacting with individual personality, if the development of many of these cases is dependent on organic processes, then very careful analysis must be made of the interaction of social and organic events. And anthropology, by both theory and field investigation, can contribute significantly to the advancement of this kind of analysis.

AN ILLUSTRATIVE PROBLEM: PIBLOKTOQ [1]

In its simplest form, the problem faced by anthropological theory in the area of mental illness can be illustrated by the syndrome *pibloktoq* among the Polar Eskimo of the Thule District of north-

---

[1] The description of the *pibloktoq* syndrome is based on a compilation of published and manuscript descriptions, both specific and generalized, by a variety of observers, from the missionary Hans Egede in 1765 to about 1940. Seventeen photographs of a woman during a *pibloktoq* attack at Etah were taken by Donald MacMillan in June 1914; we were able to use copies of these from the original negatives on file in the Photographic Division of the American Museum of Natural History. I am indebted to Mr. Robert Ackerman, my collaborator in the *pibloktoq* study, who has collected many of the data and contributed heavily to their interpretation; to Dr. Zachary Gussow, who kindly permitted use of his unpublished manuscript on *pibloktoq*; and to Dr. Gilbert Ling, who reviewed the calcium hypothesis and contributed to its refinement.

ern Greenland. The classic course of the syndrome, as judged from cases described by various travelers in the north (MacMillan 1934; Peary 1907; Rasmussen 1915; Whitney 1911) and from photographs of one attack (American Museum of Natural History 1914), is as follows:

1. *Prodrome.*   In some cases a period of hours or days is reported during which the victim seems to be mildly irritable or withdrawn.

2. *Excitement.*   Suddenly, with little or no warning, the victim becomes wildly excited. He may tear off his clothing, break furniture, shout obscenely, throw objects, eat feces, or perform other irrational acts. Usually he finally leaves shelter and runs frantically onto tundra or ice pack, plunges into snowdrifts, climbs onto icebergs, and may actually place himself in considerable danger, from which pursuing persons usually rescue him, however. Excitement may persist for a few minutes up to about half an hour.

3. *Convulsions and Stupor.*   The excitement is succeeded by convulsive seizures in at least some cases, by collapse, and finally by stuporous sleep or coma lasting for up to twelve hours.

4. *Recovery.*   Following an attack, the victim behaves perfectly normally; there is amnesia for the experience. Some victims have repeated attacks; others are not known to have had more than one.

The epidemiological parameters seem to be:

1. *Geographical.*   Pibloktoq (or, in Danish usage, *perdlerorpoq*) is known to occur among the Polar Eskimo of the Thule District. Whether the same syndrome (whatever it is called) occurs elsewhere is uncertain. Hoygaard, in a dietary and medical study of the Angmagssalik Eskimo in 1936–37, reported that "*Hysterical fits* accompanied by strong mental and physical excitation were frequent, especially in women" (Hoygaard 1941:72). It does not seem to have been noted, however, among Canadian or Alaskan Eskimo, nor is it certain that it occurs in Asia or northern Europe. Thus we can only say that it *certainly* occurs in northwest Greenland; that it *probably* occurs elsewhere in Greenland; and that it *may* occur anywhere in the world. Whether or not the syndrome is to be considered a uniquely arctic or even Polar Eskimo affliction depends on whether it is a unique disease.

2. *Seasonal.*   Reports describe cases occuring at all seasons of the year but cases are said to be fewer in the summer.

3. *Historical.*   As might be expected, since the Thule Eskimo were not visited by white men until 1818, the case notes and descriptions are recent, the best of them dating from the time of Peary's visits to the Polar Eskimo in the first decade of the twentieth century. Detailed accounts have been provided by Peary (1907), MacMillan (1934), Knud and Niels Rasmussen (1915), and Gussow (1960), and others familiar with the Polar Eskimo. It is probable, however, that the disorder is fairly ancient in the area. As early as the mid-eighteenth century, northwest Greenlanders (possibly including the Polar Eskimo) were reported to be peculiarly subject to the "falling sickness." And in the 1850's the crew of Kane's icebound ship, twice wintering north of Thule, were afflicted by a strange "epilepto-tetanoidal disease" which, in combination with scurvy, killed at least two men,

incapacitated others, and rendered their dogs worthless (Kane, 1856). "Epilepto-tetanoidal" is a reasonably accurate descriptive phrase for *pibloktoq*.

4. *Frequency*.   *Pibloktoq* can apparently reach epidemic proportions: eight of seventeen Eskimo women associated with Peary's 1908 expedition were afflicted during one winter season; other observers have claimed that at certain times cases could be seen almost every day in a single village.

5. *Racial Nonspecificity*.   As was noted above, several probable cases of *pibloktoq* among scorbutic whites were observed by Kane and Hayes in the 1850's in the same region.

6. *Possible Species Nonspecificity*.   "Fits" among sled dogs, with social withdrawal, snarling, fighting, and convulsive seizures, but usually ending in death, are said to be regarded by Eskimo as the same syndrome and are given the same name, *pibloktoq*, as the human attacks.

The Hysteria Hypothesis

The major psychological explanation of the *pibloktoq* syndrome has been psychoanalytic. In 1913 A. A. Brill, Freud's self-appointed American apostle, wrote a paper on the subject based on a reading of one of Peary's books and on personal discussion with Donald MacMillan, the naval officer who accompanied Peary (Brill 1913). Brill considered the syndrome to be classic hysteria major. Following a somewhat simplified Freudian model, he interpreted the seizures as expressions of frustration at lack of love and cited as the type case a female who displayed particularly flamboyant attacks. This attractive young woman had not succeeded in getting a husband because she was a poor seamstress; she was consequently frustrated in her emotional need for love in all but the most crudely physical sense. More recently, Gussow (1960) has extended Brill's formulation, interpreting the hysterical flight as a seductive maneuver, an "invitation to be pursued," in persons whose chronic insecurities have been mobilized by some precipitating loss or fear of loss, and who seek loving reassurance in a "primitive and infantile, but characteristically Eskimo, manner." Indeed, he feels that such reactions are a manifestation of the basic Eskimo personality. The greater frequency of *pibloktoq* in women he explains culturally as the result of "the socially subservient position of women . . . and their added helplessness in the face of culturally traumatic experiences." The nudity is in part explained by the common tendency of Eskimo to undress indoors and to chill the naked body out of doors after the sweat bath. The glossolalia, mimetic behavior, shouting, weeping, and singing sometimes observed he also explains culturally by pointing out that these behaviors are found in shamanistic performances and religious ceremonies, not only among the Eskimo, but also in Korea. The flight is considered to be a hysterically motivated invitation to be taken care of, rather than a component of an involuntary psychomotor seizure pattern, because no cases of flight have been reported in which the victim was not seen, followed, and rescued. The asserted tendency for *pibloktoq* to occur in winter is illuminated by the observation "that winter, more than other seasons, intensifies Eskimo insecurity—and hence their proneness to derangement—through increased threat of starvation, high rate of accidents, fear of the future, and so forth."

These psychoanalytic and psychocultural explanations, however, are for several reasons not entirely satisfying. Nudity, for instance, is indeed culturally prefigured, since it is the only means of reducing body temperature in persons who have no clothes to wear other than heavy furs in poorly ventilated dwellings where the temperature may rise to over 100° F. But this suggests that the denudation may be merely a response to a sudden somatic sensation of extreme heat. The fact that most reported victims of hysterical flight were rescued from danger without injury may obviously be an artifact of observation: any victims who froze, drowned, lost themselves, were carried away on drifting ice, fell and died alone in the snow, and so on, would by definition be those who were not observed. Furthermore, in at least one case, a rescued woman *was* injured; she suffered a frozen hand and breast, a serious condition in the absence of European medical technology. Two of Kane's men died and the dogs often die. Glossolalia, singing, and so forth are hardly evidence for an influence of *Eskimo* culture on the form of this hysteria, since these behaviors are virtually pandemic. The evidences of extreme physiological stress (bloodshot eyes, flushing of face, foaming at mouth, convulsive movements) and the demented behavior (attempting to walk on the ceiling, eating of feces, and ineffectual destructiveness) are not prefigured in the culture. And finally, the Eskimo are not reported to explain these fits (in contrast to psychotic disorders) by supernatural theories of disease (such as possession, witchcraft, punishment for taboo violation, or soul loss) but seem to regard them as natural ailments, experienced by dogs and men alike, comparable perhaps to the common cold, the broken limb, and other ills that the flesh is heir to. This phlegmatic response would not provide very much in the way of reward for a hysterical fit.

The Calcium Deficiency Hypothesis

An alternative, and in part biological, hypothesis can be suggested which explains *pibloktoq* with at least equal plausibility.

Low concentrations of ionized calcium in the blood (hypocalcemia) produce a neuromuscular syndrome known as tetany which is often complicated by emotional and cognitive disorganization. The neurological symptoms of tetany include characteristic muscular spasms of hands, feet, throat, face, and other musculature, and in severe attacks, major convulsive seizures. The tetanic syndrome may be precipitated by trivial stimuli and is usually brief and sporadic rather than continuous (continuous tetany may of course be fatal). Although the information available in the photographs and literature is not sufficient in itself to establish the diagnosis, the symptoms of *pibloktoq* are compatible with the clinical picture of hypocalcemic tetany, and several authorities have suggested the calcium deficiency hypothesis (Hoygaard 1941:72; Baashuus-Jensen 1935:344, 388; and Alexander Leighton in a personal communication). Observation and testing in the field would be required to confirm the hypocalcemic hypothesis and to rule out alternative diagnoses (hypoglycemic shock, hysteria, food poisoning, virus, encephalitis, etc.). It is also possible that a tendency toward epilepsy may have been genetically determined by inbreeding in this small isolated group; this is suggested by reports that epilepsy is more common in northern Greenland than elsewhere on the island. The hypocalcemia and epilepsy theories are not mutually exclusive, however, since hypocalcemia probably would tend to precipitate a latent seizure in persons prone to epilepsy. Observation and testing for differential diagnosis would require both the eliciting of neurological signs in victims during attack, or in persons with a history of attacks, and blood tests on victims and on samples of *pibloktoq*-prone and *pibloktoq*-free persons for serum calcium, serum potassium, and possibly other constituents.

The plausibility of the calcium deficiency hypothesis is supported not merely by the opinions of certain authorities and by the compatibility of the *pibloktoq* syndrome with the syndrome of hypocalcemic tetany, however. It is also suggested by indirect evidence, both medical and ecological.

Medically, the Eskimo of Greenland (including the Thule District) are characterized by a proneness to hemorrhage and slow coagulation (Hoygaard 1941:83–85, and Cook 1894:172). Such a tendency toward bleeding might conceivably be associated with low serum calcium levels (although vitamin K deficiency is more likely to lead to this condition). At Angmagssalik, convulsions in infants, suggestive of hypocalcemic tetany, were reported by Hoygaard to be frequent (Hoygaard 1941:78, 135), and Bertelsen noted in a medical report on the Greenland Eskimo that there was a high frequency of cramps, especially of the legs, even in adults (Bertelsen 1940:216). These observations are reminiscent of the account by Kane of the "strange epilepto-tetanoidal disease" which incapacitated his crew north of Smith Sound in the 1850's. He diagnosed two fatal cases of "tetanus" displaying laryngospasm (these could have been actually hypocalcemic tetany going into *status eclampticus*), two fatal cases of the "epilepto-tetanoidal disease," and numerous cases of cramps and muscular pains, sometimes accompanied by "mental symptoms" of disorientation and confusion, both in dogs and man (Kane 1856).

Ecologically, it may without hesitation be stated that the high arctic environment does not provide rich sources of nutritionally available calcium during all seasons of the year to technologically primitive populations. Hoygaard found that nearly half of the annual calcium intake at Angmagssalik was provided by dried capelin (the bones of dried capelin being edible). When dried capelin was available, the calcium intake was low but above the level asserted by medical authorities to be the minimum for maintenance of health. But without dried capelin (a circumstance which periodically occurred as a result of unavailability of the fish or unsuitability of the weather for drying them), calcium intake dropped well below the minimum (Hoygaard 1941). Rodahl also found the dietary of certain Alaskan Eskimo groups to be relatively low in calcium (Rodahl 1957). At Thule, although no careful dietary studies have been found, it is reported that little fishing is done because fish are sparse and consequently capelin is not caught in substantial quantity. Probably substituting for dried capelin, however, are birds— the "little auks"—which, after storage in seal oil, can be eaten whole, including, apparently, some of the bones (MacMillan 1918). A further ecological complication may be a product of the high latitude itself. Man requires a certain quantity of vitamin D3 in order to absorb and utilize dietary calcium efficiently (and possibly also to metabolize carbohydrate efficiently). This vitamin is formed in the human and animal skin when ultraviolet light activates certain cholesterol-containing oils. In the high arctic, however, a combination of low sun angle during summer, a long period of winter darkness, and the need for heavy clothing during most of the year, must prevent the human body from synthesizing much of its own vitamin D3. Whether sufficient vitamin D3 can be secured from sea fauna at this latitude is uncertain. Seal oil contains significant quantities of vitamin D_3 but, at Thule, the fish oils rich in vitamin D_3, such as cod liver oil, are probably not a major source of supply because of the aforementioned lightness of fishing in that region. To summarize the ecological problem briefly, even if sufficient vitamin D_3 is available to allow maximum efficiency in calcium absorption and utilization, it is still highly probable that some people, at some seasons of the year, will be unable to secure sufficient dietary calcium to meet published medical standards. If such a low calcium intake were coupled with a high protein and high potassium intake, the neurological consequences would be intensified, and the heavy meat consumption of Polar Eskimo entails a large intake of protein and potassium.

One fact, however, militates against a simple dietary calcium deficiency hypothesis: the reported extreme rarity of rickets in Eskimo infants and of osteomalacia in Eskimo adults (for example, in pregnant and lactating women) (Bertelsen 1940). These are diseases in which, as a consequence of inadequate calcium intake or utilization, or both, the bones yield their calcium to the blood and, eventually, to the urine, with the sufferer thus gradually losing calcium from the body at the expense of bony tissue. In temperate latitudes, rickets and osteomalacia are normally forestalled by milk, sunlight, and supplementary vitamin D_3 preparations in cod liver oil and vitamin pills. If one hypothesizes that the Eskimo diet is low in calcium, and perhaps in sun-formed vitamin D_3, how is it that rickets is not evident? The answer to this question requires another hypothesis concerning hormonal function. It would seem that if calcium and/or vitamin D_3 intake is chronically low in the high arctic environment, then the Eskimo physiology must for generations have been forced to "choose" between tetany and rickets—and, unlike more southerly populations, it has "chosen" tetany as the lesser of two evils. (More precisely, of course, it is the environment which has selected the better-fitted physiological alternative.) Rickets and osteomalacia would in a primitive Eskimo economy be fatal because they are physically crippling. Sporadic attacks of tetany, even if occasionally damaging or even fatal, would be by comparison merely an annoyance. Hence the hypoealcemia hypothesis requires the corollary that the Polar and perhaps other Eskimo tend to be mildly hypoparathyroid (or, more exactly, again, that in this cultural-ecological matrix, optimum parathyroid function requires a lower activity than does optimum function under the conditions of European and American medical practice). Such a mild "hypoparathyroidism" would be conceived as a product of natural selection for primitive life in an arctic environment, yielding a type of hormonal balance which retains calcium in the bones even if calcium levels in serum fall occasionally. There is, as a matter of fact, some evidence to support this hypothesis. The doomed medieval Norsemen, not preadapted to a high arctic environment, who settled along the west coast of Greenland, and who finally died out and were replaced by ricketless Eskimo, *did* suffer from rickets and osteomalacia (Maxwell 1930:20).

But if we propose a hypocalcemia hypothesis, do we ignore Eskimo culture? Certainly not. Consideration of cultural factors is, in fact, already implicit in the hypothesis as enunciated. This hypothesis rests on the assumption that the subsistence technology is "primitive," that is, in this application of the concept, that manufactured vitamins and imported or specially processed calcium-containing foods are not available and that, to hunters, a strong and undistorted skeletal structure is of greater survival value than freedom from occasional attacks of tetany. These cultural characteristics render the population vulnerable to a local dietary calcium and/or vitamin D_3 shortage and select the nervous and muscular system rather than the skeleton as the target tissue of any calcium and/or vitamin D_3 nutritional deficiency.

But Eskimo culture also functions to minimize, within the limits stated above, the frequency and severity of attacks, *via* the customs of securing, processing, and storing of large quantities of calcium-containing birds (the "little auks"); of obtaining, preserving, and making extensive use of vitamin-D_3-containing seal oils; of stripping and exposing the body to direct sunlight whenever the weather permits; of weaning children late (thus ensuring them maximal calcium intake in mother's milk during the rickets-vulnerable period of infancy); of securing to pregnant women (who are particularly vulnerable to osteomalacia) and children preferred access to fresh and stored foods high in calcium (specifically, the little auks and whatever dried fish are available) by making women and children chiefly responsible for netting the birds and collecting the eggs, and (to judge from taboos reported from Eskimo groups other than Thule) by maintaining food taboos which have the effect at certain times of substantially restricting the pregnant or lactating mother to the use of dried fish, birds, or other stored foods high in calcium.

It is possible that, apart from its role in etiology, Eskimo custom also affects the details of overt symptomatology. Conceivably the frequently reported impetuous flight from the group during the initial phases of an attack may reflect a personality trait common among Eskimo: withdrawal from, rather than aggression in, a situation when the individual's confidence in his ability to master it has been shaken. Such a tendency may be reflected in the tendency for Eskimo men to abandon kayak hunting if their confidence has once been disturbed ("kayak-phobia"); by the practice of *kiviktoq,* or "going into the mountains" to live a hermit's life, in men and women alike who feel rejected by their communities; by the reported willingness of the aged and infirm to be abandoned to die; and by the anxiousness of Eskimo parents not to disturb the confidence of their children, even when playing dangerously, by frustrating negative commands. Such a psychological interpretation— which is, in a sense, directly contradictory to the hysteria hypothesis —rests on the assumption that any incipient neurological disfunction is susceptible to different interpretations by the victim and his associates and can therefore precipitate different overt responses, depending on particular customs of the individual and group.

And finally, with regard to its handling of cases of *pibloktoq,* Eskimo custom obviously plays a very important role. An attack of *pibloktoq* is not automatically taken as a sign of the individual's general incompetency. The victim is, if necessary, prevented from injuring himself or others; otherwise he is left alone while the attack spends itself. The attack may be the subject of good-humored joking later but is not used to justify restriction of the victim's social participation. There is, in other words, little or no stigma; the attack is treated as an isolated event rather than as a symptom of deeper illness. Such a phlegmatic approach would seem well calculated once again to minimize any damage to the individual's personal confidence and thus would work to forestall the development of chronic psychological invalidism. The impact on chronicity of differential handling of such episodic disorders is well illustrated in the history of American combat psychiatry, which between World War II and the Korean War achieved a 50 per cent reduction in the rate of chronic psychoneurosis developing out of combat breakdown simply by refusing to treat the breakdown as a symptom of illness (Glass 1953).

Implications of the Alternative Theories

Two alternative armchair theories of *pibloktoq* have been presented. Although the "organic" (hypocalcemia) theory seems preferable, the organic theory is just as much concerned with analysis of cultural factors as is the "psychological" (hysteria) theory. In order to choose between the two, field investigation will be necessary. Such field investigation will have considerable significance for anthropological theories of mental illness (and professional psychiatric theory, for that matter). For not only will it contribute to the solution of a particular—and to some eyes, perhaps, an unnecessarily exotic diagnostic problem, it will also bear on two major theoretical issues.

One of these major issues is the understanding of hysteria itself. As is well known, psychoanalysis was originally conceived as a means for treating hysteria, and upon the analysis of cases diagnosed as hysteria much of its theoretical structure has been erected. Since Freud's time, hysteria has become a rare disorder in most of Europe and America. This may be the consequence of culturally determined changes in modal personality structure in Western countries and in preferences for various styles of psychosomatic expression. It may also be the result of changes in diagnostic practice (it has been suggested, for instance, that "hysteria has vanished right into the diagnosis of epilepsy" (Peterson 1950)). And it may be the result of culturally determined changes in such matters as style of dress and housing, hours of work, methods of lighting, and diet, which could affect, in particular, calcium intake and utilization in persons vulnerable to tetany and rickets. Certainly rickets has become more rare in precisely those groups once most prone to grand hysteria: the Western European urban populations. But now we are suggesting that at least one type of hysteria (the "grand hysterical attack") may not be purely psychogenic!

Such an implication demands support by way of empirical investigation—an investigation which, in fact, takes up again an abortive line of inquiry into the relationship between tetany and hysteria that began in Europe before the psychoanalytic theories of hysteria swept competing approaches from the field (Barrett 1919–1920:385–386). It is of more than antiquarian interest to recall that between 1880 and 1895 there was a veritable endemic of tetany among the working class of Vienna, Paris, and other European cities (Shelling 1935:115–116). This plague of tetany was, at the time, not understood etiologically, for the role of calcium in tetany had not been established. During the same period, the work of French and Viennese neuropsychiatrists on hysteria was being pursued most intensively, and it culminated, as everyone knows, in Freud and Breuer's *Studies in Hysteria,* which was published in 1895 after a preliminary publication in 1893. This study revealed the psychological connection between the hysterical symptom and traumatic emotional conflict and suggested a technique of "talking" therapy which soon developed into the method of psychoanalysis. We might now ask, however, whether the physiological milieu of hypocalcemia may not have been a conditioning factor in hysteria. The most serious endemics of rickets and of hypocalcemic tetany—determined by constraints of custom and/or economy on food, dress, interior lighting, working hours, and access to open spaces not only among working people but among all classes in late nineteenth century Europe—came at precisely the same time that hysteria reached its peak as a psychiatric problem. The discovery of the value of sunlight, milk, and vitamin-D_3-containing foods, and the general amelioration of social conditions, during the early twentieth century, was accompanied by a drastic reduction in the frequencies of rickets, of tetany, and of hysteria. Thus we may suggest, as a hypothesis for medicohistorical investigation, that the hysterical attack and perhaps even hysterical conversion will occur most readily in persons with low levels of serum ionized calcium and that chronically low levels may maintain a neurophysiological milieu in which either tetany, hysterical attacks, hypersuggestibility, or hysterical learning of conversion symptoms is sooner or later inevitable, the choice of disorder depending on various conditioning factors of situation, personal history, and biochemical individuality.

Suggesting that the late nineteenth century European hysterias may have been in considerable proportion undiagnosed cases of serum calcium deficiency raises a major issue in psychiatric theory, for psychoanalysis was founded on the analysis of hysterics. In view of this fact, it may be well to evaluate further the culture-historical dimensions of the issue. The late nineteenth century students of hysteria—including Freud—were aware that hysterics might display unusual physiological profiles as well as disordered behavior, and some felt that hereditary predisposition played a role in the pathogenesis of the disease. But these psychiatrists of the 1890's were in somewhat the same position vis à vis physiological explanations of hysteria as the anthropologists of the 1920's were vis à vis explanations of psychopathology in general: physiological investigations had not advanced far enough to provide a base for framing testable physiological hypotheses.

Thus the first demonstration that tetany was associated with reduced concentration of calcium in the blood was not made until 1908; hitherto the diagnosis depended on the finding of positive neurological signs. Not until 1921 did the development of micrometric methods of determining quantities of serum calcium make possible widespread testing for serum calcium level (Shelling 1935: 114–116). Differential diagnosis in certain cases between hysteria and tetany was extremely difficult, and in fact probably was arbitrary, before the development of the serum calcium and tetany hypothesis and the provision of appropriate methods of clinical chemistry. Consequently, some cases which today would probably be regarded as unequivocally tetany (e.g., the tetanic syndrome following thyroidectomy) were in 1904 diagnosed as mixtures of tetany and hysteria (*cf.* Curschmann 1904). Thus it is *impossible* that Freud could have considered the possibility that hysteria might be a symptomatic consequence of low serum calcium. The cultural milieu in which he worked had not provided him with the concepts or tools by which the question could have been asked or answered. Inasmuch as we cannot return to the nineteenth century to do serum calcium determinations on Freud's original patients, we cannot say what the results would have been, nor can we estimate the impact on the development of psychoanalysis if the findings had been positive. But at least we have still another historical answer to the question "Why has hysteria virtually disappeared in Europe and the United States?" Our (metaphorical) answer is, "It dissolved in bottles of milk and cod-liver oil"—that is to say, the cultural changes associated with an appreciation of the importance of sunlight, vitamin D3, milk, and various other factors for maintaining proper calcium balance, together with a general improvement of nutritional standards, has virtually eliminated (except in certain rare medical conditions) a total syndrome, one symptom cluster of which was once (and still is) called tetany, and another symptom cluster of which was once (but no longer is) called "grand hysterical attack."

The need for empirical evidence bearing on the hypotheses outlined above leads immediately to a consideration of the second major issue: the larger theoretical structure which should guide such an investigation. It is evident that even if it is possible to identify a specific physiological variable as the *precipitant* of the overt symptomatology, an adequate explanation of the frequency of the syndrome in the population, its geographical range, its racial and species distribution, its seasonal variation, its history, and the severity and details of form of the symptoms themselves, must depend on evaluating other variables, physiological, psychological, and cultural. It is the interaction of these other variables with the immediately precipitating physiological variable which provides the necessary and sufficient conditions for a type of mental illness to occur in a particular group with a particular frequency. We have already suggested some of these conditions in the *pibloktoq* analysis. Let us now turn our attention to the development of a frame of reference which can guide the refinement of theory and the acquisition of relevant empirical data. We shall begin, in the next section, with a further discussion of a point introduced in the *pibloktoq* analysis: the importance of the "theory of illness" in the formation of a symptomatic structure. And finally we shall attempt to generalize the line of thought represented in the *pibloktoq* analysis, and in the following discussion, into a rough model of a biocultural approach to mental illness.

THE IMPORTANCE OF CULTURALLY INSTITUTIONALIZED THEORIES OF ILLNESS AS DETERMINANTS OF RESPONSE TO ORGANICALLY BASED PSYCHOPATHOLOGY

Mental illness is an episode in a life program, usually following a more or less extended period of normalcy (as defined by both the person and his community), and terminated either by death or by a return (temporary perhaps) to normalcy. In the biocultural model, a conjunction of pathogenic, organic, and psychological events is considered to abort a life program normal to the society by crippling the victim's apparatus for cognitive organization. With the onset of the physiologically determined desemantication (reduced cognitive organization capacity) the victim is unable to organize his perceptions, his motives, and his actions meaningfully so as to satisfy his own wishes without frustrating those of others or vice versa. His more or less desperate efforts to protect himself from the consequences which he expects to follow the drastic reduction of cognitive capacity are apt to be the most conspicuous symptoms of the disorder: withdrawal, aggression, paranoid delusion, and the bizarre use of the familiar mechanisms of defense like repression, sublimation, denial, etc. And simultaneously, the victim's community is responding to this overt symptomatology with its own procedures of withdrawal, aggression, therapy, and so forth.

What will determine the victim's and the community's expectations of consequences and their choices of defensive strategy? Evidently the frequency, duration, and predictability of periods of desemantication, and their commonness in the population, will be data of extreme importance in the evaluation of self by the victim and of victim by community. If the period of desemantication is relatively brief (not more than a few days), is relatively infrequent (not more than once a month), is predictable (either by a calendrical device or by association with other scheduled events), and is commonly observed to occur in others without dire consequences, then even severe degrees of desemantication with considerable associated inconvenience and discomfort may be tolerated by the personality. Similarly, brief, infrequent, predictable, and common overt disorders may be tolerated by the community. Such situations (to give some familiar examples) are premenstrual tension, drug and alcoholic intoxication, ritually induced dissociation, exhaustion, and the Polar Eskimo *pibloktoq*. The more delayed in the life program, the more frequent, the more prolonged, the less predictable, and the less common the event, the more threatening it will be to the personality and to the community, and the more desperate and (for the victim) the more ill conceived their complementary defensive strategies will become. Where the desemantication is severe and irreversible, as in chronic brain syndromes, the victim may be so preoccupied with maintaining the former sense of competence that even trivial *contretemps* precipitate "catastrophic" reactions (Goldstein 1940). Schizophrenia and perhaps the affective psychoses (such as involutional melancholia) would appear to have an intermediate status between chronic syndromes and brief episodic attacks. The desemantication is not fully continuous and the victim is consequently able to retain for a considerable period an intermittent normalcy of function, but the episodes are sufficiently frequent, prolonged, and severe to result in an accumulation of permanent defensive strategies which eventually in themselves make adequate social participation almost impossible during the clear periods, and, sometimes, even after the desemantication phase itself has ended.

But it is not merely the timing and conventionality of the disorder which will affect the defensive response of the victim and his community. The personality of the victim and the culture of the group provide models of the experiences and symptoms of the event which assign to them definite meanings and provide recipes for handling the situation. These models are, in the individual's case, a function of the history of his learnings, and in the community's case, a function of other aspects of the culture, its social structure, and its history. They are widely variable in form and are not entirely predictable from a knowledge of the timing and conventionality of the disorder. While the anthropologist may or may not undertake the solution of problems of differential diagnosis and etiology (which, as we observed earlier, unavoidably involve questions of biological as well as psychological dynamics), he can certainly investigate the patient's and the community's theories of illness and its treatment. Thus his most immediately relevant contribution can be an analysis of how, in the society in question, symptomatology and its programming are normally conceptualized. As we have indicated above, whatever its etiology, the course of an illness occurs in a social matrix and is observed both by the victim and his associates. Their conception of what is happening will play an important part in determining what will be their response to the symptoms (see Wallace 1959). Thus, even if etiology and the primary symptoms of an illness were, except in an epidemiological inquiry, to be considered as physiological accidents and thus as largely independent of culture, the efforts of the victim and of his fellows to cope with the illness must be recognized as being highly dependent on culture, for these responses to illness are very considerably determined by what may be called the native—and, in particular, the patient's—theory of illness. In short, since the cause of illness even if physiologically initiated is progressively modified by feedback via the victim's and the community's conception of the illness, the victim's personality and the community's culture play a determining role.

Some of the recent literature in social psychiatry has directed attention to theory of illness as a significant variable. Of particular interest are the studies of psychiatric illness in New Haven summarized in Hollingshead and Redlich's book *Social Class and Mental Illness* (1958). These studies demonstrate again not only class differentials in prevalence of certain kinds of treated mental illness (for example, that schizophrenia is about nine times as prevalent in the lowest socioeconomic group as in the highest, even after standardizing for population size), but also class differentials in methods of treatment (that is, that lowest-class schizophrenics receive either organic treatment or no treatment at all, while highest-class schizophrenics receive psychotherapy and/or organic treatment). These differences are doubtless partly a function of differential access to economic resources; but, as Hollingshead and Redlich carefully show, they are also partly a function of differences in the conceptions of illness and of treatment between lower-class and higher-class patients. Specifically, the dissonance between the lower-class patients' and their middle-class physicians' theories of what illness is, how it originates, and how it is cured, interferes with free communication. These differences make mutual acceptance, liking, trust, and intelligent co-operation difficult, and often result in either mutual withdrawal or the patient's refusal to enter into a psychotherapeutic relationship at all.

Other sources have approached the problem of theory of illness from various standpoints. Cannon and others, for instance, have analyzed the phenomenon of "voodoo death" as a type of overresponse to a "realistically" trivial trauma by a victim who is convinced that he will die because he has been bewitched by an enemy or doomed for the infraction of some taboo (Cannon 1942). Comparable, if less dramatic, studies have revealed that bodily injuries and mental infirmities of one sort or another lead to different responses depending on the culturally defined meaning of the situation. For instance, in their collection of papers reporting on investigations by the National Institute of Mental Health of the impact of mental illness on the family, Clausen and Yarrow describe in some detail the differences in the "meaning" of mental illness to various persons, including the patient, and the effect of these semantic positions in shaping the path to, through, and from the mental hospital (Clausen and Yarrow 1955). In their study of thirty-three families in which the husband was the patient, they found that nearly half of the husbands were never seen by a psychiatrist before hospitalization was arranged. The difficulty, and usually the reluctance, with which the patient's family came to define his problem as one requiring psychiatric care, and the slowness and uncertainty with which they proceeded to secure that care, meant that "discontinuities of action were frequent, and paths to the hospital were beset with obstacles and traumata for husband and wife" (Clausen and Yarrow 1955:32). And in our own research at the Eastern Pennsylvania Psychiatric Institute, we have been concerned with the problem of how the patient's theory of the mechanism of hallucination affects his and his fellows' response to that experience. We have worked with cross-cultural materials in the literature and have pointed out, for instance, the contrast between the responses to mescaline intoxication of normal white volunteers and of American Indian religious peyotists (Wallace, 1959).

A Model for the Analysis of Theories of Mental Illness

We conceive that among the set (mazeway) of cognitive "maps" which each individual maintains, describing and interpreting the world as he perceives it, is his theory of mental illness. This map gives meaning to experience, by defining the possible states which a person can occupy in a mental health context, and by relating the possible states which the person can occupy to one another via various transfer mechanisms, so as to provide the rationale for decision. Such a map can therefore be conceived of as having three aspects: (1) the *states* specified; (2) the *transfer mechanisms* which are conceived to effect change from one state to another; and (3) the *program* of illness and recovery which is described by the whole system. We confine our attention here to the patient's program for the patient himself; his programs for other persons, and the program of others for him, may (or may not) be different. Thus in the following analyses the entity to which each state description refers is constant, being ego, even though ego is variable in the sense of having different properties at different stages of the program, and in the sense of being "now" at one or another of these stages in ego's own (not necessarily correct) opinion. (Interesting possibilities of programs involving multiple referent entities, because of the logical complexities of such schemas, are not considered here.)

Evidently, one can "plug in" on an individual's program at a number of different levels of abstraction. In order to minimize partly the unreliability of reporting which ensues if level of abstraction is left unspecified, we have found it useful to base analysis on five "states," which will constitute stages of every program: "normalcy," "upset," "psychosis," "in treatment," and "innovative personality." These are always to be understood as the subject's concepts of his own possible states and not as the observer's concepts of the subject's condition. The terms are unimportant; they simply label positions in the model. *Normalcy* refers to a state in which the person is performing to his own and other's satisfaction the roles appropriate to his situation in society. *Upset* refers to a state where role performance has been reduced to a level of minimal adequacy,

with noticeable personal and/or group discomfort. *Psychosis* is a
state where role performance has become so inadequate that in
order to reduce personal and group discomfort, some degree of social isolation (either self- or group-imposed) must be instituted.
In treatment is a state where the person is receiving ministrations
from specialists, designed to remove the conditions responsible for
personal and group discomfort, and to return the patient to full
social participation. *Innovative personality* is a state in which the
person is again able to perform roles to his own and group satisfaction, but roles different to a greater or lesser degree from those
performed in state N (as the difference approaches insignificance,
P approaches N). These five states may be conceived as arranged
in a graph whose starting point is N, with "goodness" of state decreasing in order of position to the right of N:

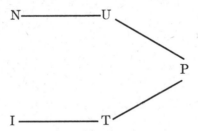

We assume that any individual classification of states will include
these five except where concept I is equivalent to N, in which case
the graph reduces to:

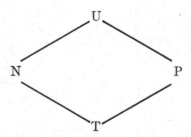

We also assume that between any two states one of four transfer
relations may be conceived: no transfer possible (symbolized by
open space); one-directional transfer ($\longrightarrow$); one-directional
transfer ($\longleftarrow$); and reversible transfer ($\longleftrightarrow$). Definition of the
states and of the transfer mechanisms can usually be best repre-
sented not on the graph but in appended tables in order to avoid
cluttering the graph with written notations. The reader will note

that any two states may stand, in relation to one another, as positive and negative goals depending on their relative position on the value dimension. For instance, U may be a negative goal for a person who is in state N, but a positive goal for a person in state P. And finally, depending on the circumstances, additional states may be added to the model if they are part of the subject individual's or culture's phenomenological world.

A given patient's theory of illness can be inferred from several types of behavior:

1. Plain statements ("It's worrying that makes people lose their minds").
2. Comparative statements ("Joan was real sick when they brought her in, but now that she's been here awhile, she's quieted down a lot").
3. Differential motor behavior (avoiding certain patients while socializing with others).
4. Case history material (information that experiencing hallucinations first convinced the patient that he was seriously ill and required psychiatric help).

These and other data, obtained from tape-recorded interviews with patient and his family and associates, records kept by social workers and therapists, direct observation on the ward, and so on, permit the classification of concepts and beliefs, and the working out of their interrelationships in the subject's mazeway. The investigator must keep constantly in mind that these belief structures can change and (this is often difficult) that it is the subject's (or the community's) belief system, and not the patient's "true" condition as perceived by the clinician, that is being studied. (And if the clinician's belief system is being studied, the validity of the clinician's beliefs is technically irrelevant.) The tediousness of the task should not be underestimated. A satisfactory case history, for instance, covering day-by-day events for months prior to hospitalization, and during the hospital stay itself, requires extensive checking and cross-checking with dozens of sources of information. The process is comparable to the compilation of data for a biography. Discrete items of information, culled from various sources, are ordered first chronologically and then by topic until an internally coherent process appears in which the subject's decisions and attitudes are demonstrably related to his current situation and past experience. Thus one source may reveal that on a certain date the patient, a ritually faithful Catholic, failed to go to Mass; another source may show that the day before, he had an interview with his priest, who counseled him to exercise will power and to cease wallowing in self-pity; a third source reveals that next week the patient went to his family doctor and received a prescription for tranquilizers; and a fourth source finally shows that some time during the week preceding the visit to the priest, the patient experienced a frightening impulse to kill his wife and child. These details fit into the pattern of a process. With increasing fear of losing self-control, the patient, who still regards his "upset" state as one of moral uncertainty, turns to the priest for help; but the priest's advice does not help to resolve the uncertainty, and he redefines his state as an "illness" requiring medical attention.

Illustration: A Zulu Theory of Mental Illness

Among the Zulu known to Canon Callaway in South Africa, about the middle of the last century, a complex and rather sophisticated theory was held which, in its formal structure, is not dissimilar to some varieties of current psychiatric theory. The structure of this theory is given in the following formula:

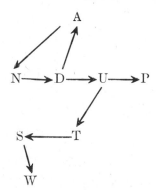

The definition of the states, as given in Callaway's translation of the Zulu text (Callaway 1931) is as follows:

N: "Robust"; good appetite; not choosy about food.
D: "Delicate, not having any real disease, but delicate."
A: "Ill"; choosy about food; loss of appetite; suffers vague pains; anxious dreams; possessed by spirits of ancestors.
U: "Ill"; choosy about food; loss of appetite; suffers vague pains; anxious dreams; possessed by a class of spirits known as *Amatongo.*
P: "A fool," "unable to understand anything," "mad," not a "man."
T: Continued ill health, sleeplessness, loss of weight, skin diseases, but hopeful of becoming a shaman.
S: Good physical health; the state of being a shaman or *inyanga,* i.e., one with a "soft head" who, with the help of his familiar spirits among the *Amatongo,* performs the respectable special role of "diviner" (finder of lost objects and physician to possessed persons).

W: "Always out of health," unable to divine, but of unusual wisdom, and able to work.

The transfer operations, to the extent that they are described in Callaway's text, are:

N ——→ D: Initial possession by either *Amatongo* or ancestral spirits.

D ——→ A: Completion of possession by ancestral spirits.

A ——→ N: Relinquishment of possession by ancestral spirits after being exorcised by sacrifice of cattle under direction of shamans.

D ——→ U: *Amatongo* increase control over victim but divide into two groups, one group (under influence of medicines and cattle sacrifice exorcism) objecting to complete possession and the other insisting on complete possession.

U ——→ P: Continued "blocking the way" of the *Amatongo* by exorcism and by medicines taken by mouth.

U ——→ T: Patient's family, patient, and community, recognize that *Amatongo* are struggling to possess patient, and terminate medicines and exorcism.

T ——→ S: Patient seeks communication with *Amatongo* in his dreams and singing; community participates in his singing and ask him questions for *Amatongo* to answer.

S ——→ W: A "great doctor" can "lay the spirit" of *Amatongo* to the extent of preventing the patient from remaining a diviner but only at the cost of leaving him chronically in state W.

Notable features of the model are, first, the importance of the differential diagnosis (by a shaman) between possession by the relatively benevolent ancestors and by the dangerous *Amatongo;* and second, the irreversible nature of *Amatongo* possession, which eventuates in a state of dementia unless the victim accepts his fate and undergoes the complete course of training as an *inyanga.*

Application to Clinical Case Material

In the application of the foregoing concepts to clinical case material, it must be born in mind that the structure and development of a patient's theory of illness may be related to, but is nevertheless distinct from, the structure and development of his conflict structure ("neurosis") and of his therapeutic regime. In one of the two cases which we have analyzed in some detail by the help of the model, we found the model to be helpful in understanding a temporary impasse, with an associated flurry of disturbed behavior, reached at a certain stage in therapy. The crucial problem in treatment, from the therapist's viewpoint, was the patient's unwillingness to accept the presence in himself of hostile feelings toward various close relatives. The therapist defined the goal of treatment (I) as a less repressive personality and he encouraged the patient to assert himself and his needs more freely and to recognize that these needs, and the hostilities generated by their frustration, were not evil but merely human. The patient was stubbornly resistant, not merely because of the psychodynamics of the situation, but also because the therapist was suggesting that he "act out" in somewhat the same way as his own psychotic father had acted out before his hospitalization some years before. The therapist thus was suggesting to the patient a state I which, in the patient's theory of illness, was hard to distinguish from P. The patient's conscious attention was, at this time, centered on a struggle to avoid entering state P; hence the therapist's suggestions were terrifying, not only because they may have aroused unconscious resistance (in the conventional psychodynamic sense), but because they pushed him toward a self-identification with a psychotic father.

The resolution of the impasse was provided by his development of a compromise, which the therapist was willing to accept, between his original theory and the therapist's theory. This compromise took the following form:

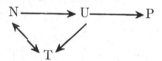

He steadfastly retained the belief that the object of his efforts was a return to his normal, presymptomatic, good-husband-and-father self (N). But he accepted T as a necessary way station on the path to N and as a means of avoiding the alternative state P. His acceptance of the existence and value of T were followed almost immediately by release to the outpatient department.

Application to the Classification of Cultures

Because of the ubiquity of the major types of mental disease, and because of the uncertainty of etiological understanding, it is hazardous to classify cultures as more or less pathogenic in respect to any particular mental illness or to mental illness in general. In all likelihood, as knowledge of the causes of mental illness is extended, it will become easier to discern the relation between culture and etiology. Thus in the future it may be possible to regard the frequency, distribution, and forms of mental illness in a society as an index of its culture. But at the present time, despite the currency of certain hypotheses based on psychodynamic assumptions about the relation between culture and mental illness, it is not feasible to establish a classification based on demonstrated etiological processes.

It is however reasonable to suggest that cultures may, even on the basis of present knowledge, be classified with respect to such culturally institutionalized responses to various types of mental illness as the society's taxonomy and definitions of mental illness, its theory or theories of illness, and its techniques of therapy and their rationale. Such a classification must, in effect, form a matrix of intersection of a constant typology of mental illness (that is, a typology defined by the investigator and used as a constant referent for controlling cross-cultural comparisons) and of alternatively possible responses available cross-culturally. The types so defined may then be investigated in order to discern whether or not a correlation exists between response type and other aspects of culture. If such correlations can be shown to exist, then at least *response to mental illness* may be considered an index of culture.

Evidently a number of possible schemes, of varying degrees of complexity and abstraction, can be created, based on different constant typologies and different panels of alternative responses. One typological system based on theoretical considerations introduced in the preceding sections will be outlined here. For the constant typology, not Western diagnostic categories, but the two dichotomous dimensions of severity and chronicity will be used (mild versus severe, and intermittent versus continuous). For the response typology, two dichotomous dimensions will be used: episodic versus symptomatic interpretations of illness, and treatment versus extrusion as a method of handling illness. These concepts may be defined further as follows: Mildness and severity refer to the degree of abnormality of the overt behavior itself and not to its duration or frequency of occurence; intermittency and continuousness refer to halves of a continuum, intermittency being the half in which the disorder can best be characterized as discrete attacks separated by intervals of normalcy, and continuousness as the half in which the disorder can be characterized as a period of uninterrupted disfunction. Episodic interpretations of illness confine attention only to the overt disorder itself and regard it as an isolated episode in an essentially normal life program, whereas symptomatic interpretations construe the overt disorder as a sign of a more serious under-lying inadequacy which threatens to recur, possibly in a more un-desirable form, on later occasions. Treatment as a method of handling illness implies a policy of attempting to cure, to improve, or to tolerate (even by ignoring the behavior) and make the best use of the victim, in contrast to the method of extrusion, which by such devices as confinement, banishment, or even execution at-tempts to rid society entirely of an incompatible participant. The suggested dichotomies are, of course, divisions of continua, and the distinctions are easier to make in extreme than in intermediate cases. Thus a series of epileptic attacks is easy to classify in the constant typology as intermittent and severe, and a case of obsessive fear of heights as mild and continuous; but a given schizophrenic psychosis may be neither clearly continuous nor notably severe, yet seem by contrast with epilepsy and the fear of heights to require the con-tinuous and severe classification.

The whole schema may be represented in the following diagram:

	Intermittent	Continuous
Mild	Episodic *or* Symptomatic Treatment *or* Extrusion	Episodic *or* Symptomatic Treatment *or* Extrusion
Severe	Episodic *or* Symptomatic Treatment *or* Extrusion	Episodic *or* Symptomatic Treatment *or* Extrusion

Thus any group, with respect to any given syndrome, may be classi-fied as episodic-treatment, episodic-extrusion, symptomatic-treat-ment, or symptomatic-extrusion, within that cell which character-izes the syndrome on the constant typology. If we consider *pibloktoq*, for instance, we would classify this as intermittent-se-vere in the constant typology, and the Polar Eskimo handling of it as episodic-treatment in the response typology. The same syn-drome in the context of, let us say, an operational wing of the U.S. Strategic Air Command would also be classified as intermittent-severe, but the handling of the condition would be classified as symptomatic-extrusion. And, again, this same intermittent-severe syndrome in the context of a liberal arts college campus would be handled either as episodic-treatment or symptomatic-treatment.

The number of possible cultural patterns established by this paradigm is quite large. Although, with regard to any single syndrome, only four types of response are considered, there are four types of syndrome, with regard to each of which these four possibilities exist. Therefore the number of possible cultural patterns is 4^4 or 256. Furthermore, of course, any *description* of the way in which a society handles mental disorders will make many distinctions, even of a classificatory kind, that cannot be included in a pattern classification scheme. Thus, for instance, with respect to the "treatment" class, it will be noted in any description whether the condition in question is ignored, is recognized but tolerated, or is directly approached by a means of therapy. If therapy is employed, it can be medical (physiological) or psychological; and if psychological, it can be secular or religious, cathartic or repressive, and so on. Rather than attempt to embrace all of the 256 patterns, let alone the further elaborations and refinements desirable for any sort of descriptive account, therefore, it would appear to be useful to note that among the large number of possible patterns, several stand out as stock patterns which may be used for the purpose of seeking to establish whether or not, in principle, correlations may exist between a group's manner of handling behavior disorder and other aspects of its culture.

Four such ideal pattern types are offered below:

	Int.	Cont.		Int.	Cont.		Int.	Cont.		Int.	Cont.
Mild	Sy Ex	Sy Ex		Ep Tr	Sy Tr		Sy Tr	Sy Tr		Sy Tr	Sy Tr
Severe	Sy Ex	Sy Ex		Ep Tr	Sy Ex		Sy Ex	Sy Ex		Sy Tr	Sy Tr
	I			II			III			IV	

It is suggested—with the hope not so much that the suggestions will convince as provoke thought and consideration in empirical studies —that these four patterns of institutionalized response to mental illness are associated with definite types of social structures. Pattern I, for instance, would seem to be characteristic of aggressive and power-seeking, self-selected, elite groups generally, whether they be kinship, military, political, economic, or religious. These elite groups extrude (screen out) all persons with visible behavioral anomalies (symptomatic of possible other disabilities as yet unrevealed) in order to maintain a maximally reliable and effective organization. Pattern II would seem to be characteristic of technologically primitive, small communities that recognize disorder as a symptom of a hidden, threatening weakness only when it is continuous, and that will resort to extrusion only when it is both continuous and severe. Pattern III would seem to be characteristic of prenineteenth century Western civilization generally: all disorders are symptomatic, and all serious disorders require extrusion. Pattern IV, on the other hand, would seem to characterize the psychodynamic tradition in twentieth century Western psychiatry, and an increasing number of other educated subgroups in Western populations, who regard all disorders as symptomatic, but also consider that all disorders should be treated rather than disposed of by extrusion.

Space does not permit further elaboration of these concepts; but enough has been said, perhaps, to indicate not only the problems in attempting to create a taxonomy of responses to mental illness with cultural index value, but also the possible value of such a taxonomy in establishing relations between responses to mental illness and other aspects of culture. To the extent that these patterns of response have a bearing on the course of various syndromes, whatever their etiology may be, a taxonomy of this kind may additionally have some utility as an evaluative index of social efficiency in handling the problems of mental illness. We may speculate, for instance, that a group whose response to a behavioral disorder is to regard it as symptomatic of an underlying and threatening chronic incompetency, rather than an episode in a normal life program, will induce in the victim a sense of his own inadequacy that is in itself directly pathogenic. We may further speculate that his anxious efforts to defend himself will markedly affect the form and course of the disorder itself. If these defensive efforts are not directed toward the securing of a validly effective therapy, then the pathogenic pressure of the culturally institutionalized definitions of and responses to mental illness will be uncompensated. In such an unhappy case, even if the etiology of the disorder were actually completely organic, the culture would be playing a contributory role in the mental disease process.

TOWARD A BIOCULTURAL THEORY OF MENTAL ILLNESS: THE INTEGRATION OF THE ORGANIC AND FUNCTIONAL APPROACHES

How can the cultural anthropologist relate his conceptions of the structuring of social behavior to biological theories of mental illness? The model of mental illness advocated in this paper as an answer to this question is essentially homeostatic. A behavior system is considered to be disturbed when an independent variable, organic in nature, passes certain boundary values; and the responses of the various components of this system can be construed as motivated efforts to restore equilibrium. These responses are prescribed by the system itself in its theory of illness. But mere lip service to the ideal of an "interdisciplinary" approach, and pleas for the recognition of the importance of biological or cultural factors, will not solve the scientific problem. Only an approach which considers the *specific nature* of the interaction between biological and cultural (psychosocial) variables can have high predictive value.

The specific nature of this biocultural interaction can best be investigated by conceiving of the total course of the psychotic episode as a single event and then analyzing it into stages. Each stage is defined by a change in one of the major relevant dimensions of the event. A number of plausible programs can be constructed by a priori reasoning from different assumptions about the identity of the initial stage. One such program derives from the assumption (not yet justified by empirical findings) that the initial event in the psychotic episode is the occurrence of an organic disfunction in a hitherto intact (even if peculiarly vulnerable) individual.

If one makes this assumption, every episode of serious mental illness can be divided into four stages (exclusive of therapeutic and rehabilitation stages).

In the first stage, the organism is functioning normally.

In the second stage, an intermittent or continuous, of greater or lesser severity, organic interference with normal brain function occurs. Presumably the oft-remarked transcultural invariance of the major clinical entities and the absence of unique ethnic psychoses result because the number of types of organic interference is limited. Many sources of such interferences are known, however: cerebral hypoglycemia or hypoxia, electrolyte disturbances, gross tissue change, hormonal autointoxication, toxic metabolites, drugs, viral invasion, anomalies of enzyme action, and so on. These immediate sources in turn can theoretically depend upon many "final" causes, including prolonged states of psychodynamically and socially determined stress (such as those revealed by psychoanalytic investigations) which may produce temporary, and conceivably sometimes even irreversible, changes in body chemistry. Genetic factors may also be responsible for differential vulnerabilities within a population to the various noxious factors. Thus even from an organismic position one can comfortably look to social and psychological processes as "final" causes, particularly if the differential incidence of disorders rather than the understanding of individual cases is of primary concern. Coincident with the neural dysfunction occurs psychological dysfunction. The quality of this dysfunction is best conceived as a relative difficulty in organizing cognitive content: difficulty in finding the "meaning" of perceptual data, difficulty in maintaining the structure of motives, difficulty in relating affect to "rational" considerations. These difficulties may be metaphorically described as desemantication: the shrinking of the semantic matrix. This kind of dysfunction can vary in severity from an almost imperceptible decrement to a decrement so catastrophic as to approximate decerebration, with attendant loss of perceptual contact with the environment, motor discharge, and release of autonomic functions. At an intermediate level between mild confusion and unconsciousness would seem to fall the experience of meaninglessness, described by some schizophrenics as a sense of unreality, depersonalization, and loss of identity. Desemantication may be briefly episodic, as in hysteriform attacks, or chronic, as (apparently) in schizophrenia. Also coincident with neural and psychological dysfunction is primary behavioral failure attendent upon the desemantication. This is failure as judged by either the victim and members of his group, or both, and may occur in a variety of sectors of life, both interpersonal and technological. While incompetence in interpersonal relations may be the most conspicuous consequence of desemantication in the eyes of the group, technical failures in performing essential routine tasks, such as walking, paddling a kayak, ironing clothes, and preparing food, may come first to the victim's own awareness. Such failures may vary in duration and in the social or individual importance of the area of behavior involved.

If negative self-evaluation by the victim follows the events of the second stage, then the third stage will occur, characterized by anxiety, depression, and other negative affects directed toward the self. All persons constantly monitor and evaluate their competence in attaining their goals, both by self-perception and by perception of others' response to their behavior. A person experiencing desemantication finds the performance of his tasks more difficult and in some instances impossible. If the desemantication is continuous and is relatively severe, he will be unable to deny the reality of his loss of competency. His evaluation of these failures, which is a complex function of his current experience, the responses of others, and past learning, will be less effective than normal precisely because of the desemantication itself. But it will be based, in every instance, in part on concepts available to him from his past learning of the culturally standardized interpretations of the specific experiences and incompetencies which he now recognizes in himself. Thus he may interpret the perplexing voices which he hears as religious revelations, as the delirium accompanying fever, as the result of overwork, as the consequence of emotional conflict, and so forth, depending on the content of the experience, the reactions of others, and the explanations offered by his own cultural background. To the extent that the self-evaluation is negative, he loses confidence in his ability to control his own behavior, to master his environment. and to relate his behavior systematically with others.

The fourth stage is cognitive damage incurred in the course of the victim's defensive response to the negative self-evaluation. The response to his own anxiety and depression is, because of the existence of physiological dysfunction, itself apt to be disorganized. But it is designed to improve the negative self-image and to protect the person from catastrophe, and may in some degree relieve the patient's anxiety and depression, albeit at the cost of cognitive damage in the form of paranoid delusions, self-limiting withdrawal from society, and so on. Part of the response may be "neurotic," in the sense of utilizing such mechanisms of defense as denial, repression, projection, paranoid oversimplification, and so on. Part of it may be impulsive fighting with, or withdrawing from, a now dangerous and exhausting world. Part of it may take the form of seeking help. The style in which the person goes about attempting to defend himself, maintain self-respect, and secure help will of course reflect his cultural learning.

Through the second, third, and fourth stages, the victim's community is also evaluating and responding to him as a "changed person." Even in a homogeneous community, the social evaluation and response may be considerably different from the victim's, both because the victim's desemantication constrains his behavior, and because his motives may be divergent from those of the group. Whether or not his motives diverge from the group will depend considerably on the nature of these beliefs. Thus, for instance, if mental illness as evidenced by hallucination is culturally defined as a degrading condition to which society responds by social extrusion, the victim will be strongly motivated to conceal his condition, to deny it, to withdraw from prying eyes, and to accuse others of conspiracy against him if the charge is made. If, on the other hand, hallucination is a sign of contact—uncomfortable perhaps—with the supernatural world, and is responded to with rituals of intensified social acceptance, the hallucinator's motives will in all likelihood not be directed toward denial, concealment, and defense, but toward maximum publicity.

This model of the process of becoming mentally ill, as an immediate consequence of neurophysiological dysfunction, in a social environment, may be succinctly represented in a paradigm. Such a paradigm, of course, represents only a canonical form or modal type. The symbols are read as follows: "O" represents level of neurophysiological function of brain; "S" represents level of semantic psychological function; "B" represents level of overt behavioral success in achieving goals in social context; "A" represents level of anxiety, depression, and other negative affect directed toward self; and "D" represents the degree of cognitive damage incurred in the course of the defensive responses of the individual to his own negative self-evaluation. The operator $\downarrow$ represents pathological change, and $\wedge$ represents "and."

Stage 0: Eufunction (O,S,B,) $\wedge$ (A) $\wedge$ (D)
   If physiological injury occurs, then

Stage 1: Primary Dysfunction ($\downarrow$ O, $\downarrow$ S, $\downarrow$ B) $\wedge$ (A) $\wedge$ (D)
   If negative self-evaluation occurs, then

Stage 2: Anxiety and Depression ($\downarrow$ O, $\downarrow$ S, $\downarrow$ B) $\wedge$ ($\downarrow$ A) $\wedge$ (D)
   If anxiety and depression are severe and prolonged, then

Stage 3: Cognitive Damage ($\downarrow$ O, $\downarrow$ S, $\downarrow$ B) $\wedge$ (A) $\wedge$ ($\downarrow$ D)

CONCLUSION

The importance of the organic factors in psychopathology has been largely ignored by anthropological theory, which has emphasized psychological factors almost exclusively. If the viewpoint is taken that organic events play a significant role in the etiology of many mental disorders, it is possible to see the role of cultural differences as particularly relevant to etiology via their influence in determining the frequency with which the pathogenic organic events occur. From this point of view also, the culturally institutionalized theories of illness and of therapy appear to be extremely important in deciding the nature of the victim's and his group's responses to the disorder. A model of mental illness as a type of event is offered which integrates the organic and psychosocial approaches.

It may be hoped that anthropologists who have occasion to make observations in the field on persons with mental illness will in the future be able to obtain and record more extensive information on the physical status and history of the victims. Data on nutrition, infectious diseases, head injuries, and autonomic symptomatology, both with regard to the individual cases and also with respect to the community as a whole, would be helpful in describing individual cases, in understanding group differences, and in putting the brakes on overly facile attributions of psychopathology to "social structure," "culture," and "basic personality."

BIBLIOGRAPHY *

AMERICAN MUSEUM of NATURAL HISTORY, PHOTOGRAPHIC DIVISION.
  1914   Photographs of the Crockerland Expedition.
BAASHUUS-JENSEN, J.
  1935   Arctic nervous diseases. Veterinary Journal (London) 91:339–350, 379–390.
BARRETT, ALBERT M.
  1919–20 Psychosis associated with tetany. American Journal of Insanity 76:373–392.
BELLAK, LEOPOLD (ed.)
  1958   Schizophrenia: a review of the syndrome. New York, Logos Press.
BERTELSEN, A.
  1940   Grønlandsk medicinsk statistik og nosografi. Meddelelser om Grønland, Bd 117, Nr. 3. Copenhagen.
BRILL, A. A.
  1913   Pibloktoq or hysteria among Peary's Eskimos. Journal of Nervous and Mental Disease 40:514–520.
CALLAWAY, CANON H.
  1931   The religion of the Amazulu of South Africa, as told by themselves. In A. L. Kroeber and T. T. Waterman, Source book in anthropology. New York, Harcourt, Brace.
CANNON, WALTER B.
  1942   Voodoo death. American Anthropologist 44:169–181.
CLAUSEN, J. A., and M. R. YARROW
  1955   The impact of mental illness on the family. Journal of Social Issues 11:(4) (whole issue).
COOK, FREDERICK A.
  1894   Medical observations among the Esquimaux. Transactions of the New York Obstetrical Society, 1893–1894, pp. 171–174.

---

* A short bibliography of other works dealing with the same subject but not referred to here is appended at the end of this chapter. A selected bibliography bearing on the mutual relationship between anthropology, psychiatry and psychoanalysis is given in the Appendix at end of the book.

CURSCHMANN, HANS
   1904 Tetanie, psuedotetanie und ihre mischformen bei hysterie. Deutsche zeitschrift für nervenheilkunde 27: article 12, 239–268.

GLASS, ALBERT J.
   1953 Psychotherapy in the combat zone. *In* Symposium on Stress, Washington, Walter Reed Army Medical Center.

GOLDSTEIN, KURT
   1940 Human nature. Cambridge, Harvard University Press.

GUSSOW, Z.
   1960 Pibloktoq (hysteria) among the Polar Eskimo: an ethnopsychiatric study. *In* W. Muensterberger, ed., Psychoanalysis and the Social Sciences. New York, Ruternational Universities Press.

HOLLINGSHEAD, A. B., and F. C. REDLICH
   1958 Social class and mental illness. New York, Wiley.

HOYGAARD, ARNE
   1941 Studies on the nutrition and physio-pathology of Eskimos. Oslo, Skrifter utgitt au Det Norske Videnskaps-Akademi i Oslo, I. Mat.-Naturv. Klasse 1940 No. 9.

HUNT, J. McV. (ed.)
   1944 Personality and the behavior disorders. New York, Ronald Press.

KALLMAN, FRANZ
   1938 The genetics of schizophrenia. New York, J. J. Augustin.

KANE, E. K.
   1856 Arctic explorations: the second Grinnell expedition. Philadelphia, Childs and Peterson.

MACMILLAN, DONALD B.
   1918 Food supply of the Smith Sound Eskimos. American Museum Journal 18:161–176.
   1934 How Peary reached the pole. Boston, Houghton.

MANDELBAUM, DAVID G.
   1949 Selected writings of Edward Sapir. Berkeley, University of California Press.

MAXWELL, J. P.
   1930 Further studies in osteomalacia. Proceedings of the Royal Society of Medicine 23:639–640.

MILBANK MEMORIAL FUND
   1952 The biology of mental health and mental disease. New York, Hoeber.

PEARY, ROBERT E.
   1907 Nearest the pole. New York, Doubleday, Page.

PETERSON, DONALD B., *et al.*
   1950 Role of hypnosis in differentiation of epileptic from convulsive-like seizures. American Journal af Psychiatry 107:428–443.

RASMUSSEN, KNUD
   1915 Foran Dagens Øje: Liv I Grønland. Copenhagen.

RODAHL, K.
   1957   Human acclimatization to cold. Arctic Aeromedical Laboratory, Technical Report 57–21.

SELYE, HANS
   1956   The stress of life. New York, McGraw-Hill.

SHELLING, D. H.
   1935   The parathyroids in health and disease. St. Louis, Mosby.

TOOTH, GEOFFREY
   1950   Studies in mental illness in the Gold Coast. London, H. M. Stationery Office.

WALLACE, ANTHONY F. C.
   1959   Cultural determinants of response to hallucinatory experience. A.M.A. Archives of General Psychiatry 1:58–69.
   1959   The institutionalization of cathartic and control strategies in Iroquois religious psychotherapy. In Marvin Opler, ed., Culture and mental health. New York, MacMillan.

WHITNEY, H.
   1911   Hunting with the Eskimos. New York, Century.

SELECTED GENERAL WORKS DEALING WITH PHYSICAL AGENTS OR PROCESSES WHICH LEAD TO PSYCHOPATHOLOGY OR REDUCE IT

ARIETI, SILVANO, ed.
   1959   American handbook of psychiatry. 2 vols. New York, Basic Books.

BELLAK, LEOPOLD, ed.
   1958   Schizophrenia: a review of the syndrome. New York, Logos Press.

BEST, CHARLES H. and NORMAN B. TAYLOR
   1955   The physiological basis of medical practice. 6th ed. Baltimore, Williams and Wilkins.

DAVIDSON, S., A. P. MEIKLEJOHN, and R. PASSMORE
   1959   Human nutrition and dietetics. Baltimore, Williams and Wilkins.

DEWAN, JOHN G. and WILLIAM B. SPAULDING
   1958   The organic psychoses. Toronto, University of Toronto Press.

DUNCAN, GARFIELD G., ed.
   1952   Diseases of metabolism. 3d ed. Philadelphia, W. B. Saunders.

GOLDSTEIN, KURT
   1940   Human nature. Cambridge, Harvard University Press.

HOSKINS, R. G.
   1946   The biology of schizophrenia. New York, W. W. Norton and Co.

KALLMAN, FRANZ
   1938   The genetics of schizophrenia. New York, J. J. Augustin.

KLINE, NATHAN S.
   1956   Psychopharmacology. Washington, D.C., American Association for the Advancement of Science.

MERRITT, H. HOUSTON and CLARENCE C. HARE, eds.
  1953   Metabolic and toxic diseases of the nervous system. Baltimore, Williams and Wilkins.

MILBANK MEMORIAL FUND
  1952   The biology of mental health and mental disease. New York, Hoeber.

PFEIFFER, JOHN
  1955   The human brain. New York, Harper & Bros.

RESEARCH PUBLICATIONS OF THE ASSOCIATION FOR RESEARCH IN NERVOUS AND MENTAL DISEASE.

SARGANT, WILLIAM
  1954   An introduction to physical methods of treatment in psychiatry. Baltimore, Williams and Wilkins.

SELYE, HANS
  1950   The physiology and pathology of exposure to stress. Montreal, Acta.
  1956   The stress of life. New York, McGraw-Hill.

WILLIAMS, ROGER J.
  1956   Biochemical individuality. New York, Wiley.

Chapter 10

ANTHROPOLOGICAL STUDIES OF DREAMS

ROY G. D'ANDRADE
Harvard University

HISTORICALLY, the investigation of dreams has occupied an interesting position in anthropological theory. From an early position of prominence in the nineteenth century, the study of dreams became more and more peripheral to the major interests of anthropologists. Perhaps this was due to the Freudian revolution, which radically altered the general conception of dreams, and also to the shift in interest away from cultural evolution. Before Freud, dreams had been considered a possible major influence on the origin and development of religion. After Freud, dreams came to be considered disguised representations of motives, and, therefore, more relevant to the analysis of the individual psyche than to an analysis of social and cultural events.

However, by 1930, anthropologists had begun to raise questions concerning the psychoanalytic theory of dreams, and especially the assumption that dream symbols had the same meaning in societies with cultural traditions very different from those of Western Europe. Since 1930, numerous dreams from non-Western peoples have been interpreted by field workers interested in the relation between culture and personality, and the psychological uses and functions of dreams in a number of non-Western societies have also been examined. Thus, dreams have again entered into the discussion of man's cultural life, although in a psychological rather than evolutionary context.

This review will attempt to bring together the anthropological findings concerning dreams, focussing on the interaction of cultural and psychological factors. First, as a historical introduction, the influence of dreams on the origin and development of culture will be discussed. Next the question of universal symbolism in dreams will be considered, followed by a review of the results of psychological interpretations of dreams from "primitive" or non-Western societies. The last two sections will consider the ways in which culture influences and utilizes dreams.

The Influence of Dreams on the Origin and Development of Culture

The cultural study of dreams begins in modern anthropology with Tylor's work on animism. Tylor considered animism, or the "doctrine of the soul," to be the basic substratum of religion, from which arose more complex forms of religious belief. In order to account for the origin of animism, Tylor turned to the ethnographic materials available to him concerning dreams, and especially the widespread belief that during dreams the soul may travel about, meet other souls, and receive injuries which may affect the health of the dreamer. From this association of dreams and beliefs about the soul, Tylor inferred that the idea of the soul arose from man's attempt to account for the phantom visitors in sleep and dreams, and to explain the differences between sleeping and waking, and life and death. This thesis has been found plausible by a wide range of scholars. Lowie stated:

His (Tylor's) theory is avowedly a psychological interpretation pure and simple, but inasmuch as it not only explains the empirical observations, but operates exclusively with facts like death, dreams, and visions, all of which demonstrably exercise a strong influence on the minds of primitive man, it must be conceded to have a high degree of probability. I for one, certainly have never encountered any rival hypothesis that could be considered a serious competitor. (1924:108)

Tylor was not the first to present this idea. Thomas Hobbes, in 1651, stated:

From this ignorance of how to distinguish Dreams and other strong fancies from Vision and Sense did arise the greater part of the religion of the Gentiles in times past that worshipped Satyres, Faunes, Nymphs, and the like; and nowadays the opinion that rude people have of Fayries, Ghosts, and Goblins, and the power of Witches. (*Leviathan,* ch. xii, quoted by Jones 1931.)

A further elaboration of this thesis from the psychoanalytic point of view has been presented by Ernest Jones, who postulates that the conceptions of werewolves, vampires, incubi, witches, and the devil, current in the Middle Ages, were also derived from dream experiences. Specifically, Jones tries to show that these supernatural figures were derived from nightmares, with which they share numerous common features, such as an identical latent content representing incestuous wishes, extreme dread, transformation of persons into animals, the occurrence of fantastic animal forms, the alternation of the imagined object between extreme attractiveness and intense repulsiveness, the idea of flying through the air, and the representation of sexual acts as torturing assaults. Also these creatures appeared frequently in nightmares, and were, at the time, considered to be a direct cause of nightmares (1931:239).

Lincoln, in the *Dream in Primitive Culture,* presents a number of ethnographic examples in which cultural items, such as curing rituals, art work, songs and dances, religious cults, and so forth, were supposedly invented in dreams. Lincoln points out that it is usually in culturally defined and expected dreams that these culture items originate, rather than idiosyncratic dreams, and that these culture items are often presented in the dream by an ancestor-like spirit. Lincoln concludes:

> . . . a large part of primitive culture is a result of the dream, or more accurately a result of the psychological and cultural processes behind the dream. These processes are given form in the dream and influence the culture directly from the latter. (1935:93)

The general thesis of Tylor, Jones, Lincoln, and others that dreams have been either a primary or secondary source of innovation is a difficult argument to prove or disprove. Generally, the argument is based on similarities between typical dream experiences and cultural items and the frequent appearance in dreams of these items. Even where there are cultural demands that an individual invent a song or myth or ritual in dreams, this process is often only a minor reworking of already existing materials, for which the dream is as much an expected means of validation as an actual source of invention. Devereux, in a careful study of Mohave dreams and rituals, finds:

> Although Mohave shamans and singers are supposed to acquire their knowledge in dreams they actually learn it in waking life and then have dreams which condense or allude to this body of knowledge. (1957:1044)

While the influence of dreams on the origin and development of culture remains obscure, these studies have clarified one aspect of the relation of dreams to culture. They document the persistent association found between dreams and beliefs about supernaturals, including other souls. Dreams have been shown to be one of the chief means of communication with supernaturals, and supernaturals have been found to have certain similarities to figures which typically appear in dreams. It appears that dreams, as a common projective experience, merge with and take material from other culturally defined projective systems, and also give the individual direct access to these projective systems, although the degree of merger and access varies from culture to culture.

Universal Symbolism in Dreams

Of the complex theory presented by Freud in the *Interpretation of Dreams,* anthropologists have discussed most frequently the problem of the universality of dream symbols. The relevance of this problem has been succinctly put forward by C. G. Seligman.

> If it can be shown that identical symbols (i.e., identical symbols with the same meaning attached to them) prevail, then we shall have to admit that the unconscious of the most diverse races is qualitatively so alike that it actually constitutes a common store on which fantasy may draw, and it becomes imperative to give full weight to this in any discussion of the origin of myths and beliefs. (1927:200)

In the *Interpretation of Dreams,* symbolization is treated as just one of the processes by which the latent content, consisting of a series of thoughts expressing a wish, may be transformed into the jumble of vivid images which comprise the manifest content of the dream. The latent dream thoughts may also be changed through condensation and displacement, that is, by the use of hints or allusion, or by the substitution of a part for the whole, or by representing words in pun-like images. Unlike the processes of condensation and displacement, however, symbolization is considered to be more limited in scope, and to refer, especially in dreams, to only a limited number of things: the nuclear family, the human body, and the biological activities of the body, such as birth, sucking, defecation, copulation, and death (Freud 1920:156–177).

While the hypothesized processes of condensation and displacement have not been subject to much question, the possibility that man uses a special vocabulary without awareness and tuition has been the subject of frequent debate. And the possibility that this vocabulary is everywhere the same, impervious to culture, has also raised questions, especially among anthropologists. It should be mentioned that the issue here is not whether dreams can be interpreted solely through symbols, but whether a certain cognitive process, symbolization, is universal. Any interpretation of dreams based on symbols alone would leave out all the other processes of dream formation, thereby omitting the analysis of a large amount of material, and resulting in an oversimplified if not incorrect analysis (Freud 1900:353, Eggan 1952, Roheim 1947:88).

Unfortunately, actual investigations of dream symbolism in non-Western cultures have been relatively rare, perhaps because of the great methodological difficulties. Those studies of non-Western dreams which have used symbols in dream interpretation have sometimes brought out impressive convergences with other personality data (Devereux 1951, Lee 1958). However, these convergences cannot be considered good evidence for the universality of dream symbols, since the conclusions derived from the interpretation of dream symbols have not been compared systematically with, nor constructed independently from, other personality data.

There is, however, some assessable evidence on the issue of symbolism in dreams. Within Western culture, supportive evidence has been reported from the studies of hypnotic dreams, in which a subject is instructed to dream of certain activities in a hidden or disguised way, and to remember the dream but to forget the instructions upon waking. Roffenstein reports the following dream by an uneducated woman told to dream of sexual intercourse with her father:

> I dreamt about my father, as if he had presented me with a great bag, a traveling bag, and with it he gave me a large key. It was a very large key. It looked like a key to a house. I had a sad feeling, and I wondered about its being so big; it couldn't possibly fit. Then I opened the bag. A snake jumped out right against my mouth. I shrieked aloud and then I woke. (1951:255)

The symbols of the key and the snake for the penis, and the traveling bag and mouth for the female genitalia, stand out clearly. While this kind of evidence supports the symbolism hypothesis, one positive instance is not a proof.

However, even if Western dreamers do use (sometimes, at least) a stereotyped set of symbols, it would be rash to then assume that these same symbols are used in the same way in all cultures. One excellent but laborious method of investigating the universality of dream symbolism is to compare interpretations based on the symbolism found in the dreams of non-Western informants with *independently* collected history materials. An example of this method has been reported by Honigman.

> It has been suggested that in dreams protrusions symbolize the male sex organ and the male's normally assertive role in copulation. Aware of this clinically derived interpretation, we implicitly predicted sexual inadequacy or impotence for a young Kaska man who reported a dream in which he was attacked by a grizzly

bear. "My gun stick. I get nervous. I try to take shot at him. My gun got no power. Goes sssss—goes out quick." When interviewed, the informant rejected the interpretation equating gun and penis. Our prediction was nevertheless confirmed when on two subsequent occasions, according to reliable testimony, the informant experienced acute impotence." (1954:158–159)

Another kind of evidence for the universality of dream symbols is found in the meaning that particular cultures assign to certain dreams. It has been found that a number of cultures, widely dispersed, attribute to certain common dreams similar meanings which correspond closely to the psychoanalytic interpretations of these dreams. C. G. Seligman has collected a number of examples of such similarities (1924, 1932), and a review of this material may be found in Lincoln (1935:107–131). Two of the most remarkable of these similarities are the interpretations that feces in a dream stand for wealth, which is reported for the Ashanti, Tikopia, Western Europeans, Thai, Tangerians, Naga, Chinese, and Sinhalese, and the interpretation that loss of a tooth in a dream indicates death, illness, or disaster, reported for the Lolo, Araucanians, Chuckchee, Western Europeans, Chiricahua, Cuna, Ashanti, Naga, Malayans, Achelenese, Japanese, Chinese, and Diegueño (Seligman 1924). Although these interpretations are not made by every culture, it seems unlikely that widely dispersed cultures should have hit upon such similar symbolism by chance.

From these bits of evidence, it would seem that some degree of universal symbolism in dreams is probable. Seligman's conclusions, set down in 1924, seem to be still adequate. He stated:

> The essential dream mechanisms of non-Europeans including savage and barbaric peoples, appear to be the same as in ourselves. Thus dreams with symbolism, sometimes elaborate and recondite, often simple and obvious, occur. These dreams may be wish-fulfillments or be provoked by conflict.
> Dreams with the same manifest content to which identical (latent) meanings are attached (type dreams) occur, not only in cognate groups, but among peoples of diverse race and in every stage of culture. (1924:46)

A complete validation of the hypothesis of universal symbolism is, of course, impossible. The important issue is the degree of probability which is to be assigned to this hypothesis. Perhaps it would be more fruitful to investigate the degree to which universal symbols, in dreams and in other fantasy materials, can be laid over with secondary cultural and individual meanings, and the degree to which culture is selective in choosing from the stock of possible symbols, than to try to document such an unwieldy issue as the universality of symbols. Lee, for example, in his study of Zulu dreams, demonstrates the way in which different dream symbols are used by women at various points along the life cycle.

Lee finds that unmarried women are more likely to have symbolic birth dreams of still water, compared to married women with few children, who are more likely to have undisguised dreams of babies. Married women with *many* children, however, are likely to have frightening symbolic birth dreams of flooded rivers (1958). This selectivity in dream symbolism supports the hypothesis that symbols are less likely to be used if the wish symbolized is acceptable, and also demonstrates something of the complex relations between cultural norms, social roles, and motivation.

PSYCHOLOGICAL INTERPRETATIONS OF NON-WESTERN DREAMS

This section will review some of the findings and basic issues involved in the psychological interpretation of dreams from non-Western societies. The theory and techniques of dream interpretation used by field workers in non-Western societies have been based on Freud's monumental *Interpretation of Dreams,* although a number of warnings about complete acceptance of the psychoanalytic methods and theory have been presented by anthropologists who have worked with non-Western dreams (Eggan 1952, Honigmann 1954).

From a scanning of the published interpretation of non-Western dreams by Lincoln (1935), Roheim (1946, 1949, 1950), Devereaux (1951), and Kluckhohn and Morgan (1951), all of whom have used psychoanalytic techniques, it appears that dreams from different cultures frequently have strikingly similar latent contents. Typically, the analysis of non-Western dreams has revealed incestuous attachments, sibling rivalry, anxiety associated with castration and maternal separation, cross-sex identification, and so forth. Roheim, a psychoanalyst and anthropologist, has used dreams consistently to illustrate Oedipal concerns in non-Western peoples. He has attempted to show, for instance, that among the Baiga such typical Oedipal concerns as castration anxiety and hostility toward the father are prominent in fantasy, although the sexual behavior of both adults and children is subject to very few restrictions.

Another man reported to Elwin the dream "I was in a rage, wrestling with my father; then a tiger knocked me down and killed me. I went below the earth, and there I turned into a tiny man only a foot high. A great snake saw me and said, "I am going to eat you." I said "Open your mouth," and in I went and came out the other end. At once I flew away; up to my own house." (Elwin 1939:432–434)

The tiger is a representation of the father. The tiny man a foot high who goes into the earth is the dreamer's penis entering Mother Earth. The snake in this dream represents both father (phallus) and mother (devouring). Entering and flying are symbols of coitus. The latent dream wish is to kill the father (tiger) and have intercourse with the mother (Roheim 1946:507).

Some of the findings about the universal characteristics of the latent content of dreams may be due to bias in the theory and methods of dream interpretation, and especially to an overreliance on symbolic interpretation. This is not the case for all of these studies, however. For example, Clyde Kluckhohn's conclusions from his study of Navaho dreams are based not only on his informants' dreams, but on observations made after years of field work. The following excerpt is taken from the analyses of a series of dreams from a five-year-old Navaho boy.

Dream 2

We were in our hogan, and a wolf came, and he had long teeth, and he frightened us and Mamie ran to the bed, and I ran outside where my mother was and I hid behind her and she scared away the wolf.

Associations

Yesterday I was playing in a deep arroyo. And above it my father was building on the adobe house. And I built some steps up the arroyo so I could climb out. The white dog and puppies came down into the arroyo. I got scared and couldn't find the steps. So I ran home.

Interpretation

The dream itself is oedipal. The general pattern is already familiar from dreams of the other children. "Father threatens children. Mother protects us." Wolf in the dream and dog in the associations seem to be equated. The long teeth may represent the penis, but they also recall the vagina dentata motif. Crawling out of the deep arroyo represents birth, and the whole of this part of the association suggests speculation about the father's part in the birth process. (Kluckhohn and Morgan 1951:130)

In the same paper Kluckhohn states:

I still believe that some of the cautions uttered by Boas and others on the possible extravagances of interpretations in terms of universal symbols, completely or largely divorced from minute examination of cultural context, are sound. But the facts uncovered in my own field work and that of my collaborators have forced me to the conclusion that Freud and other psychoanalyists have depicted with astonishing correctness many central themes in motivational life which are universal. The styles of expression of these themes and much of the manifest content are culturally determined, but the underlying psychologic drama transcends cultural differences. (Kluckhohn and Morgan 1951:120)

Since these depth interpretations of dreams tend to find universal themes, is there any reason to include such investigations in the study of particular cultures? Roheim has argued strongly that dream interpretation can be extremely useful in uncovering the unconscious meaning of various cultural practices, such as initiation ceremonies and totemism. This is to be done by analyzing the context in which aspects of these practices occur in dreams (Roheim 1932:21). For example, in the controversy over the supposed lack of knowledge of physical paternity of the Aranda, Roheim used the analyses of dreams concerning birth to indicate not only unconscious knowledge of the process of impregnation on the part of the Aranda, but also to illustrate that the official denial serves other personality needs, such as avoidance of rivalrous feelings toward the real father, and identification with the supernatural fathers, as well as disguised gratification of Oedipal wishes (Roheim 1938:359).

It should be pointed out that it is the more unconscious and primitive dream contents which seem most universal rather than the particular manner in which these impulses are expressed and defended against, and the specific reality situations which are associated with these impulses. For example, many of the dreams of Devereux's Plains Indian patient have the characteristics of moral maxims. In these dreams, significant figures often give the dreamer advice, helping him carry out his dream activities successfully. In other dreams the dreamer gives advice to himself, and to others. Here the manifest dream content shows a kind of moral life style typical of some individuals from the Plains culture area. This kind of manifest content would be most unusual in Alor where theft and lying are more prevalent dream activities.

In the last decade, there has been a shift of interest from the latent to the manifest content of dreams. The psychoanalytic concern with the functions of the ego and the potentialities of quantitative data treatment have contributed to this change in interest. Within anthropology, Dorothy Eggan has pioneered in the study of the manifest contents of dreams. Mrs. Eggan has collected more than six hundred Hopi dreams from twenty informants in five Hopi villages, including over two hundred dreams with associations from a single informant who has been the subject of an extensive life study. Mrs. Eggan presents fifteen dreams from this informant, taken over a number of years, whose manifest contents demonstrate vividly some of the less conscious motivations in this man's life (Eggan 1949). The manifest content of this informant's dreams has also been subjected to a content analysis (Eggan 1952). The high ratio of the number of dreams which the dreamer felt were "bad" compared to the number experienced as "good," and the large number of dream elements dealing with security and support on the one hand, and elements of persecution and conflict on the other, portray the conflicts and unrest in the dreamer's personality.

The shift in emphasis from latent to manifest content in the study of dreams, both Western and non-Western, has also been accompanied by the use of more explicit theory and hypothesis in the construction of content categories (Hall 1956). (Cf. Eggan 1960 for a further review of some of the current psychological research on manifest content in Western dreams.) Dittman and Moore (1957) have attempted to rate Navaho dreams for degree of emotional disturbance, comparing the dreams of members of the Peyote cult with nonmembers. They found that the members of the Peyote cult had somewhat more disturbed dreams, but only measured by the global dream ratings made by raters who had some knowledge of Navaho culture.

Based on an earlier version of Schneider's analysis of the dream of the Yir-Yoront, a small Australian tribe, (Schneider 1941), Walter Sears, in an undergraduate honors thesis, compared Navaho dreams with the dreams of the Yir-Yoront, and found that the Navaho have more threatening and terrifying dreams, fewer dreams in which aggression is directly expressed by the dreamer, fewer dreams with explicit sexual activities, and more dreams about white culture than the Yir-Yoront. Generally, it would seem that the Navaho are less free about the expression of impulses than the Yir-Yoront, and concomitantly find dreaming more unpleasant (Sears 1948).

Another comparative study, by Griffith, Miyagi, and Tago, contrasts the typical dreams of American and Japanese college students (1958). Griffith and his co-workers used the questionnaire method, requesting that the subjects check from a list of thirty-four typical dreams those which they could recall. It was found that there were great similarities between Japanese and Americans in the frequencies with which most typical dreams are recalled, with about as much agreement between the two cultures as there was between males and females within either culture. There were some small but significant differences between the Japanese and Americans, however, the Japanese reporting more dreams of being attacked or pursued, of trying to do something again and again, of school, teachers, and studying, of being frozen with fright, of flying or soaring through the air, and of wild, violent beasts. The Americans report more dreams of arriving late, of missing trains, of being locked up, of loved persons being dead, of finding money, of being inappropriately dressed, of being nude, and of lunatics or insane people. These differences can be tentatively interpreted as indicating that Americans are more concerned with time, money, physical freedom and body shame than the Japanese, but less concerned with feelings of responsibility and projected aggression.

An outline for an analysis of individual dreams, including both manifest and latent content, has been presented by Eric Erikson in a paper on the dream specimen in psychoanalysis (1954). This outline breaks up the manifest content into verbal, sensory, spatial, temporal, somatic, interpersonal, and affective qualities, and the latent content into the sleep-disturbing stimulus, the day residue, acute life conflicts, repetitive conflicts, associated basic childhood conflict, impulses, and methods of defense. Using this outline, Erikson reanalyses Freud's Irma dream (Freud 1900:106–120), illustrating brilliantly not only the sexual and aggressive impulses woven into the dream, but also how the social and emotional conflicts attendant upon intellectual creativity were pictured by Freud in the dream, and solved within the dream by an individual ritual of identification.

Adelson (1960), using a modified form of Erikson's outline for the analysis of manifest content, has contrasted the dreams of college girls who have highly rated literary creativity with the dreams of those who display little literary creativity. Creative girls tend to have dreams in which impossible events occur, often in an exotic setting, with many changes in these settings, while girls without much creative talent had dreams tied to the local, prosaic, and familiar. Also, 20 per cent of the dreams of the creative girls were marked by the absence of the dreamer, while the noncreative girls *always* appeared in their own dreams. And finally, creative girls tended to have open and even flamboyant sexual activities occur in their dreams, contrasting sharply with the vague, timid, and symbolic dreams of the noncreative girls. Generally, it would seem that creative people, at least in dreams, can tolerate, and perhaps prefer, more incoherent, illogical, and directly expressive materials, and can treat these materials more impersonally.

Recently, the study of dreams has received tremendous impetus from the psychological research on dreaming conducted by Dement, Kleitman, and others. They have found that an individual while dreaming moves his eyes much as he would if watching a play, and that such eye movements occur during light sleep, indicated by electroencephalographic records. If woken during rapid eye movement periods, an individual is able to report a dream approximately 80 per cent of the time often in considerable detail. Even habitual nondreamers, who remember less than one dream a month, are able to report dreams on almost 50 per cent of the wakenings after rapid eye movements (Goodenough, Shapiro, Holden, and Steinschriber 1959). Eye movement periods, and presumably dreams, range from 3 to 50 minutes in duration, averaging about 20 minutes, and tend to occur periodically throughout the night at intervals of 70 to 100 minutes (Dement and Kleitman 1957). The increase in both quantity and quality of dream reports made possible by this technique offers tremendous advantages in the study of dreams. Using this technique, Dement found that schizophrenics dream approximately the same amount of time as normals, but differ in their reports of dreams. Approximately half of the schizophrenic subjects frequently reported dreams of isolated, motionless, inanimate objects, apparently hanging in space. Dement rules out communication problems as the cause of this difference, but notes that although the schizophrenic subjects report motionless objects, their eyeballs were moving as if following moving objects. Dement concludes that this peculiar type of dream report is due to a "distorted schizophrenic concept of a more active visual experience" (1955:268).

Dorothy Eggan reports, concerning a series of studies at Billings Hospital using Dement-Kleitman techniques, that the manifest content of dreams may show certain regularities over the course of an evening.

Tresman, Rechtschaffen, Offenkrantz, and Wolpert studied the patterning of dream content in two subjects over several nights of dreaming, while Offenkrantz and Rechtschaffen (1960a, 1960b) submitted the dream sequences of two additional subjects to intensive clinical analysis. The results of these studies suggest the following: While there is rarely a direct continuity of manifest content from dream to dream in the course of a night, a single emotional conflict, expressed in a variety of contents, may underlie all the dreams of an evening. There is a tendency for specific elements of manifest content to be repeated at similar times on different nights. The early dreams of a night tend to deal with events of the very recent past, often the experimental situation itself. Dreams of childhood scenes occur more often later in the night. (Eggan, personal communication)

Findings based on two very different methods have been presented in this section. The first method, dream interpretation, uses symbols and associations to reconstruct the motivation which gave rise to the dream. The validity of this method obviously depends greatly on the skill and insight of the investigator. Using this method, very similar motives and conflicts have been found for peoples from different cultures.

The second method, content analysis, charts the frequency with which particular categories of dream events occur, making a comparison of large samples of dreams possible. Using this method, differences in dreams have been found between such groups as the Navaho and the Yir-Yoront, creative and noncreative girls, schizophrenics and normals, and so forth.

The difference in the type of findings reported for these two methods would seem to indicate that different levels of personality are being analyzed. It has been suggested that the individual dream interpretations have tended to refer to the more primitive and basic motivations similar in all cultures, while the content analyses have dealt more with the way in which impulses are expressed, defended against, and reintegrated, material which shows more individual and culturally distinctive patterning.

THE EFFECT OF CULTURE ON DREAMS

Dreams, like other kinds of human behavior, can be expected to show some degree of cultural patterning. In dreams, however, conscious self-control and external restraints, which serve as the two great agents of conformity with cultural norms, are almost completely absent. Cultural patterning in dreams must come from deep within the individual rather than from conscious imitation of a cultural model, or the restrictions of cultural institutions. For this reason, cultural patterning in dreams seems especially relevant to an understanding of which aspects of cultural norms are most deeply internalized.

One of the simplest and most direct ways in which culture might be expected to affect dreams is in manifest content. Certainly, peoples who have never seen automobiles are not likely to dream of them. However, there is evidence that dreams do not give a faithful point-by-point representation of the sector of culture experienced and manipulated by the individual in waking life, but instead give a selective, edited picture of the individual's cultural world.

First, some dreams seem almost completely bare of cultural items of any sort. Often these dreams are symbolic dreams of flying, body destruction, landscapes, animals, and so forth. Perhaps the cultural bareness of these dreams is due to the difficulty in translating dream images into words, and then retranslating into the ethnographer's language. I would guess that about one fifth of the dreams I have examined from non-Western cultures lack any culturally distinctive materials in manifest content, although this seems to vary by culture.

Second, certain areas of cultural life are overrepresented in the manifest content of dreams, while other areas may be considerably underrepresented. Within the United States, Calvin Hall finds that:

> Dreams contain few ideas of a political or economic nature. They have little or nothing to say about current events in the world of affairs. I was collecting dreams daily from students during the last days of the war with Japan when the first atomic bomb was exploded, yet this dramatic event did not register in a single dream. Presidential elections, declarations of war, the diplomatic struggles of great powers, major athletic contests, all of the happenings that appear in newspapers and become the major topics of conversation among people are pretty largely ignored in dreams.
>
> What then is there left to dream about? There is the whole world of the personal, the intimate, the emotional and the conflictful, and it is this world of ideas out of which dreams are formed. (1953:11–12)

Emotionally, the content of dreams seems to contain more negative feelings than waking life. In a content analysis of a large sample of Western dreams, Hall found that 40 per cent of the emotions displayed in dreams can be characterized as apprehension, 18 per cent as anger, and 6 per cent as sadness. Another 18 per cent of the emotions are characterized as neutral excitement and surprise, while only 18 per cent are characterized as happiness. In this same sample almost half of the dream persons were strangers to the dreamer, while about 20 per cent were family, of which 34 per cent were mother, 27 per cent father, 14 per cent brother and 12 per cent sister (Hall 1951).

The manifest content of dreams may also reflect the sex of the dreamer. Hall finds that men in our culture dream about males twice as frequently as about females, while women dream equally about both (Hall 1951). In Lee's study of Zulu dreams (1958), an unusual degree of difference between the manifest contents of the dreams of men and the dreams of women was found; the women dream more of babies and children, the men dream more of fighting and cattle. This difference reflects the traditional division of labor, although at the time of the study, the traditional separateness of men's and women's activities had broken down. Lee's hypothesis, that the content of dreams is laid down in the early years of life, offers an interesting avenue of exploration, which might account for the lack of political and economic activities noted by Hall.

Devereux offers a similar hypothesis about the relation between the dream content and childhood experience of a Plains Indian in psychotherapy. The items of aboriginal culture which appeared in this patient's dreams were those which "reflected most clearly both the highest traditional values of Wolf culture (pseudonym for the patient's culture), and the least rational parts thereof: i.e., medicine bundles, magic and the like" (1951:100). These aboriginal materials began to appear with greater frequency in the patient's dreams when he began to analyze his own past, and dreams with many aboriginal items were often the most significant and revealing.

Devereux speculates that the small amount of manifest content taken from the immediate present in this patient's dreams may be due to the fact that these dreams reflected life-long defense mechanisms, laid down in childhood, and also to the fact that Plains Indian children were often brought up by their grandparents, who embody the more traditional culture (1951:88).

Holmberg, in his study of the Siriono, found the manifest content of dreams to be related to one of the central features of Siriono life. The Siriono are a hunting and gathering people of the interior Amazon, who are often if not always hungry and who spend much of their time in a grim search for food. Holmberg found that more than half of a sample of fifty dreams were concerned with eating food, hunting game, and collecting edible products from the forest. One of the most common dreams is that a relative out hunting has had luck and is returning with game for the dreamer (Holmberg 1950:91). He found that "one of the striking things about food dreams is that they seem to occur just about as often when a person is not hungry as when he is hungry" (Holmberg 1950:91). This would lead one to speculate that food has come to symbolize a number of things for the Siriono besides its hunger-reducing properties.

So far some of the ways in which dreams tend to give a selective and edited picture of the dreamer's culture have been described. Schneider and Sharp, in a thorough and systematic monograph, have investigated the relation between Yir-Yoront dreams and culture. The dreams were collected by R. L. Sharp, and analyzed by D. Schneider (in manuscript). Schneider begins with the assumption that dreams portray the dreamer's view of the world, or his "definition of the situation," and that culture, as a system of norms, affects but is not identical with this definition of the situation.

In order to investigate the relation between Yir-Yoront dreams and culture Schneider has analyzed the manifest content of 149 dreams taken from 51 subjects, 43 men and 8 women. Four kinds of dream situations were studied; dreams involving sex, aggression, death, and contact with white culture. Certain striking regularities in these areas were uncovered. Nineteen dreams containing explicit material on sexual intercourse were found, all from men. The partner in these dreams is in a little more than half of the cases from the approved classificatory kinship class (mother's brother's daughter), although in only one case is the sex partner actually a wife.

Perhaps the most interesting finding from a review of the dreams of sexual intercourse is that when the sex partner is of a prohibited degree of relationship, and where no adjustment to this fact has been made in waking life, the men picture (1) a specific interruption before or during the act of intercourse which occurs as (a) an organic defect of the woman's sexual organs or (b) an overt, verbal rejection of the male dreamer's advances which have little deterrent effect in the dream. (2) The magnitude of the interruption correlates with the strength of the prohibition on sexual relations. Intercourse with FaSiDa never gets started; with the SiDa, the act is completed but with difficulty; with the SiDaDa there is merely verbal rejection of the man by the woman. (Chapter 5:2–3)

Another interesting finding involves the expression of aggression. In Yir-Yoront dreams both mother's brother and elder brother are frequent aggressors *against* the dreamer. This is quite different from the actual situation, in which a man gives gifts and shows respect towards his mother's brother, and treats his older brother with deference. Dreams involving death also show some surprising patterning. While there is no cultural belief in resurrection, in most of the dreams of death in which the dreamer himself dies, the dreamer then "stands alive" or is resurrected. However, in dreams in which someone else dies, the corpse most frequently remains dead.

These findings raise some interesting questions about the relation between any fantasy product, such as dreams, and the actual experiences of the individual. Certainly most fantasy, including dreams, contains something of a "reflection" of the individual's experiences and his "definition of the situation." Usually this "reflected" material is selected and edited according to the particular interests and concerns of the person. For example, it has already been mentioned that personal and intimate materials are more likely to appear in American dreams than public and political matters.

Selection and editing of fantasy, however, results in only mild distortions of the individual's actual experience. Sometimes the distortion is more drastic, as in obvious cases of wish fulfillment. Schneider and Sharp consider the fact that the sex partner in Yir-Yoront dreams is almost always some one other than a wife to be the result of wish fulfillment, and, in a sense, still a part of the individual's definition of the situation.

Projection is a still more drastic kind of distortion. Certainly the Yir-Yoront tendency to picture mother's brother and elder brother as hostile and aggressive, when the shoe is on the other foot, would seem to fit neatly the definition of projection. Other dream materials may also involve projection, but are less discernible because the individual's actual experiences are less clearly known. For example, it may be that the dreamer's portrayal of the woman as the source of interruption of intercourse is pure projection, or this may be an accurate portrayal of what actually happens. If it is projection, this would make some sense out of such bizarre items as the woman's clitoris falling off in one of these dreams, and the other images of the woman having damaged genitals. It would then be really the man's genitals which would become injured, or which he fears would become injured if intercourse with a forbidden woman were to take place. Here the dreamer's actual "definition of situation" is reversed, although the anxiety is still apparent as sexual in origin.

An even more elaborate kind of distortion occurs in instances of symbolization. For example, it may be that the resurrection dreams of the Yir-Yoront are symbolic dreams of repeated sexual intercourse, in which the penis dies and is then born again. The men of the Yir-Yoront "in waking life, talk as if a single act of intercourse was more unusual than four, five, or six," but in overt sex dreams rarely have more than one act of intercourse. Perhaps the same anxiety that gives rise to this kind of bragging also motivates the "stand alive" dreams. The following dream of a mature man may be a case in point, and gives something of the flavor of Yir-Yoront dreams in general.

I'm making a forked support for the corpse at Olwin-an. It is for Spear's sister (dead, unknown). I saw Yaltide's vagina. Her legs were far apart. A mob from the north (Yir Ma'as and others) speared me. I lay down alongside the corpse. I was full of spears. The North people cut me up. They took my bones out. They cut me up like a wallaby. They ate my liver and flesh after cooking it. I came alive again. I had healed up but had no bones, which had been smashed up and the marrow eaten. My brains, bones, etc. were all eaten. Wil (also was eaten). I rolled up belongings and left. I went along and died. I was buried. I heard people keening for me. Women were jabbing sticks in their vaginas so that blood would run out; they were sorry. Blood running down their legs, vaginas. I came alive again. Stretched arms and legs and back. I went off hunting. I killed two goannas, cooked them and woke up.

Inf.: Parkaia perhaps sent dream. My mother, who is Spear's sister (dead, unknown), was dead in the dream. Yaltelde, my sister, was simply mourning the corpse. I dreamed this last night. (dream 34)

If this hypothesis is correct, it would help explain why "dreams of death are noticeably lacking in intense affect," and why resurrection occurs in dreams but not as an item of cultural belief. In any case, the relation between the culture, the individual's experience, and dreams of "standing alive" is not a simple one.

To summarize so far, it seems that there is no simple relation between culture and the manifest content of dreams. This appears to be because a dream is not exclusively a cognitive act, in which things once perceived are reshuffled and reviewed in the mind's eye. Instead, the dream is a selective, edited, and sometimes highly distorted version of the individual's experience. This selectivity and distortion is generally considered to be an effect of motivation, as well as the type of special mental process involved in dreaming. The various examples of selectivity in dream content mentioned above, such as the frequent reference to food in the dreams of the Siriono, the sex differences in the dreams of the Zulu, an acculturated Plains Indian's tendency to dream about nonrational aspects of his aboriginal culture, and Hall's finding that American dreamers dream about the personal and intimate rather than the political and economic, would, therefore, be held to be due to the particular needs of individuals in these societies. More dramatic distortions seem to be due to conflict. The Yir-Yoront projection of hostility onto the mother's brother may represent such a conflict, perhaps in this case between aggressive feelings and anxiety about retaliation.

The effect of culture on dreams may be seen more directly in the "culture pattern dream." (Lincoln 1935:189). These dreams, which are specified and sanctioned by the culture, and which usually involve supernaturals or supernatural manifestations, are often considered visions (Lincoln 1935:189). The Crow, for example, gave great importance to culture pattern dreams, and success in life was considered to depend upon these visions. Lowie remarks that he never succeeded in securing a detailed narrative of an ordinary dream, because his informants would report only visions (1922:342). Typically, culture pattern dreams of this type involve a preparatory phase of fasting, isolation and self-mutilation, followed by a hallucinatory experience, in which a spirit helper, usually in human guise, adopts the dreamer as his child, and gives him specific instructions in the use of a supernatural power.

Although it might seem likely that individuals would falsify such experiences in order to gain honor and riches, Lowie reports that this was not the case. In fact, some people were never successful in obtaining a vision, and others, who thought they had received a true revelation, later became convinced through testing their supposedly acquired powers that they had been deceived by their vision (1924:8–14).

In those cases in which an individual believes that he has had a culture pattern dream, the degree to which the content of the dream has been affected by secondary elaboration, in which the dreamer unwittingly assimilates the dream experience to a previous cultural model, remains problematic. Sometimes such a process of secondary elaboration can be seen quite clearly. Erika Bourguigon notes that in Haiti a dream may be recounted as if a particular supernatural had appeared in it, although more detailed questioning would reveal that only an ordinary person with certain characteristics which might indicate a disguised supernatural had been seen in the dream. Her conclusion, based on Haitian materials, is probably representative for other societies in which culture pattern dreaming occurs.

> While it is difficult to see to what extent dreams themselves may be culturally patterned, the cultural dogma of the dreams as appearance of the gods interacts with the dream content in such a way that an interpreted version of the dream seems to be experienced by the dreamer. (E. Bourguigon 1954:268)

The effect of acculturation on culture pattern dreaming has been discussed by Radin and King. Radin presents some evidence that as a result of acculturation, the Ottawa and Ojibwa stopped having culture pattern dreams and began to have dreams concerned only with personal problems (Radin 1936). King documents the opposite case, in which an acculturated Mountain Maidu Indian (whose biological father was white) had a series of culture pattern dreams which incorporated elements of Western culture (King 1943). In this series of dreams the dreamer was able to defeat the magical attacks of malicious shamans by using both Indian and white kinds of magical power. King finds that the remarkably good adjustment of this man to Western culture is shown in these dreams, and also speculates that dreams might be fruitfully used to study psychological adjustment in acculturation.

Cultural beliefs and theories about dreams also appear to affect the content of dreams and emotional reactions to dreams. One often quoted example of the effect of dream theories is the difference between the Tikopia and the Trobriand Islanders in their emotional reactions to incest dreams (Firth 1934). The Tikopia believe that incest dreams are inspired by malignant spirits who may impersonate relatives and seduce the dreamer. The Trobriand Islanders, on the other hand, believe more in the reality of their dreams, and react with shame and guilt to incest dreams. While the Tikopia do not react with shame and guilt, they nevertheless do not completely escape the consequences of such dreams. For the Tikopia, sexual intercourse in a dream is sexual intercourse with a spirit, and intercourse with spirits results in loss of vitality and illness. In general, Tikopia dream theory demands taboo on sexual intercourse as a goal of the dream, while Trobriand dream theory involves a taboo only on certain sexual objects, a difference which may correspond to personality features characteristic of these two societies.

A somewhat more subtle effect of dream theories on dreams has been noted by Devereux, who points out that where dreams are given certain kinds of objective reality, the dreams of individuals appear to be more egosyntonic, and in such cultures dream events tend to be more similar to real life events, and also to be more useful to the individual, who may use his dreams to plan new activities, and to attempt to integrate old and painful experiences by reworking them successfully (1951:87).

Another possible effect of dream theories has been explored by Hallowell, who finds that where dreams are considered to be actual experiences of the self, as among the Objiwa, that the self may be conceived of and experienced as capable of dream-like activities, such as physical metamorphosis, separation from the body, and the ability to shift back and forth in time. As a result of such a self-conception, and the integration of dreams with waking experiences, the "behavioral environment" or "habitat" of the individual may come to have radically different qualities than the "physical environment" (1955:172–182).

The findings concerning culture pattern dreams suggests that, while it is possible for some individuals to dream as required, this is not an easy task, and for some persons even impossible. Some of the implications of this situation will be discussed below.

With respect to the ways in which cultural cognitive structures affect dreams, the findings of Firth, Devereux, and Hallowell suggest that native dream theories play a part in taming fantasy, making it more like waking life, and, reciprocally, in making waking life more like dream fantasy.

The Cultural Uses of Dreams

In the ethnographic literature a wide range of beliefs and practices concerning dreams has been reported. These beliefs and practices enter into many different aspects of culture. One important set of culture traits relates dreams to the religious system, and includes the use of dreams to contact and gain power from supernaturals, as well as the more common beliefs that the soul wanders during dreams, meets other souls, and is responsible for its actions. Another set of traits concerns the use of dreams in the social system, in which there may be formal or informal statuses and roles involving dreams, such as dream interpreters, or shamanistic dream performances, and roles which can only be assumed if the proper dream is dreamed. An almost universal set of traits involves the use of dreams to predict the future. The last major group of traits involves emotional catharsis through ritualized methods of reacting to dream experiences, in which the effect of a bad dream may be dispelled or a good dream made to come true by a more or less elaborate ritual, such as not telling the dream, or acting out the dream commands, or making a sacrifice.

These traits are not cultural monads, but have functional relations with other phenomena, cultural, social, and individual. Two examples of such relations, concerning "primitive dream psychotherapy" and "unconscious role acceptance" have been discussed in the anthropological literature.

"Unconscious role acceptance" becomes a factor in a social system when culture pattern dreams are used to determine which roles an individual will assume. The dreamer may either be obligated to assume a particular role because he has had a certain type of dream, as, for example, among the Sioux, where dreams of the moon, or a hermaphroditic buffalo, require the individual to become a *berdache,* or the dreamer may be required to dream a particular culture pattern dream before he is allowed to assume a certain role, as among the Pukapuka, where qualifications for priesthood require that a man have dream contact with supernatural powers during the initiation period.

Since dreams are not under direct conscious control, the use of culture pattern dreams to determine role taking brings factors of "unconscious choice" into consideration. A young man who is required to have a vision and obtain a spirit helper before he may have all the responsibilities and privileges of the adult role may consciously want to assume an adult role, but if on a less conscious level he feels he is not ready to become a man, dreaming the required dream would probably be an impossibility, both because of unconscious sabotage, and because typically the content of the culture pattern dream in these cases is psychologically sound, symbolizing accurately the resolution of dependency conflicts. Also, where an individual is forced into a deviant role because of his dreams, not only are unconscious factors taken into account, but a culturally legitimate excuse is given for such deviancy. Erikson, in his discussion of the Sioux, states:

A homogenous culture such as that of the Sioux, then, deals with its deviants by finding them a secondary role, as clown, prostitute, or artist, without, however, freeing them entirely from the ridicule and horror which the vast majority must maintain in order to suppress in themselves what the deviant represents. However, the horror remains directed against the power of the spirits which have intruded themselves upon the deviant individual's dreams. It does not turn against the stricken individual himself. In this way, primitive cultures accept the power of the unconscious. As psychopathologists, we must admire the way in which these "primitive" systems managed to maintain elastic mastery in a matter where more sophisticated systems have failed. (1950:137)

Another example of the use of dreams to manage psychological problems can be found in primitive psychotherapy, discussed by Wallace (1958), Devereux (1951), Kilton Stewart (1954, 1951), and Toffelmier and Luomala (1936). Generally, such therapy seems to consist of a cultural recognition that dreams reveal hidden wishes and conflicts, and a culturally prescribed method of dealing with those wishes and conflicts. The most common method of handling such wishes and conflicts seems to be to fulfill or act out the wish, once it is revealed. Anthony Wallace presents an impressive example of this method in his study of Iroquois dream theory.

Intuitively, the Iroquois had achieved a great deal of psychological sophistication. They recognized conscious and unconscious parts of the mind. They knew the great force of unconscious desires, and were aware that the frustration of these desires could cause mental and physical ("psychosomatic") illness. They understood that these desires were expressed in symbolic form by dreams, but that the individual could not always properly interpret these dreams himself. They had noted the distinction between the manifest and latent content of dreams, and employed what sounds like the technique of free association to uncover the latent meaning. And they considered that the best method for the relief of psychic and psychosomatic distress was to give the frustrated desire satisfaction, either directly or symbolically. (1958:237–238)

Among the Senoi, impulses revealed in dreams are evidently handled in an unusually sociable fashion, so that if a man dreamed he was attacked by another, he would attempt to settle the differences between them through discussion and mediation (K. Stewart 1951). The Navaho, on the other hand, use dreams not to reveal wishes, but to indicate proper curing rituals. Lincoln suggests that the Navaho curing ceremonies prescribed on the basis of the content of dreams have symbols similar to those of the diagnostic dreams, and that the particular curing ceremony is effective because it resolves symbolically the unconscious conflict in the dream. For example:

> Dreams of death, that is, of one's own death, or the death of neighbors and relatives, also dreams that your teeth have fallen out require the Hozhonju or Chant of the Restoration of the Family.
> *Suggestion.* Death dreams are generally death wishes, and the symbol of losing a tooth as often meaning castration anxiety because of death wishes is widespread. (Here again occurs the association of loss of a tooth, death of a relative as in the universal type dreams.) The Hozhonji is to restore the family, that is to protect it from death wishes towards the parents. (Lincoln 1935:180)

It has been suggested by Stewart that a therapeutic psychological effect may be obtained if the symbolic forms which emerge in trance and dream are taken as objective dangers, and group support is given to mastering these symbolic dangers. Stewart presents a vivid if journalistic account of the psychotherapeutic methods of the Phillipine Negritos. A group of shamans co-operate in placing the patient in trance, and then encourage the patient to meet and overcome the spirit that has caused the patient's illness. This spirit, which has been attacking the patient in his dreams, is made to give the patient a song, and to become the patient's spirit helper. Stewart comments that this method seems effective in curing chronic physical ailments, such as skin irritations, headache, and recurrent fever, which probably have at least a partial psychosomatic origin. In this form of therapy, conflicts are externalized as spirits, and group support is given to overcoming their symbolic representations. Also, a spirit, once faced and overcome, is made to work for the person, and a public ritual is used to displace previous anxiety (Stewart 1954).

A technique of dream therapy has been reported for the Diegueno Indians of southern California which seems to be similar to Western psychotherapy in its management of dreams. This technique is used to treat persons who appear to be afflicted with obsessive sexual fantasies. There are two recognized forms of this type of illness. The first, which is less serious, is characterized by symptoms of excessive dreaming, laziness, and social withdrawal. The second form of this malady is considered to be an advanced form of the first, and appears to be an actual psychosis, characterized by persistent hallucinations of a spirit lover, a supernatural bullet hawk which takes human form as a person of either sex. Persons afflicted with this hallucination are called "spouses of that bird."

To treat these maladies, a dream shaman is sought. The shaman attempts to get the patient to talk about his dreams and sexual life, actual and imaginary. The shaman begins by asserting that he already knows all the patient's dreams, so that there is no use in trying to conceal anything. A mild type of hypnotic trance may be used to encourage the patient's talking, except in the more severely psychotic cases, which do not respond to this kind of treatment. Along with discussion of the patient's sexual life and fantasies, the shaman also prescribes blood letting and special nourishing foods. For the unwed, marriage is recommended, apparently to help the patient shift from substitute gratification in fantasy to real life situations (Toffelmier and Loumala 1936). The technique of therapy in this example is in many ways unusual. The technique of discussing with the patient his fantasies, including dreams, rather than permitting the patient to enact his fantasies, or to create a ritual defense against them, is particularly striking. It is not surprising that in this culture shamans are selected because of their stable (rather than unstable) personalities.

To summarize the material which has been treated so far in this section, the distinctions between content, structure, function, and process in culture may provide a useful framework (Hsu 1959). The cultural uses of dreams may be considered to be a type of culture content, having relations with the structural, functional, and procedural aspects of culture and society. Dreams may affect the structure of a society in becoming the subject matter of formal and informal roles, such as that of the dream interpreter, or in becoming a prerequisite for the ascription and achievement of roles, bringing factors of unconscious choice into the process of role allocation, as well as offering justification for the choice of deviant roles. Dreams may also function to help the individual maintain psychic equilibrium, serving as an important part of non-Western and Western psychotherapy.

Dream Usages and Their Correlates

The next part of this section will present the results of a cross-cultural study of the conditions which affect the cultural uses of dreams. In this study I have attempted to find out why some societies have extensive uses for dreams, while other societies do not. On the basis of case history materials reported in the ethnographic literature, it seemed to me that anxiety about being alone and on one's own often gives rise to a strong preoccupation with dreams and fantasy. If this were true, then societies in which individuals frequently experience anxiety concerning isolation and self-reliance would be likely to place an especially strong cultural emphasis on dreams. I therefore attempted to specify the social conditions which would be most likely to subject individuals to this type of anxiety, so that it would be possible to predict the degree of emphasis placed on dreams in any given culture from these conditions.

Field workers interested in culture and personality have presented several examples of the effect of social isolation and the effect of cultural roles which demand independent and self-reliant action. Margaret Mead recounts the story of an orphaned Manus boy who felt isolated and unloved, and who, unlike the other Manus children, was preoccupied with fantasies about a guardian spirit which he took to be his own father (Mead 1932:183). A similar case has been reported by Dorothy Eggan, in a study of mythic materials in dreams (1955). One of her Hopi informants, who also felt isolated and abandoned, also turned inward to fantasy about a supernatural helper. Dorothy Eggan comments:

> Benedict has pointed out that although the Pueblo area is surrounded by the concept of a power-giving or protecting Guardian Spirit, such a concept has not been standardized in the Pueblo groups because they are dominated by the "necessity of the group ceremonial approach not that of individual experience" (Benedict 1923:36). But in Sam we find a man who, because of personal problems, although believing firmly in the "group approach," was frequently made to feel less a part of the community than he needed to feel. Consequently he has elaborated the concept of *dumalaitaka* (guide or guardian spirit), which is found among the Hopi, but which is generally rather vague and unstressed, into an ever present and active spirit who comes to him in dreams, takes him to witches' meetings and on treasure hunts, gives him strength, wisdom and advice, rescues him from dangerous situations, and always assures him that he is on the right road and that his enemies are wrong. (1955:448)

Wallace, in his study of Iroquois dream theory, also concludes that anxiety about independence is related to this kind of extensive use of dreams:

... the typical Iroquois male, who in his daily life was a brave, generous, active, and independent spirit, nevertheless cherished some strong, if unconscious, wishes to be passive, to beg, to be cared for. This unallowable tendency, so threatening to a man's sense of self-esteem, could not appear easily even in a dream; when it did, it was either experienced as an intolerably painful episode of torture, or was put in terms of a meeting with a supernatural protector. However, the Iroquois themselves unwittingly make the translation: an active manifest dream is fulfilled by a passive receiving action. The arrangement of the dream guessing rite raises this dependency to an exquisite degree: the dreamer cannot even ask for his wish; like a baby, he must content himself with cryptic signs and symbols until someone guesses what he wants and gives it to him. (1958:247).

These reports indicate that anxiety about being isolated and on one's own may give rise to preoccupation with dreams and fantasy, especially fantasy about magical helpers. The content of such fantasy seems to serve as a denial of the individual's actual isolation and helplessness, thereby partially relieving these anxieties.

In order to measure the degree of cultural preoccupation with dreams, the following traits involving dreams were coded for a sample of sixty-three societies taken from the Human Relations Area Files. No society was selected unless at least a paragraph on dreams could be found in the literature, and no more than two societies have been taken from any one culture area, using Murdock's World Ethnographic Sample (1957):

a) Supernaturals appear in dreams and give important powers, aid, ritual, and information.
b) Religious experts (priests, shamans) expected to use their own dreams in performance of their role (e.g., curing, divination).
c) Culture pattern dreams required before some roles may be assumed.
d) Dreams induced by special techniques (e.g., fasting, drugs, sleeping alone, etc.).
e) Formal or informal role of dream interpreter.
f) Undoing ritual after some dreams (e.g., sacrifice, avoidance).
g) Supernaturals appear in dreams and harm or foreshadow harm to the dreamer.

These particular traits were selected because they are neither universal nor extremely rare, and because they cover a wide range of types of uses of dreams. I had hoped that all of these traits would be positively correlated with each other; however, this proved not to be the case. Only four of these traits showed high significant correlations with each other: traits *a, b, c,* and *d.* The other three traits were uncorrelated with each other, and with these four.

If all seven traits had been strongly intercorrelated, it would have been reasonable to assume that there is a general factor of preoccupation with dreams. The findings seem to indicate, however, that rather than a general factor of preoccupation with dreams, there is a more limited complex centered about the use of dreams to seek and control supernatural powers. Traits *a, b,* and *d* involve this seeking and controlling of supernatural power quite directly. Trait *c,* involving culture pattern dreams which are required before certain roles may be assumed, is less directly related to seeking supernatural aid. However, it seems that such culture pattern dreams often consist of a visitation by a magical helper, who teaches the aspiring shaman or warrior important supernatural techniques. The other dream traits, involving dream interpretation, undoing rituals and possible supernatural harm, are unrelated to this complex, and have not been used in measuring this type of cultural preoccupation with dreams.

In view of these findings, the original hypothesis has been modified to state that anxiety about being alone and on one's own gives rise to the use of dreams to seek and control supernatural powers. The extent of this use of dreams has been measured by the number of traits *a, b, c,* and *d* reported present for each society. The median number of traits reported present for this cross-cultural sample is one. Societies with none of these four traits fall below the median, and are considered low on the use of dreams to seek and control supernatural powers. Societies with one or more traits reported present are considered high on this use of dreams.

The first condition specified as a possible cause of anxiety about isolation and independence involves residence at marriage. If, at marriage, a son or daughter moves far away from his or her parents, the loss of parental support should give rise to anxiety about being isolated and on one's own. In order to test this hypothesis, estimates of the distances that sons and daughters most usually move at marriage for each society have been taken from a cross-cultural study of residence by Whiting and D'Andrade (1959). Table 1 presents the association between the typical distances for parents and married son and the use of dreams to seek and control supernatural powers. The data in this table indicate that the further the son typically moves away from his parents, the more likely a society is to use dreams to seek and control supernatural powers. The degree of association is fairly strong, and significant at the .01 level. No table has been presented for the relation of distance between parents and married daughter and use of dreams because it was found that there is no association between these two measures. Apparently,

TABLE 1

RELATION OF MOST TYPICAL DISTANCE BETWEEN MARRIED SON AND PARENTS TO
USE OF DREAMS TO SEEK AND CONTROL SUPERNATURAL POWERS

The societies are grouped in columns on the basis of distance between married son and parents and in descending degree of extensiveness of use of dreams to seek and control supernatural powers. The letters in parentheses after each society designate the traits reported present. (See page 321 for definition of traits.)

Son Resides in Parents' Household	Son Resides in Same Village or Local Group	Son Resides in Different Village or Local Group
		Crow (a,b,c,d)
		Iroquois (a,b,c,d)
		Jivaro (a,b,c,d)
		Naskapi (a,b,c,d)
		Ojibwa (a,b,c,d)
		Omaha (a,b,c,d)
		Paiute (a,b,c,d)
	Comanche (a,b,c,d)	Andamans (a,b,c)
	Semang (a,b,c,d)	Copper Eskimo (a,b,c)
	Pukapuka (a,b,c)	Cuna (a,b,c)
	Chukchee (a,b)	Kaska (a,c,d)
	Rwala (b,d)	Lapps (a,b)
	Araucanians (b)	Yaruro (b,d)
	Azande (d)	Bemba (b)
Papago (a,b,c,d)	Fang (a)	Mundurucu (a)
Kapauku (a,b)	Nyakusa (b)	Trobriands (c)
Ifugao (c)	Wolof (b)	Yakut (d)
Bhil (−)	Ashanti (−)	Burmese (−)
Iban (−)	Aymara (−)	Callinago (−)
Lepcha (−)	Ifaluk (−)	Ganda (−)
Mataco (−)	Kurtatchi (−)	Karen (−)
Nama (−)	Marquesas (−)	
Samoa (−)	MinChia (−)	
Siriono (−)	Mossi (−)	
Tupinamba (−)	Riffians (−)	
	Somali (−)	
	Tallensi (−)	
	Tanala (−)	
	Thai (−)	
	Tiv (−)	
	Tubatulabal (−)	
	Yoruba (−)	

anxiety suffered by women does not affect this use of dreams. Perhaps this is because religion is more frequently a man's affair, or perhaps because women may turn to their spouses in order to relieve the anxiety of loss of parental support in a way that men may not.

In order to check on these findings, Murdock's residence and family classification has been used. From the findings presented above, nonpatrilocal societies should have more uses of dreams to seek and control supernatural powers than patrilocal societies, and independent families should have more uses for dreams than extended families. Both these conditions have effects in the predicted direction and are statistically significant when considered together.

TABLE 2

RELATION OF SUBSISTENCE ECONOMY TO USE OF DREAMS TO SEEK AND CONTROL
SUPERNATURAL POWERS

The societies are grouped in columns on the basis of economy in descending degree of extensiveness of use of dreams to seek and control supernatural powers. The letters in parentheses after each society designate the traits reported present. (See page 321 for definition of traits.)

Agriculture plus Animal Husbandry	Agriculture without Animal Husbandry	Hunting, Fishing, and Animal Husbandry without Agriculture
		Comanche (a,b,c,d)
		Crow (a,b,c,d)
		Naskapi (a,b,c,d)
		Ojibwa (a,b,c,d)
		Omaha (a,b,c,d)
		Paiute (a,b,c,d)
		Semang (a,b,c,d)
		Andaman (a,b,c)
	Iroquois (a,b,c,d)	Copper Eskimo (a,b,c)
	Jivaro (a,b,c,d)	Kaska (a,c,d)
	Papago (a,b,c,d)	Pukapuka (a,b,c)
	Cuna (a,b,c)	*Chukchee (a,b)
	Carib (a,b)	*Lapps (a,b)
	Azande (d)	*Rwala (b,d)
Chagga (b,c)	Bemba (b)	Wishram (a,d)
Kapauku (a,b)	Fang (a)	Yaruro (b,d)
Araucanians (b)	Ifugao (c)	Caingang (d)
Nyakusa (b)	Mundurucu (a)	Tlingit (b)
Wolof (b)	Trobriands (c)	*Yakut (a)
Aymara (–)	Ashanti (–)	Callinago (–)
Bhil (–)	Ifaluk (–)	Mataco (–)
Burmese (–)	Kurtatchi (–)	*Nama (–)
Ganda (–)	Marquesas (–)	Siriono (–)
Iban (–)	Samoa (–)	*Somali (–)
Karen (–)	Subanum (–)	Tubatulabal (–)
Lepcha (–)	Tupinamba (–)	
MinChia (–)	Yoruba (–)	
Mossi (–)		
Riffians (–)		
Tallensi (–)		
Tanala (–)		
Thai (–)		
Thonga (–)		
Tiv (–)		

* Animal husbandry societies.

A second possible source of anxiety about being isolated and on one's own involves the subsistence economy. The relation of the subsistence economy to adult roles which demand independent and self-reliant behavior has been discussed by Barry, Child, and Bacon in a study of economy and child-rearing practices (1959). They find that child-rearing practices stressing independence, self-reliance, and achievement are most typical of hunting and fishing societies, while child-rearing practices stressing obedience, responsibility, and nurturance are typical of societies with both agricultural and animal husbandry. Societies with agriculture, and without animal husbandry, fall between these extremes. The correlation between the form of economy and a combined child-training measure of relative "pressure for compliance" (composed of scores for obedience, responsibility, and nurturance training) versus "pressure for assertiveness" (composed of scores for independence, self-reliance, and achievement training) yields exceptionally strong coefficients of association of $+.94$ and $+.93$ for extreme and intermediate comparisons (1959:59). This very high degree of association is thought to be due to the functional adjustment of child-rearing practices to the type of adult roles necessary to maintain food production. That is, societies with both agriculture and animal husbandry can best assure future food supply by "faithful adherence to routine" and therefore train children to be obedient and responsible, while in hunting and fishing societies individual initiative and skill is more adaptive, along with child-rearing practices stressing independence and self-reliance (1959:52).

It is expected, then, that hunting and fishing societies will be likely to use dreams to seek and control supernatural powers, while societies with both agriculture and animal husbandry will be less likely to use dreams in this fashion. Societies with either agriculture or animal husbandry, but not both, should fall between these two extremes.[1] This result is predicted for two reasons. First, according to Barry and co-workers, hunting and fishing societies place greater pressure on the adult to be independent and self-reliant. Second,

---

[1] Barry, Child, and Bacon group together both nomadic pastoral societies and societies with a combination of animal husbandry and agriculture, evidently considering the use of animals to be the crucial determinant in accumulation of food resources. However, the combination of agriculture with animal husbandry would be more likely to produce a stable and high food output than either economy separately. For this reason the groupings of categories of economy used by Barry and his co-workers have been altered slightly in this paper, and societies with animal husbandry and no agriculture have been put in the intermediate hunting and fishing group.

hunting and fishing societies also place relatively greater pressure on the child to be independent and self-reliant.

Table 2 presents the association between type of economy and the use of dreams to seek and control supernatural powers. The ratings on economy have been taken from Murdock (1957).

The results indicate that there is a strong and significant relation between the type of economy and the use of dreams. Approximately 80 per cent of the hunting and fishing societies use dreams to seek and control supernatural powers, while only 20 per cent of the societies with both agriculture and animal husbandry use dreams this way. The intermediate societies, which have either agriculture or animal husbandry, but not both, fall between the two extremes, with 60 per cent of these societies using dreams to seek and control supernatural powers.

Unfortunately, it is not possible to decide whether this association is due to the effect of child rearing, or to the effect of role pressures on adults. A separate test, using the child-training measure of pressure for compliance versus assertiveness, results in a significant correlation of assertiveness with an extensive use of dreams. However, attempting to control the effect of economy reduces this correlation drastically, although no firm conclusion can be drawn because of the large amount of overlap between type of economy and child-rearing practices. Attempts to use other measures of child rearing involving independence training, taken from Whiting and Child (1953), and unpublished scores rated by Barry and his associates, reveal a nonsignificant tendency for early indulgence of dependency and later severe socialization of dependency to go with extensive use of dreams to seek and control supernatural powers.

Although economic conditions are related to the typical distance a son moves at marriage with the son moving further in hunting and fishing society, these two conditions seem to have clearly assessable independent effects. Within agricultural societies, the greater the distance between son and parent, the more likely a society is to use dreams to seek and control supernatural powers. The same relations hold within hunting, fishing, and pastoral societies.

In general, the findings of this cross-cultural study support the notion that anxiety about being isolated and under pressure to be self-reliant may create an involvement with a type of fantasy about magical helpers. Both the use of fantasy and dreams, rather than ritual as the means of contact with the supernatural, and the use of personal helpers, rather than impersonal forces, seem to be involved in this complex. The type of economy and the degree of isolation of the married son from his parents have been found to affect this complex strongly, with hunting and fishing societies, and societies in which the son moves far away from his parents being more likely to use dreams to seek and control supernatural powers. Based on the rather weak correlations with child-training practices, and the lack of association with the isolation of the married daughter. I suspect that this effect is mediated by what happens to adults rather than children, and what happens to men rather than women.[2]

As a final summary, the following general conclusions about the relations between dreams, personality, and culture are tentatively advanced.

1. There is a close association between dreams and the supernatural. This association consists of similarities between dream images and the conceptions of the supernatural, and also of the use of dreams to see and interact with the supernatural. This association does not necessarily indicate that dreams gave rise in the distant past to various conceptions of the supernatural, but would seem to indicate that similar psychological mechanisms may underlie both.

2. There are a number of small bits of evidence to support the thesis that symbolism in dreams is a universal phenomena. If true, this means that man either innately or due to experience establishes a set of identities or equivalences without cultural tuition, and without awareness, and that these equivalences are in constant use.

3. Dreams, it is assumed, can be used to reveal the dreamer's motives. Further, the relation between the dream content and these motives may be more or less indirect and disguised. The most basic (and usually the most disguised) motives involve obtaining direct physical gratification from members of the nuclear family. These motives can be found in the dreams of people from all societies. The modal ways in which these motives are represented and defended against, however, vary culturally.

4. It is also assumed that dreams have a cognitive as well as motivational component. The dreamer's waking life and, hence, his culture are represented in dreams. This representation is always dis-

---

[2] There is some evidence that early childhood conditions involving the identification process, whereby a young child comes to admire and wish to be like his or her parent of the same sex, also affects the use of dreams. It is thought that strong parental same-sex identification leads to fantasy about parent-like guardian spirits, and to the use of fantasy rather than ritual or acting out to relieve anxiety. This formulation is at present still tentative, and dependent upon further research. It may be that strong early same-sex parental identification is a necessary but not sufficient cause for a strong degree of cultural emphasis on dreams, with adult role stress involving isolation and independence a later "eliciting" factor.

torted, however. Sometimes the distortion is mild, involving minor editing of material and bias in selection. At other times the distortion may be drastic, involving complete reversal of normal experience. Such distortion is probably due in part to the press of motivation, and especially conflicts in motivation.

5. Culture may also specify the content which is appropriate to dreams under certain conditions. Where the individual is supposed to dream a certain dream, the retelling of these dreams is probably influenced by some degree of later elaboration. Acculturation may bring foreign material into such dreams, or completely break the pattern. The emotional reaction to dreams may be affected by the cultural definition of what is likely to take place in dreams, and in turn the cultural definition of the self may be affected by the kinds of events which occur in dreams.

6. Dreams have numerous cultural uses. Prediction of the future and contact with supernaturals are the most common of these uses. Dreams are also used in native psychotherapies and as a means of selecting and rejecting personnel for various roles. One special use of dreams, to seek and control supernatural powers, seems to be caused by anxiety about being alone and needing to be able to be self-reliant. Societies in which the economy demands self-reliant behavior on the part of the men, as in hunting, and societies in which the married son must move away from his natal family into another village are more likely to use dreams to seek and control supernatural powers.

BIBLIOGRAPHY

ADELSON, JOSEPH
    1960   Creativity and the dream. Merrill Palmer Quarterly 6:92–97.
BARRY, H., I. CHILD and M. BACON
    1959   Relation of child training to subsistence economy. American Anthropologist 61:51–63.
BENEDICT, RUTH
    1923   The concept of the guardian spirit in North America. Memoirs of the American Anthropological Association 29.
BOURGUIGON, ERIKA E.
    1954   Dreams and dream interpretation in Haiti. American Anthropologist 56:262–268.
DEMENT, WILLIAM
    1955   Dream recall and eye movement during sleep in schizophrenics and normals. Journal of Nervous and Mental Disease 122:263–269.

DEMENT, WILLIAM and N. KLEITMAN
1957 The relation of eye movements during sleep to dream activity. Journal of Experimental Psychology 53:339–346.

DEVEREUX, GEORGE
1951 Reality and dream. New York, International Universities Press.
1957 Dream learning and individual ritual differences in Mohave Shamanism. American Anthropologist 59:1036–1045.

DITTMANN, ALLEN and HARVEY MOORE
1957 Disturbance in dreams as related to peyotism among the Navaho. American Anthropologist 59:642–649.

EGGAN, DOROTHY
1949 The significance of dreams for anthropological research. American Anthropologist 51:171–198.
1952 The manifest content of dreams: a challenge to social sciences. American Anthropologist 54:469–485.
1955 The personal use of myth in dreams. *In* Myth: a symposium, T. Sebeok, ed. Journal of American Folklore 68:445–453.
1961 Dream analysis. *In* Studying personality cross-culturally, Bert Kaplan, ed. Row, Peterson and Co., Evanston, Ill.

ELWIN, VERRXER
1939 The Baiga. London, John Murray.

ERIKSON, ERIK H.
1950 Childhood and society. New York, Norton.
1954 The dream specimen in psychoanalysis. *In* Psychoanalytic psychiatry and psychology, Knight and Friedman eds., pp. 131–170. New York, International Universities Press.

FIRTH, RAYMOND
1934 The meaning of dreams in Tikopia. *In* Essays presented to C. G. Seligman, Evans-Pritchard, Firth, Malinowski, and Schapera, eds., pp. 63–74. London, Kegan Paul, Trench, Trubner and Co.

FREUD, SIGMUND
1900 The interpretation of dreams. transl. New York, Basic Books, 1958.
1920 A general introduction to psychoanalysis. transl. New York, Doubleday, Permabook edition, 1953.

GOODENOUGH, D., A. SHAPIRO, M. HOLDEN, and L. STEINSCHRIBER
1959 A comparison of "dreamers" and "nondreamers." Journal of Abnormal and Social Psychology 59:295–302.

GRIFFITH, R., O. MIYAGI, and A. TAGO
1958 The university of typical dreams: Japanese versus American. American Anthropologist 60:1173–1179.

HALL, CALVIN S.
1951 What people dream about. Scientific American, May.
1953 The meaning of dreams, New York, Harper.
1956 Current trends in research on dreams. *In* Progress in clinical psychology. New York, Grune and Stratton.

HALLOWELL, A. IRVING
    1938   Freudian symbolism in the dream of a Salteaux Indian. Man., 38:47–48.
    1955   The self and its behavioral environment. *In* Culture and experience. Philadelphia, University of Pennsylvania Press.

HOBBES, THOMAS
    1651   Leviathan. Reprint of 1st Ed. Cambridge, England, University Press 1904.

HOLMBERG, ALLAN R.
    1950   Nomads of the long bow: the Siriono of Eastern Bolivia. Smithsonian Institution: Institute of Social Anthropology Publication No. 10.

HONIGMANN, JOHN J.
    1954   Culture and personality. New York, Harper.
    1961   The interpretation of dreams in anthropological field work: a case study. *In* Studying personality cross-culturally, Bert Kaplan, ed. pp. 579–585. Row, Peterson and Co., Evanston, Ill.

HSU, FRANCIS K.
    1959   Structure, function, content, and process. American Anthropologist 61:790–805.

JACOBS, MELVILLE
    1959   The content and style of an oral literature; Clackamas Chinook myths and tales. Viking Fund Publications in Anthropology 26, New York, Wenner-Gren Foundation for Anthropological Research, Inc.

JONES, ERNEST
    1931   On the nightmare. New York, Grove Press. Evergreen edition, 1959.

KING, ARDEN R.
    1943   The dream biography of a mountain Maidu. Character and Personality 11:227–234.

KLUCKHOHN, CLYDE and WILLIAM MORGAN
    1951   Some notes on Navaho dreams. *In* Essays in honor of Geza Roheim, Wilbur and Muensterger eds. pp. 120–131. New York, International Universities Press.

LEE, S. G.
    1958   Social influences in Zulu dreaming. Journal of Social Psychology, 47: 265–283.

LINCOLN, JACKSON S.
    1935   The dream in primitive cultures. London, Cresset Press.

LOWIE, ROBERT H.
    1924   Primitive religion. New York, Liveright. Black and Gold edition reprint, 1948.
    1922   The religion of the Crow Indians. Anthropological Papers of the American Museum of Natural History 25:309-444.

MEAD, MARGARET
    1932   An investigation of the thought of primitive children with special reference to animism. Journal of the Royal Anthropological Institute 62: 173–189.

MURDOCK, GEORGE P.
    1957   World ethnographic sample. American Anthropologist 59:664–687.

OFFENKRANTZ, W. and A. RECHTSCHAFFEN

1960a Dream sequences of a patient in psychotherapy. Paper presented at the 47th Annual Meeting of the American Psychoanalytic Association, Atlantic City, New Jersey, May.

1960b Clinical studies of dreams in sequence. II Papers presented at meeting of American Psychoanalytic Association, New York, December.

RADIN, PAUL

1936 Ojibwa and Ottawa puberty dreams. *In* Essays presented to A. L. Kroeber. University of California Press.

ROFFENSTEIN, GASTON

1951 Experiments on symbolism in dreams. *In* The organization and pathology of thought, David Rapaport, ed. and translator, pp. 249–256. New York, Columbia University Press.

ROHEIM, GEZA

1932 Psychoanalysis of primitive cultural types. International Journal of Psychoanalysis 13:2–224.

1938 The nescience of the Aranda. British Journal of Medical Psychology 17:343–360.

1946 The Oedipus complex and infantile sexuality. Psychoanalytic Quarterly 15:503–508.

1947 Dream analysis and field work in anthropology. Psychoanalysis and the Social Sciences 1:87–130.

1949 The technique of dream analysis and field work in anthropology. Psychoanalytic Quarterly 18:471–479.

1950 Psychoanalysis and anthropology. New York, International Universities Press.

SCHNEIDER, DAVID

1941 Aboriginal dreams. Masters thesis, Cornell University.

SCHNEIDER, D. M. and R. L. SHARP

(n.d.) Yir-yoront dreams. In manuscript.

SEARS, WALTER E.

1948 The Navaho and Yir-Yoront, their primitive dreams. Undergraduate honors thesis, Harvard University.

SELIGMAN, C. G.

1924 Anthropology and psychology. Journal of the Royal Anthropological Institute 54:13–46.

1927 Appendix. Religion and Art in Ashanti, Rattray, R. S. pp. 197–204. Oxford, Clarendon Press.

1932 Anthropological perspective and psychological theory. Journal of the Royal Anthropological Institute 62:193–228.

STEWART, KILTON

1951 Dream theory in Malaya. Complex 6:21-33.

1954 Pygmies and dream giants. New York, Norton.

TOFFELMIER, G., and K. LUOMALA

1936 Dreams and dream interpretation of the Diegueño Indians of Southern California. Psychoanalytic Quarterly 2:195–225.

TRESMAN, H., A. RECHTSCHAFFEN, W. OFFENKRANTZ, and E. A. WOLPERT
  1961? Studies in psychophysiology of dreams III. Relation among dreams in sequence. Archives of General Psychiatry (in press).

WALLACE, ANTHONY
  1958 Dreams and the wishes of the soul: a type of psychoanalytic theory among the seventeenth century Iroquois. American Anthropologist 60:234–248.

WHITING, J. W. M. and I. L. CHILD
  1953 Child Training and personality; a cross-cultural study. New Haven, Yale University Press.

WHITING, J. W. M. and R. G. D'ANDRADE
  1959 Sleeping arrangements and social structure: a cross-cultural study. Presented at American Anthropological Association Annual Meetings, Mexico City, December.

Chapter 11

THE MUTUAL METHODOLOGICAL RELEVANCE OF ANTHROPOLOGY AND PSYCHOLOGY

DONALD T. CAMPBELL
Northwestern University

RATHER than report upon a specific technique, this chapter will deal with some general methodological problems in relating theory to data. Rather than deal solely with an interdisciplinary specialty of "culture and personality," this chapter will emphasize the mutual relevance—at a *methodological* level—of anthropology and psychology for each other. This relevance is believed to hold even when each discipline is focused upon its own pure problems, as well as when they enter into interdisciplinary collaboration. This mutual methodological relevance is emphasized as a mode of contact separate from the inevitable mutual relevance of their substantive theories. The latter, while more important, has also received more repeated attention, and is in any event not the topic treated here.

Anthropology as a Source of Discipline for Psychological Theory

There is no need to reiterate or to document here the tremendous influence which anthropology's culture-personality studies have had upon social psychology since the 1930's. From the tenor of some of the papers of this volume and from other professional stock-takings by anthropologists (for example, Bennett 1946, Kluckhohn 1954b, Honigmann 1954), it can be gathered that many anthropologists feel somewhat uneasy about this very great popularity of what may be a not-too-dependable product; that many might explain the rapid diffusion of this trait complex more as due to the extreme needs of the new converts than to the efficacy of the invention, that is, an acceptance phenomena more akin to the diffusion of the Ghost Dance Religion than to the spread of the compound bow, barbed fishhook or better mousetrap. As an academic, experimentally oriented, and methodologically anxious social psychologist, I, of course, share these misgivings. However, even when in an incomplete and fragmentary form, anthropological evidence has served as a source of discipline, as well as a source of inspiration to psychological theory.

The first, and perhaps still most needed influence is at a very general level. This is the message of cultural relativism. While recognizing that anthropologists themselves are not too happy with this slogan, and that the perspective may not be adequate for anthropology's theoretical purposes, the message it has to offer is still very much needed by academic psychologists. Implicitly, the laboratory psychologist still assumes that his college sophomores provide an adequate base for a general psychology of man. (Such assumptions of universality are automatic for any provincially enculturated ethnocentric.) For social psychology these tendencies have been very substantially curbed through confrontation with the anthropological literature. Continued confrontation, however, will be required to prevent relapse. For the general psychologist, most of the message is yet to be learned.

The message of cultural relativism is very general and nonspecific. Often it is merely a general caution against intemperate generalization. (And often it takes the extreme of a negativistic denial of the possibility of any generalization.) The central purpose of this paper is to call attention to more concrete and specific methodological relevance. As Honigmann (1952, 1954), Whiting (1954), and Child (1954) have pointed out, anthropological evidence has been, and can continue to be, of invaluable service as a crucible in which to put to more rigorous test psychology's tentative theories, enabling one to edit them and select among alternatives in ways which laboratory experiments and correlational studies within our own culture might never make possible.

While this can never be anthropology's central role, what is here argued is that anthropology provides an important part of the scientific apparatus of psychology, particularly for personality theory. This is said within a perspective upon the strategy of science which sees experimentation and the other methods of science as having essentially an editorial function. That is, scientific data serve to choose among, prune out, and in this sense, edit theories. Essential to building a science are such laboratories. Where all are lacking, no science is possible. In the absence of the possibility of experimentation with modes of child rearing and personality formation, a science of personality would be all but impossible were it not for the "laboratory" of cross-cultural comparison opened up by the anthropologist.

To illustrate this role, several condensed and oversimplified examples are offered. Note that these are organized around problems in *psychological* theory. (That such problems are not central to anthropology should not distract us from this important service.) Though the "facts" in the illustrations may in fact be controversial, it is hoped that they exemplify the possibility, if not the actuality, of the editing role of anthropological data.

1. Freud validly observed that boys in late Hapsburgian Vienna had hostile feelings toward their fathers. Two possible explanations offered themselves—the hostility could be due to the father's role as the disciplinarian, or to the father's role as the mother's lover. For reasons that can be neglected here (but see Bakan 1958) Freud chose to emphasize the role of the mother's lover. However, working only with his patient population there was no adequate basis for making the choice. The two rival explanations were experimentally confounded, for among the parents of Freud's patients the disciplinarian of little boys was usually the mother's lover. (Remember that in Freud's day it was the *morality* of one's parents more often than their immorality that drove one to choose the analyst's couch over other couches, so that Freud got a biased sample.) Malinowski (1927) studied a society in which these two paternal roles were experimentally disentangled, in which the disciplinarian of young boys and the mother's lover were not one-and-the-same person. And in this society, the boys' hostility was addressed to the disciplinarian, not to the mother's lover. This outcome makes the Oedipal hostility more easily encompassed within the framework of a simple hedonistic learning theory such as that of Thorndike or Hull. While the love-jealousy and the punishment Oedipal theories are no doubt both appropriate to some extent, Malinowski's work helps to integrate personality theory within learning theory and gives us a firmer base upon which to predict the Oedipal complex of the son of a commuting suburban father where the mother is the only source of discipline.

2. Pettitt's (1946) monograph on educational practices among North American Indian tribes serves the purpose of calling attention to the fact that our theories of learning and cognition predict trouble for the modern emancipated American family. According to learning experiments, conditioned fear and conditioned hostility are the unrational product of temporal contiguity between stimulus and pain, or between stimulus and frustration. And if we go to cognitive psychology, we find that the perception of causality, and with this the phenomenon of blaming, are likewise functions of temporal and spatial contiguity (Heider 1944, Michotte 1946). From these theories it follows that in a society such as intellectual suburbia, where the parents stand alone in representing the restraints which society passes on to children, the parents will become the stimuli for conditioned hostility on the part of the children, the children will perceive the parents

as causing, as to blame for, their frustrations. Thus, the conditioning and/or the causal perception processes predict a chronic divisive force within the modern family.

With the inevitable selective process in which, among the countless customs that are tried, some are preserved more readily than others (e.g., Keller 1931), one can expect that in stable societies preventive customs will have grown up around this inevitable parental-resentment problem. Pettitt's (1946) analysis spells out the role of shamans and kachina dancers as disciplinarians, of the avunculate, of age grade systems, all as devices serving to deflect the discipline-induced hostility of the child away from the parent, and, thus as preserving intrafamilial solidarity. Reading his monograph gives one both a greater appreciation of the relevance of learning theory for predicting intrafamilial attitudes, and parenthetically a greater sympathy for those unsophisticated parents in our own culture who attempt a similar deflection of childish hostility away from themselves through invoking the sanctions of the policeman, the boogeyman, Santa Claus, or a reified God. (On the other hand, perhaps it is well that in our culture the socialization-induced hostilities are associated with parents, for our occupational structure requires new entrants to the labor force who are willing and eager to leave home permanently. Just such a labor force is lacking in some of the underdeveloped countries, perhaps in part because of the greater "wisdom" of their intrafamilial relationships.)

3. Every practicing psychoanalyst doing therapy with parents has probably recognized that the parent contributes much of the irrational and projected attitudes that comprise the intergenerational Oedipal interaction—yet this recognition is little represented in the literature, although not totally absent (e.g., Hsu 1940, Wellisch 1954). Recently the Herskovitses (1958a, b) have not only called attention to the ubiquity of the theme of the father's hostility toward his first born son in the Oedipus-type myths of Africa and Eurasia, but have in addition hypothesized that this paternal hostility to the newborn represents a reactivation of the father's sibling-rivalry hostility, acquired in his childhood in reaction to a younger sibling who abruptly displaced him in the total attention of the mother. The Herskovitses came to this hypothesis working with the mythology of Dahomey, a polygynous society in which each wife has her own hut, and in which a newborn child is continually with the mother, at work during the day and on the sleeping mat at night, until at around the age of two or three it is displaced by a younger sibling. Corresponding to this familial pattern is a mythology exceptionally full of strife between brothers and between generations, and in which the older brother or the older generation is portrayed as the initiator of the hostility.

Once pointed out, this seems exactly what one would expect from considerations of stimulus equivalence and habit transfer. Certainly in many cultures besides Dahomey (e.g., Levy 1935, Paul 1950, Henry 1944, Spiro 1953) hostility toward younger siblings is among the most characteristic and strongest learnings of childhood. When later as an adult an older sibling is presented with the new stimulus that his own child constitutes, this novel stimulus can be expected to elicit the strongest of the response tendencies learned in the past toward a similar stimulus, that is, the responses learned toward the younger sibling as an infant. The degree of this projected hostility would presumably be correlated with the degree to which the child in its first years had the undivided attention of the mother, and, hence, was the more frustratingly displaced at the end of the infancy period. If initiation rites be taken as symptomatic of the hostility of the older generation toward the younger (as Wellisch 1954 has plausibly interpreted infanticide and the sacrificing of children to bc), then one might expect the high correlation between length and degree of infant monopoly of the mother's attention and the hostility of initiation rites, which Whiting and co-workers (1958) report. (Initiation rites could also, on the basis of the same theory, represent the still more direct expression of the hostility of the older already initiated brothers toward the younger.) It can be noted that Dahomey is included in Whiting's sample, and is scored in the very highest category for severity of initiation rites. In Kwoma, the child's displacement may be through the father's return to the sleeping mat, but this is not the pattern in Dahomey. In general, displacement by a younger sibling is probably the more usual mechanism. If the projected sibling hostility is a relevant part of the explanation, then upon examination we should find both actual and mythological sibling strife more prevalent both in cultures with the harsher initiation rites and in the cultures with the longer infant monopoly of the mother's attention in infancy.

I have recently confirmed the stimulus equivalence of offspring and younger siblings assumed in this derivation in an unpublished study of the types of confusions of names that occur on the part of parents of college sophomores: When a parent mistakenly calls a child by the name of one of the parent's own siblings, the name of a younger sibling (of the same sex as the child) is most frequently involved. This study can not, of course, confirm the hostility aspects of the interpretation. Note also that this theory predicts a relative absence of parent-originated hostility for parents who were only children or youngest in their families, except insofar as the newborn is a genuine displacer of the parent in the attentions of the spouse.

4. Freud presented psychology with an insightful, but doubly double-jointed theory relating drive fixation in childhood and adult behavior. On the one hand, the fixation could be produced by overindulgence of the drive in childhood, or by its opposite, underindulgence. As to expression in adult life, fixation could express itself in excessive preoccupation with drive-relevant things or by its opposite, a counterphobic avoidance. Such a prediction is somewhat more specific than no prediction at all, but when combined with the inevitable errors of classification, the polar-cross scatter diagram which it predicts may not be distinguishable from a zero correlation. And whereas on many points, psychoanalysis and hedonistic-associationistic learning theories agree, the learning theories predict most easily a parallelism between conditions of acquisition and those of expression and transfer, rather than compensatory or complementary relationships, since memory but not energy storage is expected to persist. Whiting and Child's (1953) study may be interpreted as confirming those aspects of the Freudian hypothesis which thus agree with the learning theory interpretation. Persons for whom a given drive had been associated with frustration in childhood show phobic reactions regarding it in adult life (negative fixation). And insofar as infantile indulgence and gratification had adult symptoms, those who found a given drive a source of gratification in childhood sought it out as a source of cure in adult life. Here, again, the result has been in the direction of integrating personality

theory with learning theory. Here, again, the anthropological data have been efficacious in selecting among alternative psychological hypotheses. And as Child (1954) shows, insofar as relationships, Freudian or otherwise, have been established between early child training and adult behavior, the confirmations have come primarily from the studies of cross-cultural breadth, rather than from studies making use of the small range of differences within our own culture.

5. Other studies using the cross-cultural method seem to confirm the positive transfer of attitudes between childhood reinforcement conditions and adult personality, the assumptions of stimulus equivalence, transfer, displacement in approach-avoidance conflicts, and so forth. Spiro's (1953, 1958) demonstration of the parallel between infant training by parents and attitudes toward spirits is interpreted as confirmatory in this regard. This may seem contradictory, since in his 1953 paper, Spiro takes his evidence as justifying a choice in favor of a perceptual rather than a learning theory. As I understand it, learning theories are silent as to the nature of conscious contents. Hence, evidence regarding conscious contents are not contradictory to learning theory. In particular, evidence regarding "perceptions of" objects cannot be interpreted as corresponding to the stimulus terms of learning theory. Usually a better translation of "perceived as" is "responded to as to." On this ground, learning theory expects the authority symbols of adult life to be responded to as (to be perceived as) were the authority figures of childhood to which the responses (perceptions) were originally learned. For more details on this mode of integrating theoretical terminologies, see Campbell (1961). For more evidence on the parallels between attitudes toward parents and toward spiritual beings, see Lambert and co-workers (1959).

In general, the evidence of social anthropology is seen as having a salutary and disciplining effect upon personality psychology, serving, paradoxically, to make personality theory more clearly a part of the learning theory of general psychology.

Some Psychological Comments on Anthropological Method

It is probably true that the testing of psychological theories must remain a very minor part of the research agenda of the anthropologist. In addition, the great difference in task must be recognized between the descriptive, humanistic task of one who seeks to record all aspects of a specific cultural instance and the task of the abstractive and generalizing "scientist" who wants to test the concomitant variation of two isolated factors across instances in general. Cooperation between these orientations is often difficult—but is helped rather than hindered by the explicit recognition of the great difference in goals: Too often those in one camp regard those in the other as the willful practitioners of a wrongheaded approach, implicitly assuming a common goal. Both orientations are represented in the present volume, in some instances both within a single person. The descriptive-humanistic rather than abstractive approach has in the past been typical of much of anthropology. On the other hand, Honigmann (1952), Whiting (1954), and Spiro (1953, 1958) have presented the abstractive, hypothesis-testing commitment. Murray (1949) and Gillin (1954) have called for such an orientation in previous symposia on culture and personality. My interests are wholly of this sort, and some of the methodological comments to follow are thus irrelevant to the more typically descriptive anthropological undertaking. Many of these comments come from an interest in a potential psychology of induction (Campbell 1958a, 1959), and in particular from an application of knowledge about human perception, learning, and biases to the calibration of the human observer as a scientific measuring instrument (for example, Campbell, Hunt, and Lewis 1957, 1958, Campbell 1958b).

Before going into these details, it may be well to note a common cause joining the abstractive-generalizing orientation central to this paper and the descriptive-humanistic orientation as it has been modally represented in anthropological research training. Both stand in opposition to the undisciplined generalizations often found in the more dramatic efforts to interpret man and culture. Both look askance at the sweeping generalizations of a Spencer, a Spengler, a Toynbee, or a Nietzsche when offered as established scientific truth. This common ground is not always noted, and, indeed, each orientation tends to attribute undisciplined generalization to the other.

In the major departments of anthropology of the 1920's and 1930's the theoretical excesses of a previous generation of anthropologists led to an emphasis upon objectivity in field work which was antitheoretical insofar as adherence to theory had in the past served to reduce the objectivity of field work. Herskovits (1960) has recently called attention to a superior objectivity for the humanistic aspects of anthropological study. Both the descriptive-humanistic orientation and the abstractive, hypothesis-testing orientation wish to avoid self-deception and bias in the data collection process. Both call for reliable, intersubjectively communicable observations. Both are ideally hardheaded, skeptical, modest, and conservative in their orientation to factual knowledge. For these reasons, many of the topics covered in what follows are of joint relevance. This point is made without weakening the appeal for the mutual recognition and respect for a separateness of task and division of labor between the two orientations, both of which are essential in the complete study of man.

The Relation of Intersubjective-Verifiability to Directness of Sense Receptor Access

It goes without saying that a science of either type cannot be built without intersubjective verifiability of observations. Psychological research on the accuracy and person-to-person agreement in independent reporting seems summarizable by the statement that the greater the direct accessibility of the stimuli to the sense receptors, the greater the intersubjective verifiability of the observation. The weaker or the more intangible, indirect, or abstract the stimulus attribute, the more the observations are subject to distortion.

It is quite conceivable that there are some aspects of culture, including its over-all pattern or ethos, that are so abstract or indirectly inferred that intersubjective verifiability is lost. If this is so, then until corrected, these aspects cannot become a part of science, and we, as scientists, should concentrate on those aspects upon which we can get agreement. Recently Holmes (1957, 1958) has reported a restudy of some of Mead's work on Samoan society, which along with the other restudies of recent years (such as Li An-Che 1937, Bennett 1946, and Lewis 1951) supports the methodological expectation of greater verifiability to the more palpable and visible. As far as the great bulk of Mead's ethnology, Holmes confirms her findings, stating "the reliability of Mead's account is remarkably high." While he reports some differences in the description of traditional political systems and other matters, on matters of material culture and observable custom, there is general agreement. This extends also to the observed absence of an adolescent disturbance on the part of the girls, and the easy transition from childhood to adult life. But upon several of the broader aspects of ethos, his findings are in complete disagreement, for example, upon the lack of specialized feeling in human relations, the lack of competitive spirit, the lack of crisis in human relations, and the importance of "Mafau-fau," or the gift of wise judgment. In the context of his presentation, one cannot easily interpret these differences as due to culture change in the intervening years, but rather one must interpret them as disagreement in the description of aspects of "the same" culture. If, as Mead has said, "in the matter of ethos, the surest and most perfect instrument of understanding is our own emotional response" (Mead and McGregor 1951:300), then ethos may indeed be beyond the realm of scientific study. This lack of intersubjective verifiability is not inevitable however. In the methodological pattern of Whiting and Child (1953) some of the relevant data are made much more directly accessible to the senses; in addition, the integrative patterning is made a matter of explicit public combinational formulas. Through the use of methodological procedures developed to control the demonstrated biases of human observers, judgments of the intangibles of ethos may be made intersubjectively confirmable, demonstrable in reliability studies.

Adaptation Level and Contrast Effects

In considering the faults of our laboratory experiments in social psychology, we have come up with a list of recurrent flaws, some of which also apply to other types of data collection. One of these has been called infelicitously "instrument decay" (Campbell 1957): When human observers are used as the measuring device their judgmental standards often change in ways that may be misinterpreted as experimental effects. A major source of such "instrument decay" is a set of phenomena in human judgment summarized by Helson (1947) under the concept of "level of adaptation." Its role in social science field work may be illustrated by the anecdote in the following paragraph.[1]

In the last several years, considerable numbers of Russian experts from American universities have been sent on visits to the U.S.S.R. In part, they have had different itineraries, some going first to Leningrad, others first to Moscow, and so forth. In comparing notes later they have found themselves in disagreement as to which Russian city (Leningrad or Moscow) was the more drab and which the more lively. These differences in opinion have turned out to be correlated with the differences in itinerary: which ever city one visited first seemed the more drab. Against the adaptation level based upon experience with familiar United States cities, the first Russian city seemed drab and cold indeed. But a stay in Russia modified the adaptation level, changed the implicit standard of reference so that the second city was judged against a more lenient standard. Such a process is what would be predicted by extrapolation from laboratory and field studies of the effect of context upon clinical psychology judgments (e.g., Campbell, Hunt, and Lewis 1957, 1958). Of course, other processes were also involved—familiarity with the Russian vernacular, sensitivity to the expressive components of voice tone and gesture, and other skills facilitating warm social contacts were increasing. All such effects were operating, however, to change the calibration of the human observer, and thus to bias his reports in a systematic way.

---

[1] I am indebted to Professors Deming Brown and Raymond Mack for this information.

How can we learn of, and correct, such bias? The anecdote is instructive in this regard. This bias would not have been noted if all of the visitors had had the same itinerary. Their actual pattern constituted a counterbalanced, observational schedule, and could have been analyzed as a crossover design (Cochran and Cox 1950) to determine the main effects of firstness versus secondness, of city, and of observer. Essential in the control were multiple observers and multiple sequences.

Today many anthropologists, as in Africa, are combining basic ethnography with acculturation studies, and are faced with the decision as to whether to study first the members of the tribe who remain in the bush, or the members living in the westernized city. Combining the principles of adaptation level with other principles of bias, particularly those involving assimilation errors or transfer (see Campbell 1958b for a survey of such biases) some predictions can perhaps be made: (1) If one compares anthropologist's impression of the indigenous bush culture under the two orders (bush-city versus city-bush), this indigenous culture would probably appear more strange and exotic under the bush-city order. This is because, under that order, the bush culture is perceived with a more divergent adaptation level than that provided when the partially westernized members of the culture have been previously studied in the city. (2) The bush data might be better in detail and intimacy of records for the city-bush order than for the bush-city order. This might be expected insofar as rapport is increased by the familiarity with the culture and the friendship bonds acquired through the city fieldwork with the partially acculturated members of the ethnic group. (3) The observation of "survivals" of the indigenous culture among the westernized urban descendents is no doubt enhanced by detailed knowledge of the relatively untouched bush culture. Thus, such "survivals" might be noted in greater number in the bush-city order. These predictions cannot, of course, be made unequivocally. But whatever the direction predicted, there are adequate grounds to expect the two sequences to produce different results, particularly on those intangible matters most relevant to the culture-personality problem.

The source of error is great enough, and a considerable remedy is near enough at hand, so that we are morally bound to request from our sources of financial support the funds to implement them—particularly since all concerned should now recognize how precious to the social sciences is our rapidly dwindling supply of novel and independent social systems. The cheapest remedy would be to schedule the field work so that it was broken up into several alternating visits to each location, bush and urban, allowing *both* conditions to be recompared several times, and both to be judged against the end-of-field-trip adaptation level. This could probably be accomplished with 10 per cent increases in the travel budgets and 50 per cent increases in the field residence budgets—certainly not impossible to promote once the importance is recognized. A more complete control would double field costs by having the field-workers work in pairs, one starting in the bush and one in the city, and trading locations from time to time. This approach would also offer an important control over the "personal equations" or idiosyncratic predilections of the observers, biases of a more permanent and less predictable sort than those due to adaptation level. There would seem no doubt but that this additional cost would be justified.

Adaptation Level and Usable Vocabulary in Cross-Cultural Interviewing

One of the emphases of the present paper is upon the desirability of some studies which collect data on a limited set of topics from many cultural units. This is advocated not as a substitute for the intensive ethnography of single peoples, but rather as a needed additional mode of data collection, particularly for those correlational types of analysis in which dozens of cultures are needed. In such multiple-culture studies the field work would be particularly dependent upon interviews with informants, the anthropologist himself not having time to observe directly all of the customs about which he inquired. In such studies the phenomenon of adaptation level creates for a class of descriptive words "translation" problems over and above the troublesome fact of language differences. That is to say, these adaptation-level problems would remain even if the heterogeneous cultures were to "speak the same language" as the anthropologist.

The words or concepts in question are those used to characterize the tribe as a whole which imply degrees of departure from a usual norm or adaptation level, this norm being itself provided by the average behavior or experience of the tribe itself. Such words are usable to denote individual differences within the tribe, but not to characterize over-all attributes of the culture. Thus, for a hypothetical "wholly isolated" tribe, lacking a range of other peoples for comparison, one could not interpret for cross-cultural comparisons answers to questions such as: "Are your people happy, intelligent, hard working, strict with children, warm, friendly, prudish, joking, able to endure pain, and so forth?"

Anthropologists, experienced with many cultures and having a common base in European cultures, may be able to make such observations and judgments reliably, particularly if the fluctuations of their own adaptation levels, as described above, be compensated for. But a completely isolated tribe would have no "lingua franca," no intertribal measuring stick against which to calibrate their use of the terms. And even though informants might reliably employ the frame of reference provided by the several adjacent tribes, given the ubiquitous tendencies toward regional similarity, this would not entirely eliminate the problem.

For some of these topics, modes of questioning are available which may avoid this problem. Such questioning may make use of internal comparisons within the tribe ("Are children happier than adults?"). More typically, the problem may be solved by reducing the question to sample behaviors from the implied syndrome, employing terms referring to qualitatively discrete and universal behaviors: "Upon what occasions do women smile and laugh." "What does a mother do when her child cries?" "What are the times during the day when a man works—or rests?" These suggestions, however, do more to raise the problem than to suggest a solution.

The Uninterpretability of Comparisons between But Two Natural Instances

In view of the importance of Malinowski's challenge to the love-jealousy interpretation of the Oedipal conflict, it is unforgivable that his observations have not been replicated. However thorough his field work on other points, his published evidence on this point is very thin indeed. While he alludes to evidence from manifest dream content, of the type that Dorothy Eggan (1952) has discussed, what we need are substantial samples of detailed records of the dreams of boys and girls and men and women.

But while there is a crying need for verifying and extending Malinowski's evidence on Trobriand intrafamilial attitudes, such a replication is of minor importance for testing the Freudian hypothesis. We who are interested in using such data for delineating process rather than exhaustively describing single instances must accept this rule: *No comparison of a single pair of natural objects is interpretable.* Between Trobriand and Vienna there are many dimensions of differences which could constitute potential rival explanations and which we have no means of ruling out. For comparisons of this pair, the *ceteris paribus* requirement becomes untenable. But data collection need not stop here. Both the avunculate and the European arrangement are so widely distributed over the world that if testing Oedipal theories were our purpose, we could select a dozen matched pairs of tribes from widely varying culture areas, each pair differing with regard to which male educates and disciplines the boy, but as similar as possible in other respects. Assuming that collections of dreams from boys showed the expected differences between each pair, then the more such pairs we had, the fewer tenable rival hypotheses would be available and, thus, the more certain would be our confirmation.

There is an analogous *ceteris paribus* problem with the use of a single measuring instrument. An established difference between two matched populations on a *single* questionnaire item is likewise uninterpretable because there are so many rival hypotheses to explain the difference—the groups may differ because of their reactions to the first word, or to the second word, or to the grammatical features of the wording rather than the semantic features, and so forth. However, if there are multiple indicators which vary in their irrelevant attributes, and if these all agree as to the direction of the difference on the theoretically intended aspects, then the number of tenable rival explanations becomes greatly reduced and the confirmation of theory more nearly certain (Campbell 1957:310, Campbell 1959, Campbell and Fiske 1959). Doob (1958) has recently demonstrated the seriousness of this problem in cross-cultural studies, in an important paper which should be read by every graduate student planning to do research on culture and personality. On this point, it has been psychologists studying college sophomores and not anthropologists who have been most guilty of a naive overdependence upon single instruments, and our critical literature on "response sets" (e.g., Cronbach 1946, 1950, Chapman and Bock 1958) shows how misleading this can be.

The Whiting and Child Studies

From this sample of content interests and methodological biases, it will come as no surprise to learn that I regard studies of the Whiting and Child type (Horton 1943; B. B. Whiting 1950; Murdock and Whiting 1951; McClelland and Friedman 1952; Whiting and Child 1953; Whiting 1954; Wright 1954; Barry 1957; Barry,

Bacon and Child 1957; Freeman and Winch 1957; Rose and Willoughby 1958; Whiting, Kluckhohn and Albert 1958; Spiro and D'Andrade 1958; Lambert, Triandis and Wolf 1959; Barry, Child and Bacon 1959; Whiting 1959) as very important steps toward a science of personality and culture, as well as one of the major events in the social sciences of the past twenty years. It can be seen why, from this perspective, the earlier studies of individual cultures such as Trobriand, Dobu, Kwakiutl, Kwoma, Ifaluk, and Brobdingnag, can be regarded more as sources of hypotheses than as confirming evidence for the purposes of a science of culture and personality.

This is stated so strongly because it is felt that until very recently anthropology has in general both rejected and neglected these studies, and that the reasons for this rejection might well be discussed. These reasons have been given little attention in the anthropological journals. The neglect has been so great that it is difficult to document the rejection. The few published references in anthropological publications are in general favorable (Gladwin 1954, Kluckhohn 1954, Honigmann 1952, Spiro 1958). The neglect is perhaps indicated by the fact that until Spiro's (1958) study appeared, none of the dozen or so prior studies had been presented in an anthropological journal. Thus, for the details of the rejection, the writer will have to depend for the most part upon informal sampling of the opinions of anthropology graduate students and faculty members at some seven universities, relying primarily on their reports as to how "anthropologists in general" felt. These are the objections heard most frequently (Gladwin 1954 and Spiro 1958 mention several of them):

1. *This is not anthropology.* This objection can be, of course, an entirely legitimate expression of differences in goals. It may reflect upon the fact that problems of psychological theory rather than anthropological theory are under test. It can express a commitment to anthropology's task, comparable to that of the historian, of documenting in detail the full complexity of single instances. But this objection is usually a concomitant of other objections which reject the studies for the abstracting-generalizing purpose also.

2. *Taking fragments of a culture and attempting to interpret them apart from the whole cultural complex is impossible or illegitimate.* Spiro (1958) has cited this widespread objection, and has correctly called it an empirical question to be answered by the final outcomes of trying the approach. Such criticisms may be right. It may be that none of the findings will stand up under cross-validation, that no correlational laws relating aspects of cultural phenomena can be established. Such laws cannot be ruled out on *a priori* grounds, however.

From the standpoint of an empirical science of induction (Campbell 1959), it must be expected that there may be many problem areas in which a science cannot be established. In the terminology of the analysis-of-variance statistics of experimentation, if in a given area one always finds significant highest-order interactions, and never finds significant main effects or lower order interactions, then a science probably never can be developed. The healthy infancy of the successful sciences seems to have been predicated upon the stimulating nourishment of crude but effective *ceteris paribus* laws. For example, the force fields of atomic nuclei extend in infinite distance in all directions. However, they decay so rapidly as a function of distance that they can be disregarded in the statement of many crude laws, such as those embodied in Archimedes' mechanics. Were this not so, were Archimedes to have had to limit himself to statements about each particular instance, then physics never could have developed. The critics of the generalizing social scientists are right in cautioning against claiming effective *ceteris paribus* laws when one hasn't got them, but pointing to the obvious idiosyncracy of every person, tribe, or swinging cathedral chandelier provides no *a priori* basis for rejecting the enterprise.

3. *The data in the Human Relations Area Files and in the research monographs available are inadequate to the purpose.* While it is obvious to every one, Whiting and Child first of all, that better data would be desirable, the incompleteness and the inaccuracy of the files cannot explain away the striking correlations obtained. Error of this sort *lowers* correlations, rather than raises them. Significant high correlations can be explained away as due to the incompetence of the ethnography *only* if a *systematic* source of error be found to be confounded with the classifications used—if, for example, all of the indulgent cultures turned out to have been described by French anthropologists and all of the high socialization anxiety cultures by German ethnologists. Such systematic sources of error have not been suggested and are extremely unlikely.

4. *A specific tribe has been misclassified, or there is another tribe which they don't report upon which doesn't fit.* The abstractive-generalizing social scientist knows that in dealing with natural groups *ceteris* are not in fact *paribus*, and he therefore expects exceptions which represent the operation of many other laws which he as yet knows nothing of. Such exceptions are repeatedly found in the law-confirming scatter diagrams of biology and psychology. If the over-all significant relationship still persists when the specific errors are corrected and the new cases plotted, the exceptions are not invalidating.

5. *The process of coding qualitative data into numerical categories offers opportunities for a subjective bias which generates the correlations.* This criticism is certainly occasionally valid, and may explain away the results of one striking relationship (McClelland and Friedman 1952, as restudied by Child *et al.* 1958). The basic Whiting and Child studies have been, however, scrupulously careful about this. They may have more trouble on this score in their new studies with their specially trained fieldworkers who can hardly remain in ignorance of the hypotheses under test.

6. *Many correlation possibilities have been inspected and only those that are high reported; thus, high values may be due to chance even if apparently statistically significant.* This criticism is in some degree appropriate to most exploratory studies that admit of reformulating hypotheses in the course of the investigation. It can be answered only by testing the relationships on new samples, and this, of course, should be done. (The social sciences differ from the

physical sciences in lacking the voluminous replication research that validates and revalidates every important new discovery.)

7. *Since cultures are not independent, the usual tests of significance are not appropriate.* I am not competent to enter into the abstruse statistical considerations that are involved here, but do want to point out some more common sense considerations. The criticism applies equally to samplings of persons and their response dispositions, where we normally use tests of significance without qualms. Cluster-sampling techniques (e.g., Kish 1956) are appropriate for computing a more accurate and larger error term. The criticism would be particularly damning if it turned out that regional areas were confounded with theoretical classifications: if, for example, most of the indulgent cultures came from the South Seas and most of the high socialization-anxiety cultures from Africa. This has not been the case, however. Furthermore, when Whiting and Child (1953:168) analyze their data so as to show that a given relationship holds *within* each of five major culture areas, the use of a number of tribes from each of several culture areas becomes a *strength* rather than a weakness, and if analyzed in terms of the logic of analysis of variance, would result in a smaller error term rather than a larger one.

SUMMARY

In the first part of this paper, the role of anthropological data in editing among the competing theories of psychology has been emphasized. Such research can never be central among the anthropologist's tasks, but can be invaluable in the consolidation of psychological theory. Anthropology is in this fashion of great methodological importance to psychology.

In the second part of the paper, the roles are reversed. Since anthropology depends upon enculturated human beings as its measuring instruments, the psychology of bias in human judgment becomes relevant to choices among methodological alternatives open to anthropologists. Several such points are discussed, as are methodological strengths and weaknesses of the statistical cross-cultural studies.

BIBLIOGRAPHY

BAKAN, DAVID
    1958   Sigmund Freud and the Jewish mystical tradition. Princeton, Van Nostrand.
BARRY, HERBERT
    1957   Relationships between child training and the pictorial arts. Journal of Abnormal and Social Psychology 54:380–383.
BARRY, HERBERT, MARGARET K. BACON and IRVIN L. CHILD
    1957   A cross-cultural survey of some sex differences in socialization. Journal of Abnormal and Social Psychology 55:327–332.

BARRY, HERBERT, IRVIN L. CHILD and MARGARET K. BACON
  1959   Relation of child training to subsistence economy. American Anthropologist 61:51–63.

BENNETT, JOHN W.
  1946   The interpretation of pueblo culture. Southwestern Journal of Anthropology 2:361–374.

CAMPBELL, DONALD T.
  1955   The informant in quantitative research. American Journal of Sociology 60:339–342.
  1957   Factors relevant to the validity of experiments in social settings. Psychological Bulletin 54:297–312.
  1958a Common fate, similarity, and other indices of the status of aggregates of persons as social entities. Behavioral Science 3:14–25.
  1958b Systematic error on the part of human links in communication systems. Information and Control 1:334–369.
  1959   Methodological suggestions from a comparative psychology of knowledge processes. Inquiry (Univ. Oslo Press) 2:152–182.
  1961   Social attitudes and other acquired behavioral dispositions. *In* Psychology: a study of a science. Vol. 6. Investigations of man as socius: their place in psychology and the social sciences. Sigmund Koch ed. New York, McGraw Hill (in press; duplicated draft 1957).

CAMPBELL, DONALD T. and DONALD W. FISKE
  1959   Convergent and discriminant validation by the multitrait-multimethod matrix. Psychological Bulletin 56:81–105.

CAMPBELL, DONALD T., WILLIAM A. HUNT and NAN A. LEWIS
  1957   The effects of assimilation and contrast in judgments of clinical materials. American Journal of Psychology 70:347–360.
  1958   The relative susceptibility of two rating scales to disturbances resulting from shifts in stimulus context. Journal of Applied Psychology 42:213–217.

CHAPMAN, LOREN J. and R. DARRELL BOCK
  1958   Components of variance due to acquiescence and content in the F scale measure of authoritarianism. Psychological Bulletin 55:328–333.

CHILD, IRVIN L.
  1954   Socialization. *In* Handbook of social psychology, Gardner Lindzey, ed. Cambridge, Mass., Addison-Wesley.

CHILD, IRVIN L., THOMAS STORM and JOSEPH VEROFF
  1958   Achievement themes in folk tales related to socialization practice. *In* Motives in fantasy, action, and society. John W. Atkinson, ed. New York, Van Nostrand.

COCHRAN, WILLIAM G. and GERTRUDE M. COX
  1950   Experimental designs. New York, Wiley.

CRONBACH, LEE J.
  1946   Response sets and test validity. Educational and Psychological Measurement 6:475–494.
  1950   Further evidence on response sets and test design. Educational and Psychological Measurement 10:3–31.

DOOB, LEONARD W.
  1957   An introduction to the psychology of acculturation. Journal of Social
          Psychology 45:143–160.
  1958   The use of different test items in nonliterate societies. Public Opinion
          Quarterly 21:499–504.
EGGAN, DOROTHY
  1952   The manifest content of dreams: a challenge to social science. Ameri-
          can Anthropologist 54:469–485.
FREEMAN, LINTON C. and ROBERT F. WINCH
  1957   Societal complexity: an empirical test of a typology of societies. Ameri-
          can Journal of Sociology 62:461–466.
GLADWIN, THOMAS
  1954   Review of Whiting and Child, Child training and personality. American
          Anthropologist 56:893–897.
GILLEN, JOHN
  1954   Methods of approach to the study of human behavior. In Aspects of
          culture and personality, Francis L. K. Hsu, ed. New York, Abelard-
          Schuman.
HEIDER, FRITZ
  1944   Social perception and phenomenal causality. Psychological Review 51:
          358–374.
HELSON, HARRY
  1947   Adaptation-level as frame of reference for prediction of psycho-
          physical data. American Journal of Psychology 60:1–29.
HENRY, JULES and ZUNIA
  1944   Doll play of Pilage Indian children. Research Monographs No. 4, Ameri-
          can Orthopsychiatric Association.
HERSKOVITS, MELVILLE J.
  1960   Humanism in anthropological science. VI International Congress of
          Anthropological and Ethnological Sciences, Paris, August 4, 1960.
HERSKOVITS, MELVILLE J. and FRANCES S.
  1958a   Sibling rivalry, the Oedipus complex, and myth. Journal of American
          Folklore 71:1–15.
  1958b   Dahomean narrative: a cross-cultural analysis. Evanston, Ill., North-
          western University Press.
HOLMES, LOWELL DON
  1957   The restudy of Manu'an culture: a problem in methodology. Unpub-
          lished Ph.D. dissertation, Northwestern University.
  1958   Ta'u: Stability and change in a Samoan village, Wellington, New Zea-
          land, Polynesian Society, Reprint No. 7.
HONIGMANN, JOHN J.
  1952   The testing of hypotheses in anthropology. American Anthropologist
          54:429–432.
  1954   Culture and personality. New York, Harper.
HORTON, DONALD
  1943   The functions of alcohol in primitive societies: a cross-cultural study.
          Quarterly Journal of Studies on Alcohol 4:199–320.

Hsu, Francis L. K.
  1940   The English wife. Chapter VI, Mother and children, Section 5, A non-
         Freudian explanation. Unpublished manuscript.
  1954   Aspects of culture and personality. New York, Abelard-Schuman.

Keller, Albert Galloway
  1931   Societal evolution (rev. ed.), New Haven, Yale University Press.

Kish, Leslie
  1956   Confidence intervals for clustered samples. American Sociological Re-
         view 22:154–165.

Kluckhohn, Clyde
  1954a Culture and behavior. *In* Handbook of social psychology, Gardner
         Lindzey, ed. Cambridge, Mass. Addison-Wesley.
  1954b Southwestern studies of culture and personality. American Anthro-
         pologist 56:685–697.

Lambert, William W., Leigh Minturn Triandis and Margery Wolf
  1959   Some correlates of beliefs in the malevolence and benevolence of super-
         natural beings: a cross-cultural study. Journal of Abnormal and Social
         Psychology 58:162–169.

Lasswell, Harold D.
  1931   A hypothesis rooted in the preconceptions of a single civilization tested
         by Bronislaw Malinowski. *In* Methods in social science, Stuart A. Rice,
         ed. Chicago, University of Chicago Press.

Levy, David M.
  1935   Sibling rivalry studies in children of primitive groups. American
         Journal of Orthopsychiatry 9:205–214.

Lewis, Oscar
  1951   Life in a Mexican village: Tepoztlan restudied. Urbana, University
         of Illinois Press.

Li An-Che
  1937   Zuni: some observations and queries. American Anthropologist 39:
         62–76.

Malinowski, Bronislaw
  1927   Sex and repression in savage society. London, Humanities Press.

McClelland, David C. and G. A. Friedman
  1952   A cross-cultural study of the relationship between child-training prac-
         tices and achievement motivation appearing in folk tales. *In* Readings
         in social psychology, Guy E. Swanson, Theodore M. Newcomb, and
         Eugene L. Hartley, eds. New York, Holt.

Mead, Margaret and F. M. C. MacGregor
  1951   Growth and culture: a photographic study of Balinese childhood. New
         York, Putnam.

Michotte, A. E.
  1946   La perception de la causalite. Louvain, Institute superior de Philosophie,
         Etudes Psychologiques vol. 6.

Murdock, George Peter, and John W. M. Whiting
  1951   Cultural determination of parental attitudes: the relationship between

the social structure, particularly family structure, and parental behavior. *In* Problems of infancy and childhood. Transactions of the Fourth Conference March 6–7, 1950, Milton J. E. Senn, ed. New York, Josiah Macy Jr. Foundation, 1951.

MURRAY, HENRY A.
1949   Research planning: a few proposals. *In* Culture and Personality, S. Stansfeld Sargent and Marian W. Smith, eds. New York, Viking Fund, 1949.

PAUL, BENJAMIN D.
1950   Symbolic sibling rivalry in a Guatemalan Indian village. American Anthropologist 52:205–217.

PETTITT, GEORGE A.
1946   Primitive education in North America. Berkeley, University of California Press, University of California Publications in American Archaeology and Ethnology Vol. 43, No. 1.

ROSE, EDWARD and GARY WILLOUGHBY
1958   Culture profiles and emphases. American Journal of Sociology 63: 476–490.

SARGENT, S. STANSFELD and MARIAN W. SMITH
1949   Culture and Personality. New York, Viking Fund.

SPIRO, MELFORD E.
1953   Ghosts: an anthropological inquiry into learning and perception. Journal of Abnormal and Social Psychology 48:376–382.

SPIRO, MELFORD D. and ROY G. D'ANDRADE
1958   A cross-cultural study of some supernatural beliefs. American Anthropologist 60:456–466.

WELLISCH, E.
1954   Isaac and Oedipus: a study in Biblical psychology of the sacrifice of Isaac, the Akedah. London, Routledge & Kegan Paul.

WHITING, BEATRICE B.
1950   A cross-cultural study of sorcery and social control. *In* Paiute Sorcery. New York, Viking Fund (Publications in Anthropology No. 15).

WHITING, JOHN W. M.
1954   The cross-cultural method. *In* Handbook of social psychology, Gardner Lindzey, ed. Cambridge. Mass., Addison-Wesley.
1959   Sorcery, sin and the superego: a cross-cultural study of some mechanisms of social control. *In* Nebraska symposium on motivation: 1959, Marshall R. Jones, ed., pp 174–195. Lincoln, University of Nebraska Press, 1959.

WHITING, JOHN W. M. and IRVIN L. CHILD
1953   Child training and personality. New Haven, Yale University Press.

WHITING, JOHN W. M., RICHARD KLUCKHOHN and ALBERT ANTHONY
1958   The function of male initiation ceremonies at puberty. *In* Readings in social psychology, 3d ed., Eleanor E. Maccoby, Theodore M. Newcomb, and Eugene L. Hartley, eds. New York, Holt.

WRIGHT, GEORGE O.
1954   Projection and displacement: a cross-cultural study of folk-tale aggression. Journal of Abnormal and Social Psychology 49:523–529.

INTRODUCTION TO PART III

SOCIALIZATION, CULTURE, AND FEEDBACK

IF PSYCHOLOGICAL characteristics of the individual, whether identified with his total personality or with the socially functioning part of it, are dependent upon the culturally conditioned child-rearing practices or socialization processes, what are the factors which determine or at least shape the patterns of culture, which in turn condition the child-rearing practices or socialization processes? If human societies are as stable and unchanging as those of ants and bees, the latter type of question, though not wholly irrelevant, would not have been important. But human societies are highly dynamic entities with extreme variability in their rates of change, just as human individuals in any society are quite capable of, and often given to, deviation.

Jules Henry, a well-known psychological anthropologist, puts it this way: "As I see it, the crucial difference between insect societies and human ones is that whereas the former are organized to achieve homeostasis, the organization of the latter seems always to *guarantee and specifically provide for instability*" ("Homeostasis, Society and Evolution: A Critique." Scientific Monthly, LXXXI, 1955: 308). While this may be an overstatement, the plain fact is that all human societies do undergo change, rapidly or slowly.

The question of individual deviation was discussed by Kaplan in Chapter 8; the question of social and cultural change was briefly touched upon by Hsu in Chapter 7. The best accepted view at present is that the individual and society-culture relationship is a two-way traffic in spiral progression. The individual's psychological characteristics are results of his socialization processes, but his psychological characteristics are, in turn, at the root of the patterns of culture, in change or in stability, which govern the socialization processes.

The three chapters in this section of the book have some important differences which the reader will do well to keep in mind. The first difference concerns approach. Whiting's approach and that of Aberle are more rigorous in methodology, with emphasis on ascertaining cross-culturally the interrelationship between a few specific variables (such as "exclusive mother-infant sleeping arrangement" and "cross sex identity," or "economic organization" and "ethics"). Hsu's approach, while likewise attempting cross-cultural generalization, is still at a more qualitative or speculative stage. The generalization attempted is perhaps for this reason more "ambitious," in that it hypothesizes the existence of a single socio-psychological axis that generates or integrates a wide range of more specific cultural features. While the Whiting and Aberle chapters in this section, as well as the other chapters of the entire book, are primarily critical appraisals of works already carried out or well under way, Hsu's chapter is launched more or less as a trial balloon, an exploration of a hypothesis which will stand or fall depending upon intensive research yet to come.

Chapter 12

SOCIALIZATION PROCESS AND PERSONALITY

JOHN W. M. WHITING
Harvard University

THE use of the comparative or cross-cultural method in studies of culture and personality has served two quite different purposes. Psychologists have tended to view this method as one by which certain assumptions about personality development may be tested. Anthropologists, on the other hand, are more likely to view such studies as a test of hypotheses concerning the way in which elements of culture can be integrated by underlying psychological processes. It is to the latter aim that this chapter will be devoted.

Most of the early studies concerned with culture and personality were intensive case studies of a single society such as Mead's *Coming of Age in Samoa* (1928) or comparisons of a series of case studies such as Ruth Benedict's *Patterns of Culture* (1934), Margaret Mead's *Sex and Temperament* (1935), Linton and Kardiner's *The Individual and His Society* (1939) and *The Psychological Frontiers of Society* (1945). This review, however, will not consider such case studies, but will be restricted to cross-cultural studies which have used a large sample of societies presumed to be in some way representative of the cultures of the world.

The studies under review can be classified essentially into two types: those which have made some assumptions about the psychological effect of certain child-rearing practices on personality as reflected in some other aspect of culture such as magic, art, or religion; and those which have concerned themselves with the effect of features of the basic economy or social structure on child-rearing practices. Fortunately, in many instances studies in these two categories may be linked by virtue of the fact that they share the same scores

355

on child-rearing practices. In the first type of study these linking child-rearing scores have the theoretical status of independent or antecedent variables; that is, they have been assumed to be determinants of personality which is assumed to be a mediating psychological process reflected in magic and religion. In the second type of study, child-rearing scores have the theoretical status of dependent or consequent variables; that is, they have been assumed to be determined by economic and social structural aspects of the culture.

The conjunction of these two kinds of studies described above permits the testing of the general hypothesis suggested by Whiting and Child (1953:310) concerning the way in which personality or psychological process may serve to integrate culture. This hypothesis was summarized by the following diagram:

| Maintenance Systems | $\rightarrow$ | Child Training Practices | $\rightarrow$ | Personality Variables | $\rightarrow$ | Projective Systems |

Maintenance systems were defined as "the economic, political, and social organizations of a society—the basic customs surrounding the nourishment, sheltering, and protection of its members." Personality was defined as "a set of hypothetical intervening variables." Projective systems include customs which are for the most part magical and unrealistic. The term "projective system" suggested by Kardiner (1945) is perhaps unfortunate since it suggests that the psychological process of projection is necessarily involved. Since "acting out," "distortion," "ritualization," "displacement," "fixation," or any other psychological process relating to personality is implied, a term such as "systems of psychological defense" or of "psychological security" might have been more appropriate. The cultural systems which reflect such processes most directly are those of magic, religion, art or any other feature that is not immediately and practically involved in the satisfaction of basic biological needs. In sum, the hypothesis implies that personality is an intervening hypothetical variable determined by child rearing which is in turn determined by maintenance systems and which finally is reflected in projective systems.

This paper, then, will review the evidence for and against this general hypothesis. The evidence will be drawn from cross-cultural studies of the two types specified above. This review could be organized by maintenance systems, child-rearing variables, intervening psychological processes, or projective variables. I have rather arbitrarily chosen to organize it by child-rearing practices which have been ordered in terms of the life line from early infancy to later childhood. I will begin, therefore, with those studies related to the treatment of infants.

Parental Image and the Nature of the Gods

For a long time psychologists, particularly those of Freudian persuasion, have assumed that the nature of the gods and their relation to man is a reflection of the parental image and, hence, could be predicted from the relation between parent and child during infancy and early childhood. Several cross-cultural studies have recently attempted to put this hypothesis to the test (Spiro and D'Andrade 1958; Lambert, Triandis, and Wolf 1959; and Whiting 1959a). Each of these studies tends to support the general hypothesis that harsh parental treatment during infancy leads to the cultural belief that the spirit world is harsh and aggressive.

Spiro and D'Andrade (1958), using the Whiting and Child (1953) "initial satisfaction of dependence" as a score [1] for estimating the degree to which infants are indulged, found that societies that were judged to be relatively high on the above score tended to believe that the behavior of the gods was contingent upon the behavior of humans and that gods could be controlled by the performance of compulsive rituals. [2] Such societies did *not* propitiate the gods. The authors argue that the adults' treatment of the gods is, therefore, a reflection of an infant's relation to his parents. In other words, infants who are treated indulgently by their parents, that is, whose parents respond to them when they cry or show discomfort, when they grow up feel they can be equally successful in controlling the supernaturals.

Lambert, Triandis, and Wolf (1959) used a score taken from Barry, Bacon, and Child (1957) for estimating the relation between an infant and his caretakers, consisting of a judgment of the degree to which they treated him harshly or painfully. They found that societies in which infants were treated relatively painfully believed in gods which were judged to be more aggressive than benevolent toward human beings. Again the gods seem to reflect the parental treatment of infants.

---

[1] This score includes such items as the encouragement of the infant's dependence, his freedom to be dependent, and the duration of this freedom. For a more complete description of this score see Whiting and Child (1953), pp. 50, 91.

[2] Unless specified the 5 per cent level of confidence or better has been used as a criterion to report a relationship. To simplify presentation *p* values will not ordinarily be reported.

Finally, Whiting (1959a), using still a different score for infant indulgence, reports a finding consistent with this hypothesis. The score in this study was also from Barry, Bacon, and Child (1957) and was an over-all judgment of the degree to which an infant was indulged by his caretakers.[3] It was reported that societies high in the over-all indulgence of infants tended not to fear ghosts at funerals. The assumption here is that funereal ghosts are, like the gods in the previous studies, a projection of the parental image.

In order to test the general hypothesis of personality as a mediator, the next problem is to discover whether or not there is any relationship between maintenance systems of a culture and the degree to which infants are indulged. It was suggested by Murdock and Whiting (1951) that the economic and ceremonial duties of the mother might have some bearing on the amount of time she could spend in caring for her child, and tentative results based on a small number of cases tended to confirm this hypothesis. They report (pp. 33–35) that societies in which mothers have few economic responsibilities and are little involved in the ceremonial life of the tribe tend to be more indulgent with their infants than in societies where mothers have such responsibilities. These results were based on a very small sample of societies and were not statistically significant and, therefore, must be judged as highly tentative. They also reported that there was a tendency for large extended families where there were many hands to care for the infant, to treat him more indulgently. Again this relationship was not strong and reached only the 10 per cent level of statistical significance. Murdock (1957), however, has recently published judgments on the family and household structure for a large number of societies. This, taken together with the ratings by Barry, Bacon, and Child (1957) on the degree of over-all indulgence described above, enables us to make a more adequate test of this hypothesis than was possible in 1951. Since household membership rather than family structure should be most relevant to our hypothesis, this has been used as our independent variable. The results of the test are presented in Table 1.

It will be seen from this table that the degree of infant indulgence is roughly proportional to the number of adults living in the household. Extended and polygynous families where there are more

---

[3] This score took account of the following items: display of affection, degree of drive reduction, immediacy of drive reduction, constancy of the presence of caretakers, and the absence of pain induced by caretakers.

Over-all Infant Indulgence	Households			
	Extended	Polygynous	Nuclear	Mother-Child
High	Araucanians (11) Cuna (12) Hopi (13) Jivaro (11) Lepcha (12) Maori (11) Nauru (11) Ontong Java (12) Papago (14) Samoans (12) Tupinamba (12) Winnebago (12) Zuni (12)	Aranda (11) Arapesh (13) Cheyenne (11) Chiricahua (12) Comanche (11) Crow (11) Kwoma (11) Omaha (12) Teton (12) Wogeo (13)	Chamorro (12) Chenchu (11) Kaska (12) Manus (12) Tikopia (12)	Lesu (11) Kurtachi (12) Bena (13) Chukchee (11)
Low	Klamath (10) Tenetehara (10)	Ojibwa (10) Paiute (10)	Alcrese (4) Aymara (6) Balinese (9) Ifugao (8) Lamba (10) Navaho (10) Pukapukans (9)	Ainu (5) Ashanti (10) Azande (10) Chagga (7) Dahomeans (7) Ganda (9) Masai (10) Mbundu (9) Tanala (9) Thonga (7) Venda (9) W. Apache (10)

TABLE 1. The relation between household structure and the over-all indulgence of infants. The numbers following the names of the societies indicates the Barry, Bacon, and Child (1957) score on over-all infant indulgence. Extended households include lineal and stem as well as large extended categories of Murdock. The two communal households in the sample—Siriono (10) and Yagua (11)—are omitted from the table.

than two adults living in the household tend to be predominantly indulgent with their infants. Nuclear households with two adults are unpredictable. Finally, in the mother-child household where one woman alone has to care for her children the probability of high indulgence is slight. The percentage of societies with high infant indulgence is as follows: extended, 87 per cent; polygynous, 83 per cent; nuclear, 42 per cent; and mother-child, 25 per cent. The probability that both extended and polygynous households will be high on infant indulgence is statistically significant at better than the 5 per cent level of confidence. Societies with nuclear households are unpredictable in this respect. Although only 25 per cent of societies with mother-child households are indulgent, this relationship does not quite reach an acceptable level of confidence.

Before we can accept the thesis that infant indulgence creates a parental image which is reflected in the gods and thus forms a link between household structure and religious beliefs, we must meet the argument that household structure and the nature of the gods are related to one another for some other reason and that they jointly affect the treatment of children. If this latter hypothesis were true, the gods could be predicted from a knowledge of the household structure when the child-rearing factors were held constant. This is not, in fact, the case. Thus, for example, the Tenetehara who, although they have an extended household, are exceptional in being rated low in the indulgence of infants, have aggressive gods, a fact which would have been predicted from their child rearing rather than from their household arrangements. Conversely, the Chukchee who, although they have mother-child households, are high in the indulgence of their children—an exception to the rule that mother-child households are low in infant indulgence—have benevolent gods.

Thus, child rearing rather than household structure seems to be the determinant of the nature of the gods. Statistically, household structure can be shown to be unrelated to the gods if infant indulgence is not taken into account.[4] Thus, although 87 per cent of extended family households are high on infant indulgence and 80 per cent of the societies with high indulgence are below average on the fear of ghosts at funerals, only 67 per cent of the extended families in the sample are below average on fear of ghosts. The relation between household and indulgence and that between indulgence and ghost fear are statistically significant at better than the 1 per cent level of confidence. Thus, it seems that the nature of the gods cannot be predicted from a knowledge of household structure alone. Child rearing with its influence on personality seems to be prerequisite.

Exclusive Sleeping Arrangements and Cross Sex Identity

The over-all indulgence of infants discussed above is concerned with how a child is treated during the day. The relation of a child to his parents at night has also been shown (Whiting *et al.* 1958) to be an important child-rearing variable. In most societies over the world infants sleep in the same bed or on the same sleeping mat

---

[4] This method of analysis is similar to that suggested by Blalock (1960). Confidence limits (Hald 1952) rather than correlation coefficients have been used to establish the relative degree relationship between the three variables.

with their mothers. Even where an infant has a cradle or cot of his own, this is generally placed next to the mother's bed within easy reach. The sleeping distance between a mother with a nursing infant and her husband, however, is more varied. In slightly over half of the societies of the world the husband sleeps either in a bed in the same room but at some distance from his wife, or in another room. This may be called an "exclusive mother-infant sleeping arrangement."

Whiting and co-workers (1958) showed that exclusive mother-infant sleeping arrangements are strongly associated with male initiation rites at puberty. They offered three different interpretations of this association. They assumed that such sleeping arrangements (1) increased the Oedipal rivalry between son and father and that initiation rites served to prevent open and violent revolt against parental authority at a time when physical maturity would make such revolt dangerous and socially disruptive, (2) lead to excessively strong dependence upon the mother which initiation rites serve to break, and (3) produced strong identification with the mother which the rites serve to counteract.

Although the first interpretation was favored by these authors, later research (Whiting 1960a; Burton and Whiting 1960; Stephens, ms.) has favored either the third or a modification of the second, the incest hypothesis to be discussed below. The first interpretation has been rejected for a number of reasons. The assumption made by Whiting and his associates (1958) that exclusive mother-infant sleeping arrangements exacerbate rivalry between father and son is not supported if one looks more closely at the facts. In the first place, since such sleeping arrangements usually occur in polygynous societies, the father has sexual access to his other wife and, hence, should not be particularly frustrated by the infant or see him as a rival. In the second place, at the time of weaning when the exclusive sleeping arrangements terminate, the father usually does not move in to sleep with the mother, since in more than half such societies a man never *sleeps* with his wife and in most of the remaining societies he sleeps with each wife in turn and, thus, sleeps with any one wife at most but half the time.

Campbell has in this volume suggested another version of the rivalry hypothesis, namely, that a younger sibling may be seen as the person responsible for the infant's fall from grace at the time of weaning. Although this hypothesis has considerable plausibility, the fact that in societies with exclusive mother-infant sleeping arrangements the mother is under a sex taboo during the nursing period should mean that the younger sibling would ordinarily not appear until at least nine months after the previous child's displacement. The mother, herself, therefore, seems to be the best candidate as the person who is perceived by the child as the one responsible for the termination of his exclusive relationship with her. It is she who at the same time both weans him and refuses to let him sleep with her.

In a recent theoretical paper Whiting (1960b) has formulated a series of hypotheses concerning identification as it relates to the control and mediation of resources. One hypothesis in this formulation has bearing upon the analysis in the preceding paragraph. This, the so-called "status-envy hypothesis," is stated by Whiting (1960b: 18) as follows: "If a child perceives that another has more efficient control over resources than he has; if, for example, he sees another person enjoying resources of high value to him when he is deprived of them, he will envy such a person and attempt to emulate him."

If the status-envy hypothesis be applied to sleeping arrangements, the father should be seen to occupy an envied position if he sleeps with the mother, particularly if the infant is in a cradle. Contrariwise with the exclusive mother-infant arrangements, when the mother withdraws this exclusive privilege at the time of weaning, she should be seen as the most envied person. This should lead a boy to see his mother's status, and that of women in general, as being all important and powerful, and, hence, lead to cross sex identification.

A preliminary test of this hypothesis was presented by Whiting (1960a) and has been summarized by Burton and Whiting (1960). A more detailed report is in preparation and will be published under the joint authorship of Whiting, Fischer, D'Andrade, and Munroe. In this study the following evidence is presented in support of the status-envy hypothesis.

First, members of the societies in which male initiation rites occur often define these rites as death and rebirth—the death of a person in a "woman-child" status and rebirth into the status of an "adult male." This suggests that an initial cross sex identification in boys is recognized.

Second, exclusive mother-infant sleeping arrangements are associated with the couvade as well as male initiation rites. The couvade can be interpreted as a cultural device which permits the acting out of the female role. Since initiation rites and couvade rarely occur in the same society, some reason must account for the choice between counteracting and permitting the expression of cross sex identity. Residence patterns serve this purpose. Societies with exclusive mother-infant sleeping arrangements and patrilocal residence tend to have initiation rites, whereas those with exclusive sleeping and matrilocal residence generally have the couvade. It has not been settled as to whether residence operates as another factor relating to status envy and identification or whether it requires a differential role for adult males.

Third, totemism was also shown to be associated with exclusive mother-infant sleeping arrangements. This fact leads to the interpretation that totemism serves to establish a male's relationship to his male progenitors where his early life creates some doubt about it.

Finally, in a recent study Bacon, Child, and Barry (ms.) showed that the rate of personal crime (assault, murder, rape, suicide, sorcery, and the making of false accusation) is highest in societies with exclusive mother-infant sleeping arrangements. They interpreted this as an attempt, in part at least, to express masculinity in societies where there is a need to deny an underlying feminine identity.

As has already been suggested, polygyny is the maintenance system variable most strongly associated with exclusive sleeping arrangements. In nearly 80 per cent of societies with strict monogamy the mother and father sleep in the same or adjacent beds, whereas this is only true of 3 per cent of those households where a husband has more than one wife. Whether polygyny has an influence upon the various projective consequences of exclusive mother-infant sleeping arrangements is now under investigation and cannot be reported upon here. Residence, however, as was reported above does, in interaction with sleeping arrangements, have a direct association with both male initiation rites and the couvade.

Infant Seduction and Mother-Son Incest

Whiting and his co-workers (1958) found that another child-rearing practice relating to infancy was strongly associated with male initiation rites at puberty. This practice consists of a prolonged postpartum sex taboo lasting for at least a year. This practice is often associated with the belief that sexual intercourse will sour or alter the mother's milk in a manner that would be dangerous to a nursing infant. The taboo is generally coterminous with the nursing period which often lasts in these societies for nearly three years.

Whiting's group (1958) interpreted this factor as having much the same effect as that of an exclusive mother-infant sleeping arrangement. Stephens (ms.), however, assumed that a mother, deprived of her normal sex life during such a prolonged period, will gain some indirect sexual satisfaction from her infant, particularly during the act of nursing. If this interpretation is correct, a strong incestuous bond between mother and son should be established in societies with a prolonged postpartum sex taboo.

Stephens (ms.) argued that since the expression of mother-son incest is not permitted in adult life in any society, this early tendency must be strongly opposed and that strong sex conflict and anxiety should be induced. As a projective index of such conflict, he chose the degree to which menstrual taboos were elaborated in a society. He established a scale which indicated the degree to which women were isolated from men while they were menstruating and argued that this measured castration anxiety in the males. He then showed that societies with a prolonged postpartum sex taboo tended to have elaborate menstrual taboos as measured by this scale. The fact that the Whiting and Child (1953) measure of the severity of sex training in later childhood was also related to Stephen's menstruation scale lends support to the interpretation that it is an indicator of sex anxiety.

These results suggest that male initiation rites serve to oppose mother-son incest as well as to counteract cross sex identification. The fact that severe menstrual taboos were not found by Stephens to be independently related to male initiation rites is puzzling, however.

Stephens and D'Andrade (Stephens, ms.) report still another consequence of a prolonged postpartum sex taboo. They showed that societies with this practice tend to have formal avoidance patterns between a woman and her daughter's husband, between a man and his son's wife, and between a brother and a sister. They argue that these avoidances result from sexual conflict produced by the seductive and incestuous relationship between mother and infant consequent upon the prolonged postpartum sex taboo.

Polygyny is again the aspect of the maintenance system which is highly predictive of a prolonged postpartum sex taboo. Stephens (ms.), however, found that polygyny alone is not significantly related to the degree of elaboration of menstrual taboos. Thus, a pattern similar to that reported for the nature of the gods emerges, where a maintenance system variable is related to a projective system variable by common linkage with a personality variable implied by a child-rearing practice.

The Age of Socialization—Guilt

Proceeding along the life line of the child, the next item that has been used in cross-cultural research concerns variations in the age at which societies begin the serious training of their children. This has in general been shown to affect the projective systems which reflect guilt. Whiting and Child (1953), taking as a measure of guilt the degree to which a patient was believed to be responsible for causing his own illness, presumably indicating his readiness to accept blame, found that societies with early weaning, early independence training, and early training in modesty and the inhibition of heterosexual play were those which tended to have high guilt. The age of toilet training was not related.

Whiting and Child (1953) tentatively concluded that this relationship was due to identification. Anticipating the status-envy hypothesis, they argued that parents should seem more powerful to a very young child than to an older one who has already learned, to a degree at least, to cope with the environment by himself. Thus, early socialization should produce stronger identification and, hence, guilt over contravening parental values.

It is again possible to relate this association to the maintenance systems. Whiting (1959b) reports that household structure is a significant determinant of the age of socialization. Nuclear households are earliest for both weaning (median age 2 years) and independence training (median age 2 years, 9 months) and mother-child households are the latest.[5] On the average they do not begin to wean their children until they are three years old nor start training them in independence until they are four and one half. Extended and polygynous households fall in between these two extremes for both weaning and independence training.

To test our hypothesis we have to ask whether nuclear households independently of child rearing have higher guilt than mother-child households. This is in fact what is reported by Whiting (1959a); 86 per cent of the nuclear households in the sample reported had high scores on patient responsibility whereas but 14 per cent of the mother-child households were high in this regard.

Although it is difficult to be sure with the relatively small num-

---

[5] The age of independence training should not be confused with the degree of infant indulgence referred to above (p. 358). Mother-child households are both low and late.

ber of cases on which data are available, it seems that in this instance households have some effect on guilt independent of child rearing. Thus, whereas it seems as if the nature of the gods is directly dependent on child-rearing practices and only indirectly upon household structure, guilt is produced by an interaction of both social structure and child rearing. Thus, Whiting (1959a) showed that the age of weaning was correlated with patient responsibility for monogamous societies. This was not true of polygynous societies. They tended to have a low score on guilt whether weaning was early or late. From this we may conclude that, while the age of socialization may be a mediating factor between social structure and magical theories of disease, it is clearly not the only one.

It was assumed above that strong identification with the mother should be induced by exclusive mother-infant sleeping arrangements which is in turn strongly associated with polygyny. But polygynous societies are low in guilt. To get around this contradiction, Whiting (1959c) has argued that guilt is derived from identification with the male rather than the female role. The basis of argument consisted of the assumption that "the role of the father and of males in general in any society tends to be more punitive, rigid and unforgiving than that of the mother and of women in general . . . . A woman could scarcely bring up a child unless, when he deviates from the familial rules, she made exceptions if the child were sick or tired or upset."

Severity of Socialization and Negative Fixation

Estimates of the severity of socialization in early childhood provide the next set of child-rearing variables to be considered. Such estimates were made by Whiting and Child (1953) with respect to five systems of behavior: oral, anal, sexual, aggression, and dependence. The presumed effect of severe training was that of "negative fixation" or the anxious preoccupation with the type of behavior or behavior system which is severely punished. The theory of negative fixation was based upon the effect of conflict rather than on the stages of psychosexual development. The hypothesis which they put forward is that conflict between habits learned in infancy and then punished during the socialization process produces persistent motivation which activates behavior in adulthood in some way related to the conflict and presumably is functionally defensive in nature.

Explanations for illness and therapeutic techniques were chosen by Whiting and Child (1953) as aspects of the projective system which might reflect fixation. A content analysis of magical beliefs and practices relating to illness was made for each society with the five behavior systems in mind. In judging the severity of socialization for each system, the following factors were taken into consideration: intensity and frequency of punishment, suddenness of the transition from behavior appropriate to infancy and that to later childhood, and signs of emotional disturbance on the part of the child.[6]

In general the fixation hypothesis was supported. The severity of weaning (oral anxiety) was strongly related to "oral explanations for illness." Such oral explanations include the belief that sickness is caused by eating or drinking magically poisoned food or by the verbal spells and incantations of sorcerers. The severity of aggression training (aggression socialization anxiety) which includes the treatment of temper tantrums, physical and verbal aggression, damage to property, and disobedience was related to explanations for illness involving aggression. These include hostility toward or disobedience to spirits, poison if it is introjected into the patient rather than being ingested, and the use of magical weapons by a sorcerer. The severity of independence training was shown to be related to dependence explanations for illness, a measure which includes the belief that illness could be caused by "soul stealing" or by "spirit possession." The negative fixation hypothesis was not confirmed in the other two systems of behavior. Toilet training did not predict the Whiting and Child score on anal explanations for illness nor did the severity of sex training predict sexual explanations for illness. However, there was some indication that relevant avoidance in these behavior systems was used as a therapeutic practice. Thus, societies with severe toilet training tend to have therapeutic practices involving washing or cleansing, the adherence to cleanliness taboos, or the retention of feces, and societies with severe sex training tended to believe that abstention from sexual intercourse by the patient would have a therapeutic effect.

In addition, as was reported above, Stephens (ms.) found that severe sex training is associated with elaborate menstrual taboos, and Ayres (1954) showed this child-rearing measure to be related to prolonged sex taboos during pregnancy. Each of these may be viewed as an index of negative fixation.

The following maintenance system variables have been reported

---

[6] It should be noted that the *age* of socialization was conceptually distinguished from the *severity* of socialization. Although in general these measures were negatively correlated (Whiting and Child 1953, p. 110), they were empirically distinct as well. In other words late socialization is not necessarily mild.

to be associated with severity of socialization in the various systems. Murdock and Whiting (1951) report that societies with sororal polygyny are significantly less severe in weaning their children than are societies with nonsororal polygyny. Monogamous societies, according to their findings, stand between these two extremes and are not significantly different from either. They explained mild weaning in sororal-polygynous societies as a consequence of the co-operation between co-wives who are sisters. The severity of sex training is associated with polygyny. Only 15 per cent of the societies which are monogamous, or in which not more than 10 per cent of the women are polygynously married, are above the median on the severity of sex training, whereas 73 per cent of the societies with a higher proportion of polygynous marriages are severe in this regard.

Finally, a strong association between the severity of aggression training and household structure has been reported by Whiting (1959b). Ninety-two per cent of the extended families in the sample used are above the median on the punishment for aggression. Nuclear households were least severe in this respect—only 25 per cent of the cases being severe. Polygynous and mother-child households were 61 per cent and 46 per cent respectively. Whiting (ms.) in an analysis of the Zuni extended family households suggests that the expression of aggression cannot be tolerated in circumstances where so many people are living in such crowded quarters. No maintenance system variable has as yet been reported to predict the severity of either toilet training or independence training. An item of interest, however, that should be followed up was reported to me by C. S. Ford. An undergraduate paper in one of his classes showed that toilet training was more severe in societies that had wooden floors and rugs than in societies with dirt floors and no rugs.

Factor analysis provides another method of estimating the effect of child-rearing practices upon projective systems. Prothro (1960) subjected the Whiting and Child (1953) fixation hypothesis to such an analysis. The first factor, which he names the "aggression-hypochondriasis factor" had high positive loadings for the severity of aggression training, and all explanations for illness and techniques of therapy save those relating to dependence. This factor was also positively loaded on sorcery and negatively on the fear of spirits. The second factor, named "orality-sexuality," had heavy negative loadings on initial indulgence for dependent and oral systems, and on the severity of sex training. It also had heavy positive loadings on oral and dependent explanations for illness and the fear of spirits. The third and final factor, "independence-anality," had a high positive loading on the severity and earliness of toilet training, and a strong negative loading on the severity and earliness of independence training. A negative loading dependence avoidance therapy was the only projective measure which seemed related to this factor.

Severity of Socialization: Projection and Displacement

Cross-cultural studies involving the importance of sorcery and witchcraft have generally interpreted this belief as one involving the psychological mechanism of projection and/or displacement. Two views of this mechanism have been put forth. One, derived essentially from behavior theory, assumes that the fear of sorcerers occurs in societies where the direct expression of aggression is strongly inhibited and, hence, must be either attributed to others or justified by being directed against criminal sorcerers. The other view is derived from psychoanalytic theory and involves the hypothesis that sorcery implies paranoia, a personality variable which is derived from sexual inhibition and involves homosexuality. Whiting and Child (1953) were unable to decide between these two hypotheses. On the basis of their evidence, sorcery was found to be an important explanation for illness both in societies where children were punished severely either for sex or aggression during childhood. The fact that severity of socialization in these two behavior systems are positively related to one another makes it difficult to disentangle their influence.

Whiting (1959a) presents some evidence in favor of the sex anxiety hypothesis, but the data are not very convincing. The most likely interpretation of the results so far is that there are in effect two kinds of projection. The distinction between these may correspond to that which has been made between sorcery and witchcraft, the former being a result of the inhibition of aggression, the latter being associated with conflict in the area of sex. That sorcerers are more often male and witches female is suggestive in this regard.

That aggression may be projected has been shown by Wright (1954) using a content analysis of folktales as an index. He showed that in societies with severe training in the control of aggression during childhood the hero in folktales does *not* direct his aggression toward friends but rather toward strangers or enemies, that a stranger rather than the hero was more likely to be the agent of aggression, and finally that the hero was less likely to be triumphant. Whiting and Child (1953) report a similar finding. Societies with severe training in the control of aggression which believe that spirits can cause illness, tend to define the spirits as animal rather than human.

The maintenance system variables relating to severe socialization for sex and aggression have already been reported—the former is associated with polygyny, the latter with the extended family household. Direct relationships between maintenance system variables and sorcery were reported in two studies. Beatrice Whiting (1950), assuming that sorcery functions as a mechanism of social control, showed that a strong belief in sorcery occurs in societies lacking in mechanisms of social control that involve the delegation of authority for the judging and punishing of crime. She also showed that this pattern tended to occur in small rather than in large societies. LeVine (1960) showed that sorcery tends to occur in societies that maximize jealousy between co-wives. In three East African societies similar in other respects, the preoccupation with sorcery was greatest among the Luo where co-wives lived in adjacent houses and virtually absent among the Kipsigis where the co-wives ordinarily live miles apart. He also reports that, cross-culturally, sorcery is a major cause of illness in 93 per cent of the societies with polygynous households, 60 per cent of the societies with mother-child households, 53 per cent of the societies with extended family households, and only 36 per cent of the societies with nuclear households. The total pattern for predicting sorcery thus seems to be small societies with no formal systems of social control with either polygynous households and severe sex training or extended family households and severe training in the control of aggression.

Independence Training and Achievement Motivation

McClelland and Friedman (1952) report cross-cultural findings supporting the hypothesis that achievement motivation is produced by early and severe training in independence. Achievement motivation was measured by applying to folktales a modification of the method used to score need achievement imagery in thematic apperception tests. Such scores were related to Whiting and Child's (1953) measures of the age and severity of independence training.

Societies with early and severe socialization of independence tended to have more achievement imagery in their folktales.

Child, Storm, and Veroff (1958) also investigated the relation of child-rearing variables to achievement imagery in folktales. They used a larger sample of societies (the McClelland and Friedman study was restricted to North American tribes) and reported essentially negative results. Scoring reliability was low and different myth episodes from a single society showed wide variation in achievement imagery. They report the curious finding that societies which are both generally severe in socialization and who punish achievement have more achievement imagery in their folktales than societies with any other combination of these child-rearing factors. They also report that positive training for achievement in later childhood is related to their folktale score if, and only if, training in self-reliance is held constant. Their score on achievement imagery was not significantly related to the Whiting and Child measures used in the McClelland and Friedman study.

Over-All Early Socialization, Decorative Art, and Asceticism

Certain consequences are reported for over-all socialization anxiety, a measure obtained by combining the scores for the five behavior systems (Whiting and Child 1953). Barry (1957) reports that the decorative art forms of societies that are generally severe in training their children tend to be complex, and Friendly (1956) shows that such societies tended to have ascetic mourning customs. The relation of maintenance systems to over-all socialization anxiety has not as yet been investigated. Fischer (1959), however, reports that complexity in social structure is reflected in the complexity of decorative art. He used the Barry (1957) score on complexity of art design and Murdock (1957) scores of complexity of social organization. The presense of status distinctions based on wealth, social class membership, or heredity tends to result in complex designs in contrast with those from no rank distinctions or those based on age alone.

Another over-all measure of the severity of socialization in early childhood is provided by the Barry, Bacon, and Child study (1957). This measure, which they call "transition anxiety," is an estimate of the degree of pressure exerted upon the child during his change of status from infancy to childhood. This measure, although not statistically significant, is positively related to the Whiting and Child (1953) measure of over-all socialization anxiety. Whiting and his co-workers (ms.) show it to be related to household structure. They report that societies with nuclear households are significantly more severe on this score than are societies with extended family households. It has already been pointed out that societies with nuclear family households begin independence training early. It now seems that they are generally severe as well, suggesting that strong pressures in child-rearing toward independence are required to enable a couple to set up an independent establishment.

Socialization in Later Childhood

An elaborate set of judgments about socialization during later childhood is provided by the Barry, Bacon, and Child study (1957). These judgments concern the manner in which a child is trained to be obedient, responsible, self-reliant, nurturant, and generally independent, as well as his training in achievement. For each of these behavior systems a separate judgment was made for the general pressure exerted upon the child, the severity of punishment for non-compliance, the difficulty of performance, the amount of conflict, and the frequency of the response.

Separate judgments on the above scales were made for the treatment of boys and girls by Barry, Bacon, and Child (1957). Significant differences in training were reported. These involved more stress upon nurturance, obedience, and responsibility for the girls and upon achievement and self-reliance for the boys. Although they did not relate these differences to any projective system, they did report that large differences in the training of the sexes occur in societies where large animals are hunted, where grain rather than root crops are grown, where large or milking animals are kept, where fishing is unimportant or absent, where the settlement is nomadic rather than sedentary, and where polygyny is high. They interpreted those results as implying that differential training for boys and girls is required where superior strength and motor skill is involved or where a large family with a high degree of co-operation is required.

Lambert, Triandis, and Wolf (1959), in the study discussed previously (see page 357) concerning the nature of the gods, report that the supernaturals are more aggressive in societies which put strong pressure upon the boys for self-reliance and independence. They also report an even stronger relationship in the same direction with a score which combines the pressures exerted in all six systems; that is, nurturance, obedience, self-reliance, achievement, responsibility, and general independence. It is interesting that they assume a reverse direction of causation to explain this relationship; that is, the belief in aggressive gods requires training a child to be independent and self-reliant so that he can cope with a hostile world as an adult.

Bacon, Child, and Barry (ms.) show that societies which severely punish their older children for disobedience, irresponsibility, lack of self-reliance, and lack of achievement are high in the frequency of theft. Since they also find that a high frequency of theft is found in societies with low infant indulgence and severe weaning, they interpret these findings as a reaction to emotional deprivation during infancy and childhood. Such anxieties, except for severe weaning, interestingly enough, are not related to the frequency of personal crime.

Barry, Child, and Bacon (1959) report some interesting relationships between socialization pressures in later childhood and various aspects of the maintenance system, in this case the basic economy. They state, "In considering the relation of economy to adult role, and hence to child training, we felt that perhaps a variable of great significance is the extent to which food is accumulated and must be cared for." To test this hypothesis they classified societies into four categories on the basis of their subsistence activities which represent the degree to which this implies an accumulation of food. Assuming that food "on the hoof" requires the greatest amount of care, societies that were mainly dependent upon animal husbandry were judged to be highest on the scale. The lowest point was represented by hunting and fishing societies. Between these extremes a distinction was made between those societies depending upon agriculture only for subsistence and those depending upon a combination of agriculture, hunting, and fishing. The former were assumed to be higher in food accumulation than the latter.

Contrasting the extremes on the scale, that is, animal husbandry versus hunting and fishing, they showed that societies with high accumulation of food put strong pressure upon their children to be responsible and obedient and were low in stressing achievement and independence in their boys and also low in stressing achievement and self-reliance in girls. They then constructed a general score which they called "pressure toward compliance versus assertion" by adding the scores on obedience and responsibility and subtracting from this sum the combined score on achievement and self-reliance. The relation of this over-all pressure toward compliance

Subsistence Economy	Percentage above Median on Compliance	
		N
Animal Husbandry	83%	(24)
Agriculture only	93	(15)
Agriculture, hunting and fishing	33	(18)
Hunting and fishing	14	(22)

TABLE 2. Relation between pressure toward compliance versus assertiveness as indicated by a subsistence economy scale. Numbers in parentheses represent the number of societies in each category. This table is adapted from Barry, Child, and Bacon 1959, P. 60.

to food accumulation is striking and shown in Table 2.

It should be noted that high points on the subsistence scale—animal husbandry and agriculture—are rather heavily weighted with cases from Africa and that perhaps pressure toward compliance is an African culture trait and, thus, the association is spurious. If, however, all African cases are omitted from the sample, the association between subsistence and pressure toward compliance is still strong. When this is done, high compliance is represented by the following percentages in order of the degree of accumulation: 70 per cent, 90 per cent, 33 per cent, and 14 per cent. Thus, the relationship, although somewhat less strong, is still substantial.

Although the direct relationship between subsistence economy and aggressive gods is not reported, Bacon, Child, and Barry (ms.) indicate that this scale is *not* related to the frequency of theft. Thus, here again a child-rearing factor seems to be a necessary link between an aspect of the maintenance system and a projective consequence. It should be noted that D'Andrade in this volume, using a scale for measuring subsistence economy essentially similar to the one described above, found this aspect of the maintenance system directly predicts a projective measure—a preoccupation with dreams—but that neither were related to child rearing.

Discussion

The general hypothesis that personality can serve as a mediator between the maintenance and projective systems of a culture has been supported by a fairly substantial amount of cross-cultural research. It should be pointed out, however, that a substantial number of specific hypotheses failed to be confirmed. Many of these have not been reported in the studies under review; furthermore, those negative findings which were reported have usually been omitted from this review. To have included them would have been too cumbersome. This decision, however, may give an exaggerated view of the importance as an integrating factor of those personality processes which are determined by child rearing. It should be noted that both Wallace and D'Andrade report in this volume cultural responses relevant to personality which are not related to child rearing, but rather to either physiological process or to social structure. Despite these cautions, it seems clear that economics and social structure do often have a determining influence upon the way in which children are brought up, and the child rearing in turn often has a predictable and determining effect upon magical belief, rituals, art forms, taboos, and even crime rates.

The direction of causation is, of course, an ever-present problem in cross-cultural research. Why cannot it be assumed that projective systems determine child rearing and that child rearing determines the maintenance systems? Such may, in fact, be the case in some or even many of the instances reported above. Although this is an important question, it is beyond the scope of this review. The position taken here has been to accept the assumptions as to the direction of causation made by the authors of the works considered.

In reviewing the relationships reported above, certain patterns or types emerge which should be noted. First, where a certain aspect of the maintenance system may be classed into discreet categories, such as household, marriage form, residence, basic subsistence economy, and so forth, some of these categories may be *determining* with respect to child rearing, whereas other categories in the same maintenance system may be *nondetermining*. A number of examples of this contrast could be drawn from the results reported above, but the relation between household structure and over-all infant indulgence shown in Table 1 will serve to illustrate this contrast. It will be seen from this table that extended and polygynous family households determine high infant indulgence but that nuclear households are nondetermining as to indulgence. Mother-child households are, by a confidence limits test (Hald 1952), almost determining of low indulgence, but the proportion does not quite reach the 5 per cent level of confidence. Thus, if a person were told that a society had an extended family or polygynous household, he could make money, even if he gave odds, that infants were treated indulgently, but if he were told that a society had nuclear households, he should not bet on how infants are treated. It is believed that this distinction between cultural categories which are determining and those which are nondetermining may apply to other features of cultural integration than child rearing and may be a distinction useful to keep in mind in describing cultural patterns.

A second general conclusion may be drawn from this review. This consists of a typology of various ways in which personality factors can serve to integrate culture. These types can perhaps best be shown in the following diagrammatic models. In these diagrams M will stand for a maintenance system variable, C for a child-rearing practice presumed to influence personality, and P for a projective system variable. The arrows stand for the assumed direction of causation.

The most common type is shown in Figure 1. Here it is assumed

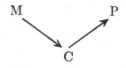

Figure 1. The mediation type.

that a certain feature of maintenance systems determines a child-training practice and that this practice determines a feature in the projective systems, but that the given feature of the maintenance systems has no directly determining influence with respect to the projective system feature. This type can be illustrated by the relation between household structure, infant indulgence, and the nature of the gods as described above: that is, extended family households predict high infant indulgence, and high infant indulgence predicts a low fear of ghosts, but household structure is unrelated to the fear of ghosts (see p. 360).

Another important type is shown in Figure 2. Here it is assumed that neither a feature of the maintenance system nor a child-rearing practice alone will determine a given feature in the projective system but that taken together they will. As an example, the age of weaning predicts guilt in monogamous but not polygynous societies (see p. 370).

Figure 2. The interaction type.

It is more likely that many more examples of this type will be discovered as research in this area becomes more sophisticated.

The third type, shown in Figure 3, assumes a direct effect of pressures from the maintenance system upon some aspect of the projective system.

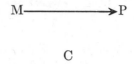

C

Figure 3. Adult pressure type.

Although this type was not considered in this review, a recent study (Field 1960) showing heavy drinking to be associated with bilateral descent, but to none of the child-rearing variables discussed above, is a good example of this type.

Figure 4 indicates the assumption of causation between a child-rearing and a projective feature in a direction opposite to that which

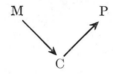

Figure 4. "Reverse" Causation.

has usually been assumed in the studies under review. The only case of this type noted is from the study by Lambert and his group (1959) where training in self-reliance and independence was interpreted as being a consequence rather than the cause of a belief in aggressive gods (see p. 357).

As a final comment it would seem to this reviewer that the cross-cultural study of personality as a mediating factor in the integration of culture is off to a good start, but still has a long way to go. The measurement of child rearing is far from satisfactory partly because ethnographic reports are often inadequate and partly because it is highly unlikely that the variables selected by Whiting and Child (1953) and by Barry, Bacon, and Child (1957) will turn out in the long run to be more than first approximations of the dimensions most crucial to personality development. Furthermore, as has been shown in this review, cross-cultural research has just begun to attack the complex problem of the effects of the interaction of several variables operating jointly—an approach which should yield interesting results in the near future if it is pursued.

BIBLIOGRAPHY

AYRES, BARBARA C.
  1954   Personality determinants of food and sex taboos during pregnancy. (Typescript, Doctoral dissertation.) Cambridge, Radcliffe College.

ANTHONY, ALBERT S.
  1955   A cross-cultural study of factors relating to male initiation rites and genital operations. (Typescript, doctoral thesis, Harvard Graduate School of Education.) Cambridge.

BACON, MARGARET K., I. L. CHILD, and HERBERT BARRY, III
    A cross-cultural study of crime in pre-literate societies. (Typescript).

BARRY, HERBERT A.
  1957   Relationships between child training and the pictorial arts. Journal of Abnormal and Social Psychology 54:380–383.

BARRY, HERBERT A., MARGARET K. BACON, and IRVIN L. CHILD
  1957   A cross-cultural survey of some sex differences in socialization. Journal of Abnormal and Social Psychology 55:327–332.

BARRY, HERBERT A., IRVIN L. CHILD, and MARGARET K. BACON
  1959   Relation of child training to subsistence economy. American Anthropologist 61:1.

BENEDICT, RUTH
  1934   Patterns of culture. Boston, Houghton-Mifflin Co.

BLALOCK, H. M., JR.
  1960   Correlational analysis and causal inferences. American Anthropologist 62:4.

BURTON, ROGER V. and J. W. M. WHITING
  1960   The absent father: effects on the developing child. Paper presented at A.P.A. Meeting, September, 1960.

CHILD, IRVIN L., T. STORM, and J. VEROFF
  1958   Achievement themes in folktales related to socialization practices. *In* Motives in fantasy, action and society, J. W. Atkinson, ed. New York, Van Nostrand.

FIELD, PETER B.
    A new cross-cultural study of drunkenness. *In* Society, culture and drinking patterns, D. J. Pittman and C. R. Snyder, eds. New York, Wiley. In press.

FISCHER, JOHN L.
  1959   Art styles and cultural cognitive maps. Paper presented at American Anthropological Association Meeting, Mexico City, December, 1959.

FRIENDLY, JOAN P.
  1956   A cross-cultural study of ascetic mourning behavior. (Typescript, Honors Thesis) Cambridge, Radcliffe College.

FORD, CLELLAN S.
  1945   A comparative study of human reproduction. Yale University Publications in Anthropology, No. 32. New Haven.

HALD, A.

1952 Statistical tables and formulas. New York, Wiley.

KARDINER, ABRAM and RALPH LINTON

1939 The individual and his society. New York, Columbia University Press.

KARDINER, ABRAM et al.

1945 The psychological frontiers of society. New York, Columbia University Press.

LAMBERT, W. W., LEIGH TRIANDIS, and MARGERY WOLF

1959 Some correlates of beliefs in the malevolence and benevolence of supernatural beings: A cross-cultural study. Journal of Abnormal and Social Psychology 58:2.

LeVINE, ROBERT A.

1960 Witchcraft and marital relations in East Africa: a controlled comparison. Paper presented at the American Anthropological Association Meeting, Minneapolis, Minnesota.

McCLELLAND, D. C. and G. A. FRIEDMAN

1952 A cross-cultural study of the relationship between child-training practices and achievement motivation appearing in folk tales. In Readings in social psychology (rev. ed.), G. E. Swanson, T. M. Newcomb, and E. H. Hartley, eds., pp. 243–249. New York, Henry Holt.

MEAD, MARGARET

1928 Coming of age in Samoa. New York, Morrow.

1935 Sex and temperament in three primitive societies. New York, Morrow.

MURDOCK, GEORGE P.

1957 World ethnographic sample. American Anthropologist 59:664–687.

MURDOCK, GEORGE P. and J. W. M. WHITING

1951 Cultural determination of parental attitudes: the relationship between the social structure, particularly family structure and parental behavior. In Problems of infancy and childhood, Milton J. E. Senn, ed. New York, Josiah Macy, Jr., Foundation.

PROTHRO, E. TERRY

1960 Patterns of permissiveness among preliterate peoples. Journal of Abnormal and Social Psychology 61:151–154.

ROBERTS, JOHN M., ROBERT R. BUSH, and MALCOLM ARTH.

1957 Dimensions of mastery in games. Stanford, California, Ford Center for Advanced Study in the Behavioral Sciences. (Mimeographed.)

SPIRO, MELFORD E. and ROY G. D'ANDRADE

1958 A cross-cultural study of some supernatural beliefs. American Anthropologist 60:456–466.

STEPHENS, WILLIAM N.

The oedipus complex: cross-cultural evidence. Glencoe, Illinois, The Free Press. (In press.)

WHITING, BEATRICE B.

1950 Paiute sorcery. Viking Fund Publications in Anthropology No. 15, New York.

WHITING, MARJORIE GRANT

1958   A cross-cultural nutrition survey of 118 societies representing the major culture areas of the world. Unpublished Ph.D. thesis, Harvard School of Public Health.

WHITING, J. W. M.

1959a   Sorcery, sin and the superego: a cross-cultural study of some mechanisms of social control. *In* Symposium on motivation, pp. 174–195. University of Nebraska Press.

1959b   Cultural and sociological influences on development. *In* Maryland child growth and development institute, June 1–5, 1959, pp. 5–9.

1959c   The male and female conscience. Paper presented at American Psychological Association Meeting, September. Cincinnati.

1960a   Social structure and identification. Mona Bronfman Sheckman Lectures delivered at Tulane University, New Orleans, Louisiana.

1960b   Resource mediation and learning by identification. *In* Personality development in children, I. Iscoe and M. Stevenson, eds. Austin, Texas, University of Texas Press.

WHITING, J. W. M., M. F. ANTONOVSKY, E. M. CHASDI, and B. C. AYRES

The learning of values. *In* Peoples of Rimrock (Vol. I.), E. Z. Vogt and J. M. Roberts, eds. Final Report of the Harvard Values Study, manuscript.

WHITING, J. W. M. and IRVIN L. CHILD

1953   Child training and personality. New Haven, Connecticut, Yale University Press.

WHITING, J. W. M., RICHARD KLUCKHOHN, and ALBERT S. ANTHONY

1958   The function of male initiation ceremonies at puberty. *In* Readings in social psychology, Eleanor E. Maccoby, T. Newcomb, and E. Hartley, eds., pp. 359–370. New York, Henry Holt.

WRIGHT, GEORGE O.

1954   Projection and displacement: a cross-cultural study of folk-tale aggression. Journal of Abnormal and Social Psychology 49:523–528.

Chapter 13

CULTURE AND SOCIALIZATION*

DAVID F. ABERLE
Brandeis University

Historical Perspective

IT WOULD be fair to say that in the field of culture and personality, child-rearing practices have been studied primarily from the point of view of their effects on the development of personality, rather than as products of other features of the culture (*cf.* Child 1954). Sometimes the inquiry about the effects of socialization stops with the attempt to demonstrate the impact of child rearing on personality. Sometimes it goes on to attempt to show that various cultural features are derived from imputed or known personality characteristics present in a given group. In either case, the child-rearing practices are viewed as causes, and personality or features of culture as effects.

* This essay owes a great deal to a series of graduate seminars on the topic of the causes of socialization which I have conducted at the University of Michigan from 1954 to the present. I am indebted to many students for discussions, research results, and papers on theoretical problems—so many that it would be invidious to select a few for mention and impossible to list them all. I am grateful to the Social Science Research Council for funds which provided me with a research assistant for one of these seminars, and to Mrs. Eviva Menkes for her able work in that capacity. I benefited by several years' stimulating meetings of a Social Science Research Council Committee on Personality Development, the other members of which were Alfred L. Baldwin, William E. Henry, Robert R. Sears, M. Brewster Smith (staff), and John W. M. Whiting. An earlier version of this essay was prepared for a conference on cross-cultural research on personality development sponsored by the SSRC committee just mentioned and held in Kansas City on May 20–22, 1955. I profited by discussions of that earlier version at the conference. I am indebted for helpful criticism and discussion to John W. Atkinson, Thomas Gladwin, my wife, E. Kathleen Gough, Francis L. K. Hsu, Alex Inkeles, the late Clyde Kluckhohn, Robert LeVine, Daniel R. Miller, Kaspar D. Naegele, and G. E. Swanson, some of whom have read one or another draft of this paper, and some of whom have discussed the general problem with me. The University of Michigan provided travel funds which made it possible for me to attend a conference with the editor of this volume and some of the authors of other chapters.

I am especially grateful to Irvin L. Child, who provided me with ratings on the socialization practices of 111 cultures, prepared by him and his co-workers, and as yet unpublished. These ratings have been used in many of the University of Michigan seminars mentioned above. Some results of this work are mentioned below.

Less effort has been made to determine the causes of the socialization practices themselves. Sometimes these causes are treated as self-evident; sometimes the problem is disregarded. This essay attempts to set forth an approach oriented to systematic inquiry into the causes of socialization patterns. It will discuss the theoretical utility of such an approach, and will outline some of the features of cultural systems which seem to be important causes of socialization patterns. It will make some mention of field techniques and comparative techniques and will allude to some results now available.

The Problem

Anthropologists have been willing to treat joking and respect relationships as the outgrowth of other features of kinship relationships (Radcliffe-Brown 1952; Eggan 1955), to examine kinship terms as reflexes of kinship groupings (Murdock 1949), to see political structure and social complexity as functions of level of productivity (White 1949), but by and large they have not been interested in accounting for socialization practices.

There are points of view in culture and personality which make attention to the causes of socialization seem unnecessary or unprofitable. One of these sees socialization as the prime cause of major features of different cultural systems, but pays no heed to the question of why the members of a particular system show uniformities in socialization, rather than randomness. A second point of view, which confines itself to relations between socialization and personality, is one or another version of the "chicken-and-egg" approach. In its simplest form, this theory would hold that people who grow up under a given socialization regime reproduce the same regime that they experienced, because the personalities they developed make it congenial to do so. In this version, antecedent and consequent pursue each other in a small circle forever, and the answer as to why the socialization pattern is as it is can only be because the socializers were reared as they were. There is no room in this system for change. A more sophisticated chicken-and-egg approach asserts that strains engendered under one socialization regime give rise to efforts by those who experienced the strains to alter the regime in rearing their own children. Presumably the result is either a new stability or a perpetual series of changes, but in this version, too, socialization and personality chase each other forever.

When we find, however, as Child and his co-workers have done, in studies discussed below, that there is sizable variation in socialization aims in different types of subsistence economies, none of these views seems particularly satisfactory. For now we see that the ecological niche of a culture affects its socialization practices. Thus factors not themselves the results of socialization can be seen to affect socialization practices and through them (as well as directly) the personalities of constituent members of the society. The task ahead is that of tracing the impact not only of ecological and technological factors, but of economic and political factors on units in which the bulk of childhood socialization occurs—the family in almost all societies, age groups where they are present, and schools in literate societies. Through their impact on social relationships in the socializing units, and on the aims of the socializers, these factors can probably be shown to account for a very large amount of the variance in socialization patterns from one society, or segment of a society, to another. It remains possible that some features of socialization cannot be so explained, but it seems heuristically valuable to treat socialization as a dependent variable, with the same close attention that has been given to a number of other cultural variables.

Previous Work

In a great deal of anthropological work quite simple explanations of socialization practices are proffered, but these fall short of what is needed. Thus it may be asserted that the Cheyenne are warlike and raise their children to be warriors, or that the Hopi are nonaggressive and trammel aggressive manifestations in their children. This is simply a special version of the chicken-and-egg formula, although it is easily converted to another point of view. Thus, if, as in Kardiner's work on the Comanche (1945), it is asserted that warfare is a necessary ingredient of Plains life, and therefore the induction of warrior skills and attitudes is required for the system to exist in its setting, we are closer to what I mean by an explanation. The simpler explanation treats the warlike characteristics of the Plains Indians as a historical happenstance, so that we might equally well find that the Cheyenne are peaceful and raise their children to be pacific. I will therefore pass over the large number of explanations to be found in the literature which treat socialization simply as a reflex of (or congruent with, or the cause of) adult values and orientations taken as given factors.

Another class of explanation takes certain important institutions of the culture as given factors and proceeds from there. This is common in the treatment of ethnic groups on the American scene. The values, family structure, and outlook of these groups as they existed in Europe are set forth, with relatively little attention to the sources of these factors; the carry-over and change on the American scene are described; and socialization is treated as a reflex of this historical continuity, with greater or less sophistication in the analysis of the position of the groups in contemporary America. Since the interest, in most such cases, is not in the causes of the socialization practices, but in having two contrasting sets of practices and in examining the results, such research cannot be criticized for failing to do what it never intended to do. Nevertheless, it must be mentioned as falling short of the goal I have in mind.

Such work merges imperceptibly with work on social class. In most of this work there is an awareness of the hard facts of stratification—of differential opportunity, differential income, differential security, and differential power, but the work runs the gamut from treating these differences almost as historically accidental variations in subcultures to a clear analysis of the class structure itself.

Rather than make invidious comments about the many studies of social class, ethnicity, and child rearing which do not meet my requirements—a procedure which would lead some social scientists to protest that their aims are not mine, and others to protest that they did a better job of explanation than this essay recognized—I would like to mention some research which does attempt an explanation of socialization practices along the lines I have in mind, even though there are doubtless other suitable examples as well. In *The Changing American Parent* (1958), Miller and Swanson deal with a change in the organization of the society, from small-scale firms and small government to large-scale firms and big government, and show how the role requirements for adults in the new large-scale organizations (bureaucratic) differ from those in the older (entrepreneurial) units. They then hypothesize that differences in orientation toward adult social life will lead to differences in child-rearing patterns and demonstrate that the "bureaucratic" portion of their sample is more permissive, more oriented to interpersonal skills and adjustment for their children, as compared with the stricter and more achievement-oriented "entrepreneurial" portion of the sample. (In this and in other illustrative cases I am not concerned with the adequacy of the theory or of the methods, but with the type of approach to the explanation of child rearing that is employed.) Here the authors have proceeded from major institutions of the society to reflections of participation in these institutions in the outlook of adults, to reflexes of parental outlook in child rearing. Furthermore, the shift from "entrepreneurial" to "bureaucratic" is itself accounted for by reference to certain general organizational and economic problems in the society at large, rather than being left as a spontaneous movement.

I shall not be concerned here with the various efforts to explain socialization patterns or contexts by reference to the idiosyncratic structures of particular families within a generally homogeneous group, since we are here concerned with fairly widespread modalities of child rearing common in groups.

Much of the work alluded to above concerns American society or other complex societies, and the bulk of it has been carried on by sociologists and psychologists, rather than by anthropologists or by psychologists interested in the primitive and the non-Western world. Some of the most interesting work on primitive and other non-Western cultures has been done by Whiting and Child and their various co-workers. I refer here not to *Child-Training and Personality* (1958), which treats child rearing primarily as a cause and is little concerned with its antecedents, but to four other pieces of research (Murdock and Whiting 1951; Whiting, Kluckhohn, and Anthony 1958; Barry, Bacon, and Child 1957; and Barry, Child, and Bacon 1959). The first of these deals, among other things, with relative indulgence as a correlate of monogamy, sororal polygyny, and nonsororal polygyny. The second deals with the relationship between prolonged nursing and polygyny, and, in addition, discusses male initiation rites as a socialization practice arising where male children are attached to the mother to an unusual degree and for an unusually long period of time. The third deals with differences between the socialization of boys and of girls, finding that in general boys are trained more for achievement, self-reliance, and independence, and girls more for obedience, responsibility, and nurturance, in a large sample of cultures. Furthermore, these differences are maximized in cultures where big game is hunted, or large animals are herded, or grain agriculture is found because of the particular demands these activities place on males. The fourth is concerned with the balance between socialization toward compliance and that toward assertion in the child-rearing practices of a similar large sample, relating this balance to what is termed "surplus"—a technical base likely to produce a generous and predictable output, rather than a meager and unpredictable output. Compliant pressures are found in the more productive group, presumably because of its greater demands for co-ordinated work, planning, and subordination of immediate gratification for long-range family goals. In all these papers a variety of other issues are considered.

Again, without reference to my own views as to the adequacy of the explanations, we find fundamental features of technology or of kinship organization used as a basis for explaining socialization. Furthermore, unlike the studies of caste, class, and ethnicity, the explanations are general and apply to a wide range of societies.

Dr. Child has provided me with copies of the ratings on various features of socialization which he and his co-workers have developed for 111 cultures, and in seminars my students and I have used these for preliminary studies illustrative of the general point of view of this essay. Thus we have found that in general there is an association between the severity of obedience training and the number of levels of political organization above the community level, the severity of the sanctions utilized by authoritative figures (other than parents disciplining their immature children), the scope of regulation imposed by authority, and so on. Unfortunately this finding cannot be disentangled from the findings of Barry, Child, and Bacon (1959) regarding surplus, since there is a close association between their measures of surplus and our measures of political organization. We have also found a simple association between age of first serious economic activity for boys, and the nature of the tasks imposed by the technology. A boy's serious economic activities are likely to begin late (often after 10 years of age) where the tasks are dangerous, where they must be performed far from home, or where they require considerable strength. In other words, when the risk to the child is great and his contribution is small, or when the nuisance value of the child is great and his contribution small, he begins his serious tasks late. This is so even when there is women's productive work which he could easily perform. This finding would seem obvious, but perhaps its corollary is less self-evident. It means that in many highly productive horticultural societies children begin work early, whereas in many hunting and gathering and some herding societies, where the supply of food is more meager and uncertain, they begin late. This, in turn, is likely to influence judgments like those made by Child and his co-workers as regards responsibility, obedience, self-reliance, and independence, so that this finding, too, overlaps with their conclusions regarding surplus.

Our work, it should be said, has been with extreme cases, using no more than 40 at a time of the cultures utilized by Child, and there has been no reliability check of the type employed in all his ratings. Hence, the findings are tentative.

This review of previous work is spotty and capricious, lighting on a few studies which are useful for present purposes and omitting many major studies of socialization antecedents. But our primary purpose here is to focus attention on the problem rather than to review findings in an effort to arrive at answers.

Socialization as a Dependent Variable

Heretofore we have used such terms as socialization and child rearing, without defining terms. Now, however, somewhat greater explicitness seems needed. In any society or subsystem of a society, socialization consists of those patterns of action, or aspects of action, which inculcate in individuals the skills (including knowledge), motives, and attitudes necessary for the performance of present or anticipated roles. As such, socialization continues throughout normal human life, insofar as new roles must be learned, but our interest here is in socialization in infancy, childhood, and early adolescence, on the assumption that what is learned in these early periods is more general and more fixed than what is learned later. This assumption is not vital, so long as it is possible to assume that what is learned early is at least important. Socialization clearly has latent as well as manifest qualities, since the definition is made from the point of view of the observer. Hence, the inculcation may be unconscious from the point of view of the socializer. As Benedict (1953) has pointed out, what is required for a present role may have to be unlearned in the future; conceivably what is learned for the future may constitute a difficulty for the present. In addition, socializers' miscalculations regarding future roles—due, for example, to major changes in the social system—can involve the learning of nonadaptive or maladaptive qualities. For all these reasons, the definition proposed does not commit us to the view that all practices labeled socialization are adaptive in character, either immediately or in the long run. On balance, however, in a society not undergoing rapid change, it can probably be assumed that the bulk of socialization is adaptive.

Child care consists of the biological maintenance of the developing human being, until the time when older generations no longer take care of his physiological needs. Hence, in childhood a concrete act performed by a parent may often have aspects of child care and of socialization. When a child is fed on a schedule so as not to spoil it, the patterns of feeding involve both care and socialization. Examples could be multiplied indefinitely. The complex of child care and socialization will be referred to as *child rearing,* a term which will be used in many contexts simply to avoid repeated use of the term *socialization. Child training* will be used as a synonym for *early socialization.*

There is a large number of ways of classifying socialization practices. For present purposes a simple classification will be used, one adapted from a mimeographed manual on the study of socialization, prepared by Whiting and his co-workers (1953). It specifies the who, why, how, and when of child rearing: the agent—who performs the activity; the aim—with what end in mind; the technique—what is done; and the timing—at what point or points in the child's life the action is performed. No theoretical justification for this classification will be attempted, except to say that these are things we normally need to know about any social act, and to say that the literature of psychology would certainly lead us to believe that variation in any one of these factors should have significance for personality development. Nevertheless, many other conceivable modes of classification and additional variables have been overlooked.

There are two different perspectives for the study of child rearing, in the context of the present discussion. One of these is an examination of particular child-rearing patterns or the total complex of such patterns, in an effort to discern its organization and the causes of that organization or parts thereof. From this perspective, for example, we might examine socialization in the American school, referring the fact that the agents of socialization in early school years are likely to be women teachers rather than men to various features of the sexual division of labor in the professional world, but referring the time-consciousness instilled in the child to the specialization and interdependence of a complex social organization—both the school and the world into which the child will later emerge. Thus the totality of agents, aims, techniques, and timing in school might be parceled out to various social antecedents, in the course of a coherent discussion of the school program. The result of this approach is to maintain a clear view of child rearing, or items thereof, but a piecemeal view of the larger social order.

The second perspective begins with a coherent analysis of the cultural order and adduces therefrom certain consequences of that order for socialization. In the course of this, although the general orientations of socialization may emerge with some clarity, the sequence is likely to be lost. It is probable that both perspectives are necessary, even though the use of both involves some repetition of data. We will use both procedures in this essay, beginning with a discussion of sources of variation of agent, aim, technique, and timing, and proceeding thereafter to show how certain segments of cultural systems affect agent, aim, technique, or timing. Thus the first section is divided by aspects of socialization, and the second by aspects or parts of the cultural system.

ASPECTS OF SOCIALIZATION

Agent

It is self-evident that the agents of socialization are products of the wider social order: that mother's brothers play a different role in socialization in matrilineal than in patrilineal societies, that schools are found in complex, literate cultures, and so on. The importance of variation in agents is generally accepted, yet relatively little work has been done to show this, except for studies in Western cultures which deal with the differential impact of mothers versus fathers trying to teach their children the same things. A number of problems in accounting for variation in agents have not been explored, or have only recently been systematically explored. Thus, for example, we do not understand the conditions under which elder siblings have relatively great autonomous authority over younger ones, in childhood, and those under which their authority is delegated, temporary, and limited. Eisenstadt's *From Generation to Generation* (1956) is an interesting attempt to account for the importance of structured peer groups in socialization, dealing, as it does, with types of societies in which age groups do and do not occur.

Methods for case study in this area are the usual observational, descriptive, and analytic techniques of ethnology; this is a topic which involves essentially the same skills as the description and analysis of work groups, kinship units, political systems, and so on. Eisenstadt's work bears witness to the possibility of hypothesis-testing comparative studies of problems in this area.

Aim

However large may be the area of child rearing that does not involve conscious planning and decisions on the part of the agent, another large area remains that does. Agents, although sometimes siblings and peers, are often members of the society occupying roles like those the children will later occupy. As Riesman (1950) and Mead (1953a and 1953b) have pointed out, agents may have important aims even when precise future roles for the child are unpredictable. Agents may aim at any given time at (1) making an immediate alteration in the child's behavior necessary in a given situation (getting the child off the floor of the supermarket and making him walk out the door); (2) training the child in the role he is now occupying; (3) training the child for the next role in a sequence; (4) training the child for more remote roles.

In the training for remote roles, the linkages with the present can be simple or complex. In some cultures where accumulation of herds by adults is important, the child is encouraged to prepare for this by being given small quantities of livestock, being told how to tend them, and being permitted to enjoy the rewards of his surplus. The relationship between long-range aim and practice here is simple and direct. On the other hand, in a group of middle-class fathers I interviewed, a number were pleased by, or anxious about their male childrens' athletic performance. It became clear that none of them expected professional athletes among their adult sons, but that all of them felt that success in athletics implied a future capacity to engage in the competitive rough and tumble of adult occupational life, in spite of the very different character of that later competition (Aberle and Naegele 1952).

An emphasis solely on socialization practices at the behavioral level is insufficient unless it is accompanied by the study of the type of adult, and the type of child the agents hope to create. Anthropological literature abounds in sensitive descriptions of these aims, yet the topic is sometimes omitted in the very monographs which deal most intensively with socialization practices. There must be wide variations in the clarity and generality with which such goals are formulated. We know from life histories that in some primitive cultures, children are given quite broad and general descriptions by members of the older generation of what constitutes a "good" Navaho or Hopi (Kluckhohn 1945; Dyk 1938; Simmons, 1942). Yet Riesman (1950) has the impression that in many primitive tribes what is taught is particular skills and behaviors. In still other tribes the aims may be cloudy. Yet somehow the picture of these aims must be built up. Traditional techniques of interviewing are at least the starting point for field work in this area. Comparative work has already begun, as manifested by the two papers by Barry, Bacon, and Child cited earlier. The work indicates clearly that certain general aims are associated with subsistence patterns, whatever the variables that intervene between subsistence techniques and socialization aims.

The linkage of aims with the adult roles and values of the socializers is extraordinarily easy, in a certain sense, as I have pointed out earlier in the discussion of training for the warrior role on the Plains. But only when the nature of the wider system is understood, and the adults' roles are seen not merely as cultural givens but themselves as cultural products, can the requiredness of the aims of the socializers be adequately comprehended.

Technique

The literature of socialization is full of suggestions and demonstrations that techniques, singly or in combination, are responsible for major variations in personality: corporal punishment and non-conditional love; conditional love and consistent behavior; capricious indulgence and corporal punishment, and so forth. But in this area, systematic efforts to relate the techniques of socialization to cultural antecedents are few and far between, save for work on Western societies, where the research of Riesman, and of Miller and Swanson may stand as representative of vigorous efforts along these lines. Generalizations of wider scope are rare, and we do not at present know why one system emphasizes rewards, another punishments, one loss of love, and another fear of beating. I will provide one suggestive case and one example of cross-cultural comparative work in this area. Among the Kalmuk Mongols, according to my informants, it is thought that a father should bind his children to him by ties of love and gratitude. Parents may be stern and authoritative, they may scold and reprove, but they use little physical punishment. When we note that the adult son may take his livestock and leave the family group, and that support in old age is achieved through children, this absence of harshness and use of affection seems sensible. It would seem that the child's future independence and the parents' subsequent dependence are foreshadowed by the father's need to build a strong emotional bond with his child, and hence to forego harshly authoritative discipline.

Two students at Michigan have used small samples of cultures from the Human Relations Area Files (about 20) to examine the relationship between the use of bogeymen, the use of physical punishment, and the level of political organization. They find that, in general, use of bogeymen is more likely where physical punishment is little used, and that bogeymen are used most heavily where there is a low level of political integration. It is only fair to add that two other students, using slightly different samples, found no such relationships, that there was no reliability check, and that the criteria for "use of bogeymen" varied from term paper to term paper. As in many other instances, however, the example is used mainly for illustration of an approach. The theory underlying this is that where parents are not themselves severely subordinated, they do not seem to see their children as appropriate objects for severe subordination. Whether they simply do not envisage this possibility, or whether they envisage it and reject it, is unknown. Faced with the need to control their children, they refer the sanction source to an outside agency, the bogeymen, rather than attempting direct coercion of the child.

A number of lines of inquiry as respects techniques suggest themselves; the two most obvious ones are the authoritative relationships in which the parents are involved, and the future meaning of the children to the parents. Inquiry in the field about the "why" of techniques may yield little useful information on this score; it is at least as likely to elicit valuable information regarding aims. Thus, if we asked American parents of a few decades ago why they put their childrens' arms in cardboard tubes to prevent thumbsucking we would, I think, ultimately elicit anxiety about dependent, babyish behavior and values respecting independence and maturity. We would still be left with the problem of cardboard tube versus bitter aloes versus slapping the hands, which would lead to still other considerations.

Timing

Why there are changes in agents, aims, or techniques at particular times in different cultures constitutes a problem still largely unsolved. We have mentioned the work of Whiting, Kluckhohn, and Anthony, on delay of weaning and its association with general polygyny and the spacing of births, Eisenstadt's regarding movement into age groups, and my own seminars' work on age of first serious economic responsibility. Due attention has been given to weaning, toilet training, and various features of responsibility and independence training in various groups in Western society. But systematic efforts in field work, or on a comparative basis to account for the timing of various features of socialization, is still largely in the future. The two most promising areas for work seem to be an adequate analysis of age grading in childhood as a feature of social organization, and due attention to material conditions. Thus toddlers may find their lives more circumscribed if they live surrounded by dangers or valuables than under other conditions; women who work in the fields may take unweaned children with them or leave them behind, depending on the distance from home and the conditions of life for children in the fields, and so on.

FEATURES OF CULTURES IN THEIR IMPACT ON SOCIALIZATION

We have previously attempted to suggest that much work remains to be done regarding the cultural variability of agent, aim, technique, and timing in the process of socialization. We now turn to take the perspective of the cultural system—or rather certain features of it—as cause of this variability. In general, our analysis of the causes of socialization cannot be much better than our understanding of the operation of cultural systems, since through this understanding we come to see the requiredness of various features of socialization for particular kinds of systems. I shall touch on some major cultural features which seem promising antecedents for socialization practices.

Technology

The specific demands of various technical operations in a culture seem to afford one major, significant, and obvious source of variability in socialization. It has already been said that this may influence the age of the assumption of major economic responsibility for males. Barry, Bacon, and Child have shown that differences in the socialization practices for boys and for girls are maximized (boys' socialization stressing independence, achievement, and self-reliance in such instances), where hunting, grain agriculture (there is no separate consideration of plough agriculture), and care of large herded animals are found. The authors consider the task itself as imposing demands for this type of training; my own findings would suggest that in some of these instances boys' training is delayed and they are given a good deal of freedom—so that they spend much time away from home in play groups where just these qualities are enhanced. Both factors may be operative. Movement to serious economic activities may result in a shift in the major agent of socialization from mother to father or mother's brother, and the nature of the activities may determine the time of the shift. What associations between task and technique there may be, I do not know. At any rate, agent, aim, and timing are probably influenced directly by task, if current findings are any guide.

It can also be assumed that the work groups dictated by the task are significant matrices for socialization.

Economic Organization

Among the dominant types of extrafamilial systems of distribution of goods and services in premarket economies are reciprocity and redistribution. Reciprocity involves an exchange where A gives goods or services to B with the expectation of a subsequent return from B. Haggling over the terms of the exchange is not found; instead, A attempts by his generosity to make a future claim on B— rather than attempting to sell his services as dearly as possible. As a subtype of reciprocity, for present purposes, I will include cases where a hunter who kills a large animal distributes it to his fellows, rather than giving it to one person, expecting that when they, in turn, kill large animals they will reciprocate.

Under redistribution I include cases where goods or services are channeled upward to a central authority (individual or group), which funnels the same or other goods downward to the followers (*cf.* Sahlins 1958).

Market economies involve a relatively free market in land, labor, and goods, with bargaining, a supply crowd and a demand crowd, and the possibility of risk taking, profit making, and reinvestment (*cf.* here and earlier Polanyi 1957, and Polanyi *et al.* 1957).

These three systems, only the first two of which are found in the primitive world, have fundamentally different ethics. The ethic of reciprocity is mutual generosity (however often it is transgressed); the ethic of redistribution in its less exploitative forms is obligation on the part of the follower and generosity in the form of *noblesse oblige* on the part of the central authority; the ethic of the market under various conditions has been delineated by Fromm (1947), Riesman (1950), and Miller and Swanson (1958), among others, and need not concern us here. These ethics are fundamental requirements of these systems—or at least are so under most conditions. It must be assumed that they affect parental orientations, and hence ultimately the socialization practices associated with these different economies. This sort of chain affords the possibility of getting beyond values as primary causes, since it permits us to go from social organizational antecedents to values to socialization. I have, in addition, an impression that under similar technical and environmental conditions, the presence of a redistributive system in one case and its absence in another increases the actual production of the group in the redistributive case and hence makes it likely that children will be pulled into the work group at an earlier age. (These remarks should be qualified by noting that the scope of the redistributive system—village-wide, chiefdom-wide, or kingdom-wide—is more important than its mere presence or absence.)

Much of the work on achievement and affiliation, as well as on other features of American child rearing by class and by time period can probably be ultimately related to the nature of the market system in the modern world, but our concern at present is with large-scale comparisons and not merely with the present epoch of our own culture.

I have here suggested, then, some connections between socialization aims and economic systems, without adverting to agents, techniques, or (except in passing) timing.

Political Systems

Needless to say, there is a close connection between the type of economic integration and the level of political integration. Bands, which lack any clear-cut authoritative structure, and tribes, which consist of sets of small territorial units cross-cut by sodalities or clans, but lacking either strong local authority or overarching authority above the local unit, are likely to have well-developed systems of reciprocity. Chiefdoms, where there is some centralized authority but no ultimate central control of legitimate use of force, and preindustrial states, where legitimate use of force is the property of the government, are the domain of various kinds of redistributive systems. Market-dominated societies, by contrast, seem to belong par excellence to the period of mechanized industry. But here we are concerned with the impact of authority or its absence on socialization. In tribes and bands, two conditions normally prevail: individuals are highly interdependent and leaving the group is difficult, or family units are relatively autonomous and egress is easy. With no central control of aggression, the former situation seems to promote inhibition of aggression; the latter permits or encourages it. If this impression is correct, the aims of socialization with respect to aggression should vary with these conditions. Weak chiefdoms should resemble the first type of bands and tribes with respect to aggression. Beyond that I cannot carry these assumptions. I have already suggested that obedience training varies directly with level of political integration, but the causes of this are not clear. Is it the parents' anticipation of the authority the child must later meet? Is it the parents' fear of being called to account for the child's later behavior as a young adult? Is it simply automatic reflection of the parents' own subordination? Is it association with level and type of productivity and a demand imposed by day-to-day tasks, as suggested by Barry, Child, and Bacon (1959)?

General Comments

It would be possible to continue indefinitely with kinship units, religious groupings, secret societies, age groups, types of community structure, housing, crowding, and so on, as factors having influence on socialization. I will stop at this point, however, since the examples chosen do proceed from major cultural features to socialization, even if the explanations and suggestions remain largely hypothetical. They remain so because we are so far from understanding the causes of socialization.

METHODS OF RESEARCH

I have already suggested that the major methods available to us for the study of socialization are the type of analysis of single cases and the comparative techniques which permit us to demonstrate covariation which have succeeded in other domains of ethnology (*cf*. Whiting 1954). Field techniques include usual observation, interviewing, and record keeping, but may have to be supplemented by a large battery of special techniques. The publications to be expected from Whiting, Lambert, Child, and their co-workers on the studies they have completed of six cultures can be expected to enrich our methodology, our substantive materials, and our systematic understanding.

One special method deserves particular mention, however, if only because it has received so little systematic attention for so long. That is the detailed exploration of the transition rituals from birth to marriage. It is hard to find a modern example of comparative work in this area, except for the study of male initiation rituals by Whiting, Kluckhohn and Anthony, and Eisenstadt's study of age grouping. Case studies are relatively perfunctory, on the whole, although clues to many features of socialization and its attendant values are to be found in these rituals.

There has been no discussion here of methods of the study of the results of socialization. This is so for three reasons. First, this is not the task I set myself. Second, it is my impression that personality evaluation has become far too specialized a task for the anthropologist to expect to be both a competent clinical, personality, or social psychologist and a competent anthropologist. Field teams seem to be the answer here. Finally, accounting for socialization practices does seem to me to be a task well within the province and competence of the anthropologist, interesting in its own right, and feasible through the same techniques that permit us to understand other cause and effect relationships in the cultural realm.

BIBLIOGRAPHY

ABERLE, DAVID F., and KASPAR D. NAEGELE
  1952 Middle-class fathers' occupational role and attitudes toward children. Amer. J. Orthopsychiatry 22:366–378.

BARRY, HERBERT III, MARGARET K. BACON, and IRVIN L. CHILD
  1957 A cross-cultural survey of some sex differences in socialization. J. Abnormal and Social Psych. 55:327–332.

BARRY, HERBERT III, IRVIN L. CHILD, and MARGARET K. BACON
  1959 Relation of child training to subsistence economy. Am. Anthropologist 61:51–63.

BENEDICT, RUTH F.
  1953 Continuities and discontinuities in cultural conditioning. *In* Personality in nature, society, and culture. Clyde Kluckhohn, Henry A. Murray, and David M. Schneider, eds., pp. 522–531. New York, Alfred A. Knopf.

CHILD, IRVIN L.
  1954 Socialization. *In* Handbook of social psychology. Gardner Lindzey, ed., pp. 655–692. Reading, Mass., Addison-Wesley Publishing Co., Inc., Vol. II.

DYK, WALTER, ed.
  1938 Son of Old Man Hat. New York, Harcourt, Brace and Co.

EGGAN, FRED
  1955 The Cheyenne and Arapaho kinship system. *In* Social anthropology of North American Tribes. Fred Eggan, ed., pp. 35–95. Chicago, University of Chicago Press.

EISENSTADT, S. N.
  1956 From generation to generation: age groups and social structure. Glencoe, The Free Press.

FROMM, ERICH
  1947   Man for himself, an inquiry into the psychology of ethics. New York, Rinehart and Company, Inc.

KARDINER, ABRAM, et al.
  1945   The psychological frontiers of society, pp. 81–100. New York, Columbia University Press.

KLUCKHOHN, CLYDE
  1945   A Navaho personal document with a brief Paretian analysis. Southwestern Journal of Anthropology 1:260–283.

MEAD, MARGARET
  1953a Social change and cultural surrogates. In Personality in nature, society, and culture. Clyde Kluckhohn, Henry A. Murray, and David M. Schneider, eds., pp. 651–662. New York, Alfred A. Knopf.

MEAD, MARGARET
  1953b Administrative contributions to democratic character formation at the adolescent level. In Personality in nature, society, and culture. Clyde Kluckhohn, Henry A. Murray, and David M. Schneider, eds., pp. 663–670. New York, Alfred A. Knopf.

MILLER, DANIEL R., and GUY E. SWANSON
  1958   The changing American parent. New York, Wiley and Co.

MURDOCK, GEORGE P.
  1949   Social structure. New York, The MacMillan Company.

MURDOCK, GEORGE P., and JOHN W. M. WHITING
  1951   Cultural determination of parental attitudes: the relationships between the social structure, particularly family structure, and parental behavior. In Problems of infancy and childhood: transactions of the fourth conference March 6–7, 1950, New York, sponsored by Josiah Macy, Jr. Foundation, ed. Milton J. E. Senn. New York, Josiah Macy, Jr. Foundation. Paper, pp. 13–34; discussion, pp. 34–80.

POLANYI, KARL
  1957   The great transformation. Boston, Beacon Press.

POLANYI, KARL et al., eds.
  1957   Trade and market in the early empires. Glencoe, the Free Press.

RADCLIFFE-BROWN, A. R.
  1952   On joking relationships. In Structure and function in primitive society, by A. R. Radcliffe-Brown, pp. 90–104. Glencoe, The Free Press.

RIESMAN, DAVID
  1950   The lonely crowd. New Haven, Yale University Press.

SAHLINS, MARSHALL D.
  1958   Social stratification in Polynesia. Seattle, University of Washington Press.

SIMMONS, LEO
  1942   Sun Chief, the autobiography of a Hopi Indian. New Haven, Yale University Press.

WHITE, LESLIE A.
  1949   Energy and the evolution of culture. In The science of culture, by Leslie A. White, pp. 363–393. New York, Farrar, Straus and Co.

WHITING, JOHN W. M.
   1954   The cross-cultural method. *In* Handbook of social psychology, Gardner Lindzey, ed., pp. 523–531. Reading, Mass., Addison-Wesley Publishing Co., Inc. Vol. I.

WHITING, JOHN W. M. *et al.*
   1953   Field manual for the cross cultural study of child rearing, prepared for Committee on Social Behavior. New York, Social Science Research Council. Mimeo.

WHITING, JOHN W. M., and IRVING L. CHILD
   1953   Child training and personality. New Haven, Yale University Press.

WHITING, JOHN W. M., RICHARD KLUCKHOHN, and ALBERT ANTHONY
   1958   The function of male initiation ceremonies at puberty. *In* Readings in Social Psychology, Eleanor E. Macoby, Theodore M. Newcomb, and Eugene L. Hartley, eds., pp. 359–370. New York, Henry Holt and Company.

Chapter 14

KINSHIP AND WAYS OF LIFE: AN EXPLORATION*

FRANCIS L. K. HSU
Northwestern University

To THE individual in all societies the importance of other human beings, as compared with that of nonhuman elements in his environment, is supreme. This factor can even overshadow his basic desire for self-preservation, for it is not hard to find individuals in any culture who will give their lives because of their parents, spouses, tribe, or nation. Whether the custom is head-hunting or potlatch, whether the economic activity is agriculture, nomadism, or mechanized industries, and whatever the individual's status or interest, the prime mover of the individual's behavior lies in the nature of his relationship with other members of his society. The extent to which he will exert himself is in direct ratio to the degree to which he feels he has attained a proper place among his fellow men. That is to say, he tends to experience a greater urge to strive toward improvement of his position if he pictures himself to be in a wrong or lower place from where he ought to be, whereas he tends to be more satisfied with the status quo if he feels the reverse. The specific methods he resorts to are, of course, as varied as they are culturally given, but the basic objects he strives for may be summarized into three categories: sociability, security, and status. The meanings of these basic social needs of the individual, and how they compare with needs postulated by other scholars, have been discussed elsewhere (Hsu

* In preparing this chapter, I am particularly indebted to Dr. Paul J. Bohannan for going over the entire manuscript and making many valuable comments and suggestions, especially with reference to the relationship between kinship structure and kinship content. I am also indebted to Dr. G. P. Murdock for his constructive comments when the basic ideas of the paper were first presented at the annual American Anthropological Association meetings at Tucson, Arizona, in 1953 and to Drs. W. R. Bascom and Fred Eggan for going over the early version of the manuscript and materially helping its birth.

1961, Chapter VIII). Suffice it to point out here that whether the individual has achieved his proper place among his fellow human beings is measured by two interrelated yardsticks: on the one hand, by what Mead, Sullivan, and others, describe as the *attitudes toward himself* (M. H. Kuhn 1954); on the other hand, the attitudes toward him on the part of those fellow men to whom he is bound or with whom he is identified.

Thus, whether the individual attempts to improve himself by getting married, by conquest of air and sea, by acquisition of wealth, or by elaboration of the imaginary, his primary concern is his place among fellow men. The place of the individual among his fellow men refers, of course, not only to the present. It could be keyed to the past, so that this concern is chiefly centered in his elders and, by extension, his departed ancestral spirits; or it could be keyed to the future, so that this concern is primarily aimed at his descendants, and, by extension, those yet to be born; or it could be keyed to both past and future.

Nor is the place of the individual among his fellow men static. It is subject to the changing circumstances in which the individual finds himself. For example, in spite of the most serene childhood experiences, a majority of individuals will not feel secure when faced by later economic, social, or political uncertainty. Regardless of early histories, a majority of human beings in any crowd escaping from a fire will become panicky and trample one another.

The relative importance of early versus later experiences is immaterial to the arguments of this chapter. The crucial point here is the great importance of kinship as the primary web of relationships connecting every new-born individual with his fellow men and through them, with the over-all pattern of thought and action prevailing in the society of which he forms a part.

The connection between a kinship system and the over-all pattern of thought and action of a people may be seen from two angles. On the one hand, some kinship systems enable the individuals reared in them to achieve their appropriate places in terms of sociability, security, and status with greater ease than do other kinship systems. The inference is that the individuals who grow up and live in the former type of kinship system may be expected to bestir themselves far less than those who grow up and live in the latter type of kinship systems. Hence, the societies with the former type of kinship systems are likely to be more dynamic than those with the latter type.

On the other hand, the individual can be expected to strive more not only when his self-attitude is higher than accorded it by his fellow human beings but also when the people related to him cause him to feel that he has some chance of success and much to gain after his success. Conversely, he is unlikely to strive very hard when the people related to him give him reason to believe that he has little chance of success or little to gain even with success. Therefore, the individual's tendency to adventure, conquest, and expansion no less than his tenacity to face terrible disasters like epidemic, drought, or foreign conquest depends greatly, in the first place, on whether or not his society demands such heroic actions on his part in order for him to keep his membership in it as a self-respecting man, and in the second place, on whether or not his group provides him with social-psychological support for prolonged efforts and concerted action. This hypothesis makes no assumption on the uniformity of behavior in any society. A few individuals may be aggressive where most others in the same society are docile; a few may fight a last-ditch battle where most others have given up; but the behavior of the majority is strongly affected by the forces just described.

The Hypothesis

However, existing results of kinship studies would seem to show that varieties of kinship have no connection with the diverse ways of life in different societies.[1] There does not seem to be any way of avoiding this conclusion when we note that the Eskimo "type" of "kinship organization" is also characteristic of the highly industrialized Yankees of New England, the peasant Ruthenians of eastern Europe, the simple agriculturalists of Taos Pueblo in the southwestern United States, and the Andamese pygmies of the tropical forest as well as many others (Murdock 1949:226–228); and that the Dakota type of kinship organization is also characteristic of such diverse peoples as the Fijians, the Tallensi, the Manchus, and the Chinese (Murdock 1949:236–238). For in spite of the similarity or even the identity of the kinship structures in question, the ways of life of the diverse societies in which they are found bear no resemblance one to another.

What has happened so far is that most students of kinship from Murdock, Steward (1937), Spoehr (1947), Goldschmidt (1948)

---

[1] The term "way of life" is used to denote the characteristic manner in which the people of a given society look at things and express their outlook in concrete actions. It is, therefore, the same as "national character," a term used in Chapters 6 and 7, except that "national character," by custom, is applicable to large and literate societies, while "way of life" here applies to all societies. For a fuller exposition of what the "way of life" means, see Hsu 1953:2–17.

to Levi-Strauss (1949), Eggan (1950), Leach (1952), and others have concentrated on certain aspects of kinship structure. They attempt to answer in one way or another the following questions: What factors are correlated with the development of kinship groups such as clan, phratry, dual organization, or their shift from one emphasis to another? What factors affect the change of kinship usages such as relationship terms, mother-in-law avoidance, and forms of marriage? But there has been little or no serious attempt to deal with kinship content which can go far to help us with another question: What effects do certain types of kinship organization have on the pattern of thought and behavior of individuals reared in them?

Answers bearing on such a question have been sought by some students of psychological anthropology with the central focus on child-rearing practices (see Whiting in Chapter 12). But even some students of kinship have not been completely oblivious of this question. For example, it may have been implicit in parts of works by Eggan when he spoke of the "sociological correlates" of the kinship systems of the Western Pueblo (1950:292). It had been skirted by Malinowski when he attempted to show the effect of matrilineal inheritance in Trobriand Islands on the nature of father-son relationship (1929, 1933), and by Fortune (whatever we think of his conclusions) when he related the Dobuan world view with their kinship usage of alternative residences (1932). The only more extensive examination of this question is a work of Firth (1951), but this volume, though sometimes stimulating and insightful, comes to little more than the general observation that human behavior is intimately intertwined with social organization.

However, armed by an untenable antithesis between psychological and sociological explanations, students of kinship have not only seen no necessary connection between their work and the culture-and-personality studies but often reacted to them with frank hostility. The task of a systematic exploration of the exact relationship between kinship variation and specific ways of life in different societies remains to be attempted. This line of inquiry seems imperative if the study of kinship is to attain a truly significant place in the total perspective of the science of man. For if kinship is the web through which human beings are woven together from birth to death, it most certainly must, *a priori*, be related not only to matters such as kinship terms or mother-in-law avoidance but also to the formation, organization, and operation of the most essential patterns of thought and behavior.

The purpose of this chapter is to show that a very real correlation exists between kinship and ways of life. This hypothesis is based on three interrelated propositions: (1) The failure to perceive this correlation thus far is due to concentration on structure to the neglect of content, (2) kinship structure is less clearly related to the thought and action patterns of the individual than kinship content, and (3) kinship content is, in the last analysis, rooted in kinship structure.

Kinship Structure and Kinship Content Differentiated

Kinship structure describes those features which govern the formal patterns of arrangement among individuals standing in reciprocal categories of kinship. It comprehends rules of descent, residence, inheritance; in-law avoidances; conjugal or joint families; and so forth. Kinship content pertains to the characteristics which govern the tenacity, intensity, or quality of interaction among individuals related through kinship. It crystallizes itself into such values as individualism and self-reliance, romantic love in marriage, emphasis on youth, or on the importance of ancestors.

To illustrate, a new-born infant may have coming early into his life only his parents or mother and mother's brothers plus a few siblings and an occasional contact with others; or he may have coming early into his life relatives including not only his parents or mother and mother's brothers as well as siblings, but also a vast array of other relatives and nonrelatives. These are matters of kinship structure. They spell the differences between the conjugal family and some larger unit, or between patrilocal or matrilocal residence.

However, two infants who have the same number and kind of individuals come into their respective lives may be affected differently because these individuals may act as though they each possess them and can order their lives separately; or these individuals may act as though they are mere spectators and that their own mothers are the real powers that lay down all laws. These are matters of kinship content. They are rooted in the difference between mutual dependence and individualism, both terms to be explained below.

The differences between structure and content have been explored in another publication (Hsu 1959). What needs to be pointed out here, however, is that the content of a kinship system is to a great extent determined by the emphasis given one or another particular primary relationship in the kinship structure.

Eight basic relationships are to be found in every kinship system. They are those of husband-wife, father-son, mother-son, mother-daughter, father-daughter, sister-sister, brother-brother, and brother-sister. No matter how much more extensive the kinship system is, the relationships between more remotely situated individuals in it (designated in this chapter as secondary relationships) are, with few exceptions, extensions of one or another of these primary relationships. However, these eight primary relationships are not given the same emphasis by different societies. Furthermore, when a kinship system gives emphasis to one of these relationships, it does so not only by reducing the importance of other relationships, but also by modifying their contents, so that the resulting kinship systems vary greatly in attributes and in their influences on the individuals reared in them.

To pursue this hypothesis I propose to examine, in the balance of this chapter, four types of kinship systems, each dominated by one structural relationship, and see how they may be related to many outstanding characteristics in thought and behavior among the peoples living in them. The hypothesis presupposes that each structural relationship possesses inherent and distinctive attributes. When one relationship is elevated over other relationships in a given kinship system, the attributes of the dominating relationship tend to modify, eliminate, or at least reduce the importance of the attributes of other structural relationships. The hypothesis further presumes that the total effect of the dominance of the attributes of one structural relationship leads to a particular kind of kinship content which in turn strongly conditions the pattern of thought and behavior of the individual reared in it. The four types of kinship content and their structural connections are given below:

A. Mutual dependence among members of kin and community, which is rooted in the emphasis on father-son axis at the expense of all other relationships.
B. Self-reliance on the part of the individual which is rooted in the supremacy of husband-wife axis at the expense of all other relationships.
C. Supernatural reliance which is found where the mother-son axis tends to have more primary importance over other relationships.
D. A degree of mutual dependence together with the emphasis on brother-brother axis and practically no worship of the ancestors.

It is understood, of course, that no typology covers all the facts or puts all of them into perfectly neat compartments (J. H. Steward 1954). First, every typology is a matter of abstraction, and the level of abstraction determines what facts must be included and what must be excluded. Second, even the facts covered by any one statement are never as uniform as the statement would indicate. Consider such an observation as "American society is founded on the ideas of equality, freedom and fair play." Surely any reader can find many historical and contemporary facts as well as the outlook of individual Americans which obviously negate the high-sounding principles. Yet, to conclude that the American society is not founded on these ideas is to be blind to the fundamental trend of development of American society and culture and, therefore, to be very wide of the mark. Even a statement such as "Universal education prevails in American society" is not without exception. In World War II, at least 2 per cent of American males were rejected because of illiteracy. Yet, no one can dispute the fact that universal education is firmly established in this society both as a matter of conviction and as a matter of practice. Third, every type enumerated below contains internal variations which, in more elaborate treatments, may merit description as subtypes.

With these qualifications in mind let us, then, examine in some detail the characteristics of behavior in the four types of societies that are associated with the four different kinds of kinship content.[2]

TYPE A SOCIETIES

Included in this group are those of a majority of the Oriental peoples, including Chinese, Japanese, Koreans, Siamese, and others, but excluding the major inhabitants of India: the Hindus and the Moslems.

Kinship

The structural characteristics of these kinship systems are simple: they are patrilineal, patrilocal, and by and large patriarchal. The basic unit in which the infant finds himself is generally the patrilineal extended family. Among the lower classes this unit is smaller, approximating the individual family of parents and unmarried children, but in higher classes, it is sometimes enormous. However, even among the poor, the child's grandparents and in-laws are likely to be much in evidence.

---

[2] The sequence of A, B, C, and D given the four types of society discussed in this chapter has no ranking significance. It really follows the sequence of my academic acquaintance with these societies. I began my studies of the Chinese culture as a student in 1934; then came my introduction to English culture in 1937; this was followed by my residence and work in the U.S. since 1945; and a period of 18 months' field work in India from 1955 to 1957. My serious reading and reflection on Africa had only begun in 1959.

The structural relationship most elevated is that of the father-son. All other relationships are either extensions of this central axis, or are subordinated to and modified by it. The boldest example of this type is found among the Chinese and the weakest among the Siamese. The first attribute of the father-son relationship is inclusiveness. There is only one father but there are usually many sons. In fact, even when there is only one son the parents as a rule hope for more. The other attribute of it is continuity. Every father-son relationship is a link in an endless chain of father-son relationships. For every father is a son and every son, in the normal course of events, will be a father.

The characteristic kinship content correlated with the emphasis on father-son axis is mutual dependence. Enmeshed in a network of continuous relationships, the individual is conditioned to orient himself lineally, and, in a secondary way, laterally within a well-defined group; he is naturally the product of his forebears before him as he is automatically the progenitor of his descendants yet to some. His place in that line is specific and inalienable. Superficially the relationship seems to be one sided, namely, sons owe much more to their fathers than their fathers do to them. The obligations are actually quite mutual. The son owes his father all services as desired, unquestioned obedience, extreme respect, and complete support in life as in death. But the father owes to the son marital arrangement, protection, and all his inheritance. (In Japan the inheritance rules are governed by primogeniture.) The ideal son is sensitive to every whim on the part of his father. The father's every wish is his command. But the ideal father takes every precaution to see that his sons are well married, well educated, well connected, and well provided for. Death and torture are often endured willingly by sons and fathers in fulfilling some of these obligations. The mother, by virtue of her marriage to the father, her assumption of his clan membership, and the biological relationship with the son, in an integral part of this core relationship: whatever is due to the father is equally due to the mother, except that she is not expected to have the means to support her son.

Starting from this basic father-son axis, similar relationships extend both vertically and horizontally. Vertically each father-son axis is a necessary link in a chain connecting one's lineal forebears, living or dead, with one's lineal descendants already born or yet to be born. Horizontally it is the model against which are measured one's attitudes, duties, and obligations toward all agnatic male kinsmen and their wives in the ascending or the descending generations.

In this web of kinship the individual has no freedom; he is hedged in on all sides. But he also has little fear of being left out, for he can count on help from all sides just as he is expected to give help. This is at the root of the well-known Oriental nepotism, except in Japan (Hsu 1954). Symptomatic of this solidarity is the fact that ancestor worship, going back for many generations, is the rule among them. The living descendants have the duty of providing for the ancestors who have departed and of glorifying them. In turn, the departed members of the family as a matter of course look after the interests of the living descendants. So great is this sense of solidarity that, unlike the ancestor cult found in any other part of the world, these peoples do not believe that the departed ancestors will do them harm as spirits. There does not seem to be any Oriental society in which ancestral spirits are prayed to for forgiveness during emergencies such as sickness, floods, or epidemics.

The great importance given to the father-son axis reduces, modifies, or dominates all other relationships, including that between husband and wife. Indeed the married woman's primary duties are not those to her husband but to her husband's parents or her sons. Similarly the married man's duties to his parents and to his sons take precedence over those to others. For this reason romantic love as an ideal is absent and public expressions of intimacy, whether by a man and his wife before his parents or by a man and his wife before their children, are taboo. A son can be required by parents to divorce his wife if she fails to please them, just as he is duty-bound to take a concubine if his wife fails to provide a son. The need for vertical continuity and horizontal solidarity within the kinship group practically eliminates individual privacy. Consequently, children are raised to enter into the adult world as soon as they are physically and mentally capable to do so. In fact, mutual dependence requires that children share the vicissitudes of the adult world from infancy onward. Discipline (punishment, reward, rules) tends to be inconsistent for it is never exclusively in the hands of mother or parents. For not only grandparents, but in-laws, neighbors and friends can actively interfere with it.

The clan is seen as an extension of the father-son axis to all male agnates. Clan is usually present among most of these peoples. This clan is not a mere device to regulate marriage. It is usually an organized body which regulates the members' behavior, settles their disputes, and defends them against outside oppressors or enemies. So strong is the patrilineal emphasis in the clan that all women married into it assume its identity, a trait not found elsewhere so far except among the Gusii of Kenya (Mayer 1949).

General Characteristics

People living in this type of kinship pattern will be satisfied with the status quo and are conservative. There is no urge within the society toward fission. On the contrary, there are deep-seated centripetal tendencies. Since the place of the individual in the web of kinship is inalienable and perpetual, his need for striving to prove himself is not great. And since the individual's growing up experiences are multiple-centered, he tends to view the world not in absolute terms of black and white but in relativistic fashion with many compromises. Consequently, there are fewer chances for men to be pulled asunder by abstract issues or by the desire for all or none. Even faced with famine, they tend to tighten their belts and eat less instead of moving to new lands. The small minority of them who do emigrate tend to make up an elaborate duplication of the way of life that they had known before, and/or maintain their solidarity with the home society and/or return physically to the home society at some later date. With few exceptions, they wish to die at the places of their birth and to be buried in their ancestral graveyards. Most of them do so.

From this point of view we may see the relation between language and culture in a new light. Some scholars have tended, as did Whorf later, to conclude that the Chinese had not developed science because Chinese thought would have been incongruous with Western logic based upon Indo-European grammar (Granet 1934 and Chang 1939). Our analysis here makes it clear that the Chinese lack an interest in abstraction because their anchorage in the web of human relations foredoomed the development of any scientific spirit and inquiry, in spite of an early history of science and invention. Elsewhere I have already detailed this point (Hsu 1953). What we need to point out here is that the Chinese language, especially the written version, instead of being the cause of Chinese lack of science, was probably shaped by the same restraining forces which limited the development of Chinese science. Chinese is the only completely nonalphabetical language in the modern world; it is more difficult to learn and use than the alphabetical ones. What is more, while Japan, Korea, and Annam of Indo-China (until the French conquest) each has its own separate set of alphabet, all have tenaciously retained the Chinese characters which they borrowed before they acquired their alphabets, to be concurrently used with their own alphabetically derived words, even though this is not only unnecessary, but also a source of great inconvenience. Their conservatism is, therefore, great. A final fact indicating that language does not limit the development of science is that Japan, after her Meiji Restoration which propelled her to a position of world prominence, did not even attempt to eliminate the parallel use of Chinese language. After World War II the teaching of Chinese in Japanese schools was suspended on order of General MacArthur, but was resumed after the end of the American occupation.

Their literature is voluminous. And their art works, especially those of China and Japan, are regarded as among the best in the world. But because of the individual's security and submersion among fellow human beings, their literature and art delve very little into emotion or into the unseen. Their music is characterized by melodious elaboration of a simple nature, albeit they have many more kinds of musical instruments than most nonliterate peoples. Yet no matter how many instruments are played together, the result is unison, not harmony of different chords or melodies. The music is often functional, to be played on social, ceremonial and religious occasions and is at best tied to acting such as in operas.

Central Government

These peoples tend to develop over-all national states with centralized governments. Submission to parental authority and to long lines of ancestors is consistent with ties with the wider government. Rank is ubiquitous and consciously acknowledged by the highly placed as well as by those inferior in situation, much as that which prevails in the kinship organization. The rulers, therefore, will be frankly autocratic but not authoritarian. Their autocracy is expressed in their unconcealed claim to superiority over their subjects. They and their subjects both admit that their decrees are, at least in theory, absolute. They maintain their unabashed ranking distinctions by their almost complete separation from their subjects. They tend to have no direct contact with their subjects, either bodily or even by sight. In fact, a majority of Orientals have been traditionally forbidden to possess a likeness of their rulers.

But they cannot be authoritarian for two reasons. First, their power, however absolute, is invariably hampered by their parents, wives, concubines, or parents of their wives or concubines, or eunuchs and their parents, or powerful ministers or their relatives, or the ruler's relatives' relatives. The ruler cannot deal with these and other related individuals effectively even if he objected to what they do because, in a framework of mutual dependence, he is consciously dependent upon them as much as they are upon him.

The other reason why the ruler cannot be authoritarian is that while the ruler-subject relationship is a projection of the basic kinship model, there is one difference. The latter lies in the fact that, in the normal course of events, the security of the common man is found in solidarity with his parents and other primary circles of relatives. The ruler in such a situation does not easily achieve the sort of determined and vehement following often achieved by many of his counterparts in Type B societies (Western). Consequently, the function of the Oriental ruler is to maintain, by and large, the status quo. (Even Japan is no real exception, to be noted below.) He is less the leader of the people than the keeper of the existing tradition and social order. He cannot arouse his subjects easily to march with him because their support of him lacks the necessary zeal.

This lack of zeal explains why, unless a ruler is grossly incompetent or has behaved contrary to the established customs and ways of the people, he would have no trouble with the problem of dissension. Even when an established reign has tumbled and when many war lords are fighting for supremacy some new dynastic founder tends to emerge with relative ease within a short period of time. The lack of positive zeal for the leader and the need for preserving the kinship group taught Oriental lords to fight no battle of desperation unless there was absolutely no escape from death. As soon as one faction looked like a winner, the inclination of the other contenders was to jump on the band wagon and find themselves a comfortable but secondary place through subordination. This picture holds true even if the new ruler happens to be alien. Unless the changes imposed by the alien rulers touch the fundamentals, peoples of this type are not likely to resist subordination by violence. In fact, being relativistic in their view of life, they will not be ashamed to adjust by passive acquiescence to, and even by a degree of active cooperation with, the enemy. They may try with amazing speed even to assume the external patterns of action of the conqueror.

These are perhaps some of the reasons why Oriental states usually were able to maintain unity for longer periods of time than those of the West. The idea of an opposition as a normal feature to check on the dominant power is unknown in Oriental tradition. But for the same reason the unity of Oriental states was generally without the kind of active solidarity of strength characteristic of their counterparts in the West. For the real solidarity lay in the kinship organization, so that changes in the wider political overlordship did not concern the individual except when the new ruler actively interfered too much with his private life and relations. Therefore, when faced with modern Western states, the Oriental political organizations generally appear to be powerless.

Religion

Polytheistic.   The core is usually ancestor worship. But, in addition, there are a multitude of personified gods. They have a large number of gods. They will borrow "gods" from other peoples freely so long as these gods can coexist with each other and with previously established gods. The deities may be arranged hierarchically, and there may be one supreme deity over all others. However, there is no idea that one god only is true and others are false or that all deities are diverse expressions of the same supreme being. This is perfectly in harmony with their relativistic view of life based on the fact that all males, and even females, will in due course achieve their greatness in a continuum along the father-son axis of long lines of ancestors and descendants. Their lack of concern for the unseen and the abstract manifests itself clearly. The gods are worshipped by the peoples for the express purpose of seeking solutions to specific problems such as disease, longevity, fertility, epidemics, and so forth. Their good will is maintained through offerings, sacrifices, verbal exaltation, recitation of some portions of scriptures by the devotees themselves or hired priests, or good deeds among men. Their religious dogma, in spite of their long written histories and literacy, tends to be simple and matter-of-fact, similar to those found among nonliterate peoples, and usually offers common sense solutions to their problems. Some of their faiths may have a systematic theology running into volumes. But these concern only a minority of the believers. Hence, followers of all cults tend to mix up with each other in rituals and beliefs. In fact it is usually difficult to describe them as followers of any particular cult. Religious "persecution" may flare up on rare occasions with sudden impact of a foreign cult, but such persecution is inevitably tied up with political insecurity and is neither long lasting nor widespread. For they have no idea of an all-or-none struggle between "good" and "evil." They know no religious wars. Some of them may be "converted" to monotheistic faiths, but few of the converts exhibit anything approaching the religious fervor and devotion of many of their Western brethren. For they have no missionary zeal and are not interested in converting nonbelievers. In keeping with the pattern of mutual dependence, merits and demerits are transferable along kinship lines. Individuals could soar to fame or fortune, or their souls could be rescued from hell, by virtue of the deeds of their ancestors or descendants.

Impetus to Change

The individual tends to be highly competitive for traditional goals. A man can, and is in fact encouraged to, exhibit initiative in getting up more costly and pompous funerals for his parents, or in going to some extreme to please his parents in filial piety, to glorify his ancestry, or, in Japan, to show devotion to the emperor. But he is unlikely to exercise his imagination by doing things which are not traditionally given, such as for a scholar to go into business. Internal impetus to change within these societies is generally lacking. For the individual can, in the main, reach his proper station among fellow men through the kinship framework. But forces limiting change have a snowballing effect on the aggrandizement of tradition. Thus, a tradition, whether it be footbinding or the contempt for soldiers, tends to become stronger and even goes to extremes as time goes on. Footbinding in China began as a frivolity among some court dancers who wrapped their bare feet with white satin to please the emperor. By the early twentieth century, many women deformed their feet into such small points that they could hardly walk. The higher the social class, the greater the competitive tendency and the smaller the feet.

Most individuals are automatically assured of honorable places in the social organization, in life as well as after death. Ancestor worship provides a complete continuity between the dead and the living, the past and the present. Therefore, while the tendency to excel in glorification of the lineage and ancestry is great, the tendency to preserve everything traditional, from duties and obligations to mores and customs, is also great. The very close and permanent human ties serve as a drag on initiative so that people are prevented from venturing out into untrodden paths, intellectually, emotionally, and physically (except Japan; see Hsu 1954). The social organization is such as softly but unremittingly to nip in the bud a majority if not all internal efforts to change the scheme of things. There is a general lack of interest in associations other than those based on kinship, marriage, locality, and occupation. For the vast majority there are not even age groups or hunting organizations and rarely any sort of sport which requires the competition between two organized bodies. Overthrow of the ruling dynasty was reported (except Japan), but revolution was unknown before impact of the West. Since they have little urge to elaborate the unseen, their utopias, never numerous, tend to be close copies of the actual worlds in which they live, minus such disturbing elements as war, banditry, and dishonesty. There may be different indigenous philosophies, but these have never become bases for contending factions in any irreconcilable way for the simple reason that the majority of peoples in this type of society have a tendency not to get actively involved in ideologies which are abstract and remote from the immediately accepted reality.

Over long periods of time there seem to be only two conditions which are the mainsprings for change in these societies. One condition is the increase of population which precipitates some inevitable expansion, even though the peoples entertain no great dream about new frontiers. But, as pointed out before, the expansion is slow and is not accompanied by any noticeable desire to cultural, political or economic independence of the newly acquired territory. The other condition for change is external pressure or invasion. Such societies have successfully withstood external forces, military or cultural, by their basic cohesion. But they may be overrun, although they seem to have the ability to modify ultimately the alien forces in their midst, and they usually recover by achieving new syntheses between their traditional and the alien elements. They tend to render the alien-imposed programs ineffective not by armed opposition (though this occasionally occurs) but chiefly by emasculating them through unobtrusive persistence. The strength of their way of life lies in its permanent solidarity between the dead, the living, and the unborn. This kinship relationship provides the individual with great resilience toward environmental problems so that he is not easily given to despair or loss of heart.

In the process of their persistence, they cannot but change a little. But such changes, especially the more spectacular and speedier ones, do not easily take deep root. It has been said that while China had successfully absorbed her foreign conquerors in the past, she may not be able to do it with Western powers. This remains to be seen. From this analysis, it seems certain that neither China nor Japan will be basically threatened or altered very easily by the West, even though the West, including the Communist West, certainly has caused them great disturbances.

No society in this type is likely either to die out physically through conquest or loss of resources or even to lose the continuation of its way of life such as is found in many parts of the nonliterate world or the West.

TYPE B SOCIETIES

Type B includes the societies of a majority of the Western peoples—Europeans and the peoples of European origin throughout the world.

Kinship

The kinship structure of these peoples is usually patrilineal, patrilocal or neolocal, and in many instances, nominally patriarchal. The basic unit in which the infant finds himself is the individual family, consisting of parents and unmarried children. In some parts of Europe, especially in premodern times, the joint family prevailed more than the individual family, and even in modern times some of these peoples have more affines living under the same roof than others. Among the lower and upper classes, the number of children is generally larger, while among the middle classes, the trend is in reverse.

The structural relationship most elevated is that of the husband-wife axis. All other relationships are either subordinated to this central axis or are patterned after and modified by it. The strongest example of this type is found among modern Americans of the United States, and the weakest, among the eastern Europeans.

Unlike those of the father-son axis, the attributes of the husband-wife axis are exclusiveness and discontinuity. It is discontinuous over the generations because each husband-wife relationship is ended when one or both of the partners die. It is exclusive of other individuals because each husband-wife relationship is not only complete by itself but is intolerant of intrusion by any third party. It must, therefore, insist on monogamy as an absolute ideal. Among the peoples constituting Type B there is, of course, variation in the nature of the husband-wife axis. In Eastern Europe the husband-wife axis is unquestionably husband-dominated, and in the United States the wife so equals her husband in nearly every way that it gives the impression of being wife-dominated. But whichever case we refer to, the central and dominating position of the husband-wife axis over all others in this type of kinship system is obvious. In contrast to Type A societies, the husband-wife union is the only relationship which is expressly and elaborately sanctioned, guaranteed and safeguarded by the church as well as by the law. It is so elevated above all other relationships and so freed from their encumbrances, that it is glorified by, and only supposed to be founded, on romantic love, an expression which embodies unaccountableness of the choice, exclusive possession between the partners of each other, freedom from interference by other human beings, and complete lack of definite ties with other relationships whether they be parent-child or fraternal. In Type A societies the father-son axis symbolizes all that is "forever." In Type B the husband-wife axis is the only relationship which is "forever."

Given this central emphasis it is easy to see how the other relationships in this type of system are either subordinate or thoroughly unimportant. The parent-child relationship is given great importance only before the son or daughter reaches majority. Even during this period, once the parental consent for marriage is given the parents no longer have control over anything. Support of children by parents is limited by the same factor. Support of parents by children is, even where the law insists on it, highly conditional and no child has to keep a parent under the same roof with his or her spouse. Generally speaking, parents have complete freedom in bequest.

Polygamy of any variety is incongruous with the emphasis on husband-wife axis. Mistresses and gigolos may be kept on the side by men and women who have the means. They may be connived by the public and in the church, but these relationships have never been made truly legitimate as they have in Types A, C, and D. Divorce rested at first with the church and has gradually been shifted into the hands of the two married partners, but at no time has it been a matter of the authority of the parents. Sibling relationships, uncle-niece relationships, uncle-nephew relationships, mother-in-law and daughter-in-law relationships all are reduced more or less to matters of friendship. If the parties concerned like each other, they may develop very great solidarity with each other. But if they do not happen to enjoy the sight of each other, one can die without knowing where the others live. They have no definite legal and social obligations to each other. Their economic relationships are limited to voluntary gift making or certain claims on assets left by the intestate dead. This is the only type of kinship system in which all sorts of public display of erotic expressions between lovers and spouses is encouraged, pictorialized, glorified as though they could be separated from physical sex, and played up so that they can almost stop traffic in the busiest thoroughfare.

While emphasis on the father-son axis leads naturally to the social importance of extended relationships along the male line and the formation of the clan, the emphasis on husband-wife axis cuts each married couple adrift to itself. The family starts with a man and a woman. They beget children and the family may be enlarged to a size of ten or even fifteen or more, but as the youngsters are married and move away, the family shrinks back to where it began. In contrast to the child in Type A, that in Type B grows up under the monolithic hands of the parents, usually the mother. Right and wrong, reward and punishment, tend to be absolute and clear cut. Before reaching majority children are the exclusive charges of the parents. Any interference in discipline of the child from any source (even grandparents) is resented unless the parents ask for it. At the same time the value of individual privacy leads the parents to foster in their children a childhood world of their own, divorced from that of their elders. The tendency is to make this childhood as simple as possible, as consistent as possible, as angelic as possible, so that the little ones will be free from frustration. Since parents tend not to divulge their own affairs to their children and since children's activities have little or no reference to the adult world (such as making a living), the youngsters are likely to be unaware of the inconsistencies in adult life, in which honor and dishonesty, triumph and tragedy may occur simultaneously or intermixed, sometimes without rhyme or reason. On the contrary, the children tend to be conditioned to a black or white picture of life, in which all good men are rewarded and all bad ones punished.

The kinship content most commensurate with the emphasis on husband-wife axis is individualism or self-reliance. Having to seek a mate on his or her own merits or demerits, and having to establish and nurture such a new relationship by cutting himself adrift from those who have been so dear and so close, the individual is conditioned to think in terms of the first person singular, here and now; his own rights, his own pleasures, and his own privacy; his own status, and his own chances for advancement or dangers of regression. For he is trained to regard the human world around him as impermanent. He has no inalienable place in the scheme of things except that scheme he himself initiates and constructs.

Here one must enter a note of caution about the use of the term "individualism." This term has been used so loosely to describe the pattern of behavior of many nonliterate societies (see, for example, Mead 1937) that it has lost all significance. Individualism is neither the same as individual differences nor as self-interest or egotism. Individual differences exist in all societies, as demonstrated by Gillin years ago (1939) and reiterated by Hart more recently (1954). Self-interest is never absent even among peoples who are said to value "giving for the sake of giving" (Hsu 1943), and self-interest can certainly vary in degree from society to society. But individualism is that conception of each human being as unique and as possessing God-given rights which cannot be taken away from him by men, society, or tradition. To express this uniqueness he must have freedom and, to safeguard his right, his due is equality. Individualism so defined was only initiated and exemplified by Occidental peoples of our Type B and was unknown among all other peoples before the impact of the West. Self-reliance is the American variety of individualism where it has reached its widest and most extreme expression so far (Hsu 1953).

The peculiarity of this kinship content is the primary emphasis given to the uniqueness of the individual rather than relationships between individuals, and to the likes and aspirations of the individual rather than the duties and obligations of one individual to another—for parents and children tend to be equal before the law and certainly before the supernatural. There is, therefore, an inherent tendency to conflict between the generations not known in other types of kinship systems. On the one hand parents view their children as their exclusive possession, since they are given unbridled authority to order the youngsters' lives. On the other hand, privacy and self-reliance keep parents and children apart even before the latter reaches majority in ownership of property, correspondence, relationship with friends, romance, and in the choice of life partners. Therefore, parents often find it hard to let their children go their own way as the youngsters advance in age, while children often find it necessary to reject their parents as the most important sign of maturity and independence. As a result the parent-child tie is not only terminated legally upon the youngster's reaching majority, it may be socially and psychologically broken long before.

Ancestor "worship," even when present, is never more than the mere pride in a distinguished genealogy and is never calculated to benefit the dead. In fact, death severs the relationship among men, for the spirits of the dead have no more interest in the living, while the living remember the dead only if there is individual affection. Clan is generally not an active organization, and wherever present, as in Scotland or Ireland today, of little more than nominal value.

General Characteristics

The emphasis on the uniqueness and independence of each individual cannot but encourage creativity (that is, change and deviation from the established norms) in general. Given a blackest black or whitest white pattern of approach, these cannot but cause those who desire change to champion their ends as absolute and with finality. Such individuals at once threaten those who do not see eye to eye with them and who are committed to other positions with equal absoluteness and finality.

There is an eternal struggle. Those who desire to change what has so far been held as true will be vehement about their intentions and often violent in their techniques. Others who think they have the truth already will inevitably feel compelled to defend themselves as vehemently and violently. Consequently, in this type of society, we obtain ultraconservatives and ultraradicals, arch-racists and arch-lovers-of-all-mankind, extreme isolationists and extreme one-worlders, each, being armed by the absolute truth, bent on a showdown with and complete conquest of the other. The net result is a type of society full of exuberance. It is characterized, on the one hand, by convulsions, purges, and revolutions, and, on the other, by initiative, emigration, science and technology, idealism, and new frontiers. Even without significant internal turmoil, the tendency of the individual in this type of society is centrifugal. Many of them cannot wait to move out to somewhere else or to move up the social or economic ladder. In any event, the desire to change may come about as a means of climbing the social ladder or be precipitated by the need to better the older generation or by the differences of opinion within the primary groups. And when there is significant failure in the natural resources, such as the failure of Irish potatoes in the late eighteenth century, or when there is a significant strife between those who entertain different beliefs, such as that which underlay the tensions between the early American pioneers and their other Anglican brethren, emigration tends to be on a large scale. Moses led the Jews out of Egypt, and the White Russians dispersed all over the world after 1917. It is interesting to note that even where there was still an unlimited frontier nearer to home, a considerable number of

Southerners moved from the United States to Brazil and elsewhere as a result of the Civil War.

When peoples from this type of society move to a new area, their intrinsic tendency is to set up a new society that is independent from their old. This tendency is founded on two factors. One is that, lacking permanent kinship ties, they will as a whole have little urge to return to their home society. Second, they are likely to be fired by an idealism that is not often present among peoples from societies of other types. Children who are raised apart from the vicissitudes of adult life tend to be freer with their imagination. But since the children are at the same time under the complete control of their parents, they are likely often to use their fantasy world as a reaction against the elders. Personal independence is often inextricably interwoven with the idea of doing something different. This was why all the independent immigrant republics were formed by Westerners, from Australia to the New World. Conversely, no Chinese immigrant groups in historical times and no Japanese colonizers in modern times have ever even suggested a separatist movement from their respective home countries (except for one Chinese group in Borneo for a few years). Under conquest, people of this type of society will tend to resist with violence either in open rebellion or in underground movement. Many of them would rather die than conform to the new rule. And the population is likely to be sharply divided between those who accommodate to the conquerors and those who do not. The ultimate result is likely to be either that the conquerors are overthrown by force or that the resistors are overcome and driven out by force. This does not mean that the ways of life of the conquerors or the conquered will not in the end become intermixed, but there will be persistent efforts to root out the suppressed elements.

They all have alphabetical languages of probably the same origin. Their written languages have changed from society to society and from period to period. Both of these changes tend to be much more pronounced than with the Oriental peoples belonging to Type A. The archaic form of Chinese writing found inscribed on oracle bones over 3,700 years ago has more in common with modern Chinese writing than does Latin with French or even Chaucerian English with modern English.

Part of the reason may, of course, be that the Indo-European written languages are phonemic while the Chinese written language is ideographic, but that is certainly not the whole story. As we noted earlier, the Japanese and Koreans are unwilling to give up the more inconvenient Chinese ideographs even after adoption of the alphabet. The conservatism of Japanese and Koreans with reference to their written languages is obviously based on other reasons than the relative ease with which their written languages can or cannot change.

Their literature is more voluminous than that found in the societies of Type A in spite of the fact that they came upon printing much later than the Chinese. Their literature is infinitely richer in the imaginative and emotional qualities than the Orientals or non-literate peoples, but not peoples of Type C such as the Hindus. Their art is great for the same reason. Since the uniqueness of the individual is best displayed in creativity, art for art's sake has developed to an extent unknown elsewhere. Their music is truly one of the greatest gifts bestowed upon mankind; even the great music of the Hindus and Indian Moslems cannot surpass it. They have developed harmony systematically and intensively; they have a wider variety of instruments, more precise instruments, and instruments which are able to cover a wider musical range than all other peoples except, perhaps, the Hindus. Unlike the peoples of Type A, they have much music that is played simply as music, not as accompaniment to some thematic plot or dance. With their urge to explore the unseen and the unknown, these peoples have advanced science both qualitatively and quantitatively to a height undreamed of by the rest of the world.

Central Government

These peoples tend to develop national states whether in modern or premodern times. These states tend to be either extremely authoritarian or pronouncedly democratic. In both forms, the rulers feel compelled to make personal appearances before the people for the purpose of solidarity, since the people, having no mooring in their primary groups, are always in search of wider circles of solidarity. The authoritarian rulers have to be guarded heavily, while the democratic ones have less need to be so. The techniques are somewhat different, but allegiance to the system as well as allegiance to the leader is important in both. Both types of government will be heavily organized and in both the primary relationships of man are of far less importance than either the impersonal law or the impersonal state. Universal military service and later universal education tend to be the rule and not the exception. In these and other ways, the state tends to enter into the private lives of the average individuals whether they like it or not. This type of society gives rise to modern nationalism which underlies its strong solidarity at given points of time, especially in the face of dangerous enemies, either human or natural. But in the long run, the organizations of such societies tend to be unstable or undergo rapid changes from time to time because they are subject constantly to attack from within, either by recognized opposition or by unrecognized foes, and to threat from without by other societies similarly constituted. This is, perhaps, one of the reasons why Europe was never united under one government, while large societies like China were marked by long periods of peace under one ruler interspersed only by short periods of interdynastic chaos.

Religion

The monolithic family constellation is concordant with a monotheistic view of the supernatural. Even before Christianity came into being, disputes over gods and efforts to suppress creeds other than those adhered to by the ruler were not unfamiliar in Rome and in the Middle East. We mentioned the fact that there is as a rule no ancestor worship. When and if more than one supernatural being is believed in, the tendency is for the ones other than God to be regarded as parts of God's expression, and prayer to them is only justified on the ground that they will intercede with God for the benefit of the believer. On the other hand, though believing in the same God, they will be irretrievably and continuously divided as to faith. The extent to which the church is divided tends to go hand in hand with the development of individualism. New sects and denominations will appear not only when there is a theological difference but even when no such differences exist. This greater tendency on the part of the freer branches of the church to subdivide is closely related to the sharper division among men under stronger individualism. Thus in Catholicism and Eastern Orthodoxy, prevalent in southern Europe, eastern Europe, and Latin America, the clerical hierarchy is important while in the Protestantism prevailing in northern Europe and North America, it becomes less important or of no consequence as far as the relationship of the worshipper and his God is concerned. Then, as we move from Catholicism to Protestantism the other-worldly punishment goes from being somewhat relative to irretrievable. In the Catholic purgatory the soul still has hope, since the good works of his kinsmen as well as his own devotion can raise him, but when the Protestants removed the belief in purgatory they severed all permanent relationships between the individual and his kin.

Lacking any permanent relationship among men, the individualist has to compensate it with attachment to some other objects: faith, creed, dogma, and so forth. He tends, therefore, to be hostile toward, or persecute, those who do not share his faith or his version of the fundamentally same faith. Since polytheists will not fight about or for their supernaturals, the monotheists will inevitably have their most trouble with other monotheists. They must missionize the nonbelievers as well as other monotheists, for the individualists must "advance" personally as a way to salvation or they will surely lag far behind or even be engulfed by the others. To buttress themselves they must have not only systematic theology but many techniques in organization and indoctrination. They need more and more interpretation and reinterpretation of the theology, but in spite of such theological erudition, the core of the dogma tends to remain unchanged and uncompromising, thus requiring more theology in turn.

Religious prejudice, ranging all the way from outright persecution, inquisition, and burning of heretics to occupational and social discrimination, is common. The religious wars of the world were practically all fought by monotheists. Even when religion is not the outstanding issue, the monotheists cannot but inject religious elements into any struggle that each group makes with another. While both parties in a combat may worship the same god, each will consider its own war a struggle of the good against the evil. An eternal struggle is inherent in monotheism. Their religious men may preach dependence upon God, but the worshippers usually waste no time in doing it themselves.

Impetus to Change

Over any period of time, this type of society tends to propel itself toward incessant change. There will be, as pointed out above, extreme conservatives and extreme radicals. But since those who do not wish to change do not hesitate to force a showdown with those who desire extremely to change, the result is usually a major or minor explosion. And when the remains of an explosion are gathered and reintegrated together, they are never the same as before. In any case, the average individual in this type of society is encouraged to show initiative or he will lose his self-respect. This is the psychological background of free enterprise as a way of life. This is the reason why associations of all descriptions, based on both abstract and concrete goals, are countless. This is the crucial force giving societies of this type a degree of internal impetus to change undreamed of by all other types.

In one sense, the technological development and changes are most noticeable and are usually described as being most characteristic of this type of society. But changes in other areas of life are no less colossal. Thus, in religion, this type of society has changed from early polytheism to Catholicism, and from Catholicism to Protestantism; or from polytheism to Mohammedanism and then branching out into such creeds as Bahaism. The family has changed from being extremely authoritarian in form through being equalitarian to that of America in which the family ties even between parents and children are based on ideals of friendship. There are drastic changes in laws, in the treatment of criminals, and so forth. Most prominent of all are the revolutions which are unique to this type of society. The revolutions, though primarily directed to a change in the form of government, always have had much wider effects, partly because Western forms of government affect the people's way of life much more than do the Oriental ones, and partly because each revolution is always based on some ideology which envisages a new society that it hopes to realize. Utopias are numerous and most of them very different in form from existing reality.

Such societies tend to be able to develop strong internal solidarity to withstand external pressure, military or cultural. But because of their strong solidarity and of the solidarity of those who hope to conquer or are opposed to them, the resulting conflagration and destruction are sometimes irreparable. In addition to the more severe nature of the explosion, many, perhaps most, individuals in this type of society tend to be brittle psychologically and lack elasticity to deal with ambiguity, having been trained in a kinship pattern to insist on all or none, black or white, completely right or completely wrong. They will be hilarious in their triumphs and extremely depressed in their failures. They may go on to greater achievements and greater glories, but they may also sicken at heart and die out, in the Toynbeean sense.

TYPE C SOCIETIES

Societies in this group include those of the Hindus in India and possibly the Moslems of this subcontinent as well.

Kinship

The center of the kinship structure of the Hindus is the joint family ideal like that in China and Japan. It is patrilineal, patrilocal, and generally patriarchal. It has a nominal clan (Gotra, etc.) that is mainly a negative means of regulating marriage, but is not organized as a whole and not based on blood (genetic) relationships.

In one respect the kinship pattern is similar to that in Type A. Children tend to live in the adult world and are actively initiated into adult roles as soon as they are physically and mentally capable of doing so without waiting for the official age of majority (Mandelbaum 1949 and Murphy 1953). But the most important structural relationship is that of mother-son. The mother-son axis distinguishes itself from both the father-son and husband-wife relationships by several attributes. Like the father-son axis but not the husband-wife axis it is inclusive. There is usually more than one son, and there is the perpetual desire on the part of the parents for more than one son. In the Orient and in India, high infant mortality is especially conducive to the usually conscious feeling that there is security in numbers. Unlike the father-son axis, but like the husband-wife axis, the mother-son relationship is discontinuous. No mother is a son and no son is a mother. A mother-son relationship is not, therefore, a link in a chain of a continuous mother-son line.

A third attribute of the mother-son relationship makes it totally dissimilar to both of the other axes. It is more one-sidely dependent, and more all-inclusively so, than either of the other two. An infant after birth is undifferentiated in its reaction to its surroundings, whether human, animal, or material. Watson, reporting the studies of Bridges, states that the emotional differentiations in the infant begin at about three weeks of age "when distress characterized by muscular tension, trembling, crying, and checked breathing can be distinguished from excitement" in general (Watson 1959:199–201). The mother-son relationship begins essentially with complete emotional and physical dependence on the part of the son upon the mother. As the infant grows in years he learns more and more to differentiate between persons, things, and ideas, as well as between different persons, different things, and different ideas. Paralleling with these processes the infant experiences another process: while external stimuli are undifferentiated, all things are translatable into all things. But with differentiation of them into categories, he finds that some categories are translatable, or more nearly so, into each other while others are absolutely immutable into each other. For example, a toy dog and a toy duck are far more easily translatable into each other, from the point of view of the child, while a toy dog and an actual dog are far less translatable into each other. For some time a toy dog and an actual dog may be the same to a child, but as he matures, he is going to perceive a greater immutability between inanimate and animate things. Similarly, as he grows in his power of perception he is likely to become aware of the differences between a toy dog and a toy duck even though this pair will remain more translatable into each other than the other pair. Later on baby sitters are usually translatable into each other. As the child is more used to one baby sitter than another, he may develop a higher degree of preference for one over the other, thus developing a feeling that some baby sitters are not translatable into others. But in the majority of cases, the younger the infant the more dependent he is upon his mother, since she is the answer to all his troubles and needs, and the more all categories of stimuli which come to him are translatable into each other (or undifferentiable).

In the father-son axis, the son does not come into close relationship with the father at first,[3] but is more likely to do so from one year of age or when he is weaned upon the birth of the next sibling. In the husband-wife axis, the son may come into close relationship with both parents at the same time, though his relationship with the mother is likely to be more intense at first. His possibly close contacts with both parents from the beginning of life may enable him to have from the start a greater experience of differentiated stimuli than in the case of the father-son axis. In the mother-son axis, since the son retains a close contact with the mother till he is much older than in the case of the father-son axis or the husband-wife axis, the individual is conditioned to retain more of the thought pattern of mutability between all categories of stimuli than would be the case in the other two types of kinship system.

The characteristic kinship content correlated with the emphasis on mother-son axis is what may be described as supernatural dependence. The most basic quality of the content of supernatural dependence is that, instead of solving life's problems by self-reliance, external safeguards and conquests as in Type B, and instead of looking to mutual dependence with other human beings as in the case with Type A, the individual is encouraged to seek supernatural help

---

[3] The picture may be different in societies where the custom of *convade* prevails. But what is said here certainly applies to the Type A peoples specified in this chapter.

either by passivity or by active elaboration of rituals to control or at least influence the gods. Passivity often leads to reduction and even the elimination of many or all of the individual's desires and wants. (Popularly this pattern has been associated with Buddhism. What is less well known is that Buddhism is merely a protestant movement of Hinduism and that self-negation has always been part of the essence of traditional Hinduism as well.)

The importance of the mother-son axis is not rooted in the cultural design. It is not the traditional ideal. Wherever mentioned in the scriptures, the father-son and mother-son relationships are given nearly equal importance, with a slight edge in favor of the former. However, the actual pattern of life in the Hindu kinship system is such as to produce the unintended effect of increasing the importance of the mother-son axis and of decreasing the importance of the father-son axis.

The Hindu culture, even more so than the cultures in Type A, is male-oriented. For example, where the Hindu scriptures and ritual practices are concerned, the males are the primary beneficiaries or sufferers. Females are mentioned sometimes. They may suffer in the other world as a result of certain things; but if and when they benefit somewhere, such benefit primarily comes through men. Otherwise they seem to have the role of accumulating spiritual merits for men. They observe fasting days for their husbands and sons; they practice austerities so that their deceased husbands can fare better in the nether world; and they jump on their husband's funeral pyres so that all members of their husband's families in many generations can go up to heaven. They have no part in the major rituals of any worship. They cannot wear the sacred thread except in a modified form among smaller protestant sects such as the Lingayats.

The clearest statement of the male-centered nature of Hindu culture is to be found in the four stages (ashramas) of life which every individual should *ideally* pass through: brahmacharya (studentship), grhastha (life of a married man), vanaprastha (life of disinterested hermit, in which familial ties and social relations are renounced) and samnyasa (life of the ascetic). I am not aware of any Hindu scripture or even its modern expositions which attempts to apply this or any similar scheme to women. It is simply designed for men.

Despite the male-centered nature of Hindu kinship and culture, the mother-son axis exerts far greater influences on the Hindu individual for a variety of reasons. In the first place, the Hindu household is one in which adult males and females are much more segregated from each other than in Type A and Type B societies. The higher the caste and the socioeconomic status, the closer the family tends to approximate complete segregation. Male children, before puberty or adolescence, tend, therefore, to be under the protective and guiding hands more of females such as mothers and grandmothers than of males such as fathers and grandfathers. This seems not only to be true of individuals like Indrasingh, who grew up in his mother's village because his father passed away when he was fifteen months old, as reported by Gitel Steed (1950 and 1955) but also of numerous other men, in general as reported by G. Morris Carstairs (1957).

> Although it is particularly through his participation in the adult male world of caste and family discussion that a child receives the imprint of his community's values, the process has begun even before this, during his earliest years when he spent more time in the women's side of the household than in the men's. Brahmans commonly mentioned that it was their mother, or their grandmother, who first impressed upon them the need to bathe if they touched a low-caste person, until the response became second nature to them. It is women, also who give a boy his early toilet training. . . . From his mother and his substitute mothers, a boy also learns how and what to eat, how to dress, what constitutes good manners and what is to be avoided as indecent or shameful.
>
> From his mother, grandmothers and aunts a child learns the concrete details of religious observance at all the multitude of holy days in the calendar. . . . A part of the experience of every child in Deali is to be taken by his mother to a bhopa when he is sick. . . .
>
> The child's sources of verbal instruction can now be viewed as a series of concentric circles, the innermost representing the women's world; then that of the extended family in which his father, if he himself is a younger son, may seem to play a minor part. (Carstairs 1957:148–149).

In the second place, the relationship between Hindu fathers and their sons is less close than that between their Oriental or Occidental counterparts. Mrs. Murphy observes in her chapter on "Roots of Tolerance and Tensions in Indian Child Development" that Hindu children "are carried easily, first in cradled arms which do not grasp them possessively . . . later they straddle a hip of a sister or a brother, father or mother, balancing comfortably" (Murphy 1953:49). In different parts of India, from Punjab to Cape Comorin, Bengal to U.P., a child may be carried in this way most frequently by a mother, or sister, less frequently by a young brother, but rarely by a father. I think part of the reason is the Hindu male's strong aversion against pollution by the bodily functions of infants and children. But another part of the reason is that the Hindu fathers are also likely to be more preoccupied with some aspect of the ritual activities, such as pilgrimage, designed to bring them closer to their deities or the Truth.

It is not implied that all Hindus live strictly according to the injunctions of the ancient scriptures, any more than all Americans live strictly according to the spirit of the Declaration of Independence and the Christian concept of universal love or turning the other cheek. But many Americans have undoubtedly been motivated by the high principles which form part of their heritage. Likewise, it is among Hindus, and not among Japanese, Chinese, or Germans, that we find hundreds of thousands of devout human beings carrying out various forms of asceticism or doing penance up the Himalayas and other centers of pilgrimage; and we find also the great popularity of such leaders as Gandhi with his supernatural-centered philosophy and ascetic practices. Furthermore, Hindu children in their home environments are taught much more about the importance of the great ultimate than the children in other societies (Mukerji 1923 and Chaudhuri 1953). Therefore, even though many Hindu fathers do not leave their homes to become hermits and ascetics as they grow older, most of them cannot but in many ways be affected by or attracted to their religious ideal and practices especially away from home.

It is a well-known fact that, even without the Hindu's supernatural orientation, older individuals in any culture tend to gravitate more toward religion than younger ones. As the Hindu ages, he is more likely to devote much time and attention to pilgrimages and, if he can read, scriptures. Furthermore, my personal observation and Dr. Steed's show it is not at all necessary to be aged for the Hindu to turn to seclusion and gods. Indrasingh, whom we have met in a previous paragraph, a man 26 years old with two wives but no children, turned from opium smoking, one form of institutionalized retreat, to "goddess-worship which will change a man's present and future." Yet, "by other members of Kasandra society, Indrasingh's reactions were not regarded as socially deviant." (Steed 1955:141–143). I have seen again and again where men with children conducted themselves in a way quite similar to what Indrasingh did.

Whatever the cause, the lack of close relationship between the Hindu father and son is also documented by other students. (See Carstairs 1957:67–70). Dube's description of a Hyderabad village confirms Carstairs' findings except that it is more cursory (Dube 1955:148–150).

One other fact is worth noting. While the father-son relationship in Type A societies is, as in the Hindu scene, also marked by greater formality than the mother-son relationship, it is far more continuous in nature than the latter. The Hindu father-son relationship does not seem to go much beyond life since ancestor worship is of no great importance. The over-all tendency of the people is to look to the ultimate station of reaching oneness with the universe through religious devotion rather than the maintenance of entities of individual ancestors and lineages. Thus, while each father-son axis in the Chinese kinship system is one link in a perpetual line of ancestors and descendants fortified by an organized clan, the Hindu father-son relationship has no such significance and is not so fortified. The Hindus tend to keep no genealogical records except in Rajasthan and, as we noted earlier, have no organized clan (Hsu 1961), though the recognized circles of relatives are greater than in Type B. At the same time the absence of individualism does not encourage the Hindu children to any great desire for independence from their parents which, under the circumstances, means their mothers more than their fathers. Hindu mothers, in contrast to American mothers, do not have to worry about resentment on the part of their grown sons, because Hindu sons, in contrast to American sons, do not have to regard acceptance of their mothers' affection and control as signs of immaturity or weakness. The result is a closer mother-son tie than is found in either of the other two types of kinship systems analyzed before.

It is, of course, difficult to determine whether the kinship content of supernatural-dependence or the structural elevation of mother-son relationship came first. That is not a scientifically profitable question to be dealt with. But given the cultural tradition of supernatural-dependence, the influence of mother-son relationship generates the appropriate psychological material in the individual for it. Ramakrishna, the greatest Hindu saint in modern times, asked: "Why does the God lover find such pleasure in addressing the deity as Mother?"

And he answered himself: "Because the child is more free with its mother, and consequently she is dearer to the child than anyone else." (Muller 1898: No. 89).

Sister Nivedita, one of Ramakrishna's European disciples, nee M. E. Noble, who was a pillar of the Vedanta movement after the death of the master, experienced the following episode and sentiment:

Shortly after her arrival in Calcutta, she heard a cry in a quiet lane. Following her ears, she traced it to a little Hindu girl who lay in her mother's arms dying. The end came soon, and for a while the mother wept inconsolably. After a while she fell back into Sister Nivedita's arms and turning to her said: "Oh, what shall I do? Where is my child now?" "I have always regarded that as the moment when I found the key," says Sister Nivedita. "Filled with a sudden pity, not so much for the bereaved woman as for those to whom the use of some particular language of the Infinite is a question of morality, I leaned forward. 'Hush, mother,' I said, 'Your child is with the Great Mother. She is with Kali.' And for a moment, with memory stilled, we were enfolded together, Eastern and Western, in the unfathomable depth of consolation of the World Heart." (Nivedita 1904:17ff.)

These narrations, given by Ernest A. Payne in his book on *The Saktas* (1933:128–129) as evidence for the psychological foundation of Mother Goddess worship are, from what we know of child development today, actually at the psychological root of all religions, whether the deities in question are male or female. Undoubtedly Mother Goddess worship is one of the most prevalent forms of worship in India, but there is no need to restrict our consideration to it. The complete dependence of the child upon the mother is a universal human fact. To the child, the mother is the magical source of all power, gratification, and punishment. This is the psychology that makes the widespread appeal of the creation story in Genesis or other forms possible. In Type A societies this mother dependence is soon tempered by the authority of the father and later altered by the individual's integration into a network of human relationships, with specific duties, responsibilities, and privileges with reference to ascendants including deceased ancestors and descendants both born and unborn. The adult individual's place in the scheme of things is measured by concrete points of reference, and no longer submerged under the unexplainable power of the mother. In Type B societies growing up means independence not only from the mother but also from the father, self-reliance in food and sex quest, and ability to make decisions and bear consequences. It is not surprising to find that Type A peoples are close only to their ancestral spirits and make offerings to other gods primarily for ulterior motives, while Type B peoples believe that God only helps him who helps himself.

The mother-dependence relationship of Type C peoples generates the psychological material which feeds a cultural orientation of supernatural dependence, continued and elaborated generation after generation. The difference between supernatural dependence and self-reliance is obvious, but the difference between supernatural dependence and mutual dependence is equally significant. For one thing, in contrast to mutual dependence, it is one-sided. The worshipper-dependent expects much more from the gods than they give to the gods, just as the child does with the mother. For another thing it is all demanding and, therefore, the objective realities tend to be less differentiated and more mutable. The worshipper-dependent expects simple boons to solve all problems however difficult, just as the child demands of his mother. And finally, unlike mutual dependence, it is loaded with diffuse sexuality. Type A peoples relegate sex into a few social compartments and see sex as having no relevance to their relationship with the supernatural. Type B peoples repress sex so that they must have a God-child who is born without sex. Type C peoples neither relegate sex into separate compartments nor eradicate it. As a whole, they approach the supernatural through sexuality, an element which is at times blatant, and at other times thinly veiled, but at all times more or less present. When demands or supplication fails, the strongest step on the part of the worshipper-dependent is extreme passivity, fasting, abstention, and other forms of austerity, just as many a child can, or thinks he can, bring his mother to her knees by refusing to eat or to get up. The Hindu approach to the supernatural, from complicated ritualism to extreme forms of Samadhi, will be touched on below. The Hindu way in penance and austerity to achieve power has been made famous by Gandhi in India's long history of struggle against British colonialism, but also by the martyrs and would-be martyrs in many an internal struggle (for example, the struggle for linguistic states) since Independence.

General Characteristics

There will be more emigration from this type of society than from those of Type A because the people will not only be propelled by hunger, but also motivated by pilgrimage. However, Type C peoples disperse less easily than Type B because the Hindu society has no inherent tendency to explosion as has its Western counterparts. When peoples from this type of society move to a new area, they tend not to set up a new society that is completely independent from their old. On the other hand, there is also no such great urge as exhibited by the Chinese and the Japanese to return to their homeland for retirement or death. Under conquest peoples in this type of society tend to act like those of Type A, except that, because of the centrifugal tendencies inherent in their supernatural orientation, the conquerors will find them more difficult to administer than Type A peoples.

At home they will show more dissatisfaction with the status quo than the Chinese or Japanese, and will be more vociferous about their dissatisfaction. Most religions embody contradictions, but the Hindus see little or no necessity to reconcile highly obvious incongruities in their religious beliefs as well as in their secular life which is governed by religion. Hence, historical changes in their society due to internal impetus are as insignificant as among Type A peoples.

Their art and literature tends to be richer than that of China or Japan in the imaginative and emotive qualities, but poorer than those of the Occidental societies in the logical and rationalistic qualities. Their music is neither Oriental nor Occidental, being based on the most refined and complicated rhythmic patterns and tonal elaborations the world has ever seen. Unlike the Chinese music, all Hindu music, like Hindu art and literature, is religious. In science the Hindus made more theoretical contributions than the Chinese or Japanese, but the volume is not great and the practical application of it is insignificant.

Central Government

These peoples tend to develop multiple national states. In essence, the states are not authoritarian or democratic as in the West, but are essentially autocratic as among Type A peoples. Political and other relationships are secured either by exaggerated external signs of differentiation between those who are in power or superior and those who are not or inferior (caste is an example), or on the basis of brutal power (conquest) or by supernatural qualities (austerity). The rule of man in the name of the supernatural overshadows the impersonal laws on the state. Universal education and universal military service were unknown before contact with the West, but there tends to be more direct interaction between the ruler and the people than in Type A societies. The discontinuity of the primary grouping and the supernatural orientation propel the individual toward wider alliances. Therefore, political leaders in India can exert a greater active influence over their followers than can their counterparts in Type A societies. In spite of and probably also because of this, the stability of the central authority is always in question. The diffused outlook and the many diverse issues, objects and personalities enjoying great separate public enthusiasms tend to make large and tight organization difficult. Hence, their written languages tend to change much more in time and space than do those of their Chinese or Japanese counterpart.

Religion

Since they are supernatural-oriented and diffused in their efforts in seeking help, their gods multiply much more freely than in Type A societies. The Hindus have more gods than any other known people on earth. Yet, there is also an opposite tendency to view the multitude of gods as diverse expressions or part and parcel of the same Supreme Being.

Hindus, more than the Chinese and Japanese, are occasionally divided somewhat in religion. There is, however, no irreconcilable schism among the believers. In fact, even those who call themselves Vaishnavats (worshippers of Vishnu) or Saivats (worshippers of Shiva) tend not to neglect, and certainly not to be contemptuous toward, the other gods.

Theology is more important than in Type A societies but much less important than in Type B. The central dogma is obscure. Where clarified, it comes to no more than the negative ideas of "action with nonattachment," or extreme "devotional love." Theological literature increases largely through the increase of rituals and to a lesser extent through protestant movements. But religious truths tend to be relative, so that the elites and the common men are understood to possess different grades of knowledge about God and different experiences with Him, which are considered equally valid. There will be far more reform or protestant movements in Hinduism than in the religion of the Chinese and the Japanese, but such protestant movements do not seem to succeed in really dividing the believers. This is why the remnants of Buddhism in India were merely absorbed by Hinduism instead of existing as a rival creed. Jainism, Sikkhism, and so forth remained in India but have become caste groups in the same Hindu fold. Contrary to popular misconception, riots between the Hindus and Moslems are of post-British origin and very recent. It is a well-known fact that Hindus and Moslems lived and still live peacefully in close proximity in the villages (Murphy 1953). The Hindus are probably as difficult to convert to any monotheistic belief as peoples of Type A, except for specific reasons of social and economic improvement. One of the basic reasons for Hindu conversion to Mohammedanism was the lowly position of the untouchables who hoped to better themselves.

Over and above these general characteristics, the Hindu approach to religion, like those of the Chinese and the Westerners, reflects even more clearly the basic content in the Hindu kinship system. The Type A peoples, with their father-son axis and their permanent web of vertical and horizontal kinship relationships, need their gods and goddesses for functional and utilitarian purposes. They cannot get excited about their supernaturals unless the latter can satisfy their materialistic requests. Type B peoples with their husband-wife axis and their impermanent human relationships in the long run need their gods to be masculine, stern, single minded, and exclusive, though this stress on masculinity applies more to Western Protestants than Western Catholics.

The gods of Type C peoples, though represented bisexually, are basically more feminine than masculine. No other people worship as many female deities as the Hindus. Not only did recent popular revolutionary writers like Bankim Chandra Chatterjee sing of India's aspirations to Mother and not only do modern Indians refer to Bharat Mata (Mother India), but also the mother goddess in the form of Kali, Durga, Radha, Sita, Parvati, Chumundeshvari, or the wife of Ramakrishna, founder of the modern Protestant movement bearing his name, is worshipped in every part of India. Moreover, in Indian popular mythology the gods sometimes change themselves into females for sexual purposes.

One famous tale concerns Vishnu and Siva, who were so intoxicated by the scenery they saw together that Vishnu changed himself into a female so that the two could have a sexual union on the spot to enjoy themselves. Today, there are temples in West and South India in which are worshipped gods each representing half of one and half of the other sex. Finally, the Hindu devotee's approach to the supernatural is predominantly what, for want of a better term, may be described as "feminine."

I am aware that Margaret Mead in her classic work on *Sex and Temperament* has stressed the notion that cross-culturally, psychological characteristics are not peculiar to either sex. Whether we call the Hindu devotee's approach "feminine" or not is immaterial. What is relevant is that this approach is characterized by traits which traditionally in the West have been subsumed under the term "femininity." I mention this term here to help me clarify my position on the subject. Like other people the Hindus resort to all sorts of rituals to coerce or channelize many gods and spirits according to their wishes, but one age-old and most widespread

Hindu approach to the supernatural is austerity (fasting, abstention, suffering, and so forth) to get what one wants. This method is so frequently used in Indian mythology, history, and contemporary belief, not only by men to coerce gods, but also by one god to coerce other gods, that it is sheer redundancy to mention it more than in passing.

The more modern version of the same approach is represented by the Bhakti movement begun by Chaitanya of Bengal about 250 years ago, the central theme of which is to love God (the Lord Krishna) as though the worshipper is the God's illicit sweetheart (Radha). In South India an outstanding devotee using this approach would be Kshetranja, the composer and performer of God-love songs and dances. Foreign visitors and observers have often been shocked by the proliferation of sexual representation in Hindu temples that they read in it much that is profane but nonexistent. Some Hindus, scholars and others, have understandably been defensive about this by trying to explain the sexual elements away from them altogether. The truth of the matter is that the Hindu approach to the supernatural is sexual only in the Freudian sense. For every major Hindu deity has one or more consorts, both of whom are worshipped by males and females. Even the temple Lingam is not a static symbol: it is often described as representing the male and female organs in active sexual congress. What we can say is that the Hindu attitude is characterized by passivity, submissiveness, diffused eroticism which, if not feminine in character, is certainly different from that found among Type A and Type B peoples.

Prejudice

The structural characteristics of exclusiveness and discontinuity of Type B seem to be related to the greatest exhibition of prejudice, in contrast to those of inclusiveness and continuity in the kinship system of Type A, which seem to be related to the least exhibition of prejudice. This contrast has been more fully dealt with in a previous chapter (Chapter 7, American Core Values and National Character). The Hindu kinship system, being dominated by the mother-son axis, occupies in this regard an intermediary position. It is more inclusive than that of type B but less so than that of type A; it is more continuous than that of type B but less so than that of type A. This would seem to be connected with the fact that prejudice, though strongly present in the form of caste, untouchability, and Hindu-Moslem riot, is without finality. That is to say, there are obvious and above-board mechanisms for crossing the caste lines or for raising the statuses of entire castes. For example, even the extremists in casteism accept the premise that the lower castes and higher castes are one in the reincarnation scheme. Then, the caste of meritorious individuals had often been changed by edicts of kings and princes. Finally, the place of entire low castes, such as the Reddy of Andbra and Kayastha of Bengal, were raised by reason of their numbers or occupation. The entire question of caste in India is treated in a separate publication (Hsu 1961) and need not be detailed here. There is some witchhunting in Type C societies but it is moderate, like that in nonliterate societies of Type D.*

Impetus to Change

To the extent that there is more internal dissatisfaction with the status quo in such societies than in Types A and D, there should have been more internal tendency toward change. But this pressure for change is greatly undercut by the diffuseness of its direction and objectives. Over a long period of time, there tend to be changes in appearance but not in substance. This is probably a partial explanation for the fact that of all the large status-oriented societies of the East and West, only India built up a caste system, the numerous princely states, and the highly differentiated nature of the endogamic circles within each caste. The Hindu caste system is an accommodation between the two opposites: change and no change (Hsu 1961). There have always been many centrifugal tendencies but there have never been any revolutions and/or utopias which aimed at achieving a new way of life on this earth. These types of societies are less likely to die out than the Western variety, either from loss of resources or from external conquest. The peoples of this type of societies have a similar ability to endure suffering as those of Type A, even though they may appear more unhappy about it because of their tendency to voice their dissatisfaction with the status quo. The peoples in this type of societies are somewhat more likely to take to changes than their brethren in Type A, once they are under the pressure of, and given direction by, the West, though the permanency of the new changes is questionable.

TYPE D SOCIETIES

In type D societies are to be found the majority of the Africans south of the Sahara.

* The complex psycho-cultural basis of caste in India is treated intensively in my forthcoming book, *Clan, Caste and Club, a Comparative Study of Chinese, Hindu and American Ways of Life* (Princeton, N.J.: D. Van Nostrand Co., Inc., in press).

Kinship

The kinship structures are varied and the basic unit in which the infant finds himself may be large or small. There is no ideal of individualism or supernatural dependence as a road to personal salvation. The structural element in systems of kinship which seems to have a great deal of dominance over others is brother-brother axis, across lines of descent, inheritance, and succession. Their kinship content may be described as fraternal equivalence.

Similar to the father-son and mother-son axes, brother-brother relationship is inclusive. But similar to the husband-wife and mother-son axes, it is discontinuous. There is always more than one brother, but the brothers of each generation have no intrinsic relationship with the brothers of another generation. To the extent that the individual tends to be oriented little toward the past and the future but much toward the present, the brother-brother axis is similar to the husband-wife axis. And to the extent that the individual is conditioned to be mutually dependent among the peers, the brother-brother axis is similar to the father-son axis. But the feature which distinguishes the brother-brother relationship from all other axes, including the husband-wife axis, is its inherent competitiveness. Where there is acknowledged unequalness between the parties of a relationship, there is little potential source of competitiveness. This is the situation of the father-son and mother-son axes. The father and the son or the mother and the son are not equal. In the husband-wife axis the relationship may be equal in conception but never really equal in reality, for men and women are different and they are bound to perform different roles, however such differences are minimized by other factors. The brother-brother axis is one in which the parties to the relationship are more equal and more similar than the parties to any of the other three axes and, therefore, more competitive with each other.

The kinship content correlated with the brother-brother relationship is fraternal equivalence. But before I go into the characteristics of fraternal equivalence I must enter a word of caution for my readers.

In the analysis of the African situation I am on far less certain ground than in what has gone before. My views on the previous systems are based on my own field observations as well as extensive acquaintance with works of my colleagues. I have had no field experience in Africa, having visited parts of it for only short periods of time; and my acquaintance with anthropological works on Africa is far more limited. Nevertheless, what I have read so far has emboldened me to make this exploration, following the same trend of analysis which I have pursued so far, and to hope that the results will stimulate further works in this direction.

In analyzing Types A, B and C peoples, I have first examined the characteristics of a particular structural relationship which dominates the kinship system; then proceeded to relate those characteristics to the kinship content; and finally extended the latter characteristics to the attitudes and ideas underlying the wider culture as a whole. In analyzing Africa I shall reverse the first two, by discussing first content of the kinship system and then stating my case for expecting the dominance of the particular structural relationship in question.

Like Type A and C societies, Type D peoples raise their children to enter into adult worlds as soon as they are physically and mentally capable of doing so. They do not attribute great value to individual privacy. These two facts favor a community of interest between the generations. But in spite of such resemblances to Type A societies, the kinship content is one in which the ties between generations are overshadowed by those between males of the same generation.

First, the claims to dependence between parents and their children seem to require constant reiteration or open gestures to meet with satisfaction. The fear against overclaim and against nonfulfillment of expected claims is indicated by the almost universal belief in sorcery or witchcraft among close family members, especially between parents and children (between mother's brother and sister's son in matrilineal systems), and between other individuals, who are related as seniors and juniors, but almost none between brothers and others, who are related as equals.

Secondly, though some African societies—Dahomey, Yoruba, many Bantu tribes, and others—maintain rites designed to deal with the dead, they and their ancestral spirits do not have unquestioned reliance upon one another. The living may regard the dead as possible sources of benevolence but more constantly suspect them as possible sources of harm; while the dead always enforce their demand on the living for sacrifices and offerings by means of disasters such as epidemics and personal accidents imposed on their descendants.

Thirdly, in many instances the African word translated into

English as ancestors simply means spirit or god. In most cases there is a tendency for ancestral spirits to lose their identity and connection with their own descendants, so that ancestral spirits are simply one of the several mechanisms (equally important) for human beings to reach the supernatural, or the connection with the past is simply a means for vindicating the status of the present.

Fourthly, strong age-grading customs prevail in most parts of Africa except among people like Dahomean and Bantu of North Kavirondo (Wagner 1949) so that the youngsters, after reaching a certain age, leave their parental houses for their own separate quarters and/or by the well-known phenomenon of secret societies in which members maintain strong bonds outside of kinship. The children may or may not be directly dependent upon initiatory rites, but such rites are undoubtedly as important in Africa as they are insignificant in Asia. The relationship among the youngsters so separated from their parents may range from that of intimate friends, such as the "best friend" institution in Dahomey (Herskovits 1938a), to what has been described as a kind of "Communist" order such as found among the Umbundu (Childs 1949:114–115).[4]

Fifth, although parents and other elders can exercise an authoritative hand over members of the younger generation, the latter seem to exhibit much more independence of thought and action than in Type A societies. In some African societies the pattern is even described as "respect" for the personality of the children (Childs 1949:120–121). In practically all known African societies the young tend to have to work for the establishment of their own homes and their own marriages, as well as to exercise rather decisive influences over the choice of their own spouses. In addition there is much evidence indicating a linkage in the marriage payments and obligations between brothers and sisters (Radcliffe-Brown 1950: 52–53).

Sixth, while the institution of blood-brotherhood (that is, a group of unrelated men usually of similar age swearing themselves into a brotherhood by rites involving letting or exchanging of blood) is found sporadically in diverse parts of the world including Europe and Asia, its prevalence in Africa south of the Sahara and outside of Ethiopia is well known. It is said that a blood brother is a

---

[4] In a comprehensive treatise on age groups all over the world Eisenstadt's examples from the "Primitive" and "Semihistorical" societies are all taken from Africa (over 40 tribes and groups of tribes) except for ancient Sparta, five of the Plain Indian groups in North America, Irish peasants, some tribes in India, and some vague allusions to ancient Inca and Aztec empires (Eisenstadt 1956).

"much better friend than a real brother" (Tegnaeus 1952:13ff.).

Finally, while the problem of royal succession is nowhere on earth near a perfect solution, it seems to assume extraordinary proportions in many parts of Africa. Tor Irstam of the Ethnographical Museum of Sweden has made a study of the sacral kingship in Africa in which he surveys many traits (he calls them "institutions") connected with the coronation, life, and death of the king in 103 tribes from existing ethnographic reports. Four of the traits are particularly relevant to the question of succession: (1) "The announcement of the king's death was followed by a period of anarchy"; (2) "the king's death was kept secret for a certain time"; (3) "the king's brothers were killed"; and (4) the king was challenged to a "ritual combat" (Irstam 1944:78–166).

We have, of course, to exercise much caution in ascertaining the meanings given to each fact by the particular people among whom it occurs. Thus, among the Ganda the king's ritual combat sometimes led to actual fighting which was "continued until only one of the rival princes was left alive," but among the Nyoro, as far as the ethnographer was able to determine, "only actual fighting for the throne occurred" (Irstam 1944:62). Again, the custom of the newly crowned king going into a certain period of solitude was practiced "to avoid his brothers' envy and conspiring" but the same sentiment was not reported for the other tribes with a similar custom. For this reason, this last-mentioned usage is not included in our list of traits considered as supporting our contention that the problem of royal succession seems extraordinary, and the magnitude of this problem is related to the importance of the kinship content of fraternal equivalence which undermines the vertical continuity.

From Irstam's study we have 62 tribes (or over 60 per cent of his total) in which at least one of the four traits or customs indicating succession difficulties was found. Trait No. 2 ("The king's death was kept secret for a certain time") was found among the largest number of tribes (32). Trait No. 1 ("The announcement of the king's death was followed by a period of anarchy") was found among the second largest number of tribes (19). The other two traits are found among 7 (Trait No. 3) and 10 (Trait No. 4) tribes, respectively. From the logical point of view the four traits are obviously interrelated. The fraternal contention for the throne will lead to suppression of the news of the King's death, which when released leads to a period of anarchy, and for both of which the killing of the king's brothers seems to be a reasonable solution. The ritual combat to which the king is challenged could be considered a formalized version of the actual fight which frequently occurs among the contenders.

A tabulation of the occurrence of these traits shows a high degree of correlation among them and indeed supports this thesis. The correlation is less pronounced between Trait No. 2 and others (out of 51, 19 are correlated with one or more other traits) than between Trait No. 1 and others (out of 19, 17 are so correlated). (See the accompanying table.)

DISTRIBUTION OF TRAITS AMONG TRIBES *

Trait or Trait Combination	Tribe	Total Number of Tribes in Category
No. 1	Kabinda, Ha	2
Nos. 1 & 2	Dahomey, Konde, Kuba, Luba, Lunda, Mbundu, Nyamwezi, Pare, Shambala	9
Nos. 1 & 3	Wydah (Wadai) (?)	1
Nos. 1, 2 & 3	Abyssinia	1
Nos. 1, 2, & 4 . . .	Congo, Loango, Ruanda, Shilluk	4
Nos. 1, 2, 3 & 4 . .	Ganda, Nyoro	2
No. 2	Ashante, Bena, Camba, Comendi, Daka, Djaga, Gbande, Gissi, Gogo, Hona, Igara, Yoruba, Jukun, Kam, Kanakuru, Kimbu, Konongo, Kpelle, Mbum, Ngoni, Safwa, Sango, Saramo, Shona, Soga, Sove, Temne, Tikai, Toma, Vende, Zeguha, Zulu	32
Nos. 2 & 3	Kaffitsho	1
Nos. 2 & 4	Tonga, Nkole	2
No. 3	Limmu, Koki, Benin	3
Nos. 3 & 4	Rundi	1
No. 4	Umundri, Mossi, Ziba, Toro	4
	Total	62

* Greater statistical sophistication is not attempted at this stage of the analysis. This will be done in a later paper when more precise data may be obtained from the literature and field work.

It is on the basis of the foregoing facts that I expect the dominance of the brother-brother relationship in a majority of African kinship structures over other relationships. I frankly admit that I have as yet insufficient direct data except in a few African societies, such as the Nyakyusa age-set villages as reported by Monica Wilson (Radcliffe-Brown and Forde [ed.] 1950:111–138). However, I feel strongly that if future students of African tribes will explore this hypothesis, their chances of being rewarded are likely to be good. Furthermore, the theory of tribal and lineage segmentation developed by Africanists like Evans-Pritchard and Fortes in which the peoples are said to live in "ordered anarchy" (Evans-Pritchard 1940b:181) and in which corresponding segments oppose each other, suggests that horizontal or fraternal solidarity and opposition are actually far more important in African kinship system than are parent-child and other relationships.

General Characteristics

In contrast to Type B societies the individual here will have less urge to leave home because there is no need to prove his worth elsewhere. But in contrast to Type A societies the individual here will also be more easily forced to do so by nature (population pressure, epidemics, and so forth), or by human enemies (war, conquest, and so forth), because of lack of strong anchorage with the past. The kinship content of fraternal equivalence makes possible larger expansion of human relationships than in Type A. That is to say, whereas in Type A societies the individual is encouraged to think lineally and to regard himself as a link in an endless chain connecting the past with the future, in Type D societies he is encouraged to think horizontally and to gravitate toward contemporaries far and near. Therefore, once forced to move they tend to be more ready than Type A peoples to give up much of the past and make *new* adjustments on *new* bases. Some of them, like the Masai, might resist innovation in their modes of livelihood but some have gone from dry cultivation of rice to wet cultivation of rice (Linton 1939). Others might start with a well-defined monarchial system and disintegrate into a context of contending nobles, none of whom has any central authority (Evans-Pritchard 1940a:51–61). In Southern Rhodesia, there are ruins of one or more rock cultures of perhaps only 1,500 or 1,000 years ago, or less which are probably ancestral to the cultures of some of the modern Bantu groups (such as Ba Vanda) but with which the latter today claim no psychocultural affiliation (Caton-Thompson 1931). On the other hand, in the nonliterate world, Africa is one of the continents where trade contacts, team work, and group dances (ritual and otherwise) were most extensive and impressive. The magnitude of their messianic-movements against conquest and oppression, within or without the Christian Church, in Africa or in the New World (Herskovits 1938b), is without parallel among other peoples in similar circumstances.

Compared with Type A peoples, they have less determination to resist external cultural pressures or to absorb the invaders and to restore their past glory; but compared with other nonliterate peoples they are much more indomitable because of their tendency to group themselves horizontally. They do not easily give up the struggle for political independence. However, their fraternal solidarity is undermined by much opposition which some psycho-analysts could easily designate as a sort of "sibling" rivalry. The Type B peoples form many effective nonkinship groups to revolt against the past. Type A peoples form few effective nonkinship groups because they have solidarity with the past. But the most important attributes of Type D peoples' kinship content is rooted in the fact that the brother-brother relationship is discontinuous with both past and future at the same time that it is internally competitive. The difficulties of the horizontal groupings of Type D peoples are due, outside of foreign domination, primarily to the fact that they are their own worst enemies.

As a rule they have no written languages even though they must have at one time or another come into contact with either the Egyptian hieroglyphics or the Indo-European alphabets. My inference is that the assumption of a written language, even though its elements may have been borrowed, as were those of a majority of mankind who have written languages, depends upon a strong need for a wide circle of communication and for a permanent preservation of the relationships with the past, and requires a concerted and continuous group exertion. Most peoples of Type D obviously did not feel the need and were not willing or prepared to make the necessary efforts.

Central Government

Though some of these peoples have developed centralized national states, or at any rate some forms of externally recognized chieftainship, the political domains are not likely to reach the extent of some of those found among Types A or B, nor are they likely to be as stable. We have already related the succession difficulties of African chieftainship. A reverse support for this thesis is seen in the degree of correlation in Africa between more centralized political organizations under autocratic kings or chiefs, and a somewhat more well-defined ancestor cult in Africa. A preliminary survey, without meaning to be exhaustive, shows the correlation to hold in the following African tribes: Bemba, Lozi, Ngoni, Nyakyusa (Colson and Gluckman 1951:1–93, 164–291), Dahomey (Herskovits 1938a), Kikuyu (Kenyatta 1939), Yoruba (Bascom 1944), Tanala (Linton 1933), Jukun (Meek 1931) Shilluk (Hofmayr 1925 and Seligman 1932), Baganda (Roscoe 1911), Fanti

(Christensen 1954), Kgatla (Schapera 1941), Ankole, Zulu, and Mgwato (Fortes and Evans-Pritchard (ed.) 1940:25–82, 121–164).

The following African tribes seem to have little belief in ancestral spirits coupled with unclear, vague or lack of centralized tribal organization: Tonga, Yao, Shona tribes (Colson and Gluckman 1951:94–163, 292–395), Lango (Driberg 1923), and Anuak (Evans-Pritchard 1904a).[5] The few tribes known to me in which this correlation does not seem to obtain are Tallensi (Fortes and Evans-Pritchard 1940:239–271), and several tribes composing the Bantu Kavirondo (Fortes and Evans-Pritchard 1940:197–236, and Wagner 1949:277–288), which have a somewhat more well defined ancestor cult but no centralized tribal organization. The clearest negative cases are those of the Nuer and the Tiv who have no belief in ancestral spirits and no centralized tribal organization of any kind (Evans-Pritchard 1940; Fortes and Evans-Pritchard 1940;272–296; and Laura and Paul Bohannan 1953).[6]

The reason for this correlation between more centralized political authority and better-defined ancestor cult has already been sug-

---

[5] A well defined ancestor cult includes the following basic elements: a. the belief in the existence of ancestral spirits; b. the belief that all ancestral spirits are interested only in their own living descendants and can affect their welfare; c. shrines, sacred places or tombs where offerings and sacrifices are made to the ancestors regularly or on special occasions from facts already noted. Ancestor cult in most African societies cannot be described as well-defined. The usual African pattern is that only a few of the ancestors are remembered and made offerings to, that the ancestral spirits so honored tend to be merged with other gods, and, therefore, not necessarily worshipped only by their own descendants because the spirits' interest is wider and vaguer.

[6] Both Fortes and Evans-Pritchard speak elaborately of political organization when in fact only some kinship or lineage system prevails. This problem has been dealt with elsewhere (Hsu 1959). One group, the Ngoni, has a centralized political organization but about whom the ethnographer reports no present evidence of ancestor cult (Colson and Gluckman 1951:194–252). Judging by the case of Nupi (and probably that of Kede, a formerly independent group within the Nupi kingdom) who have well-defined political organization but are presently Moslems (Fortes and Evans-Pritchard 1940:165–195, and Nadel 1946), complete absence of ancestor cult among the Ngoni is inconclusive. For the Nupi, though converted to Islam, hold to their mythical ancestor-king, Tsoede, as of basic importance to whom annual sacrifices are made, recite long lists of illustrious ancestors of noblemen at public functions, and consider the Tsoede's grave and relics as the most sacred treasures they possess (Nadel 1946:66–67, 72, 85, 130, and so forth). In addition, we find: "We shall see that the ruling house of Nupe crystallized in three dynasties, which trace their descent from different sons of the founder of the ruling house, and divide between them the rights and duties vested in the ruling house. The ancestors of the three dynasties lived only two or three generations back; but already certain religious observances (prayers on their grave) mark them off from all subsequent royal ancestors. In this rigidly defined system of reckoning descent in the father's line back to these almost sanctified 'first ancestors' and in the relationship with one another which is in the nature of mutual obligations for the sake of the larger unit, the royal house itself, the three dynasties correspond, from kinship point of view, to incipient "clans"—the only analogy to clan structure which we find in Nupe." (Nadel 1946:33). It is probably, therefore, not unreasonable to suggest that in pre-Islam days the Nupi did have some sort of ancestor cult.

gested with reference to Type A peoples: submission to parental authority and to long lines of ancestors paves the way to ties with the wider government.

In line with the fact that the kinship content is fraternal equivalence, the centralized governments tend to be somewhat "democratic." The word "democratic" is used to denote the fact that, while at any given time the ruler of such a government may have the power of life and death over his subjects, he tends to remain in touch or in direct contact with them and to be at their mercy. In Type A societies, the ruler will not be in any close contact with the people and there tends to be no occasion on which the people can as a matter of convention turn out to see the ruler in person. In Type B societies, the people demand to see the ruler in person, whether upon his return from the Crusades or from the victory at Verdun, essentially to admire him as a hero for what he has done, for his shining armor, or for his stately bearing and good looks. The modern Western tendency of criticizing their heads of states for poor taste or calling them by shortened names like "Ike" or "Jack" is but a variety of the same underlying attitude. The ruler-subject relationship in Type D societies differs from either in some respects but combines both in other ways. Here the ruler can and must maintain direct contact with his subjects under specified conditions. In order to maintain his power among psychological equals he must awe and exact obedience from them. His person is surrounded with taboos and restrictions, and as a rule his subjects treat him with great ceremony often including prostration before him so as to avoid his sight (Bascom 1951; Gluckman 1951; Herskovits 1938: Vol. II; Meek 1931; Oberg 1940; and others.).[7]

The other feature in which the ruler-subject relationship in Type D societies distinguishes itself is that the ruler seems always to be very much at the mercy of his subjects, or at any rate many of them. The despotic position of the rulers of Lozi (Gluckman 1951) or Dahomey (Herskovits 1928: Vol. 2, Chap. XXIII) may appear absolute enough. But in most Type D societies the power of the ruler is basically diffused, residing in the hands of his chief councils, min-

---

[7] The King of Ife in Yorubaland makes, for example, according to W. R. Bascom, two public appearances before his subjects every year. One is for the worship of the deity Orishanla and the other for the worship of two other deities. On the first occasion no subject is allowed to see him. Everybody is required to go home and lock their windows and doors, and if caught peeking, will be beaten. On the second occasion the King appears with great fanfare and the whole town turns out prostrating before him. At all other times the king is not even supposed to leave the palace (personal communication).

isters, Queen Mother, lesser dignitaries, and even the commoners. In 50 per cent of the 103 African tribes surveyed by Irstam, the king was killed under various stipulations (1944:146). Even where the custom of killing the physically weakening king does not prevail, the ruler is likely to be subject to election and deposition by the courtiers and/or by many of the people (Fortes and Evans-Pritchard 1940; Colson and Gluckman 1951; and Bascom: personal communication). The fact is that if a considerable number of the people are opposed to the ruler in a Type D society, or even show no interest in him, there is very little that such a man can do to force the obedience of the people. He will simply be unable to find instruments for the implementation of his rule. The rulers in Types A and B, though limited by their subjects in the long run, are much more secure and, therefore, more absolute in their rule at any given point of time.

Religion

The beliefs in Type D societies will range from simple animism to personified gods. Their religious mythology tends to be matter of fact, which offers common sense answers to problems of origin or of daily life. Their supernatural beings, often mixed with ancestral spirits, are valued more or less for concrete ends. There is no missionary zeal or movement. There is no systematic theology as the West knows it. Jealousy between rival priests is reported, but religious strife on theological or denominational basis cannot be expected. Like Type A peoples they do not fight religious wars. New gods are introduced as in Types A and C societies, but having little feeling for vertical continuity with the past or with the unfathomable Ultimate Reality, gods are much more replaceable than in Types A and C societies. In fact, Africa is the only continent outside Europe in which entire societies such as the Basuku simply gave up their own gods wholesale and without a struggle in favor of the missionary's holy water (Igor Kopytoff 1960).

Prejudice

There tends to be no racial or religious prejudice of the Western kind, except that learned from their present or former colonial masters. Rivalry among medicine men or priests will exist as it will wherever there is conflict or practical interests. African societies believe in witches and conduct witch hunts. But what has so far escaped the attention of students who have made specific contributions on the subject (Evans-Pritchard 1937; Kluckhohn 1944) and the students who contributed to one special number of *Africa* (1935, Vol. VIII, No. 4) is that witch hunting in all nonliterate and Type A and C societies is relativistic while its counterpart in the West is absolutistic. For example, Western "witches," convicted or suspected, were rarely spared, while "witches" in all other societies can be freed from such punishment by material compensation from their families. In nonliterate societies there are always counterwitchcraft measures or white magics which are essentially the same sort of acts as those employed (alleged or actual) by the witches or the sorcerers, but which are greatly valued by the people (Wolfe 1954a:853–856). Possessors of such counterwitchcraft measures may even achieve positions of influence (Browne 1929; Hogbin 1934:216; Firth 1954:103 and 113–115). The question has been dealt with elsewhere (Hsu 1960).

Impetus to Change

Because the individual can more or less reach his proper station among fellow men through the kinship framework, there is, as in Type A, little internal impetus to change. But since the solidarity within the kinship groups is far less than that in Type A, there is not the same centripetal force to resist deviation. In fact, there is evidence that a daring member of the society, if he is really determined, can actually break some of the traditional rules by personal initiative. Witness the way in which incest taboos can be and are actually broken in spite of the threat of death penalty, which is rarely carried out to the extent that they are formally threatened (Hsu 1940). But although they tend to have more nonkinship groupings than in Type A societies, such as age-grade villages and secret societies, which seriously claim the individual's allegiance and attention, such ties remain concrete but not idealistic in nature. Therefore, customs, whether considered by the West as good or evil, tend to perpetuate themselves since no individuals or groups will take it upon themselves to eradicate them. Too, although they have many more revolts against their rulers than would be the case among Type A societies, they also know no such thing as revolution of an internal origin, which aims at not only changing the ruler but also the social order. Having no written languages, their opportunities for accumulation of knowledge and ideas from the past and for stimulation within the society are much more limited than among

Type A, B, and C peoples. This fact actually gives such societies, in spite of their greater instability, fewer internal chances for cultural evolution than Type A societies.

Concluding Remarks

This chapter is no more than a preliminary exploration of the hypothesis. It is offered in the spirit of a Chinese proverb: "Throw the bricks to lead in the jade." In the first place, there are, of course, many facts which cannot be squeezed into the categories postulated, although as pointed out before, no scientific classification covers all the facts. In the second place, many differences do exist within each of the types postulated. Take prejudice for example. Obviously, not all societies in Type B are equally prejudiced. The pattern of variation in prejudice coincides roughly with that of variation in individualism. In Europe, racial prejudice is more pronounced in Britain and Germany, where individualism is stronger, than in Spain and Italy where it is weaker. This difference becomes magnified when European peoples settle in colonies. As a matter of fact, there is almost a complete dichotomy with Protestant colonies, including the United States, Canada (the word "colony" is applied to these independent countries in a historical and cultural sense), Union of South Africa, East Africa, and Australia, showing more racial prejudice than Catholic colonies from French Equatorial Africa, Portuguese East Africa, to Mexico and all South American republics.[8]

The differences between China and Japan (both being Type B) are perhaps even more spectacular. Elsewhere I have advanced one reason why Japan had actively and successfully met the modern challenge of the West while China remained politically, economically, and militarily prostrate for a whole century. I found the presence of the kinship usage of primogeniture in Japan and the absence of it in China to be one of the most relevant factors (Hsu

---

[8] New Zealand is a possible exception so far. There the relationship between the Protestant whites and the Maoris shows greater harmony than that between the indigenous populations and white settlers elsewhere. There are some peculiar but complex reasons for this which are not as yet systematically explored. One of these reasons is the the Europeans never scored decisive victories over the Maoris in battle. Another rason is that Maori values seem to have a great deal of affinity to those of the European settlers. Judging by the white New Zealanders' prejudicial attitude toward other nonwhites, the significance of the nature of their relationship with the Maoris remains inconclusive. According to recent reports, the situation in Angola seems to be one other exception. But the usual defect in such reports is their failure to distinguish politically and militarily oppressive actions from the continued and tenacious prejudice in day-to-day life. A truer picture must await more intensive researches.

1954). The diversity in patterns of life among nonliterate tribes, even of one in sub-Sahara Africa, is both great and obvious.

The relationship between kinship structure, kinship content, and way of life postulated in this chapter must be seen as circular or spiral, with all variables boosting or limiting each other in time, rather than in the manner of a straight line, with one variable being the ultimate cause of another. The circular or spiral relationship in the four types of societies may be crudely represented in the following diagrams:

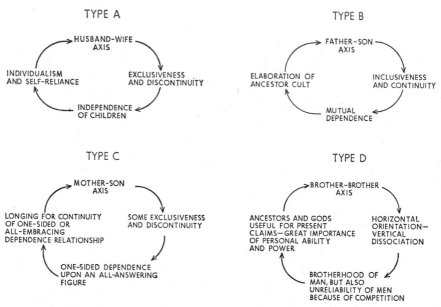

The peoples belonging to each of the four types of kinship systems presented here enjoy some obvious advantages and suffer from some obvious drawbacks. Continuity in Type A is an advantage because it provides the individual with psychological security, but it also can be a drawback because it restrains the individual's initiative. With reference to the discontinuity of Type B, the order of advantage versus disadvantage is exactly the reverse. Type C peoples may be more diffused in outlook than others but among them we find more individuals reaching great heights of spirituality than among others. Type D peoples may fight more among themselves, but their kinship content is the only one of the four which seems truly consistent with universal brotherhood of man.

Finally, the kinship structure and content of a people obviously form only one of the variables, though a most important one, affecting its development. The physical facts of size of population and ecology may have a great deal to do with it. Firth's description of Tikopian family, clan, and ancestor cult (Firth 1936) bears great resemblance to what we find in China, but factors other than kinship (for example, life on isolated islands as compared with that on a vast continent) obviously have some important bearing on why the Tikopia did not develop vast empires such as those of the Chinese. Other important factors in the development of peoples are the presence or absence of external threats of conquest, of intertribal or international communication and stimulation, and perhaps even climatic conditions and biological compositions.

The error of some students lies in their attempt to produce final explanations for all by one factor. But the error of some others lies in reluctance to explore any hypothesis to its logical conclusion for fear of the accusation of being biased. Neither of these approaches, if carried to the extreme, is likely to be fruitful in the long run.

What I have tried to do in this chapter is probably to raise many more questions to be settled by further research than I have answered. My purpose is to show that the patterns of kinship content, which have been neglected in systematic kinship studies, are demonstrably rooted in those of kinship structures, and that both have strong bearing on the patterns of personality and culture in different societies. In the preliminary results, I plead guilty to having lumped numerous peoples together whom many will certainly regard as being incongruous. But I am no more guilty than the zoologist who puts fish, chickens, crocodiles, monkeys, and humans together into the single category of vertebrata and attributes to all of them a number of common characteristics. If differences alone are stressed, I am positive that no two human societies are identical. For that matter we can go further and note that no two individuals are completely alike. At a certain level, it is important to ascertain the exact cultural differences between two particular tribes just as at a certain other level it is relevant to see the mental differences between two individual leaders. But before those who are interested in diamonds attempt to ascertain the differences between diamonds and pebbles, they must first make sure that they know what separates, on the one hand, the diamonds and pebbles (which are both stones), and, on the other, cabbages and turnips (which are both vegetables).

BIBLIOGRAPHY

BASCOM, W. R.
   1944   The sociological role of the Yoruba cult-group. American Anthropo-
          logical Association. Memoir, 63.
   1951   Social status, wealth and individual differences among the Yoruba.
          American Anthropologist (Part I) 53:490–505.

BOHANNAN, LAURA and PAUL
   1953   The Tiv of Central Nigeria. Ethnographic Survey Series, International
          African Institute, London.

BROWNE, C. R.
   1929   Maori witchery. London, J. M. Dent and Sons, Ltd.

CARSTAIRS, G. MORRIS
   1957   The twice born. London, The Hogarth Press.

CATON-THOMPSON, G.
   1931   The Zimbabwe culture ruins and reactions. London, Oxford University
          Press.

CHANG, TUNG-SUN
   1952   A Chinese philosopher's theory of knowledge. Yenching Journal of
          Social Studies, I.

CHAUDHURI, NIRAD C.
   1951   The autobiography of an unknown Indian. New York, McMillan Co.

CHILDS, GLADWYN M.
   1949   Umbundu kinship and character. London, Oxford University Press.

CHRISTENSEN, J. B.
   1954   Double descent among the Fanti. New Haven, Human Relations Area
          Files.

COLSON, E. AND M. GLUCKMAN (ed.)
   1951   Seven tribes of British Central Africa. London, Oxford University Press.

DRIBERG, J. H.
   1923   The Lango. London, T. F. Unwin, Ltd.

DUBE, C. S.
   1955   Indian village. Ithaca, New York, Cornell University Press.

EGGAN, FRED
   1950   Social organization of the western Pueblos. Chicago, University of
          Chicago Press.

EISENSTADT, S. N.
   1956   From generation to generation: age groups and social structure. Glencoe,
          Ill., The Free Press.

EVANS-PRITCHARD, E. E.
   1937   Witchcraft, oracles and magic among the Azande. London, Oxford
          University Press.
   1940a The political system of the Anuak of the Anglo-Egyptian Sudan.
          London, P. Lund, Humphries & Co., Ltd.
   1940b The Nuer. London, Oxford University Press.

FIRTH, R.
    1936   We the Tikopia. London, Routledge & Kegan Paul.
    1951   Elements of social organization. London, Watts & Co.
    1954   The sociology of 'magic' in Tikopia, Sociologus, 14, 2, New Series,
            97–116.

FORTES, M. and E. E. EVANS-PRITCHARD
    1940   African political systems. London, Oxford University Press.

FORTUNE, R.
    1932   Sorcerers of Dobu. London, G. Routledge & Sons, Ltd.

GILLIN, J.
    1939   Personality in pre-literate societies. American Sociological Review
            4:681–702.

GLUCKMAN, MAX
    1951   The Lozi of Barotzeland. *In* Colson and Gluckman, Seven Tribes of
            British Central Africa, pp. 1–93. London, Oxford University Press.

GOLDSCHMIDT, WALTER
    1948   Social organization in native California and the origin of clans. Ameri-
            can Anthropologist 50:444–456.

GRANET, MARCEL
    1934   La pensee Chinoise. Paris, La Renaissance du Livre.

HART, C. W. M.
    1954   The sons of Turimpi. American Anthropologist 56:242–261.

HERSKOVITS, M. J.
    1938a   Dahomey. 2 Vols. New York, J. J. Augustin.
    1938b   Acculturation. New York, J. J. Augustin.

HOFMAYR, WILHELM
    1925   Die Schilluk. Vienna, St. Gabriel, Modling bei Wien. Admistration
            des Anthropos.

HOGBIN, IAN H.
    1934   Law and order in Polynesia. New York, Harcourt, Brace & Co.

HSU, FRANCIS L. K.
    1940   The problem of incest tabu in a North China village. American An-
            thropologist 42:122–135.
    1943   Incentives to work in primitive communities. American Sociological
            Review 8:638–642.
    1953   Americans and Chinese: two ways of life. New York, Abelard-Schuman.
    1954   Cultural factors. *In* Williamson and Buttrick (ed.), Economic De-
            velopment. New York, Prentice-Hall.
    1959   Structure, function, content and process. American Anthropologist
            (Part I) 61:790–805.
    1960   A neglected aspect of witchcraft studies. Journal of American Folklore
            73:287.
    1961   Clan, caste and club: a comparative study of Chinese, Hindu and Amer-
            ican ways of life. Princeton, Van Nostrand and Co.

IRSTAM, TOR
    1944   The King of Ganda, studies in the institutions of sacral kingship in

IRSTAM, TOR (cont'd)
> Africa. Stockholm, The Ethnological Museum of Sweden, New Series, Publication 8.

KENYATTA, J.
> 1939 Facing Mount Kenya. London, Routledge & Kegan Paul.

KLUCKHOHN, C.
> 1944 Navaho witchcraft. Cambridge. Peabody Museum Papers, XXII, 2.

KOPYTOFF, IGOR
> 1960 Suku religion: A study in internally induced reinterpretation. Evanston, Ill., Northwestern University doctoral dissertation.

KUHN, MANFORD H.
> 1954 Factors in personality: socio-cultural determinants as seen through the Amish. In Francis L. K. Hsu (ed.), Aspects of Culture and Personality, pp. 43–45. New York, Abelard-Schuman.

LEACH, E. R.
> 1951 The structural implications of matrilateral cross-cousin marriage. Journal of Royal Anthropological Institute of Great Britain (Part I & II) 81:23–55.

LEVI-STRAUSS, CLAUDE
> 1949 Les structures elementaires de la parente. Paris, Presses Universitaires de France.

LINTON, R.
> 1933 Tanala, a hill tribe of Madagascar. Chicago Field Museum Series, XXII.
> 1939 In A. Kardiner, The individual and his Society. New York, Columbia University Press.
> 1940 A neglected aspect of social organization. American Journal of Sociology 45:870–866.
> 1945 The Comanche. In A. Kardiner, The psychological frontiers of society, pp. 47–48. New York, Columbia University Press.
> 1955 The tree of culture. New York, Alfred Knopf.

MALINOWSKI, B.
> 1929 Sexual life of savages. 2 vols., London, G. Routledge & Sons, Ltd.
> 1933 Sex and repression in a savage society. London, G. Routledge & Sons, Ltd.

MANDELBAUM, DAVID G.
> 1949 The family in India. In R. N. Anshen, ed., The family, its function and destiny. New York, Harper Bros.

MAYER, PHILIP
> 1949 Lineage principle in Gusii society, Memorandum XXIV, International African Institute, London.

MEAD, MARGARET (ed.)
> 1937 Cooperation and competition among primitive peoples. New York, McGraw Hill Book Co., Inc.
> 1939 Coming of age in Samoa. In From the South Seas. New York, Morrow & Co.

MEEK, C. K.
1931 A Sundanese kingdom. London, Kegan Paul, Trench, Trubner & Co., Ltd.
MUKERJI, D. GOPAL
1923 Case and outcaste. New York.
MULLER, F. MAX
1938 Ramakrishna, his life and sayings. London.
MURDOCK, GEORGE PETER
1949 Social structure. New York, McMillan & Co.
MURPHY, GARDNER
1953 In the minds of men. New York, Basic Books, Inc.
MURPHY, LOIS B.
1953 Roots of tolerance and tensions in child development, chap. IV, *In* Gardner Murphy: In the minds of men. New York, Basic Books, Inc.
NIVEDITA, SISTER (Miss M. E. Noble)
1904 The web of Indian life. London & Bombay, Longmans, Green & Co.
OBERG, K.
1940 The Kingdom of Ankole in Uganda. *In* Fortes and Evans-Pritchard, eds., African political systems. London, Oxford University Press.
PAYNE, ERNEST A.
1933 The Saktas. Calcutta & London, Oxford University Press.
RADCLIFFE-BROWN, A. R.
1950 Introduction. *In* African systems of kinship and marriage, edited by A. R. Radcliffe-Brown and Daryll Forde, pp. 1–85. London, Oxford University Press.
RADCLIFFE-BROWN, A. R. and DARYLL FORDE, (ed.)
1950 African systems of kinship and marriage. London, Oxford University Press.
ROSCOE, J.
1911 The Baganda. London, MacMillan & Co., Ltd.
SCHAPERA, I.
1941 Married life in an African tribe. New York, Sheridan House.
SELIGMAN, C. G. and B. Z.
1932 Pagan tribes of the Nilotic Sudan. London, G. Routledge & Sons, Ltd.
SPOEHR, ALEXANDER
1940 Changing kinship systems. Anthropological Series. Field Museum of Natural History, vol. 33, No. 4.
STEED, GITEL P.
1950 Life history documents, I (Indrasingh). New York, Columbia University Research in Contemporary India Project (hectographed).
1955 Personality formation in a Hindu village in Gujarat. *In* McKim Marriott (ed.): Village India, pp. 102–144. Chicago, University of Chicago Press.
STEWARD, JULIAN
1954 Types of types. Discussion of Ford, The type concept revisited. American Anthropologist 56:42–54, 55–57.
1955 Theory of Cultural change. Urbana, University of Illinois Press.

TEGNAEUS, HARRY
    1952   Blood brothers, Stockholm, The Ethnological Museum of Sweden, New
          Series, Publication 10.
WAGNER, G.
    1949   The Bantu of North Kavirondo. London, Oxford University Press.
WATSON, R. I.
    1959   Psychology of the child. New York, John Wiley & Sons.
WOLFE, ALVIN W.
    1954   The institution of demba among the Ngonje Ngombe. Zaire (Belgian
          Congo Review) 8:843–856.

INTRODUCTION TO PART IV
ASSESSMENT

IN THIS final section Spiro gives us an integrated picture of the whole field of psychological anthropology. He touches on some of the chapters of this book which have gone before but he also takes into consideration other works not specifically dealt with by the contributors to this volume. The reader will note that in certain areas Spiro's views do not agree with those of some of his colleagues. To take but a few examples: He opines that anthropology cannot claim to be a synthetic science of man because "vast dimensions of human behavior and experience," from "British folklore, American politics, Greek archaeology" to "Chinese economy," do not "come within our purview." But quite a few anthropologists specialize wholly or partially in "national character" studies of large and literate societies.

Then the term "primitive," which Spiro uses liberally and which the other contributors use only rarely or not at all, is meeting with increasing disfavor among anthropologists. Apart from other considerations, such as the fact that in our fast-changing world most former colonies now enjoy equal diplomatic relationship with the great powers, there are grave doubts, from the purely scientific point of view, concerning the lumping together of diverse peoples from Australia and Polynesia to Africa and the Americas into this one category.

Finally, Spiro's characterization that psychological anthropologists "have been primarily concerned with explaining personality" neglects the fact that even the Kardiner-Linton studies emphasize folklore and religion as projections of personality.

In spite of these and a few other points on which there is possible disagreement, the main thesis of Spiro's chapter is as important as it is likely to meet with hearty approval by psychological anthropologists. After having discussed the fact that psychological anthropologists have so far been "primarily concerned with explaining personality" by focusing our studies on "those aspects of social systems and culture which putatively are determinants of personality," he goes on and devotes the rest of his chapter to the problem of "maintenance of persistence of social systems" and "the problem of their internal change." In other words, he is emphasizing the view, as the Editor does in Chapter 1, that psychological anthropology not only must deal with "the origin of psychological characteristics as they are molded by the patterns of child rearing, social institutions, and ideologies but must also account for the origin, development and change in these child-rearing practices, institutions, and ideologies." Spiro indicates that there are at least three situations in which the potential conflict between personal desires and cultural norms is not resolved and the motivation for noncompliance with cultural norms is stronger than the motivation for compliance. He then proceeds to examine these in detail and hypothesizes on the dynamics of how such conflicts and their eventual resolution in each of the three situations—psychologically, structurally, and culturally induced—not only enable the social systems to persist but also to change.

Some readers will note, however, one point of discord between Spiro and the Editor. In Chapter 1 the Editor had indicated some possible distinctions between cultural anthropology, social anthropology, and psychological anthropology. Spiro, on the other hand, concludes that psychological anthropology should "conceive of itself as part of . . . social anthropology." The difference of opinion between Spiro and the Editor is, however, more superficial than real. The Editor's distinctions between the three subdisciplines are purely a matter of points of view, which cannot and should not prevent the territories of the three from overlapping with each other.

Chapter 15

AN OVERVIEW AND A SUGGESTED REORIENTATION

MELFORD E. SPIRO
University of Washington

The Emergence of Culture-and-Personality

AN examination of textbooks in general anthropology, of symposia such as *Anthropology Today,* of compendia such as the recently inaugurated *Annual Review of Anthropology,* of the classification of book reviews in the *American Anthropologist,* or of much of the empirical and theoretical work which is labeled as "culture-and-personality"—an examination of all of these yields the unambiguous impression that for most anthropologists culture-and-personality is a substantive field within the larger domain of anthropological science. Since anthropology as a collective enterprise audaciously pursues an imperialistic course consistent with its etymological meaning—I say, "collective'," because with Kroeber's recently lamented demise no single anthropologist pursues the study of man in all its dimensions—we easily and naturally slice up our field into *physical* anthropology, *linguistic* anthropology, *cultural* anthropology, *social* anthropology, *historical* anthropology, and finally— in the case of culture-and-personality—*psychological* anthropology. When we are challenged by some of our academic colleagues to explain the meaning of "anthropology" in each of the above expressions, we are often embarassed in our attempts to provide a satisfactory response because, of course, other sciences are centrally concerned with man's soma, his society, his psyche, and so forth. We sometimes attempt to explain "anthropology" in these expressions —and at the same time to justify our imperialism—by claiming that "anthropology" connotes a concern for all of these dimensions of man's existence in a synthetic or holistic manner.

459

Unfortunately this claim cannot be seriously defended. There are vast dimensions of human behavior and experience with which we have little or no concern. Seldom, for example, do British folklore, American politics, Greek archaeology, Chinese economy—to take but a few examples—come within our purview. On the other hand, we do study Navaho folklore, Nuer politics, Iroquois archaeology, and Samoan economy. In short, not Man, but primitive man, has been our concern. It must be admitted, of course, that in some important instances, the development of theoretical models and analytic schemes has proceeded without special concern for the uniquely primitive. But when this has occurred, progress has been made by eschewing the holistic approach. Thus in those fields where advance has been most spectacular, such as population genetics or structural linguistics, the anthropologist has become indistinguishable from his nonanthropological colleagues working in these vineyards.

These comments concerning the anthropological concern with primitive peoples are not intended as a criticism, but rather as a characterization, of the nature of our discipline, which in turn provides the historical context within which culture-and-personality studies developed. These studies emerged, I believe it is fair to say, as a result of a serious crisis with which anthropology was confronted beginning, roughly, about 1920. One might almost characterize this crisis, as Erik Erikson characterizes the typical adolescent crisis, as one of "identity."

When anthropology first arose as a separate discipline, its primary concern was with the origin, evolution, and distribution of man and his cultures. Holding this aim as its charter, armed with the older comparative method as its main research tool, and accepting as a methodological premise the approximate equation of primitive and prehistoric peoples, its rationale for the study of primitive peoples was axiomatic. With the growth and development, however, of American anthropology and its disparagement of both the aims and methods of the various evolutionary schools, the rationale for the focus on primitive peoples lost much of its force. If, according to the American school, the study of American or Australian aborigines could shed little light on the origin and evolution of culture, what interest, for other than an antiquarian curiosity, could aboriginal peoples have for modern science? And if, in accordance with the emerging conception of cultural relativism, the cultures of aboriginal peoples (like our own culture) were to be viewed as so many variants of a universal culture pattern, rather than as different stages in an evolutionary scheme or as different points on some scale—of progress, or development, or complexity, or any other measure—why bother to study them? To provide further documentation for the thesis of variability and of relativism? But were anthropologists then to become like those, of whom Pierce (1935:233) complained, who

. . . seem to love to argue a point after all the world is fully convinced of it. But no further advance can be made. When doubt ceases, mental action on a subject comes to an end; and, if it did go on, it would be without a purpose.

In general, American anthropologists justified their preoccupation with primitive cultures by arguing that ethnographic facts—when they were all in—would constitute vital data for the reconstruction of culture history, and, perhaps, provide the evidence for an inductive construction of cultural "laws" (presumably, laws of change, invention, diffusion, and so forth). Hence, like the older evolutionists—but for different reasons—anthropologists continued to collect ethnographic facts. They differed from the evolutionists in that their facts were collected at first hand in the field, rather than from the reports of missionaries and travelers. They differed too in their antitheoretical bias. Since science was "objective," ethnographic science was to be descriptive, assiduously avoiding all theoretical entanglements; and the immediate if not the ultimate aim of ethnographic research was to be the meticulous observation, collection, and classification of facts—in the spirit of Ranke's historiography: *wie es eigentlich gewessen ist.* Only after this essentially descriptive task was performed in a fairly large number of societies could the anthropologist (if he were so inclined) attempt to discover cultural laws. And even then, as Boas (1936: 257) cautioned, "cultural phenomena are of such complexity that it seems doubtful . . . whether valid cultural laws can be found."

This approach to the study of primitive peoples—the approach of radical empiricism—which, I believe, represented a serious attempt to solve our identity crisis, had at least two important consequences for anthropological theorizing. On the one hand, it led to the proliferation of speculative, nontestable theory. On the other, it led to an extreme skepticism concerning the possibility of any theory. As one wit put it, it led to the generalization that the only valid anthropological generalization is the generalization that there are no valid generalizations.

That a method which insisted on the divorce of theory and data should have resulted in a proliferation of speculation was, though ironical, inescapable. If theoretical generalizations are to emerge *from* research, they must be used *in* research. And if theory is divorced from research, it necessarily leads an independent existence, neither affecting the nature of inquiry, nor being affected by the results of inquiry. Removed in effect from any empirical context, it remains in the realm of speculation—and of fruitless controversy. This state of affairs can cease only when theory exists in a correlative relationship with fact, when, that is, it generates hypotheses to be tested in inquiry. Only then are its concepts formulated operationally and its predicted consequences confirmed or disconfirmed empirically. But the method of radical empiricism precluded the empirical resolution of theoretical controversy. Since theory was not employed in research, facts adduced for the support of theories were, at best, illustrative; and equally good illustrations could be found for almost any theory and its antithesis.

Facts can become data only when they are used as evidence for the testing of scientific hypotheses, only when, that is, they are expected to solve theoretical problems. For it is a theory, in the form of a hypothesis to be tested, that determines which facts out of a potentially infinite number are to be collected—those facts, namely, which are believed to constitute evidence for the inquiry at hand. Dewey (1938:497) put it much better when he observed that:

> All competent and authentic inquiry demands that out of the complex welter of existential and potentially observable and recordable material, certain material be selected and weighed *as* data or the "facts of the case." This process is one of adjudgment, of appraisal or evaluation . . . An idea of an end *to be* reached, and end-in-view, is logically indispensable in discrimination of existential material as the evidential and testing facts of the case. Without it, there is no guide for observation; without it, one can have no conception of what one should look for or even is looking for. One "fact" would be just as good as another—that is, good for nothing in control of inquiry and formation and in settlement of a problem.

That the method of radical empiricism should have led, too, to scientific agnosticism is not at all surprising. Cultural phenomena are indeed complex, as Boas rightly cautioned; but this method could hardly have decreased the impression of their complexity. The fact is, of course, that the phenomenal world—the physical no less than the cultural—is always complex; it is, as William James put it, a "booming, buzzing, confusion." Hence, it is at least arguable that the order and simplicity now perceived to characterize the physical world are conceptual rather than phenomenal, and that the absence of order and of simplicity that seems to characterize the cultural world may similarly be conceptual rather than phenomenal. For we anthropologists are no exception to a universal law of perception: *viz.*, that any stimulus field becomes a perceptually meaningful field only when it is structured. But having decided to collect all the ethnographic facts, and to collect them as objectively as possible—that is, without explicit theory—anthropology was confronted with an enormous corpus of unstructured ethnographic material. And, as in any other unstructured situation, the resultant perception was one of enormous complexity.[1]

It is against this background and within this context that culture-and-personality studies emerged.[2] In an era of radical empiricism and scientific agnosticism, it is probably inevitable that the desire of some scholars for a different methodological charter and a satisfying theoretical orientation should lead to new approaches. For anthropologists this desire was satisfied in two quite dissimilar ways and by two seemingly dissimilar schools: the British school of social anthropology and the American school of culture-and-personality. Despite the important differences that divided these schools, it should be observed that they also had much in common. First, in contrast to the earlier historical schools, both displayed almost systematic indifference to problems of a historical nature. This is not to say, as is sometimes charged, that they dismissed historical variables as irrelevant, but rather that they viewed the task of anthropology as something other than historical reconstruction. Second, in contrast to an older trait-list approach, both emphasized

---

[1] In this connection the following statements, one by an eminent physical, and the other by an eminent social, anthropologist, are relevant. In an article on social structure Levi-Straus (1953: 549) observes: "Surprisingly enough, it is at the very moment when anthropology finds itself closer than ever to the long-awaited goal of becoming a true science that the ground seems to fail where it was expected to be the firmest: the facts themselves are lacking, either not numerous enough or not collected under conditions insuring their comparability." Washburn, writing in the same volume (1953:714–715) on physical anthropology, states: "After more than a century of intensive fact-finding there is less agreement among informed scientists on the evolution of man to other primates than there was in the latter part of the nineteenth century."

[2] Since these studies have historical roots both in eighteenth century thought and in nineteenth century scholarship, I do not mean to imply that culture-and-personality represented an unprecedented innovation. Indeed, in addition to its deeper historical roots, it will be remembered that Edward Sapir, Ruth Benedict, and Margaret Mead were all students of Franz Boas, whose psychological interests are well known. But continuity is not identity, and these three pioneers are sufficiently distinct from their intellectual predecessors to warrant our reference to their work as a "new approach."

the primacy of context, pattern, configuration, and structure. Third, instead of a descriptivist approach, both were theoretically oriented. Primitive societies were to be studied for the light they could shed on theoretical issues: in the one case—and here they differed—sociological, in the other, psychological. The one was interested in the forms of society, the other in the dynamics of behavior. And this difference in turn led to still another fundamental difference. The one either dismissed culture as irrelevant to its interests (for example, Radcliffe-Brown), or else concentrated on an examination of its properties (for example, Malinowski); the other viewed it as of crucial importance, but as an independent rather than as a dependent variable. That is, its interest was in demonstrating the importance of culture as an efficient cause in the development of personality and in the patterning of behavior. In any event, both innovations—social anthropology and culture-and-personality—represented important attempts to salvage anthropology as a theoretically informed discipline, concerned with discovering laws or principles that would explain classes of phenomena, whether these phenomenal classes be social, cultural, behavioral, or psychological.

For culture-and-personality, the phenomenal class to be explained was personality and its cross-cultural variability. This school, like the older historical schools, was deeply interested in culture—and, like the older schools, it conceived of culture as a holistic concept, including social structure, material goods, social norms, values and ideas, and so forth; in short, the "man-made part of the environment." But this school, as has already been stated, was interested in culture as an independent, rather than as a dependent, variable. Instead of asking—as did the older schools—what historical, environmental, or biological variable(s) produced certain cultural variables or even a total culture, culture-and-personality asked what cultural variables produced certain personality variables or a total personality. Culture-and-personality, focusing on personality but stemming from general anthropology, was concerned with demonstrating that almost all behavior was cross-culturally variable rather than constant; that this variability was a function (primarily) of environment rather than biology (race); that the crucial environmental variable was culture; and that culture was learned rather than innate.

The Copernican revolution in anthropology which was sponsored by culture-and-personality did not consist (as the threadbare cliche has it) in the promotion of the study of the individual, in contrast to social or cultural anthropology which studied the group (as if it were possible to do either without the other!). It consisted, rather, in the change from the traditional focus on culture as *explanandum* to culture as *explanans*, and in the substitution of personality as *explanandum*. Indeed even a cursory examination of the early literature of culture-and-personality will reveal how false is the claim that culture-and-personality was—or is— a "study of the individual in culture." Although some autobiographies were collected, the autobiography was exploited to the end of discovering not individual differences, but cultural influences on the individual. The "individual" was of concern not in those characteristics which differentiated him from other individuals in his group—not, that is, as an idiocyncratic person—but as a social person, as an example of a culturally molded psychological or personality type. The question to be examined was how this individual, viewed as a prototypical Hopi or Samoan or Alorese acquired a Hopi, rather than an Alorese or Samoan personality. Culture-and-personality students became, in short, the personality psychologists of primitive societies —comparative human psychologists—attending always to the crucial importance of culture for personality: its development, its structure, and its functions. And since there were many new theories to be tested, culture-and-personality studies were, from their inception, strongly theoretical—if not always systematic—in orientation.

Nevertheless, and despite its theoretical emphasis, culture-and-personality did not—and in some quarters does not, even today— receive an entirely favorable reception even among theoretically oriented anthropologists. Many—perhaps most—of the pioneering articles in culture-and-personality were published in nonanthropological journals—sometimes, to be sure, because psychologists replaced anthropologists as the reference group of certain members of this school, but more frequently because their work did not receive the imprimatur of anthropology. In general, those anthropologists who were dissatisfied with the older intellectual styles in anthropology turned, not to culture-and-personality, but to British social anthropology for new directions. Despite some of the dramatic changes introduced by this school, it was not the *terra incognita* of culture-and-personality. Kinship and economics, divination and totemism, government and law—rather than shame and guilt, projection and displacement, hostility and repression—continued to comprise its basic vocabulary. In short, if British structuralism[3] constituted a revolution in anthropology, it was certainly not Copernican; for however radical its departure from the more conventional anthropological tradition, British structuralism remained, like the latter, a social science. Culture-and-personality, on the other hand, entered anthropology—and was eventually legitimized—as its behavioral science branch. Its unique contribution to the understanding of behavior was the culture concept of traditional anthropology. By conceiving of culture as an efficient cause which could not only, like other putative efficient causes, explain behavior but which could also, unlike some other putative causes, explain its cross-cultural variability, culture-and-personality not only commanded serious—if not always respectful—attention among the other behavioral sciences, but it also provided the anthropological concern for primitive peoples with triumphant vindication. Instead of satisfying essentially exotic, quixotic, or romantic curiosity, anthropology—according to the more partisan supporters of culture-and-personality—was pursuing a scientific enterprise of the first magnitude: it was engaged, almost uniquely, in an "experimental" study of human behavior. Whereas the other behavioral sciences were studying the same highly restricted sample of behavior drawn from an atypical segment of the total universe of behavioral samples, the study of primitive peoples allowed anthropology to sample the total universe. Since anthropology had already shown that behavioral differences within the class of primitive societies were even greater than the differences between primitive societies as a class and nonprimitive societies as a class, primitive societies could acquire new interest for the behavioral sciences not because they were alike but because they differed. Since all societies were members of the same universe, each society—including primitive—represented a variation on the same human theme.

With this new rationale and this new approach, the study of primitive peoples, for many anthropologists who had viewed the more traditional approach as having entered an intellectual *cul-de-sac,* received new and important justification. Primitive peoples, it was claimed, were important, not because they could contribute

---

[3] Here, and elsewhere in this chapter, the term "social anthropology" is not intended to be synonymous with British social anthropology: the latter is to the former what the part is to the whole. I use the term "British structuralism" or "pure structuralism" to refer to that school within social anthropology which views the discovery of "structural principles" as its major analytic task, and which systematically excludes psychological variables from its modes of analysis.

to an understanding of a separate class of behavior, the class of *primitive* behavior, but because they could contribute to the understanding of a larger behavioral class, the class of *human* behavior. From this point of view, each primitive society was thought to constitute, as it were, a natural laboratory for the study of different dimensions of behavior. And since these laboratories seemed to be the special preserve of anthropologists, they alone, it was alleged, were able to study the complete content, and to test the full limits, of human behavioral variability.

Toward a Reorientation of Culture-and-Personality

It is not my task to evaluate this charter, or to assess the culture-and-personality studies which have been conducted in many parts of the world within its provisions: the latter task is admirably accomplished in other chapters in this volume. I am concerned rather with assessing the future contribution which such studies may make to the furtherance of the theoretical aims of anthropological science. It is, of course, both difficult and hazardous to draw hard and fast distinctions among the various sciences; and it is even more hazardous to fix the frontiers of any discipline and, thus, to declare as alien all research concerns that fall beyond those frontiers. I do not intend to do either. At the same time, within the present system of scientific specialization it is obvious that anthropology and sociology have been traditionally concerned with the analysis of cultural and social systems, while other disciplines (personality psychology, psychiatry, and so forth) are centrally concerned with personality. I would suggest that anthropology, including culture-and-personality, persist in its traditional concern—not because I believe that cultural or social systems are of greater scientific interest or importance than personality systems, but because the theoretical problems which they pose are still for the most part unsolved; and if anthropologists (as well as sociologists) eschew them, they may never be solved. Hence, I am suggesting that, as anthropologists, the important task for culture-and-personality theorists today is the analysis of sociocultural systems rather than personality systems.

This suggested reorientation of the focus of culture and personality is not intended to imply that our past efforts have been wasted, misguided, or misdirected. Quite the contrary! I believe they were crucially important and highly desirable, both for anthropology as well as for personality psychology. Their importance for the latter discipline has been marked. The relevance of socio-cultural variables in the process of personality development and formation, though acknowledged in part prior to the work of culture-and-personality, was seldom incorporated systematically into personality theory. This is no longer the case. Most personality theorists—from psychoanalytic, to stimulus-response—are now systematically aware of the relevance of sociocultural variables for personality development and persistence. This is not to say that culture-and-personality was solely responsible for this change. Many currents in the social, behavioral, and psychiatric sciences contributed to this growing awareness of the importance of sociocultural variables. (Indeed, it is possible, as Wallace implies in his chapter in this volume, that the importance of sociocultural determinants has been exaggerated, and that it might be well to take another look at genetic and other biological variables.) Nevertheless, the documentation of the importance of cultural determinants in personality formation was a major—though not exclusive—intellectual achievement of culture-and-personality studies, and it represents the major contribution of anthropology to personality theory.

The importance of culture-and-personality has been, if anything, even more important for anthropology than for psychology. By focusing on personality dynamics and on social behavior (rather than on culture traits or social structure) these studies have impressed upon some anthropologists, at least, the realization that cultures and/or social systems do not lead an independent existence of their own; that their operation and maintenance are dependent to a marked degree on their internalization (either as cognitive or as affective variables) within the personalities of the members of society; and that for many—but by no means for all—problems of both structure and process, a studied indifference to the psychological dimensions of behavior can only lead to truncated, if not false, theories.

Indeed it is precisely because it has been so successful that I am suggesting a reorientation of culture-and-personality. Having succeeded in its attempts to induce personality psychology to incorporate sociocultural concepts within its conceptual apparatus, and having succeeded in legitimizing the use of personality concepts by anthropology, it might be argued that its original mission has come to its end. For if, on the one hand, the study of personality is *not* the focal concern of anthropology, I can see no grounds for pursuing something which others can do better than we; or are we content to become for personality theory what medieval philosophy was for theology, its handmaiden?—in this case, a handmaiden in exotic places. If, on the other hand, the study of culture and of social systems *is* the focal concern of anthropology, I can see no grounds for abandoning this concern to other anthropologists whose conceptual apparatus does not systematically include what for us is a key concept: the concept of personality.

For those *au courant* with the literature of culture-and-personality (if only from having read the previous chapters in this volume), this suggestion for a reorientation of the focus of our interest will not be received as a new or original suggestion. Much of the research and theory in culture-and-personality, even that of its pioneers—Mead, Hallowell, Henry, Kluckhohn, and others—exemplifies the approach which is proposed in this chapter. This proposal, therefore, is intended not as a radical departure from, but rather as a strengthening of, a trend which already has distinguished practitioners. But this trend must be broadened as well as strengthened. Because, as comparative personality theorists, we have been primarily concerned with explaining personality, our studies have in general focused on those aspects of social systems and culture which putatively are determinants of personality. And since, in the main, our theories have stressed the primacy of primary groups and the crucial importance of the socialization system, we have tended to ignore other social groups and other systems. In saying this I am not concerned here with evaluating the validity of our theories concerning the importance of primary groups or of socialization, but rather with explaining the relative neglect of other systems—political systems, as Inkeles rightly observes in his chapter in this volume, are a notable case in point—in culture-and-personality studies.

It is at least debatable, of course, that even as comparative personality theorists we have been negligent in our relative neglect of other systems; perhaps political systems, for example, are important determinants of personality formation. If this is so, our theories of personality development must be revised. But this is not the brunt of this discussion. Even if it were established that political and other institutions have no bearing on personality formation, my proposal for a reorientation of culture-and-personality would nevertheless demand that these institutions, instead of personality as such, become our major concern.

In suggesting that we abandon the Copernican revolution of culture-and-personality, I do not intend to imply that we abandon our concern for personality. On the contrary! The introduction of personality concepts has been our unique contribution to anthropology, and the retention of personality as a crucial variable is our very *raison d'être*. My suggestion implies, rather, that its conceptual status be changed from *explanandum* to *explanans*, from a concept to be explained to an explanatory concept. Hence, though we would share a common focal concern—social system and culture—with our fellow social anthropologists, we would differ from them in our emphasis on personality and personality-derived concepts as our central analytical tools.

Restricting the discussion to social systems, I think it can be shown that current anthropological theories of social systems which explicitly preclude personality concepts from the domain of anthropological modes of explanation—pure structural theories—frequently fail to deal adequately either with the problem of the maintenance or persistence of social systems, or with the problem of their internal change. With respect to change, the strategy of pure structural analysis almost necessarily precludes the possibility of dealing with internally derived sociocultural change. The analysis of social structure is, of course, the first task in the analysis of social and cultural systems, and any theorist—psychological and antipsychological alike—must derive his structural variables by abstraction from the behavior of psychobiological organisms. The pure structuralist differs from other theorists, however, in insisting that these structural variables are the only legitimate data for anthropological analysis, and in denying other variables which can be derived from the behavior of these psychobiological organisms the status of legitimate anthropological concern. Since psychological variables are *not* structural variables, they are relegated to the psychologists. Having thus excluded the very variables which comprise a constant and persistent source of internal (in contrast to external) change—the needs and drives of the psychobiological organisms whose frustrations exert a continuous innovative strain—pure structural theories must necessarily adopt models of stable equilibrium, models which are almost inherently incapable of dealing with internally derived change.

Yet personality variables are as important for the maintenance of social systems as for their change. Without the use of personality concepts, attempts fully to explain the operation of these systems, either in terms of efficient causes or in terms of functional consequences, are seldom convincing. (Indeed the frequent recourse to psychological explanation, albeit in disguised form, at crucial points in many "antipsychological" structural analyses attests to the validity of this thesis.) Thus, although no one could take issue with Radcliffe-Brown's assertion (1950:82) that "the social function of any feature of a system is its relation to the structure and its continuance and stability, not its relation to the biological needs of individuals,"—although no one could take issue with this assertion (because, of course, no one would commit the semantic fallacy of confusing *social* with *biological* functions), and although we might even concede that our task as social anthropologists is the discovery of social rather than biological functions, we might still want to ask whether in some instances at least an understanding of the biological functions of some structural unit may not be necessary for an understanding of its social functions. Or are we to say that the satisfaction of biological needs or their frustration have no consequences —even crucially important consequences—for the operation of a social system? If a negative answer to this question is the obviously correct answer, it is certainly not obvious to me.

Similarly although we might agree with Professor Firth (1956: 224) that in studying religious ritual the anthropologist "is concerned primarily with the kinds of social relations that are produced or maintained, rather than with the inner state as such of the participants," we would ask whether it is at all possible to understand the nature of a "social relation" without having some understanding of the "inner state" of the participants? Whether, indeed, the different "kinds" of social relations are not, among other things, a function of different "kinds" of "inner states."

Theories which attempt to explain the operation of social institutions, either in terms of their efficient causes or of their functional (particularly their latent) consequences, must necessarily include personality variables as explanatory concepts because, as I have attempted to show elsewhere (Spiro, 1961), these institutions provide culturally approved and/or prescribed means for the satisfaction of personality needs, and these, in turn, provide the motivational bases for the performance of the roles which comprise these institutions. Hence, if the *social* function of personality—it has others—consists in the contribution it makes to the maintenance or persistence of a society, and if the *psychological* function of social systems—they have others—consists in the contribution they make to the maintenance of personality, the unique task of culture and personality, as a theory of social systems, is to explain their operation in terms of personality dynamics, and to explain their social (not merely their psychological) functions by reference to their capacity for the gratification and frustration of personality needs.

This is, however, a most difficult task. Human social systems are necessarily culturally constituted systems; and although culture may be viewed, in evolutionary perspective, as man's unique and crucial mechanism for adapting to nature and adjusting to other men, it is at the same time a new environment to which man must adapt and adjust. In short, culture is both an instrument and an object; it contributes to social adaptation and adjustment and at the same time it constitutes an object for adjustment. Hence, any analysis of human, that is, culturally constituted, social systems must explain how man adapts to the demands of culture—with all the conflict attendant upon the process—at the same time that he uses culture for the purpose of adaptation. Analyses which ignore or are unacquainted with the dynamics of behavior—including such unconscious mechanisms as psychological defenses—cannot perform this task satisfactorily. This is the thesis to be examined in the next section.

Culture-and-Personality Theory and the Operation of Social Systems [4]

On the basis of our present knowledge, it is probably safe to compile at least a partial list of both personal and social functional requirements. In this short compass we shall be concerned merely with those which are germaine to the relatively narrow focus of this discussion—some of the problems posed by cultural conformity and social control. With respect to the functional requirements of personal adjustment and integration, at least the following must be mentioned: (a) the gratification of drives, both acquired and innate; (b) their gratification by means which comply with cultural norms; (c) their gratification by means that preclude pain for the actor, whether imposed by others (in the form of social sanctions) or by the self (in the form of shame or of moral anxiety). These functional requirements are fulfilled by the organization and operation of personality. Similarly, the functional requirements for the adaptation and integration of society include at least the fol-

---

[4] Isolated paragraphs, scattered in various parts of this section, have been taken from Spiro 1960.

lowing: (*a*) the gratification of the drives of its members; (*b*) the performance of those tasks which achieve commonly accepted group ends; (*c*) the protection of its members from aggression and other socially disruptive acts. For the most part these functional requirements are fulfilled by the organization and operation of social systems.

If social systems be conceived as configurations of reciprocal roles which are shared by the members of a group in virtue of their inheritance from a prior generation—innovations do not become part of a social system until or unless they are accepted, that is, shared, and thereafter transmitted to succeeding generations—then, in the most inclusive comparison of societies, from insect to human, we can distinguish three broad types of social systems. First, there are those whose constituent roles are inherited but not learned. These, of course, are the insect social systems whose shared roles are inherited through some process of biological determination, either by genetic inheritance or by postpartum nutrition. The persistence of these systems poses no special problem for the theorist of insect social systems: a worker ant must do whatever it is that worker ants *do* do; her status is defined by her role, and her role is determined by her nature. Second, there are social systems whose constituent roles are inherited, at least to some extent, through learning. These are the mammalian, and especially the primate, social systems. Third, there are social systems whose roles are not only inherited through learning, but whose roles are *prescribed*. These are human social systems.

Whereas the second type of social systems is found in those biological species characterized by a relatively small degree of plasticity, and, hence, by a relatively narrow range of behavioral variability, the third type is found in a species—*homo sapiens*—which exhibits an enormous degree of plasticity and, hence, a broad range of behavioral variability. Thus, holding the physical environment constant, all societies within the same infrahuman mammalian species have, more or less, the same social system; and within each society the system persists with little change over time. This homogeneity in space and time suggests that although many, if not all, of the social roles in these societies are learned, the behavioral repertoire of the typical member of these societies is not significantly broader than the learned behavior patterns that comprise this group's social system. Hence, in these societies what any member has learned to do in order to satisfy his needs is little different from what he is able to do and it, therefore, corresponds (more or less) to what he would like to do.

For the human species, even when the environment is held constant, different societies have different social systems and, for any society, social systems change over time. Since, therefore, the actual range of behavioral variability within the species is much broader than the permitted range of variability within any society of the species—since, that is, humans are capable of doing many things in addition to those they are expected to do—it is obvious that for human societies it is not sufficient that social roles be inherited, shared, and learned; they must also be *prescribed*. Hence, if human social systems differ from those of other mammals in that only the former are cultural, the crucial difference between cultural and noncultural systems is not—as we anthropologists have always, and I now believe wrongly, maintained—a difference between learned and nonlearned systems. Recent work in comparative animal sociology (Beach and Janes 1954; Schneirla 1950; Carpenter 1958) shows convincingly that learning is an important mechanism in the social behavior not only of man, but of all social mammals. With Hallowell (1960), Parsons (1951), and others, I believe that the distinctive feature of culture resides, rather, in its normative or prescriptive dimension.[5]

This prescriptive, or normative, dimension of culturally constituted social systems is for human societies what narrow plasticity and biological determination are, respectively, for mammalian and insect societies: it reduces the range of intragroup behavioral variability and, thus, helps make social order possible. Without this technique for reducing the range of potential variability inherent in any status, the long-range adaptive value of flexibility—which is made

---

[5] In a previous publication (Spiro 1951) I argued that culture and personality were interchangeable concepts, since culture, if it had any ontological status, was internalized by the individual. This extreme position was adopted in opposition to various superorganicist theories which seemed to postulate a reified entity, culture, which was empirically as well as analytically divorced from its "carriers," and was assigned an independent existence in its own ontological realm. It has long been obvious to me that this extreme position is no more tenable than the position it had attempted to counter. In the first place, although it may be cognized, culture need not be internalized; and even when internalized, it comprises only one dimension of the personality: the superego. I would now argue, in agreement with the Parsonian tripartite classification, that culture consists, among other things, of the norms which govern social relationships; that these norms are to be distinguished analytically from that system of social relationships which may be termed the social system of a society; and that both are to be distinguished from personality, by which I understand the motivational system (including internalized norms) that characterizes individuals. It is obvious, from this classification, that much so-called "culture and personality research" is really concerned with social systems rather than with culture, or with culture rather than with personality.

possible by wide plasticity—would have had to be sacrificed for the short-run superiority of social order achieved through narrow plasticity. Hence, the invention of culture allowed man to achieve both flexibility and order; in short, *almost* to have his cake and to eat it too. Almost, but not quite; for since what a person *must* learn to do in order to participate in his social system is not the same as what he *can* learn to do, it may conflict with what he would *like* to do.

This is, however, not the only conflict which may exist between personal desires and cultural norms. Cultural norms may be proscriptive as well as prescriptive. The former not only function to reduce the range of potential variability in a society, but also to preclude the expression of those activities which are, or are deemed to be, socially disruptive. In short, in human societies *par excellence* there exists, potentially, persistent conflict between cultural norms and personal desires. But since cultural conformity—whether in the form of the performance of socially prescribed tasks or in the form of the inhibition of socially prohibited acts—is a functional requirement of society,[6] this conflict must be resolved in such a way as to achieve compliance with the cultural norms. On the other hand, since the gratification of drives is a functional requirement for personal adjustment, this conflict must be resolved in such a way as to permit at least a minimum degree of drive gratification. In short, the conflict must be resolved so as to satisfy the functional requirements of the individual and of society simultaneously. How can this be done?

If it be granted that behavior is motivated, it is obvious that the mere learning of the cultural norms is not sufficient to induce compliance. For if behavior is motivated, cultural conformity can be achieved only if, in addition to the learning of the norms, the motivation for compliance with their demands is stronger than the motivation for the performance of competing behavior patterns that comprise the behavioral repertoire of the actors. With respect to the performance of social roles (compliance with prescriptive norms) there is one obvious way in which this can be achieved. If motivated behavior is goal-oriented behavior, and if we conceive of goals as objects, events, or conditions which gratify drives, the performance of roles can be ensured if, in the first place, the goals

---

[6] It is not the maintenance of *the* social system, but of *a* social system that is a functional requirement. It is not cultural change but *anomie* that is dysfunctional, so that new roles may fulfill the functional requirements just as well if not better than the old ones. But change in a social system does not alter the problem with which we are concerned: potential conflict between compliance with the new norms and gratification of drives.

which are achieved by their performance are cathected by and, hence, serve to gratify personality drives, and if, secondly, the roles are perceived to be efficient means for their achievement. When this occurs, not only are the functional requirements of individual and society satisfied simultaneously, but the functional requirement of each is satisfied by an attribute of the other; that is, personality drives serve to instigate the performance of social roles, and the performance of roles serves to gratify personality drives.

There are, as far as I can tell, only two types of objects, conditions, and events which can become cathected as goals for the gratification of drives, and which, therefore, can serve to instigate the performance of roles which attain them. These are (a) the functions which comprise the culturally defined *raison d'être* of a status, and (b) the social rewards, or incentives,[7] which societies offer to the occupants of statuses. To use the esteem drive as an example, those individuals for whom the culturally prescribed functions of health or economic productivity are cathected as goals for the gratification of this drive will be motivated, respectively, to occupy the statuses of doctor or entrepreneur. Frequently, however, a status is occupied, even though its social function is not cathected, because of the cathexis of those rewards which societies offer to the occupants of the status. Thus, the statuses of doctor and entrepreneur may be occupied because of the incentives provided by a prestigeful title or a high income. If, then, occupants of a status perform its prescribed role in order to obtain either or both of these goals, the motivation for their performance may be termed "function oriented" and "incentive oriented" respectively.[8]

To summarize, if the culture of a society provides goals which gratify drives, and if its social system consists of roles whose performance is instrumental in achieving these goals, the functional requirements both for successful personal adjustment as well as for social adaptation and integration are satisfied. Although potential conflict between personal desires and cultural norms is frequently resolved in this way, there are at least three situations—psychologically, structurally, and culturally induced—in which this type of resolution is not achieved, in which, on the contrary, the motivation for noncompliance with cultural norms is stronger than the motivation for compliance. In each of these situations other means for

---

[7] "Social rewards" is used instead of the conventional "positive sanctions."

[8] This is a deliberate oversimplification. It is obvious that role performance is almost always motivated by a congeries of conscious and unconscious needs (*cf.* Spiro 1961).

ensuring cultural conformity—means which are usually referred to as "techniques of social control"—are required. We may begin with the least disruptive of these situations, that which is psychologically induced.

Although the performance of social roles may attain drive-gratifying goals, some of their constituent norms may be sufficiently irksome to lead to a psychologically induced preference for noncompliance with these norms. Thus, a teacher may prefer not to comply with a five-day teaching schedule, although in general he is otherwise content with his role. Compliance with norms of this type must be achieved by some technique other than function-oriented or incentive-oriented role motivation.

A second situation of potential violation of norms obtains even though the performance of roles is an efficient means for the attainment of drive-gratifying goals, because the social structure prevents certain social strata from occupying the statuses in which these roles are performed, so that drive gratification requires other—perhaps proscribed—means for the attainment of the goals. Hence, unlike the first situation in which cultural conformity (compliance with prescriptive norms), however irksome, produces drive gratification, the second situation is one in which cultural conformity (compliance with proscriptive norms) leads to drive frustration. Thus, if Negroes are prevented from occupying those achieved economic statuses in which role performance attains prestige-gratifying goals, they may acquire a structurally induced motivation for proscribed techniques of gratification. I say "may" because often, as we shall see below, a frustrated drive is free to seek gratification by other approved techniques, as well as by those which are proscribed. Only if these alternative means are not attempted or, if attempted, prove to be unsuccessful, can it be predicted that the frustration of the drive will become a powerful basis for the motivation of proscribed behavior. And in order to preclude these proscribed motives from seeking overt expression, techniques of social control are required.

The third basis for nonconformity—one which is culturally induced—obtains when a drive can find no sanctioned means of gratification because the drive itself is culturally disapproved. This is almost universally true with respect to such interpersonal drives as hostility and dependency. That any expression of these drives should be deemed socially undesirable is not difficult to understand. Although the minimal satisfaction of a child's initial dependency is a necessary condition for the survival of society, the persistence of childhood dependency into adulthood is a sufficient condition of its extinction. Similarly uncontrolled aggression against the in-group would ultimately eventuate in a Hobbesian state of war of all against all. Culturally viewed, these drives are entirely different therefore from, for example, the esteem drive. Although cultural norms may differ concerning the desirability of the latter drive— cross-culturally the norms may vary from permission to encouragement to applause—there is no society to my knowledge in which every undisguised expression of this drive is prohibited. And in those societies in which this drive is widely frustrated, it is not because the drive itself is deemed undesirable, but because, as we have seen, the social roles by which it may be gratified are not available to large segments of the population. Hence, where a conflict exists between the esteem drive and proscriptive norms, the conflict is between cultural norms and certain motives for the gratification of the drive, rather than between cultural norms and the drive itself. In the case of hostility and dependency, however, there is a conflict between the cultural norms and the drives themselves because, since they are socially disruptive, all motives for their gratification are proscribed. But since these are powerful drives, techniques of social control are required to prevent their overt expression.

In sum, the psychologically induced bases for nonconformity require techniques of social control to ensure the performance of socially required tasks, while the structurally and culturally induced bases for nonconformity require techniques of social control to protect society from socially disruptive activities.

It would seem that there are two techniques of social control— provided by the social system—which may be employed for the fulfillment of these functional requirements of society. One technique consists of social sanctions, that is, socially administered punishments,[9] which induce the members of society to perform prescribed activities or to suppress (or inhibit) proscribed activities. If these sanctions—which consist either of physical or emotional punishment (prison terms or public censure, for example), and which may be administered either by constituted authority (natural or supernatural) or by peers—are cathected as negative goals (because their imposition frustrates important drives), the resultant motivation to comply with cultural norms may be termed "sanction oriented."

But social sanctions may not be sufficient to ensure compliance

---

[9] "Social sanctions" is used here in place of the traditional, "negative social sanction."

with all cultural norms for the obvious reason that many activities occur at times and in places which are temporarily inaccessible either to authority figures (super alters) or to peers (alter egos). If the social system, through its socialization institutions, produces personalities in which the norms themselves are cathected as goals— personalities, that is, that have acquired a superego—cultural conformity may be achieved by what may be termed "norm-oriented" motivation. In this technique of social control—one whose universality is still a matter of dispute among anthropologists (Spiro 1961)—compliance with cultural norms itself becomes a goal (which gratifies the drive of self-esteem). In short, norm-oriented motivation differs from the other motivational bases for cultural conformity in that the norms are internalized as ends as well as means. By providing these techniques of social control, social systems satisfy two functional requirements of society: they assure the performance of those tasks which achieve commonly accepted group ends, and they protect society from socially disruptive activities.

Although they arrive by somewhat different routes, most theories of social systems—psychologically oriented and antipsychological, alike—converge at this point. That is, almost all theorists agree that the potential conflict between the normative demands of cultural systems and the personal desires of psychobiological systems presents all societies with one of their crucial maintenance problems. Almost all theorists agree, too, that this potential conflict is resolved by various techniques of conflict resolution that are built into the very fabric of the social system: on the one hand, by socialization mechanisms which, at least to some extent, create personalities whose desires are consistent with cultural norms; on the other hand, by techniques of social control which serve to preclude the expression of those desires that remain in conflict with cultural norms. Thus, by these (and other) maintenance mechanisms, the potentially disruptive forces inherent in any society are contained.

Yet it is precisely at this point of convergence that psychologically and nonpsychologically oriented theorists diverge most dramatically. The typical pure structural theorist would now conclude that with the resolution of conflict equilibrium is achieved, and society can now go about its business. For the culture-and-personality theorist, on the other hand, it is only at this point that the problem of social control becomes truly vexatious. For though the techniques of social control described above are adequate to handle what are

termed the psychologically induced bases for nonconformity, t
are most definitely inadequate to handle, except temporarily,
structurally and culturally induced bases for nonconformity. T
is, the desire to achieve goals by means less onerous than those
turally prescribed (psychologically induced nonconformity) can
easily be held in check by ordinary techniques of social control because the culturally prescribed means of attaining cathected goals,
however sufficient or irksome, do in fact lead to drive gratification.
This is not true of the other two bases for nonconformity. Although
forbidden motives (proscribed means for gratifying the sanctioned
esteem drive, for example, and all means for gratifying the forbidden hostility or dependency drives) may be *inhibited* by the fear
of superego or of social sanction punishment, the drives which acti-
vate these motives are not *extinguished*. On the contrary, they persist and they continue to demand gratification. Hence, although
the expression of the forbidden motive may be effectively contained
by techniques of social control, the conflict between cultural norms
and personal drives remain unresolved. In short, although they may
satisfy a functional requirement of society by discouraging the expression of forbidden motives, techniques of social control may
prevent the satisfaction of a functional requirement of personal adjustment when, as in the case of culturally and structurally induced
forbidden motives, they not only contain the expression of forbidden motives, but they also prevent the gratification of personal
drives. And since these drives demand gratification, they must either
be gratified by some approved technique whose existence eludes the
conceptual framework of pure structural analysis, or else their continued frustration will lead either to serious dysfunctional consequences for personality—which, in turn, is bound to have serious
dysfunctional consequences for society—or to the breakdown of
social control (that is, the motives for noncompliance will be
stronger than those for compliance).

To summarize, techniques of social control serve to contain the
expression of socially disruptive motives without producing ill effects on personal adjustment or social integration if the drives which
instigate the performance of the motives are gratified in other ways
—ways which the more conventional anthropological theories have
not systematically explored because of their exclusion of personality
variables from their conceptual formulations. Culture-and-personality theory, cognizant of the importance of frustrated drives, and
realizing that these drives must be handled in some way, can make a

unique contribution to the analysis of social system by an investigation of this problem. Not only unique, but important! For however these drives are handled, their expression has important consequences for the maintenance, change, or disruption of social systems. Here we can offer only some preliminary suggestions.

Frustrated drives, in the first place, provide one motivational source for social-cultural change. Thus, in the case of structurally induced drive frustration, the frustrated drive, which cannot be gratified by the performance of social roles, is free to seek gratification, as we have already indicated, by other approved means. For example, individuals whose esteem drive is frustrated may seek satisfaction in the invention or borrowing of new means for the achievement of blocked goals, means which, though not proscribed, are different from the prescribed roles. Should these instrumental innovations, however bizarre, fall within the limits of variability permitted by the cultural norms, they are socially acceptable; and should they be broadly imitated by others, they become the basis of cumulation and/or change in the social system. If, on the other hand, new means are not available or if they do not succeed in attaining the blocked goals, the pain of drive frustration may lead to a substitution of new goals for the gratification of the drive (nativistic and utopian movements provide extreme examples). Sometimes this may be achieved by the conversion of the norms themselves into goals. If, for example, the sanctioned norms are conceived to have been instituted by the gods, compliance with the norms may become the goal whereby esteem is gratified. This is frequently the stance taken by movements of religious protest and sectarianism.

Secondly, frustrated drives provide an important motivational basis for the disruption of social systems. Thus, from the data now available there is abundant reason to believe that frustrated drives— whether culturally or structurally induced—constitute at least one important motivational basis for delinquency, crime, and political revolution. And such frustration must surely be a powerful basis for the *anomie* that is said to characterize certain sectors of industrial society, as well as for the frequently observed disruptive consequences of acculturation.

Our concern in this discussion is with the persistence of social systems. And here it would appear that the most important means by which forbidden motives are handled consist of the various mechanisms of ego defense described in the personality literature.

These mechanisms have been viewed by personality theorists as techniques for defending the ego against pain—the pain of shame, of moral anxiety, of guilt, and of social sanctions. For the social system theorist, however, their significance resides in their social functions. That is, by resolving the conflict between cultural norms and personal drives in ways which are satisfactory to both personality and society, they not only protect the ego from the pain of inner conflict, but they may also—as we shall see—contribute importantly to the maintenance of social systems. Among the various types of defense, three are of special importance to us here because of the additional light they may shed on this thesis. These are repression, displacement, and sublimation.

Repression—the rendering of the awareness of a drive or of its frustration unconscious—although an important means of ensuring cultural conformity is, at best, an unsatisfactory defense mechanism. The persistence of an unconscious, because forbidden, motive may, for example, lead to guilt and depression. Moreover, the energy required for persistent repression may result in continuous enervation and fatigue. Or, perhaps, the motive may break through the repressive forces only to find expression in some hysterical symptom. Alternatively, as in the case of unconscious hostility, it may be turned against the self and result in suicide. Depression, hysteria, and so forth, are unlikely candidates for indices of good mental health; and, should they become widespread, they would hardly (except in certain special circumstances) provide the psychological basis for a viable social system. In brief, a successful defense mechanism must not only protect the individual from the inner conflict and pain produced by the motive in question, but it must also allow him to gratify it in some form. But is this possible for such drives as hostility and dependency, all of whose motives are prohibited?

The answer is, of course, that although proscribed drives are not permitted direct gratification, they may be gratified in disguised ways. Thus, since it is the meaning of a motive, rather than the motive itself, that renders it acceptable or unacceptable, a change in any of its four dimensions—the drive, or its goal, the act, or its agent—may sufficiently alter its meaning so that it may re-enter consciousness and, in its disguised form, seek gratification. Each of these dimensional distortions produces each of the well-known defense mechanisms which need not be described here. Although these mechanisms may resolve inner conflict (between norm and desire) and promote drive gratification, not all of their expressions are equally desirable, either for the individual or for society. Indeed, using the latter qualification as a criterion, we can distinguish three types of defenses: (*a*) those that are *culturally prohibited*, and socially and psychologically disruptive; (*b*) those that are *culturally approved*, and socially and psychologically integrative; (*c*) those that are *culturally constituted*, and socially and psychologically integrative.

Let us begin with the first type. If the distortion of a forbidden aggressive motive, for example, should lead to paranoid projection and therefore to acting-out behavior, on the one hand, or to its displacement onto other members of the in-group, on the other, the defensive behavior (in-group aggression) encounters the same cultural disapproval and meets the same social sanction as the original motive. The resolution of inner conflict is achieved at the price of mental illness and/or social punishment for the individual, or of the breakdown of social control for society. This is hardly a satisfactory type of defense.

The second type of defense does not require the payment of such a high price. In any society, everyone uses defenses of this type all the time, and they serve them, their society, and their social system very well. Thus, for example, the kicking of a tree instead of attacking a kinsman; the killing of animals for sport, instead of assassinating a chief; the temporary dependence upon a wife during illness, instead of the permanent dependence upon mother—these and scores of other defenses are used by individuals in all societies. They protect individuals from inner conflict and, at the same time, permit them to satisfy, albeit in a disguised form, forbidden needs; they achieve compliance with cultural prohibitions and thereby protect society from the expression of forbidden motives. Their importance both for the student of personality and for the student of social systems cannot be overestimated. For the latter they provide an important conceptual tool for the analysis of cultural conformity. They enable him to understand how techniques of social control can frustrate proscribed motives without producing dysfunctional consequences for the members of society or for their social system.

But defense mechanisms are of even greater importance to the social system theorist than has thus far been suggested; and this brings us to our third type of defenses. Defense mechanisms, like other behavior patterns, are both idiocyncratic and culturally patterned. That is, some defense mechanisms—the ones to which we have already alluded—are developed by the individual through his own personality resources; others are developed by groups of individuals, and even by an entire society by means of resources which are provided by their social system or their culture. In short, if social systems and cultures are analyzed by an array of conceptual tools—psychological as well as structural—it would appear that many of their component parts (values, norms, beliefs, roles, and so forth) are used by the typical member of society as the bases for defense mechanisms. Indeed, their use as important ingredients of defense mechanisms may sometimes be their crucially important (latent) function. These mechanisms of defense, to be described below, which are based on beliefs, practices, and roles, and other constituent parts of cultural or social systems, comprise that type which I have termed "culturally constituted," in contrast to the other two types which consist of privately constituted defense mechanisms. The analysis of these culturally constituted defense mechanisms is, in my opinion, one of the vital tasks of culture-and-personality as a theory of social systems. Although this task has still to be undertaken, I should like to suggest a preliminary classification of culturally constituted defenses.

One type of culturally constituted defense is the functional equivalent for society of the private defense of repression. Like repression—but by other means to be explained below—it serves to preclude the expression of socially disruptive motives. A second type—analogous to displacement—utilizes materials from the social or cultural system for the distortion of a forbidden motive and, hence, its disguised gratification. Both of these types are essentially techniques of social control; they serve, that is, to contain the potential expression of disruptive motives. A third type—analogous to sublimation—not only serves to contain socially disruptive motives, but it uses these very motives as an important basis for the performance of social roles. This type, in short, not only protects society from the expression of proscribed motives, it also provides an important motivational basis for the performance of prescribed roles. Space permits only a brief description of each of these types. We shall begin with the first.

I would suggest that various types of avoidance behavior, based on avoidance taboos, may be viewed as culturally constituted defenses which serve to prevent the expression of forbidden motives. These are the functional equivalents of the private defense of repression. This suggestion has been made by Freud (1919, ch. 1) and Murdock (1949:273) with respect to sexual avoidance, when they observe that patterned avoidance of relatives of opposite sex—mother-in-law and son-in-law, for example—is a means of preventing incest. Similarly, other motives which are deemed socially disruptive—aggression against a same-sex in-law, for example—may be denied expression by separating (physically or emotionally) the motivated individual from the source of temptation. Other customs may have the same function. For example, the couvade—shorn of its cultural elaborations—has the objective consequence of separating a mother from her offspring for a certain period after its birth. If we assume that fathers are initially hostile to their offspring of either sex (because they are competitors for his wife's affection, nurturance, and so forth), either repression of the hostility or institutionalized avoidance (or some third functional equivalent) would serve to preclude the overt expression of the motive. To be sure, since avoidance behavior serves only to contain the motive rather than to gratify the drive, we would expect to find other means of disguised or symbolic gratifications—either in private or cultural fantasy (religion, myth, and so forth) or in one of the other culturally constituted defenses.

The differences between this type of analysis and a typical "structural" analysis of the Radcliffe-Brown type—in which in-law avoidance is interpreted as symbolic expression of friendship (1952:92), and postpartum fatherhood rituals as symbolic expressions of paternal concern (1952:150)—are threefold. First, hypotheses of the former type are deduced from fairly well established, empirically grounded, principles of behavior, while those of the latter type are based on certain assumptions concerning human nature—in this case, the necessity to symbolize certain types of interpersonal relationships—whose validity is merely assumed. (Both types, be it noted, are "psychological.") Second, hypotheses of the first type are based on a functionalist conception of social systems which views them as (in the long run) instrumental to a variety of personal and social adaptive and integrative ends, while those of the latter type view them as essentially serving the one end of maintaining the social structure. Third, and most important, hypotheses of the first type are empirically testable: they can be confirmed or disconfirmed. Those of the latter type are essentially nontestable. What kinds of empirical data could either confirm or disconfirm the hypothesis that sentiments of friendship between in-laws must be institutionalized and symbolically expressed, and that avoidance does in fact constitute such an expression?

The second type of culturally constituted defense uses materials provided by the social or cultural systems, not for the containment of forbidden motives, but for their distortion and, hence, for their disguised gratification. This type, which is most frequently exemplified by culturally constituted displacement mechanisms, has a number of subtypes. Thus social systems which include headhunting raids permit the displacement of aggression from in-group to out-group. Similarly, cultural systems that postulate the existence of malevolent supernaturals permit the projection and displacement of aggression from in-group to out-group. In both these subtypes, a forbidden motive (in-group aggression) is allowed disguised gratification by a cognitive distortion of either its object and/or its agent—a distortion which is based on culturally constituted beliefs or behavior patterns. By allowing for the disguised and culturally approved gratification of a forbidden motive, this defense reduces the probability of its undisguised gratification, and thus protects society from its disruptive consequences. "Rituals of rebellion," as Gluckman terms them, exemplify still a third subtype of culturally constituted displacement mechanisms. Here again, it is instructive to contrast a psychologically oriented analysis with a nonpsychologically oriented analysis. According to Gluckman (1956:ch. 5) these rituals, in which the politically subservient symbolically rebel against authority figures, strengthen rather than weaken loyalty to the political order, because "they assert acceptance of common goals despite these hostilities." Viewed as a culturally constituted defense, however, the performance of these rituals would be said to achieve this end *because of*, rather than *despite*, "these hostilities." This seemingly trivial substitution of adverbs contains an entirely different mode of explanation.

In Gluckman's structuralist point of view, these rituals are essentially expressive; their performance "asserts" or symbolizes a state of affairs which exists prior to their performance—the acceptance of common goals. From a culture-and-personality point of view these rituals are essentially instrumental; their performance is a means for the attainment and/or persistence of a state of affairs—the acceptance of common goals. Gluckman's mode of analysis is, of course, paradigmatic of almost all structural analyses—at least those that derive from Radcliffe-Brown: practice *a* symbolizes the solidarity of the lineage, practice *b* reflects the structure of the clan, practice *c* symbolizes both the conjunctive and disjunctive dimensions inherent in a social relationship, and so forth. But even if it were granted that certain practices are symbolic, for example, of solidarity, why, it may be asked, is it necessary or important either from a social system point of view or from a personality point of view to symbolize that which, *ex hypothesi*, exists prior to its symbolization? Thus, in the case at hand, if rituals of rebellion merely express a state of affairs—the acceptance of common goals—which already exists, then, from a social system point of view, what possible functions can these rituals have? Certainly not the strengthening of the political order since, so it is argued, the acceptance of the political order exists prior to their performance. And, even if it be argued that they have some function of which we are not aware, we still have the problem, from a personality point of view, of accounting for their motivation. That their performance is highly motivated is an obvious conclusion from Professor Gluckman's graphic descriptions. Yet, unless we postulate some personality "need" to symbolize political loyalty, we are at a loss to account for their motivation. And even if we were to grant the existence of such a dubious need, we would ask why this need is symbolized in this peculiar form.

If, on the other hand, these rituals be viewed as culturally constituted displacement mechanisms, their motivation is explicable in terms of personality theory, and their functions become explicable in terms of the functional requirements of any society. For since, as Gluckman describes very clearly, those who are politically subservient are hostile to those who hold political power, and since the expression of this hostility in acts of aggression is in conflict with norms which prohibit such expression, we may conclude that (*a*) the performance of these rituals is motivated by hostility to authority; (*b*) their performance serves the personal function of gratifying the hostility drive—in a socially approved and nondisruptive (symbolic) manner; (*c*) in serving this personal function, these rituals serve the adaptive social function of preserving political order because by gratifying this hostility drive in a symbolic manner, their performance reduces the probability of its gratification in ways (such as revolution) that would be disruptive of this order; and (*e*) by serving this personal function, these rituals also serve the integrative social function of strengthening political loyalty because in draining off these hostile emotions, their performance permits the commitment to "common goals" to reassert itself over those emotional forces which militate against this commitment.

It may be noted that in the first two subtypes of culturally constituted displacement mechanisms, a forbidden motive finds disguised gratification through a distorted expression of the motive; in this third subtype, a forbidden motive finds direct gratification through a symbolic (ritualized) expression of the motive.

The third type of culturally constituted defense—that which is analogous to the private defense of sublimation—is even more important than the first two. For in this type, society is not only protected from the possible dysfunctional consequences of socially disruptive drives, but these very potentially disruptive drives are used as the motivational bases for the performance of social roles. This may be illustrated by a brief examination of a universally prohibited drive—dependence—and its vicissitudes on the atoll of Ifaluk. The Ifaluk, like all people, must both express and gratify their dependency drive in a disguised manner; and, in my opinion, the disguise by which they express this drive takes the form of obedience and subservience *to* their chiefs, while the disguise by which they gratify the drive takes the form of affection and food *from* their chiefs.

The desire for love from the chiefs and the fear of its loss is in Ifaluk the primary basis for chiefly authority and, hence, for cultural conformity. Indeed, if love from the chiefs were not of primary importance for the Ifaluk, it would be difficult to understand how their authority could persist. For Ifaluk chiefs can neither reward nor punish; they possess neither punitive sanctions nor the means to implement them. Since they possess no means of enforcing their authority, it must be delegated to them; and the primary basis for its delegation seems to reside in the almost magical significance for emotional well-being with which their love, expressed in praise and in kindly understanding, is invested by the people. The Ifaluk say that if the chiefs "talk good," the people will live long, but if they "talk bad," the people will perish. In the former instance the people, as they say, are *eratu dipei*—that is, their stomachs are "good"; in the latter, they are *engau dipei*, their stomachs are "bad." In short, in this society, in which food—from the earliest age and in almost all anxiety-producing contexts—is used for comfort and nurturance, the kind talk of these chiefs who—as it is said in pidgin, are "all same pappa this place"—is symbolic of nurturance, their harsh talk of its withdrawal.

This symbolism of good stomachs and bad stomachs provides a possible explanation for the otherwise inexplicable, but ubiquitous,

Ifaluk ritual of food distribution. At the completion of almost any collective activity—and in Ifaluk they are frequent—the chiefs distribute food and tobacco. Since, except for a small quantity of tobacco, both the food and the tobacco distributed by the chiefs has been offered to them by the people, and since the amount received by any one household is of the same quantity and quality as they had brought, and since in any event the economic value of a few coconuts, a taro pudding, and a few ounces of tobacco is negligible, the eagerness and expectancy with which the Ifaluk await its distribution is manifestly inexplicable. Indeed, for the Ifaluk themselves the entire ritual is inexplicable. To an inquiry into its meaning, the Ifaluk retort with *musuwe, musuwe* ("before, before"); that is, "this is a tradition, and we cannot know why we perform it." But if food is a symbol of nurturance (as it is in Ifaluk), and if the chiefs are perceived by the Ifaluk as nurturant parent figures (as I believe them to be), their eager and expectant attitudes may be explained in terms of the meaning of the ritual as an instrument for the gratification of their dependency drive. (This ritual, of course, has other functions as well.)

Since the chiefs gratify the Ifaluk dependency drive, by providing them with love and nurturance, the expectation of gratifying this potentially dysfunctional drive becomes an important motivational basis for obeying the chiefs, which in effect ensures the maintenance of the political system and the body of cultural norms which it supports. This function of Ifaluk chieftainship was cogently articulated by the paramount chief:

> The chiefs are like fathers here. Just as an empty canoe is tossed about by the waves and finally sinks, so, too, a society without chiefs is tossed about by conflict and strife and is destroyed. If a father asks his son not to behave badly the latter may not obey him since he may not respect him highly. But all people obey the words of the chiefs, since they are feared and respected by all. The chiefs' duty is to see that the people behave well. The chiefs must constantly tell the people to be good, or else the society, like the canoe, would be destroyed.

Notice, then, the important functions, both personal and social, that are served by this type of culturally constituted defense mechanism. By utilizing elements of the social system as a means for disguising and thereby gratifying a forbidden drive (*a*) this type—like the second type—permits the members of society to resolve conflict between a cultural norm and a forbidden drive in a way that precludes psychotic distortion of the drive; (*b*) it protects them from punitive sanctions or punitive superego, since the disguised drive is gratified in socially prescribed activities; (c) society is protected from the socially disruptive influence of the direct gratification of the forbidden drive; (d) finally—and this function is served only by the third type—a potentially disruptive drive is transmuted into a powerful force for the maintenance of the social system.

Conclusion

I have suggested that, rather than persist as a distinctive sub-discipline within the total range of the anthropological sciences, culture-and-personality conceive of itself as part of that subdiscipline—social anthropology—which is concerned with the analysis of social and cultural systems. Thus the contributions of culture-and-personality theory can be combined with the important contributions of structural theory (notably those of British social anthropology) and of role theory (notably those of American sociology and social psychology) to advance our understanding of human society and culture. As a partner in this venture, culture-and-personality can make (indeed, has made) a unique contribution.

Rooted as it is in an instrumental approach to behavior, culture-and-personality necessarily looks at social systems from the perspective of ends to be achieved, functions to be served, and requirements to be satisfied. Given this perspective, its important theoretical goal is to discover the ways in which personality systems enable social and cultural systems to serve their social functions. These functions, it is obvious, are not served by the mere *existence* of these systems, but by their *operation*. And their operation is, in the last analysis, a motivational problem. Hence, culture-and-personality—always mindful that human behavior is the empirical datum from which all systems, all structures, and all sociocultural variables are ultimately abstracted—insists that the operation of social and cultural systems cannot be understood without reference to the empirically demonstrable or inferential needs whose expected gratifications constitute the motivational basis for human behavior, and which, therefore, comprise the immediate antecedent conditions for the operation of these systems. Hence, if the gratification of needs constitutes the personal function of social and cultural systems, their social functions cannot be served unless their personal functions are served. In short, although social and cultural systems develop—through a process of adaptive selection—as a response to various functional requirements of human social life, they persist because of their ability to satisfy the functional requirements of human personal life.

Despite the importance of motivation in the operation of social and cultural systems, an understanding of their operation could proceed without the benefit of culture-and-personality analysis if culture and personality always existed in a one-to-one relationship so that conformity with cultural norms always gratified personal needs, and personal needs were always gratified by means of culturally prescribed or approved behavior. If this were the case, motivation could be taken for granted by the social anthropologist; and though the social functions of these systems could be served only if their personal functions were served, the anthropologist would not require an understanding of the latter in order to understand the former. But conformity with cultural norms—alas—does not always gratify needs. Conformity often leads to the frustration of needs; and it is because of this frequent conflict between need gratification and cultural conformity that an understanding of personality dynamics is crucial for an understanding of cultural conformity, social control, and the operation of social systems. For, although social sanctions and superegos may, as control mechanisms, induce conformity, they do not extinguish culturally proscribed desires and, hence, they do not reduce intrapersonal conflict (between cultural norm and personal desire). It is one of the tasks of culture-and-personality to discover how this intrapersonal conflict is resolved in such a way that functional requirements both of the individual and of social life are satisfied simultaneously. The analysis of culturally constituted defense mechanisms offers one such avenue of investigation.

BIBLIOGRAPHY

BEACH, FRANK and E. JANES
    1954   Effects of early experience upon the behavior of animals. Psychological Bulletin 51:239–263.

BOAS, FRANZ
    1938   Race, language and culture. Boston, Heath.

CARPENTER, C. R.
    1958   Naturalistic behavior of the non-human primates. Handbuch der Zoologie. Berlin, Walter de Gruyter.

DEWEY, JOHN
    1938   Logic. The theory of inquiry. New York, Holt.

FIRTH, RAYMOND
1951   Elements of social organization. London, Watts.

FREUD, SIGMUND
1919   Totem and taboo. New York, Moffat, Yard.

GLUCKMAN, MAX
1956   Custom and conflict in Africa. Glencoe, Free Press.

HALLOWELL, A. IRVING
1960   Self, society, and culture in phylogenetic perspective. *In* the evolution of man. Sol Tax, ed. Chicago, University of Chicago Press.

LEVI-STRAUSS, CLAUDE
1953   Social structure. *In* Anthropology today. A. L. Kroeber, ed. Chicago, University of Chicago Press.

MURDOCK, GEORGE PETER
1949   Social structure. New York, Macmillan.

PARSONS, TALCOTT
1951   The social system. Glencoe, Free Press.

PIERCE, CHARLES
1935   Collected papers Vol. 5. P. Weiss and C. Hartshorne, eds. Cambridge, Harvard University Press.

RADCLIFFE-BROWN, A. R.
1950   Introduction. *In* African systems of kinship and marriage. A. R. Radcliffe-Brown and Daryll Forde, eds. London, Oxford University Press.

SCHNEIRLA, T. C.
1950   A consideration of some problems in the ontogeny of family life and social adjustment in various infrahuman animals. *In* Problems of infancy and childhood. M. Senn, ed. New York, Josiah Macy Fd.

SPIRO, MELFORD E.
1951   Culture and personality, the natural history of a false dichotomy. Psychiatry 14:19–46.
1959   Culture heritage, personal tensions, and mental illness in a South Sea culture. *In* Culture and mental health. M. K. Opler, ed. New York, Macmillan.
1960   Social control, socialization, and the theory of social systems. Presented at the Berkeley Conference on Personality Development in Childhood.
1961   Social systems, personality, and functional analysis. *In* Studying personality cross-culturally. Bert Kaplan, ed. Evanston, Rowe-Peterson.

WASHBURN, S. L.
1953   The strategy of physical anthropology. *In* Anthropology today. A. L. Kroeber, ed. Chicago, University of Chicago Press.

APPENDIX

A Selected Bibliography Bearing on the Mutual
Relationship between Anthropology,
Psychiatry, and Psychoanalysis

Though Chapter 9 deals with the subject of mental illness from the point of view of an anthropologist, it is not intended as a comprehensive assessment of the anthropological uses of psychiatry and psychoanalysis. The selected bibliography given here is intended to help those readers who are particularly interested in this area. Of the bibliographical items listed here, Margaret Mead's article on "Psychiatry and Ethnology" (forthcoming) covers nearly all the existing literature, though the results of many studies she touches on are not spelled out.

Aberle, D.
   1951   Analysis of a Hopi life-history, Comparative Psychology Monographs, 21, No. 1. Berkeley, University of California Press.
Adorno, T. W., et al.
   1950   The authoritarian personality. Studies in Prejudice Series. New York, Harper Bros.
Bateson, G.
   1943   Cultural and thematic analysis of fictional films. Transactions, New York Academy of Sciences, Ser. 2, 5:72–78.
   1947   The frustration-aggression hypothesis. In Readings in social psychology, T. M. Newcomb, E. L. Hartley, et al., eds., pp. 267–269. New York, Henry Holt.
   1953   An analysis of the Nazi film Hitlerjunge Quex. In The study culture at a distance, M. Mead and R. Metraux, eds., pp. 302–314. Chicago, University of Chicago Press.
Bateson, G. and M. Mead
   1942   Balinese character. New York, Special Publications of the New York Academy of Sciences, 2.
Bateson, G., et al.
   1956   Toward a theory of schizophrenia. Behavioral Science 1:251–264.
Beaglehole, E. and P. Beaglehole
   1941   Personality development in Pukapuka children. In Language, culture and personality, L. Spier, A. I. Hallowell, and S. S. Newman, eds., pp. 282–298. Menasha, Wisc., Sapir Memorial Publication Fund.

BELO, J.
  1960   Trance in Bali. New York, Columbia University Press.
BENEDICT, R.
  1934   Anthropology and the abnormal. Journal of General Psychology, 10.
BOWLBY, J.
  1951   Maternal care and mental health, WHO Technical Monograph Series, 2. Geneva, World Health Organization.
  1958   The nature of the child's tie to his mother. International Journal of Psychoanalysis 39:310–373.
CARSTAIRS, G. M.
  1957   The twice born. London, Hogarth Press.
CAUDILL, W.
  1952   Japanese American personality and acculturation. Genetic Psychology Monographs 45:3–102.
  1958   The psychiatric hospital as a small society. The Commonwealth Fund. Cambridge, Harvard University Press.
DAVIS, A., and J. DOLLARD
  1940   Children of bondage. Washington, American Council on Education.
DEVEREUX, G.
  1951a   Logical status and methodological problems of research in clinical psychiatry. Psychiatry 14:327–330.
  1951b   Reality and dream: the psychotherapy of a Plains Indian. New York, International Universities Press.
  1953   Psychoanalysis and the occult. New York, International Universities Press. (ed.)
  1956   Normal and abnormal: the key problem of psychiatric anthropology. *In* some uses of anthropology: theoretical and applied, J. B. Casagrande and T. Gladwin, eds., pp. 23–48. Washington, Anthropological Society of Washington.
  1957   Psychoanalysis as anthropological field work: data and theoretical implications. Transactions, New York Academy of Sciences, Series 2, 19:457–472.
DOLLARD, J.
  1935   Criteria for the life history, New Haven, Yale University Press. (Reprinted, New York: Peter Smith, 1949.)
  1937   Caste and class in a southern town. New Haven, Yale University Press.
DOLLARD, J., *et al.*
  1939   Frustration and aggression. New Haven, Yale University Press.
ERIKSON, E. H.
  1950   Childhood and society. New York, Norton.
FRANK, L. K.
  1948   Society as the patient. New Brunswick, N. J., Rutgers University Press.
FREUD, S.
  1918   Totem and taboo, trans. A. A. Brill. New York, Moffat, Yard and Company.
FROMM, E.
  1941   Escape from freedom. New York, Farrar and Rinehart.

GOLDHAMER, H. and A. W. MARSHALL
   1949   The frequency of mental disease: long term trends and present status. Santa Monica, Calif., Rand Corporation.
HALLOWELL, A. I.
   1955   Culture and experience. Philadelphia, University of Pennsylvania Press.
HENRY, J.
   1957a   The culture of interpersonal relations in a therapeutic institution for emotionally disturbed children. American Journal of Orthopsychiatry 27:725–734.
   1957b   Types of institutional structure. Psychiatry 20:47–60.
HENRY, J. and Z.
   1944   Doll play of Pilaga Indian children. Research Monographs of the American Ortho-Psychiatric Association, 4.
HOLLINGSHEAD, A. B. and F. C. REDLICH
   1958   Social class and mental illness: A community study. New York, Wiley.
HORNEY, K.
   1937   The neurotic personality of our time. New York, Norton.
HSU, FRANCIS L. K.
   1949   Suppression versus repression: a limited psychological interpretation of four cultures. Psychiatry 12:223–242.
   1952   Anthropology or psychiatry—a definition of objectives and their implications. Southwestern Journal of Anthropology 8:227–250.
HSU, FRANCIS L. K., B. WATROUS and E. LORD
   1961   Culture pattern and adolescent behavior. The International Journal of Social Psychiatry 7:33–53.
KARDINER, A., et al.
   1945   The psychological frontiers of society. New York, Columbia University Press.
KARDINER, A. and L. OVESEY
   1951   The mark of oppression. New York, Norton.
KLUCKHOHN, C.
   1944   The influence of psychiatry on anthropology in America during the past one hundred years. In One hundred years of American psychiatry, J. K. Hall, G. Zilboorg, and H. A. Bunker, eds., pp. 589–618. New York, Columbia University Press.
LaBARRE, W.
   1938   The Peyote cult. Yale University Publications in Anthropology, 19. New Haven, Yale University Press.
   1958   The influence of Freud on anthropology. American Imago 15:275–328.
LEIGHTON, A. H.
   1961   The Stirling County studies in psychiatric disorder and sociocultural environment. Vol. I: My Name is Legion. New York, Basic Books.
LEIGHTON, A. H. and D. C. LEIGHTON
   1944   The Navaho door. Cambridge, Harvard University Press.
LEITES, N.
   1953   A study of Bolshevism. Glencoe, Ill., Free Press.

LERNER, D., *et al.*
  1951   The Nazi elite. Stanford, Stanford University Press.

LEVY, D. M.
  1937   Studies in sibling rivalry. Research Monographs of the American Ortho-
          psychiatric Association, 2.
  1943   Maternal overprotection. New York, Columbia University Press.
  1946   The German Anti-Nazi: A case study. American Journal of Ortho-
          psychiatry 16:507–515.

LIFTON, R. J.
  1956a   Thought reform of Chinese intellectuals: A psychiatric evaluation.
          Journal of Asian Studies 16:75–88.
  1956b   Thought reform of western civilians in Chinese Communist prisons.
          Psychiatry 19:173–195.

LIFTON, R. J., *et al.*
  1957   Chinese Communist thought reform. *In* Group processes: transactions
          of the third conference, ed. B. Schaffner, pp. 219–312. New York,
          Josiah Mach, Jr., Foundation.

LINTON, R.
  1956   Culture and mental disorders, G. Devereux ed. Springfield, Ill., Thomas.

LOWENFELD, M.
  1939   The world pictures of children—A method of recording and studying
          them. British Journal of Medical Psychology 18:65–101.

MALINOWSKI, B.
  1927   Sex and repression in savage society. New York, Harcourt, Brace.

MEAD, M.
  1942   And keep your powder dry. New York, Morrow.
  1947   The concept of culture and the psychosomatic approach. Psychiatry
          10:57–76.
  1954   The swaddling hypothesis: Its reception. American Anthropologist
          56:395–409.
  1960   Mental health in world perspective. *In* Culture and mental health, M. K.
          Opler, ed. New York, Macmillan.
  (Forthcoming) Psychiatry and ethnology. *In* Psychiatrie Der Gegenwart, III,
          Heidelberg, Springer-Verlag.

MEKEEL, H. S.
  1937   A psychoanalytic approach to culture. Journal of Social Philosophy
          2:232–236.

METRAUX, R. and M. MEAD
  1954   Themes in French culture. Stanford, Stanford University Press.

MUENSTERBERGER, W.
  1955   On the biopsychological determinants of social life. *In* Psychoanalysis
          and the social sciences, W. Muensterberger and S. Axelrod, eds., pp.
          7–25. New York, International Universities Press.

OPLER, MARVIN K.
  1959   Culture and mental health. New York, MacMillan and Company.

RADIN, P.
  1936   Ojibway and Ottawa puberty dreams. *In* Essays in anthropology presented to A. L. Kroeber., pp. 233–264. Berkeley, University of California Press.

RICHARDSON, H. B.
  1945   Patients have families. New York, Commonwealth Fund.

RIVERS, W. H. R.
  1920   Instinct and the unconscious. Cambridge, Cambridge University Press.
  1923   Conflict and dream. New York, Harcourt, Brace.
  1926   Psychology and ethnology, G. E. Smith, ed. New York, Harcourt, Brace.

RODNICK, D.
  1948   Postwar Germans. New Haven, Yale University Press.

ROHEIM, G.
  1934   The riddle of the sphinx. London, Hogarth.

RUESCH, J. and G. BATESON
  1951   Communication: the social matrix of psychiatry. New York, Norton.

SAPIR, E.
  1927   The unconscious patterning of behavior in society. *In* the unconscious: a symposium, E. S. Dummer, ed., pp. 114–142. New York, Knopf.

SELIGMAN, C. G.
  1923   Anthropology and psychology: a study of some points of contact. Journal of the Royal Anthropological Institute 54:13.

SIMMONS, OZZIE G. and JAMES A. DAVIS
  1957   Interdisciplinary collaboration in mental illness research. The American Journal of Sociology, 63:297–303.

SODDY, K.
  1955   Mental health and infant development, 2 Vols. ed. London, Routledge and Kegan Paul.

SPIRO, M. E.
  1958   Children of the Kibbutz. Cambridge, Harvard University Press.

STOUFFER, S. A., *et al.*
  1949–   The American soldier: studies in social psychology in World War II,
  1950   4 Vols. Princeton, Princeton University Press.

SULLIVAN, H. S.
  1947   Conceptions of modern psychiatry, 2d ed. Washington, D.C., William Alanson White Psychiatric Foundation.

THOMPSON, L. and A. JOSEPH
  1944   The Hopi way. Chicago, University of Chicago Press.

WALLACE, A. F. C.
  1956   Revitalization movements. American Anthropologist 58:264–281.

WHITING, J. W. M. and I. L. CHILD
  1953   Child training and personality: a crosscultural study. New Haven, Yale University Press.

WILBUR, G. B. and W. MUENSTERBERGER, eds.

1951   Psychoanalysis and culture: essays in honor of Geza Roheim, pp. 455–462. New York, International Universities Press.

WOLFENSTEIN, M. and N. LEITES

1950   The movies. Glencoe, Ill., Free Press.

Human ideas and feeling tones are hard to convey in pictures. In addition the photographs of the different peoples assembled here are not strictly comparable in subject matter. Ideally we need pictures of different ways of life in action as they express themselves in similar situations. Nevertheless, these photographs, a majority of which are taken from the personal collections of some of the contributors to this volume, are reproduced here to serve as a relatively superficial but useful introduction to some of the peoples whose psychocultural characteristics are discussed here. The chapter number following each caption indicates where reference to that particular people is most likely to be found.

Boy of an Inland Sea fishing community in hot weather clothing, with strips of squash drying in background. The loincloth, once a common hot season garment for males of all ages in fishing communities, is disappearing as changing Japanese ideas of bodily modesty of the past century have come to demand more clothing. (Chapter 2)

Fisherman of Takashima, Okayama Prefecture, bringing in a net for drying and repair. In rural Japan, a serious, unsmiling countenance is considered appropriate for even informal photographs of adults. (Chapter 2)

Buddhist festival dancers at the village of Shiraishi, Hiroshima Prefecture, semiprofessionals performing for fellow villagers and Japanese tourists. Once a principal form of communal recreation for people of all ages, religious festivals tend increasingly to be family observances and community dancing is disappearing. (Chapter 2)

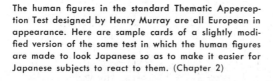

The human figures in the standard Thematic Apperception Test designed by Henry Murray are all European in appearance. Here are sample cards of a slightly modified version of the same test in which the human figures are made to look Japanese so as to make it easier for Japanese subjects to react to them. (Chapter 2)

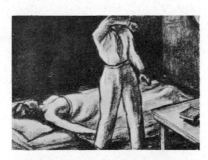

The Gusii of Kenya expect boys to display unflinching bravery during circumcision. This young initiate, the son of a chief, was made to believe he would be speared to death by the older men should he cry out or try to escape. (Chapter 3)

Clitoridectomy is practiced in many parts of Kenya. This operation, which is part of the girls' initiation among the Gusii, is performed by middle-aged and old women. The woman wearing a cowrie shell necklace is typical of those skilled in the operation. (Chapter 3)

Gusii infants are never left alone; they are usually close to their mothers and fed as soon as they cry. Even while dancing in an initiation celebration, a young mother nurses her child. (Chapter 3)

In sub-Saharan Africa, belief that death, disease, and misfortune are caused by witches is often combined with a faith in the practitioner who claims to counteract or prevent the evil effects of witchcraft. Mochama, a Gusii witchsmeller, is followed by his assistant in a frenzied chase to unearth some medicine allegedly buried by witches. (Chapter 3)

A Kaska husband and wife team is the most popular music-maker. They play for dances held in summer when the tribe assembles around the trading post. (Chapter 4)

A Kaska Indian grandfather plays with his daughter's child. (Chapter 4)

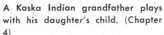

Kaska Indians subordinate external necessity, duty, and hurry to personal inclination. (Chapter 4)

Emotional aloofness is an outstanding characteristic of the Kaska Indians. It can already be discerned in this young girl who is imitating her mother as she back-packs her doll. (Chapter 4)

Kaska Indians gamble in traditional fashion to the accompaniment of a drum made of a discarded tin. (Chapter 4)

The Kaska are fur trappers and hunters. Moosehide is a commodity they prepare themselves and fashion into moccasins for wear and sale. (Chapter 4)

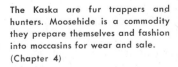

Truk: Young men and women singing and dancing. It is the breadfruit season, a time of plenty, and the dancing will be followed by an island feast for which large bowls of food have been prepared and are waiting. The dance form is widely distributed, with local variants, in Micronesia. However, it is of comparatively recent, probably European, derivation. (Chapter 5)

Truk: A mother with three of her children. Characteristically, the mother tends the baby while the slightly older child is in charge of his older sister. Modesty is irrelevant until a child can talk, and rather perfunctory, especially for boys, for some years thereafter. (Chapter 5)

Truk: Interisland baseball games are big events. These women have accompanied their team from an island some 15 miles distant to cheer their men, and incidentally to gossip with friends and relatives. Baseball was introduced by the Japanese when they controlled the islands. Games such as this could be interpreted as functional substitutes for the interisland warfare of old. (Chapter 5)

Truk: Same dance as at left. A young man who is one of the more graceful and accomplished dancers on his island. In those few dances in which young women participate they play a secondary role, with a limited array of restrained steps and gestures. In contrast the men show off to the best of their ability. Until they were discouraged by missionaries the dances traditional for festive occasions were frankly erotic. However, contemporary dancers still strive primarily to impress the opposite sex by more subtle means. (Chapter 5)

Truk: Funeral for a respected woman of a large lineage. She died after a long illness, thus allowing time for her relatives to avoid the anger of her departed spirit through their attentiveness during her last days. For the funeral their ranks are swelled by those who bear any relationship to the household or lineage. The funeral sermon is just concluding. The deceased's daughter and principal mourner sits with bowed head by the coffin (at left). The coffin will now be covered and lowered into the grave. (Chapter 5)

Truk: Women returning from fishing on the reef. Women wade in a line in the shallow water on the coral reef, holding a large dip net in each hand ready to scoop up a fleeing fish. Deep water fishing from boats is reserved for men. The women have used the canoes here only for transportation to and from a rather distant fishing site. (Chapter 5)

A group of Nunivak Island Eskimo, not all related, traveling between the village and the landing "field" on the river. Two teams have linked up, impromptu fashion. The children are riding since they could not run fast enough to keep up with the teams. (Chapter 4)

Man building old-style semisubterranean house at Mekoryuk, Nunivak Island Eskimo village. The children watch him. (Chapter 4)

Pibloktoq is a form of so-called "arctic hysteria" and seems to occur most frequently among the Polar Eskimo in the high latitudes of northwest Greenland. This photograph and the one below were taken in 1914 by Commander Edward Macmillan during a single attack suffered by a Polar Eskimo woman and were reproduced by courtesy of the American Museum of Natural History. (Chapter 9)

Inah-loo pibloctoq, Greenland, Etah. (Courtesy of the American Museum of Natural History)

Dancing is a form of religio[us]
worship in India, as is mu[sic]
and even wrestling. Here M[r.]
U. S. Krishna Rao and M[rs.]
Chandrabhaga Devi (Mrs. [U.]
S. Krishna Rao), two of t[he]
best interpreters of the clas[si-]
cal Bharat Natya, are pose[d]
in a dance scene as the Lo[rd]
Krishna and his divine lo[ve]
Radha. (Chapter 14)

A dancing class in session under Mr. U. S. Krishna Rao in Bangalore. (Chapter 14)

Worshippers at a Vishnu temple (where the deity is represented in the form of Vitoba) in Bangalore, India, receiving fire from a priest. Each worshipper in turn puts one or both hands over the fire for a second and then runs them over his or her face, hair, and back of the head. (Chapter 14)

Durga Puja (Durga worship) in Bengal. During the festival, which occurs in early fall and lasts over a week, many hundreds of pandals with images of the goddess in a warring posture against demons and her four children, for public or private worship. (Chapter 14)

Car Festival, worshipping Lord Jaganath (a form of Vishnu) in Serampore, near Calcutta. Once a year the images of the god and his two siblings are taken from their usual temple in this four-story, nearly 70-feet-high "car" for a ride of about half a mile down the street to another temporary abode. Seven days later they are returned to their own temple in another ceremony. During each trip, the "car" is pulled by a crowd of about 150 persons, who proceed a few feet at a time, accompanied by much music and dancing. Each trip lasts four to five hours and is attended by a crowd of at least 100,000 men, women, and children, most of whom come for the darshan, or spiritual radiation, of the gods. (Chapter 14)

Representation of Lakshmi drawn by the young college student in previous photo, Delhi. (Chapter 14)

Divali Festival (festival of lights) in Delhi. A young college student is seen here painting one form of symbolic representation of Lakshmi (goddess of wealth) on a wall in his father's house to serve as object of family worship later in the evening. (Chapter 14)

The central concern in Chinese ancestor worship is the benefit the rites will provide for the deceased. Here a Hawaiian-born Chinese father and his young son stand in front of a list of ancestors posted on the inside wall of a Chinese temple in Honolulu. The list contains names of ancestors submitted by living descendants of many families who have paid for the rituals and scripture recitation for the benefit of these ancestors during the annual public ancestral festival. (Chapter 14)

According to Chinese custom the dead should be buried in his ancestral graveyard near his place of birth. If he dies away from home, it is the duty of his sons to see that this is done. In this picture Mr. Francis Hiu, a prominent business man, born in Hawaii, examines jars containing the ashes of his deceased parents temporarily stored in a temple in Honolulu. These jars, and many others, were waiting to be shipped back to China in 1949. (Chapter 14)

The Chinese, like many other non-Western peoples, are polytheistic. These three images are from a single temple in Kunming, Southwestern China. Some of the gods are obviously of Indian origin with certain Chinese modifications. (Chapter 14)

A farmer and his young son in a village near Kunming, Southwestern China. As a son grows up, he enters into closer relationship with his father though he retains his warm ties with his mother. In time of trouble he takes for granted the help of his father or his older brother. (Chapter 14)

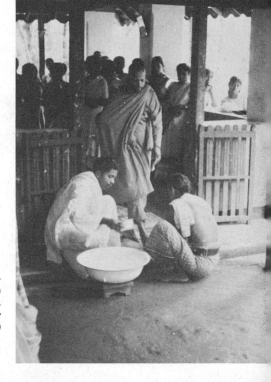

Native doctor in upper Burma village, near Mandalay. Burmese peasants, like those in other countries, combine traditional conceptions with those derived from modern science. Psychological security is obtained by recourse to the ritual techniques of traditional doctors. (Chapter 14)

Ceylon villagers washing the feet of a hermit (Buddhist) monk. Ceylon is a major center of Theravada Buddhism. The reverence shown for Buddhist priests, especially those living in jungle retreats, is deeply imbedded in Singhalese personality. (Chapter 14)

Vedda school children in jungle village, Ceylon. The Veddas of Ceylon were, until recently, a famous example of primitive hunters and gatherers. These children are the first generation of this particular village to face the psychological readjustments demanded by a sedentary, food-producing existence.

Young woman holding neighbor's baby in Ifaluk. Infants are highly prized in Ifaluk. The experience of being handled and nurtured by a variety of people is modal. (Chapter 15)

Ifaluk child at a public meeting. Ifaluk children participate in almost all public gatherings. This child has recently suffered from the birth of a sibling. (Chapter 15)

Religious ceremony in Ifaluk. The Ifaluk of Micronesia propitiate many types of spirits. Similar attitudes are evoked by elders, chiefs, and benevolent spirits. (Chapter 15)

An NYU freshman gets the feel of water as he is dunked in a horse trough dubbed "The Fountain of Knowledge" at the rear of the Hall of Fame on the New York University campus in New York City. Other pajama-clad freshmen join in the fun during traditional orientation of new students. (*Wide World Photos*) (Chapters 6 and 7)

Demonstration at segregationist meeting. Demonstrators in front of audience sound off and wave signs at start of Citizens' Council of New Orleans meeting in New Orleans. Thousands attended the meeting to hear segregation leaders of the state speak regarding the integration of two New Orleans elementary schools. (*Wide World Photo*) (Chapters 6 and 7)

All was bedlam on the floor of the Los Angeles Sports Arena during a demonstration for Senator Stuart Symington of Missouri after he was nominated as Democratic candidate for President on July 13, 1960. (*Wide World Photo*) (Chapters 6 and 7

Anti-American demonstration in Moscow. This is part of the estimated 100,000 people in Moscow, July 18, 1958, protesting American action in the Middle East as they march in front of the U.S. Embassy in the Soviet capital. In the second straight day of anti-American and anti-British demonstrations, the demonstrators smashed nearly 300 windows in the Embassy and stained the building with ink hurled in bottles. Some of the banners read, "Hands off Iraq," and "Long life, freedom for Iraq and Lebanon." (*Wide World Photo*) (Chapters 6 and 7)

Russian Communist Party chief Nikita Khrushchev, left, Soviet Premier Nikolai Bulganin, center, and Deputy Premier Anastase I. Mikoyan chat with an unidentified woman at the Kremlin, February 20, 1956, during a reception for delegates to Moscow's 20th Communist Party Congress. Delegates heard leaders pledge continued Soviet "collective leadership"—as opposed to one-man rule—and approve a massive new 5-year plan calling for sharp boosts in heavy industry and agriculture output. (*Wide World Photo*) (Chapters 6 and 7)

Demonstrators on Red Square during 1959 May First celebrations in Moscow. (*Sovfoto*) (Chapters 6 and 7)

INDEXES

AUTHOR INDEX

A

Abel, Theodora M., 187, 203, 241, 252
Aberle, David, 12, 117, 128, 390, 397, 493
Adcock, C. J., 236, 252
Adelson, Joseph, 306, 328
Adler, Alfred, 251
Adorno, T. W., 187, 203, 493
Albert, E. M., 114, 128, 346
Albino, R. C., 57, 85, 88
Allport, Gordon, 191, 198, 204, 214, 221, 229
Almond, Gabriel A., 174, 178, 203
Anthony, Albert, 59, 60, 65, 92, 352, 360, 361, 363, 364, 378, 380, 385, 388, 392, 396, 399
Arieti, Silvano, 294
Arth, Malcolm, 379
Atkinson, John, 199
Aubert, Villem, 192, 203
Ayres, Barbara C., 368, 378

B

Baashus-Jensen, J., 266, 292
Babcock, Charlotte, 36, 42
Bacon, Margaret K., 63, 88, 114, 128, 325, 326, 328, 346–349, 357–359, 363, 371–374, 378, 385, 386, 391, 393, 396, 397
Bain, Read, 212, 229
Bakan, David, 335, 348
Barnouw, V., 102, 128
Barrett, Albert M., 271, 292
Barry, Herbert III, 63, 88, 114, 128, 325, 326, 328, 345, 347–349, 357–359, 363, 371–374, 377, 378, 385, 386, 391, 393, 396, 397
Bascom, W. R., 444, 446, 447, 452
Bateson, Gregory, 140, 141, 146, 147, 158, 164, 165, 165, 493, 497
Bauer, Raymond A., 180, 203
Beach, Frank, 474, 491
Beaglehole, Ernest, 138, 147–149, 151, 158, 159, 164, 165, 167, 168, 493
Beier, H., 185, 186, 244, 252
Bellah, Robert N., 39, 42
Bellak, Leopold, 292, 294
Belo, J., 494
Bender, L., 155
Benedict, Ruth, 12, 19, 21, 23, 42, 93, 97, 98, 112, 128, 144, 146, 150, 168, 174, 175, 179, 180, 183, 203, 328, 355, 378, 387, 397, 463, 494
Bennett, John, 21, 42, 100, 128, 333, 340, 349
Berger, H., 259
Berger, S., 237, 254
Berndt, R. M. and C. H., 137, 168
Bertelsen, A., 267, 268, 292

Best, Charles H., 294
Biesheuvel, Dr. S., 51, 52, 62, 67, 71, 72, 88
Billig, O., 113, 128, 241, 252
Blalock, H. M., Jr., 360, 378
Bleuler, M. and R., 186, 187, 203
Boas, Franz, 179, 181, 203, 461, 463, 491
Bock, R. Darrell, 345, 349
Bogardus, E. E., 12, 14
Bohannon, Laura, 445, 452
Bohannon, Paul, 85, 88, 400, 445, 452
Bourguignon, Erika E., 314, 328
Bowlby, J., 494
Brelsford, W. V., 79, 88
Brickner, Richard M., 175, 203
Brill, A. A., 264, 292
Brogan, D. W., 172, 174, 203
Browne, C. R., 448, 452
Bruner, Edward M., 78, 88
Buchanan, D. C., 41
Buchanan, W., 191, 192, 203
Bunzel, R., 150
Burrows, Edwin G., 155, 156, 168
Burt, Cyril, 97, 129
Burton, Roger V., 361, 362, 378
Bush, Robert R., 379

C

Callaway, Canon H., 281, 282, 292
Campbell, Donald T., 12, 203, 333–349, 361
Cannon, Walter B., 277, 292
Cantril, H., 191, 192, 203
Carothers, J. C., 48, 49, 88
Carpenter, C. R., 474, 491
Carstairs, G. M., 187, 203, 248, 249, 252, 428, 429, 494, 452
Caton-Thompson, G., 443, 452
Cattell, R. B., 7, 14
Caudill, William, 31, 32, 34–36, 38, 42, 102, 129, 494
Chang, Tung-Sun, 409, 452
Chapin, F. S., 101, 129
Chapman, Loren J., 345, 349
Chaudrui, Nirad C., 428, 452
Chesky, J., 108, 131
Child, Irvin L., 60, 63, 88, 114, 121, 128, 134, 325, 326, 328, 332, 334, 337, 338, 341, 345–349, 352, 356, 363–375, 377, 378, 381, 385–387, 391, 393, 396, 397, 399, 497
Childs, Gladwyn M., 440, 452
Christensen, J. B., 445, 452
Christie, Richard, 188, 203
Clausen, J. A., 277, 292

501

SUBJECT INDEX

A

Abnormal, 10, 11; *see also* Mental illness; Psychopathology

Abortion, 55, 75

Abyssinia, 442

Accra (Ghana), 64, 70, 71

Acculturation, 95, 100–102, 108, 115, 125; in Africa, 69–73, 85; and expressions in projective techniques, 248, 249; of Japanese abroad, 33–36, 39, 40, 41; and mental illness, 80, 82, 83, 342; reflected in dreams, 314; and stress among *Kibei, Nisei,* 34–36, 41; *see also Kibei, Nisei*

Achelenese, 301

Achievement, and independence training, 370, 371; Japanese drive toward, 27, 34–37, 39, 40; and projective systems, 371

Acquisitive culture patterns, 53

Acting out, 261

Action, national character as, 174

Adaptation, level, 341–344; socialization viewed as adaptive, 387

Adjustment, 102; of Japanese to foreign cultures, 33–36

Adolescents, 49, 86, 87, 340; and delinquency in Japan, 32; Hopi, 111; Japanese, responses to Rorschach tests, 26

Adrenal cortex, 259, 260

Adult-child relations, 335–337; communication in, 144; *see also* Mother-child relationship

Africans, 437–449; *see also* tribal names

Age grades, 336; in Africa, 76

Aggression, 100, 102, 103, 105, 124, 274, 367; among Africans, 27, 53, 73, 74; among the Comanche, Plains, Cheyenne, 383; Dakota, 102; Eskimo, 120; Japanese, 27, 28, 32, 37; Kaska, 105; Menomini, 116; Ojibwa, 100; reflected in dreams, 312; training, 62, 63

Ainu, projective tests of, 25

Aitutaki, 149, 165

Akan, 84, 85

Alaskan Eskimo, 263, 267

Alcohol, 102, 105

Algonkian hunters, 257

Alienation, 178, 188, 193

Allport-Vernon Scale of Values, 177, 192

Alor, 150, 151, 304

Amami Ōshima Islanders, personality of, 36

Amatongo, possession by, 281, 282

Ambition; *see* Achievement, Japanese drives toward

American character, 190–192, 194, 195, 209–229

American Indians, 78, 336; Southwest, 64; use of peyote by, 278; *see also* tribal names, Indians

American national character, difficulties in studying, 209–212

American society and socialization, 384, 385

Amhara, 83

Ancestor cult, 53, 412–413, 422, 430, 447; *see also* Supernatural

Andamese, 402

Angmagssalik Eskimo, 263, 266

Animism, 111; dreams as genesis of, 297–299, 447; in reasoning, 143

Ankole, 445

Annam, 409

Anomie, 178, 188, 193

Anthropology, applied, 108, 109; contribution of, in studies of socialization, 397; cultural, 93, 97; evolutionary school of, 460, 461; relationship to psychology in socialization, 397; scope of, 450, 459; and theory, 461, 462, 464

Anuak, 445

Anxiety, 102, 112, 113, 116, 249; in middle-class Africans, 72; as reflected in dreams regarding isolation and independence, 320–327; resulting from social roles, 74; in socialization, 364, 374; in Zulus, 81

Apollonian, 98, 112

Arabs of Algeria, compared with Japanese-Americans, 35

Araucanians, 301

Archaeology, in Oceania, 135

Arctic hysteria, 263, 264; *see also* Pibloktoq

Aristotle, 177, 178, 181, 196

Art, 410, 421, 433

Arthritis, 260

Ashanti, 64, 71, 83, 84, 87, 442; dreams, 301

Asia, 263

Asians; *see* Chinese, Koreans, etc.

Assimilation, 109

Associations; *see* Relationships

Attitudes, toward mental illness, 260

Australians, 139, 145

Authoritarian personality, 182, 187–189; 198

Authoritarianism, 178, 188, 189, 193, 194; rulers, 63, 64, 86; *see also* F Scale

Authority, attitude toward, 180, 183, 189, 190, 193, 196, 197, 199, 200, 202; Japanese patterns of, 28, 39; symbols of, 338

Autocracy; *see* Rulers

Autonomy, personal, 196

Avoidance, 484, 485

Avunculate, and Oedipus complex, 335, 345

Azande, 59

B

Bahaism, 424

Baiga, dreams of, 302, 303

Balinese, 141, 143, 147, 160

Bantu, 66, 81, 439, 440

Bapende, 68

Barotseland, 49

Basic personality, 235

Basuku, 68, 447

Bathing, Japanese, 31, 32

BaVanda, 443

Bemba, 49, 65, 74, 444

Bena, 442

Benedict, Ruth, 258

Benin, 442

Bias, in judgment and methodology, 339, 341, 343, 347; *see also* Bigotry, Prejudice

Bibliographies, Oceania, 137

Bigotry, religious, and insecurity, 219, 220, 222–225; and racial prejudice, 222, 223; as values, 226–228; *see also* Prejudice, Psychological attitudes

Biology, and mental illness, 109; in personality, 143, 161

Birds, as a source of calcium, 267

Birth, order of, 337

Blood, chemical analysis of, 259, 262, 266

Brazil, Japanese in, 36

Bridewealth, in Africa, 53

Britain, 180, 181, 449

British Columbia, Japanese in, 36

British social anthropology, 49–51

Buddhism, as basis of Japanese psychotherapy, 38

Bureaucratic roles and socialization, 384, 385

C

Calcium, 266–268, 272, 273

Camba, 442

Canadian Eskimo, 263

Capelin, as a source of calcium, 267

Capitalism and socialization, 384, 385, 395

Caste, 224, 436–437

Catholicism, 422–424; and prejudice, 449

Causality, problems of inferring, regarding socialization practices, 375–377, 382, 383

Central Africa, 55, 65

Central Asia, 81

Central Nyanza (Kenya), 71

Cerebral arteriosclerosis, 256

Cerebral cortex, 259

Ceteris paribus laws, 345, 347

Cewa, 78, 79

Ceylon; *see* Sinhalese

Chagga, 59, 62

Change, centrifugal, 419, 432, 433, 437; centripetal, 409; conservatism, 490–411; cultural, 117; and cultural pressure, 414, 437, 443, 451; imitative, 413, 424; impetus toward, 413–415, 423, 424, 437, 448, 449; instability, 449; migration, 409, 419, 420, 432; and natural pressure, 414, 437, 443, 451; restrictions on, 413; revolutions, 414, 424, 437, 448; *see also* Culture change, Rulers

Character structure, 148; Japanese, described, 21–24

Character types, 177, 178, 182, 183, 194, 195; *see also* Psychological characteristics, Paranoia, American character, etc.

Cheyenne, socialization and values, 383

Child care, defined, 387, 388

Childhood, 107, 335–338; and adult world, 404, 408, 409, 417, 418, 424, 425, 439; and discipline, 417; dreams, 310; identification in, 335; mother dominance, 427, 428, 430, 431; rivalry in, 336, 337; significance of, 104; socio-psychological environment, 417, 425; *see also* Child-training, Infancy, Socialization

Child rearing, defined, 338; *see also* Socialization

Child spacing, in Africa, 56

Child training, in Africa, 62–64, 439–441; in China, 407–409; cultural influences on (in Africa), 53; defined, 335–338, 388; and economy, 326; in Euro-America, 417–419; in Hindu India, 425–432; Japanese, 28–33, 37, 38; Japanese and American compared, 29–32; Japanese class differences in, 29, 30; Japanese, Hindu, French, and Canadian child relations, Childhood, Socialization

Children's paintings, 64, 65

China, 192, 218, 219, 224, 229

Chinese, 301, 402, 406–415, 420, 422, 425, 429, 430, 433–435, 451; in foreign countries, 226, 409

Chiracahua, 301

Christianity, 103, 220; contradictions in, 220–222; and persecution, 220–222

Chū, Japanese concept of, 21

Chuckchee, 301

Circumcision, 53, 59, 65, 66

Citizenship, 187, 191, 194, 195

Class, American middle-class fathers, 390

Class conflict; *see* Intercultural relations

Class differences in personality, Japanese, 19–23, 26, 28, 38

Clinical chemistry, development of, 262

Clitoridectomy, 53, 65, 66

Coding, bias, 347

Cognition, nature of, 142, 143, 145, 146, 148, 149, 164, 166; psychology, 335

Cognitive process, 260, 274

Comanche, socialization and adult roles, 383

Combat neuroses, 259

Combat psychiatry, 270

Comendi, 442

Q

R

Truth, nature of, 107, 108
Trypanosomiasis, 257
Tshikapa (Congo), 68
Tsonga, 67
Tswana, 66
Turkey, 179
Typology, 404, 405

U

Ufufunyana, 81
Uganda, 54, 69, 71
Ulithians, 156, 157
Umbundu, 440, 442
Umundri, 442
United States, 79, 210, 220, 222, 225, 229, 415, 418, 420, 430
Urban and rural differences in personality, Japanese, 21–23, 28–30, 36, 37
Urbanization in Africa, 69–72, 86, 87

V

Values, 114, 115; African students, 70, 71; causes for conflict of, 213–220; conflict of values in America, 209–213; internalization of, 26, 27, 35, 37; of Japanese, 21, 23, 26, 27, 34–37; Japanese internalization of, 26, 27, 35, 37; of Ngomi, 63; operative, conceived, and object, 226; relation to political orientation, 190, 191; role in observation, 100; in U.S., India and China, 192
Variables, 356
Vende, 442
Vienna, 335, 344
Virus encephalitis, 266
Vitamin D3, 267–269, 272
Vocational aspirations, comparison of American and Japanese school children's, 35

Volksgeist school, 96
Voodoo death, 277

W

Weaning, 109, 110, 365, 367; in Africa, 49, 54–58, 85; delayed and socialization, 385; in Japan, 29, 30, *see also* Socialization
West Africa, 52, 64, 73
Western peoples, 412, 415–424, 431–433, 435, 443, 444, 446–449; American dreams, 305–307, 309; dreams, 300, 301
White Russian, 419
Windigo psychosis, 257
Witchcraft, 112, 437, 439, 447, 448; in Africa, 53, 75, 76, 78, 79, 84, 87
Withdrawal, 275
Work therapy, 259
World view, 107; *see* Character structure
World War II, effect on research on Japanese culture and personality, 19, 20, 34
Wydah, 442

X

Xosa, 52, 66, 67

Y

Yankee, 402
Yao, 445
Yir-Yoront, dreams of, 310–313
Yoruba, 439, 442, 444, 446
Youth, 190; *see* Adolescents

Z

Zeguha, 442
Ziba, 442
Zulu, 52, 56, 66, 67, 71, 77, 78, 81, 281, 282, 442, 445; dreams of, 301, 309, 310

This book has been set on the Linotype in 12 point and 10 point Garamond, leaded 1 point. Part numbers and titles and chapter titles are in 18 point Garamont, chapter numbers are in 14 point Garamont. The size of the type page is 27 by 46½ picas.